11/03

Fodor's 7th Ed

D0380757

New Zealand

The Guide
for All Budgets

Completely
Updated

Where to Stay, Eat,
and Explore

On and Off
the Beaten Path

When to Go,
What to Pack

Maps, Travel Tips,
and Web Sites

Fodor's Travel Publications • New York, Toronto, London, Sydney, Auckland
www.fodors.com

Fodor's New Zealand

EDITOR: Jennifer Paull

Editorial Contributors: Stu Freeman, Michael Gebicki, Satu Hummasti, Tania Inolowcki, Doug Johansen, Bob Marriott, Jan Poole, Mere Wetere
Maps: David Lindroth, *cartographer;* Rebecca Baer and Bob Blake, *map editors*
Design: Fabrizio La Rocca, *creative director;* Guido Caroti, *art director;* Jolie Novak, *senior picture editor;* Melanie Marin, *photo editor*
Cover Design: Pentagram
Production/Manufacturing: Yexenia (Jessie) Markland
Cover Photo (South Island, Kaikoura Ranges): Larry Ulrich/Stone/Getty Images

Copyright

Seventh Edition

ISBN 1–4000–1074–8

ISSN 1531–0450

Important Tip

Although all prices, opening times, and other details in this book are based on information supplied to us at press time, changes occur all the time in the travel world, and Fodor's cannot accept responsibility for facts that become outdated or for inadvertent errors or omissions. So **always confirm information when it matters,** especially if you're making a detour to visit a specific place.

Special Sales

Fodor's Travel Publications are available at special discounts for bulk purchases for sales promotions or premiums. Special editions, including personalized covers, excerpts of existing guides, and corporate imprints, can be created in large quantities for special needs. For more information, contact your local bookseller or write to Special Markets, Fodor's Travel Publications, 1745 Broadway, New York, NY 10019. Inquiries from Canada should be directed to your local Canadian bookseller or sent to Random House of Canada, Ltd., Marketing Department, 2775 Matheson Boulevard East, Mississauga, Ontario L4W 4P7. Inquiries from the United Kingdom should be sent to Fodor's Travel Publications, 20 Vauxhall Bridge Road, London SW1V 2SA, England.

PRINTED IN THE UNITED STATES OF AMERICA

10 9 8 7 6 5 4 3 2 1

CONTENTS

On the Road with Fodor's *v*
How to Use This Book *v*
Smart Travel Tips A to Z *ix*

Maps

ON THE ROAD WITH FODOR'S

A trip takes you out of yourself. Concerns of life at home completely disappear, driven away by more immediate thoughts—about, say, what marvels will beguile the next day, or where you'll have dinner. That's where Fodor's comes in. We make sure that you know all your options, so that you don't miss something that's around the next bend just because you didn't know it was there. Mindful that the best memories of your trip might have nothing to do with what you came to New Zealand to see, we guide you to sights large and small all over the country. You might set out to see some fantastic volcanic peaks, try a bungy jump, and do some wine tasting, but back at home you find yourself unable to forget an unearthly glacier; a succulent lamb dish at a small, friendly restaurant; or your experience fishing at a remote lodge. With Fodor's at your side, serendipitous discoveries are never far away.

About Our Writers

Our success in showing you every corner of New Zealand is a credit to our extraordinary writers. Although there's no substitute for travel advice from a good friend who knows your style, our contributors are the next best thing—the kind of people you *would* poll for travel advice if you knew them.

Stu Freeman, like most other Kiwis, loves to get out into the bush on a regular basis, watch rugby, and toss back a pint every now and then. He escaped the life of a daily newspaper journalist in the early 1980s, threw a pack on his back, and tramped through Asia and Europe. Since then he's been freelance writing about New Zealand and the South Pacific; he also publishes an incentive travel magazine and a freight-and-transport-industry magazine. For this edition, he covered Auckland and the North, Portraits, and the all-important Essential Information section.

Doug Johansen and **Jan Poole,** who contributed to our Adventure Vacations chapter, are owner-operators of Kiwi Dundee Adventures, Ltd., which offers a variety of tours and off-the-beaten-path hiking trips on the Coromandel Peninsula and around New Zealand. They are two nature-loving Kiwis who have a deep respect for the mountains, forests, and coastlines of their country. Doug is known as one of New Zealand's pioneers of nature tourism and in 1992 won the inaugural New Zealand Eco-tourism Award. Both are recipients of Queens medals for their work in tourism.

Bob Marriott was born in Nottingham, England, but has made his home in New Zealand since 1966. His passion for travel led him to freelance writing and photography. His travels have taken him all over the world, and his work has been widely published in New Zealand, Australia, the United States, Britain, Malaysia, and on the Web. His own photographs illustrate most of his feature articles. Bob has previously contributed to Fodor's guide to Southeast Asia; for this book he updated the Rotorua to Wellington and Upper South Island chapters.

Mere Wetere brings to her writing the perspective of her Māori heritage. For this edition she updated Christchurch and Lower South Island.

We'd also like to thank Simone Flight of the Tourism New Zealand office in Santa Monica, California; Shantini Ramakrishnan of Spring, O'Brien & Co. in New York; and the staffs of the New Zealand regional tourist offices for their generous help with questions big and small.

You can rest assured that you're in good hands—and that no property mentioned in the book has paid to be included. Each has been selected strictly on its merits, as the best of its type in its price range.

How to Use This Book

Up front is Essential Information, arranged alphabetically by topic and loaded with tips, Web sites, and contact information. Destination: New Zealand helps get you in the mood for your trip. All regional chapters are divided geographically; within each area, towns are covered in logical geographical order, and attractive stretches of road between them are indicated by the designation En Route. To help you decide what you'll have time to visit, all chapters begin with our writers' favorite itineraries. (Mix itineraries from several chapters, and you can put together a really exceptional trip.) The A to Z section that ends every chapter lists additional resources. At the end of the book you'll find Portraits, which includes a rundown on native flora and fauna, a Books and Movies section, a chronology, and a glossary of Kiwi and Māori vocabulary.

Icons and Symbols

★   Our special recommendations
✕   Restaurant
🏠   Lodging establishment
✕🏠   Lodging establishment whose restaurant warrants a special trip
⚑   Campground
☺   Good for kids (rubber duck)
☞   Sends you to another section of the guide for more information
✉   Address
☎   Telephone number
🕐   Opening and closing times
💰   Admission prices (those we give apply to adults; substantially reduced fees are almost always available for children, students, and senior citizens)

Numbers in white and black circles ③ ❸ that appear on the maps, in the margins, and within the tours correspond to one another.

For hotels, you can assume that all rooms have private baths, phones, TVs, and air-conditioning unless otherwise noted. We always list a property's facilities but not whether you'll be charged extra to use them, so when pricing accommodations, do ask what's included. For restaurants, it's always a good idea to book ahead; we mention reservations only when they're essential or are not accepted. All restaurants we list are open daily for lunch and dinner unless stated otherwise; dress is mentioned only when men are required to wear a jacket or a jacket and tie. Look for an overview of local dining-out habits in Essential Information and in the Pleasures and Pastimes Dining section that follows each chapter introduction.

Don't Forget to Write

Your experiences—positive and negative—matter to us. If we have missed or misstated something, we want to hear about it. We follow up on all suggestions. Contact the New Zealand editor at editors@fodors.com or c/o Fodor's, 1745 Broadway, New York, NY 10019. And have a fabulous trip!

Karen Cure

Karen Cure
Editorial Director

North Island

NORTH ISLAND

Cape Reinga
Kerr Point
Te Kao
Ninety Mile Beach
Bay of Islands
Kaitaia
Russell
① NORTHLAND
Whangarei
Dargaville
Matakohe
Great Barrier Island
Port Jackson
Coromandel
Coromandel Peninsula
Hauraki Gulf
Whitianga
Coroglen
Auckland
Tapu
Tairua
Firth of Thames
Thames
Whangamata
Waiuku
Paeroa
Tauranga
Cape Runaway
Te Araroa
Port Waikato
①
Te Puke
Bay of Plenty
Hamilton
Whakatone
Opotiki
Cambridge
EAST CAPE
Raglan
③
Rotorua
Tokomaru Bay
Waitomo Caves
UREWERA N.P.
Gisborne
Marakopa
Awakino
Lake Taupo
Taupo
North Taranaki Bight
TONGARIRO
Tasman Sea
④
HAWKE'S BAY
Hawke Bay
New Plymouth
TONGARIRO N.P.
Mt. Egmont
Inglewood
Cape Egmont
Stratford
Mt. Ruapehu
Taihape
Napier
③
WANGANUI
Hastings
Wanganui
㊾
Bulls
②
Palmerston North
ABEL TASMAN NATIONAL PARK
MANAWATU
Farewell Spit
TARARUA FOREST PARK
WAIRARAPA
Cape Farewell
Golden Bay
Waikane
Masterton
Tasman Bay
Upper Hutt
Martinborough
KAHURANGI NATIONAL PARK
Picton
Motueka
Lower Hutt
Cook Strait
Wellington
NELSON BAYS
Nelson
Blenheim
Seddon
⑥
MARLBOROUGH
Cape Foulwind
Murchison
NELSON LAKES FOREST PARK
Kekerengu
①
Punakaiki
Grey R.
Kaikoura
Greymouth
Hanmer Springs
LAKE SUMMER FOREST PARK
ARTHUR'S PASS N P
AORAKI/ MT. COOK N.P.
⑥ ①
Christchurch
SOUTH PACIFIC OCEAN

N

KEY
--- Ferry routes

0   100 miles
0   150 km

SOUTH ISLAND

Cape Egmont

Mt. Egmont

Inglewood

Stratford

③

Wanganui

ABEL TASMAN NATIONAL PARK

Cape Farewell

Farewell Spit

Golden Bay

TARARUA FOREST PARK

Waikane

Upper Hutt

Wellington

KAHURANGI NATIONAL PARK

Tasman Bay

Picton

Cook Strait

Motueka

Nelson

NELSON BAYS

Blenheim

Seddon

⑥ MARLBOROUGH

Cape Foulwind

Murchison

NELSON LAKES FOREST PARK

Kekerengu

①

Punakaiki

Grey R.

Kaikoura

Greymouth

LAKE SUMMER FOREST PARK

Hanmer Springs

WEST COAST

Hawarden

Hokitika

ARTHURS PASS N.P.

CANTERBURY

Christchurch

Franz Josef

AORAKI/ MT. COOK N.P.

Ashburton

Okains Bay

Fox Glacier

Akaroa

Lake Moeraki

⑥

Aoraki/Mt. Cook Village

LakeTekapo

Haast

Southern Alps

Lake Pukaki

Fairlee

Haast River

⑧

AORANGI

Timaru

Mt. Aspiring

Lake Wanaka

Milford Sound

Wanaka

Oamaru

Arrowtown

Lake Wakatipu

Queenstown

Doubtful Sound

Lake Te Anau

OTAGO

COASTAL- NORTH

Te Anau

Lake Manapouri

Lumsden

⑧ OTAGO

Dunedin

SOUTHLAND

SOUTH PACIFIC OCEAN

⑥

①

Balclutha

FIORDLAND N.P.

Invercargill

Foveaux St

Halfmoon Bay

Muttonbird Islands

Stewart Island

N

KEY

– – – Ferry routes

0   100 miles

0   150 km

ESSENTIAL INFORMATION

AIR TRAVEL

BOOKING

When you book **look for nonstop flights** and **remember that "direct" flights stop at least once.** Try to avoid connecting flights, which require a change of plane. Two airlines may operate a connecting flight jointly, so ask if your airline operates every segment of the trip; you may find that the carrier you prefer flies you only part of the way. To find more booking tips and to check prices and make on-line flight reservations, log on to www.fodors.com.

CARRIERS

Air New Zealand and **Qantas** fly from Los Angeles to New Zealand, nonstop and direct. **United** and **Air Canada** connect from points in North America with flights of their own out of Los Angeles. Air New Zealand is the only carrier with direct flights from North America to Christchurch as well as Auckland.

British Airways, Cathay Pacific, Garuda Indonesia, Japan Airlines, Malaysia Airlines, Qantas, and **Singapore Airlines** operate between London and Auckland, with a stopover in Asia. **Air New Zealand** and **United** operate between London and Auckland by way of the United States.

Within New Zealand, **Air New Zealand** and **Qantas** compete on intercity trunk routes. Air New Zealand serves a wide network of provincial and tourist centers, while Qantas works with local airline **Origin Pacific** to cover a number of secondary routes.

➤ To AND FROM NEW ZEALAND: **Air Canada** (☎ 800/776–3000, WEB www. aircanada.ca). **Air New Zealand** (☎ 310/615–1111; 800/262–1234 in the U.S.; 800/663–5494 in Canada; 020/8741–2299 in the U.K.; WEB www. airnewzealand.co.nz). **British Airways**

(☎ 0345/222–111, WEB www. britishairways.com). **Cathay Pacific** (☎ 020/7747–8888, WEB www. cathaypacific.com). **Garuda Indonesia** (☎ 09/366–1855, WEB www.garuda-indonesia.com). **Japan Airlines** (☎ 0345/747–700, WEB www.jal.com). **Malaysia Airlines** (☎ 09/379–3743, WEB www.malaysiaairlines.com.my). **Qantas** (☎ 800/227–4500 in the U.S. and Canada; 0345/747–767 in the U.K.; WEB www.qantas.com.au). **Singapore Airlines** (☎ 020/7439–8111, WEB www.singaporeair.com.sg). **United** (☎ 800/241–6522 in the U.S.; 020/8990–9900 in the U.K.; WEB www. ual.com).

➤ WITHIN NEW ZEALAND: **Air New Zealand** (☎ 09/357–3000, WEB www. airnewzealand.co.nz). **Origin Pacific** (☎ 0800/302–302, WEB www. originpacific.co.nz). **Qantas** (☎ 0800/808–767, WEB www.qantas.com.au).

CHECK-IN AND BOARDING

Always **ask your carrier about its check-in policy.** Plan to arrive at the airport about 2 hours before your scheduled departure time for domestic flights and 2½ to 3 hours before international flights. For domestic flights within New Zealand, check in at least half an hour before departure. Assuming that not everyone with a ticket will show up, airlines routinely overbook planes. When everyone does, airlines ask for volunteers to give up their seats. In return, these volunteers usually get a certificate for a free flight and are rebooked on the next flight out. If there are not enough volunteers, the airline must choose who will be denied boarding. The first to get bumped are passengers who checked in late and those flying on discounted tickets, so **get to the gate and check in as early as possible,** especially during peak periods.

Always **bring a government-issued photo ID to the airport;** even when it's not required, a passport is best.

CUTTING COSTS

The least expensive airfares to New Zealand are priced for round-trip travel and must usually be purchased in advance. Airlines generally allow you to change your return date for a fee; most low-fare tickets, however, are nonrefundable. It's smart to **call a number of airlines and check the Internet;** when you are quoted a good price, **book it on the spot**—the same fare may not be available the next day. Always **check different routings** and look into using alternate airports. Also, price off-peak flights, which may be significantly less expensive than others. Travel agents, especially low-fare specialists (☞ Discounts and Deals, *below*), are helpful.

Consolidators are another good source. They buy tickets for scheduled international flights at reduced rates from the airlines, then sell them at prices that beat the best fare available directly from the airlines. Sometimes you can even get your money back if you need to return the ticket. Carefully read the fine print detailing penalties for changes and cancellations, purchase the ticket with a credit card, and **confirm your consolidator reservation with the airline.**

When you **fly as a courier,** you trade your checked-luggage space for a ticket deeply subsidized by a courier service. There are restrictions on when you can book and how long you can stay. Some courier companies list with membership organizations, such as the Air Courier Association and the International Association of Air Travel Couriers; these require you to become a member before you can book a flight.

Many airlines, singly or in collaboration, offer discount air passes that allow foreigners to travel economically in a particular country or region. These visitor passes usually must be reserved and purchased before you leave home. Information about passes can be difficult to track down on airline Web sites, which tend to be geared to travelers departing from a given carrier's country rather than to those intending to visit that country. Try typing the name of the pass into a search engine, or search for "pass" within the carrier's Web site.

While budget air travel within New Zealand is still expensive compared with the cost of bus or train travel, you can **save a substantial amount of money if you buy multitrip tickets.** Air New Zealand (☞ Carriers, *above*) offers a **New Zealand Travelpass** entitling you to a certain number of point-to-point flights, or sectors. Travelpasses are available for between three and eight sectors, starting from $515 for a three-sector pass and adding roughly $150 for each additional sector. (The price varies somewhat according to sector.) The pass is valid for the duration of your stay in New Zealand and should be purchased prior to arrival to avoid the New Zealand sales tax. While using a Travelpass, you can change your travel dates without a penalty fee, but you will be charged extra if you change your route. If you hold an international student identification card, you'll save even more (☞ Students in New Zealand, *below*).

In 2002 Air New Zealand introduced a no-frills domestic service with lower fares; these are worth inquiring about. As with standard fares, you'll save more by booking in advance.

➤ CONSOLIDATORS: **Cheap Tickets** (☎ 800/377–1000 or 888/922–8849, WEB www.cheaptickets.com). **Discount Airline Ticket Service** (☎ 800/576–1600). **Unitravel** (☎ 800/325–2222, WEB www.unitravel.com). **Up & Away Travel** (☎ 212/889–2345, WEB www.upandaway.com). **World Travel Network** (☎ 800/409–6753).

➤ COURIER RESOURCES: **Air Courier Association** (☎ 800/282–1202, WEB www.aircourier.org).

➤ DISCOUNT PASSES: **Boomerang Pass,** Qantas (☎ 800/227–4500; 0845/774–7767 in the U.K.; 131–313 in Australia; 0800/808–767 in New Zealand; WEB www.qantas.com). **Pacific Explorer Airpass,** Hideaway Holidays (☎ 61–2/9743–0253 in Australia; FAX 530/325–4069 in the U.S.; WEB www.hideawayholidays.com.au). **Polypass,** Polynesian Airlines (☎ 800/264–0823 or 808/842–7659; 020/8846–0519 in the U.K.; 1300/653737 in Australia; 0800/800–993 in New Zealand; WEB www.polynesianairlines.co.nz).

ENJOYING THE FLIGHT

State your seat preference when purchasing your ticket, and then repeat it when you confirm and when you check in. For more legroom, you can request one of the few emergency-aisle seats at check-in, if you are capable of lifting at least 50 pounds—a Federal Aviation Administration requirement of passengers in these seats. Seats behind a bulkhead also offer more legroom, but they don't have under-seat storage. Don't sit in the row in front of the emergency aisle or in front of a bulkhead, where seats may not recline.

Ask the airline whether a snack or meal is served on the flight. If you have dietary concerns, **request special meals when booking.** These can be vegetarian, low-cholesterol, or kosher, for example. It's a good idea to pack some healthy snacks and a small (plastic) bottle of water in your carry-on bag. On long flights, try to maintain a normal routine, to help fight jet lag. At night, **get some sleep.** By day, **eat light meals, drink water** (not alcohol), and **move around the cabin** to stretch your legs. For additional jet-lag tips consult *Fodor's FYI: Travel Fit & Healthy* (available at bookstores everywhere).

Smoking policies vary from carrier to carrier. Many airlines prohibit smoking on all of their international flights; others allow smoking only on certain routes or certain departures. Ask your carrier about its policy. All New Zealand domestic flights and flights between New Zealand and Australia are nonsmoking. Air New Zealand has banned smoking on all of its flights worldwide.

FLYING TIMES

From New York to Auckland (via Los Angeles) flights take about 19 hours; from Chicago, about 17 hours; from Los Angeles to Auckland (nonstop), about 12 hours. From the United States and Canada, you will have to connect to a New Zealand–bound flight in L.A.

Flights from London to Auckland take about 24 hours, either via the United States or via Southeast Asia. Flights between Sydney and Auckland take about three hours. These are all actual air hours and do not include ground time.

HOW TO COMPLAIN

If your baggage goes astray or your flight goes awry, complain right away. Most carriers require that you **file a claim immediately.** The Aviation Consumer Protection Division of the Department of Transportation publishes *Fly-Rights,* which discusses airlines and consumer issues and is available on-line. At PassengerRights.com, a Web site, you can compose a letter of complaint and distribute it electronically.

➤ AIRLINE COMPLAINTS: **Aviation Consumer Protection Division** (✉ U.S. Department of Transportation, Room 4107, C-75, Washington, DC 20590, ☎ 202/366–2220, WEB www.dot.gov/airconsumer). **Federal Aviation Administration Consumer Hotline** (☎ 800/322–7873).

RECONFIRMING

Check the status of your flight before you leave for the airport. You can do this on your carrier's Web site, by linking to a flight-status checker (many Web booking services offer these), or by calling your carrier or travel agent. Always confirm international flights at least 72 hours ahead of the scheduled departure time. It is not required that you reconfirm outbound flights from or within New Zealand.

AIRPORTS

The major airport is **Auckland International Airport** (AKL). It is usually a bit cheaper to fly into and out of this airport, but the supplemental fees for flights to Wellington or Christchurch are quite reasonable. New Zealand's airports in general are relatively compact and easy to negotiate.

➤ AIRPORT INFORMATION: **Auckland International Airport** (☎ 09/275–0789, WEB www.auckland-airport.co.nz). **Christchurch International Airport** (☎ 03/374–7100, WEB www.christchurch-airport.co.nz). **Wellington International Airport** (☎ 04/385–5123, WEB www.wellington-airport.co.nz).

DUTY-FREE SHOPPING

The international airports in Auckland and Christchurch have some of the best duty-free deals (on liquor, cigarettes, and cosmetics) in the South Pacific and even compare favorably with those in many Asian countries.

BIKE TRAVEL

New Zealand is a sensational place to take cycling tours. For information on multiday trips throughout the country, *see* Chapter 6. Major cities are increasing their biking facilities, such as cycling lanes in central areas.

Bike rental shops can be found in all larger cities and other tourist centers. Pedaltours NZ, for instance, has bike rental outlets in both Auckland and Christchurch. They can get you in touch with bike rental companies in other New Zealand spots and even customize tour itineraries for special-interest groups.

➤ BIKE MAPS: *The New Zealand Cyclers' Guide to Cycle Touring* by J. B. Ringer has North Island and South Island editions and is available in some bike shops and major bookstores around the country.

➤ BIKE RENTALS: **Pedaltours NZ** (✉ 45 Tarawera Terr., Kohimarama, Auckland, ☎ 09/302–0968, WEB www. pedaltours.co.nz).

BIKES IN FLIGHT

Most airlines accommodate bikes as luggage, provided they are dismantled and boxed; check with individual airlines about packing requirements. Airlines sell bike boxes, which are often free at bike shops, for about $15 (bike bags start at $100). International travelers often can substitute a bike for a piece of checked luggage at no charge; otherwise, the cost is about $100. Domestic and Canadian airlines charge $40–$80 each way.

BOAT AND FERRY TRAVEL

To travel between North Island and South Island take **Tranz Scenic's Interislander** ferry or the faster, slightly more expensive **Lynx** ferry between Wellington and Picton. Both ferries carry cars. They also connect with Tranz Scenic's trains, and a free shuttle is available between the railway station and ferry terminal in both Wellington and Picton. The Interislander travels five times a day; the Lynx, two to three times. Standard one-way fare can be as much as $52, but there are off-peak deals to be had. The fare for a medium-size sedan costs $179. Be sure to ask about specials, including ferry-train deals, when you book.

FARES AND SCHEDULES

Schedules are available at train stations and visitor information centers around the country. Most will arrange Interislander ferry bookings. Be sure to reserve in advance, especially during holiday periods.

➤ BOAT AND FERRY INFORMATION: **Tranz Scenic** (☎ 0800/802–802, WEB www.interislandline.co.nz).

BUSINESS HOURS

BANKS AND OFFICES

Banks are open weekdays 9–4:30, but trading in foreign currencies ceases at 3.

GAS STATIONS

Gas stations are usually open, at the least, from 7 AM to 7 PM. Large stations on main highways are commonly open 24 hours.

MUSEUMS AND SIGHTS

Museums around the country do not have standard hours, but many are open daily from 10 AM to 5 PM.

PHARMACIES

Pharmacies are open from 9 AM to 5 PM. In larger cities, you will find basic nonprescription drugstore items in supermarkets, many of which are open until 8 PM. During off-hours there will usually be emergency-hour pharmacies in the major cities. Phone the local hospital for details.

SHOPS

Shops are generally open Monday–Thursday 9–5:30, Friday 9–9, and Saturday 9–noon (until 5 in main cities). Sunday trading is becoming more common but still varies greatly from place to place. Most Auckland shopping centers are open at least Sunday mornings. Liquor stores are often open daily.

BUS TRAVEL

New Zealand is served by an extensive bus network; for many travelers, buses offer the optimal combination of cost and convenience. **InterCity** and **Newmans** are the main bus lines and are owned by the same company. Fares vary greatly, depending on how much flexibility you have in terms of days and times traveled. A standard full fare between Auckland and Wellington is $94 but can be obtained for as low as $47. There's no smoking on any bus lines.

➤ BUS INFORMATION: **InterCity** (☎ 09/913–6100, WEB www.intercitycoach.co.nz). **Newmans** (☎ 09/913–6200, WEB www.newmanscoach.co.nz).

CUTTING COSTS

A range of flexible passes allows coach travel over a set route in a given time frame, usually three or six months. You can travel whenever you like, without paying extra, as long as you stick to the stops covered by your pass. There is also the InterCity Travelpass, which allows unlimited travel on all InterCity buses and trains and on the Interislander ferries that link the North and South Islands (☞ Train Travel, *below*). Both **Newmans** and **Intercity** offer a 20% discount to students and Youth Hostel members. Identification cards are required. A 30% discount is available for passengers over the age of 60.

PAYING

Credit cards and traveler's checks are accepted by the major bus companies.

RESERVATIONS

Reservations are recommended.

CAMERAS
AND PHOTOGRAPHY

New Zealanders are usually happy to have their photograph taken, but if you're getting up close, it pays to ask permission first.

If you are taking photos of mountains and lakes, avoid the glare of the afternoon—dusk and dawn are the best times. In the North Island, the West Coast has some spectacular sunsets. In the South Island, particularly in Fiordland, thick fog wraps itself around moss-laden trees on winter mornings, providing for eerie-looking photographs. For a spectacular wide-angled photograph, be sure to travel to the top of Bob's Peak by the Skyline Gondola and take a shot of Queenstown and the Remarkables mountain range. For a close-up, attend a Māori dance performance in Rotorua and take a photo of a tattooed warrior as he thrusts his tongue out during the *haka*. For an evocative urban shot, head to the Auckland waterfront and take a picture of the joggers, skaters, and cyclists, with the Rangitoto Island in the background. The *Kodak Guide to Shooting Great Travel Pictures* (available at bookstores everywhere) is loaded with tips.

➤ PHOTO HELP: **Kodak Information Center** (☎ 800/242–2424, WEB www.kodak.com).

EQUIPMENT PRECAUTIONS

Don't pack film and equipment in checked luggage, where it is much more susceptible to damage. X-ray machines used to view checked luggage are becoming much more powerful and therefore are much more likely to ruin your film. Try to **ask for hand inspection of film,** which becomes clouded after repeated exposure to airport X-ray machines, and **keep videotapes and computer disks away from metal detectors.** Always **keep film, tape, and computer disks out of the sun.** Carry an extra supply of batteries, and **be prepared to turn on your camera, camcorder, or laptop** to prove to airport security personnel that the device is real.

FILM AND DEVELOPING

Film is readily available in airport duty-free shops, pharmacies, department stores, tourist shops, and gas stations. **Kodak** and **Fuji** are widely available. A roll of 36-exposure film costs about $13. Twenty-four-hour film developing is available even in smaller towns, and some pharmacies and photo shops will develop in an hour or two.

VIDEOS

The local standard for videotape is PAL; a three-hour tape will cost around $8.

CAR RENTAL

Japanese brands dominate rental agencies in New Zealand. Cars in the "economy" ranges are likely to include Honda Logos, Honda Civics,

Toyota Corollas, or similar types. They are suitable for two or three people. At the luxury end of the scale you will find Honda Legends. **For some local flavor, rent a Holden Commodore,** a popular car in New Zealand. Most major agencies will have this as a luxury option.

Rates in New Zealand begin at $70 a day and $350 a week for an economy car with unlimited mileage. This does not include tax on car rentals, which is 12.5%.

➤ MAJOR AGENCIES: **Alamo** (☎ 800/522–9696, WEB www.alamo.com). **Avis** (☎ 800/331–1084; 800/879–2847 in Canada; 0870/606–0100 in the U.K.; 02/9353–9000 in Australia; 09/526–2847 in New Zealand; WEB www.avis.com). **Budget** (☎ 800/527–0700; 0870/156–5656 in the U.K.; WEB www.budget.com). **Dollar** (☎ 800/800–6000; 0124/622–0111 in the U.K., where it's affiliated with Sixt; 02/9223–1444 in Australia; WEB www.dollar.com). **Hertz** (☎ 800/654–3001; 800/263–0600 in Canada; 020/8897–2072 in the U.K.; 02/9669–2444 in Australia; 09/256–8690 in New Zealand; WEB www.hertz.com). **National Car Rental** (☎ 800/227–7368; 020/8680–4800 in the U.K.; WEB www.nationalcar.com).

➤ LOCAL AGENCIES: **Mauitours** (☎ 800/351–2323 in the U.S.; 800/663–2002 in Canada; 01737/843242 in the U.K.; 0800/651–080 in New Zealand) rents cars as well as the popular campervans.

CROSS-ISLAND RENTALS

Most major international companies have a convenient service if you are taking the ferry between North and South islands and want to continue your rental contract. You simply drop off the car in Wellington and on the same contract pick up a new car in Picton, or vice versa. It saves you from paying the considerable fare for taking a car across on the ferry (and it's easier for the company to keep track of its rental fleet). Your rental contract is terminated only at the far end of your trip, wherever you end up. In this system, there is no drop-off charge for one-way rentals, making an Auckland–Queenstown rental as easy as it could be.

CUTTING COSTS

For a good deal, **book through a travel agent who will shop around.** If you're renting a car in New Zealand, **check for special rates based on a south-to-north itinerary**; it may be less expensive this way, as it's against the normal flow. Special rates should be available whether you book from abroad or within New Zealand.

INSURANCE

When driving a rented car you are generally responsible for any damage to or loss of the vehicle. You may also be liable for any property damage or personal injury that you may cause while driving. Before you rent, **see what coverage you already have** under the terms of your personal auto-insurance policy and credit cards.

In New Zealand, it is usual to have the insurance included in the rental price, but you will almost certainly be expected to pay what Kiwis call an "excess" if you badly damage the car. This will be about $1,200. Since deductibles are very high with the most basic coverage, you may want to opt for total coverage. Be sure to get all of the details from the rental agent before you decide.

REQUIREMENTS AND RESTRICTIONS

In New Zealand your own driver's license is acceptable. An International Driver's Permit is a good idea; it's available from the American or Canadian Automobile Association, and, in the United Kingdom, from the Automobile Association or Royal Automobile Club. These international permits are universally recognized, and having one in your wallet may save you a problem with the local authorities.

The minimum age for renting a car in New Zealand is 25. This requirement is waived if the driver has held a driver's license for one year or more. Even then, the young driver is liable for an extra "underage driver's fee" of $25 plus the 12.5% general sales tax (GST) in addition to the quoted rates. Children's car seats are mandatory for kids under five years old. Car rental companies may ask drivers not to take their cars onto certain roads, but this is rare and tends to only apply in the rough and rugged hill country around the Southern Alps.

SURCHARGES

Before you pick up a car in one city and leave it in another, **ask about drop-off charges or one-way service fees,** which can be substantial. Note, too, that some rental agencies charge extra if you return the car before the time specified in your contract. To avoid a hefty refueling fee, **fill the tank just before you turn in the car,** but be aware that gas stations near the rental outlet may overcharge. It's almost never a deal to buy the tank of gas in the car when you rent it; the understanding is that you'll return it empty, but some fuel usually remains.

CAR TRAVEL

Nothing beats the freedom and mobility of a car for exploring. Even for those nervous about driving on the "wrong" side of the road, motoring here is relatively easy.

Remember this simple axiom: **drive left, look right.** That means keep to the left lane, and when turning right or left from a stop sign, the closest lane of traffic will be coming from the right, so look in that direction first. By the same token, pedestrians should **look right before crossing the street.** Americans and Canadians can blindly step into the path of an oncoming car by looking left as they do when crossing streets at home. So repeat this several times: drive left, look right. You'll find yourself in a constant comedy of errors when you go to use directional signals and windshield wipers—in Kiwi cars it's the reverse of what you're used to. You won't be able to count how many times those wipers start flapping back and forth when you go to signal a turn (it'll happen in reverse when you get back home). You can be sure it's time to call it a day when you reach over your left shoulder for the seat belt and grab a handful of air.

AUTO CLUBS

➤ IN AUSTRALIA: **Australian Automobile Association** (☎ 02/6247–7311).

➤ IN CANADA: **Canadian Automobile Association** (CAA; ☎ 613/247–0117).

➤ IN NEW ZEALAND: **New Zealand Automobile Association** (☎ 09/302–1825, WEB www.nzaa.co.nz).

➤ IN THE U.K.: **Automobile Association** (AA; ☎ 0990/500–600). **Royal Automobile Club** (RAC; ☎ 0990/722–722 for membership; 0345/121–345 for insurance).

➤ IN THE U.S.: **American Automobile Association** (☎ 800/564–6222).

EMERGENCY SERVICES

In the case of serious accident, immediately pull over to the side of the road and **phone 111.** Emergency phone boxes are not common; you may have to rely on a cellular phone. You will find New Zealanders quick to help if they are able to, particularly if you need to use a phone. Minor accidents are normally sorted out in a calm and collected manner at the side of the road. However, "road rage" is not unknown. If the driver of the other vehicle looks particularly angry or aggressive, you are within your rights to take note of the registration number and then report the accident at the local or nearest police station.

The New Zealand Automobile Association offers emergency road service and is associated with the American Automobile Association (AAA). If you are an AAA member, you will be covered by the service as long as you register in person with a NZAA office in New Zealand and present your membership card.

➤ CONTACTS: **New Zealand Automobile Association** (✉ 99 Albert St., Auckland, ☎ 09/302–1825, WEB www.nzaa.co.nz).

GASOLINE

On main routes you'll find stations at regular intervals. However, if you're traveling on back roads where the population is sparse it's best not to let your tank get too low—it can be a long walk to the nearest helpful farmer if you run out of gas.

The price of gas (Kiwis say "petrol") in New Zealand is more volatile than the fuel itself. At press time prices had recently rocketed from 82¢ per liter to about $1 a liter. Credit cards are widely accepted, though not necessarily at small country gas stations, so ask before you fill up.

Unleaded gas is widely available and is often referred to as 91. High-octane unleaded gas is called 96. The 91 is usually a couple of cents cheaper than 96; most rental cars run on 91. Leaded fuel is no longer sold widely in New Zealand, and cars that still run on this require a special additive, available from gas stations. Virtually all gas stations will have staff on hand to pump gas or assist motorists in other ways; however, they tend to have self-service facilities for anyone in a hurry. These are simply operated by pushing numbers on a console to coincide with the dollar value of the gas required. When you pump the gas, the pump will automatically switch off when you have reached the stated amount. Pay at the counter inside the station. For gas station opening hours, *see* Business Hours, *above*.

ROAD CONDITIONS

Roads are well maintained and generally uncrowded, though signposting, even on major highways, is often poor. (On highways, navigating is easiest using the names of towns along the way rather than route numbers.) Because traffic in New Zealand is relatively light, there has been little need to create major highways, and there are few places where you get straight stretches for very long. So don't plan on averaging 100 kph (62 mph) in too many areas. Expect two or three lanes on main highways; major roads frequently have passing lanes. Rural areas still have some one-lane roads.

Most roads pass through beautiful scenery—so much in fact that you may be constantly agog at what you're seeing. The temptation is strong to look at everything, but keep your eyes on the road. Rest areas, many in positions with great views, are plentiful. Some roads are incredibly windy; others, like the road from Wanaka to Arrowtown outside of Queenstown, are off-limits for rental cars. Ask your rental company in advance where you can and cannot

drive if you plan to go off the beaten path. One-lane bridges are common and are sometimes used by trains as well as cars; signs indicate which driver needs to give way.

The only city with a serious congestion problem during rush hour is Auckland, particularly on inner-city motorway on and off ramps. Avoid driving between 7:30 AM and 9 AM, and 5 PM and 6:30 PM. Traffic around other cities, such as Wellington and Christchurch, builds up at these times, too, and it is worth taking this into account if you have important appointments or a plane to catch. Give yourself a spare 15 or 20 minutes to be on the safe side.

New Zealanders are seldom as good at driving as they think they are, so the best policy is just to keep at a safe distance. Dangerous overtaking, speeders, lack of indication, and slow drivers in passing lanes are all afflictions you will have to suffer on New Zealand highways. In saying that, driving has improved over recent years due to increased education about speeding and drunk driving and bad driving in general.

ROAD MAPS

Road maps are widely available in gas stations, at airports, and in bookshops around the country; AA maps are reliable bets. Car rental companies will hand you a road map on request, and local city guidebooks available at airports and information centers usually have passable maps on the back pages. In the unlikely event you can't find what you want, contact the **New Zealand Automobile Association** (☞ Auto Clubs, *above*).

RULES OF THE ROAD

The speed limit is 100 km per hour (62 mi per hour) on the open road and 50 kph (31 mph) in towns and cities. A circular sign with the letters LSZ (Limited Speed Zone) means speed should be governed by prevailing road conditions but still not exceed 100 kph. **Watch out for speed cameras,** particularly in city suburbs and on approaches to and exits from small towns. The police force (not to mention the money counters) has taken to them with relish. Fines start at about $60 for speeds 10 km (6 mi) over the speed limit.

Right turns are not permitted on red lights. The law states that **you must always wear a seat belt** in New Zealand, whether you are driving or a passenger in a car. If you are caught without a seat belt and you are clearly not a New Zealander, the result is likely to be a friendly but firm warning.

Drunk drivers are not tolerated in New Zealand. The blood alcohol limit is 0.05, and it's safest to **avoid driving altogether if you've had a drink.** If you are caught driving over the limit you will be taken to the nearest police station to dry out and required to pay a high fine. Repeat offences or instances of causing injury or death while under the influence of alcohol are likely to result in jail terms.

When driving in rural New Zealand, **cross one-lane bridges with caution**— there are plenty of them. A yellow sign on the left will usually warn you that you are approaching a one-lane bridge, and another sign will tell you whether you have the right-of-way. A rectangular blue sign means you have the right-of-way, and a circular sign with a red border means you must pull over to the left and wait to cross until oncoming traffic has passed. Even when you have the right-of-way, slow down and take care. Some one-lane bridges in South Island are used by trains as well as cars. Trains always have the right-of-way.

The usual fine for parking over the time limit on meters is $10–$15. In the last few years "pay and display" meters have been put up in cities. You'll need to drop a couple of dollars' worth of coins in the meter, take the dispensed ticket, and put it in view on the dashboard of your car. The fine for running over the time for these meters runs about $12, but if you don't display your ticket at all, the fine will be at least $40 and you may risk being towed. So **carry a few coins at all times**—any denomination will usually do. Make sure to observe all "no parking" signs. If you don't, your car will almost certainly be towed away. It will cost about $100

to have the car released, and most tow companies won't accept anything but cash.

CHILDREN IN NEW ZEALAND

New Zealand may not have the high-tech theme parks of many other destinations, but the big appeal for children here is the same as it is for adults: wide, open spaces. The forests are safe to explore (there are no poisonous snakes, spiders, or even poison ivy); remote beaches have secret coves to discover; and there are lakes to kayak on and cool, clear rivers to swim in. Many city attractions are child-friendly as well, with museums adding "discovery" centers where young people can have hands-on learning experiences. These and other sights and attractions of special interest to children are highlighted in this book by a 🌀 icon. New Zealand is a safe place for children, but don't get careless. Especially around water, make sure you accompany children at all times. And like adults, children who wander off marked paths and tracks in forested or mountainous areas can get lost for a long time.

If you are renting a car, don't forget to **arrange for a car seat** when you reserve. For general advice about traveling with children, consult *Fodor's FYI: Travel with Your Baby* (available in bookstores everywhere).

BABY-SITTING

Most hotels and resorts have baby-sitters available at a charge of around $10–$15 per hour. Baby-sitting services are also listed in the yellow pages of city telephone directories.

FLYING

If your children are two or older, **ask about children's airfares.** As a general rule, infants under two not occupying a seat fly at greatly reduced fares or even for free. When booking, **confirm carry-on allowances** if you're traveling with infants. In general, for babies charged 10% of the adult fare you are allowed one carry-on bag and a collapsible stroller; if the flight is full, the stroller may have to be checked or you may be limited to less.

Experts agree that it's a good idea to use safety seats aloft for children weighing less than 40 pounds. Airlines set their own policies: U.S. carriers usually require that the child be ticketed, even if he or she is young enough to ride free, since the seats must be strapped into regular seats. Do **check your airline's policy about using safety seats during takeoff and landing.** Safety seats are not allowed everywhere in the plane, so get your seat assignments as early as possible.

When reserving, **request children's meals or a freestanding bassinet** (not available at all airlines) if you need them. But note that bulkhead seats, where you must sit to use the bassinet, may lack an overhead bin or storage space on the floor.

FOOD

New Zealand children are included in most of their parents' social activities. Children are welcome in all restaurants throughout the country. However, they are rarely seen in those restaurants that appear in Fodor's very expensive (**$$$$**) and expensive (**$$$**) price categories. These restaurants may not have high chairs or be prepared to make special children's meals.

LODGING

Most hotels in New Zealand allow children under a certain age to stay in their parents' room at no extra charge, but others charge for them as extra adults; be sure to **find out the cutoff age for children's discounts.**

In hotels, roll-away beds are usually free, but few hotels have otherseparate facilities for children.

Home hosting provides an ideal opportunity for visitors to stay with a local family, either in town or on a working farm. For information on home and farm stays, home exchange, and apartment rentals, *see* Lodging, *below.*

SIGHTS AND ATTRACTIONS

Places that are especially appealing to children are indicated by a rubber duckie icon (🐥) in the margin.

SUPPLIES AND EQUIPMENT

Baby products such as disposable diapers (ask for napkins or nappies), formula, and baby food can be found in chemists' shops (pharmacies). They are less expensive in supermarkets.

➤ STROLLER AND BASSINET RENTAL: **Royal New Zealand Plunket Society** (✉ 5 Alexis Ave., Mt. Albert, Auckland, ☎ 0800/933–922 or 09/849–5652).

COMPUTERS ON THE ROAD

Traveling with a laptop does not present any problems in New Zealand, where the electricity supply is reliable. However, you will need a converter and adapter as with other electronic equipment (☞ Electricity, *below*). It pays to **carry a spare battery and adapter,** since they're expensive and can be hard to replace.

City hotels and even provincial hotels and motels are well equipped to handle computers and modems. You may get a little stuck in family-run bed-and-breakfasts and farm stays in remote areas, but even these places will probably be able to sort something out for you.

CONSUMER PROTECTION

Whether you're shopping for gifts or purchasing travel services, **pay with a major credit card** whenever possible, so you can cancel payment or get reimbursed if there's a problem (and you can provide documentation). If you're doing business with a particular company for the first time, **contact your local Better Business Bureau and the attorney general's offices** in your state and (for U.S. businesses) the company's home state as well. Have any complaints been filed? Finally, if you're buying a package or tour, always **consider travel insurance** that includes default coverage (☞ Insurance, *below*).

➤ BBBs: **Council of Better Business Bureaus** (✉ 4200 Wilson Blvd., Suite 800, Arlington, VA 22203, ☎ 703/276–0100, FAX 703/525–8277, WEB www.bbb.org).

CRUISE TRAVEL

Auckland's bright new cruise depot, opened in 2001, reflects the upswing in the cruising industry in recent years. Since the 1990s more companies have been drawn to Auckland's superb harbor, as well as to the gorgeous scenery in places such as the Bay of Islands and Marlborough Sounds. New Zealand is now included on world cruise itineraries by vessels such as *QEII* and *The Amsterdam,* but some of the best cruising programs are those that concentrate entirely on the South Pacific and combine New Zealand with destinations such as Fiji, New Caledonia, Tonga, and Samoa. Generally, such cruises start and finish in Auckland and visit South Pacific islands in between. **P&O Holidays** operates *Pacific Sky,* which runs about six cruises out of Auckland from May to July, as well as fly-and-cruise packages out of Auckland with Sydney as the ship's departure point. The "Land of Legends" cruise covers New Zealand most thoroughly, visiting Auckland, Tauranga, Christchurch, Dunedin, and Milford Sound. Another choice is the **Holland America Line** vessel *Prinsendam,* with its 16-day cruises around New Zealand and Australia between late November and mid-February. The cruises visit eight or nine New Zealand ports, plus three or four in Australia.

To learn how to plan, choose, and book a cruise-ship voyage, consult *Fodor's FYI: Plan & Enjoy Your Cruise* (available in bookstores everywhere).

➤ CRUISE LINES: **Holland America Line** (✉ Level 2, 10 Northcote St., Takapuna, Auckland, ☎ 09/489–1363, WEB www.hollandamerica. com). **P&O Cruises** (✉ Level 11, 6B Crawley St., Ellerslie, Auckland, ☎ 0800/441–766, WEB www.pocruises. com.au).

CUSTOMS AND DUTIES

When shopping abroad, **keep receipts** for all purchases. Upon reentering the country, **be ready to show customs officials what you've bought.** If you feel a duty is incorrect, appeal the assessment. If you object to the way your clearance was handled, note the inspector's badge number. In either case, first ask to see a supervisor. If the problem isn't resolved, write to the appropriate authorities, beginning with the port director at your point of entry.

IN AUSTRALIA

Australian residents who are 18 or older may bring home A$400 worth of souvenirs and gifts (including jewelry), 250 cigarettes or 250 grams of tobacco, and 1,125 ml of alcohol (including wine, beer, and spirits). Residents under 18 may bring back A$200 worth of goods. Prohibited items include meat products. Seeds, plants, and fruits need to be declared upon arrival.

➤ INFORMATION: **Australian Customs Service** (Regional Director, ✉ Box 8, Sydney, NSW 2001; ☎ 02/9213–2000 or 1300/363263; 1800/020504 quarantine-inquiry line; FAX 02/9213–4043; WEB www.customs.gov.au).

IN CANADA

Canadian residents who have been out of Canada for at least seven days may bring in C$750 worth of goods duty-free. If you've been away fewer than seven days but more than 48 hours, the duty-free allowance drops to C$200. If your trip lasts 24 to 48 hours, the allowance is C$50. You may not pool allowances with family members. Goods claimed under the C$750 exemption may follow you by mail; those claimed under the lesser exemptions must accompany you. Alcohol and tobacco products may be included in the seven-day and 48-hour exemptions but not in the 24-hour exemption. If you meet the age requirements of the province or territory through which you reenter Canada, you may bring in, duty-free, 1.5 liters of wine *or* 1.14 liters (40 imperial ounces) of liquor *or* 24 12-ounce cans or bottles of beer or ale. If you are 19 or older you may bring in, duty-free, 200 cigarettes and 50 cigars. Check ahead of time with the Canada Customs and Revenue Agency or the Department of Agriculture for policies regarding meat products, seeds, plants, and fruits.

You may send an unlimited number of gifts (only one gift per recipient, however) worth up to C$60 each duty-free to Canada. Label the package UNSOLICITED GIFT—VALUE UNDER $60. Alcohol and tobacco are excluded.

➤ INFORMATION: **Canada Customs and Revenue Agency** (✉ 2265 St. Laurent Blvd. S, Ottawa, Ontario K1G 4K3, ☎ 204/983–3500, 506/636–5064, or 800/461–9999, WEB www.ccra-adrc. gc.ca/).

IN NEW ZEALAND

New Zealand has stringent regulations governing the import of weapons, foodstuffs, and certain plant and animal material. Anti-drug laws are strict and penalties severe. In addition to personal effects, nonresidents over 17 years of age may bring in, duty-free, 200 cigarettes or 250 grams of tobacco or 50 cigars, 4.5 liters of wine, one bottle containing not more than 1,125 ml of spirits or liqueur, and personal purchases and gifts up to the value of US$440 (NZ$700).

Don't stash any fruit in your carry-on to take into the country. The agricultural quarantine is serious business. So if you've been hiking recently and are bringing your boots with you, clean them before you pack. Since the foot-and-mouth-disease outbreak in the United Kingdom and Europe in 2000–2001, as well as terrorist attacks in the United States, airport officers have become even more vigilant and all bags coming into the country are X-rayed. The authorities for very good reason don't want any nonnative seeds haplessly transported into the country. It's a small and fragile ecosystem, and Kiwis rightfully want to protect it.

IN THE U.K.

From countries outside the European Union, including New Zealand, you may bring home, duty-free, 200 cigarettes or 50 cigars; 1 liter of spirits or 2 liters of fortified or sparkling wine or liqueurs; 2 liters of still table wine; 60 ml of perfume; 250 ml of toilet water; plus £145 worth of other goods, including gifts and souvenirs. Prohibited items include meat products, seeds, plants, and fruits.

➤ INFORMATION: **HM Customs and Excise** (✉ Portcullis House, 21 Cowbridge Rd. E, Cardiff CF11 9SS, ☎ 029/2038–6423 or 0845/010–9000, WEB www.hmce.gov.uk).

IN THE U.S.

U.S. residents who have been out of the country for at least 48 hours may bring home, for personal use, $400 worth of foreign goods duty-free, as long as they haven't used the $400 allowance or any part of it in the past 30 days. This exemption may include 1 liter of alcohol (for travelers 21 and older), 200 cigarettes, and 100 non-Cuban cigars. Family members from the same household who are traveling together may pool their $400 personal exemptions. For fewer than 48 hours, the duty-free allowance drops to $200, which may include 50 cigarettes, 10 non-Cuban cigars, and 150 ml of alcohol (or perfume containing alcohol). The $200 allowance cannot be combined with other individuals' exemptions, and if you exceed it, the full value of all the goods will be taxed. Antiques, which the U.S. Customs Service defines as objects more than 100 years old, enter duty-free, as do original works of art done entirely by hand, including paintings, drawings, and sculptures.

You may also send packages home duty-free, with a limit of one parcel per addressee per day (except alcohol or tobacco products or perfume worth more than $5). You can mail up to $200 worth of goods for personal use; label the package PERSONAL USE and attach a list of its contents and their retail value. If the package contains your used personal belongings, mark it PERSONAL GOODS RETURNED to avoid paying duties. You may send up to $100 worth of goods as a gift; mark the package UNSOLICITED GIFT. Mailed items do not affect your duty-free allowance on your return.

➤ INFORMATION: **U.S. Customs Service** (for inquiries, ✉ 1300 Pennsylvania Ave. NW, Washington, DC 20229, WEB www.customs.gov, ☎ 202/354–1000; for complaints, ✉ Customer Satisfaction Unit, 1300 Pennsylvania Ave. NW, Room 5.5A, Washington, DC 20229; for registration of equipment, ✉ Office of Passenger Programs, 1300 Pennsylvania Ave. NW, Room 5.4D, Washington, DC 20229, ☎ 202/927–0530).

DINING

The restaurants we list are the cream of the crop in each price category. Properties indicated by an ✕▣ are lodging establishments whose restaurant warrants a special trip and welcomes non-overnight guests.

Some restaurants offer a fixed-price dinner, but the majority are à la carte. It's wise to make a reservation and inquire if the restaurant has a liquor license or is "BYOB" or "BYO" (Bring Your Own Bottle)—many places have both.

Attire countrywide is pretty casual; unless you're planning to dine at the finest of places, men won't need to bring a jacket and tie. At the same time, the most common dinner attire is usually a notch above jeans and sports shirts.

MEALS AND SPECIALTIES

When in New Zealand, **try lamb.** Restaurants offer it roasted, grilled, barbecued, or almost any other way you could think of. *Cervena,* or farm-raised venison, is a local delicacy available all over New Zealand. Of course, seafood is a specialty in this island country, and one of the tastiest fish around is snapper. Orange roughy and salmon are other favorites. As for shellfish: don't miss the wonderful Bluff oysters (in season March–August), Greenshell mussels (also known as green-lipped or New Zealand green mussels), scallops, crayfish (spiny lobster), and two local clamlike shell-fish, *pipi* and *tuatua.* Whitebait (known to Māori as *inanga*), which are the juvenile of several fish species, are featured in many restaurants in the springtime. They are eaten whole, usually in an omelet-like fritter. Be sure to try *kūmara,* a local sweet potato that's sacred to the Māori. If you see *pavlova* on the dessert menu, give it a go. It's a large slice of meringue, usually stuffed with cream and garnished with fruit.

MEALTIMES

Restaurants serve breakfast roughly between 7 and 9:30. Lunch usually starts up at about noon and is over by 2. Dinners are usually served from 5 PM onward, but the most popular dining time is around 7. Restaurants in cities and resort areas will serve dinner well into the night, but some places in small towns or rural areas still shut their doors at around 9.

Unless otherwise noted, the restaurants listed in this guide are open daily for lunch and dinner.

PAYING

Credit cards are widely accepted in restaurants and even small cafés. You may find exceptions to this rule, so check first.

RESERVATIONS AND DRESS

Reservations are always a good idea; we mention them only when they're essential or not accepted. Book as far ahead as you can, and reconfirm as soon as you arrive. (Large parties should always call ahead to check the reservations policy.) We mention dress only when men are required to wear a jacket or a jacket and tie.

WINE, BEER, AND SPIRITS

New Zealand's wine industry has leaped forward over the last decade. Best known for its white wines, particularly sauvignon blanc, riesling, and chardonnay, the country is now gaining a reputation for red wines such as cabernet sauvignon, pinot noir, and merlot. The main wine-producing areas are West Auckland, Hawke's Bay, Martinborough, Marl-borough, and Nelson. Emerging regions include Canterbury and central Otago. Restaurants almost without exception feature New Zealand products on their wine list. For a rundown on New Zealand's wine industry, *see* "News from the Grapevine" *in* Chapter 4.

Only 10 or 15 years ago people ordering a beer in New Zealand had a choice of two—Lion Red or DB Draught. Now those two breweries have substantially improved their range, and small microbreweries have added to the mix. Monteith Breweries and Macs are South Island–based breweries that distribute around the country and have a strong local following. Steinlager, probably the most famous of New Zealand beers, is brewed by Lion Breweries and is widely available. Most restaurants and liquor stores sell beers from Australia, the United States, Europe, and other parts of the world.

The only spirit New Zealand can really call its own is Wilson's Whisky, distilled in Dunedin—a city with a strong Scottish heritage.

Since 1999 it has been possible to purchase beer and wine in supermarkets as well as specialized shops and to do so seven days a week. People under 18 are not permitted by law to purchase alcohol, and shops, bars, and restaurants strictly enforce this. If you look younger than you are, carry photo identification to prove your age.

DISABILITIES
AND ACCESSIBILITY

The **New Zealand Tourism Board** publishes *Access: A Guide for the Less Mobile Traveller,* listing accommodations, attractions, restaurants, and thermal pools with special facilities.

➤ LOCAL RESOURCES: **New Zealand Tourism Board** (☎ 04/472–8860, WEB www.purenz.com).

AIR TRAVEL

In addition to making arrangements for wheelchair-using passengers, **Qantas** accommodates trained dogs accompanying passengers with sight and hearing impairments. On **Air New Zealand,** wheelchairs for in-flight mobility are standard equipment; seatbelt extensions, quadriplegic harnesses, and padded leg rests are also available. Ask for the company's brochure "Air Travel for People with Disabilities."

CAR RENTAL

Budget offers cars fitted with hand controls, but these are limited. **Hertz** will fit hand-held controls onto standard cars in some cities. *See* Car Rental, *above.* **New Zealand CCS** (www.ccs.org.nz) can provide the temporary disabled parking permits needed for using specified parking places.

LODGING

In New Zealand, all accommodations are required by law to provide at least one room with facilities for guests with disabilities. Even independent lodgings with more than eight rooms should provide at least one room with such facilities. The major hotel chains provide three or four rooms with facilities for guests with disabilities in most of their properties. In Auckland, the **Crowne Plaza** and the **Carlton** are recommended, and in Rotorua, the **Royal Lakeside Novotel** is a good option.

RESERVATIONS

When discussing accessibility with an operator or reservations agent, **ask hard questions.** Are there any stairs, inside *or* out? Are there grab bars next to the toilet *and* in the shower/tub? How wide is the doorway to the room? To the bathroom? For the most extensive facilities meeting the latest legal specifications, **opt for newer accommodations.** If you reserve through a toll-free number, consider also calling the hotel's local number to confirm the information from the central reservations office. Get confirmation in writing when you can.

TAXIS

Companies have recently introduced vans equipped with hoists and floor clamps, but these should be booked several hours in advance if possible; contact the **Plunket Society** (☞ Children in New Zealand, *above*) for more information.

TRAIN TRAVEL

Passengers on mainline passenger trains in New Zealand can request collapsible wheelchairs to negotiate narrow interior corridors. However, compact toilet areas and platform-access problems make long-distance train travel difficult.

TRANSPORTATION

➤ COMPLAINTS: **Aviation Consumer Protection Division** (☞ Air Travel, *above*) for airline-related problems. **Departmental Office of Civil Rights** (for general inquiries, ✉ U.S. Department of Transportation, S-30, 400 7th St. SW, Room 10215, Washington, DC 20590, ☎ 202/366–4648, FAX 202/366–3571, WEB www.dot. gov/ost/docr/index.htm). **Disability Rights Section** (✉ NYAV, U.S. Department of Justice, Civil Rights Division, 950 Pennsylvania Ave. NW, Washington, DC 20530; ☎ ADA information line: 202/514–0301, 800/ 514–0301, 202/514–0383 TTY, 800/ 514–0383 TTY, WEB www.usdoj. gov/crt/ada/adahom1.htm).

TRAVEL AGENCIES

In the United States, the Americans with Disabilities Act requires that travel firms serve the needs of all travelers. Some agencies specialize in working with people with disabilities.

➤ TRAVELERS WITH MOBILITY PROB-
LEMS: **Access Adventures** (✉ 206
Chestnut Ridge Rd., Scottsville,
NY 14624, ☎ 716/889–9096,
dltravel@prodigy.net), run by a for-
mer physical-rehabilitation counselor.
Flying Wheels Travel (✉ 143 W.
Bridge St. [Box 382, Owatonna,
MN 55060], ☎ 507/451–5005,
FAX 507/451–1685, WEB www.
flyingwheelstravel.com).

DISCOUNTS AND DEALS

Be a smart shopper and **compare all
your options** before making decisions.
A plane ticket bought with a promotional coupon from travel clubs,
coupon books, and direct-mail offers
or purchased on the Internet may not
be cheaper than the least expensive
fare from a discount ticket agency.
And always keep in mind that what
you get is just as important as what
you save.

DISCOUNT RESERVATIONS

To save money, **look into discount
reservations services** with Web sites
and toll-free numbers, which use their
buying power to get a better price on
hotels, airline tickets, even car rentals.
When booking a room, always **call
the hotel's local toll-free number** (if
one is available) rather than the
central reservations number—you'll
often get a better price. Always ask
about special packages or corporate
rates.

When shopping for the best deal on
hotels and car rentals, **look for guaranteed exchange rates,** which protect
you against a falling dollar. With your
rate locked in, you won't pay more,
even if the price goes up in the local
currency.

➤ AIRLINE TICKETS: ☎ 800/AIR–
4LESS.

➤ HOTEL ROOMS: **Turbotrip.com**
(☎ 800/473–7829, WEB www.
turbotrip.com).

PACKAGE DEALS

Don't confuse packages and guided
tours. When you buy a package, you
travel on your own, just as though
you had planned the trip yourself.
Fly-drive packages, which combine
airfare and car rental, are often a
good deal.

ECOTOURISM

For anyone passionate about the
natural world, a journey to New
Zealand offers the chance to step
back in time to a primeval era. Isolated from other landmasses for at
least 80 million years, New Zealand
has enormous biological diversity.

Learn about local flora and fauna
with eco-sensitive tour operators from
the 100% Pure Nature network, a
group that works with Tourism New
Zealand to promote nature tourism.
These are knowledgeable tour operators who are actively involved in
conservation.

When visiting national parks, remember that you will need to pack out
your garbage.

➤ 100% NATURE ECO-TOURISM
OPERATORS: **Akaroa Harbour Cruises**
(✉ Akaroa, ☎ 03/304–7641, WEB
www.blackcat.co.nz). **Bush & Beach**
(✉ Auckland, ☎ 09/575–1458, WEB
www.bushandbeach.co.nz). **Dolphin
Discoveries** (✉ Bay of Islands, ☎ 09/
402–8234, WEB www.dolphinz.co.nz).
Guided Nature Walks (✉ Queenstown, ☎ 03/442–7126, WEB www.
nzwalks.com). **Heritage Expeditions
Ltd.** (✉ Christchurch, ☎ 03/338–
9944, WEB www.heritage-expeditions.
com). **Kiwi Dundee Adventures**
(✉ Coromandel, ☎ 07/865–8809,
WEB www.kiwidundee.co.nz). **Monarch Wildlife Cruises** (✉ Dunedin,
☎ 03/477–4276, WEB www.wildlife.
co.nz). **Mt. Bruce National Wildlife
Center** (✉ Masterton, ☎ 06/375–
8004, WEB www.mtbruce.doc.govt.nz).
Nature Connection (✉ Rotorua, ☎
07/347–1705). **Nature Guides Otago**
(✉ Dunedin, ☎ 03/454–5169, WEB
www.nznatureguides.com). **100%
Pure Nature Network** (WEB www.
purenz.com). **Otago Peninsula Trust**
(✉ Dunedin, ☎ 03/478–0497).
Penguin Place (✉ Dunedin, ☎ 03/
478–0286, WEB www.penguin-place.
co.nz). **Waimangu Valley** (✉ Rotorua,
☎ 07/366–6137, WEB www.waimangu.
com). **Whalewatch Kaikoura** (✉
Kaikoura, ☎ 03/319–5045, WEB www.
whalewatch.co.nz). **Wilderness Lodge
Arthur's Pass** (✉ Canterbury, ☎ 03/
318–9246, WEB www.wildernesslodge.
co.nz).

ELECTRICITY

To use your U.S.-purchased electric-powered equipment, **bring a converter and adapter.** If you forget to pack one, you'll find a selection on sale at duty-free shops in Auckland's airport and at electrical shops around the city. The electrical current in New Zealand is 240 volts, 50 cycles alternating current (AC); wall outlets take slanted three-prong plugs (but not the U.K. three-prong) and plugs with two flat prongs set at a "V" angle.

If your appliances are dual-voltage, you'll need only an adapter. Don't use 110-volt outlets, marked FOR SHAVERS ONLY, for high-wattage appliances such as blow-dryers. Most laptops operate equally well on 110 and 220 volts and so require only an adapter.

EMBASSIES

➤ AUSTRALIA: (✉ 72-78 Hobson St., Wellington, ☎ 04/473–6411).

➤ CANADA: (✉ 61 Molesworth St., Wellington, ☎ 04/473–9577).

➤ U.K.: (✉ 44 Hill St., Wellington, ☎ 04/472–6049).

➤ U.S.: (✉ 29 Fitzherbert Terr., Wellington, ☎ 04/472–2068).

EMERGENCIES

For either fire, police, or ambulance services, **dial 111.**

➤ CONTACTS; ☎ 111.

ETIQUETTE

Kiwis are generally friendly and accommodating, but there are a few etiquette points to keep in mind. People try to be right on time for meetings, and call ahead if they're running late. First-name usage is the norm. If you're visiting someone's house, take along a small gift. Among gestures, avoid the "V" symbol with the first two fingers with the palm facing in—an offensive vulgarity. For Māori customs, it's best not to use hongi (touching foreheads and noses) unless someone initiates it.

GAY AND LESBIAN TRAVEL

Discrimination on the grounds of sexual orientation is illegal in New Zealand, and Kiwis in general are accepting of gays and lesbians. As in North America, Britain, and Australia, gay and lesbian travelers may feel comfortable in many urban areas but might want to be more cautious in rural areas. Helpful Web sites include www.nzglta.org.nz, www.gaytourismnewzealand.com, and www.gayNZ.com. NZGLTA, for instance, posts listings for gay-friendly accommodations and events.

➤ GAY- AND LESBIAN-FRIENDLY TRAVEL AGENCIES: **Different Roads Travel** (✉ 8383 Wilshire Blvd., Suite 902, Beverly Hills, CA 90211, ☎ 323/651–5557 or 800/429–8747, FAX 323/651–3678, lgernert@tzell.com). **Kennedy Travel** (✉ 314 Jericho Turnpike, Floral Park, NY 11001, ☎ 516/352–4888 or 800/237–7433, FAX 516/354–8849, WEB www.kennedytravel.com). **Now, Voyager** (✉ 4406 18th St., San Francisco, CA 94114, ☎ 415/626–1169 or 800/255–6951, FAX 415/626–8626, WEB www.nowvoyager.com). **Skylink Travel and Tour** (✉ 1006 Mendocino Ave., Santa Rosa, CA 95401, ☎ 707/546–9888 or 800/225–5759, FAX 707/546–9891, WEB www.skylinktravel.com), serving lesbian travelers.

HEALTH

Nutrition and general health standards in New Zealand are high, and it would be hard to find a more pristine natural environment. There are no venomous snakes, and the only native poisonous spider, the *katipo,* is a rarity. The whitetail spider, an unwelcome and accidental import from Australia, packs a nasty bite and can cause discomfort but is also rarely encountered.

DIVERS' ALERT

Do not fly within 24 hours of scuba diving.

FOOD AND DRINK

One of New Zealand's rare health hazards involves its pristine-looking bodies of water; **don't drink water from natural outdoor sources.** While the country's alpine lakes might look like backdrops for mineral-water ads, some in the South Island harbor a tiny organism that can cause "duck itch," a temporary but intense skin irritation. The organism is found only on the shallow lake margins, so the chances of infection are greatly reduced if you stick to deeper water. Streams can be infected by giardia, a waterborne protozoal parasite that can cause gastrointestinal disorders, including acute diarrhea. Giardia is most likely contracted when drinking from streams that pass through an area inhabited by mammals (such as cattle or possums). There is no risk of infection if you drink from streams above the tree line.

PESTS AND OTHER HAZARDS

The major health hazard in New Zealand is sunburn or sunstroke. Even people who are not normally bothered by strong sun should cover up with a long-sleeve shirt, a hat, and pants or a beach wrap. At higher altitudes you will burn more easily, so apply sunscreen liberally before you go out—even for a half hour—and wear a visor or sunglasses.

Dehydration is another serious danger that can be easily avoided, so be sure to carry water and drink often. Limit the amount of time you spend in the sun for the first few days until you are acclimatized, and avoid sunbathing in the middle of the day.

One New Zealander you will come to loathe is the tiny black sand fly, common to the western half of South Island, which inflicts a painful bite that can itch for several days (some call it the state bird). In other parts of the country, especially around rivers and lakes, you may be pestered by mosquitoes. Be sure to use insect repellent.

HOLIDAYS

On Christmas Day, everything closes down in New Zealand except for a few gas stations, some shops selling essential food items, and emergency facilities. On other public holidays (often referred to as bank holidays) many museums and attractions will stay open, as will transportation systems, though on a reduced schedule. Local anniversary days, which vary from region to region, pop up as once-a-year three-day weekends in each particular area; some businesses close but hotels and restaurants stay open. Around Christmas and New Year's Kiwis pack up and go to the beach, so seaside resorts will be difficult to visit unless you have booked well in advance. You'll get plenty of sunshine and far fewer crowds if you visit from late January through to the colder period of late March. Cities such as Auckland and Wellington are quite pleasant over Christmas and New Year's. Fewer cars are on the road, and you'll get good prices from hotels trying to make up for the lack of corporate guests. *See* Festivals and Seasonal Events, *below,* for more information on public holidays.

INSURANCE

The most useful travel-insurance plan is a comprehensive policy that includes coverage for trip cancellation and interruption, default, trip delay, and medical expenses (with a waiver for preexisting conditions).

Without insurance you will lose all or most of your money if you cancel your trip, regardless of the reason. Default insurance covers you if your tour operator, airline, or cruise line goes out of business. Trip-delay covers expenses that arise because of bad weather or mechanical delays. Study the fine print when comparing policies.

If you're traveling internationally, a key component of travel insurance is coverage for medical bills incurred if you get sick on the road. Such expenses are not generally covered by Medicare or private policies. U.K. residents can buy a travel-insurance policy valid for most vacations taken during the year in which it's purchased (but check preexisting-condition coverage). British and Australian citizens need extra medical coverage when traveling overseas.

Always **buy travel policies directly from the insurance company**; if you buy them from a cruise line, airline, or tour operator that goes out of business you probably will not be covered for the agency or operator's default, a major risk. Before making any purchase, **review your existing health and home-owner's policies** to find what they cover away from home.

➤ TRAVEL INSURERS: In the United States: **Access America** (✉ 6600 W. Broad St., Richmond, VA 23230, ☎

800/284–8300, FAX 804/673–1491 or 800/346–9265, WEB www. accessamerica.com). **Travel Guard International** (✉ 1145 Clark St., Stevens Point, WI 54481, ☎ 715/ 345–0505 or 800/826–1300, FAX 800/ 955–8785, WEB www.travelguard. com).

➤ INSURANCE INFORMATION: In the United Kingdom: **Association of British Insurers** (✉ 51 Gresham St., London EC2V 7HQ, ☎ 020/7600–3333, FAX 020/7696–8999, WEB www. abi.org.uk). In Canada: **RBC Travel Insurance** (✉ 6880 Financial Dr., Mississauga, Ontario L5N 7Y5, ☎ 905/791–8700 or 800/668–4342, FAX 905/813–4704, WEB www. rbcinsurance.com). In Australia: **Insurance Council of Australia** (✉ Level 3, 56 Pitt St., Sydney, NSW 2000, ☎ 02/9253–5100, FAX 02/ 9253–5111, WEB www.ica.com.au). In New Zealand: **Insurance Council of New Zealand** (✉ Level 7, 111–115 Customhouse Quay [Box 474, Wellington], ☎ 04/472–5230, FAX 04/ 473–3011, WEB www.icnz.org.nz).

LANGUAGE

To an outsider's ear, Kiwi English can be mystifying. Even more so, the Māori (pronounced *moh*-ree) language has added to the New Zealand lexicon words that can seem utterly unpronounceable. It is still spoken by many New Zealanders of Polynesian descent, but English is the everyday language for all people. A number of Māori words have found their way into common usage, most noticeably in place-names, which often refer to peculiar features of the local geography or food supply. The Māori word for New Zealand, Aotearoa, means "land of the long white cloud." The South Island town of Kaikoura is famous for its crayfish—the word means "to eat crayfish." Whangapiro (fang-ah-*pee*-ro), the Māori name for the Government Gardens in Rotorua, means "an evil-smelling place," and if you visit the town you'll find out why. A Polynesian word you'll sometimes come across in Māori churches is *tapu* ("sacred"), which has entered the English language as the word "taboo." Another Māori word you will frequently encounter is *Pākehā*, which means you, the non-Māori.

The Māori greeting is *kia ora*, which can also mean "good-bye," "good health," or "good luck." *See* the Kiwi and Māori glossaries *in* Chapter 7.

LODGING

The **New Zealand Tourism Board** (☞ Visitor Information, *below*) publishes an annual "Where to Stay" directory listing more than 1,000 properties.

The lodgings we list are the cream of the crop in each price category. We always list the facilities that are available—but we don't specify whether they cost extra: when pricing accommodations, always ask what's included and what costs extra. Properties are assigned price categories based on the range from their least-expensive standard double room at high season (excluding holidays) to the most expensive. All rooms listed have private bath unless otherwise noted.

Assume that hotels operate on the **European Plan** (EP, with no meals) unless we specify that they use the **Continental Plan** (CP, with a Continental breakfast), **Breakfast Plan** (BP, with a full breakfast), **Modified American Plan** (MAP, with breakfast and dinner), or the **Full American Plan** (FAP, with all meals).

Properties marked ✕🏨 are lodging establishments whose restaurants warrant a special trip and welcome non-overnight guests.

BED-AND-BREAKFASTS

There are some helpful resources on the Web for researching and booking bed-and-breakfast choices. On Web sites such as those maintained by SelectionsNZ and Jasons Travel Media, you'll find hundreds of listings and advertisements for bed-and-breakfasts throughout the country.

Once in New Zealand you will find the *New Zealand Bed and Breakfast Book* in most major bookstores. It lists about 1,000 bed-and-breakfasts, but be aware that the editorial copy in the book has been provided by the property owners themselves, rather than providing independent assessments as this Fodor's guide does.

➤ CONTACTS: **Jasons Travel Media** (WEB www.jasons.com). **SelectionsNZ** (www.selections.co.nz).

CAMPING

There are more than 950 backcountry huts in New Zealand. They provide basic shelter but few frills. Huts are usually placed about four hours apart, although in isolated areas it can take a full day to get from one hut to the next. They are graded 1 to 4, and cost varies from nothing to $14 per person per night. Category 1 huts (the $14 ones) have cooking equipment and fuel, bunks or sleeping platforms with mattresses, toilets, washing facilities, and a supply of water. At the other end of the scale, Category 4 huts (the free ones) are simple shelters without bunks or other facilities. Pay for huts with coupons, available in books from Department of Conservation (DOC) offices. If you plan to make extensive use of huts, an annual pass giving access to all Category 2 and 3 huts for one year is available for $65.

In addition to the huts, the DOC runs more than 250 campsites on protected lands. These range from campgrounds with hot showers, flush toilets, and powered sites to bare-bones spots. Rates run between $2 and $10 a night. For more information on huts and campgrounds, contact the appropriate regional DOC bureau.

➤ CONTACT: **Department of Conservation** (WEB www.doc.govt.nz).

HOME AND FARM STAYS

Home and farm stays, which are very popular with visitors to New Zealand, offer not only comfortable accommodations but a chance to get to know the countryside and its people—a great thing to do because Kiwis are so naturally friendly. Most operate on a bed-and-breakfast basis, though some also offer an evening meal. Farm accommodations vary from modest shearers' cabins to elegant homesteads. Guests can join in farm activities or explore the countryside. Some hosts offer day trips, as well as horseback riding, hiking, and fishing. For two people, the average cost is $90–$150 per night, including all meals. (See "Farm Stays and Rural New Zealand" in Chapter 5 for more information on farm stays.) Home stays, the urban equivalent of farm stays, are less

expensive. Most New Zealanders seem to have vacation homes, called *baches* on North Island, *cribs* on South Island, and these are frequently available for rent.

➤ CONTACT: **Homestay NZ Ltd.** (✉ Box 25–115, Auckland, ☎ 09/411–9166).

HOSTELS

No matter what your age, you can **save on lodging costs by staying at hostels.** In some 4,500 locations in more than 70 countries around the world, Hostelling International (HI), the umbrella group for a number of national youth-hostel associations, offers single-sex, dorm-style beds and, at many hostels, rooms for couples and family accommodations. Membership in any HI national hostel association, open to travelers of all ages, allows you to stay in HI-affiliated hostels at member rates; one-year membership is about $25 for adults (C$35 for a two-year minimum membership in Canada, £13 in the United Kingdom, A$52 in Australia, and NZ$40 in New Zealand); hostels run about $10–$30 per night. Members have priority if the hostel is full; they're also eligible for discounts around the world, even on rail and bus travel in some countries.

In addition to the International Youth Hostels, a network of low-cost, independent backpacker hostels operates in New Zealand. They can be found in nearly every city and tourist spot, and they offer clean, twin- and small-dormitory-style accommodations and self-catering kitchens, similar to those of the Youth Hostel Association (or YHA, the Australian version of IYH), with no membership required.

Qualmark, New Zealand's official tourism quality assurance company, has added ratings for backpacker hostels. Backpacker lodgings are given one- to five-star ratings. As this is Qualmark's newest category the coverage is not yet comprehensive, but reviews are being steadily compiled. You can check ratings on the company's Web site, www.qualmark.co.nz.

➤ ORGANIZATIONS: **Hostelling International—American Youth Hostels** (✉ 733 15th St. NW, Suite 840,

Washington, DC 20005, ☎ 202/783–6161, FAX 202/783–6171, WEB www.hiayh.org). **Hostelling International—Canada** (✉ 400–205 Catherine St., Ottawa, Ontario K2P 1C3, ☎ 613/237–7884 or 800/663–5777, FAX 613/237–7868, WEB www.hihostels.ca). **Youth Hostel Association of England and Wales** (✉ Trevelyan House, Dimple Rd., Matlock, Derbyshire DE4 3YH, U.K., ☎ 0870/870–8808, FAX 0169/592–702, WEB www.yha.org.uk). **Youth Hostel Association Australia** (✉ 10 Mallett St., Camperdown, NSW 2050, ☎ 02/9565–1699, FAX 02/9565–1325, WEB www.yha.com.au). **Youth Hostels Association of New Zealand** (✉ Level 3, 193 Cashel St. [Box 436, Christchurch], ☎ 03/379–9970, FAX 03/365–4476, WEB www.yha.org.nz).

HOTELS

When looking up hotel information, you'll often see a reference to Qualmark, New Zealand's official tourism quality assurance agency. Qualmark grades hotels on a one- to five-star rating system; participation is voluntary. These ratings are generally fair gauges of each property's cleanliness and security. You can check a hotel's Qualmark rating on the Web site www.qualmark.co.nz.

➤ TOLL-FREE NUMBERS: **Best Western** (☎ 800/528–1234, WEB www.bestwestern.com). **Choice** (☎ 800/424–6423, WEB www.choicehotels.com). **Holiday Inn** (☎ 800/465–4329, WEB www.sixcontinentshotels.com).

MOTELS

Motels are the most common accommodations, and most offer comfortable rooms for $70–$120 per night. Some motels have two-bedroom suites for families. All motel rooms come equipped with tea- and coffee-making equipment; many have toasters or electric frying pans and full kitchen facilities. Air-conditioning is rare in small-town or rural motels.

MOTOR CAMPS

The least expensive accommodations in the country are the tourist cabins and flats in most of the country's 400 motor camps. Tourist cabins offer basic accommodation and shared cooking, laundry, and bathroom facilities. Bedding and towels are not provided. A notch higher up the comfort scale, tourist flats usually provide bedding, fully equipped kitchens, and private bathrooms. Overnight rates run about $6–$20 for cabins and $25–$70 for flats.

SPORTING LODGES

At the high end of the price scale, a growing number of luxury sporting lodges offer the best of country life, fine dining, and superb accommodations. Fishing is a specialty at many of them, but there is usually a range of outdoor activities for nonanglers. Tariffs run about $350–$800 per day for two people; meals are generally included.

MAIL AND SHIPPING

Airmail should take around six or seven days to reach the United Kingdom or the United States and two or three days to reach Australia.

OVERNIGHT SERVICES

Overnight services are available between New Zealand and Australia, but to destinations farther afield "overnight" will in reality be closer to 48 hours. Even to Australia, truly overnight service is only offered between major cities and can be subject to conditions, such as the time you call in. A number of major operators are represented in New Zealand and the services are reliable, particularly from cities.

➤ MAJOR SERVICES: **DHL World Express** (✉ corner of Hope and Lawrence Stevens Dr., Mangere, ☎ 09/976–2800 or 0800/800–020, WEB www.dhl.co.nz). **Federal Express** (✉ Airport Freight Centre, Auckland Airport, ☎ 0800/733–339, WEB www.fedex.com). **TNT International Express** (✉ 1 Joseph Hammond Pl., Mangere, ☎ 09/255–0500, WEB www.tnt.com).

POSTAL RATES

Post offices are open weekdays 9–5. The cost of mailing a letter within New Zealand is 40¢ standard post, 90¢ fast post. Sending a standard-size letter by airmail costs $1.50 to North America, $1.80 to Europe, and $1 to Australia. Aerograms and postcards are $1 to any overseas destination.

RECEIVING MAIL

If you wish to receive correspondence, have mail sent to New Zealand held for you for up to one month at the central post office in any town or city if it is addressed to you "c/o Poste Restante, CPO," followed by the name of the town. This service is free; you may need to show ID.

SHIPPING PARCELS

You can use the major international overnight companies listed above or purchase packaging and prepaid mail services from the post office. Major duty-free stores and stores that deal frequently with travelers will be able to help with international shipping, but if you purchase from small shops, particularly in country areas, **arrange shipping with a company in the nearest city.**

MEDIA

New Zealand has its share of scandal sheets and gossip magazines, but in general the standard of journalism is high. Because it is a small and isolated country, you'll find the interest in international news greater than you may expect. Any major stories coming out of the United States and the United Kingdom—or major sports events around the world—are likely to receive full coverage.

NEWSPAPERS AND MAGAZINES

There are daily metropolitan newspapers in all cities (two in Wellington), smaller local dailies in provincial towns, and many community and local papers. The *New Zealand Herald* is the daily with the country's largest circulation. Although it has a distinctly Auckland slant to it, the *Herald* does a good job on national and international news. The *Dominion Post* is Wellington's morning paper and is the best source for the nation's political events. In Christchurch, the *Press* is highly regarded. On Sunday the *Sunday Star Times* and the *Sunday News* vie for readership; both are available nationally.

The country has a massive array of locally published magazines—there are more local magazine titles per capita than in any other country in the world.

Women's Weekly, Women's Day, and *New Idea* will keep you current with royal scandals from Britain and who's doing what to whom among the local celebrities. For more serious reading, pick up a copy of *North & South* (monthly) or *Listener* (weekly). Both have in-depth articles on issues facing New Zealand. The monthly *Metro* magazine is slightly more lighthearted and concentrates on Auckland issues. *Pavement,* another monthly, pitches to the hip.

RADIO AND TELEVISION

For news, views, and talk back (talk radio) try Newstalk ZB at AM 1080, and for sports coverage (including American sports events in the middle of the night New Zealand time) tune to AM 1332. There's a good array of music stations. For the latest hits, go to the ZM network (FM 91 in Auckland).

New Zealand has four main television channels: TV 1, 2, 3, and 4, plus other free channels (Prime and Triangle) that you'll find in main centers. Channels 1 and 3 have news at 6 PM. Channels 2 and 4 are targeted at the youth market, and this is where you'll find popular U.S. programs.

Most hotels have Sky TV, including the news channel that takes a feed from CNN.

MONEY MATTERS

For most travelers, New Zealand is not an expensive destination. The cost of meals, accommodation, and travel is slightly higher than in the United States but considerably less than in Western Europe. At about $1 per liter—equal to about US$2.10 per gallon—premium-grade gasoline is expensive by North American standards but not by European ones.

The following were sample costs in New Zealand at press time:

Cup of coffee, $2.50; glass of beer in a bar, $2.50–$4; take-out ham sandwich or meat pie, $2.50; hamburger in a café, $5–$8; room-service sandwich in a hotel, $12; a 2-km (1-mi) taxi ride, $5.

Prices throughout this guide are given for adults. Substantially reduced fees are almost always available for children, students, and senior citizens. For information on taxes, *see* Taxes, *below.*

ATMS

ATMs are widely found in city and town banks and in some shopping malls. The number of ATMs is growing all the time. All the major banks in New Zealand (Bank of New Zealand, Westpac, and Auckland Savings Bank) accept cards in the Cirrus and Plus networks. The norm for PINs in New Zealand is four digits. If the PIN for your account has a different number of digits, you must **change your number before you leave for New Zealand.**

CREDIT CARDS

Throughout this guide, the following abbreviations are used: **AE,** American Express; **DC,** Diners Club; **MC,** MasterCard; and **V,** Visa.

➤ REPORTING LOST CARDS: **American Express** (☎ 09/367–4247 or 0800/ 263–936). **Diners Club** (☎ 09/359–7797). **MasterCard** (☎ 0800/449–140).**Visa** (☎ 0800/445–594).

CURRENCY

All prices quoted in this guide are in New Zealand dollars.

New Zealand's unit of currency is the dollar, divided into 100 cents. Bills are in $100, $50, $10, and $5 denominations. Coins are $2, $1, 50¢, 20¢, 10¢, and 5¢. At press time the rate of exchange was NZ$2.17 to the U.S. dollar, NZ$1.46 to the Canadian dollar, NZ$3.26 to the pound sterling, and NZ$1.27 to the Australian dollar. Exchange rates change on a daily basis.

CURRENCY EXCHANGE

For the most favorable rates, **change money through banks.** Although ATM transaction fees may be higher abroad than at home, ATM rates are excellent because they are based on wholesale rates offered only by major banks. You won't do as well at exchange booths in airports or rail and bus stations, in hotels, in restaurants, or in stores. To avoid lines at airport exchange booths, **get a bit of local currency before you leave home.**

➤ EXCHANGE SERVICES: **International Currency Express** (☎ 888/278–6628

orders). **Thomas Cook Currency Services** (☎ 800/287–7362 orders and retail locations, WEB www.us. thomascook.com).

TRAVELER'S CHECKS

Do you need traveler's checks? It depends on where you're headed. If you're going to rural areas and small towns, go with cash; traveler's checks are best used in cities. Lost or stolen checks can usually be replaced within 24 hours. To ensure a speedy refund, buy your own traveler's checks—don't let someone else pay for them: irregularities like this can cause delays. The person who bought the checks should make the call to request a refund.

OUTDOORS AND SPORTS

As if prompted by the thrilling extremes of its landscape, New Zealanders have pushed the envelope of extreme sports and adventures. If you want to bungy jump off a bridge, speed close to rocks in a jet-boat, or brave rapids with nothing but a bodyboard, you'll be able to try it here. Queenstown gets the lion's share of attention for its extreme-sports outfitters, but there are plenty of opportunities all over the country. For information on tamer guided bicycling, cross-country skiing, diving, fishing, hiking, horseback riding, rafting, sailing, and sea-kayaking tours and tour operators, *see* Chapter 6. To find links to all kinds of sports organizations, including team sports, hit the Web site www.sportnz.co.nz.

FISHING

Wherever you fish, and whatever you fish for, you will profit immensely from the services of a local guide. On Lake Taupo or Rotorua, a boat with a guide plus all equipment will cost around $150 for two hours. In South Island, a top fishing guide who can supply all equipment and a four-wheel-drive vehicle will charge about $400 per day for two people. In the Bay of Islands region, an evening fishing trip aboard a small boat can cost as little as $45. For a big-game fishing boat, expect to pay between $600 and $1,000 per day. There are also several specialist lodges that provide guides and transport to wilderness streams sometimes accessible only by helicopter. Note that while you can bring clean fishing gear with you, you cannot bring home-made flies into the country. The New Zealand Fish and Game Council Web site, www.fishandgame.org.nz, has thorough guidelines, along with information for experts, beginners, and everyone in between.

GOLF

Generally speaking, clubs can be rented, but you'll need your own shoes. Greens fees range from $10 at country courses to $60 at exclusive city courses. The better urban courses also offer resident professionals and golf carts for rent.

➤ CONTACT: **NZ Golf Association** (✉ Box 11–842, Wellington, WEB www.nzga.co.nz).

HIKING

There are hiking trails of all kinds and grades of difficulty in New Zealand, helpfully grouped by the Department of Conservation. The nine Great Walks are the cream of the crop; they go through the country's most spectacular scenery and take at least two or three days. Kiwi Walks are shorter walks on well-maintained tracks, suitable for most ages and fitness levels. Heritage Walks visit points of historical interest identified by local communities. DOC Walk-ways are generally relatively easy and tend to be close to urban centers.

The traditional way to hike in New Zealand is freedom walking. Freedom walkers carry their own provisions, sleeping bags, food, and cooking gear and sleep in basic huts. A more re-fined alternative—usually available only on more popular trails—is the guided walk, on which you trek with just a light day pack, guides do the cooking, and you sleep in heated lodges. If you prefer your wilderness served with hot showers and an eiderdown on your bed, the guided walk is for you.

If you plan to walk the spectacular Milford or Routeburn Track in De-cember or January, book at least six months in advance. At other times, three months is usually sufficient. (If you arrive without a booking, there may be last-minute cancellations, and parties of one or two can often be accommodated.) The Milford Track is closed due to snowfall from the end of April to early September.

Plan your clothing and footwear carefully. Even at the height of sum-mer weather can change quickly, and hikers must be prepared—especially for the rainstorms that regularly drench the Southern Alps. (The Mil-ford Sound region, with its average annual rainfall of 160 inches, is one of the wettest places on earth.) The most cost-effective rain gear you can buy is the U.S. Army poncho.

Wear a hat and sunglasses and put on sunblock to protect your skin against the sun. Keep in mind that at higher altitudes, where the air is thinner, you will burn more easily. Sun reflected off of snow, sand, or water can be especially strong. Apply sunscreen liberally before you go out—even if only for a half hour.

Also, be careful about heatstroke. Symptoms include headache, dizzi-ness, and fatigue, which can turn into convulsions and unconsciousness and can lead to death. If someone in your party develops signs of heatstroke, have one person seek emergency help while others move the victim into the shade, and wrap him or her in wet clothing (is a stream or lake nearby?) to cool him or her down.

Temperatures can vary widely from day to night. Be sure to bring enough warm clothing for hiking and camp-ing, along with wet-weather gear. Exposure to the degree that body temperature dips below 35°C (95°F) produces the following symptoms: chills, tiredness, then uncontrollable shivering and irrational behavior, with the victim not always recogniz-ing that he or she is cold. If someone in your party is suffering from any of this, wrap him or her in blankets and/or a warm sleeping bag immedi-ately and try to keep him or her awake. The fastest way to raise body temperature is through skin-to-skin contact in a sleeping bag. Drinking warm liquids also helps.

Avoid drinking from streams or lakes, no matter how clear they may be. Giardia organisms can turn your stomach inside out. And in South

Island a tiny organism found on the shallow margins of lakes can cause "duck itch," a temporary but intense skin irritation. The easiest way to purify water is to dissolve a water purification tablet in it. Camping equipment stores also carry purification pumps. Boiling water for 15 minutes is always a reliable method, if time- and fuel-consuming.

For information on camping, *see* Lodging, *above.*

PACKING

In New Zealand, be prepared for temperatures varying from day to night and weather that can turn suddenly, particularly at the change of seasons. The wisest approach to dressing is to wear layered outfits. You'll appreciate being able to remove or put on a jacket. Take along a light raincoat and umbrella, but remember that plastic raincoats and nonbreathing polyester are uncomfortable in the tropics. Don't wear lotions or perfume in the tropics either, since they attract mosquitoes and other bugs; carry insect repellent. Bring a hat with a brim to provide protection from the strong sunlight (☞ Health, *above*) and sunglasses for either summer or winter; the glare on glaciers can be intense. You'll need warm clothing for South Island; a windbreaker is a good idea wherever you plan to be.

Dress is casual in most cities, though top resorts and restaurants may require a jacket and tie. In autumn, a light wool sweater and/or a jacket will suffice for evenings in coastal cities, but winter demands a heavier coat—a raincoat with a zip-out wool lining is ideal. Comfortable walking shoes are a must. You should have a pair of running shoes or the equivalent if you're planning to trek, and rubber-sole sandals or canvas shoes are needed for walking on reef coral.

In your carry-on luggage, **pack an extra pair of eyeglasses or contact lenses and enough of any medication** you take to last a few days longer than the entire trip. You may also ask your doctor to write a spare prescription using the drug's generic name, since brand names may vary from country to country. In luggage to be checked, **never pack prescription drugs or valuables.** And don't forget to carry with you the addresses of offices that handle refunds of lost traveler's checks. Check *Fodor's How to Pack* (available in bookstores everywhere) for more tips.

To avoid customs and security delays, carry medications in their original packaging. Don't pack any sharp objects in your carry-on luggage, including knives of any size or material, scissors, manicure tools, and corkscrews, or anything else that might arouse suspicion.

CHECKING LUGGAGE

You are allowed one carry-on bag and one personal article, such as a purse or a laptop computer. Make sure that everything you carry aboard will fit under your seat or in the overhead bin. Get to the gate early, so you can board as soon as possible, before the overhead bins fill up.

If you are flying internationally, note that baggage allowances may be determined not by piece but by weight—generally 88 pounds (40 kilograms) in first class, 66 pounds (30 kilograms) in business class, and 44 pounds (20 kilograms) in economy.

Airline liability for baggage is limited to $2,500 per person on flights within the United States. On international flights it amounts to $9.07 per pound or $20 per kilogram for checked baggage (roughly $640 per 70-pound bag) and $400 per passenger for unchecked baggage. You can buy additional coverage at check-in for about $10 per $1,000 of coverage, but it excludes a rather extensive list of items, shown on your airline ticket.

Before departure, **itemize your bags' contents** and their worth, and label the bags with your name, address, and phone number. (If you use your home address, cover it so potential thieves can't see it readily.) Inside each bag, **pack a copy of your itinerary.** At check-in, **make sure that each bag is correctly tagged** with the destination airport's three-letter code. If your bags arrive damaged or fail to arrive at all, file a written report with the airline before leaving the airport.

PASSPORTS AND VISAS

When traveling internationally, **carry your passport** even if you don't need one (it's always the best form of ID) and **make two photocopies of the data page** (one for someone at home and another for you, carried separately from your passport). If you lose your passport, promptly call the nearest embassy or consulate and the local police.

U.S. passport applications for children under age 14 require consent from both parents or legal guardians; both parents must appear together to sign the application. If only one parent appears, he or she must submit a written statement from the other parent authorizing passport issuance for the child. A parent with sole authority must present evidence of it when applying; acceptable documentation includes the child's certified birth certificate listing only the applying parent, a court order specifically permitting this parent's travel with the child, or a death certificate for the non-applying parent. Application forms and instructions are available on the Web site of the U.S. State Department's Bureau of Consular Affairs (www.travel.state.gov).

ENTERING NEW ZEALAND

U.S., Canadian, and U.K. citizens need only a valid passport to enter New Zealand for stays of up to 90 days.

PASSPORT OFFICES

The best time to apply for a passport or to renew is in fall and winter. Before any trip, **check your passport's expiration date,** and, if necessary, renew it as soon as possible.

➤ AUSTRALIAN CITIZENS: **Australian State Passport Office** (☎ 131–232, WEB www.passports.gov.au).

➤ CANADIAN CITIZENS: **Passport Office** (to mail in applications: ✉ Department of Foreign Affairs and International Trade, Ottawa, Ontario K1A 0G3; ☎ 800/567–6868 toll-free in Canada; 819/994–3500; WEB www.dfait-maeci.gc.ca/passport).

➤ U.K. CITIZENS: **London Passport Office** (☎ 0870/521–0410, WEB www.passport.gov.uk).

➤ U.S. CITIZENS: **National Passport Information Center** (☎ 900/225–5674, 35¢ per minute for automated service or $1.05 per minute for operator service, WEB www.travel.state.gov).

REST ROOMS

Shopping malls in cities, major bus and train stations, gas stations, and many rest areas on main highways have public toilets. Look for a blue sign with white figures (ladies and gents) for directions to a public toilet. New Zealanders often use the word "loo."

Most New Zealand public rest-room facilities are clean and tidy and often have a separate room for mothers with young children.

Some gas stations, shops, and hotels have signs stating that only customers can use the rest room. Kiwis are generally fair-minded folk, so if you're genuinely caught short and explain the situation you will probably not be turned away.

Most gas stations in New Zealand have toilet facilities, but their standard is variable. As a rule of thumb, the newer and more impressive the gas station, the cleaner and better the toilet facilities.

SAFETY

New Zealand is safe for travelers, but international visitors have been known to get into trouble when they take their safety for granted and let their guard down. Use common sense, particularly if walking around cities at night. Stick around other people and avoid deserted alleys. Although New Zealand is an affluent society by world standards, it has its share of poor and homeless (often referred to as "street kids" if they are young). Avoid bus and train stations or city squares late at night. The crowds in some pubs can get a bit rough late at night, so if you sense irritation, leave.

Hotels offer safes for guests' valuables, and it pays to use them. Don't flash your wealth, and remember to lock doors of hotel rooms and cars. Unfortunately, opportunist criminals stake out parking lots at some popular tourist attractions. Put valuables out of sight under seats before you arrive at the destination.

If traveling in the countryside, you're safer as a couple. Remember, most visitors have no trouble and find the New Zealand people among the friendliest in the world. Nine times out of ten, offers of help or other friendly gestures will be genuine.

WOMEN IN NEW ZEALAND

Women will not attract more un-wanted attention than in most other Western societies, nor will they be immune from the usual hassles. In cities at night, stick to well-lit areas and avoid being totally alone. Hotel staff will be happy to give tips on any areas to avoid, and the times to avoid them. New Zealand is relatively safe for women, but don't be complacent.

Don't wear a money belt or a waist pack, both of which peg you as a tourist. If you carry a purse, choose one with a zipper and a thick strap that you can drape across your body; adjust the length so that the purse sits in front of you at or above hip level. Store only enough money in the purse to cover casual spending. Distribute the rest of your cash and any valu-ables (including credit cards and your passport) between a deep front pocket, an inside jacket or vest pocket, and a hidden money pouch. Do not reach for the money pouch once in public.

SENIOR-CITIZEN TRAVEL

To qualify for age-related discounts, **mention your senior-citizen status up front** when booking hotel reservations (not when checking out) and before you're seated in restaurants (not when paying the bill). Be sure to have identification on hand. When renting a car, ask about promotional car-rental discounts, which can be cheaper than senior-citizen rates.

➤ EDUCATIONAL PROGRAMS: Elderhos-tel (✉ 11 Ave. de Lafayette, Boston, MA 02111-1746, ☎ 877/426–8056, FAX 877/426–2166, WEB www. elderhostel.org).

SHOPPING

New Zealand is not widely regarded as a shopping destination for tourists. However, the state of the Kiwi dollar at press time means that visitors from the United States and Europe will find plenty of bargains. Duty-free shopping is particularly good, and at Auckland International Airport you'll find prices to rival anywhere else in the world. Most cities and towns have outdoor markets at least once a week. You'll often find local arts and crafts at these, as well as secondhand clothing and assorted knickknacks. Ask at local visitor information centers for dates, times, and locations of markets.

If you have a car and want to meet Kiwis in a slightly unusual way, pick up a Friday-morning newspaper and look in the classified ads for Satur-day- and Sunday-morning garage sales. Sometimes you'll find five or six garage sales in the space of a few suburban miles—especially in places west and south of Auckland. Some of your fellow buyers will be "profes-sionals" who pick up bargains and resell them in secondhand stores; others are just people out looking for a good deal.

New Zealand shops have set prices, but you'll be able to bargain a bit in antiques and secondhand stores, or markets. Don't expect to be able to knock more than a few dollars off the stated price though. A "toi iho Māori Made Mark" label indicates that the product was made by Māori.

KEY DESTINATIONS

Aucklanders shop in their suburbs, and a number of these have developed excellent shopping centers. Among the best are St. Lukes, Lynmall (New Lynn), Onehunga, and Manukau City. The most accessible shopping district in Auckland is Queen Street. Wellington's Lambton Quay has a comprehensive selection of shops. Christchurch has shops stretching off in all directions from Cathedral Square, and Dunedin's best shops are around the Octagon.

SMART SOUVENIRS

A rugby jersey, especially for the All Black team, can look more fashion-able than it sounds. Expect to pay about $100.

A bottle of sauvignon blanc from the Marlborough District, particularly the attractively labeled Cloudy Bay, is a tasty souvenir and will cost between $20 and $30. It's fun to buy from the vineyard, but you can also buy New Zealand wine at general stores and in city wine shops.

Greenstone (jade) is available in tourist and souvenir shops. It's beautiful stone and is best when carved and polished. Prices vary greatly depending on the size and quality of the item.

WATCH OUT

Buy a sheepskin rug if you must, but don't do it from an inner-city souvenir shop unless you want to pay more than its worth. Look at a few shops before making a decision. New Zealand tourist shops have taken to selling toy koalas. They're adorable, so buy one if it makes you happy, but they have absolutely nothing to do with New Zealand. You won't even find koalas in the zoos here because the leaves they eat grow widely only in Australia. A much more appropriate choice, if you are buying for kids, is a fluffy toy kiwi bird.

SIGHTSEEING GUIDES

At some tourist attractions around Rotorua local boys will offer their services as guides. Negotiate the price at a few dollars and they will probably add a bit of color to your experience. Still, you'll find out much more about the place if you hire an official guide through a visitor information center.

STUDENTS IN NEW ZEALAND

Many attractions and activities in New Zealand offer discounts to students holding a current academic identification card. Students holding a New Zealand Travelpass (☞ Air Travel, *above*) can save 50% on the normal economy-class domestic airfare with Air New Zealand. The drawback is that such tickets are on a standby basis.

A couple of New Zealand's larger universities have good student Web sites with useful links. Check out Auckland University's student association site, www.ausa.org.nz, or University of Canterbury's www.ucsa. canterbury.ac.nz.

➤ IDs AND SERVICES: **STA Travel** (☎ 212/627–3111 or 800/781–4040,

FAX 212/627–3387, WEB www.sta. com). **Travel Cuts** (✉ 187 College St., Toronto, Ontario M5T 1P7, ☎ 416/ 979–2406 or 888/838–2887, FAX 416/ 979–8167, WEB www.travelcuts.com).

TAXES

AIRPORT

Visitors exiting New Zealand must pay a departure tax of $22.

VALUE-ADDED TAX

A goods and services tax (GST) of 12.5% is levied throughout New Zealand. It's usually incorporated into the cost of an item, but in some hotels and some restaurants it is added to the bill.

TELEPHONES

AREA AND COUNTRY CODES

The country code for New Zealand is 64. When dialing from abroad, drop the initial "0" from the local area code. Main area codes within New Zealand include 09 (Auckland and the North), 04 (Wellington), and 03 (South Island). Dialing from New Zealand to back home, the country code is 1 for the United States and Canada, 61 for Australia, and 44 for the United Kingdom. The prefixes 0800 and 0867 are used for toll-free numbers.

CELLULAR PHONE RENTALS

Cell phones can be rented at Auckland, Wellington and Christchurch airports, starting at $5 a day. Look for a Vodafone stand at the arrival area of each airport. Prior reservations are a good idea, though not absolutely necessary.

➤ CONTACT: **Vodaphone** (☎ 09/275– 8154, WEB www.vodarent.co.nz).

DIRECTORY AND OPERATOR ASSISTANCE

Dial 018 for New Zealand directory assistance. For international numbers, dial 0172. To call the operator, dial 010; for international operator assistance, dial 0170. To find phone numbers within New Zealand on-line go to www.whitepages.co.nz.

INTERNATIONAL CALLS

To make international calls directly, dial 00, then the international access code, area code, and number required.

LONG-DISTANCE SERVICES

AT&T, MCI, and Sprint access codes make calling long distance relatively convenient, but you may find the local access number blocked in many hotel rooms. First ask the hotel operator to connect you. If the hotel operator balks, ask for an international operator, or dial the international operator yourself. One way to improve your odds of getting connected to your long-distance carrier is to travel with more than one company's calling card (a hotel may block Sprint, for example, but not MCI). If all else fails, call from a pay phone.

➤ ACCESS CODES: **AT&T Direct** (☎ 000–911). **MCI WorldPhone** (☎ 000–912). **Sprint International Access** (☎ 000–913).

PUBLIC PHONES

Most pay phones now accept PhoneCards or major credit cards rather than coins. PhoneCards, available in denominations of $5, $10, $20, or $50, are sold at shops displaying the green PhoneCard symbol. To use a PhoneCard, lift the receiver, put the card in the slot in the front of the phone, and dial. The cost of the call is automatically deducted from your card; the display on the telephone tells you how much credit you have left at the end of the call. A local call from a public phone costs 20¢ per minute. Don't forget to take your PhoneCard with you when you finish your call. You may end up making some very expensive calls by leaving it behind.

TIME

Trying to figure out just what time it is in New Zealand can get dizzying, especially because of cross-hemisphere daylight saving times and multi-time-zone countries. Without daylight saving times, Auckland is 17 hours ahead of New York; 18 hours ahead of Chicago and Dallas; 20 hours ahead (or count back 4 hours and add a day) of Los Angeles; 12 hours ahead of London; and 2 hours ahead of Sydney.

From Canada and the States, **call New Zealand after 5 PM.** From the United Kingdom or Europe, it isn't quite as complicated: call early in the morning or very late at night. When faxing, it's usually not a problem to ring discreet fax numbers at any time of day.

TIPPING

Tipping is not as widely practiced in New Zealand as in the United States or Europe but many city restaurants and hotels now expect you to show your appreciation for good service with a 10% tip.

Taxi drivers will appreciate rounding up the fare to the nearest $5 amount, but don't feel you have to do this. Porters will be happy with a $1 or $2 coin. Most other people, like bartenders, theater attendants, gas station attendants, or barbers, will probably wonder what you are doing if you try to give them a tip.

TOURS AND PACKAGES

Because everything is prearranged on a prepackaged tour or independent vacation, you'll spend less time planning—and often get it all at a good price.

BOOKING WITH AN AGENT

Travel agents are excellent resources. But it's a good idea to collect brochures from several agencies, as some agents' suggestions may be influenced by relationships with tour and package firms that reward them for volume sales. If you have a special interest, **find an agent with expertise in that area**; the American Society of Travel Agents (ASTA; ☞ Travel Agencies, *below*) has a database of specialists worldwide.

Make sure your travel agent knows the accommodations and other services of the place being recommended. Ask about the hotel's location, room size, beds, and whether it has a pool, room service, or programs for children, if you care about these. Has your agent been there in person or sent others whom you can contact?

Do some homework on your own, too: local tourism boards can provide information about lesser-known and small-niche operators, some of which may sell only direct.

BUYER BEWARE

Each year consumers are stranded or lose their money when tour operators—even large ones with excellent reputations—go out of business. So **check out the operator.** Ask several travel agents about its reputation, and try to **book with a company that has a consumer-protection program.** (Look for information in the company's brochure.) In the United States, members of the National Tour Association and the United States Tour Operators Association are required to set aside funds to cover your payments and travel arrangements in the event that the company defaults. It's also a good idea to choose a company that participates in the American Society of Travel Agents' Tour Operator Program (TOP); ASTA will act as mediator in any disputes between you and your tour operator.

Remember that the more your package or tour includes the better you can predict the ultimate cost of your vacation. Make sure you know exactly what is covered, and **beware of hidden costs.** Are taxes, tips, and transfers included? Entertainment and excursions? These can add up.

➤ TOUR-OPERATOR RECOMMENDATIONS: **American Society of Travel Agents** (☞ Travel Agencies, *below*). **National Tour Association** (NTA; ✉ 546 E. Main St., Lexington, KY 40508, ☎ 859/226–4444 or 800/682–8886, WEB www.ntaonline.com). **United States Tour Operators Association** (USTOA; ✉ 275 Madison Ave., Suite 2014, New York, NY 10016, ☎ 212/599–6599 or 800/468–7862, FAX 212/599–6744, WEB www.ustoa.com).

TRAIN TRAVEL

New Zealand's Tranz Scenic trains travel, as a rule, north and south along the main trunk of New Zealand. If you want to crisscross the country, then you'll have to abandon the country's rail network. There are some exceptions, most notably the famous Tranz-Alpine Express, a spectacular scenic ride across Arthur's Pass and the mountainous spine of South Island between Greymouth and Christchurch.

Even the most popular services tend to run only once daily. They do leave and arrive on time as a rule. Trains have one class, and they have standard, comfortable seats, and a basic food service offering light meals, snacks, beer, wine, and spirits. Special meals (diabetic/wheat free/vegetarian) can be arranged, but you have to order at least 48 hours before you board the train. Most carriages have large windows from which to view the spectacular passing scenery, and some routes have a commentary on points of interest. Most trains also have a special viewing carriage at the rear.

CUTTING COSTS

To save money, **look into rail passes.** But be aware that if you don't plan to cover many miles you may come out ahead by buying individual tickets.

It's worth looking into Air New Zealand's South Pacific Pass fares; you can snag discounted rates for flights within New Zealand, but these must be prebooked from outside the country. Travelers can purchase a New Zealand Travelpass for unlimited travel by train, bus, and Interislander ferry for a variety of periods. For Youth Hostel Association members, the InterCity Youth Hostel Travel Card ($75 for 14 days, $99 for 28 days) gives a 30% discount on most train service, all InterCity coach service, and on Interislander ferries. Students with an International Student Identity Card (ISIC) get a 20% discount. Senior citizens (over 60) get a 30% discount with proof of age.

➤ BUYING PASSES: **ATS Tours** (☎ 310/643–0044 or 800/423–2880 in the U.S., WEB www.atstours.com). **InterCity Travel Centres** (☎ 09/639–0500 in Auckland; 03/379–9020 in Christchurch; 04/472–5111 in Wellington).

FARES AND SCHEDULES

You can obtain both schedules and tickets at visitor information centers and at train stations.

➤ TRAIN INFORMATION: **Tranz Scenic** (☎ 0800/802–802, WEB www.tranzscenic.co.nz).

PAYING

Major credit cards are accepted, as are cash and traveler's checks.

RESERVATIONS

Reservations are advised, particularly in the summer months. **Book at least 48 hours in advance.**

TRANSPORTATION
AROUND NEW ZEALAND

Trains provide a relaxing mode of travel in New Zealand but stick very much to the beaten track and have limited schedules. Buses cover the country far more extensively and depart more frequently (especially from main centers). If you really want to see New Zealand properly you'll have to grit your teeth and be prepared to drive on the left side of the road. Even so, it is a good idea to combine driving with some scenic public transport and tour opportunities, such as a ferry trip on the Auckland Harbour or the journey across the Southern Alps by train.

TRAVEL AGENCIES

A good travel agent puts your needs first. Look for an agency that has been in business at least five years, emphasizes customer service, and has someone on staff who specializes in your destination. In addition, **make sure the agency belongs to a professional trade organization.** The American Society of Travel Agents (ASTA)—the largest and most influential in the field with more than 24,000 members in some 140 countries—maintains and enforces a strict code of ethics and will step in to help mediate any agent-client disputes involving ASTA members if necessary. ASTA (whose motto is "Without a travel agent, you're on your own") also maintains a Web site that includes a directory of agents. (If a travel agency is also acting as your tour operator, *see* Buyer Beware *in* Tours and Packages, *above*.)

➤ LOCAL AGENT REFERRALS: American Society of Travel Agents (ASTA; ✉ 1101 King St., Suite 200, Alexandria, VA 22314, ☎ 800/965–2782 24-hr hot line, FAX 703/739–3268, WEB www.astanet.com). Association of British Travel Agents (✉ 68–71 Newman St., London W1T 3AH, ☎ 020/7637–2444, FAX 020/7637–0713, WEB www.abtanet.com). Association of Canadian Travel Agents (✉ 130 Albert St., Suite 1705, Ottawa, Ontario K1P 5G4, ☎ 613/237–3657, FAX 613/237–7052, WEB www.acta.ca). Australian Federation of Travel Agents (✉ Level 3, 309 Pitt St., Sydney, NSW 2000, ☎ 02/9264–3299, FAX 02/9264–1085, WEB www. afta.com.au). Travel Agents' Association of New Zealand (✉ Level 5, Tourism and Travel House, 79 Boulcott St. [Box 1888, Wellington 6001], ☎ 04/499–0104, FAX 04/499–0827, WEB www.taanz.org.nz).

VISITOR INFORMATION

➤ NEW ZEALAND TOURISM BOARD: In the United States (✉ 501 Santa Monica Blvd., Los Angeles, CA 90401, ☎ 310/395–7480 or 800/388–5494, FAX 310/395–5454, WEB www.purenz.com). In Canada (✉ 888 Dunsmuir St., Suite 1200, Vancouver, BC V6C 3K4, ☎ 800/888–5494, FAX 604/684–1265). In the United Kingdom (✉ New Zealand House, Haymarket, London SW1Y 4TQ, ☎ 020/7930–1662, FAX 020/7839–8929).

➤ U.S. GOVERNMENT ADVISORIES: U.S. Department of State (✉ Overseas Citizens Services Office, Room 4811, 2201 C St. NW, Washington, DC 20520, ☎ 202/647–5225 interactive hot line or 888/407–4747, WEB www.travel.state.gov); enclose a business-size SASE.

WEB SITES

Do check out the World Wide Web when planning your trip. You'll find everything from weather forecasts to virtual tours of famous cities. Be sure to **visit Fodors.com** (www.fodors.com), a complete travel-planning site. You can research prices and book plane tickets, hotel rooms, rental cars, vacation packages, and more. In addition, you can post your pressing questions in the "Travel Talk" section. Other planning tools include a currency converter and weather reports, and there are loads of links to travel resources.

Tourism New Zealand's site, www.purenz.com, includes city and regional overviews as well as features such as travel journals, information on major events like the America's Cup, and cultural background. If you have an interest in a specific facet of New Zealand life, a little Web browsing should turn up relevant sources. **Wine OnLine** (www.wineonline.co.nz), for instance, posts updates on some of the country's top wineries, while **NZ Gardens Net** (www.

gardens.net.nz) cultivates information on New Zealand's public and private gardens. At www.maori.org.nz, of **Māori Organisations of New Zealand,** you can find answers to cultural FAQs.

For detailed information on New Zealand's wilderness areas, visit the **Department of Conservation'**s site, www.doc.govt.nz, which covers all the national parks, major walking tracks, campgrounds and huts, safety tips, and so forth. **Snowco** (www.snow.co.nz) provides country-wide snow reports; the **New Zealand Alpine Club** (www.nzalpine.org.nz) focuses on all kinds of climbing. To get up to speed on the all-consuming rugby news, check out the **New Zealand Rugby Union'**s www.nzrugby.co.nz or the comprehensive **Planet Rugby** at www.planet-rugby.com.

WHEN TO GO

New Zealand is in the southern hemisphere, which means that seasons are reversed—it's winter down under during the American and European summer. The ideal months for comfortable all-round travel are October–April, especially if you want to participate in adventure activities. Avoid school holidays, when highways may be congested and accommodation is likely to be scarce and more expensive. Summer school holidays (the busiest) fall between mid-December and the end of January; other holiday periods are mid-May to the end of May, early July to mid-July, and late August to mid-September.

CLIMATE

Climate in New Zealand varies from subtropical in the north to temperate in the south. Summer (December–March) is generally warm, with an average of seven to eight hours of sunshine per day throughout the country. Winter (June–September) is mild at lower altitudes in South Island, but heavy snowfalls are common in South Island, particularly on the peaks of the Southern Alps. Strong southerly winds bring a blast of Antarctica. Rain can pour at any time of the year. (Some areas on the west coast of South Island receive an annual rainfall of more than 100 inches.)

The following are average daily maximum and minimum temperatures for some major cities in New Zealand.

➤ FORECASTS: **Weather Channel Connection** (☎ 900/932–8437), 95¢ per minute from a Touch-Tone phone.

AUCKLAND

Jan.	74F	23C	May	63F	17C	Sept.	61F	16C
	61	16		52	11		49	9
Feb.	74F	23C	June	58F	14C	Oct.	63F	17C
	61	16		49	9		52	11
Mar.	72F	22C	July	56F	13C	Nov.	67F	19C
	59	15		47	8		54	12
Apr.	67F	19C	Aug.	58F	14C	Dec.	70F	21C
	56	13		47	8		58	14

CHRISTCHURCH

Jan.	70F	21C	May	56F	13C	Sept.	58F	14C
	54	12		40	4		40	4
Feb.	70F	21C	June	52F	11C	Oct.	63F	17C
	54	12		36	2		45	7
Mar.	67F	19C	July	50F	10C	Nov.	67F	19C
	50	10		36	2		47	8
Apr.	63F	17C	Aug.	52F	11C	Dec.	70F	21C
	45	7		36	2		52	11

QUEENSTOWN

Jan.	72F	22C	May	52F	11C	Sept.	56F	13C
	49	9		36	2		38	3
Feb.	70F	21C	June	47F	8C	Oct.	61F	16C
	50	10		34	1		41	5
Mar.	67F	19C	July	46F	8C	Nov.	65F	18C
	47	8		34	− 1		45	7
Apr.	61F	16C	Aug.	50F	10C	Dec.	70F	21C
	43	6		34	1		49	9

FESTIVALS AND SEASONAL EVENTS

Sport features heavily in New Zealand's festival calendar. Horse and boat races, triathlons, and fishing competitions are far more prominent than celebrations of the arts. Just about every town holds a yearly agricultural and pastoral (A and P) show, and these proud displays of local crafts, produce, livestock, and wood-chopping and sheep-shearing prowess provide a memorable look at rural New Zealand. An annual calendar, *New Zealand Special Events,* is available from government tourist offices.

➤ DEC. 25–26: On **Christmas Day** and **Boxing Day** the country virtually closes down.

➤ JAN. 1: **New Year's Day** is a nationwide holiday.

➤ LAST MON. IN JAN.: For the **Auckland Anniversary Day Regatta** (☎ 09/979–7070), Auckland's birthday party, the City of Sails takes to the water.

➤ MID-FEB.: The **Festival of Romance** (☎ 03/379–9629) is held in Christchurch—the city where lovers can stroll through an old English garden and enjoy a punt ride on the Avon River.

➤ FEB. 6: **Waitangi Day,** New Zealand's national day, commemorates the signing of the Treaty of Waitangi between Europeans and Māori in 1840. The focus of the celebration is, naturally enough, the town of Waitangi in the Bay of Islands.

➤ FEB. 7–8: **Speights Coast to Coast** (☎ 03/326–5493, WEB www. coasttocoast.co.nz) is the ultimate iron-man challenge—a two-day, 238-km (148-mi) marathon of cycling, running, and kayaking that crosses South Island from west to east.

➤ FEB. 8–9: **The Devonport Food and Wine Festival** (☎ 09/446–0685, WEB www.devonportwinefestival.co.nz) showcases some of the country's best restaurants and is easily reached by a ferry trip from Auckland city.

➤ MID-FEB.: Christchurch's **Garden City Festival of Flowers** (☎ 03/379–9629, WEB www.festivalofflowers.co.nz), the country's largest flower show, finds the city bursting with blossoms and activity, with plenty of related events, displays, and exhibitions.

➤ LATE FEB.: Napier's **Art Deco Weekend** (☎ 06/835–1191, WEB www.hb.co.nz/artdeco/weekend/) celebrates the city's style with house tours, vintage car displays, and more.

➤ FEB. 26: The **Pacifika Festival** (☎ 09/979–7070) highlights the many Pacific Island cultures found in Auckland with plenty of color, music, and dance. The main activity is at Western Springs lakeside, near the Auckland Zoo. The festival is extremely popular and crowded, so don't try to find parking. Check local newspapers for special bus services on the day.

➤ 1ST THURS.–SAT. OF MAR.: **Golden Shears International Shearing Championship** (☎ 06/378–7373, WEB www.wairarapanz.com) is a three-day event that pits men armed with shears against the fleecy sheep in Masterton, north of Wellington.

➤ EARLY MAR.: Screw up your courage to try some unusual bush tucker like grubs and "Westcargots" (local snails) at Hokitika's **Wildfoods Festival** (☎ 03/755–8321).

➤ MID-MAR.: Most people take the wine tasting along the route of the **Martinborough Round the Vines Fun Run** (☎ 06/306–8228, WEB www.roundthevines.martinborough.co.nz.) much more seriously than the running. Fancy dress is not compulsory, but you'll feel far more part of the proceedings if you at least wear a funny hat.

➤ LATE MAR.: Auckland's **Round the Bays Run** (☎ 09/979–7070) is one of the world's largest 10-km (6-mi) fun runs. A few people take it seriously, but thousands of others run, walk, or ride about the course in their own time. The run starts in the city, follows Tamaki Drive around the waterfront, and finishes in the plush suburb of St. Heliers.

➤ LATE MAR.: About 30 hot-air balloons from around the world take part in the **Genesis Wairarapa International Balloon Festival** (☎ 04/473–8044, WEB www.wairarapanz.com). The event finishes with a night glow in Masterton's Solway Showgrounds.

➤ MAR. OR APR.: The **Easter** holiday weekend lasts from Good Friday through Easter Monday. Dates change each year and generally fall in March or April. The **Royal Easter Show** (☎ 09/638–9969) is held in Auckland over the holiday.

➤ LATE APR.: The **Bluff Oyster and Southland Seafood Festival** (☎ 0800/768–843, WEB www.bluffoysterfest.co.nz) stars the local specialty, the Bluff oyster.

➤ APR. 25: **Anzac Day** honors the soldiers, sailors, and airmen and women who fought and died for the country. This public holiday is marked by dawn parades around the country.

➤ EARLY MAY: The **Fletcher Marathon** (☎ 07/348–5179) around Lake Rotorua is New Zealand's premier long-distance event.

➤ 1ST MON. IN JUNE: The **Queen's Birthday** is celebrated nationwide.

➤ MID- TO LATE JULY: At the **Queenstown Winter Festival** (☎ 03/442–5746, WEB www.winterfestival.co.nz) the winter-sports capital hits the slopes for a week of competition by day and entertainment by night.

➤ MID-SEPT.: Tickets to Nelson's free-spirited **Montana World of Wearable Art Awards** (☎ 03/548–3083, WEB www.worldofwearableart.com) sell like hotcakes.

➤ OCT. 31–NOV. 3: **Dunedin Rhododendron Festival** (☎ 03/474–3300) opens the city's gardens for tours and offers lectures and plant sales.

➤ OCT. 23: **Labour Day** is observed throughout the country.

➤ LATE OCT.–EARLY NOV.: **Taranaki Rhododendron Festival** (☎ 0800/809–050, WEB www.rhodo.co.nz) in and around New Plymouth is a major event. One hundred–plus private gardens are open to the public, there are lectures, and the vast Pukeiti Rhododendron Trust holds a series of cultural events and festivities.

➤ 2ND WEEK IN NOV.: The **Canterbury Agricultural and Pastoral Show** (☎ 03/379–9629, WEB www.bethere.org.nz) spotlights the farmers and graziers of the rich countryside surrounding Christchurch.

➤ 2ND WEEKEND IN NOV.: The city of Blenheim's **Garden Marlborough** (☎ 03/577–5523) has local garden tours and a fête with products for sale. The festival follows Auckland's Ellerslie Flower Show, which gives the international experts who attended the Auckland event time to get to South Island and give excellent lectures and workshops.

➤ LATE NOV.: **Ellerslie Flower Show** (☎ 09/309–7875, WEB www.ellerslieflowershow.co.nz) in Auckland is one of the headline events on New Zealand's gardening calendar. It is modeled on London's Chelsea Flower Show. In a confusing twist, the show moved from the suburb of Ellerslie to the Botanic Gardens at Manurewa, farther south, while retaining its old name.

1 DESTINATION: NEW ZEALAND

The Eden Down Under

What's Where

Pleasures and Pastimes

Fodor's Choice

THE EDEN DOWN UNDER

FIRST LAID EYES on New Zealand in 1967, near the end of an ocean voyage from Los Angeles to Australia. For a long morning, we skirted the New Zealand coastline north of Auckland, slipping past a land of impossibly green hills that seemed to be populated entirely by sheep. When the ship berthed in Auckland, I saw parked along the quay a museum-quality collection of vintage British automobiles, the newest of which was probably 15 years old. The explanation was simple enough: the alternative would be new imports, and imports were taxed at an enormous rate. But to a teenager fresh from the U.S.A., it seemed as though we had entered a time warp. When we took a day tour into the hills, the bus driver kept stopping for chats with other drivers; in those days it seemed possible to know everyone in New Zealand.

Since then, Auckland has caught up with the rest of the world. Its cars, its cellular-phone-toting execs, its waterfront restaurants with sushi and French mineral water all exist, unmistakably, in the 21st century. Yet the countryside still belongs to a greener, cleaner, friendlier time. Nostalgia is a strong suit in New Zealand's deck—second, of course, to its incomparable scenery. You'll still find people clinging sentimentally to their Morris Minors, Wolseley 1300s, VW Beetles, or Austin Cambridges—even though inexpensive used Japanese imports have flooded the market in recent years. So if you travel in search of glamorous shopping, sophisticated nightlife, and gourmet pleasures, this may not be the place for you. For some of New Zealand's most notable cultural achievements have been made in conjunction with nature—in the spectacular displays of its gardens, the growing reputation of its wineries, the fascinating lives and artifacts of the Māori (pronounced *moh*-ree), even the respect for nature shown in its current ecotourism boom. Auckland, Christchurch, and Wellington may never rival New York, Paris, or Rome, but that's probably not why you're considering a trip to New Zealand. And when you are in the cities, you're likely to find just as much warmth, calm, and graciousness as you will in rural areas.

Humanity was a late arrival to New Zealand. Its first settlers were Polynesians who reached its shores about AD 850, followed by a second wave of Polynesian migrants in the 14th century. These were not carefree, grass-skirted islanders living in a palmy utopia but a fierce, martial people who made their homes in hilltop fortresses, where they existed in an almost continual state of warfare with neighboring tribes. That fierceness turned out to ensure them more respect from the *Pākehā*—the Māori word for Europeans—than that received by many other native groups around the world in their encounters with colonial powers. The first Europeans to come across New Zealand were on board the Dutch ships of explorer Abel Tasman, which anchored in Golden Bay atop the South Island on December 16, 1642. Miscommunication with a local Māori group the next day resulted in the death of four Europeans. The famous Captain James Cook was the next to explore New Zealand, in the 18th century, but it wasn't until the 1840s that European settlers, primarily from England, arrived in numbers.

Compared with other modern immigrant societies such as the United States and Australia, New Zealand is overwhelmingly British—in its love of gardens, its architecture, its political system, and its food. Even so, changes are afoot. Momentum is gathering toward New Zealand's becoming a republic, though it would undoubtedly remain within the British Commonwealth. In 1993, the country held a referendum that threw out the "first past the post" electoral system inherited from Westminster, adopting instead a mixed-member proportional election, the first of which was held in 1996. This means that each voter now casts two votes, one for a local representative and the other for the party of his or her choice. To govern, a party (or combination of parties) must have at least 50% of the actual vote—not just 50% of parliamentary seats. So rather than being dominated by just two strong parties, with various minor political entities filling out the numbers, New Zealand is now governed by party coalitions.

The Māori remain an assertive minority of 9%, a dignified, robust people whose oral tradition and art bear witness to a rich culture of legends and dreams. That culture comes dramatically to life in performances of songs and dances, including the *haka,* or war dance, which was calculated to intimidate and demoralize the enemy. It's little wonder that the national rugby team performs a haka as a prelude to its games. It would be a mistake, however, to feel that the Māori people's place in New Zealand is confined to history and cultural performances for tourists. They are having considerable impact in a modern political sense, reclaiming lost rights to land, fisheries, and other resources. You'll see Māori who are prominent television newscasters, literary figures, government members, and major athletes, at the same time keeping their cultural traditions alive.

The New Zealand landmass consists of two principal islands, with other outlying islands as well. Most of the country's 3.42 million people live on the North Island, while the South Island has the lion's share of the national parks (more than one-tenth of the total area has been set aside as park land). In a country about the size of Colorado—or just slightly larger than Great Britain—nature has assembled active volcanoes, subtropical rain forests, geysers, streams now filled with some of the finest trout on earth, fjords, beaches, glaciers, and some two dozen peaks that soar to more than 10,000 ft. The country has spectacular scenery from top to bottom, but while the North Island often resembles a pristine, if radically hilly, golf course, the South Island is wild, majestic, and exhilarating.

Experiencing these wonders is painless. New Zealand has a well-developed infrastructure of hotels, motels, and tour operators—but the best the country has to offer can't be seen through the windows of a tour bus. A trip here is a hands-on experience: hike, boat, fish, hunt, cycle, raft, and breathe some of the freshest air on earth. If these adventures sound a little too intrepid for you, the sheer beauty of the landscape and the clarity of the air will give you muscles you never knew you had.

— Michael Gebicki

WHAT'S WHERE

New Zealand consists of three main islands: the North Island (44,197 square mi), the South Island (58,170 square mi), and Stewart Island (676 square mi). There are also Antarctic islands and the Chatham Islands, some 800 km (500 mi) east of Christchurch in the South Pacific. If New Zealand were stretched out along the west coast of the United States, the country would extend from Los Angeles to Seattle. No point is more than 112 km (70 mi) from the sea, and owing to the narrow, hilly nature of the country, rivers tend to be short, swift, and broad.

About 3,737,000 people live on the islands of New Zealand, and population density is very low. It is less than half that of the United States (with all of its open land in the west) and about 5% of the United Kingdom. New Zealanders are very friendly people—they seem to go out of their way to be hospitable. Some would argue that the low population takes away many of the stresses that people in more densely occupied areas experience. True or not, you're likely to be charmed by Kiwi hospitality.

More than 70% of the total population lives on the North Island, where industry and government are concentrated. The South Island is dominated by the Southern Alps, a spine of mountains running almost two-thirds the length of the island close to the West Coast.

North Island
The mighty 1,200-year-old kauri (*cow*-ree) trees, ferny subtropical forests, and miles of island-strewn coastline of Northland and the Coromandel Peninsula are a perfect foil for the bustle and sprawl of Auckland, New Zealand's largest city. Mid-island, sulfuric Rotorua bubbles and oozes with surreal volcanic activity. It is one of the population centers of New Zealand's pre-European inhabitants, the Māori—try dining at one of their *hāngi* (a traditional feast). Great hiking abounds in a variety of national parks, while glorious gardens grow in the rich soil of the Taranaki Province. Charming, art deco Napier and the nation's cosmopolitan capital, Wellington, make friendly counterpoints to the countryside.

South Island

Natural wonders never cease—not on the South Island. Nor do the opportunities for adventure: sea-kayaking, glacier hiking, trekking, fishing, mountain biking, rafting, bungy jumping, and rock climbing. If you'd rather have an easier feast for your senses, fly over brilliant glaciers and snowy peaks, watch whales from on deck, and taste some of Marlborough's delicious wine. South of urbane Christchurch you'll head straight into picture-postcard New Zealand, where the country's tallest mountains are reflected in crystal-clear lakes and sheer rock faces tower above the fjords. You can enjoy some of the world's most dramatic views in complete peace and quiet, or leap—literally, if you'd like—from one adrenaline rush to the next. Take the four-day Milford Track walk or another less-touristed but still spectacular track. Or opt for the remote isolation of pristine Stewart Island. Add New Zealand hospitality to all of that, and you can't go wrong.

PLEASURES AND PASTIMES

As much as or more than any other country's residents, New Zealanders love sports—professional, amateur, and any variety of weekend sports. You'll see a number of them listed below. If you are interested in a particular adventure activity, be sure to consult Chapter 6 for specific guided trips. If you want to do it yourself, Chapter 6 can also point out desirable regions where you can strike out on your own.

Beaches

The list of unique and outstanding New Zealand beaches is almost endless—including the dramatic Karekare Beach in West Auckland shown in Jane Campion's film *The Piano*. There are no private beaches and no risks from pollution. The greatest danger is sunburn and, in some cases, strong currents.

Most New Zealanders prefer beaches along the east coast of the North Island, where the combination of gentle seas and balmy summers is a powerful attraction during January holidays. Sand on the west coast of the North Island is black as a result of volcanic activity.

South Island beaches are no less spectacular, particularly those in the northwest in Abel Tasman National Park and down the west coast. In summer popular beaches close to cities and in major holiday areas are patrolled by lifeguards. Swim with caution on unpatrolled beaches.

Bicycling

Despite its often precipitous topography, New Zealand is great for biking. A temperate climate, excellent roads with relatively little traffic, and scenic variety make it a delight for anyone who is reasonably fit and has time to travel slowly. The most common problem for cyclists is buckled wheel rims: narrow, lightweight alloy rims won't stand up long to the rigors of the road. A wide-rimmed hybrid or mountain bike with road tires is a better bet for extensive touring.

If two-wheel touring sounds appealing but pedaling a heavily laden bicycle doesn't, consider a guided cycle tour. Tours last from 2 to 18 days; bikes are supplied, and your gear is loaded on a bus or trailer that follows the riders. And you have the option of busing in the "sag wagon" when your legs give out.

Boating

The country's premier cruising regions are the Bay of Islands, Auckland's Hauraki Gulf, Marlborough Sounds, and the coast around Abel Tasman National Park, near the northern tips of North and South Islands, respectively. Both areas have sheltered waters, marvelous scenery, and secluded beaches. The Bay of Islands enjoys warmer summer temperatures, while Marlborough Sounds has a wild, untamed quality. Both areas have opportunities for sea-kayaking as well.

In Auckland, the City of Sails, it is easy to rent a yacht and go out bareboat for the day or to hire a skipper along with the vessel. Keen and experienced "yachties" could even try turning up at a yacht club along Westhaven Drive and asking if anyone is looking for crew that day. If you want a less active role, there are ferries and cruise boats with half- and full-day trips around Auckland's Hauraki Gulf and its islands.

The Whanganui River, flowing from the western slopes of Mt. Tongariro on the North Island to meet the sea at the west-coast town of Whanganui, is New Zealand's premier canoeing river. The longest navigable waterway in the country, this captivating river winds through native bushland with occasional rapids, cascades, and gorges. The most popular canoe trip begins at Taumarunui, taking four to five days to get downstream to Pipriki. Do this in warmer months, between November and March.

For thrills and spills, white-water rafting on the Shotover River near Queenstown is hard to beat. For something challenging in the North Island, the Kaituna River near Rotorua has the highest commercially rafted waterfall in the southern hemisphere.

Country Life

In New Zealand rural settings are never far away from even the largest cities. To really get a taste of Kiwi life, don't confine your stay to tourist spots, towns, and cities. Many farms are open to visitors, either for a day visit or an overnight stay. You are usually welcome to try your hand at milking a cow or taking part in other activities. *See* Essential Information for information on farm stays.

Another way to get insight into the rural scene is to attend an agricultural and pastoral (A and P) fair. These are held at various times of the year by communities large and small, but the best time to see them is during summer. Check at information centers to find out where the nearest show is being held during your stay. These events are an opportunity for farmers to bring their chickens, cattle, goats, sheep, and other stock into town and compete for ribbons. The farmers are only too happy to chat about their live exhibits to anyone who will ask. A and P shows are great for kids, who are usually welcome to pat and stroke the animals. Other favorites include wood-chopping contests, sheep shearing, and crafts displays. One tip: many of these shows go on for two or three days, one of which is declared a local holiday so that families in the area can attend. If possible, avoid such times and go on quieter days.

Dining

Old New Zealand, new New Zealand—what you'll find culinarily on your trip spans the centuries, from traditional farmers' fare to very contemporary preparations. Auckland, Wellington, Christchurch, and Dunedin offer cosmopolitan dining, and an ever-expanding roster of restaurateurs are opening high-caliber places elsewhere in the country. That said, much country cooking still follows the meat-and-two-veg school of English cuisine. The number of vineyards with noteworthy cafés or restaurants continues to grow; at these establishments, meals are carefully paired with the wine.

The waters around New Zealand are some of the cleanest in the world, so local seafood is sensational. The New Zealand crayfish, essentially a clawless lobster, is delicious, and succulent white-shelled Bluff oysters, available from March to about July, are rated highly by aficionados. Watch for orange roughy, a delicate white-fleshed fish best served with a light sauce. And don't miss *pipi* (clams), scallops (with delicious roe in spring), green-lipped mussels, *paua* (abalone) with their iridescent shells, the small seasonal fish called whitebait (usually served in fritters), and very fine freshwater eel.

Back on land, lamb and venison are widely available, and many chefs are preparing exciting dishes using *cervena,* a leaner, lighter deer raised on farms. The *kūmara* (koo-mer-ah) is a tasty, yellow-fleshed sweet potato that the Māori brought with them from Polynesia. It grows in warmer North Island soil. Don't confuse entrées with main courses—entrées are part of the appetizer course that comes before the main course. Pudding generally speaking is dessert, and one New Zealand favorite is *pavlova,* also called pav, a white meringue pie named after ballerina Anna Pavlova.

A native specialty is the *hāngi,* a Maori feast of steamed meat and vegetables. Tour operators can take you to a hāngi at a Maori *marae* (meetinghouse). Several hotels in Rotorua offer a hāngi, usually combined with an evening of Māori song and dance. Unfortunately, these days it's often unlikely that food will be cooked by steaming it in the traditional earthen oven.

For inexpensive lunches, the standard takeout is meat pies and fish-and-chips. But keep in mind that there are more and more contemporary cafés and ethnic restaurants opening up in unexpected places. Occasionally, you'll also find good vegetarian restaurants. Most country pubs serve reasonable cooked lunches and sometimes a selection of salads. In season, stock up on fruit from roadside stalls that are scattered throughout the country's fruit-growing areas.

Fishing

Considering that trout were introduced from California little more than a hundred years ago, today's population of these fish in New Zealand's lakes and rivers is phenomenal. One reason for this is that commercial trout fishing is illegal, which means you won't find trout on restaurant menus. You can, however, bring your own catch for a chef to prepare.

Getting back to fishing, the average summer rainbow trout taken from Lake Tarawera, near Rotorua, weighs 5 pounds, and 8- to 10-pound fish are not unusual. In the North Island lakes, fingerlings often reach a weight of 4 pounds nine months after they are released. Trout do not reach maturity until they grow to 14 inches, and all trout below that length must be returned to the water.

Trout fishing has a distinctly different character on the two islands. In the Rotorua-Taupo region of the North Island, the main quarry is rainbow trout, which are usually taken from the lakes with wet flies or spinners. Trolling is also popular and productive. On the South Island, where brown trout predominate, there is outstanding dry-fly fishing. It's best in the Nelson region and in the Southern Lakes district, at the top and bottom ends of the South Island, respectively. Trout season lasts from October through April in most areas, though Lakes Taupo and Rotorua are open all year.

Salmon are found in rivers that drain the eastern slopes of the Southern Alps, especially those that reach the sea between Christchurch and Dunedin. Salmon season runs from October to April, reaching its peak from January to March.

The seas off the North Island's east coast are among the world's finest big-game fishing waters. The quarry is mako, hammerhead, tiger shark, and marlin—especially striped marlin, which average around 250 pounds. For light tackle fishing, bonito and skipjack tuna and *kahawai* (sea trout) offer excellent sport. Many anglers maintain that kahawai are better fighters, pound for pound, than freshwater trout. Bases for big-game fishing are the towns of Paihia

and Russell, which have a number of established charter operators. The season runs from January to April, although smaller game fishing is good all year.

You need a license to fish in New Zealand's rivers, lakes, and streams. You can purchase these in sports shops, fishing guides, tourist offices, and other outlets around the country. No license is necessary for sea and ocean fishing. *See* Chapter 6 for more fishing information.

Glorious Gardens

New Zealand is rapidly becoming a major destination for garden lovers on vacation. Since the first British settlers arrived with seeds from their homeland, Kiwis have looked toward Great Britain for horticultural inspiration. However, as in other parts of the world, gardeners here are discovering the unique beauty of their native plants and are gradually welcoming them into their gardens, successfully mixing them with exotics and creating a look that couldn't be achieved anywhere else.

So while northern hemisphere gardens are dormant for the winter, head to New Zealand to see nature in full bloom. The climate couldn't be more accommodating to the plant life, with cool summers, mild winters, and abundant rainfall. The rich, spongy, alluvial soil readily absorbs the rain, and with few stresses, plants respond by growing to enormous proportions. Trees are taller, flowers more abundant, perfumes stronger.

Equally delightful are the gardeners themselves—a large part of the population that appears to include all economic and social groups. In true New Zealand fashion, they're enthusiastic, hospitable, and only too glad to show off their hearts' delights. As a result, hundreds of private gardens, in addition to public gardens, are open to visitors. Check local papers and tourist offices for seasonal garden tours and shows. With the foresight of a phone call, not only can a beautiful garden be visited, but a passion can be shared—an exchange that makes the world feel like a smaller, friendlier place.

Golf

Most of New Zealand's hundreds of courses welcome visitors, and you'll find the options to be of an extremely high standard, such as Titirangi, Formosa, Gulf

Harbour, and Millbrook. However, keen golfers should also take the time to enjoy a country course, where the main hazards include sheep droppings and friendly locals who will keep you chatting until the sun goes down if you let them. With a little bit of effort you can find courses in spectacular settings, with greens fees of $20 or less. (For more isolated courses, ask whether you'll need to bring your own clubs and bag.) You can play year-round; winter is the major season.

Hiking

If you want to see the best of what New Zealand has to offer, put on a pair of hiking boots and head for the bush—the Kiwi word for the great outdoors. Range upon range of mountains; deep, ice-carved valleys; wilderness areas that have never been farmed, logged, or grazed; and a first-class network of marked trails and tramping huts are just some of the reasons that bushwalking (read: hiking) is a national addiction.

The traditional way to hike in New Zealand is freedom walking. Freedom walkers carry their own provisions, sleeping bags, food, and cooking gear and sleep in basic huts. A more refined alternative—usually available only on more popular trails—is the guided walk, on which you trek with just a light day pack, guides do the cooking, and you sleep in heated lodges. If you prefer your wilderness served with hot showers and an eiderdown on your bed, the guided walk is for you.

The most popular walks are in the Southern Alps, where the South Island's postcard views of mountains, wild rivers, mossy beech forests, and fjords issue a challenge to the legs that is hard to resist. Trekking season in the mountains usually lasts from October to mid-April. The best known of all New Zealand's trails is the Milford Track, a four-day walk through breathtaking scenery to the edge of Milford Sound.

Although the Milford gets the lion's share of publicity, many other walks offer a similar—some would say better—combination of scenery and exercise. The Routeburn Track is a three-day walk that rises through beech forests, traverses a mountain face across a high pass, and descends through a glacial valley. The Kepler and the Hollyford are both exceptional, and the Abel Tasman, at the South Island's

northern end, is a spectacular three- to four-day coastal track that can be walked year-round.

By all means don't rule out tramping on the North Island, which has plenty of wonders of its own. The Coromandel Peninsula has tremendous forests of gigantic 1,200-year-old kauri trees, 80-ft-tall tree ferns, a gorgeous coastline, and well marked tracks. You can hike among active volcanic peaks in Tongariro National Park. And on a nub of the west coast formed by volcanic activity hundreds of years ago, the majestic, Fuji-like Mt. Taranaki, also known as Mt. Egmont, is positively mystifying as it alternately dons cloaks of mist and exposes its brilliant, sunlit snowy cap. In fact, there are few areas in the North or South Islands that don't have their own intriguing geological eccentricities worth exploring on foot.

If time is short, at least put aside a few hours for trekking in the Waitakerei Ranges, just a short drive from Auckland city.

Shopping

New Zealand produces several unique souvenirs, but these seldom come at bargain prices. Sheepskins and quality woolens are widely available. Bowls hewn from native timber and polished to a lustrous finish are distinctive souvenirs, but a fine example will cost several hundred dollars. Greenstone, a type of jade once prized by the Māori, is now used for ornaments and jewelry—especially the figurines known as *tiki,* often worn as pendants. The two major areas for crafts are the Coromandel Peninsula close to Auckland and the environs of Nelson at the South Island's northern tip; those areas also have local potters. Kerikeri in Northland and Katikati on the coastal Bay of Plenty are also emerging as arts-and-crafts centers. The Parnell area of Auckland and the Galleria in the Christchurch Arts Centre are the places to shop for souvenirs.

Skiing

New Zealand has 27 peaks that top the 10,000-ft mark, and the June–October ski season is the reason many skiers head "down under" when the snow melts in the northern hemisphere. The South Island has most of the country's 13 commercial ski areas, and the outstanding runs are at Treble Cone and Cardrona, near the town of Wanaka, and Coronet Peak and the Remarkables, close to Queenstown. The

North Island has two commercial ski areas, Whakapapa and Turoa, both near Lake Taupo on the slopes of Mt. Ruapeu. Mt. Taranaki also has a short season, with limited facilities.

What New Zealand ski slopes lack are the connections that mark European skiing. By international standards the slopes are comparatively small, and they lack extensive interlocking lift systems. There are few lift-side accommodations. On the other hand, if you avoid weekends and school holidays you'll find the slopes pleasantly uncrowded, with ski facilities particularly well suited for beginners and families.

Heli-skiing is very popular. Harris Mountains Heliski, the second-largest heli-ski operation in the world, gives access from the town of Wanaka to more than 200 runs on more than 100 peaks accessible to skiers by no other means. The ultimate heli-ski adventure is the 13-km (8-mi) run down Tasman Glacier.

Swimming with Marine Life

Dolphins and seals are plentiful off many parts of New Zealand, and you're likely to spot them from regular cruises and ferry trips. It's not unusual to see dolphins or even orcas (killer whales) on a cruise in and beyond Auckland's Hauraki Gulf.

If you want to get even closer, a number of operators now have swim-with-dolphins—or-seals—tours. The best places from which to access these are Paihia in Northland, Tauranga and Whakatane in the coastal Bay of Plenty, and Kaikoura in the South Island. Most tours run daily, and gear is included in the price. Many of them also guarantee at least a sighting of marine mammals and offer a free trip the next day if the animals are not spotted. Check on these details before you hand over your money.

To swim or snorkel with large numbers of fish at no cost, go to Goat Island, an hour and a half's drive north of Auckland.

Wine

New Zealand is one of the wine world's latest upstarts, and Kiwi grapes and vignerons are producing first-class wine. Sauvignon blanc was the first New Zealand varietal to win an international award—that was Hunter's 1985 vintage, from the Marlborough region. Dry rieslings and rich chardonnays are also excellent, and some *méthode champenoise* sparkling wines are coming into their own as well. As for reds, pinot noir tends to be the most refined.

New Zealand wine makers more often than not have food in mind when they create their wine, and you should plan to try sauvignon blanc alongside scallops or crayfish, chardonnay with salmon, or some of the bold reds with lamb or venison. You'll discover just how well those audacious flavors work with local cuisine.

You won't have to go out of your way to try New Zealand wine—licensed restaurants are extremely loyal to Kiwi wineries—but you might want to. If you've come from Australia or the United Kingdom, chances are you've seen more Kiwi wine back home. Not so for Americans: the California wine industry has acted as a barrier to the importation of New Zealand wine, and New Zealand's production isn't high enough to allow mass distribution in the U.S. market.

Of the major Kiwi wine routes, we cover four: Hawke's Bay and its well-known chardonnay, cabernet sauvignon, cabernet franc, and merlot grapes; Gisborne–East Cape, often overshadowed by nearby Hawke's Bay but arguably stronger in the chardonnay category; Wairarapa-Martinborough, with its esteemed pinot noir; and Marlborough, where sauvignon blanc reigns supreme.

If you aren't familiar with New Zealand wine, you're sure to find plenty of wine that isn't available at your local vintner. Bring back as much as you can—sauvignon blanc to drink soon, chardonnay to let stand for a year or two, and the red of choice to age longer.

FODOR'S CHOICE

Dining

Antoine's, Auckland. For more than 25 years, it has balanced tradition and invention. $$$$

Bell Pepper Blue, Dunedin. The setting may be somewhat casual, but the contemporary cooking is decidedly serious. $$$–$$$$

Cin Cin on Quay, Auckland. Snag a harbor-view table and don't be shy about ordering the pizza. *$$$–$$$$*

50 on Park, Christchurch. Of the three daily meals served here, breakfast may be the most tempting. *$$$–$$$$*

Hunter's Vineyard Restaurant, Blenheim. Local produce is whipped into sophisticated dishes to match this vintner's wines. *$$$*

Crayfish shacks, Kaikoura. Stop at a roadside stand to try the region's namesake delicacy. *$$*

The Back-Bencher Pub & Café, Wellington. Politicians roll out of Parliament and into this restaurant for a hearty meal and a dash of levity. *$–$$*

Main Street Café and Bar, Christchurch. The meals at this boho vegetarian spot are creative and delicious from start to finish. *$*

Lodges

Huka Lodge, Lake Taupo. With Queen Elizabeth on its guest list, this lodge epitomizes flawless luxury—for a king's ransom. *$$$$*

Lake Brunner Sporting Lodge, near Greymouth. For a fly-fishing retreat, this is a terrific bet, with very reasonable rates to boot. *$$$$*

Wharekauhau, Palliser Bay. Surrounded by 5,000 acres of farmland, you can enjoy a fascinating, remote coastline. *$$$$*

Wilderness Lodge Lake Moeraki, West Coast. At this rain forest site, you can join naturalists on guided walks and excursions. *$$$$*

Lodging

Charlotte Jane, Christchurch. This 19th-century former school is now a model of genteel luxury. *$$$$*

Hotel Inter-Continental, Wellington. The rooms here are crisply stylish, the restaurant divine. *$$$$*

Hyland House, Devonport, Auckland. Photos from the owner's world travels may scratch your travel itch during a stay in this 1907 B&B. *$$$$*

Stafford Villa, Auckland. Graciousness suffuses this B&B, from the decor to the evening cocktails. *$$$$*

The Flying Fox, Whanganui River. This pair of riverside cottages, reached by cable car, is staunchly eco-friendly. *$$$*

Saltwater Lodge, Bay of Islands. The kitchen and exercise facilities make this budget option a standout. *$–$$$*

Auckland Central Backpackers, Auckland. With a Queen Street location, fresh rooms, an Internet café, and other amenities, this urban choice makes your dollar go remarkably far. *$*

Raglan Backpackers & Waterfront Lodge, Raglan. This outdoor-living proponent fits right in with this mellow surf town. *$*

Memorable Moments

Digging out your own thermal bath at Hot Water Beach, Coromandel Peninsula

Your first glimpse of Mt. Taranaki, be it in sunshine or cloud

Experiencing a simulated earthquake or a bungy jump at Te Papa–Museum of New Zealand, Wellington

Kayaking with dolphins off of Abel Tasman National Park

Marveling at blue-ice formations on Franz Josef or Fox Glacier, West Coast of the South Island

Braving an adventure sport, whether it's bungy jumping, white-water sledging, or hurtling along in a jet-boat

National Parks and Natural Wonders

The Piano's Karekare Beach, West Auckland

Taking one of Kiwi Dundee's wilderness hikes on the Coromandel Peninsula

Gurgling, slopping, bubbling volcanic activity in Rotorua

Fishing in the lakes and rivers around Rotorua and Taupo

The wild landscapes of volcanic Tongariro National Park

Glaciers grinding down 12,000-ft peaks into the rain forests of the West Coast

Mt. Cook and Tasman Glacier in Aoraki/Mount Cook National Park

The Remarkables viewed as a backdrop to Lake Wakatipu, Queenstown

Fiordland National Park's Milford Track, Mitre Peak, and Milford Sound

The isolation and night skies of southernmost Stewart Island

Wildlife Viewing

Diving in the Bay of Islands

Night watch for kiwis in the Waipoua State Forest or on Stewart Island

Birding in Tongariro National Park

The gannet colony at Cape Kidnapper, south of Napier

Swimming with dolphins at Whakatane

Cruising with sperm whales off Kaikoura

Fiordland crested penguins and fur seals at Wilderness Lodge Lake Moeraki, West Coast

The royal albatrosses, Taiaroa Head, Otago Peninsula

2 AUCKLAND AND THE NORTH

The mighty 1,200-year-old kauri trees, ferny semitropical forests, and miles of island-strewn coastline of Northland and the Coromandel Peninsula are the perfect counterpoint to Auckland, New Zealand's largest city, and its neighborhood bustle and sprawl.

By Michael
Gebicki and
Stu Freeman

A S YOU FLY INTO AUCKLAND, New Zealand's gateway city, you might wonder where the city is. Most people arriving for the first time, and even New Zealanders coming home, are impressed by the seascape and green forest that dominate the view on the approach to the airport.

The drive from the airport does little to dispel the clean, green image so many people have of the country. The scenery is commanded by some of the city's 46 volcanic hills, their grass kept closely cropped by those four-legged lawn mowers known as sheep. And reading the highway signs will begin to give you a taste of the unusual and sometimes baffling Māori place-names around the country.

Yet a couple of days in this city of about 1.1 million will reveal a level of development and sophistication that belies first impressions. Since the early 1990s, Auckland has grown up in more ways than one. Many shops are open seven days, central bars and nightclubs welcome patrons well into the night, and a cosmopolitan mix of Polynesians, Asians, and Europeans all contribute to the cultural milieu. (In fact, Auckland has the world's largest single population of Pacific Islanders.) Literally topping things off is the 1,082-ft Sky Tower, dwarfing everything around it and acting as a beacon for the casino, hotel, and restaurant complex that opened early in 1996. This is the newest, if least pervasive, face of modern New Zealand.

In the midst of the city's activity, you'll see knots of cyclists and runners. Like all other New Zealanders, Aucklanders are addicted to the outdoors—especially the water. There are some 70,000 powerboats and sailing craft in the Greater Auckland area—about one for every four households. And a total of 102 beaches lie within an hour's drive of the city center. The city has enhanced its greatest asset, Waitemata Harbour—a Māori name meaning "sea of sparkling waters." The city staged its first defense of the America's Cup in the year 2000, and the regatta was a catalyst for major redevelopment of the waterfront. The area is now known as Viaduct Basin or, more commonly, Viaduct and has some of the city's most popular bars, cafés, and restaurants. The Cup energized the area again in 2003 as Auckland hosted the Louis Vuitton Challenger Series in October 2002 to determine the challenger to the home team for the America's Cup in February 2003. Around race time, the Viaduct is a great place to see super yachts and other major craft up close.

Auckland is not easy to explore. Made up of a sprawling array of neighborhoods (Kiwis call them suburbs), the city spreads out on both shores of Stanley Bay and Waitemata Harbour. It's best to have a car for getting around between neighborhoods, and even between some city-center sights. If you are nervous about driving on the left, especially when you first arrive, purchase a one-day Link Pass or, for a circuit of the main sights, an Explorer Bus Pass, and get acquainted with the city layout. One good introduction to the city, particularly if you arrive at the end of a long flight and time is limited, is the commuter ferry that crosses the harbor to the village of Devonport, where you can soak up the charming suburb's atmosphere on a leisurely stroll.

As you put Auckland behind you, you'll find yourself in the midst of some of the great open space that defines New Zealand. North of the city, the Bay of Islands is both beautiful, for its lush forests, splendid beaches, and shimmering harbors, and historic, as the place where Westernized New Zealand came into being with the signing of the Treaty of Waitangi in 1840. Southeast of Auckland is the rugged and exhilarating Coromandel Peninsula, with mountains stretching the length of its middle and a Pacific coastline afloat with picturesque islands.

Note: For more information on bicycling, diving, deep-sea fishing, hiking, and sailing in Auckland and the north, *see* Chapter 6.

Pleasures and Pastimes

Beaches

When the sun comes out, Aucklanders head to the beach. With seas both to the west and the east, few people in the city live more than a 15-minute drive from the coast. Generally speaking the best surfing is at the black-sand beaches on the west coast, and the safest swimming is on the east coast. Beaches that have a reputation for large waves and rips are patrolled in the summer, so play it safe and swim between the flags. The only other danger is from the sun itself. The ozone layer is weak above New Zealand, so slap on the sunscreen and resist the temptation to bake.

Boating

Auckland is dubbed "City of Sails," and for good reason. The population is crazy about boating and any other recreation associated with the sea. A variety of ferries and high-speed catamarans operate on Waitemata Harbour. Even better, go for a sail on the *Pride of Auckland*. Northland, the area above Auckland with the ravishing Bay of Islands, also has a choice of boat and sailing trips, and taking a small boat out to Cathedral Cove on the Coromandel Peninsula is a great way to see its stunning coastline.

Dining

Auckland is one of the great dining cities of the Pacific Rim, with a cosmopolitan mix of cafés, restaurants, brasseries, and bars spreading from the city center to the closest suburbs. Appropriately enough, given the maritime climate, the local style leans to the Mediterranean, with a strong sideways glance toward Asia. Seafood abounds. Don't miss such delicacies as Bluff oysters (in season March–August), salmon from Marlborough, Greenshell mussels (also known as green-lipped or New Zealand green mussels), scallops, crayfish, and two clamlike shellfish, *pipi* and *tuatua.* In spring, many restaurants will feature whitebait, known to Māori as *inanga,* which are the juvenile of several fish species. They are eaten whole, usually in an omelet-like fritter. You'll also encounter plenty of opportunities to try *kūmara,* a local sweet potato and staple of the Māori diet.

The downtown waterfront area was extensively rebuilt for the America's Cup yachting series that straddled the millennium changeover. Princes Wharf and adjoining Viaduct Quay, an easy stroll from the city's major thoroughfare, Queen Street, now burst at the seams with dozens of eateries in every style from cheap-and-cheerful to superposh. Names and chefs are constantly changing, so ask the locals for recommendations—or simply follow the crowds. High Street, running parallel to Queen Street on the Albert Park side of town, has developed into a busy café and restaurant strip over the last few years. You can get between Queen and High streets via Vulcan Lane, which has some attractive bars itself.

Away from the city center, the top restaurant areas are Ponsonby and Parnell roads, both a 10-minute bus or cab ride from the city center. Dominion and Mt. Eden roads in the city, as well as Hurstmere Road in the suburb of Takapuna, over the Harbour Bridge, are also worth exploring. The mix is eclectic—Indian, Chinese, Japanese, and Thai eateries sit comfortably alongside casual taverns, pizzerias, and high-end restaurants. At hole-in-the-wall spots in and around the city center a few dollars will buy you anything from fish-and-chips to nachos, noodles, or nan bread. Ponsonby Road leads the field in outdoor dining, but Hurstmere Road is catching up fast.

To the west, out toward the Waitakere Ranges, the suburb of Titirangi earns a reputation as a dining village, with everything from low-key pizza, Middle Eastern, and Southeast Asian places to wine bars and upscale restaurants with harbor views. Heading north from Auckland, you'll find small towns like Albany, Orewa, and Warkworth with cafés and restaurants to keep hunger at bay. In Northland itself, Paihia claims the best selection of restaurants, though Russell and Kerikeri also have an improving roster of places to eat.

CATEGORY	COST*
$$$$	over $25
$$$	$20–$25
$$	$15–$20
$	under $15

*per person for a main course at dinner

Lodging

Around Auckland and the north, a great variety of accommodation is available, from flashy downtown hotels to comfortable B&Bs to mom-and-pop motels. Because Kiwis are so naturally hospitable, it's hard not to recommend lodgings where you have a chance to talk with your hosts—unless you prefer anonymity.

CATEGORY	COST*
$$$$	over $200
$$$	$125–$200
$$	$80–$125
$	under $80

*All prices are for a standard double room.

Volcanoes and Vistas

Auckland is built on and around 48 volcanoes, and the tops of many of them provide sweeping views of the city. One Tree Hill, the largest of Auckland's extinct volcanoes, was the site of an early Māori settlement. The hill is not as distinctive as it once was; its signature lone pine was attacked several times by activists who saw it as a symbol of colonialism and in 2000 it had to be taken down. Mt. Eden is probably the most popular, and several bus tours include this central site. Rangitoto Island has an even better vista. This volcano emerged from the sea just 600 years ago, no doubt much to the wonder of the Māori people living next door on Motutapu Island. Take a ferry to the island; then either a short ride or an hour's walk to the top will give you a 360-degree view of the city and the Hauraki Gulf islands. The best views from the city itself are, not surprisingly, from the Sky Tower. The main observation deck turns under its own power so you'll get a 360-degree view without having to budge.

Walking and Hiking

There is superb bushwalking (hiking) around Auckland, Northland, and the Coromandel Peninsula. New Zealand's largest city is fringed by bush (wilderness) to the west, and the Waitakere Ranges are an ideal way to experience the country's flora if you have limited time. The Northland and Coromandel bush is full of impressive ancient kauri trees (a local species of pine) and interesting birds, such as *tūī* (*too*-ee), fantails, and wood pigeons. The flightless kiwi is making a comeback; visitors are reporting flashlight sightings, particularly in the north.

Exploring Auckland and the North

Northland and the Coromandel Peninsula have beautiful countryside, coasts, and mountains—some of the finest in the North Island. Auckland is a thoroughly modern, car-oriented metropolis, with good restaurants and a handful of suburbs to poke around. Interestingly enough, Aucklanders seem to talk as much about what surrounds the city as what's in it: the beaches, the Waitakere Ranges, and the vineyards of Waiheke Island. To get to most of these and to happening suburbs like Ponsonby, you will need a car, which you can then use to go farther afield: up to Northland and southeast to the Coromandel Peninsula.

Great Itineraries

Numbers in the text correspond to numbers in the margin and on the maps.

IF YOU HAVE 3 DAYS

Spend your nights in ⊞ **Auckland** ①–⑮, and divide your days between the city's attractions and nearby destinations. Take a full day to see the best of Auckland. Next day, head west to the Waitakere Ranges and explore the bush or west-coast beaches with their volcanic black sand. Or take the day and visit the beaches and vineyards of Waiheke Island. Be sure to work in a short foray (at the least) to charming ⊞ **Devonport,** taking in the harbor views on the ferry.

IF YOU HAVE 5 OR MORE DAYS

Spend the first day or two looking around ⊞ **Auckland** ①–⑮, then head either to the popular Bay of Islands or the less-trodden Coromandel Peninsula. With more than a week, you could see both, but the drive connecting the two is more than six hours, making it more sensible to choose one of the two places. Heading north to the Bay of Islands, stop in **Warkworth** ⑰ for a look at some great old kauri trees. ⊞ **Whangarei** ⑱ is also on the way—a good place for a picnic by the harbor or at the waterfall. Continue north and spend a couple of days exploring the beaches, water sports, and history of ⊞ **Paihia and Waitangi** ⑲, the nearby Waitangi Treaty House, and the historic port of ⊞ **Russell** ⑳. When you return south, take the western route to **Waipoua State Forest** ㉓, and stop farther down at the **Matakohe Kauri Museum** ㉔ to learn about the area's incredible native trees. If you want to stay off the main road dropping back into Auckland, go past the scenic Kaipara Harbour, then through Helensville.

The Coromandel Peninsula is an easy two-hour drive south and east of Auckland. Historic ⊞ **Thames** ㉕ is a logical first stop; then wind your way up the Firth of Thames coast to the town of ⊞ **Coromandel** ㉖, a good base for exploring the upper peninsula. Turning to the east coast, you'll find some of the best Coromandel beaches. **Hot Water Beach** ㉙ is a combination of thermal activity and surf—dig a hole in the sand, and you've got a hot bath—and you can overnight in nearby ⊞ **Tairua** ㉚. A range of mountains runs in a line up the Coromandel, and from just about any point you can head into the hills for great hiking through lush, ferny forests. To the south are the popular surf beaches of **Whangamata** ㉛ and Waihi. If you have extra time, you could linger here or even head toward the coastal Bay of Plenty. The most charming town in the area is ⊞ **Katikati** ㉜, and ⊞ **Tauranga** ㉝ is a handy base for exploring the surrounding bush and beach. The best swimming beaches are found at **Mt. Maunganui** and **Whakatane** ㉞.

When to Tour Auckland and the North

Snow doesn't fall on this part of New Zealand, and the weather doesn't exactly get frigid. Still, to see these areas at their finest, mid-November through mid-April are the beautiful months, with December through March being the highest season for tourism. If you plan to come around the Christmas holidays, reserve well in advance, especially in seaside places. The Bay of Islands is a summertime hot spot for vacationing Kiwis, and the Coromandel town of Whangamata, for example, gets overrun by surfies (surfers) around New Year's.

AUCKLAND

According to Māori tradition, the Auckland isthmus was originally peopled by a race of giants and fairy folk. When Europeans arrived in the early 19th century, however, the Ngāti-Whatua tribe was firmly in control of the region. The British began negotiations with the Ngāti-Whatua in 1840 to purchase the isthmus and establish the colony's first capital. In September of that year the British flag was hoisted to mark the township's foundation, and Auckland remained the capital until 1865 when the seat of government was moved to Wellington. Since then development has been haphazard and the urban sprawl has made this city of approximately 1.1 million people one of the largest geographically in the world.

These days, Auckland is considered too bold and brash for its own good by many Kiwis who live in other parts of the country. The glass towers, crawling rush-hour traffic, and cell-phone culture set it apart from points north and south. Visitors will see beyond all that. Indeed, much of Auckland's charm lies in the fact that you can enjoy a cappuccino in a downtown café watching the city bustle pass you by—knowing that within 30 minutes' driving time you could be cruising the spectacular harbor, playing a round at a public golf course, or even walking in subtropical forest while listening to the song of a native tūī.

Exploring Auckland

Auckland isn't the easiest place to figure out in a couple of days, the way you can get a sense of the character of other New Zealand cities. It has built out, rather than up, and the sprawl makes the greater city close to impossible to explore on foot. What might look like reasonable walking distances on maps can turn out to be 20- to 30-minute treks, and stringing a few of those together can get frustrating. If you want to see the city center close to the harbor, Devonport, and Parnell, you can get around by walking, busing, and ferrying between places. To explore suburbs farther afield, it's best to rent a car.

What Aucklanders consider the city center stretches from the waterfront up around Queen Street, including the Viaduct. The neighborhoods known as Parnell and Ponsonby take their names from their major streets. Parnell has a wealth of historic buildings and chic restaurants, while Ponsonby is a cheerfully cheaper place to hang out. Newmarket, south of Parnell, brims with more upscale boutiques.

City Center and Parnell

Auckland's city center includes the port area, much of it reclaimed from the sea in the latter half of the 19th century. You can start exploring by walking along Queen Street toward the waterfront, making detours from this main drag. Turn right to head to the Albert Park and university side of town, left to reach Sky Tower. Just keep going straight ahead to reach the Ferry Building, the Maritime Museum, and downtown shopping malls. The Auckland Domain and Parnell areas are where you'll find the city's largest museum as well as historical homes and shops. Parnell was Auckland's first suburb, established in 1841, and is a good place to look for arts and crafts or sample some of Auckland's most popular cafés, bars, and restaurants.

It's relatively easy to travel around the main inner-city sights with a combination of short bus and ferry trips and some shoe leather. Auckland is a harbor city, and the following tour gives plenty of opportunity for views both out to and back from the sea.

Start at the **Civic Theatre** ①, a restored mid-city landmark close to most major hotels and the Visitor Information Centre. Right next door is the **Force Entertainment Centre** ②. Step in to check out its futuristic architecture and eclectic shops. Walk out of the complex onto Queen Street, face down toward the harbor, and then turn immediately right into Wellesley Street East. A short walk will get you to the two buildings that compose the **Auckland Art Gallery** ③. For historic works, look around the Heritage Art Gallery, but for more modern art spend time at the New Art Gallery. At the main entrance to the gallery you are right on the edge of **Albert Park** ④, which divides the city from the university. It's a good place to take a break and watch the students studying and chatting under the trees.

Walk back to the park's western edge and make a right onto Kitchener Street. Make your first left onto Victoria Street East. Head downhill toward Queen Street and past a bevy of student-oriented shops and cafés. Continue across Queen Street and up the other side of Victoria Street to the **Sky Tower** ⑤ at Sky City. Before ascending, take a moment to glance up from the base. It's an awesome experience but nothing compared with the view from the top. And these days you can even take the quick way down on the Sky Jump, a controlled leap from a platform far above ground.

Leave Sky City and double back to Queen Street and turn left, toward the waterfront. Malls, travel agents, and myriad shops line both sides of the road. Walk all the way to the end, cross QEII square, and you'll be at the **Ferry Building** ⑥. Follow the signs to the Devonport Ferry but, instead of buying a ticket for that trip alone, spend the same amount of money ($7) on a full-day pass, good on Link buses as well. The ferry crosses between Auckland city and Devonport regularly, and the round-trip only takes 20 minutes. It's the best way to get onto the harbor if you're pressed for time and gives great views of the city, the Harbour Bridge, the North Shore, and Rangitoto Island.

Back in Auckland, walk out of the Ferry Building, turn right, and walk a few minutes along Quay Street to the **National Maritime Museum** ⑦, which is dedicated to New Zealand's seafaring past and present.

To continue this tour of Auckland, catch an Explorer Bus ($25 for a full day) in front of the museum or at the better-marked stop back at the Ferry Building. Once on the Explorer Bus go to the left side of the top level for the best views. After the bus passes some industrial ports, you'll get excellent views of Devonport, Rangitoto Island, and the Hauraki Gulf. A little farther along is Okahu Bay—the closest swimming beach to the city. The Explorer Bus travels to Mission Bay, a popular swimming and picnic spot, and then stops at **Kelly Tarlton's Underwater World and Antarctic Encounter** ⑧, where you view sharks, giant stingrays, and other species. Continue by Explorer Bus to the **Parnell Rose Gardens** ⑨. You'll have to tell the driver if you want to disembark here, as it is a "request stop." In flowering season (November to March) you should make the effort, but if it's wintertime you can continue straight on to the **Auckland Museum** ⑩ to view the most comprehensive collection of Māori artifacts in the country. The museum is set in the attractive parklands known as **Auckland Domain** ⑪.

Head away from the museum by foot, back down Maunsell Road; then cross the road and turn left on Parnell Road. Take a right onto Ayr Street where you'll find the historic **Ewelme Cottage** ⑫. Walk back up Ayr Street, turn right into Parnell Road, and you will quickly reach the Church of the Holy Trinity and **Cathedral Church of St. Mary** ⑬, a Gothic-style church built in 1886. Walk down the hill just a bit and you'll reach charming **Parnell Village** ⑭. The last Explorer Bus passes through Parnell at 4:35 PM, but if you prefer to stay in Parnell for dinner, you can head back downtown later by taxi or on a Link bus. Catch a bus at any Link bus stop on the left-hand side of the road as you face the sea. They run every 10 minutes. A convenient stop is at the corner of Parnell Road and Birdwood Crescent.

TIMING

This tour can be done in a full day, but you'd be restricting your gallery, museum, and Kelly Tarlton's visits to about an hour each. If you have two days, it would make sense to walk the first part of this tour on day one, and get off the ferry at Devonport, spending some time in this quaint, seaside suburb. On the second day, you could head to Kelly Tarlton's first and then explore the Auckland Museum and Parnell area in a more leisurely manner. You might want to pack a picnic lunch to eat in the Domain. Another way to have more museum time is to save Kelly Tarlton's for an evening visit, since the last admission is 8 PM. At that time of night you would have to drive or take a taxi both to and from Kelly Tarlton's. Most sights are open daily, with the exception of Ewelme Cottage.

Sights to See

❹ **Albert Park.** These 15 acres of formal gardens, fountains, and statue-studded lawns are a favorite for Aucklanders who pour out of nearby office blocks and the university and polytechnic to eat lunch on sunny days. The park is built on the site of a garrison from the 1840s and 1850s that was used to protect settlers from neighboring Māori tribes. There are still remnants of its stone walls (with rifle slits) behind university buildings on the east side of the park. ⊠ *Bounded by Wellesley St. W, Kitchener St., Waterloo Quad, city center.*

❸ **Auckland Art Gallery.** The country's finest collection of contemporary art hangs here as well as paintings of New Zealand dating from the time of Captain Cook. The older **Heritage Art Gallery** houses many of the historic paintings while the **New Art Gallery** across the street shows the modern work. In the Heritage, look for works by Frances Hodgkins, New Zealand's best-known artist. ⊠ *5 Kitchener St., at Wellesley St. E, city center,* ☎ *09/307–7700,* WEB *www.aucklandcity. govt.nz/around/places/artgallery.* ⊠ *Heritage Gallery free, except for special exhibits; New Gallery $4.* ☉ *Daily 10–5.*

⓫ **Auckland Domain.** Saturday cricketers, Sunday picnickers, and every-day morning runners are three types of Aucklanders who you'll see enjoying the rolling, 340-acre Domain. Watch the local paper for free summer weekend-evening concerts, which usually include opera and fireworks displays. Take a bottle of wine and a basketful of something tasty and join in with the locals—up to 300,000 of them per show. Within the Domain, the domed **Wintergardens** house a collection of tropical plants and palms and seasonally displayed hothouse plants—a good stop for the horticulturally inclined. ⊠ *Entrances at Stanley St., Park Rd., Carlton Gore Rd., and Maunsell Rd.* ⊠ *Free.* ☉ *Wintergardens daily 10–4.*

★ ☙ ❿ **Auckland Museum.** Dominating the Domain atop a hill, the Greek Revival museum is known especially for its Māori artifacts, the largest

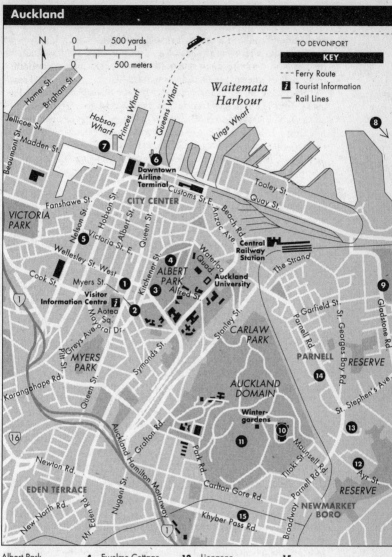

Auckland

KEY
- - - Ferry Route
ℹ️ Tourist Information
— Rail Lines

TO DEVONPORT

Waitemata Harbour

N

0   500 yards
0   500 meters

Homer St.
Brigham St.
Jellicoe St.
Beaumont St.
Madden St.
Hobson Wharf
Princes Wharf
Queens Wharf
Kings Wharf

7
6
Downtown Airline Terminal
Customs St. E.
Beach Rd.
Anzac Ave.
Tooley St.
Quay St.

Fanshawe St.
CITY CENTER

VICTORIA PARK

Nelson St.
Hobson St.
Albert St.
Queen St.

5
Victoria St. E.
Wellesley St. West

Central Railway Station

The Strand

9

8

Cook St.
Myers St.
1
Kitchener St.
4
Waterloo Quad

ALBERT PARK
3
Alfred St.
Auckland University

Visitor Information Centre ℹ️
2
Aotea Sq.

Grey's Ave
Mayoral Dr.

MYERS PARK

Symonds St.

Stanley St.

CARLAW PARK

Garfield St.
Parnell Rd.
St. Georges Bay Rd.
Gladstone Rd.

PARNELL

RESERVE

Pitt St.
Karangahope Rd.
Queen St.

16

1

Auckland Hamilton Motorway
Grafton Rd.

AUCKLAND DOMAIN

Winter-gardens
10
11

14

St. Stephen's Ave.

13

Newton Rd.

EDEN TERRACE

New North Rd.
Mt. Eden Rd.
Nugent St.

Park Rd.
Carlton Gore Rd.

Tilaki St.
Maunsell Rd.
Parnell Rd.
Broadway

12
Ayr St.

RESERVE

NEWMARKET BORO

Khyber Pass Rd.
15

1

Albert Park **4**	Ewelme Cottage **12**	Lionzone **15**
Auckland Art Gallery **3**	Ferry Building **6**	National Maritime Museum **7**
Auckland Domain . . .**11**	Force Entertainment Centre **2**	Parnell Rose Gardens **9**
Auckland Museum **10**	Kelly Tarlton's Underwater World and Antarctic	Parnell Village **14**
Cathedral Church of St. Mary **13**	Encounter **8**	Sky Tower **5**
Civic Theatre **1**		

collection of its kind. Be sure to see the *pātaka,* or storehouse; these structures were a fixture in Māori villages, and the pātaka here is one of the finest known examples. Portraits of Māori chiefs by C. F. Goldie give splendid character studies of a fiercely martial people. To delve further into this culture, hit one of the Māori performances held three times daily. Other exhibits address natural history, geology, and local history, including a reconstructed streetscape of early Auckland. Also check out the **Discovery Centres,** two interactive displays for kids of all ages. The "Weird and Wonderful" section was revamped for the museum's 150th anniversary; reopened in 2002, it covers everything from fossils to the water cycle. ⊠ *Auckland Domain, Park Rd.,* ☎ *09/ 309–0443,* ⊞⊞ *www.akmuseum.org.nz.* ⊠ *$5; $15 for Māori cultural performance.* ⊘ *Daily 10–5.*

⓭ **Cathedral Church of St. Mary.** Gothic Revival wooden churches don't get much finer than this one. Built in 1886, it's one of a number of churches commissioned by the early Anglican missionary Bishop Selwyn. The craftsmanship inside the church is remarkable, as is the story of its relocation. St. Mary's originally stood on the other side of Parnell Road, and in 1982 the entire structure was moved across the street to be next to the new church. Photographs inside show the progress of the work. The church now forms part of the Cathedral of the Holy Trinity. ⊠ *Parnell Rd. and St. Stephen's Ave., Parnell.* ⊘ *Daily 8–6.*

❶ **Civic Theatre.** This extravagant Art Nouveau movie theater was the talk of the town when it opened in 1929, but just nine months later the owner, Thomas O'Brien, went bust and fled, taking with him the week's revenues and an usherette. During World War II a cabaret show in the basement was popular with Allied servicemen in transit to the battlefields of the Pacific. One of the entertainers, Freda Stark, is said to have appeared regularly wearing nothing more than a coat of gold paint. The building reopened in late 1999 after being closed for extensive refurbishment. To see the best of the Civic, don't restrict your visit to standing outside. Sit down to a show or movie, look up to the ceiling, and you'll see a simulated night sky. ⊠ *Queen and Wellesley Sts., city center,* ☎ *09/307–5075.*

⓬ **Ewelme Cottage.** Built by the Reverend Vicesimus Lush from 1863 to 1864 and inhabited by his descendants for more than a century, this historic cottage stands behind a picket fence. The house was constructed of kauri, a resilient timber highly prized by the Māori for their war canoes and later by Europeans for ship masts. The home contains much of the original furniture and personal effects of the Lush family. ⊠ *14 Ayr St., Newmarket,* ☎ *09/379–0202.* ⊠ *$3.* ⊘ *Fri.–Sun. 10:30– noon and 1–4:30.*

❻ **Ferry Building.** This magnificent Edwardian building continues to stand out on Auckland's waterfront. The 1912 building is still used for its original purpose, and it's here that you can catch the ferry to Devonport as well as to Waiheke and other Huaraki Gulf islands. The building also houses bars and restaurants—more recent additions. Nearby, and easily seen from the Ferry Building, is Marsden Wharf, where French frogmen bombed and sank the Greenpeace vessel *Rainbow Warrior* in 1985. On Friday and Saturday after 7 PM, the regular Devonport boat is replaced by the M.V. *Kestrel,* a turn-of-the-20th-century ferry with restored wood and brass and fitted with a bar and a jazz band. ⊠ *Quay St., city center.*

❷ **Force Entertainment Centre.** With design concepts that could be from a science-fiction movie (actually, some of them are), the Force is worth a walk even if you don't intend to partake in its entertainment and eclectic shopping. Spiral staircases, bridges designed to look like film, and elevators in the shape of rockets regularly attract design and architecture students and enthusiasts. The Force incorporates an Internet café, a 12-screen cineplex, an international food court, and several bars, including the **Playhouse Pub,** an English-style tavern with a Shakespearean theme. A video arcade, bookstore, and photo developer add to the diverse mix. ✉ *291–297 Queen St., city center,* ☎ *09/303-3346.* ☉ *Daily 8 AM–midnight.*

⑧ Kelly Tarlton's Underwater World and Antarctic Encounter. The creation of New Zealand's most celebrated undersea explorer and treasure hunter, this harborside marine park offers a fish's-eye view of the sea. A transparent tunnel, 120 yards long, makes a circuit past moray eels, lobsters, sharks, and stingrays. In Antarctic Encounter, you enter a replica of explorer Robert Falcon Scott's 1911 Antarctic hut at McMurdo Sound, then circle around a deep-freeze environment aboard a heated Sno-Cat (snowmobile) that winds through a penguin colony and an aquarium exhibiting marine life of the polar sea. You emerge at Scott Base 2000, where you can see a copy of the Antarctic Treaty and flags of all the countries involved, as well as some scientific research equipment currently used in Antarctica. ✉ *Orakei Wharf, 23 Tamaki Dr., 5 km (3 mi) west of downtown Auckland,* ☎ *09/528–0603,* WEB *www. greatsights.co.nz/KellyTarltons.* ✉ *$24.* ☉ *Oct.–Easter, daily 9–9 (last admission at 8); Easter–Sept., daily 9–6 (last admission at 5).*

⑮ Lionzone. Lion Beer doesn't have the international reputation of brews like Guinness or Budweiser, but it's a Kiwi icon all the same. A tour takes you through the brewing process, recounting the history of Lion Brewery through interactive computer displays. Of course, there's a chance to taste the company's Lion Red or Steinlager at the end of the tour. ✉ *380 Khyber Pass Rd., Newmarket,* ☎ *09/358–8366,* WEB *www. lionzone.co.nz.* ✉ *$15.* ☉ *Tours daily at 9:30, 12:15, and 3.*

⑦ National Maritime Museum. You can plunge into New Zealand's rich seafaring history in this marina complex on Auckland Harbour. Experience what it was like to travel steerage class in the 1800s or check out a replica of a shipping office from the turn of the last century. There are detailed exhibits on early whaling and a collection of outboard motors, yachts, ship models, and Polynesian outriggers—not to mention *KZ1,* the 133-ft racing sloop built for the America's Cup challenge in 1988. A scow conducts short harbor trips twice a day on Tuesday, Thursday, and weekends. The museum also hosts workshops, where traditional boatbuilding, sail making, and rigging skills are kept alive. ✉ *Eastern Viaduct, Quay St., city center,* ☎ *09/373–0800,* WEB *www. nzmaritime.org.* ✉ *$12, harbor trip $15 extra.* ☉ *Oct.–Easter, daily 9–6; Easter–Sept., daily 9–5.*

⑨ Parnell Rose Gardens. When you tire of boutiques and cafés, take a 10-minute stroll to gaze upon and sniff this collection of some 5,000 rosebushes. The main beds contain mostly modern hybrids, with new introductions being planted regularly. The adjacent **Nancy Steen Garden** is the place to admire the antique varieties. And don't miss the garden's incredible trees. There is a 200-year-old *pohutukawa* (puh-hoo-too-*ka*-wa) whose weighty branches touch the ground and rise up again and a *kanuka* that is one of Auckland's oldest trees. The Rose Garden Restaurant serves lunch (closed Saturday). ✉ *Gladstone and Judges Bay Rds., Parnell,* ☎ *09/302–1252.* ✉ *Free.* ☉ *Daily dawn–dusk.*

⑭ Parnell Village. The pretty Victorian timber villas along the slope of Parnell Road have been transformed into antiques shops, designer boutiques, street cafés, and restaurants. Parnell Village is the creation of Les Harvey, who saw the potential of the old, run-down shops and houses and almost single-handedly snatched them from the jaws of the developers' bulldozers by buying them, renovating them, and leasing them out. Harvey's vision has paid handsome dividends, and today this village of trim pink-and-white timber facades is one of the most delightful parts of the city. At night its restaurants, pubs, and discos attract Auckland's chic set. Parnell's shops are open Sunday. ⊠ *Parnell Rd. between St. Stephen's Ave. and Augustus Rd., Parnell.*

⑤ **Sky Tower.** The joke among Auckland residents is that your property value rises if you *can't* see this 1,082-ft beacon. Yet it's also the first place Aucklanders take friends and relatives visiting from overseas in order to give them a view of the city. Up at the main observation level, the most outrageous thing is the glass floor panels—looking down at your feet, you see the street hundreds of yards below. Adults usually step gingerly onto the glass, and kids delight in jumping up and down on it. More educational are the audio guides to Auckland and touch-screen computers that you'll find on the deck. There's also an outdoor observation level. For an adrenaline rush you can even take a controlled leap off **Sky Jump**, a 630-ft observation deck, for a steep $195. ⊠ *Victoria and Federal Sts., city center,* ☎ *09/912–6000.* 🎫 *$15.* ☉ *Sun.–Fri. 8:30 AM–11 PM (last elevator 10:30 PM), Sat. 8:30 AM–midnight (last elevator 11:30 PM).*

Devonport

The 20-minute ferry to Devonport across Waitemata Harbour provides one of the finest views of Auckland. The first harbor ferry service began with whaleboats in 1854. Later in the century the Devonport Steam Ferry Co. began operations, and ferries scuttled back and forth across the harbor until the Harbour Bridge opened in 1959. The bridge now carries the bulk of the commuter traffic, but the ferry still has a small, devoted clientele.

Originally known as Flagstaff, after the signal station on the summit of Mt. Victoria, Devonport was the first settlement on the north side of the harbor. Later the area drew some of the city's wealthiest traders, who built their homes where they could watch their sailing ships arriving with cargoes from Europe. These days, Aucklanders have fixed up and repopulated its great old houses, laying claim to the suburb's relaxed, seaside atmosphere.

The Esplanade Hotel is one of the first things you'll see as you leave the ferry terminal. It stands at the harbor end of Victoria Road, a pleasant street for taking a stroll; stopping at a shop, a bookstore, or a café; or for picking up some fish-and-chips to eat next to the giant Moreton Bay fig tree on the green across the street.

Mt. Victoria. Long before the era of European settlement, this ancient volcano was the site of a Māori *pā* (fortified village) of the local Kawerau tribe. On the northern and eastern flanks of the hill you can still see traces of the terraces once protected by palisades of sharpened stakes. Don't be put off by its name—this is more molehill than mountain, and the climb isn't much. Mt. Victoria is signposted on Victoria Road, a few minutes' walk from the Esplanade Hotel. ⊠ *Kerr St. off Victoria Rd.*

Naval Museum. New Zealand's navy is hardly a menacing global force, but this small collection has interesting exhibits on the early exploration of the country and information on its involvement in various conflicts. The museum is five blocks west of Victoria Wharf. ⊠ *Queens Parade.* 🎫 *Small donation.* ☉ *Daily 10–4.*

North Head. The position of this ancient Māori defense site, jutting out from Devonport into Auckland's harbor, was enough to convince the European settlers that they, too, should use the head for strategic purposes. Rumor has it that veteran aircraft are still stored in the dark, twisting tunnels under North Head, but plenty of curious explorers have not found any. You can still get into most tunnels, climb all over the abandoned antiaircraft guns, and get great views of Auckland and the islands to the east. North Head is a 20-minute walk east of the ferry terminal on King Edward Parade, left onto Cheltenham Street, and then out Takarunga Road. ⊠ *Takarunga Rd.*

Around Auckland

Ⓒ **Auckland Zoo.** Since the 1990s, this zoo has focused on providing its animals with the most natural habitats possible, as well as on breeding and conservation. The primates area, sea lion and penguin shores, and the Pridelands section best exemplify this approach. To catch a glimpse of New Zealand flora and fauna, spend time in the New Zealand Aviary, where you walk among the birds, and the Kiwi and Tuatara Nocturnal House, which are at opposite ends of the zoo. By car, take Karangahape Road (which turns into Great North Road) west out of the city, past Western Springs. Take a right onto Motions Road. ⊠ *Motions Rd., Western Springs, 6 km (4 mi) west of Auckland,* ☎ *09/360–3819,* ⓌⒺⒷ *www.aucklandzoo.co.nz.* 💳 *$13.* ☉ *Daily 9:30–5:50 (last entry at 5).*

★ **Beaches.** Auckland's beaches are commonly categorized by area— east, west, or north. The eastern beaches, such as those along Tamaki Drive on the south side of the harbor, are closer to the city and don't have heavy surf. They usually have playgrounds and changing facilities. **Judge's Bay** and **Mission Bay** are particularly recommended for their settings. The best swimming is at high tide.

West-coast black-sand beaches are popular in summer. They tend to have bare-bones facilities, but many have changing sheds near the parking areas. However, the sea is often rough, and sudden rips and holes can trap the unwary. Lifeguards are on duty, and the safe swimming areas are marked with flags. The most visited of these beaches is **Piha,** some 40 km (25 mi) west of Auckland, which has pounding surf as well as a sheltered lagoon dominated by the reclining mass of Lion Rock. **Whatipu,** south of Piha, is a broad sweep of sand offering safe bathing behind the sandbar that guards Manukau Harbour. **Bethells,** to the north, often has heavy surf. In the vicinity, **Karekare** is the beach where the dramatic opening scenes of Jane Campion's *The Piano* were shot. To get to the west-coast beaches, head to Titirangi and take the winding road signposted as "The Scenic Drive." Once you are on that road, the turnoffs to individual beaches are well marked— and, as advertised, there are lots of beautiful harbor views. Across Waitemata Harbour from the city, a chain of magnificent beaches stretches north as far as the Whangaparoa Peninsula, 40 km (25 mi) from Auckland. Taking Highway 1 north and keeping an eye peeled for signs, for instance, you'll reach **Cheltenham,** just north of Devonport.

Ⓒ **Museum of Transport and Technology.** This fascinating collection of aircraft, telephones, cameras, locomotives, steam engines, and farm equipment is a tribute to Kiwi ingenuity. One of the most intriguing exhibits is the remains of an aircraft built by Robert Pearse, who made a successful powered flight barely three months after the Wright brothers first took to the skies. The flight ended inauspiciously when his plane crashed into a hedge, but Pearse, considered a wild eccentric by his farming neighbors, is recognized today as a mechanical genius. The museum is near the Auckland Zoo; a tram ($2) shuttles between the two. ⊠

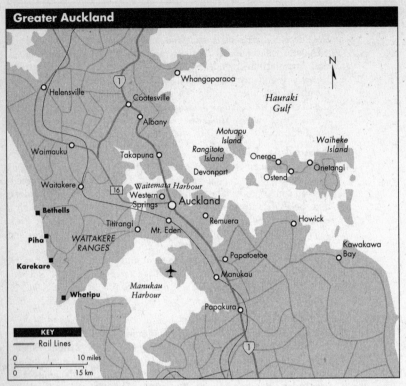

825 Great North Rd., off Northwestern Motorway, Rte. 16, Western Springs, 6 km (4 mi) west of Auckland, ☎ 09/846–0199. ▣ $10. ◷ Daily 10–5.

Rangitoto Island. When Rangitoto Island emerged from the sea in a series of fiery eruptions 600 years ago, it had an audience. Footprints in the ash on its close neighbor Motutapu Island prove that Māori people watched Rangitoto's birth. It is now the largest and youngest of about 50 volcanic cones and craters in the Auckland volcanic field, though scientists are confident that it will not blow again. During the 1920s and 1930s hundreds of prisoners built roads and trails on the island, some of which are still used as walkways. Small beach houses were also erected on the island in the early 20th century, but it now has no permanent residents.

The most popular activity on the island is the one-hour summit walk, beginning at Rangitoto Wharf and climbing through lava fields and forest to the peak. At the top, walkers are rewarded with panoramic views of Auckland and the Hauraki Gulf. Short detours will lead to lava caves and even to the remnants of a botanical park planned in 1915, and you can walk around the rim of the crater. **Fullers Cruise Centre** (☎ 09/367–9111, 🆆🅴🅱 www.fullers.co.nz) operates ferries to Rangitoto daily at 9, 11, and 1. The fare is $20 round-trip; boats leave from the Ferry Building. Fullers also arranges Volcanic Explorer tours, which include a guided ride to the summit in a covered carriage; the total cost is $49.

Waiheke Island. Once a sleepy suburb of Auckland, Waiheke was mainly used as a weekend and summer vacation retreat, with beach houses dotting its edges. Since the late 1980s more people have moved to the island as a lifestyle choice, commuting each day by ferry to the city. The island is also earning an international reputation for its vineyards, and local cafés sometimes stock wines that aren't available on the mainland—vintners make them purely for island enjoyment. Ferries make the trip from the Ferry Building at least a dozen times a day, even on Sunday. However, it pays to phone first (☎ 09/367–9111), as crossings can be canceled if the seas are rough.

The ferry lands at **Matiatia Wharf.** Buses meet ferries at the terminal and make a loop around the island. Or you can walk five minutes to the small town of **Oneroa.** Another minute's walk gets you to **Oneroa Beach,** one of the island's finest and most accessible beaches. Another great beach on Waiheke is **Onetangi,** on the north side of the island, 20 minutes from Matiatia by bus. **Whakanewha Regional Park** is on the south of the island and has hiking and picnic options.

There are around 30 vineyards on Waiheke Island, but because most are rather new, only about a dozen are producing wine. First to plant grapes were Kim and Jeanette Goldwater, whose eponymous wines have earned a reputation for excellence. The **Goldwater Estate** (✉ 18 Causeway Rd., Putiki Bay, ☎ 09/372–7493, WEB www.goldwaterwine.com) cabernet sauvignon–merlot blend is outstanding, and the Esslin Merlot has been hailed as the best Kiwi interpretation of this popular variety. The winery is open for tastings in late December through early January only, daily between 11 AM and 4 PM. It's best to call ahead. Stephen White's **Stonyridge Vineyard** (✉ 80 Onetangi Rd., Ostend, ☎ 09/372–8822, WEB www.stonyridge.co.nz) has the island's highest profile, and his Stonyridge Larose, also made from the classic Bordeaux varieties, is world class—and priced accordingly. Stephen gets faxed orders months before release and is usually sold out hours later. Call before you visit—he may have nothing left to taste or sell. A good place to try wines that never make it to the mainland is **Mudbrick Vineyard and Restaurant** (✉ Church Bay Rd., Oneroa, ☎ 09/372–9050, WEB www.mudbrick.co.nz), which produces a small portfolio of whites and reds of its own and serves them and those of other tiny producers alongside food generally regarded as the island's best.

If you're planning on going farther afield on the island, you can purchase an all-day bus pass from **Fullers Cruise Centre** (☎ 09/367–9111). The basic $38 pass includes the ferry trip and bus travel on regular services to Oneroa, Palm Beach, Onetangi, and Rocky Bay. To use the pass, you need to take the 8:15, 10, or noon ferry. Return time is optional. Fullers also offers a couple of tours that include the ferry fee. The Island Explorer tour, for $46, stops at Onetangi Beach. The Waiheke Vineyard Explorer itinerary takes 5½ hours and costs $66. After either tour, on the same day, passengers may use their ticket to travel free on regular island buses to visit additional attractions. Reservations for Waiheke tours are essential during the summer. You can also take a shuttle to beaches or vineyards; **Waiheke Island Shuttles** (☎ 09/372–7262) has reliable service. The best way to get to Whakanewha Regional Park is by shuttle.

Waitakere Ranges. This scenic mountain range west of Auckland is a favorite walking and picnic spot for locals. The 20-minute **Arataki Nature Trail** is a great introduction to kauri and other native trees. The highlight of another great trail, **Auckland City Walk,** is Cascade Falls. The **Arataki Visitors Centre** (☎ 09/817–4941) displays modern Māori carvings and has information on the Waitakeres and other Auckland parks. To get to the Waitakeres, head along the Northwestern Motorway, Route 16, from central Auckland, take the Waterview turnoff, and keep heading west to the gateway village of Titirangi. A sculpture depicting fungal growths tells you you're heading in the right direction. From here the best route to follow is Scenic Drive, with spectacular views of Auckland and its two harbors. The visitor center is 5 km (3 mi) along the drive.

Dining

City Center

$$$$ ✕ **Harbourside Seafood Bar and Grill.** Overlooking the water from the upper level of the restored ferry building, this sprawling, modish seafood restaurant is great for warm-weather dining. Some of the finest New Zealand fish and shellfish, including tuna, salmon, snapper, pipi, and tuatua, appear on a menu with a fashionably Mediterranean accent. Lobster fresh from the tank is a house specialty. Non-fish–eaters have their choice of *cervena* (farmed venison), lamb, and poultry. On warm nights, reserve ahead and request a table outside on the deck. ⊠ *Auckland Ferry Bldg., 99 Quay St.,* ☎ *09/307–0486. AE, DC, MC, V.*

$$$$ ✕ **SBF.** Once called the Steam Biscuit Factory, this restaurant kept the initials and now offers one of Auckland's most diverse buffets. At the centerpiece noodle bar, you can select the raw ingredients, give them to the chef, and watch him stir-fry your choices with a touch of ginger, chili, and soy. Take a do-it-yourself approach with a Caesar salad, or choose from sushi or other fish dishes. You can finish up with a cool sorbet or New Zealand cheese and fruit. ⊠ *Sheraton Auckland Hotel and Towers, 83 Symonds St.,* ☎ *09/379–5132. AE, DC, MC, V.*

$$$–$$$$ ✕ **Cin Cin on Quay.** Auckland's original seaside brasserie is still one of
★   the best. Look for innovative pizza—tandoori chicken with avocado-mango chutney and red onion has been here since day one—and clever selections like rare, peppered yellowfin tuna with a green-tea noodle salad and sesame dressing. The wine list includes several vintages of local icons like Kumeu River Chardonnay and Stonyridge Larose, If you're in town on the weekend, reserve an outside table overlooking the harbor for the good-value breakfast. ⊠ *Auckland Ferry Bldg., 99 Quay St.,* ☎ *09/307–6966. AE, DC, MC, V.*

$$–$$$ ✕ **Kermadec.** This complex's two restaurants are owned by a major fishing company, so naturally, the chefs lean on seafood. Both places have harborside views and dramatic Pacific-theme decor. In the more casual brasserie, start with shellfish, and then seek the kitchen's advice on the best way to enjoy the catch of the day. The adjacent **Ocean Fresh** restaurant prepares great sushi and sashimi, or you could try herb-crusted orange roughy (a mild fish) on citrus and kūmara *rösti* (sweet potato fritters). Can't decide? Share a platter—it will probably include smoked salmon, scallops, prawns, mussels, smoked eel, scampi, John Dory, and snapper. Desserts are equally imaginative. ⊠ *1st floor, Viaduct Quay Bldg., Quay and Lower Hobson Sts.,* ☎ *09/309–0413 brasserie; 09/309–0412 restaurant. AE, DC, MC, V.*

$$–$$$ ✕ **Number 5 Wine Bistro.** The sign outside declares "Life is too short to drink bad wine." Accordingly, the New Zealand wine list here is equipped to prevent such a mishap, with a vast selection by the glass as well the bottle. Unlike most high-end restaurants, they're happy to serve just a small dish with a glass of wine if that's all you feel like eating. But there are some tasty main courses, too, like the veal with rustic potato salad and marinated tomatoes. ⊠ *5 City Rd.,* ☎ *09/309–9273. AE, DC, MC, V. Closed Sun. No lunch.*

$$ ✕ **Mexican Café.** The worn red paint on the steps leading to this lively favorite says it all. Get to this restaurant at least half an hour ahead of time and join the crowds at the bar. Over the years, this spot has grown from 24 seats to 140. People go as much for the noisy, friendly atmosphere as they do for the food—though the dishes aren't chopped liver. The menu is packed with traditional choices such as nachos, tacos, and enchiladas. Don't get tucked away in a corner table unless you want

Auckland Dining and Lodging

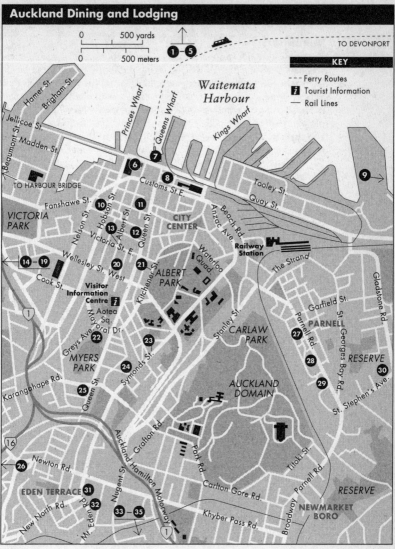

Dining

Akdeniz	5
Antoine's	29
Atomic Café	14
Burger Wisconsin	15
Cin Cin on Quay	7
Dizengoff	16
The French Café	31
Galbraith's Ale House	32
GPK	17
Harbourside Seafood Bar and Grill	8
Iguaçú	28
Kermadec	6
The Long Drop	26
Mexican Café	13
Non Solo Pizza	27
Number 5 Wine Bistro	24
Oyster Blue	4
Provence	18
SBF	23
Vinnie's	19

Lodging

Ascot Metropolis Hotel	21
Ascot Parnell	30
Auckland Central Backpackers	12
Auckland City YHA	25
Brooklands Country Estate	33
Carlton	22
Crowne Plaza	20
Devonport Villa Inn	1
Florida Motel	9
Heritage Auckland	10
Hotel du Vin	34
Hyland House	3
Sedgwick-Kent Lodge	35
Stafford Villa	2
Stamford Plaza	11

to linger and soak up the atmosphere. ⊠ *67 Victoria St. W,* ☎ *09/373–2311. AE, DC, MC, V.*

Devonport

$$$–$$$$ ✕ **Oyster Blue.** Devonport's main street is chock-full of casual cafés and delicatessens, but it's worth leaving the shopping strip and heading up the hill to this popular place. The bright blue exterior makes it easy to spot; the color scheme continues inside with blue seats and tablecloths. The menu emphasizes seafood, with dishes ranging from simple panfried snapper with garlic mashed potatoes to pricier crayfish and shrimp. You could also try the lamb, such as seared loin baked in red-currant jelly, tarragon, and red wine, with a root vegetable tart. ⊠ *58 Calliope Rd., Devonport,* ☎ *09/445–0309. AE, DC, MC, V. Closed Sun. No lunch.*

Parnell

$$$$ ✕ **Antoine's.** Owners Tony and Beth Astle have run this stately insti-
★   tution for more than a quarter century, and it still enjoys a reputation as *the* special-occasion spot in town. The decor is old-style stately, the service immaculate, and the food classy—and expensive. Tony is still at the stove, and his menu reads as if it were designed by a chef half his age. You'll find classics such as braised lamb shanks and creamy tripe along with inventive dishes such as seaweed and garlic flan topped with oysters, whitebait, and flying-fish roe, or a tuna trio presenting the rich red flesh sliced thinly as carpaccio, chopped as tartare, and sliced, seared, and tucked inside a spring roll. The wine list is extensive and international. ⊠ *333 Parnell Rd.,* ☎ *09/379–8756. AE, DC, MC, V. Closed Sun. No lunch Sat.*

$$–$$$$ ✕ **Iguaçú.** With flares blazing near the entrance, a terra-cotta tiled floor, enormous mirrors in Mexican metalwork frames, a glass ceiling, and a pair of chandeliers made from copper tubing, the decor borrows from several cultures, and the vast menu follows suit. The kitchen goes nationalistic with fritters based on tuatua (shellfish) and kūmara, served with mayo flavored with *kina* (sea urchin) roe. Or you might find yellowfin tuna, crusted with sesame seeds, seared, and arranged over Malaysian noodles and a papaw salsa. Locals come to see and be seen as much as to enjoy the food. ⊠ *269 Parnell Rd.,* ☎ *09/309–4124. AE, DC, MC, V.*

$$–$$$$ ✕ **Non Solo Pizza.** The name means "not only pizza," and that tells it
★   like it is. This uncompromisingly Italian eatery offers pasta as a single serving or in table-sharing bowls that feed four or more. Try the eggplant, panfried and layered with mozzarella, tomato, basil, and Parmesan, or look for spaghetti with fresh cockles. And there's always pizza with traditional toppings followed by a masterfully prepared green salad. The same team runs Toto, on the other side of town, so if you can't get a seat here, ask if the sister restaurant is also full. ⊠ *259 Parnell Rd.,* ☎ *09/379–5358. AE, DC, MC, V.*

Ponsonby

$$–$$$$ ✕ **Provence.** You'll think you've swapped continents when you step into this small but perfectly formed restaurant. Chef Laurance Brunacci's food is thoroughly Gallic. Snails, brains, rabbit, pig's trotters, duck—you'll find them all in various guises, and they will all be delicious. The wine list, too, has French leanings, but nationalism is sensibly suspended to give New Zealand bottles pride of place. ⊠ *44 Ponsonby Rd.,* ☎ *09/376–8147. AE, DC, MC, V.*

$$–$$$ ✕ **GPK.** The initials stand for Gourmet Pizza Kitchen or Gourmet Pizza Konnection—take your pick. This corner eatery was the city's pioneer posh-pizza place and soon afterward spawned a sister establishment at 234 Dominion Road, Mt. Eden. Some of the toppings would

make a traditionalist squirm (tandoori chicken with banana and yogurt), but there are plenty of offerings more typically Italian. The wine and beer list is impressively comprehensive. ✉ *262 Ponsonby Rd.,* ☎ *09/360–1113. Reservations not accepted. AE, DC, MC, V.*

$–$$ ✗ **Dizengoff.** The food is Jewish, though not strictly kosher, and with owner-chef Brendan Turner at the helm, it's right up to the minute. The most popular breakfast dish is a combination of eggs, lox, and butter sauce on a brioche. At lunch try the beet salad—Brendan mixes baby beets with fava beans in a balsamic dressing, then layers on extra flavor with pesto and shaved Parmesan. ✉ *256 Ponsonby Rd.,* ☎ *09/ 360–0108. AE, DC, MC, V. No dinner.*

$ ✗ **Atomic Café.** Chris Priestley was a Ponsonby pioneer, and he still runs one of the best coffee bars on the strip. There's food for vegetarians, vegans, macrobiotics, meat-eaters—and even children. Young ones are catered to in the outside courtyard, where scattered toys and other distractions keep them amused while you nibble on rice bowls or eclectic salads, followed by coffee made from beans roasted on the premises. The decor is bohemian, and the service is supercasual and friendly. ✉ *121 Ponsonby Rd.,* ☎ *09/376–4954. No credit cards. BYOB. No dinner Sat.–Wed.*

$ ✗ **Burger Wisconsin.** Traveling Americans consistently rate Wisconsin's five Auckland outlets the best burger joints in town. The bunned delights include chicken breast with cream cheese and apricot sauce, Malaysian *satay* (marinated, grilled meat skewers), bacon and beef with coconut mayonnaise, and a vegetarian soy and sesame-seed burger. At this branch—if the weather's warm—you can order your burger to go, then wander over to nearby Western Park. ✉ *168 Ponsonby Rd.,* ☎ *09/360–1894. AE, DC, MC, V.*

Other Suburbs

$$$$ ✗ **The French Café.** It's not really a café, and it's not particularly ★ French, but don't let the inaccurate nomenclature put you off—the food's great. Simon Wright has a light touch that translates to clean, focused flavors. Order classic New Zealand specialties like *paua* (black abalone), Greenshell mussels, crayfish, or spring lamb. In season, you can't beat the whitebait fritter. The wine list includes a few finds, and the staff can make strong recommendations. ✉ *210B Symonds St., at Khyber Pass,* ☎ *09/377–1911. AE, DC, MC, V.*

$$$ ✗ **Vinnie's.** Serious foodies rate David Griffith's food the best around. ★ The fresh decor in this shop-front suburban restaurant has just a hint of Paris bistro, but the food leans more toward the gutsy styles of Provence and southern Italy—with a glance toward Asia. You'll be tempted with the likes of prosciutto-wrapped quail with mortadella stuffing, Chinese five-spice duck confit with pineapple-sherry vinegar dressing and wild greens, or thyme-roasted lamb rack with summer ratatouille and goat cheese tortellini. ✉ *166 Jervois Rd., Herne Bay,* ☎ *09/376–5597. AE, DC, MC, V. No lunch Jan.–Nov.*

$$–$$$ ✗ **The Long Drop.** Perched on a steep hillside, this restaurant stands out with its corrugated iron and polished timber exterior. The menu undergoes radical changes from time to time, but you'll always find a Thai salad and an Indian curry, plus a vegetarian selection; look for the pumpkin, spinach, and lentil stew. This suburb is particularly popular for weekend brunch, and the Long Drop fills the bill with large servings of bacon and eggs, French toast, and the like. You don't have far to go if you want to walk it off in the Waitakere Ranges. ✉ *421 Titirangi Rd., Titirangi,* ☎ *09/817–5057. AE, DC, MC, V.*

$$ ✗ **Akdeniz.** "Mediterranean" stretches to its widest sense at this North Shore restaurant. Greek salad and Turkish dishes join the pizzas and pasta. Best of all is the seafood *guvech*: fish, mussels, calamari, and

prawns cooked in a clay dish in the wood-fired oven, topped with tomato sauce and grilled mozzarella. If it's a cold night, reserve a table near the open fire. ⊠ *34 Anzac St., Takapuna,* ☎ *09/486–4900. AE, DC, MC, V.*

$–$$ ✕ **Galbraith's Ale House.** Brew lovers and Brits craving a taste of home head straight for Keith Galbraith's traditionally decorated ale-house. The English-style ales are made on the premises and served at proper cellar temperature, i.e., not too cold. Keith learned the art of brewing in the United Kingdom, and he sticks religiously to the style. Order a half or dig into pub classics like pea-pie-pud—steak pie topped with mashed potatoes, minted green peas, and gravy—or bangers and mash (seriously good sausages atop creamy mashed potatoes). Well-prepared salads, steaks, and poultry satisfy less medieval palates. ⊠ *2 Mt. Eden Rd., Grafton,* ☎ *09/379–3557. AE, MC, V.*

Lodging

City Center

$$$$ 🏨 **Ascott Metropolis Hotel.** Auckland's old magistrate's court house has
★ been converted to provide an elegant lobby, restaurant, and bar for this all-suite hotel. The guest rooms are all in a new tower built just behind the court. Though most rooms have decent views, the best sea views are available higher up on the east side of the hotel. On a clear day you'll be able to see right across the harbor to the Coromandel Peninsula. Units are either one- or two-bedroom; most have balconies, and all come with a kitchenette and washing machine and dryer. ⊠ *1 Courthouse La.,* ☎ *09/300–8800,* 𝔽𝔸𝕏 *09/300–8899,* 𝕎𝔼𝔹 *www.theascott. com. 315 suites. Restaurant, kitchenettes, indoor pool, 2 hot tubs, sauna, health club, bar. AE, DC, MC, V.*

$$$$ 🏨 **Carlton.** Its proximity to the Aotea Centre performance venue and downtown makes the Carlton a favorite with business travelers. Guest rooms are spacious and elegantly furnished, with particularly well-equipped bathrooms. The best views are from the rooms that overlook the parklands and the harbor to the east. Polished granite and warm, earthy tones have been used liberally throughout the building. The hotel's restaurants have occasional food festivals and cooking classes. ⊠ *Mayoral Dr. and Vincent St.,* ☎ *09/366–3000,* 𝔽𝔸𝕏 *09/366–0121,* 𝕎𝔼𝔹 *www. carlton-auckland.co.nz. 455 rooms, 14 suites. 2 restaurants, coffee shop, in-room data ports, minibars, tennis court, 2 bars. AE, DC, MC, V.*

$$$$ 🏨 **Heritage Auckland.** Transforming one of Auckland's landmark buildings, the Farmers Department Store, this hotel opened in 1998 and quickly earned a reputation as one of the finest in the city. Since then it has added a tower wing, making it New Zealand's largest hotel as well. The size hasn't detracted from its character—the main building has retained its original 1920s Art Deco design, including high ceilings, large jarrah-wood columns, and native timber floors. The tower wing is more contemporary and includes New Zealand art especially commissioned for the rooms and public areas. Ask for a harbor-view room. ⊠ *35 Hobson St.,* ☎ *09/379–8553,* 𝔽𝔸𝕏 *09/379–8554,* 𝕎𝔼𝔹 *www. heritagehotels.co.nz. 224 rooms, 243 suites. 2 restaurants, in-room data ports, in-room safes, minibars, tennis court, indoor lap pool, pool, sauna, spa, health club, 2 bars, meeting rooms. AE, DC, MC, V.*

$$$$ 🏨 **Stamford Plaza.** Constant upgrades, noteworthy service, and attention to detail keep this mid-city hotel at the top of its game. Standard rooms are large and furnished extensively with natural fabrics and native woods in an updated art deco style. The best rooms are on the harbor side—the higher the better. Make sure you check out the rooftop area, with its expansive views over Auckland's harbor, or, on a rainy day, take high tea in the lobby. If you've got something to celebrate, head to the Yanrepé champagne bar. ⊠ *Albert St. and Swanson St.,* ☎ *09/309–8888,* FAX *09/379–6445,* WEB *www.stamford.com.au. 332 rooms. 2 restaurants, in-room data ports, in-room safes, minibars, pool, bar. AE, DC, MC, V.*

$$$ ⊞ **Crowne Plaza.** Rooms at this city landmark equal those in just about any of Auckland's leading hotels, but cutting down on facilities and glossy public areas has reduced prices substantially. Accommodations begin on the 16th floor. The suites on the 28th floor have great views and bigger bathrooms for just a slightly higher price. Service is keen and professional. ⊠ *128 Albert St.,* ☎ *09/302–1111,* FAX *09/302–3111,* WEB *www.crowneplaza.co.nz. 252 rooms. Restaurant, gym, bar. AE, DC, MC, V.*

$$ ⊞ **Ascot Parnell.** While the accommodations in this sprawling guest house are comfortable, space and character have been sacrificed to provide rooms with private bathrooms at a reasonable price. The room with the attached sunroom at the back of the house is small but pleasant. The house stands on a relatively busy street, within easy walking distance of the shops and nightlife of Parnell Village. Smoking is not permitted inside. ⊠ *36 St. Stephens Ave., Parnell,* ☎ *09/309–9012,* FAX *09/309–3729,* WEB *www.ascotparnell.com. 9 rooms. AE, MC, V. BP.*

$ ⊞ **Auckland Central Backpackers.** The best-equipped budget place in
★ town, this hostel manages to keep the lid on its rates despite a Queen Street locale. Opened in 2002, it includes features such as air-conditioning and a security system that you would normally expect to pay a lot more for. Accommodation varies from a six-bed bunk room to family rooms with bath. The lounge and Internet-café area act as the hostel's social hub, where you'll also find a travel center and even a New Zealand job-search service should you be looking for temporary work. ⊠ *229 Queen St.,* ☎ *09/358–4877,* FAX *09/358–4872,* WEB *www. acb.co.nz. 71 rooms, 23 with bath. Restaurant, café, kitchen, bar, laundry facilities, travel services. AE, DC, MC, V.*

$ ⊞ **Auckland City YHA.** Hotels with much higher room rates must envy this hostel's location just behind upper Queen Street. It's a few minutes' walk to the lively area of Karangahape Road and close to the bus circuit. Most rooms have a view over Auckland toward the harbor, but the best outlook is from the sun deck and common room. All share bathrooms. You can arrange for meals at the in-house restaurant; luggage storage and tour booking are available. ⊠ *City Rd. at Liverpool St.,* ☎ *09/309–2802,* FAX *09/373–5083,* WEB *www.yha.org.nz. 160 beds. Restaurant, travel services; no a/c. AE, MC, V.*

Devonport/North Shore

$$$$ ⊞ **Hyland House.** New Yorker Hodi Poorsoltan visited New Zealand
★ six times before deciding to stay for good. Now wonderful photographs from his world travels hang in his B&B, a 1907 home with a pair of guest rooms. The downstairs Atea Suite has an antique clawfoot tub in its bathroom. The Provence room, upstairs, has a French sleigh bed and a lounge-library area. Be sure to check out the guest lounge's ornate original ceiling and cornice. ⊠ *4 Flagstaff Terr.,* ☎ *09/445–9917,* FAX *09/445–9927,* WEB *www.hyland.co.nz. 2 rooms. Pool. AE, MC, V. BP.*

$$$$ ⊞ **Stafford Villa.** Once a missionary's home, this early 1900s home is
★ now an elegant B&B filled with Asian antiques and other artworks. Each room has a thematic bent, such as Papillon's butterfly-decorated wallpaper and China Blue's Asian inflection. The latter is a honeymoon favorite, with a four-poster bed and an antique Chinese chest. There are plenty of gracious touches, from chocolates and fresh flowers to sherry in the guest rooms and evening gin and tonics. Two rooms have showers instead of full baths, but there's an additional bathroom with

a clawfoot tub for these rooms to share. ✉ *2 Awanui St., Birkenhead Point, North Shore,* ☎ *09/418–3022,* 🖷 *09/419–8197,* 🌐 *www. staffordvilla.co.nz. 3 rooms. Library, Internet. AE, MC, V. BP.*

$$ 🏨 **Devonport Villa Inn.** This gracious timber villa combines tranquil,
★ historic surroundings and fresh sea air. The decor varies a bit, but all rooms have handmade quilts, queen-size beds with Edwardian-style headboards and lace curtains. It's a short walk to either Cheltenham Beach, a safe place for swimming, or Devonport village. Arriving guests can be collected from the Devonport ferry terminal. ✉ *46 Tainui Rd., Devonport,* ☎ *09/445–8397,* 🖷 *09/445–9766,* 🌐 *www. devonportvillainn.co.nz. 4 rooms. Library; no smoking. AE, V. BP.*

Other Suburbs and Auckland Environs

$$$$ 🏨 **Brooklands Country Estate.** A 90-minute drive south of Auckland, Brooklands is ideal if you are short of time and want a taste of rural hospitality. The turn-of-the-last-century homestead is set among gardens and surrounded by forest. Drink in the homey atmosphere in the library and lounge, where you will find plenty of leather furnishings, and books from the owner's family. An open fire is the centerpiece of the dining room in cooler months, and in summer, dinner is often served outside by the pool. Antique oak furniture and Persian rugs on the old kauri floors make the rooms welcoming. ✉ *Hwy. 22, R.D. 1, Ngaruawahia,* ☎ *07/825–4756,* 🖷 *07/825–4873,* 🌐 *www.brooklands.net. nz. 10 rooms. Dining room, pool, tennis court, croquet, billiards, lounge, library, helipad; no a/c. AE, DC, MC, V.*

$$$$ 🏨 **Hotel du Vin.** There can be no finer introduction to New Zealand
★ than to head south from Auckland to this smart, luxurious hotel, surrounded by native forests and the grapevines of the de Redcliffe estate. Standard rooms are palatial, and the newer rooms at the far end of the resort are the best. The decor is crisp and modern; the central restaurant and reception areas glow with honey-color wood and rough stone fireplaces. The restaurant has an excellent reputation, though prices are high. If you're not staying overnight, you can still stop over for a wine tasting or dinner—a great way to break the journey between Auckland and the Coromandel region. ✉ *Lyons Rd., Mangatawhiri Valley, 64 km (40 mi) south of Auckland,* ☎ *09/233–6314,* 🖷 *09/233–6215,* 🌐 *www.hotelduvin.co.nz. 46 rooms. Restaurant, tennis court, indoor pool, spa, gym, bicycles, archery, bar; no a/c. AE, DC, MC, V.*

$$$–$$$$ 🏨 **Sedgwick-Kent Lodge.** On a quiet street in the suburb of Remuera,
★ between the airport and downtown, this single-story Edwardian villa is a wonderful retreat from the city. You'll enter through a lovely garden courtyard; inside, native timber trims doorways that open onto rooms fitted with writing desks and antique bedsteads. Hosts Wout and Helma van der Lans take good care of guests and offer delightful breakfasts as well as candlelit dinners by arrangement. ✉ *65 Lucerne Rd., Remuera,* ☎ *09/524–5219,* 🖷 *09/520–4825,* 🌐 *www.sedgwick. co.nz. 5 rooms, 1 apartment. AE, DC, MC, V. BP.*

$$ 🏨 **Florida Motel.** In a harborside suburb a 15-minute drive east of the city center (and close to a major bus route into the city), this motel offers exceptional value. Rooms come in three versions: studios or one- or two-bedroom units. The units have a lounge room separate from the bedroom, and the two-bedroom units are particularly good for families. All rooms have separate, fully equipped kitchens and a few nice touches, such as wall-mounted hair dryers, French-press coffeemakers, and irons with ironing boards. As the motel is immaculately maintained and extremely popular, rooms must be booked several months in advance. ✉ *11 Speight Rd., Kohimarama,* ☎ *09/521–4660,* 🖷 *09/ 521–4662. 8 rooms. Kitchens. AE, DC, MC, V.*

Nightlife and the Arts

The Arts

For tickets, **Ticketek** (☎ 09/307–5000, WEB www.ticketek.com) is the central agency for all theater, music, and dance performances, as well as for major sporting events.

ART GALLERIES AND STUDIOS

A group of 30 artists living and working in Waitakere, west of Auckland, have set up the **Art Out West Trail,** by which visitors can view and purchase art in artists' private studios. Many of the studios require advance notice, and you'll need a car if you want to really explore the trail. Brochures are available at the Auckland Travel and Information Centre (☞ Visitor Information *in* Auckland A to Z, *below*).

For a one-stop sample of West Auckland art, visit **Lopdell House Gallery** (⊠ Titirangi and S. Titirangi Rds., Titirangi, ☎ 09/817–8087). The gallery shows local works but also has regular exhibitions by national and international artists.

MUSIC AND OPERA

The **Aotea Centre** (⊠ Aotea Sq., Queen and Myers Sts., city center, ☎ 09/309–2677 or 09/307–5060, WEB www.the-edge.co.nz) is Auckland's main venue for music and the performing arts. The **Auckland Philharmonia Orchestra** performs regularly at the center, and the **New Zealand Symphony Orchestra** performs both at the Town Hall and at the Aotea Centre. For general inquiries check by the information desk in the Owens Foyer, Level Two of the complex.

Nightlife

After sunset the liveliest area of the city is Parnell, which has several restaurants, bars, and nightclubs. For a late-night café scene, head to Ponsonby Road, southwest of the city center off Karangahape Road, where you will find street-side dining, small dessert-only restaurants, and intimate bars. If you prefer to stay in the city center, the place to be for bars and late-night dancing is High Street and nearby O'Connell Street and Vulcan Lane. At the Queen Street end of Karangahape Road (just north of Highway 1) you'll find shops, lively bars, cafés, and nightspots, but as you head toward Ponsonby Road these give way to strip clubs and sex shops. Auckland usually has three or four lively nightclubs running at any one time, but they are transient animals with names and addresses changing as young Aucklanders follow the trend of the day. From Sunday to Wednesday most bars close at 10 PM and nightclubs at about midnight or 1 AM. From Thursday to Saturday, many city bars close at 11 PM or midnight but some do have 24-hour licenses. Nightclubs keep rocking until at least 2 AM and some for a couple of hours after that. For the latest information on nightclubs get your hands on *What's On Auckland,* a pocket-size booklet available at all visitor information bureaus. *Metro* magazine can also give you a helpful nightlife scoop.

BARS AND LOUNGES

At the heart of the city center, the **Civic Tavern** (⊠ 1 Wellesley St., ☎ 09/373–3684) houses three bars. The **London Bar** has a vast selection of beer and an impressive variety of Scotch whiskey. The **London Underground Bar** is a sports bar with 8-ball pool tables and casino-style poker machines. For a glass of Irish stout, stay on the ground floor and visit **Murphy's Irish Bar.**

Classic Comedy & Bar (⊠ 321 Queen St., city center, ☎ 09/373–4321) is housed in what used to be an X-rated movie theater, so if you get a funny look when you ask for directions, you'll know why. These days it is Auckland's only regular venue for live comedy. The caliber of the acts varies, and you'll find a mix of well-known Kiwi comedians, new faces, and the occasional international act.

Part of the Viaduct Village development, the **Loaded Hog** (✉ 104 Quay St., city center, ☎ 09/366–6491) has a vaguely nautical feel. This popular brewery and bistro has indoor and outdoor dining and drinking and can get crowded late in the week, so try to arrive early. Jazz musicians perform most evenings.

Vulcan Lane has long been an after-work favorite with the suit-and-tie set of downtown Auckland. The lane has been tidied up in recent years, and the **Occidental Belgian Beer Cafe** (✉ 6 Vulcan La., city center, ☎ 09/300–6226) is one of the places that got a face-lift. Pair a pint of Belgian beer with a deep pot of mussels.

An atmospheric brewpub, the **Shakespeare Tavern** (✉ Albert and Wyndham Sts., city center, ☎ 09/373–5396) has beer with colorful names like Willpower Stout and Falstaff's Real Ale.

NIGHTCLUBS

Pappa Jacks Voodoo Lounge (✉ 9 Vulcan La., city center, ☎ 09/358–4847) spins disco music late into the night. You'll find things slightly quieter in the adjacent **Dragon Bar** if you want a break from the dancing.

Rakinos (✉ 35 High St., city center, ☎ 09/358–3535) has live jazz in an easy-to-miss upstairs location. It's open Thursday to Saturday, and music ranges from the soft and gentle to stomping blues.

Outdoor Activities and Sports

Biking
Auckland is good for cycling, especially around the waterfront. **Adventure Cycles** (✉ 36 Customs St. E, ☎ 09/309–5566) rents touring bikes for $12 for a half day, $18 for a full day. Mountain bikes run $25. The rental fee includes helmets.

Golf
Chamberlain Park Golf Course (✉ Linwood Ave., Western Springs, ☎ 09/815–4999) is an 18-hole public course in a parkland setting a five-minute drive (off Northwestern Motorway, Route 16) from the city. The club shop rents clubs and carts. Greens fees are $20 on weekdays, $22 on weekends.

Titirangi Golf Course (✉ Links Rd., New Lynn, ☎ 09/827–5749), a 15-minute drive south of the city, is one of the country's finest 18-hole courses. Nonmembers are welcome to play provided they contact the course's professional in advance and show evidence of membership at an overseas club. Clubs and golf carts can be rented; the greens fee is $75.

Running
Auckland's favorite running track is **Tamaki Drive**, a 10-km (6-mi) route that heads east from the city along the south shore of Waitemata Harbour and ends at St. Heliers Bay. The **Auckland Domain** is popular with executive lunchtime runners.

Swimming
The **Tepid Baths** (✉ 102 Customs St. W, city center, ☎ 09/379–4794) has a large indoor swimming pool, a whirlpool, saunas, and a steam room. It's open weekdays 6–9, weekends 7–7; admission is $4.50.

Tennis
ASB Tennis Centre (✉ 72 Stanley St., ☎ 09/373–3623) has 12 hard courts indoors and outdoors, 1 km (½ mi) east of the city center. Rental equipment is available.

Spectator Sports

Eden Park is the city's major stadium for sporting events. This is the best place in winter to see New Zealand's sporting icon, the rugby team All Blacks, consistently among the world's top three teams. More frequently, it sees the Auckland Blues, a Super 12 rugby team that plays professional franchise opponents from Australia, South Africa, and other parts of New Zealand. Cricket teams arrive in summer. For information on sporting events, check out *What's On Auckland,* a monthly guide available from the Auckland Travel and Information Centre (☞ Visitor Information *in* Auckland A to Z, *below*). Tickets can be booked through **Ticketek** (☎ 09/307–5000).

Shopping

Department Store

Smith and Caughey Ltd. (✉ 253–261 Queen St., city center, ☎ 09/377–4770) extends over four floors and is a comprehensive department store with a conservative bent. There are plenty of local brands to browse through, and you'll even find a hairdresser.

Districts

Ponsonby is known for its antiques shops and fashion boutiques. Auckland's main shopping precinct for clothes, outdoor gear, duty-free goods, greenstone jewelry, and souvenirs is **Queen Street**. **O'Connell and High streets** also have a good smattering of bookstores, crafts boutiques, and other specialty shops.

Mall

Dress-Smart (✉ 151 Arthur St., Onehunga, ☎ 09/622–2400) is a whole mall of factory outlets and is the place to go for quality, low-priced goods. As the name suggests, it started as a clothing mall but has recently doubled in size and diversified. You'll now find books, records, children's toys, bags, jewelry, and housewares. Expect to pay 30%–50% less than you would retail. Take the inexpensive **shuttle service** (☎ 0800/188–988) or, if you're driving, take the Penrose turnoff from the Southern Motorway; then follow the signs to Onehunga. This is the heart of Auckland suburbia, so a detailed road map will help. Dress-Smart is close to Onehunga Mall.

Specialty Stores

BOOKS AND MAPS

Legendary Hard to Find (but worth the effort) Quality Second-hand Books, Ltd. (✉ 171–175 The Mall, Onehunga, ☎ 09/634–4340) has a name that pretty much says it all. It's a local favorite and very large. Its smaller sister in Devonport, **Hard to Find North Shore** (✉ 81A Victoria St., ☎ 09/446–0300), is a great spot for browsing.

Unity Books (✉ 19 High St., city center, ☎ 09/307–0731) is a general bookstore that specializes in travel, fiction, science, biography, and New Zealand–related books.

SOUVENIRS

Follow elephant footprints down an alley in Parnell Village to **Elephant House** (✉ 237 Parnell Rd., ☎ 09/309–8740) for an extensive collection of souvenirs, many unavailable elsewhere.

The sign hanging above **Pauanesia** (✉ 35 High St., city center, ☎ 09/366–7282) sets the tone for this gift shop—the letters are shaped from paua shell, which resembles abalone. You'll find bags, place mats, picture frames, and many other items.

RUGBY: A NATIONAL OBSESSION

WHEN NEW ZEALAND lost the right to co-host the 2003 Rugby World Cup through what was seen as an administrative blunder, it seemed the whole nation was in an uproar. The resulting debates and inquiries dominated the media, pushing even news of the new coalition government into second place in the newspapers and on the airwaves. But how did a sport invented half a world away in Europe—which has become popular in few other countries—develop into such an integral part of the nation's culture?

Rugby evolved out of soccer in 19th-century Britain. It was born at the elitist English school of Rugby, where in 1823 a schoolboy by the name of William Webb Ellis became bored with kicking a football and picked up the ball and ran with it. Rugby developed among the upper classes of Britain, while soccer remained a predominantly working-class game. Since rugby was was primarily fashionable among British gentlemen, its following remained small. However, in colonial New Zealand, a country largely free from the rigid class structure of Britain, the game developed as the nation's number one sport. From early on, New Zealanders felt such passion about rugby that in many ways their national identity was formed around it. One reason for this was undoubtedly the success of New Zealand teams in the late 19th and early 20th centuries. This remote outpost of the British empire, with a population of only 750,000 in 1900, was an impressive force at rugby, and this became a source of great national pride. Today, in a country of nearly 4 million, the national sport is played by 250,000 New Zealanders at club level and embraced by huge numbers with an almost religious fervor.

The top-class rugby season in the Southern hemisphere kicks off in March with the Super 12, which pits professional teams from provincial franchises in New Zealand, South Africa, and Australia against each other. New Zealand's matches are generally held in main cities, and you should be able to get tickets without too much trouble. The international season runs from June to late August. This is your best chance to see the national team, the All Blacks, and the major cities are again the place to be. National provincial championship games hit towns all over the country from late August to mid-October. A winner-take-all game decides who will attain the domestic rugby Holy Grail, the Ranfurly Shield. If you can't catch a live game, you can always count on a crowd watching the televised match at the local pubs.

The sport is very similar to American football, except that players are not allowed to pass the ball forward and they wear no protective gear. Like American football, rugby is not a worldwide sport; only a handful of countries play it at a high level. But despite its limited worldwide following, rugby administrators have organized a world cup for the sport every four years since 1987, which New Zealand has won once. The New Zealand team was a hot favorite to win the World Cup played in Britain in 1999. So when the All Blacks not only failed to win the trophy, but failed to reach the final, the national team's failure sparked off a huge bout of introspection about what went wrong with not just the national sport but with the country as a whole. More soul-searching arose during the 2002 hosting debacle, after which most of the union board members were replaced. At press time, the country's hopes were pinned on the All Blacks's reclaiming the trophy.

Kathmandu (✉ 151 Queen St., city center, ☎ 09/309–4615) stocks New Zealand–made outdoor clothing and equipment, with everything from fleece jackets to sleeping bags to haul-everything packs.

One of a nationwide chain of stores, **Outdoor Heritage** (✉ 75 Queen St., city center, ☎ 09/309–6571) sells high-quality outdoor clothing.

The extensive range of gear at **Tisdall's Outdoors** (✉ 176 Queen St., city center, ☎ 09/379–0254) is made especially for New Zealand conditions.

Street Markets

The beautiful countryside of the Waitakere Ranges has attracted artists seeking an alternative lifestyle, close to a major population (and customer) base but away from the hustle and bustle. Many of their wares are on sale at the **Titirangi Village Market** (✉ Titirangi Memorial Hall, S. Titirangi Rd., ☎ 09/817–3584). It is held on the last Sunday of each month.

Auckland's main bazaar, **Victoria Park Market** (✉ Victoria and Wellesley Sts., city center, ☎ 09/309–6911, WEB www.victoria-park-market. co.nz), consists of 2½ acres of clothing, footwear, sportswear, furniture, souvenirs, and crafts at knockdown prices. It's housed in the city's former garbage incinerator.

Auckland A to Z

AIR TRAVEL

➤ CARRIERS: **Air Nelson** (☎ 09/379–3510). **Air New Zealand** (☎ 0800/737–000). **Cathay Pacific** (☎ 09/379–0861). **Qantas** (☎ 09/ 357–8900). **Singapore Airlines** (☎ 09/379–3209). **United Airlines** (☎ 09/379–3800).

AIRPORT

Auckland International Airport (AKL) lies 21 km (13 mi) southwest of the city center, about a 30-minute drive away.

A free Interterminal Bus links the international and domestic terminals, with frequent departures in each direction 6 AM–10 PM. Otherwise, the walk between the two terminals takes about 10 minutes along a signposted walkway. Luggage for flights aboard the two major domestic airlines, Air New Zealand and Qantas Airways, can be checked at the international terminal.
➤ CONTACT: **Auckland International Airport** (✉ Fred Thomas Dr., Manukau, ☎ 09/256–8899, WEB www.auckland-airport.co.nz).

The Airbus costs $12 one-way and $20 round-trip and leaves the international terminal every 20 minutes between 6:20 AM and 8:20 PM. The fixed route between the airport and the Downtown Airline Terminal, on the corner of Quay Street and Albert Road, includes a stop at the railway station and, on request, at any bus stop, hotel, or motel along the way. Returning from the city, the bus leaves the Downtown Airline Terminal at 20-minute intervals between 6:20 AM and 9 PM. Travel time is 35–45 minutes.

Hallmark Limousines and Tours operates Ford LTD limousines between the airport and the city for approximately $65.

Super Shuttle has service between the airport and any address in the city center. The cost is $18 for a single traveler and $6 extra for each additional person.

Taxi fare to the city is approximately $38.

➤ CONTACTS: **Airbus** (☎ 0508/247–287, WEB www.airbus.co.nz). **Hall-mark Limousines and Tours** (☎ 09/629–0940). **Super Shuttle** (☎ 09/275–1234).

BUS TRAVEL

The Sky City Coach Terminal is Auckland's hub for InterCity Coaches and Newmans Coaches. Auckland is also a jumping-off point for several of InterCity's special travel pass routes, with daily departures for trips like "Forests, Islands and Geysers" and "New Zealand Pathfinder."
➤ BUS DEPOT: **Sky City Coach Terminal** (✉ 102 Hobson St., city center).
➤ BUS LINES: **InterCity Coaches** (☎ 09/913–6100, WEB www.intercitycoach.co.nz). **Newmans Coaches** (☎ 09/913–6200, WEB www.newmanscoach.co.nz).

BUS TRAVEL WITHIN AUCKLAND

The easily recognizable white Link Buses circle the inner city, including many of the most popular stops for visitors, every 10 minutes between 6 AM and 6 PM weekdays, and then every 20 minutes until 10 PM. The weekend service is every 20 minutes from 7 AM to 11 PM. The route includes the Downtown Bus Terminal at the Britomart Centre between Customs Street and Quay Street. The buses stop at Queens Street, Parnell, Newmarket (near the Auckland Museum), Ponsonby, and Karangahape Road among other places. The fare anywhere on the route is $1.20, payable as you get onto the bus. To travel farther afield you'll need to get onto a Stagecoach Bus, which is run by the same company and has services as far north as Orewa on the Hibiscus Coast and south to Pukekohe. A one-day Auckland Pass at $8 for unlimited travel is easily the best value for anyone planning extensive use of the buses (both Link and Stagecoach), particularly because it is also valid for travel on Link ferries between the city and the North Shore.
➤ INFORMATION: **Information Kiosk** (✉ Britomart Centre, at Commerce St. and Galway St., city center). **RideLine** (☎ 09/366–6400, WEB www.rideline.co.nz).

CAR RENTAL

MAJOR AGENCIES
Avis, Budget, and Hertz have offices inside the Auckland International Airport.
➤ CONTACTS: **Avis** (☎ 09/275–7239). **Budget** (☎ 09/256–8451). **Hertz** (☎ 09/256–8692).

CAR TRAVEL

By the standards of many cities, Auckland traffic is moderate, parking space is inexpensive and readily available, and highways pass close to the heart of the city. Local rush hours last from 7 to 9 AM and 4:30 to 6:30 PM. Getting used to driving on the left, if you'll be traveling by car, can be especially difficult when trying to figure out where to get onto motorways. Take a close look at a city map before you set out. The main motorways all have convenient city turnoffs, but watch the signs to make sure you are in the correct lane. When changing lanes, flick on your indicator promptly, as New Zealanders are not always the most obliging when it comes to merging. City-center parking meters are cheaper than the covered lots, but make sure you have a wide selection of coins on hand and be aware that the meters are well policed. If you go over the time limit you'll probably end up paying a fine. Meter time is generally limited to an hour in the city center, two hours in outer areas.

CONSULATES

While the Australian and Canadian consulates are open from 8:30 until just before 5 on weekdays, the British and U.S. consulates open only from 9:30 until around 12:30 on weekdays.

➤ Australia: **Australian Consulate** (✉ Union House, 132–138 Quay St., ☎ 09/303–2429).

➤ Canada: **Canadian Consulate** (✉ Jetset Centre, 48 Emily Pl., ☎ 09/309–3690).

➤ United Kingdom: **British Consulate** (✉ Fay Richwhite Bldg., 151 Queen St., ☎ 09/303–2973).

➤ United States: **U.S. Consulate** (✉ General Assurance Bldg., Shortland and O'Connell Sts., ☎ 09/303–2724).

EMERGENCIES

➤ Dentists: **St. John's Ambulance** (☎ 09/579–9099) for local referrals.

➤ Emergency Services: **Fire, police, and ambulance** (☎ 111).

➤ Hospitals: **Auckland Hospital** (✉ Park Rd., Grafton, ☎ 09/379–7440). **Southern Cross Central** (✉ 122 Remuera Rd., Remuera, ☎ 09/524–5943 or 09/524–7906).

➤ Late-Night Pharmacy: **Late-Night Pharmacy** (✉ 60 Broadway, ☎ 09/520–6634, ◷ weekdays 5:30 PM–7 AM, weekends 9 AM–7 AM).

FERRY TRAVEL

Various companies serve Waitemata Harbour; one of the best and least expensive is the Devonport commuter ferry, run by the Fullers company. The ferry terminal is on the harbor side of the Ferry Building on Quay Street, near the corner of Albert Street. Boats leave here for Devonport Monday–Thursday 6:15 AM–11 PM, Friday and Saturday 6:15 AM–1 AM, and Sunday 7 AM–11 PM. On weekdays they depart on the hour between 10 and 3, and at half-hour intervals during the morning and evening commuter periods; on Saturday and Sunday they leave every hour. The cost is $8 round-trip. Ferries also make the 35-minute run to Waiheke Island approximately every two hours, beginning at 6:30 AM, at a cost of $24 round-trip. Return ferries leave about every two hours on odd-numbered hours.

➤ Contact: **Devonport Commuter Ferry** (✉ Ferry Bldg., Quay St. at Albert St., ☎ 09/367–9118, WEB www.fullers.co.nz).

MONEY MATTERS

Two Bank of New Zealand branches inside the international terminal of Auckland International Airport are open for all arriving and departing flights. In the city, there are several currency-exchange agencies on Queen Street between Victoria and Customs streets offering the same rate as banks. Foreign currency may also be exchanged at the cashier's office above Celebrity Walk at the Drake Street entrance of Victoria Park Market. A 24-hour exchange machine outside the Downtown Airline Terminal will change notes of any major currency into New Zealand dollars, but the rate is significantly less than that offered by banks.

➤ Currency Exchange: **Bank of New Zealand** (✉ Auckland International Airport). **Downtown Airline Terminal** (✉ Quay and Albert Sts.). **Thomas Cook Travelex** (✉ 34 Queen St., ☎ 09/377–2666). **Victoria Park Market Cashier's Office** (☎ 09/309–6911).

TAXIS

Taxis can be hailed in the street but are more readily available from taxi stands throughout the city. Placards with "Taxi Sign" in red letters mark the stands. Auckland taxi rates vary with the company but are listed on the driver's door. Most taxis will accept major credit cards.

➤ Taxi Companies: **Alert Taxis** (☎ 09/309–2000). **Auckland Cooperative Taxi Service** (☎ 09/300–3000). **Eastern Taxis** (☎ 09/527–7077).

TOURS
BOAT TOURS

Fullers Cruise Centre has a variety of cruises around the harbor and to the islands of Hauraki Gulf. The two-hour Auckland Harbor cruise ($30) departs daily at 10:30 and 1:30, with an extra afternoon cruise from late December to April. Boats leave from the Ferry Building.

The Pride of Auckland Company sails for lunch and dinner on the inner harbor. The 1½-hour lunch cruise ($65) departs at 11 and 1, and the three-hour dinner cruise ($90) departs at 7. An Experience Sailing trip ($45) departs at 11. Boats leave from the National Maritime Museum, near Princes Wharf.

➤ Contacts: **Fullers Cruise Centre** (☎ 09/367–9111, WEB www.fullers. co.nz). **Pride of Auckland Company** (☎ 09/373–4557, WEB www. sailwithpride.co.nz).

BUS TOURS

An Explorer Bus trip is a convenient introduction to Auckland. The blue-and-gray double-decker bus travels in a circuit, stopping at eight of the city's major attractions; you can leave at any stop and reboard any following Explorer bus. The loop begins at the Downtown Airline Terminal every hour between 9 and 4 daily; tickets are available from the driver. A one-day pass is $25.

The Gray Line runs a Morning Highlights tour, which includes admission to Kelly Tarlton's Underwater World. This tour departs daily from the Downtown Airline Terminal on Quay Street at 9 and costs $51.

Scenic Tours operates a three-hour City Highlights guided bus tour, which takes in the main attractions in the city and Parnell and the view from the lookout on Mt. Eden. Tours leave from Quay Street, just across from the Ferry Building, at 9:30 and 2, and tickets are $35.

➤ Contacts: **Explorer Bus** (☎ 09/360–0033 or 0800/439–756, WEB www.explorerbus.co.nz). **Gray Line** (☎ 09/377–0904). **Scenic Tours** (☎ 09/307–7880, WEB www.scenictours.co.nz).

WILDERNESS TOURS

Red Feather Expeditions Ltd. is run by expat American Beth Coleman, who has built up a love for the wilderness and culture of New Zealand. Tours are tailor-made and can be restricted to the greater Auckland area (Beth has a special knowledge of the Waitakere Ranges) or extended farther afield. Itineraries can include soft-adventure sports or a focus on ecology, Māori culture, or other topics; all include walking or hiking.

➤ Contact: **Red Feather Expeditions Ltd.** (✉ Box 60243, Titirangi, ☎ 09/309–1911, WEB www.ecotoursnz.com).

TRAIN TRAVEL

The terminal for all intercity train services is the Auckland Central Railway Station, about 1½ km (1 mi) east of the city center. A booking office is inside the Auckland Travel and Information Centre. Train service throughout New Zealand is in flux, however, and service is becoming increasingly limited.

➤ Contacts: **Auckland Central Railway Station** (✉ Beach Rd., near Ronayne St., ☎ 0800/802–802). **Auckland Travel and Information Centre** (✉ 287 Queen St., ☎ 09/979–2333).

TRAVEL AGENCIES

➤ Agency: **Thomas Cook** (✉ 107 Queen St., ☎ 09/379–3924).

VISITOR INFORMATION

The main bureau of Auckland's visitor center is open on weekdays 8:30 to 5:30, on weekends from 9 to 5. The branch in the airport opens daily at 5 AM and stays open until the last flight arrives.

The Thursday *Auckland Tourist Times* is a free newspaper with the latest information on tours, exhibitions, and shopping. The paper is available from hotels and from the Travel and Information Centre.

➤ TOURIST INFORMATION: **Auckland International Airport Visitor Centre** (⊠ Ground floor, International Airport Terminal, ☎ 09/275–6467, FAX 09/256–8942). **Auckland Travel and Information Centre** (⊠ 287 Queen St., ☎ 09/979–2333, FAX 09/979–2334, WEB www.aucklandnz. com). **Devonport Visitor Information Centre** (⊠ 2 Victoria Rd., ☎ 09/ 446–0677, WEB www.devonport.co.nz).

NORTHLAND AND THE BAY OF ISLANDS

Beyond Auckland, the North Island stretches a long arm into the South Pacific. This is Northland, an undulating region of farms, forests, and marvelous beaches. The Bay of Islands is the main attraction, an island-littered seascape with a mild, subtropical climate and some of the finest game-fishing waters in the country—witness its record catches of marlin and mako shark. Big-game fishing is expensive, but small fishing boats can take you out for an evening of trawling for around $60.

It was on the Bay of Islands that the first European settlement was established and where modern New Zealand became a nation with the signing of the Treaty of Waitangi in 1840. The main town is Paihia, a strip of motels and restaurants along the waterfront. If you plan to spend more than a day in the area, the town of Russell, just a ride or short ferry trip away, makes for a more atmospheric and attractive base.

You can explore Northland in an easy loop from Auckland, driving up Highway 1 and returning on Highway 12 with little revisiting of sights on the way back. Bay of Islands is a favorite vacation spot for Kiwis, particularly from mid-December to the end of January, when accommodations are often filled months in advance.

Albany

16 *12 km (7 mi) north of Auckland.*

If you're driving up to the small village of Albany in December, you'll see scarlet blossoms blazing along the roadside. These are pohutukawa trees in flower, turning crimson in time for the Kiwi Christmas, hence their *Pākehā* (European) name—"the New Zealand Christmas tree." To the Māori, the flowers had another meaning: the beginning of shellfish season. The spiky-leaved plants that grow in clumps by the roadside are New Zealand flax. The fibers of this plant, the raw material for linen, were woven into clothing by the Māori. The huge tree ferns—common throughout the forests of the North Island, where they can grow as high as 30 ft—are known locally as *punga*. From Highway 1 you'll need to take the well-signposted Albany turnoff. It's worth it, if have a bit of time to spare, to get away from the main highway and onto more scenic country roads.

Dining

$–$$$ ✕ **Quattro at the Albany Inn.** Break your journey north at this country pub, run by a couple of big-city weekend refugees who also operate a café in trendy Ponsonby. The food is generous, with an emphasis

Northland and the Bay of Islands

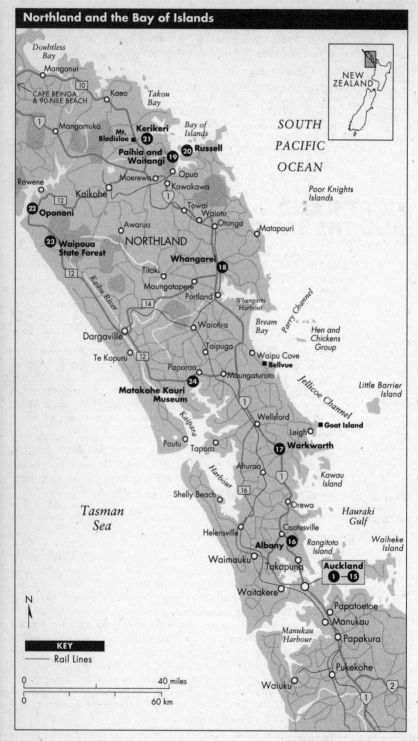

on casseroles and slow-cooked meats in winter, grilled food and salads in summer. The wine and beer lists are wide-ranging and generally well priced. Dine indoors or out—although the only view is of a parking lot. ⊠ *276 Main St.,* ☎ *09/415–9515. AE, DC, MC, V.*

Warkworth

🟠 *47 km (29 mi) north of Albany.*

One of the great natural features of the north half of the North Island is one native pine species, the kauri tree. Two giants stand in Warkworth, near the Warkworth Museum. The larger one, the **McKinney Kauri,** measures almost 25 ft around its base, yet this 800-year-old colossus is a mere adolescent by kauri standards. Kauri trees, once prolific in this part of the North Island, were highly prized by Māori canoe builders, because a canoe capable of carrying a hundred warriors could be made from a single trunk. Unfortunately these same characteristics—strength, size, and durability—made kauri timber ideal for ships, furniture, and housing, and the kauri forests were rapidly depleted by early European settlers. Today the trees are protected by law, and infant kauri are appearing in the forests of the North Island, although their growth rate is painfully slow.

The **Warkworth Museum** contains a collection of Māori artifacts and farming and domestic implements from the pioneering days of the Warkworth district. The museum also has a souvenir shop with kauri bowls and other wooden items. ⊠ *Tudor Collins Dr.,* ☎ *09/425–7093,* WEB *www.wwmuseum.orcon.net.nz.* ⊠ *$5.* ☉ *Daily 9–4.*

En Route Even if you aren't a hortomaniac, come to Daniel and Vivian Papich's **Bellvue** for its spectacular views of the Pacific Ocean. The Hen and Chickens Islands lie right off the coast, and on clear days you can even see the Poor Knights Islands, a good 70 km (45 mi) away. The bold foliage of agaves, bromeliads, succulents, and *puka* trees is abundant and sets off the more delicate exotics. Vivian's container plantings—300 at last count—are everywhere, even hanging from the trees. Conceived as a way to keep more demanding plants from struggling in the hard clay soil here, the containers have evolved into an art form. They are often composed of unconventional materials and used in inventive seasonal displays. Birders, keep your eyes and ears open for the fantails, whiteyes, and *tūī* that frequent the garden. ⊠ *Coastal Hwy., Langs Beach, 55 km (34 mi) north of Warkworth,* ☎ *09/432–0465.* ⊠ *Small entry fee.* ☉ *By appointment.*

For a glimpse of what the New Zealand coast must have been like 200 years ago, take a trip to the **Goat Island** marine reserve. Fishing is prohibited here, and marine life has returned in abundance, with prominent species including blue *maomao,* snapper, and cod. You can put on a snorkel and easily glide around the island, just a little ways offshore. You can rent mask, snorkel, and flippers ($12) at the beach from **Seafriends** (☎ 09/422–6212). **Habitat Explorer** (☎ 09/422–6334, WEB www.glassbottomboat.co.nz) has a glass-bottom boat that runs around the island ($18). But you needn't get even this serious to see plenty of fish. Just walk into the water up to your waist and look around you. To drum up more action, throw some bread or noodles into the sea and watch the fish congregate just inches from you. The beach area is good for a picnic as well.

To get to Goat Island head toward Leigh, 21 km (13 mi) northeast of Warkworth. From Leigh, take a left turn and follow the signs for a couple of miles. The area can get crowded, but if you arrive by 10 AM or earlier, you should avoid the masses. Department of Conservation leaflets detailing Goat Island can be obtained from the Warkworth Visitor Information Centre (☞ Visitor Information *in* Northland and the Bay of Islands A to Z, *below*).

Whangarei

⓲ *127 km (79 mi) north of Warkworth, 196 km (123 mi) north of Auckland.*

Many people on the way to the Bay of Islands bypass Whangarei (*fahng*-ar-ay), but it is well worth taking the turnoff from the main highway, especially since the area known as the **Whangarei Town Basin** has been improved. Here you will find **Ahipupu Maori and Pacific Arts and Crafts,** which has both traditional and contemporary works.

Just about every conceivable method of telling time is represented in the Basin's **Claphams Clock Museum.** The collection of more than 1,500 clocks includes everything from primitive water clocks to ships' chronometers to ornate masterworks from Paris and Vienna. Some of the most intriguing examples were made by the late Mr. Clapham himself, like his World War II air-force clock. Clockwork also shows up in a selection of music boxes. Ironically, the one thing you won't find here is the correct time. If all the bells, chimes, gongs, and cuckoos went off together, the noise would be deafening, so the clocks are set to different times. ⊠ *Quayside Whangarei,* ☎ *09/438–3993.* ☞ *$7.* ☉ *Daily 9–5.*

The oldest kauri villa in Whangarei, **Historical Reyburn House** contains the Northland Society of Arts exhibition gallery, which hosts monthly exhibitions. It is separated from the Town Basin by a playground. ⊠ *Lower Quay St.,* ☎ *09/438–3074.* ☞ *Donation.* ☉ *Tues.–Fri. 10–4, weekends noon–4.*

You'll find a lovely picnic spot at **Whangarei Falls** on Ngunguru Road, 5 km (3 mi) northeast of town. There are viewing platforms atop the falls and a short trail through the local bush.

Early settlers eager to farm the rich volcanic land around Whangarei found their efforts constantly thwarted by an abundance of rock in the soil. To make use of the stuff they dug up, they built walls—miles of walls. The current settlers at **Greagh,** Kathleen and Clark Abbot, have carried on this tradition, giving their gardens the Celtic name for "land among the stone." The walls form a handsome framework for perennials and roses, and the plantings, in turn, emphasize the beauty and strength of the stone on terraces and in five separate walled gardens. ⊠ *Three Mile Bush Rd.,* ☎ *09/435–1980.* ☞ *Small entry fee.* ☉ *Oct.–mid-Dec., daily 10–4; mid-Dec.–Apr. by appointment.*

Dining and Lodging

$$$ ✕ **Tonic.** Owner chef Brad O'Connell's seasonal menu can set you up with interesting seafood choices like fish with truffles, mashed peas, and crab tortellini. If you're in luck, the warm blackberry and almond crumble tart will be on the dessert list. ⊠ *239 Kamo Rd.,* ☎ *09/437–5558. AE, DC, MC, V. No lunch.*

$$$ ☷ **Parua House.** From this spot on the edge of Parua Bay, you can explore the towering Whangarei Heads that enclose the bay. The house dates from 1882 and retains much of its colonial feel, enhanced by antiques brought over from England by the owners. You can take a walk through the nearby bush or even help milk their cow. ⊠ *Whangarei Heads Rd. (R.D. 4, Parua Bay), 17 km (11 mi) from Whangarei,* ☎ *09/436–5855,* FAX *09/436–5105,* WEB *www.paruahomestay.homestead.com. 2 rooms. Dining room, hot tub. MC, V. BP. Closed June–July.*

MĀORI HISTORY AND THE WAITANGI TREATY

THE HISTORY OF COLONIALISM is rife with broken promises, and New Zealand's legacy is no different. The first recorded contact between a European and the indigenous people of New Zealand was in 1642 by Dutch explorer Abel Tasman. In October 1769, Captain James Cook landed at Poverty Bay and claimed the country for Britain. When the first Europeans arrived, the indigenous New Zealanders—who had arrived between AD 850 and 1300—had settled most of what they called Aotearoa ("land of the long white cloud"). A rich culture had developed: the family and hapū (tribe) were the central units of society. Tribal ancestors were venerated along with gods representing elemental forces. Complex systems for health, education, justice, spirituality, ecological preservation, art, and governance were in place.

The initial settlement by European whale and seal traders and missionaries was welcomed by Māori chiefs. They enjoyed the trade and quickly adapted the religion and literacy brought by missionaries. But settlers also arrived with diseases and demonstrated a growing need for more land. In the face of these conditions, North Island Māori chiefs banded together to set up a regulated system for land sales and laws to contain unruly settlers. They also desired opportunities to trade across the Tasman and farther afield.

On February 6, 1840, a confederation of North Island chiefs signed the Treaty of Waitangi with England. But there were significant differences between the Māori and English translations of this first treaty. In the first article, the English version said Māori would cede sovereignty to Queen Victoria. But the Māori version used the word kāwanatanga (governorship), which did not mean that the Māori were ceding the right to mana (self-determination).

The second article in English and Māori versions guaranteed the chiefs the "full, exclusive and undisturbed possession of their lands, estates, forests, fisheries and other properties" and allowed the Crown the right to buy and sell land from Māori. The third article granted Māori protection as British citizens, though the English version said they were British subjects.

On top of the problems of translation, basic breaches of the treaty began almost as soon as it was signed. What wasn't confiscated after the 1861 New Zealand Land Wars was taken by legislation. In 1877 Chief Justice Prendergast ruled that the treaty was "a simple nullity" that lacked legal validity because one could not make a treaty with "primitive barbarians." At first European contact, 66.5 million acres of land was under Māori control, but by 1979 only 3 million remained—of mostly marginal lands.

But the battle to have the treaty honored has continued despite the government assimilation policies through which Māori language and cultural practices were actively discouraged or banned. And the Māori population, which had been decimated by 1900, began to resurge over the course of the 20th century.

By the 1970s some urban Māori were pushing for policies to allow Māori language to be taught in schools and for Māori to have greater say in social services and government. Under the Labour Government, the Waitangi Tribunal was established in 1975 to allow Māori to rule on alleged breaches of the treaty, and in 1985 the tribunal's powers were made retrospective to 1840. Today, Māori have over 15 representatives in Parliament, including seven dedicated Māori seats, and Māori hold key government portfolios.

Many would agree that the key issue facing the country is what to do about the claims for alleged grievances under the Treaty of Waitangi. The Māori are a growing political force. Some predict that by 2040 50% of the country's population will be of Māori or Polynesian descent. Despite many economic and social troubles, Māori are making inroads into participating in New Zealand society at every level. And the government is, finally, grappling with how to implement the partnership.

Paihia and Waitangi

⑲ *69 km (43 mi) north of Whangarei.*

As the main vacation base for the Bay of Islands, Paihia is an unremarkable stretch of motels at odds with the quiet beauty of the island-studded seascape and the rounded green hills surrounding it. Nearby Waitangi, however, is one of the country's most important historic sites. It was near here that the Treaty of Waitangi, the founding document for modern New Zealand, was signed.

Waitangi National Reserve is at the northern end of Paihia. Inside the visitor center a 23-minute video, shown every hour on the hour, sketches the events that led to the Treaty of Waitangi. The center also displays Māori artifacts and weapons, including a musket that belonged to Hone Heke Pokai, the first Māori chief to sign the treaty. After his initial display of enthusiasm for British rule, Hone Heke was quickly disillusioned, and less than five years later he attacked the British in their stronghold at Russell. From the visitor center, follow a short track (trail) through the forest to **Nga Toki Matawhaorua** (ng-ga to-ki mata-*fa*-oh-*roo*-ah), a Māori war canoe. This huge kauri canoe, capable of carrying 150 warriors, is named after the vessel in which Kupe, the Polynesian navigator, is said to have discovered New Zealand.

Treaty House in Waitangi National Reserve is a simple white timber cottage that has a remarkable air of dignity despite its size. The interior is fascinating, especially the back, where exposed walls demonstrate the difficulties that early administrators faced—such as an acute shortage of bricks (since an insufficient number had been shipped from New South Wales, as Australia was known at the time) with which to finish the walls.

The Treaty House was prefabricated in New South Wales for the British Resident James Busby, who arrived in New Zealand in 1832. Busby had been appointed to protect British commerce and put an end to the brutalities of the whaling captains against the Māori, but Busby lacked either the judicial authority or the force of arms necessary to impose peace. On one occasion, unable to resolve a dispute between Māori tribes, Busby was forced to shelter the wounded of one side in his house. While tattooed warriors screamed war chants outside the windows, one of the Māori sheltered Busby's infant daughter, Sarah, in his cape.

The real significance of the Treaty House lies in the events that took place here on February 6, 1840, the day that the **Treaty of Waitangi** was signed by Māori chiefs and Captain William Hobson, representing the British crown. Under the treaty, the chiefs agreed to accept the authority of the Crown; in return, the British recognized the Māori as the legitimate landowners and granted them all the rights and privileges of British subjects. The treaty also confirmed the status of New Zealand as a British colony, forestalling French overtures in the area, and legitimized—at least according to European law—the transfer of land from Māori to European hands. In recent years the Māori have used the treaty successfully to reclaim land that they maintain was misappropriated by white settlers.

The Treaty House has not always received the care its significance merits. When Lord Bledisloe bought the house and presented it to the nation in 1932, it was being used as a shelter for sheep.

Whare Runanga (fah-ray roo-nang-ah) is a Māori meetinghouse with an elaborately carved interior. Inside, an audio show briefly outlines traditional Māori society. The house is on the northern boundary of Waitangi National Reserve. ⊠ *Waitangi Rd., Waitangi,* ☎ *09/402–7437.* 🎟 *$5.* ⊙ *Daily 9–5.*

🐣 The *Tui,* high and dry on the banks of the Waitangi River, is a historic kauri sailing vessel that was built to carry sugar to a refinery in Auckland. Below decks is an exhibition of artifacts recovered from shipwrecks by the famous New Zealand salvage diver Kelly Tarlton. In addition to the brass telescopes, sextants, and diving helmets that you can try on for size, there is an exquisite collection of jewelry that belonged to Isidore Jonah Rothschild (of the famous banking family), which was lost when the S.S. *Tasmania* sank in 1897. Rothschild was on a sales trip to New Zealand at the time. ✉ *Waitangi Bridge, Paihia,* ☎ 09/402–7018. 🎫 *$5.* 🕐 *Daily 10–5.*

Mt. Bledisloe offers a splendid view across Paihia and the Bay of Islands. The handsome ceramic marker at the top showing the distances to major world cities was made by Doulton in London and presented by Lord Bledisloe in 1934 during his term as governor-general of New Zealand. The mount is 3 km (2 mi) from the Treaty House, on the other side of the Waitangi Golf Course. From a small parking area on the right of Waitangi Road, a short track rises above a pine forest to the summit.

Dining and Lodging

$$–$$$ ✕ **Saltwater Café.** If the sea air's given you a serious appetite, head to this casual spot to grab a steaming pizza. The Kiwi Pizza, a local favorite, is loaded with salsa, onions, herbs, and ham. A Greek pie with feta cheese and spinach and a meat lover's version are also worth trying. ✉ *Kings Rd., Paihia,* ☎ 09/402–6080. *AE, DC, MC, V. Licensed and BYOB.*

$–$$ ✕ **Tides.** The sun streams into this central café in the morning, making it a great place to enjoy a plate of bacon, eggs, and hash browns. Lunch and dinner take on an unusual but tasty Asian-Mex flavor, with dishes such as the Asian Chicken Tortilla, a sweet soy chicken tortilla with stir-fried vegetables, black bean sauce, and sour cream. If you're looking for a local wine, go for something from the Cottle Hill vineyard. ✉ *Williams Rd., Paihia,* ☎ 09/402–7557. *AE, DC, MC, V.*

$ ✕ **Waikokupu Café.** With a view straight out to sea, this pleasant spot has a lot going for it. Chunky sandwiches, delicious cakes, and other goodies are available through the day, but things get more serious in the evening. Try the tuna infused with lemongrass, pink ginger, and sesame or the tortilla-wrapped spiced lamb loin with roasted corn, grilled bell peppers, and bean salsa. ✉ *Tau Henare Dr., Waitangi,* ☎ 09/402–6275. *MC, V. Licensed and BYOB. No dinner May–Sept.*

$$$–$$$$ 🏨 **Abri.** These studio apartments take advantage of the bush setting just behind the Paihia beachfront, offering lovely sea views. The two units feature *rimu* flooring and *macrocarpa* timber walls and jet baths; their large living-room areas open onto outside decks. The apartments have their own kitchen facilities, even a small barbecue on the deck, but most guests take the short walk to the restaurants in town for meals. The owners know the little touches that make visitors feel welcome, and you'll find fresh fruit and flowers in your room daily. Listen for the "resident" kiwi bird, and if you do hear some shuffling outside at night, grab a flashlight and attempt some bird spotting. ✉ *10 Bayview Rd., Paihia,* ☎ 09/402–8003, 🌐 *www.abri-accom.co.nz. 2 studios. In-room hot tubs, in-room VCRs, kitchens. MC, V.*

$$$–$$$$ 🏨 **Copthorne Resort Waitangi.** The biggest hotel north of Auckland and a favorite with tour groups, this complex sprawls along a peninsula within walking distance of the Treaty House. Garden-facing rooms are decorated in a French provincial style, with yellows and blues and wrought-iron light fixtures. Ask for one of the more recently refurbished rooms, which have a courtyard-breakfast area, giving the room a far more open feeling. ✉ *Waitangi Rd., Waitangi,* ☎ 09/402–7411, 📠 09/

402–8200. 138 rooms, 7 suites. 3 restaurants, minibars, pool, 2 bars, laundry facilities. AE, DC, MC, V.

$–$$$ 🏨 **Saltwater Lodge.** Backpackers and budget travelers tend to congregate
★ in Paihia's Kings Road area, near most of the town's hostels. This is
the best of the bunch, as both cleanliness and comfort are top priori-
ties. The hostel rooms start at $19 a night, and even the cheapest beds
have duvets supplied. Bunk-bed dormitories all have en-suite bathrooms
with shower, storage facilities, and reading lights over the beds. The
second-floor motel units come with double beds and bunks, plus a fridge
and a small TV. The communal kitchen is probably the best equipped
you'll find in the whole country, with everything from a wok to egg
beaters. There's even a small gym, as well as kayaks and bikes for use
at no extra charge. ✉ *14 Kings Rd., Paihia,* ☎ *09/402–7075,* FAX *09/*
402–7240, WEB *www.saltwaterlodge.co.nz. 10 motel units, 9 dorm*
rooms. Dining room, kitchen, some refrigerators, gym, laundry facil-
ities. AE, DC, MC, V.

$$ 🏨 **Austria Motel.** The large, double-bed rooms here are typical of
motel accommodations in the area—clean and moderately comfortable
but almost totally devoid of charm. The motel also has a family unit
on the ground level of the two-story wing. The shops and waterfront
at Paihia are a two-minute walk away. ✉ *36 Selwyn Rd.,* ☎ FAX *09/*
402–7480. 7 rooms. Kitchenettes. AE, DC, MC, V.

Outdoor Activities and Sports

BOATING

Carino NZ Sailing and Dolphin Charters (✉ Box 286, Paihia, ☎ 09/402–
8040, FAX 09/402–8661) gets as close as practical to sea life such as dolphins and penguins. Passengers can just relax or help with sailing. A
catamaran operated by **Straycat Day Sailing Charters** (✉ Doves Bay Rd.,
Kerikeri, ☎ 09/407–7342 or 025/96–9944) makes one-day sailing trips
in the Bay of Islands from Russell and Paihia at $60 per person.

DIVING

The Bay of Islands has some of the finest scuba diving in the country,
particularly around Cape Brett, where the marine life includes moray
eels, stingrays, and grouper. The wreck of the Greenpeace vessel *Rainbow Warrior,* sunk by French agents, is another Bay of Islands underwater highlight. Water temperature at the surface varies from 16°C (62°F)
in July to 22°C (71°F) in January. From September through November, underwater visibility can be affected by a plankton bloom. **Paihia
Dive Hire and Charter** (✉ Box 210, Paihia, ☎ 09/402–7551, WEB www.
divenz.com) offers complete equipment rental and regular boat trips
for accredited divers for about $145 per day.

FISHING

The Bay of Islands is one of the world's premier game-fishing grounds
for marlin and several species of shark. **NZ Billfish Charters** (✉ Box
416, Paihia, ☎ 09/402–8380) goes for the big ones. A far less expensive alternative is to fish for snapper, kingfish, and John Dory in the
inshore waters of the bay. **Skipper Jim** (☎ 09/402–7355) organizes a
half day of fishing, including bait and rods, for about $50 per person.
M.V. Arline (☎ 09/402–8511) is another resource for a half-day trip
with gear included.

Russell

⑳ *4 km (2½ mi) east of Paihia by ferry, 13 km (8 mi) by road and car
ferry.*

Russell is regarded as the "second" town in the Bay of Islands, but it
is far more interesting, and pleasant, than Paihia. Hard as it is to be-

lieve these days, sleepy little Russell was once dubbed the "Hellhole of the Pacific." In the early 20th century (when it was still known by its Māori name, Kororareka) it was a swashbuckling frontier town, a haven for sealers and for whalers who found the east coast of New Zealand to be one of the richest whaling grounds on earth. Tales of debauchery were probably exaggerated, but British administrators in New South Wales were sufficiently concerned to dispatch a British Resident in 1832 to impose law and order. After the Treaty of Waitangi, Russell was the national capital, until in 1844 the Māori chief Hone Heke attacked the British garrison and most of the town burned to the ground. Hone Heke was finally defeated in 1846, but Russell never recovered its former prominence, and the seat of government was shifted first to Auckland, then to Wellington. Today Russell is a delightful town of timber houses and big trees that hang low over the seafront, framing the yachts and game-fishing boats in the harbor. The atmosphere can best be absorbed in a stroll along the Strand, the path along the waterfront.

Pompallier House, at the southern end of the Strand, was named after the first Catholic bishop of the South Pacific. Marist missionaries built the original structure out of rammed earth (mud mixed with dung or straw—a technique known as *pise* in their native France), since they lacked the funds to buy timber. For several years the priests and brothers operated a press here, printing bibles in the Māori language. The original building forms the core of the elegant timber house that now stands on the site. ⊠ *The Strand,* ☎ *09/403–7861.* ⌑ *$5.* ☉ *Daily 9–5.*

The **Russell Museum** houses a collection of Māori tools and weapons and some fine portraits. The pride of its display is a ⅕-scale replica of Captain Cook's ship, HMS *Endeavour,* which entered the bay in 1769. A short video recounts the history of the region. The museum is set back slightly from the waterfront, some 50 yards north of Pompallier House. ⊠ *York St.,* ☎ *09/403–7701.* ⌑ *$3.* ☉ *Daily 10–4.*

Christ Church is the oldest church in the country. One of the donors to its erection in 1835 was Charles Darwin, at that time a wealthy but unknown young man making his way around the globe on board the HMS *Beagle.* Behind the white picket fence that borders the churchyard, gravestones tell a fascinating and brutal story of life in the early days of the colony. Several graves belong to sailors from the HMS *Hazard* who were killed in this churchyard by Hone Heke's warriors in 1845. Another headstone marks the grave of a Nantucket sailor from the whaler *Mohawk.* As you walk around the church, look for the musket holes made when Hone Heke besieged the church. The interior is simple and charming—embroidered cushions on the pews are examples of a folk-art tradition that is still very much alive. ⊠ *Church and Robertson Sts.* ☉ *Daily 8–5.*

You can drive all the way between Russell and Paihia, but the road is long and windy—hard driving, and thus not recommended. The quickest and most convenient route is by ferry. Three passenger boats make the crossing between Paihia and Russell, with departures at least once every 30 minutes in each direction from 7:30 AM to 11 PM. The one-way fare is $3. It's also easy to take the short drive to Opua, about 5 km (3 mi) south of Paihia, to join the car ferry. This ferry operates from 6:40 AM to 8:50 PM (Friday until 9:50 PM), with departures at approximately 20-minute intervals from either shore. The last boat leaves from Russell at 8:50 (Friday 9:50), from Opua at 9 (Friday 10). The one-way fare is $7 for car and driver plus $1 for each adult passenger.

Dining and Lodging

$$$$ ✕ **Kamakura.** A Buddha statue stands at the back of this waterfront restaurant, offsetting the minimalistic, black-and-white decor—but a glance at the menu may tempt you to indulge rather than seek the middle way. You can't go wrong with seafood dishes such as fresh snapper panfried in lemon butter with a pinot noir sauce. There's always a lamb choice, too, such as rack of lamb with smoked bacon. ⊠ *The Strand,* ☎ 09/403–7761. *AE, DC, MC, V. BYOB.*

$$$–$$$$ ✕ **Sally's.** Overlooking Kororareka Bay from the pretty cream-and-green timber Bay of Islands Swordfish Club building, this restaurant aims to please seafood lovers. The dishes are mostly old-fashioned, but the kitchen does them well. Oysters are served raw, or topped with bacon and cheese and grilled. The fish medley is a bit more adventurous—it spikes bacon-wrapped scallops, shrimp, and fish onto bamboo skewers; sits them on lemon couscous; and drizzles them with hollandaise sauce. Ask for a window table, or dine outdoors when it's sunny. ⊠ *The Strand,* ☎ 09/403–7652. *MC, V. Licensed and BYOB.*

$$$$ 🏠 **The Homestead at Orongo Bay.** Tucked away in gardens off the road between the car-ferry landing and Russell, this lodge, built in 1865, soothes with peace and quiet. The style of the half dozen rooms varies. The small Oyster Bay room, for instance, has a tasteful green-and-blue color scheme and a shared bath, while a pair of bi-level Barn rooms, set back from the main building, are more contemporary, with angled roofs and skylights. Four-course dinners or light suppers are available by prior arrangement. ⊠ *Aucks Rd. (R.D. 1, Russell),* ☎ 09/403–7527, FAX *09/403–7675,* WEB *www.thehomestead.co.nz. 6 rooms, 4 with bath. Dining room, lounge. AE, MC, V.*

$$$$ 🏠 **Kimberley Lodge.** From the large windows and sunny verandas of
★ this splendid white timber mansion, you'll have terrific views overlooking Russell and Kororareka Bay. Below, terraced gardens fall away down a steep hillside to the sea. The house is opulently furnished in contemporary style, and the bathrooms are very well equipped. Only one bedroom at the rear of the house—Pompallier—lacks impressive views. The best room in the house is the Kimberley Suite, which costs more than the standard suites. The management team has a number of innovative ideas, including events like a winter ball to add appeal outside of the summer months. Smoking is not allowed indoors. ⊠ *Pitt St.,* ☎ 09/403–7090, FAX *09/403–7239,* WEB *www.lodges.co.nz. 4 rooms, 1 suite. Pool, massage; no-smoking rooms. AE, DC, MC, V. BP.*

$$$$ 🏠 **Okiato Lodge.** Okiato is high up on Okiato Point, looking out on Opua, Paihia, and other Bay of Islands locales—on Wednesday evenings, you may even see vessels from the local yacht club sailing by below. Spacious rooms include step-down lounge areas, with high-vaulted ceilings and large windows with great views. Rates include drinks and a four-course dinner, which emphasizes New Zealand produce such as scallops, venison, and lamb. ⊠ *Okiato Point (R.D. 1),* ☎ 09/403–7948, FAX *09/403–7515,* WEB *www.okiato.co.nz. 8 rooms. Dining room, in-room data ports, minibars, pool, bar, lounge. AE, DC, MC, V. MAP.*

$$ 🏠 **Duke of Marlborough Hotel.** This historic hotel is a favorite with the yachting fraternity, for whom ready access to the harbor and the bar downstairs are the most important considerations. Antiques and contemporary art add character; in the stairwell up to the rooms you'll find a 1780s clock and the family coat of arms on a stained-glass window. The rooms are bright, with plenty of yellows and floral designs. The front rooms with harbor views are the priciest, fairly small, and can be noisy, especially on weekends. Best in the house, especially if you like a bit of room, are the suites (rooms 7 and 8). ⊠ *The Strand,* ☎ 09/403–7829, FAX *09/403–7760,* WEB *www.theduke.co.nz. 25 rooms, 2 suites. Restaurant, bar. DC, MC, V.*

$ ⚅ **Russell Lodge.** Surrounded by quiet gardens two streets back from the waterfront, this lodge—owned and operated by the Salvation Army—offers neat, clean rooms in several configurations. Family units have a separate bedroom with two single beds and either a double or a single bed in the main room. The largest room is Unit 15, a two-bedroom apartment with a kitchen, which will sleep six. Backpacker-style rooms sleep four; towels and sheets are not provided in these rooms but may be rented. Five rooms have kitchen facilities. ⊠ *Chapel and Beresford Sts.,* ☎ *09/403–7640,* FAX *09/403–7641. 14 rooms, 9 dorm rooms, 1 apartment. Pool, kitchen, laundry facilities. AE, MC, V.*

Outdoor Activities and Sports

FISHING

Bay of Islands Sportsfishing (⊠ Box 78, Russell, ☎ 09/403–7008) represents several operators who can meet most sportfishing requirements. John Gregory of **Primetime Charters & Gamefishing** (⊠ Conifer La., Kerikeri, ☎ FAX 09/407–1299, WEB www.primetimecharters.co.nz) has more than 20 years' experience at sea. Primetime is prepared to go after everything from tuna to marlin, and it specializes in broadbill swordfish. Overnight trips can be arranged.

Kerikeri

㉑ *20 km (12 mi) north of Paihia.*

Kerikeri is often referred to as the cradle of the nation because so much of New Zealand's earliest history, especially in terms of interaction between Māori and Europeans, took place here. The main town itself is small but is gaining a reputation for its crafts and specialty shops.

The **Historic Kerikeri Basin,** just north of the modern town, is where most of the interest lies. Missionaries arrived in this area in 1819, having been invited to Kerikeri by its most famous historical figure, the great Māori chief Hongi Hika. The chief visited England in 1820, where he was showered with gifts. On his way back to New Zealand, during a stop in Sydney, he traded many of these presents for muskets. Having the advantage of these prized weapons, he set in motion plans to conquer other Māori tribes, enemies of his own Ngapuhi people. The return of his raiding parties over five years, with many slaves and gruesome trophies of conquest, put considerable strain between Hongi Hika and the missionaries. Eventually his warring ways were Hongi's undoing. He was shot in 1827 and died as a result of complications from the wound a year later.

The 1821 **Kemp House,** otherwise known as Mission House, has gone through many changes since 1821, but ironically a major flood in 1981 inspired its "authentic" restoration. The flood washed away the garden and damaged the lower floor, and during repair much information about the original structure of the house was revealed. As a result, its ground floor and garden have been restored to the style of missionary days, and the upper floor, which remained unharmed by the flood, is still presented with its Victorian decoration. ⊠ *Kerikeri Historic Basin, Kerikeri Rd.,* ☎ *09/407–9236.* ☑ *$5.* ☉ *Nov.–Apr., daily 10–5; May–Oct., Sat.–Wed. 10–5.*

Across the road from the Basin's Stone Store is a path leading to the historic site of **Kororipo Pa,** the fortified headquarters of chief Hongi Hika. Untrained eyes will have a bit of difficulty working out exactly where the *pā* (hilltop fortification) was, as there are no structures left. Information boards and drawings aid the imagination. The pā was built on a steep-sided promontory between the Kerikeri River and the Wairoa Stream. You'll still get a fine view over both.

Rewi's Village museum re-creates a *kāinga* (unfortified fishing village) where local Māori would have lived in peaceful times. (In times of siege they would have taken refuge in nearby Kororipo Pā.) The village-museum was built in 1969, when the local community wanted to save the area from threatened urban development. A video plays near the entrance, with a history of chief Hongi Hika. In the village itself are replicas of the chief's house, the weapons store, and the family enclosure, as well as two original canoes dug up from local swamps and original hāngi stones (used to cook traditional Māori feasts) found on-site. ⊠ *Kerikeri Historic Basin, Kerikeri Rd.*, ☎ 09/407–6454. ☎ *$3.* ⊙ *Nov.–Apr., daily 9–5; May–Oct., daily 10–4.*

The **Stone Store** is Kerikeri's most picturesque attraction and is the most striking building in the historic basin. Built between 1832 and 1836, it is New Zealand's oldest existing stone building. It was part of the Kerikeri Mission Station and was built to hold stores for the whole New Zealand mission of the time. In November 1998, after a three-year-long renovation, it opened in what is close to its original state. The shop is more interesting than the average tourist trap, with historical items such as tripod bulge pots, musket flint, slash hooks, and old English felling axes for sale. ⊠ *Kerikeri Historic Basin, Kerikeri Rd.*, ☎ 09/407–9236. ☎ *$2.50.* ⊙ *Nov.–Apr., daily 10–5; May–Oct., Sat.–Wed. 10–5.*

Lodging

$$$ ⊞ **The Summer House.** Hosts Christine and Rod Brown both come from artistic families, a background that infuses this B&B. The prints are Christine's mother's, Rod's sister provided the impressive sculpture at the main doorway, and his father supplied the watercolors. The downstairs room, slightly detached from the house, is done in browns and creams. It has the most space, a kitchenette, and a higher room rate. The two upstairs rooms in the main house share a guest lounge. One room has an 1860 French bed with furniture to match, and the other has a Victorian brass bedstead. Christine's breakfasts are wonderful, including fresh or poached fruits, Greek yogurt, and homemade muesli. The tropical garden surrounding the house attracts doves and monarch butterflies. ⊠ *Kerikeri Rd. (south end)*, ☎ 09/407–4294, ℻ 09/407–4297, ⓦ *www.thesummerhouse.co.nz. 3 rooms. Kitchenette, lounge. MC, V. BP.*

$$ ⊞ **Kauri Park.** This small cluster of chalets is a notch above the usual, with modern decor and a beautiful setting among fruit trees adjacent to farmland. Owners Alexander Gramse and Helene Henriksen have combined a touch of European hospitality—a free drink on arrival, a guest lounge—with the usual Kiwi warmth. Each unit has a veranda and colorful furnishings. Kauri Park is a little bit out of town, which gives it a rural feeling, but it's still only a few minutes' drive from the historic sights. ⊠ *Kerikeri Rd. (south end)*, ☎ 09/407–7629, ⓦ *www.kauripark.co.nz. 7 rooms. In-room data ports, lounge. AE, DC, MC, V.*

Opononi

㉒   *85 km (53 mi) west of Paihia.*

Opononi is a small town near the mouth of the Hokianga Harbour. It is the place where Opi, a tame dolphin, came to play with swimmers in the mid-1950s, putting the town on the national map for the first and only time in its history. There is a statue in front of the pub commemorating the much-loved creature. If you're driving and approaching the town from the south, be sure to check out some of the signposted lookouts en route.

㉓ **Waipoua State Forest** contains the largest remnant of the kauri forests that once covered this part of the country. A short path leads from the parking area through the forest to **Tane Mahuta,** "Lord of the Forest," standing nearly 173 ft high and measuring 43 ft around its base. The largest tree in New Zealand, it's said to be 1,200 years old. The second-largest tree, but older by some 800 years, is **Te Matua Ngahere.** It takes about 20 minutes to walk to it from the road. There are other trees of note in the forest, among them the **Four Sisters,** four trees that have grown together in a circular formation. If you have three hours to spare, hike the Yakas Track, which links the Four Sisters to the **Department of Conservation Visitor Centre** (☎ 09/439–0605). It's possible to camp in the forest, as long as you check at the visitor center before you pitch a tent. Facilities include toilets, hot showers, and a communal cookhouse. When it's wet, you may spot some large kauri snails in the forest. Also, the recent successful eradication of predators such as weasels and stoats has led to a rise in the number of kiwis in the forest. Visitors are beginning to report sightings, but it's still very much a case of being in the right place at the right time. You'll need a flashlight to spot one, because the birds only come out at night.

Dining and Lodging

$$$ ✕🏠 **Waipoua Lodge.** Owners Raewyn and Tony Lancaster have taken what were once working farm buildings and turned them into lovely guest lodgings. The names of the rooms record their past lives: the Calf Pen, the Wool Shed, and the Stables. All the rooms have plenty of space and natural light. The original farmhouse is now the reception area and restaurant and is packed with antiques such as an old pedal organ, photographs, and saws. Raewyn's cooking is legendary; she sparks up country fare in dishes such as rack of lamb with braised summer fruits and wild berry sauce. Tony, a fish-and-game ranger, can advise you on fly-fishing, bushwalks, and other outdoor activities in the area. The lodge is just a kilometer (½ mi) south of Waipoua Forest. ⊠ *State Hwy. 12, Waipoua,* ☎ *09/439–0422,* 🕿 *09/439–0422,* 🌐 *www.waipoualodge. co.nz. 3 rooms. Restaurant, bar. MC, V.*

$ 🏠 **Kauri Coast Holiday Park.** With a stream running through its grounds and the Trounson Kauri Park marking its northern boundary, this spot is as close to nature as you can get. Owners Herb and Heather Iles can point you in the right direction for several outdoor activities, but perhaps the biggest draw is after-dark exploration. The Department of Conservation gives guided tours of the kauri park nightly if demand warrants; guests frequently spot kiwis on the walks. The various lodging configurations—cabins with or without kitchens, backpackers' bunkhouses, apartments—are all kept spotless, and there's a camp kitchen and barbecue area. If you are travelling from the north, you'll need to turn left off the state highway and onto Trounson Park Road, 3 km (2 mi) before the small village of Kaihu. The holiday park is clearly signposted. ⊠ *Trounson Park Rd., 70 km (43 mi) south of Opononi,* ☎ 🕿 *09/439–0621. 2 motel units, 3 apartments, 4 cabins, 2 backpacker cabins, extensive campsites. Dining room, grocery, some kitchens, playground, laundry facilities. MC, V.*

En Route Once a thriving river port, **Dargaville** these days is a good place to stock up if you're planning to camp in any of the nearby forests. You can also linger in its few small crafts shops and cafés. The surrounding region is best known for its main cash crop, the purple-skinned sweet potato known as kūmara. You'll see field after field dedicated to this root vegetable and plenty of shops selling it cheaper than you'll find anywhere else.

Matakohe

95 km (59 mi) south of Opononi.

★ ㉔ **Matakohe Kauri Museum** is one of the most intriguing museums in the country. Its vast collection of artifacts, tools, photographs, documents, and memorabilia tells the story of the pioneers who settled this part of the country in the second half of the 19th century—a story interwoven with the kauri forests. Here you'll find superb examples of craftsmanship: furniture and a complete kauri house, as well as an early example of an American-built Caterpillar bulldozer, which was used to drag logs from the forest. One of the most fascinating displays is of kauri gum, the transparent lumps of resin that form when the sticky sap of the kauri tree hardens. This gum, which was used to make varnish, can be polished to a warm, lustrous finish that looks remarkably like amber—right down to the insects that are sometimes trapped and preserved inside. At one time collecting this gum was an important rural industry. **Volunteers Hall** contains a huge kauri slab running from one end of the hall to the other, and there is also a Women in the Bush display, a replica of a cabinetmaker's shop, a chain-saw exhibit, and an area dedicated to fishing in Kaipara Harbour. The Steam Saw Mill illustrates how the huge kauri logs were cut into timber. The life-size mannequins in the exhibit, like others in the museum, are modeled on living descendants of the actual pioneers of the region. If you like the whirring of engines, the best day to visit is Wednesday, when much of the museum's machinery is started up. ⊠ *Church Rd.,* ☎ *09/431–7417,* WEB *www.kauri-museum.com.* ▨ *$10.* ◷ *Daily 9–5.*

Northland and the Bay of Islands A to Z

BUS TRAVEL

InterCity, Newmans, and Northliner Express buses run several times daily between Auckland and Paihia. Once you're in the region, you'll find that the bus network is quite extensive; as long as you're not too pressed for time, bus travel is an easy way to get around. For instance, there are at least four daily buses between Paihia and Kerikeri, and at least one daily bus even to whistle-stop towns like Dargaville.

➤ BUS DEPOTS: **Paihia** (⊠ Paihia Travel Centre, Maritime Bldg., ☎ 09/ 402–7857). **Whangarei** (⊠ Northland Coach and Travel Bldg., 11 Rose St., ☎ 09/438–2653).

➤ BUS LINES: **InterCity** (☎ 09/358–4085, WEB www.intercitycoach.co. nz). **Newmans** (☎ 09/913–6200, WEB www.newmanscoach.co.nz). **Northliner Express** (☎ 09/307–5873, WEB www.nzinfo.com/northliner).

CAR TRAVEL

Taking your own car is the most convenient way to explore the Northland. The main route from Auckland is Highway 1. Leave the city by the Harbour Bridge and follow signs to Whangarei. Driving time for the 250-km (150-mi) journey to Paihia is about 3½ hours. Highway 12 is longer and winds more than the 1, but it's more scenic. The view over Hokianga harbor as you drive north into Omapare is especially beautiful.

EMERGENCIES

➤ EMERGENCY SERVICES: **Fire, police, and ambulance** (☎ 111).

TOURS

ADVENTURE TOURS

The 4x4 Dune-Rider is a novel way to get to Cape Reinga—via the vast strip of 90 Mile Beach. The company uses four-wheel-drive vehicles for small groups and makes slightly unusual stops, such as a visit to the "world-famous" Mangonui fish-and-chips shop. The drive gives you a chance to dig for the shellfish known as tuatua and goes to the dramatically set Cape Reinga Lighthouse. Tours depart Paihia daily at 7:30 AM, Kerikeri at 8:15, and cost $75.

➤ CONTACT: **4x4 Dune-Rider** (✉ Box 164, Paihia, ☎ 09/402–8681, WEB www.dunerider.co.nz).

BOAT TOURS

Fullers Bay of Islands runs cruises and sea-based adventure trips departing daily from both Paihia and Russell. The most comprehensive sightseeing trip is the Supercruise ($85) aboard a high-speed catamaran. You'll follow the Cream Trip route and see the Hole in the Rock, a massive rock jutting from the sea with a hole through the middle.

➤ CONTACT: **Fullers Bay of Islands** (✉ Bay of Islands Travel Centre, Shop 2, Downtown Shopping Centre, Customs St., Auckland, ☎ 09/358–0259, WEB www.nzinfo.co.nz/fullersboi).

SIGHTSEEING TOURS

Great Sights, based out of Auckland, leads one-, two-, and three-day trips to the Bay of islands. The one-day tour stops at Warkworth for morning tea and goes on to visit the Waitangi Treaty House and cruise out to the Hole in the Rock. You can opt for a tour of historic Russell instead of the cruise. Taking the two-day tour allows you both to cruise and visit Russell, while the three-day itinerary adds a trip along 90 Mile Beach to Cape Rienga, the northernmost tip of the country. Rates start at $195 for the one-day trip.

➤ CONTACT: **Great Sights** (✉ The Sightseeing Centre, 180 Quay St., Auckland, ☎ 09/375–4700).

VISITOR INFORMATION

The main Bay of Islands visitor bureau, in Paihia, is open daily, as is the Warkworth tourist information center.

In addition to the tourism Web site listed below, there are some helpful community Web resources, including www.russell.net.nz, www.kerikeri.co.nz, and www.paihia.co.nz. Destination Northland, a regional tourism organization, maintains www.northland.org.nz; the Northlands Museums Association runs www.northland-museums.co.nz.

➤ TOURIST INFORMATION: **Bay of Islands Visitor Information Centre Paihia** (✉ Marsden Rd., Paihia, ☎ 09/402–7345, WEB www.bay-of-islands.co.nz). **Warkworth Visitor Information Centre** (✉ 1 Baxter St., Warkworth, ☎ 09/425–9081, FAX 09/425–7584).

THE COROMANDEL PENINSULA

New Zealand has countless pockets of beauty that are not included in standard itineraries. One of the most accessible is the Coromandel Peninsula, which juts out like a hitchhiker's thumb east of Auckland. As with so many other lands "discovered" by Europeans, the peninsula was looted for its valuable resources: kauri trees, then kauri gum, and finally gold in the 1870s. Relative quiet since the 1930s has allowed the region to recover a little, and without question natural beauty abounds.

The center of the peninsula is dominated by a craggy spine of volcanic peaks that rises sharply to a height of almost 3,000 ft. The west coast cradles the Firth of Thames, and along the east coast the Pacific has carved out a succession of beaches and inlets separated by rearing headlands. Due to its rich volcanic soil, the peninsula has many spectacular gardens, several of which are open to the public. From the town of Thames, the gateway to the region, Highway 25 and the 309 Road circle the lower two-thirds of the peninsula—an exhilarating drive with

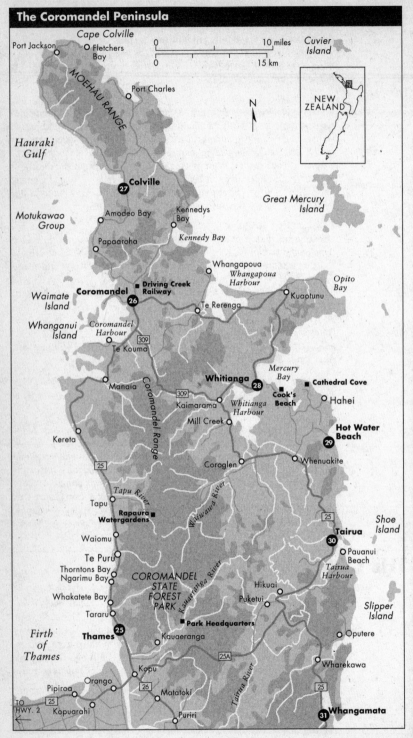

The Coromandel Peninsula

Cape Colville

Port Jackson

Fletchers
Bay

Port Charles

MOEHAU RANGE

*Cuvier
Island*

NEW
ZEALAND

0   10 miles

0   15 km

N

*Hauraki
Gulf*

27 Colville

*Great Mercury
Island*

*Motukawao
Group*

Amodeo Bay

Kennedys
Bay

Papaaroha

Kennedy Bay

*Opito
Bay*

Whangapoua

*Whangapoua
Harbour*

Kuaotunu

*Waimate
Island*

Coromandel

Driving Creek
Railway

26

Te Rerenga

*Whanganui
Island*

*Coromandel
Harbour*

309

Te Kouma

Manaia

Coromandel Range

309

Kaimarama

Whitianga **28**

*Mercury
Bay*

Cook's
Beach

■ Cathedral Cove

Hahei

*Whitianga
Harbour*

Mill Creek

**Hot Water
Beach**

29

Kereta

25

Coroglen

Whenuakite

Tapu River

Tapu

■ Rapaura
Watergardens

Waiomu

Te Puru

Thorntons Bay
Ngarimu Bay

Whakatete Bay

Tararu

COROMANDEL
STATE
FOREST
PARK

Waiwawa River

Kauaeranga River

■ Park Headquarters

25

Thames

Tairua **30**

Pauanui
Beach

*Shoe
Island*

*Tairua
Harbour*

Hikuai

Puketui

*Slipper
Island*

25

Kauaeranga

25A

Oputere

*Firth
of
Thames*

Kopu

Orongo

Pipiroa

25

26

Matatoki

Tairua River

Wharekawa

25

TO
HWY. 2

Kopuarahi

Puriri

31 Whangamata

the sea on one side and great forested peaks on the other. Hiking in the peninsula's lush forest is a great pleasure, and the east-coast beaches are breathtaking. Especially considering the Coromandel's proximity to Auckland, it would be difficult to find a finer introduction to the wonders of New Zealand.

Thames

②⑤ *120 km (75 mi) southeast of Auckland.*

Since the 1920s, the historic town of Thames has changed from a gold-mining hotbed to a center for local agriculture. Locals have a saying that when the gold ran out, "Thames went to sleep awaiting the kiss of a golden prince—and instead it awoke to the warm breath of a cow." At the **Historical Museum** you can look into earlier ways of life in the town. ⊠ *Pollen and Cochrane Sts.,* ☎ *07/868–8509.* 🖾 *$2.50.* ☉ *Daily 1–4.*

Meanwhile, the **Mineralogical Museum** (⊠ Brown and Cochrane Sts., ☎ 07/868–6227) gives a geologic take on the area's history. If you want to learn even more about early gold-mining efforts in the Coroman-del, stop in at the **stamper battery,** north on the way out of town, and take a brief underground tour of the old Golden Crown Claim, which was first worked in 1868. Five hundred feet below this site, the Cale-donia strike was one of the richest in the world. A guide will describe the geological and historical interest of the mine. ⊠ *State Hwy. 25, north of Waiotahi Creek Rd.,* ☎ *07/868–8514.* 🖾 *$5.* ☉ *Daily 9–5.*

To soak up a bit of goldmining atmosphere, head to the 1868 **Brian Boru Hotel.** Stop for a cold drink and check out the mining paraphernalia and historic photographs on the walls of the bar, reception, and dining area. ⊠ *200 Richmond St.,* ☎ *07/868–6523.*

You might also want to take a quick look into **St. George's Anglican Church,** at Willoughby and MacKay streets. The interior is unpainted, and the kauri wood used to build it is gorgeous.

Meonstoke is probably New Zealand's most unusual garden, and nothing printed here will quite prepare you for it. For more than 35 years, Pam Gwynne has been working every square inch of her ¼-acre lot. Numerous paths wind through a junglelike space; there are no look-outs or vistas to distract you from the lush surroundings. Pam collects found objects and ingeniously incorporates them into surreal and often humorous tableaux with the plantings. On one path, a row of a ce-ramic pitchers is suspended from a rod, while elsewhere, tiny winking porcelain Asian figures festoon bonsai plants. Although the garden is small, allow yourself plenty of time to peer at the details. The small entry fee goes to local charities. ⊠ *305 Kuranui St.,* ☎ *07/868–6560 or 07/868–6850.* ☉ *By appointment only.*

The **Tropical Butterfly Garden** is just a few minutes' drive north on the way out of Thames, but it's easy to miss unless you're specifically look-ing for the signs. Owners Roger and Sabine Gass have brought some color to the Coromandel with a flock of butterflies from Australia. Up to 12 species and 250 butterflies may be on view at any time, includ-ing large birdwing butterflies. Look for the chrysalis box at the entrance to the garden and the glassed-in display of the massive gum emperor moth kept near the garden's waterfall. Exotic birds such as finches, doves, and quails join the butterflies, plus about 100 different plant species. The orchids are particularly stunning. ⊠ *Dickson Holiday Park, Vic-toria St.,* ☎ *07/868–8080,* FAX *07/868–5648.* 🖾 *$9.* ☉ *Mid-Oct.–mid-Apr., daily 10–4; mid-Apr.–mid-July and Sept.–mid-Oct., daily 10–3.*

Dining and Lodging

$ ✕ **Pipiroa Country Kitchen.** Sweet treats made this café's reputation. You'll be tempted with brownies and lemon cookies, but best of all is the raspberry tart with a dollop of yogurt. For lunch, try one of the burgers, the most spectacular being the Mountain, topped with cheese, onion, egg, ham, tomato, apricot, and lettuce. Add to all this a sauce of your choice: peanut, plum, spicy tomato, or just plain ketchup. A playground that's easy to see from the tables makes this a particularly good stopover if you're traveling with kids. ✉ *1492 State Hwy. 25, Pipiroa, 6 km (4 mi) southwest of Thames,* ☎ *07/867–7599. MC, V. No dinner Mon.–Thurs.*

$$–$$$ ⊞ **Tuscany on Thames.** Alison and Peter Fitzgerald fell in love with Tuscany on a visit to Italy and decided to bring a bit of its style back to their New Zealand motel. The details—flowers in the rooms, custom-made pottery cups—make this stand out from other area hotels. For extra space, ask for Room 1, a two-bedroom suite with access to a small courtyard. The two rooms without a full bath have showers instead. ✉ *Jellicoe Crescent and Bank St.,* ☎ *07/868–5099,* FAX *07/868–5080,* WEB *www.tuscanyonthames.co.nz. 13 rooms, 11 with bath; 1 suite. In-room data ports, pool; no a/c. MC, V.*

$–$$ ⊞ **Te Kouma Harbour Farmstay.** A little off the beaten track, this set of single-story wooden chalets set on a deer farm is excellent for families, with outdoor options like kayaking, nearby bushwalking, and a soccer field, *pétanque* (the French game *boules*), and pool on-site—enough to keep you busy for a couple of days. Large, bright multiroom cabins have contemporary furniture and kitchen areas with cooking facilities. Breakfast is available by arrangement, but most guests cook for themselves. There are also barbecue areas on the grounds. The cabins are down a long drive that is well signposted from Highway 25 north out of Thames. ✉ *Te Kouma Harbour,* ☎ *07/866–8747. 6 cabins. Picnic area, kitchens, pool, boating, recreation room. No credit cards.*

Outdoor Activities and Sports

Coromandel State Forest Park has more than 30 walking trails, which offer anything from a 30-minute stroll to a three-day trek, overnighting in huts equipped with bunks. The most accessible starting point is the delightful Kauaeranga Valley Road, where the **Coromandel Forest Park Headquarters** provides maps and information (☎ 07/868–6381). The office is open weekdays 8–4. Keep in mind that the park can be very busy from late December to mid-January. If you're traveling then, plan to visit the park midweek. To reach the Kauaeranga Valley, head south from Thames and on the outskirts of the town turn left on Banks Street, then right on Parawai Road, which becomes Kauaeranga Valley Road.

En Route   The Coromandel Ranges drop right down to the seafront Highway 25 as it winds up the west coast of the peninsula. Turn upon turn makes each view seem more spectacular than the last, and when you top the hills north of Kereta on the way to Coromandel, mountains, pastures, and islands in the Firth of Thames open out before you—stunning.

Tapu–Coroglen Road

25 km (16 mi) north of Thames.

The unpaved Tapu–Coroglen Road turns off Highway 25 in the hamlet of Tapu to wind into the mountains. It's a breathtaking route where massive tree ferns grow out of the roadside hills. About 6½ km (4 mi) from Tapu you will come to the magical **Rapaura Watergardens.** Travel another 3½ km (2 mi) along the road and pull over to climb the 178 steps up to the huge, 1,200-year-old **Square Kauri,** so named for the shape that a cross section of its trunk would have. At 133 ft tall and 30 ft around, this is only the 15th-largest kauri in New Zealand. From a tree-side platform there is a splendid view across the valley to Mau Mau Paki, one of the Coromandel Ranges peaks. Continuing east across the peninsula, the road passes through forests and sheep paddocks—a shimmeringly beautiful ride in sun or mist.

Rapaura Watergardens, full of native and exotic flowering species, has been sculpted from the wilderness in a 65-acre sheltered valley in the Coromandel Ranges. Rapaura (running water) is a wonderful example of water's use in New Zealand gardens. In the garden's various streams, waterfalls, fountains, and 14 ponds, fish and ducks swim among colorful water lilies and other bog plants while songbirds lilt overhead. Paths wind through collections of grasses, flaxes, gunneras, rhododendrons, and camellias, all organically gardened. (The camellias and rhododendrons usually flower between late June and October.) Giant tree ferns and rimu, *rata,* and kauri trees form a lush canopy overhead. The combination of delicacy and rugged grandeur may have been what inspired the philosophic messages that you'll find painted on signs around the garden, such as KEEP YOUR VALUES IN BALANCE AND YOU WILL ALWAYS FIND HAPPINESS. Be sure to take the easy 10-minute walk to the cascading falls known as Seven Steps to Heaven, especially if you aren't planning on spending much time in the native bush. Rapaura has a tearoom and a crafts shop with work by Coromandel artisans. ⊠ *Tapu–Coroglen Rd., 6 km (4 mi) east of Tapu,* ☎ ℻ *07/868–4821.* 🖭 *$6.* ⊙ *Daily 10–5.*

Coromandel

㉖ *60 km (38 mi) north of Thames, 29 km (18 mi) northwest of Whitianga.*

Coromandel became the site of New Zealand's first gold strike in 1852 when sawmiller Charles Ring found gold-bearing quartz at Driving Creek, just north of town. The find was important for New Zealand, since the country's workforce had been severely depleted by the gold rushes in California and Australia. Ring hurried to Auckland to claim the reward that had been offered to anyone finding "payable" gold. The town's population soared, but the reef gold could be mined only by heavy and expensive machinery. Within a few months Coromandel resumed its former sleepy existence as a timber town—and Charles Ring was refused the reward. Nowadays, Coromandel is touristy in a low-key way, with 19th-century buildings lining both sides of its single main street.

ⓒ **Driving Creek Railway** is one man's magnificent folly. Barry Brickell is a local potter who discovered that clay on his land was perfect for his work. The problem was that the deposit lay in a remote area at the top of a steep slope; so he hacked a path through the forest and built his own miniature railroad to haul the stuff. Visitors to his studio began asking if they could go along for a ride, and Brickell now takes passengers on daily tours aboard his toy train. The diesel-powered, narrow-gauge locomotive's route incorporates a double-decker bridge, three tunnels, a spiral, and a switchback. The round-trip takes about 50 minutes. The "station" is 3 km (2 mi) north of Coromandel township. ⊠ *410 Kennedy's Bay Rd.,* ☎ *07/866–8703,* 🆆🅴🅱 *www.drivingcreekrailway. co.nz.* 🖭 *$12.* ⊙ *Late Oct.–Apr., daily 10–5, with trains running on the hr; May–mid-Oct., daily 10–5, with trains at 10 and 2.*

Dining and Lodging

$–$$ ✕ **Pepper Tree Restaurant and Bar.** Coromandel seafood takes precedence on the menu here. Locally farmed oysters are served simply on the half shell, and Greenshell mussels are steamed open and piled into bowls, or turned into fritters and offered with a dipping sauce. Organic produce, including meat, is used whenever possible. Nachos, potato wedges, and other easygoing nibbles dominate the all-day menu, but things get more serious after sundown with dishes like local lamb shanks with a sauce based on dark beer. ✉ *Kapanga Rd.,* ☎ *07/866–8211. AE, DC, MC, V.*

$ ✕ **Coromandel Cafe.** Seek out the best breakfast in town at this main-street café. The menu may not be extensive or adventurous, but the substantial servings of tried-and-true choices like pancakes with maple syrup or bacon and eggs come piping hot. What's more, you won't miss out if you sleep in, as breakfast runs right through late afternoon. ✉ *Kapanga Rd.,* ☎ *07/866–8495. MC, V. No dinner mid-Apr.–late Oct.*

$$$$ ★ ✕ **Buffalo Lodge.** Perched on a hillside and surrounded by bush just out of Coromandel town, this lodge looks across the Hauraki Gulf toward Auckland. The owner's own artwork hangs at the lodge's entrance and in guest rooms, and wood is used lavishly in the ceilings, floors, and furnishings. The restaurant's prix-fixe dinner ($90) hones in on New Zealand specialties such as king salmon, venison, and locally caught fish. With a limit of six people staying at any one time, you'll never feel crowded. ✉ *Buffalo Rd.,* ☎ FAX *07/866–8960,* WEB *www.buffalolodge.co.nz. 4 rooms. Restaurant. AE, DC, MC, V. Closed May–Sept. BP.*

$$ ★ **Coromandel Colonial Cottages.** These eight immaculate timber cottages offer spacious and comfortable self-contained accommodations for about the same price as a standard motel room. Six of the units have two bedrooms; a living room with convertible beds; a large, well-equipped kitchen; and a dining area. The two newer units have only one bedroom but still feel spacious. Arranged with military precision in two ranks, the cottages face each other across a tailored lawn surrounded by green hills on the northern outskirts of Coromandel. For vacation periods book several months in advance. ✉ *Rings Rd.,* ☎ *07/866–8857,* WEB *www.corocottagesmotel.co.nz. 8 cottages. Some kitchens, pool, playground. AE, DC, MC, V.*

$$ **Coromandel Court Motel.** Tucked behind the Coromandel Information Centre, these clean units are newer and more spacious than those of the area's average motel. You'll get a friendly welcome at reception; guest rooms are well equipped with kitchenettes (including microwaves) and dining-room tables. All have showers instead of full baths. ✉ *365 Kapanga Rd.,* ☎ *07/866–8402,* FAX *07/866–8403,* WEB *www.coromandelcourtmotel.co.nz. 9 units. Kitchenettes, microwaves. DC, MC.*

En Route On your way south from Coromandel, stop at **Harmony Gardens** for a quiet walk among the rhododendrons. From Coromandel, drive down Highway 25 for about 4 km (2½ mi) and turn inland where a sign points to WHITIANGA—309 ROAD. After about 2 km (1 mi), this road passes the gardens. ✉ *Rte. 309,* ☎ *07/866–8487.* *$4.* *Sept.–May, daily 10–4.*

Colville and Beyond

27 *30 km (19 mi) north of Coromandel.*

If you find yourself possessed with the urge to reach land's end on the wilds of the peninsula—with more rugged coastline, beautiful coves, beaches, and pasturelands—follow the paved road up to Colville. Beyond that, a gravel road will take you to the **Mt. Moehau** trail that climbs to the peninsula's highest point (2,923 ft); to the sands at **Port Jackson**; or all the way to the tip, at **Fletcher's Bay** (60 km [38 mi] from

Coromandel). Colville's classic counterculture **General Store** (☎ 07/866–6805) sells foodstuffs, wine, and gasoline and has a café with vegetarian meals. It is the northernmost supplier on the peninsula, so don't forget to fill up before you move on.

Whitianga

㉘ *46 km (29 mi) southeast of Coromandel.*

As you descend from the hills on the east coast of the Coromandel, you'll come to the long stretch of Buffalo Beach, lined with motels and hostels. Just past this beach is Whitianga, the main township on this side of the peninsula. Most people use the town as a base for fishing or boating trips, while others stock up for camping at nearby beaches.

$$$ ⊞ **Mercury Bay Beachfront Resort.** Stepping out of this family-run resort's garden takes you straight onto a beautiful beach. The downstairs rooms claim the best beach access, but upstairs you'll have great views and the most sun. Either way, seven of the eight rooms have beach views. The hosts keep things comfortable and casual, and there's plenty of sports equipment, including kayaks, fishing gear, golf clubs, and body boards, available for use at no extra charge. Note that only one room has a full bath; the rest have showers. ⊠ *111–113 Buffalo Beach Rd.,* ☎ *07/866–5637,* 𝔽𝔸𝕏 *07/866–4524,* 𝕎𝔼𝔹 *www.beachfrontresort.co.nz. 8 rooms, 1 with bath. Spa; no a/c. AE, DC, MC, V.*

Around Hahei

14 km (9 mi) northeast of Whenuakite on Hahei Beach Rd., 57 km (35 mi) southeast of Coromandel, 64 km (40 mi) northeast of Thames.

The beaches and seaside land formations in and around Hahei make for a great day of exploring—or lounging. Past Hahei on Pa Road, **Te Pare Historic Reserve** is the site of a Māori *pā* (fortified village), though no trace remains of the defensive terraces and wooden spikes that ringed the hill. (A much larger pā was on the hilltop overlooking this site.) At high tide, the blowhole at the foot of the cliffs will add its booming bass note to the sound of waves and the sighing of the wind in the grass. To reach the actual pā site, follow the red arrow down the hill from the parking area. After some 50 yards take the right fork through a grove of giant pohutukawa trees, then through a gate and across an open, grassy hillside. The trail is steep in places and becomes increasingly overgrown as you climb, but persist until you reach the summit, and then head toward more pohutukawas off to your right at the south end of the headland.

Cathedral Cove is a beautiful white-sand crescent with a great rock arch. It is only accessible at low tide, about a 45-minute walk each way. To get there, travel along Hahei Beach Road, turn right toward town and the sea, and then, just past the shops, turn left onto Grange Road and follow the signs. From the parking lot you will get excellent views over Mahurangi Island, a marine reserve.

Cook's Beach lies along Mercury Bay, so named for Captain James Cook's observation of the transit of the planet Mercury in November 1769. The beach is notable because of the captain's landfall here—it was the first by a European, and it is commemorated by a beachside plaque. The beach itself is one of the less attractive ones in the area.

★ **㉙** The popular **Hot Water Beach** is a delightful thermal oddity. A warm spring seeps beneath the beach, and by scooping a shallow hole in the sand, you can create a pool of warm water; the deeper you dig, the hotter the water becomes, but the phenomenon occurs only at low to mid-tide, so time your trip accordingly. Hot Water Beach is well sign-posted off of Hahei Beach Road from Whenuakite (fen-oo-ah-kye-tee). Do not swim in the surf at Hot Water Beach itself, as it's notorious for drownings. However, nearby, at the end of Hahei Beach Road, you'll find one of the finest protected coves on the coast, with sands tinted pink from crushed shells; it's safe to swim here.

NEED A BREAK?
Colenso Orchard and Herb Garden (⊠ Main Rd., Whenuakite, ☎ 07/866-3725), on Highway 25 just south of the Hahei turnoff, is a relaxed cottage café that you might find yourself wishing would franchise across rural New Zealand. Set in a garden full of lavender and kitchen herbs, Colenso serves fresh juices (from its own orchards), daily soups, focaccia sandwiches, those addictive chocolate fudge biscuits (also called slices) that are a real Kiwi treat, and Devonshire teas. Before getting back on the road, buy a bag of the freshly harvested fruit at the roadside stand. Colenso is open from 10 to 5 daily, September through July.

Tairua

30 *28 km (18 mi) south of Hahei, 37 km (23 mi) north of Whangamata.*

A town that you'll actually notice when you pass through it, Tairua is a harborside center where you can find food stores and a seafood joint or two. The twin volcanic peaks of Paku rise up beside the harbor.

Dining and Lodging

$$$$ ✕🏨 **Puka Park Resort Mercure Grand.** This stylish hillside hideaway, which attracts a largely European clientele, lies surrounded by native bushland on Pauanui Beach, at the seaward end of Tairua Harbour on the east coast of the peninsula. Timber chalets are smartly furnished with black cane tables and wooden Venetian blinds. Sliding glass doors lead to a balcony perched among the treetops. The restaurant's sophisticated daily menu merits perusal; keep an eye out for the seared fish with grilled vegetables and coconut-lime sauce. The turnoff from Highway 25 is about 6 km (4 mi) south of Tairua. ⊠ *Private Bag, Pauanui Beach,* ☎ *07/864–8088,* FAX *07/864–8112,* WEB *www.mercure. co.nz. 48 rooms. Restaurant, pool, spa, tennis court, bicycles, bar. AE, DC, MC, V.*

$$–$$$ 🏨 **Pauanui Pines.** The light, bright decor of this modern motor lodge suits a beach vacation; even the crockery fits into the color scheme. The units are self-contained, with French-press coffeemakers a nice extra. You can arrange for a Continental breakfast, but for other meals guests cook their own or wander into town. Portable gas barbecues are available as well. ⊠ *168 Vista Paku, Pauanui Beach,* ☎ *07/864–8086,* FAX *07/864–7122,* WEB *www.pauanuipines.co.nz. 15 one-bedroom units, 3 two-bedroom units. Kitchenettes, pool, putting green, tennis court. AE, DC, MC, V.*

En Route On the road between Tairua and Whangamata you'll pass the mountainous wilderness around the second branch of the Tairua River, which is the remarkable domain of Doug Johansen. Over the past 20 years he has cut his own trails in the valley's lush rain forest—not that you could find them even if you were walking on one. Their minimal invasiveness is uncanny. Heading into the woods with a knowledgeable, and in this case entertaining, guide to point out native plants and their uses can make later hikes on your own even more rewarding. *See* Kiwi Dundee Adventures *in* The Coromandel Peninsula A to Z, *below.*

While on the road between Tairua and Whangamata, you can also stop at Oputere Beach and the Wharekawa (fah-ray-ka-wa) Wildlife Refuge for a 15-minute stroll through the forest to another great stretch of white sand. The long beach is bounded at either end by headlands, and there are stunning views of Slipper Island. An estuary near the parking lot is a breeding ground for shorebirds. In the late afternoon waterfowl are often present as the sun slants across the Coromandel Ranges to the west. A handsome bridge arches over the river to the forest walk.

Whangamata

③ *37 km (23 mi) south of Tairua, 60 km (38 mi) east of Thames.*

The Coromandel Ranges back Whangamata (fahng-a-ma-*ta*), another harborside village. While the modest houses and main strip of this town of 4,000 won't exactly bowl you over, its harbor, surf beaches, mangroves, and coastal islands are glorious. It is a great spot for deep-sea fishing, and its bar break brings in some of the best waves in New Zealand. Around the Christmas holidays and into January, it's a favorite for throngs of surfers.

Dining and Lodging

$ ✕ **Vibes Café.** This café boasts of being the friendliest place in town,
★ and the daylong crowds support the claim. Paintings by local artists cover the walls (not surprisingly, a beach theme predominates), and magazines and newspapers are on hand for a quick read over your espresso. Of the light meals, the vegetarian dishes are the most exciting, with choices like kūmara stuffed with pesto and sun-dried tomatoes. ⊠ *638 Port Rd.,* ☎ *07/865–7121. AE, DC, MC, V. No dinner.*

$$$ ⌂ **Brenton Lodge.** Looking out over Whangamata and the islands in
★   its harbor from your hillside suite, you'll have no trouble settling into a luxurious mood. Fresh flowers and a tray of fruit and muffins greet you on arrival, as do cheerful furnishings and comforts like terry robes. The lodge's only rooms are two suites on the second floors of attractive outbuildings. Stroll around the garden, peep at the birds in the aviary, and in springtime breathe in the scent of orange and jasmine blossoms. ⊠ *1 Brenton Pl. (Box 216),* ☎ *07/865–8400,* WEB *www.brentonlodge. co.nz. 2 suites. Pool, laundry service. AE, MC, V. BP.*

The Coromandel Peninsula A to Z

BUS TRAVEL

InterCity links Whitianga and Thames with Auckland daily. Bus travel within the region is reliable, if not frequent. An InterCity bus makes the trip between Coromandel and Thames once each way daily. A daily InterCity bus also connects Coromandel and Whitianga.

➤ BUS DEPOTS: **Coromandel** (⊠ Coromandel Visitor Information Centre, 355 Kapanga Rd., ☎ 07/866–8598). **Thames** (⊠ Thames Information Centre, 206 Pollen St., ☎ 07/868–7284). **Whitianga** (⊠ Whitianga Visitor Information Centre, 66 Albert St., ☎ 07/864–7575). ➤ BUS LINE: **InterCity** (☎ 07/868–7251, WEB www.intercitycoach.co.nz).

CAR TRAVEL

It's easiest to get around this area by car. From Auckland take the Southern Motorway, following signs to Hamilton. Just as you get over the Bombay Hills, turn left onto Highway 2; then take the turnoff to Highway 25, signposted between the small towns of Maramarua and Mangatarata. Follow the signs to Thames. Allow 1 to 2½ hours for the 118-km (73-mi) journey.

Highway 25 is the peninsula's main loop, and though the road is windy it's in good condition. If you've heard reports of extensive stretches of gravel, don't be put off; at this writing the road was expected to be paved by the end of 2002. Route 309, which crosses the peninsula between

Coromandel and the east coast, can be challenging. It's narrow, windy, and unpaved for about half of its 33 km (21 mi). The well-maintained, paved Highway 25A, to the south, is a quicker way to reach the east coast from Auckland. You'll miss Thames and Coromandel but will get to Buffalo, Whangamata, and Waihi beaches much more quickly.

EMERGENCIES
➤ EMERGENCY SERVICES: **Fire, police, and ambulance** (☎ 111).

TOURS
BOAT TOURS

Mercury Bay Safaris has a swim-with-the-dolphins program ($90), plus a glass-bottom boat trip ($40) and a journey around islands in the area ($75). Departures from Whitianga Wharf are subject to weather conditions.

➤ CONTACT: **Mercury Bay Safaris** (✉ Whitianga Visitor Information Centre, Whitianga, ☎ 07/866–5555, FAX 07/866–2205).

WILDERNESS TOURS

A trip to New Zealand really wouldn't be complete without a day or more with Doug Johansen and Jan Poole or one of their expert associate guides from Kiwi Dundee Adventures. Their total enthusiasm for the region inevitably rubs off on anyone who takes a Kiwi Dundee tour. There are one- to five-day or longer experiences of the majesty of the Coromandel, or all of New Zealand if you'd like. The spectacular natural phenomena that they know intimately and respect deeply and the odd bits of history and bush lore are all rolled into their hikes and walks. They have a great time as conservationists and guides, and you're sure to have one with them in their beautiful neck of the woods.

➤ CONTACT: **Kiwi Dundee Adventures** (✉ Box 198, Whangamata, ☎ FAX 07/865–8809, WEB www.kiwidundee.co.nz).

VISITOR INFORMATION
The peninsula's visitor centers in are all open daily, though from spring through fall Whitianga's bureau has half days on weekends. For tidal information, check the back page of the *New Zealand Herald* newspaper.

➤ TOURIST INFORMATION: **Coromandel Visitor Information Centre** (✉ 355 Kapanga Rd., ☎ 07/866–8598, FAX 07/866–7285, WEB www.coromandeltown.co.nz). **Thames Visitor Information Centre** (✉ 206 Pollen St., Thames, ☎ 07/868–7284, WEB www.thamesinfo.co.nz). **Whangamata Information Centre** (✉ 616 Port Whangamata, ☎ FAX 07/865–8340). **Whitianga Visitor Information Centre** (✉ 66 Albert St., ☎ 07/866–5555, WEB www.visitor.net.nz).

THE BAY OF PLENTY

Explorer Captain James Cook gave the Bay of Plenty its name for the abundant sources of food he found here; these days it is best known for its plentiful supply of beaches. Places like Mt. Maunganui and Whakatane overflow with sunseekers during peak summer-vacation periods (especially over Christmas and New Year's), but even at the busiest times you only need to travel a few miles to find a secluded stretch of beach.

The gateway to the region is the small country town of Katikati, but the central base for the area is Tauranga, which has managed to retain its relaxed vacation-town atmosphere despite its recent spurts of development. From Tauranga you can take day trips to beaches, the nearby bush, and offshore attractions such as Mayor Island marine reserve and the volcanic White Island.

Katikati

③ *62 km (39 mi) southeast of Thames, 35 km (22 mi) northwest of Tauranga.*

In its early days, the Katikati area was heavily populated by Māori, and many pā (fortified village) sites have been found—an indication of frequent tribal warfare. These days, fruit growing keeps the economy afloat. Katikati's most noticeable features are the 26 murals that locals have painted on buildings around town. Look for the Returned Servicemen's Association's *Those Who Served* murals and those that depict the arrival of the Māori by *waka* (canoe).

Waihi Beach, 19 km (12 mi) north of Katikati, is ideal for swimming and surfing and has access to numerous walkways. At low tide, people dig in the sand looking for tuatua and pipi—delicious shellfish that you boil until they open. Don't miss the drive to the top of the Bowentown heads at the southern end of Waihi Beach. This is an old Māori pā with stunning views. A short but steep walk from here leads to Cave Bay directly below the view point. Don't swim here, as there are dangerous currents.

You'll find great views over the Bay of Plenty at the **Lindemann Road Lookout** a couple of minutes north of Katikati on State Highway 2. The only sign pointing to the lookout is right at the turnoff, so you might come upon it fairly suddenly. The road is good but narrow in parts. Once at the lookout (where the road ends) you'll find a map embedded in rock to help orient you. Look for Mayor Island just to the north and Mt. Maunganui to the south.

On the main road just out of Katikati township to the south you'll spot the Cape Dutch design of the **Morton Estate** winery building. Wine maker Evan Ward produces a large range and has won a stack of awards over the years. He has also talked the company's accountants into letting him hold some bottles back until he thinks they're drinking at their best, so you are likely to find earlier vintages here than you will in most wineries. Most of the grapes come from Hawke's Bay, but Evan also occasionally uses Marlborough fruit. The top-of-the-line Black Label Chardonnay is particularly recommended. ⊠ *Main Rd. Katikati,* ☎ *0800/667–866.* ⊙ *Daily 10:30–5.*

Dominating Moffat Road in the town of Bethlehem, the impressive **Mills Reef Winery** stands out from the local farmland. Owner–wine maker Paddy Preston used to make kiwi-fruit wine, but he hasn't looked back since he turned to the real thing. The complex includes a classy tasting room and a reliable restaurant, open for lunch all year, and dinner for most of it. ⊠ *Moffat Rd., Bethlehem, 29 km (18 mi) south of Katikati,* ☎ *09/576–8800,* WEB *www.millsreef.co.nz.* ⊙ *Tastings daily 10–5.*

Dining and Lodging

$$$$ ✕ **Somerset Cottage.** The name says it all—Somerset is a genuine country cottage, and many locals consider it the region's best restaurant. The menu is modern and eclectic, with dishes like panfried squid with lemon zest, chili, and roasted peanuts. The wine list is moderately comprehensive, but you're welcome to take your own bottle—perhaps one you've just purchased nearby. ⊠ *30 Bethlehem Rd., 29 km (18 mi) south of Katikati,* ☎ *07/576–6889. AE, DC, MC, V. Licensed and BYOB. No lunch Sat.–Tues.*

$$$$ ☷ **Fantail Lodge.** Expat Harrie Geraerts has brought some European flair to the region with his lodge's Bavarian-style exterior. His enthusiasm for his adopted country is infectious, though, and even locals are likely to advise you to "ask Harrie" if you have questions about the Katikati area.

The Bay of Plenty

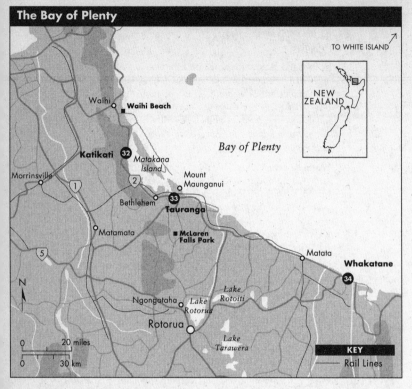

TO WHITE ISLAND

NEW ZEALAND

Waihi
Waihi Beach

Katikati **32**
Matakana Island

Bay of Plenty

Morrinsville

Mount Maunganui

Bethlehem
33 **Tauranga**

Matamata
■ McLaren Falls Park

Matata

Whakatane
34

N

Ngongotaha
Lake Rotorua

Lake Rotoiti

Rotorua

Lake Tarawera

0 ___ 20 miles
0 ___ 30 km

KEY
Rail Lines

His friendships and alliances with local landowners mean he can get you places (like a nearby glowworm grotto) that you wouldn't find alone. If you're planning a few days' stay, consider one of the two-bedroom villas. Each has two bathrooms, a kitchenette, and a private terrace. Rooms in the main lodge are all done in natural colors with timber ceilings. Fresh flowers in your room on arrival usually come from the lodge's garden. ⊠ *117 Rea Rd.,* ☎ *07/549–1581,* FAX *07/549–1417,* WEB *www.fantaillodge. co.nz. 11 rooms, 2 two-bedroom villas. Restaurant, some kitchenettes, pool, tennis court, bar. AE, DC, MC, V.*

Tauranga

33 *216 km (134 mi) southeast of Auckland, 88 km (55 mi) north of Rotorua.*

The population center of the Bay of Plenty, Tauranga is a pleasant town—one of New Zealand's fastest growing, thanks to retirees and young families escaping the bustle (and housing prices) of Auckland. To explore the town center, start at the **Strand,** an attractive tree-lined street that separates the shops from the sea. You'll find bars, restaurants, and cafés along this road and its side streets.

The **Compass Community Foundation** is a watered-down version of what was once a more impressive historic museum. It's worth a visit though, if just to check out the **House of Bottles Wood Museum** where Keith Godwin takes old fence posts originally used in New Zealand's pioneering farms, and turns them into handcrafted bottles. They make unusual and attractive souvenirs. ⊠ *17th Ave. W,* ☎ *07/571–3700.* ☜ *Free.* ☉ *Daily 9–5.*

The formerly volcanic **Mt. Maunganui** is the geological icon of the region, with its conical, rocky outline rising 761 ft above sea level. Regarded as one of the best beach and surfing areas in New Zealand, "the Mount" gets quite crowded around Christmas and New Year's Eve. To see it at its best, come in November, early December, or between mid-January and late March. A system of trails around Mauao—Maunganui's local Māori name—includes an easy walk around its base and the more strenuous Summit Road from the campground by the Pilot Bay boat ramp.

McLaren Falls Park is just a 15-minute drive south of Tauranga off State Highway 29. You can take the 10-minute easy bushwalk to the falls, or tackle the more strenuous walks to Pine Tree Knoll or the Ridge, where your efforts will be rewarded with great vistas across the park. ⊠ *State Hwy. 29,* ☎ *07/578–8103.*

Dining and Lodging

$$–$$$$ ✕ **Harbourside Brasserie and Bar.** The Oregon timber floor of this Tauranga institution is supported by piles sunk into the seabed. The building began as a yacht club back in the 1930s, but it's been better known as a restaurant for much of its life. The menu keeps things simple and tasty; for a delicious spin on fish-and-chips, try the tarakihi in crispy beer batter. ⊠ *Strand Extension,* ☎ *07/571–0520. AE, DC, MC, V.*

$$$ ✕ **Spinnaker's.** This pleasant indoor-outdoor restaurant has great views of Mt. Maunganui across a sea of pleasure craft in one direction and Tauranga township in the other. The emphasis is on seafood, with at least three fish-of-the-day options. Seared yellowfin tuna is one popular choice, but despite the nautical leaning, roast lamb loin with sweetbreads often outsells it. ⊠ *Tauranga Bridge Marina,* ☎ *07/574–4147. AE, DC, MC, V.*

$$–$$$ ✕ **Bella Mia.** The Roman owner succeeded in re-creating a little piece of home in this cozy suburban eatery. The decor hits the classic notes, with red-and-white checked tablecloths and grapes hanging from the ceiling. The food is equally traditional; much of the pasta is homemade, and the flavorful pizzas are thin-crusted. Be sure to leave room for dessert—Bella Mia makes its own gelato, sorbets, and tiramisu. ⊠ *73A Devonport Rd.,* ☎ *07/578–4996. MC, V. BYOB. No lunch Sun.*

$$$–$$$$ ☷ **Taiparoro House.** This restored Victorian villa has the best views in town, overlooking Tauranga harbor, and it's also close to the shopping and dining district. The owners collected "pre-loved" furniture to match the colonial atmosphere they were after. The bedrooms are furnished differently and are on the top floor, with slanting ceilings. A favorite for honeymooners is the pricier Harbourview Suite, which has the best views, a superb clawfoot bath, a (decorative) mosquito net over the bed, and an old kauri dresser. The house can be hard to find if you're coming from the harbor, so call for directions. ⊠ *11 5th Ave.,* ☎ *07/577–9607,* FAX *07/577–9264. 1 room, 1 suite. Lounge. MC, V. BP.*

$$–$$$ ☷ **Puriri Park Tauranga.** If you're seeking modern accommodations close to town, this is easily the best of Tauranga's mass of lodging choices. This all-suites establishment is priced just above motels in the vicinity but is still less expensive than its location and facilities would suggest. The rooms are spacious, with kitchen facilities, private balconies, and solid oak work tables. For lunch and dinner, guests can walk to a selection of nearby restaurants that have a "charge back" arrangement with the hotel. ⊠ *32 Cameron Rd.,* ☎ *07/577–1480,* FAX *07/577–1490,* WEB *www.puriripark.co.nz. 21 suites. Kitchenettes, pool, bar. AE, DC, MC, V.*

Outdoor Activities and Sports

SWIMMING (WITH AND WITHOUT DOLPHINS)

Dolphin Seafaris will take you out for a dolphin encounter. Wet suits, dive gear, and towels are included in the $100 price tag. Phone ahead for daily departure times from the Bridge Marina in Mt. Maunganui. ✉ *90 Maunganui Rd., Mt. Maunganui,* ☎ *07/575–4620,* WEB *www. nzdolphin.com.*

The **Mt. Manganui Hot Pools** include a cool pool with marked lanes for anyone who wants some serious exercise, but most visitors prefer to soak in the hotter saltwater pools. ✉ *Adams Way,* ☎ *07/575–0868.* ✉ *$3.* ☉ *Mon.–Sat. 6 AM–10 PM, Sun. 8 AM–10 PM.*

Whakatane

④ *100 km (62 mi) southeast of Tauranga.*

For yet another chance to laze on the beach, **Whakatane** (fah-kah-*tah*-nee) claims to be the North Island's sunniest town. This was landfall on New Zealand for the first migratory Māori canoes, and the fertile hinterland was the first part of the country to be farmed. The most popular and safest swimming beach in the area is Ohope beach, east of Whakatane.

Whakatane is also a base from which to explore **White Island,** where you can deep-sea fish or swim with dolphins. The island is an active volcano, and whether you see it by plane, boat, or on foot, its billowing steam makes for a typically awesome Pacific Rim geothermal experience.

The least expensive way to get to White Island is by boat. Options include tours on the *Te Kahurangi* (☎ 07/323–7829), a 37-ft SuperCat vessel that only carries small groups. The cost is $85 and includes lunch and a two-hour tour of White Island. **Vulcan Helicopters** (☎ 0800/804–354, WEB www.vulcanheli.co.nz) has a nine-seat helicopter; pilot-owner Robert Fleming is an authority on the island. Two-hour flights cost $375 and include a landing. **East Bay Flight Centre** (☎ 07/308–8446, WEB www. ebfc.co.nz) has aircraft that fly over the island's crater; 50-minute trips cost $150.

For closer aqueous encounters of the mammalian kind, **Dolphins Down Under** (✉ 2 The Strand East, ☎ 07/308–4636, FAX 07/308–0359, WEB www.dolphinswim.co.nz) has four-hour cruises during which you can swim with or simply view dolphins. Wet suits and snorkels are provided. Cruises leave at 7:30 AM and cost $100.

The Bay of Plenty A to Z

BUS TRAVEL

InterCity links Auckland, Thames, Waihi, Katikati, Mt. Maunganui, and Tauranga daily. InterCity links Auckland to Whakatane through Rotorua.

InterCity's Pacific Coast Highway Traveller pass follows the Pacific Coast Highway tourist route from Auckland through to Napier in Hawke's Bay. The pass allows for stops in Tauranga and Whakatane and nicely links these towns to the Coromandel Peninsula, Rotorua, and Gisborne. It costs $209.
➤ BUS DEPOTS: **InterCity Tauranga Depot** (✉ 97 Willow St., ☎ 07/571–3211). **InterCity Whakatane Depot** (✉ Pyne St., ☎ 07/308–6169).
➤ BUS LINE: **InterCity** (☎ 09/913–6100, WEB www.intercitycoach.co.nz).

CAR TRAVEL

Car travel is the easiest way to get around the area; roads are generally well maintained and many follow the coast. From Auckland take the Southern Motorway, following signs to Hamilton. Just past the narrowing of the motorway, turn left onto Highway 2, and travel through Paeroa. Stay on Highway 2 all the way to Tauranga, driving through Waihi and Katikati on the way. The driving time between Auckland and Katikati is around 2 hours, 40 minutes. Between Auckland and Tauranga, it is 3 hours, 15 minutes.

EMERGENCIES
➤ EMERGENCY SERVICES: **Fire, police, and ambulance** (☎ 111).

TOURS
BOAT AND FISHING TOURS
Blue Ocean Charters operates three vessels and offers both half- and full-day trips, plus overnight excursions. A day of reef fishing will cost about $50, but if you want to get serious and go for a large hapuka, the cost will increase to more than $100. Equipment is provided.
➤ CONTACT: **Blue Ocean Charters** (✉ Coronation Pier, Wharf St. [Box 13-100, Tauranga], ☎ 07/578–9685, FAX 07/578–3499, WEB www. ubd-online.co.nz/blueocean).

VISITOR INFORMATION
The Katikati, Tauranga, and Whakatane visitor centers are all open daily; the Mt. Maunganui bureau opens on weekdays only.
➤ TOURIST INFORMATION: **Katikati Visitor Information** (✉ Centre Main Rd., ☎ 07/549–1658). **Mt. Maunganui Visitor Information Centre** (✉ Salisbury Ave., ☎ 07/575–5099). **Tauranga Visitor Information Centre** (✉ 97 Willow St., ☎ 07/578–8103). **Whakatane Visitor Information Centre** (✉ Boon St., ☎ 07/308–6058).

3 ROTORUA TO WELLINGTON

Sulfuric Rotorua bubbles and oozes with surreal volcanic activity. It's one of the population centers of New Zealand's pre-European inhabitants, the Māori—and thus the best place to participate in a traditional *hāngi* feast. Great hiking abounds in a variety of national parks, and glorious gardens grow in the rich soil of the Taranaki Province. The nation's capital, Wellington, and charming, art deco Napier are friendly urban counterpoints to the countryside.

NORTH AND SOUTH ISLANDS have different sorts of natural beauty. The South Island's better-known heroic landscapes are generally flat or precipitous. The North Island's rolling pasturelands have a more human scale—some think of Scotland. Parts of the North Island do break the rhythm of these verdant contours: the majestic, Fuji-like Mt. Taranaki, the rugged wilderness areas of Te Urewera and Tongariro national parks, the gorges of the Whanganui river region, the rocky forms in the Wairarapa district, and the bizarre geological plumbing around Rotorua.

Updated by
Bob Marriott

Rotorua is the mid-island's population center, and it has been a tourist center since Europeans first heard of the healing qualities of local hot springs. All around, you'll find a gallery of surreal wonders that include limestone caverns, volcanic wastelands, steaming geysers, and hissing ponds. From the shores of Lake Taupo—the country's largest lake and the geographic bull's-eye of the North Island—Mt. Ruapehu, the island's tallest peak, is plainly visible. Site of New Zealand's largest ski area, the mountain is the dominant feature of Tongariro National Park, a haunting landscape of craters, volcanoes, and lava flows that ran with molten rock as recently as 1988 and were throwing up some threatening clouds in 1996.

Southeast of Lake Taupo, on the shores of Hawke Bay, the town of Napier has an interesting aggregation of art deco architecture. Around Napier, the Hawke's Bay region is one of the country's major wine routes. A diversion to the north will take you to relatively isolated Gisborne and Eastland, which are often overlooked but extremely rewarding: the largely agricultural East Cape juts out above Gisborne, coursing with trout-rich streams and ringed with stunning beaches and coves.

The lush Taranaki region literally sprang from the ocean floor in a series of volcanic blasts, forming that odd hump down the west coast of the North Island. The now-dormant cone of Mt. Taranaki is the breathtaking symbol of the province and the site of great hiking tracks (trails). Agriculture thrives in the area's volcanic soil, and Taranaki's gardens are some of the country's most spectacular. The local Māori mythology and historical sites deepen any experience of the area.

More and more people are finding their way to Wellington—New Zealand's capital—by choice rather than necessity. Arguably the country's most cosmopolitan city, it is gaining a reputation for fostering the arts and preserving its culture in a way that the more brash Auckland to the north does not. Charming and small enough to explore easily on foot, Wellington has an excellent arts complex, the popular Te Papa–Museum of New Zealand, and scores of fashionable cafés. Because it is perched at the southern tip of the North Island, Wellington is the jumping-off point for the ferry south—but don't jump south too quickly. It's worth considering taking a side trip east to the Wairarapa, a rugged coastal area with some of the country's finest wineries, or north to the isolated settlements of the Whanganui river region.

Note: For more information on bicycling, fishing, hiking, kayaking, and rafting in central North Island, *see* Chapter 6.

Pleasures and Pastimes

Dining

Between Rotorua and Wellington, you'll come across a number of small towns with little more than a country-style pub or a dairy (convenience store) to satisfy the appetite. They may lack big-city sophistication, but they're certain to be friendly. If you're lucky, the pub might have an attached restaurant offering honest home cooking, but mostly you'll have to settle for a sandwich and a sweet bun from the dairy. Two sandwich fillings that never fail to fascinate visitors are spaghetti and baked beans, both from a can. You'll find this weird combination only in New Zealand and Australia.

Rotorua is the best place to try the Māori feast known as a hāngi. Traditionally, meat and vegetables placed in flax baskets were gently steamed in an earth oven lined with heated stones and wet leaves— lamb, pork, chicken, and seafood along with potatoes, pumpkin, and *kūmara* (sweet potato), a staple of the Māori diet that holds spiritual significance to some tribes. Nowadays, the food may well be prepared aboveground, but when it's done well, it doesn't lose much in the translation. Almost without exception, a Rotorua hāngi will be followed by a Māori concert, usually a commercialized but entertaining performance of traditional songs and dances, with often hilarious audience participation.

In the central North Island, particularly around Taupo, you might be lucky enough to taste freshly caught trout. Laws prohibit trout from being sold commercially, so you'll probably have to hook one for yourself, then ask your host or a local chef to cook it. (Not long ago, an enterprising restaurateur tried to bypass the law by offering the trout free and charging $28 for the sauce. Nice try, but he didn't get away with it.) Also look for game such as wild boar, venison (the farmed version is usually called *cervena*), and hare. On the Whanganui River, the local catch is eel—try it smoked at the Flying Fox.

CATEGORY	COST*
$$$$	over $32
$$$	$25–$32
$$	$15–$24
$	under $15

per person for a main course at dinner

Fishing
Central North Island is trout country. You can get out on any of the designated lakes and waterways if you have your own gear and a fishing license. It is worthwhile, however, to engage a local guide to take you to the right spots. On the lakes around Rotorua, and perhaps even more on Lake Taupo, few people leave disappointed. For more information on central North Island fishing, *see* Chapter 6.

Lodging
New Zealand's lodges are often small and exclusive, set in places of great beauty. Some of the best are in central North Island, the most famous being Huka Lodge, just outside Taupo, near Rotorua. They tend to attract people keen on fishing, hunting, or other outdoor activities. Decor and ambience vary greatly from lodge to lodge, but the best places combine a relaxed country-house atmosphere—perhaps mixing antique furniture and contemporary design—with excellent dining; high-quality, unobtrusive service; and exhaustive facilities. If your budget allows, even one night at one of these lodges will be an experience you won't soon forget.

The up-and-down fortunes of New Zealand's rural communities over the last decade or so have persuaded farming families to supplement their incomes by offering farm-stay accommodations. Farm stays usually aren't luxurious, but the best provide hands-on involvement with the working life of the farm. Standards can vary, as the hosts have often not had extensive hospitality training, but you will be safe sticking to farm stays recommended in this book. Or ask for guidance at the nearest information center.

In Rotorua and Taupo there are many more hotel beds than visitors for much of the year, and a number of hotels and motels offer significant discounts on their standard rates in the off-season. The exception is school holidays, for which you should book well in advance. Also note that peak season in Tongariro National Park and other ski areas is winter (June–September), which means summer visitors can always find empty beds and good deals.

CATEGORY	COST*
$$$$	over $200
$$$	$125–$200
$$	$80–$125
$	under $80

*All prices are for a standard double room.

Soaking

In Rotorua and Taupo, thermal springs are literally on tap. You can soak in your own thermal bath in even the cheapest hotels in Rotorua, or take advantage of public facilities such as Polynesian Spa. Many Taupo motels and hotels also have their own thermal baths or pools. Lie back and close your eyes. You'll be amazed how relaxed you feel afterward.

Tramping and Walking

Central North Island doesn't have the world-famous walking tracks of the South Island, but it does have equally serious bushwalking and plenty of pleasant trails. Excellent longer trails circle Mt. Taranaki or climb through the alpine areas in Tongariro National Park. Some of the most rugged bush in the country is in Te Urewera National Park southeast of Rotorua, and hiking opportunities abound around Rotorua, Taupo, and the Wairarapa.

Exploring Central North Island and Wellington

You could easily spend a month traveling between Auckland and Wellington and still touch on only the major sights. Realistically, you're most likely to travel either straight through the middle or down the east or west coast. The difficulty comes in deciding which coast and which smaller areas to explore. If you're interested in the bizarre thermal activity of Rotorua, start there. If you're a garden lover, starting in Taranaki to the west and stopping at other spots on the way to Wellington is the way to go. If wine routes are more appealing, you can take in three on the east coast: Gisborne, Hawke's Bay, and Wairarapa. If you want to get into some astonishing backcountry, Tongariro and Te Urewera national parks are unbeatable, as are parts of the Wairarapa. And Wellington is a charming city for refreshing yourself for a couple of days before hopping over to the South Island.

Great Itineraries

Numbers in the text correspond to numbers in the margin and on the Central North Island, Napier, Wellington, and Greater Wellington and Wairarapa maps.

IF YOU HAVE 3 DAYS
Three days will only allow you to see one of the major areas covered in the chapter or to scratch the surface of two—especially taking travel time into account. If you do have only three days, spend all of them either in ⚐ **Rotorua** ④, popping over to **Waitomo Caves** ③ for the glowworm spectacle and spending all or part of a day fishing; or in ⚐ **Napier** ⑧–⑰, with a day in the city and two days in the surrounding

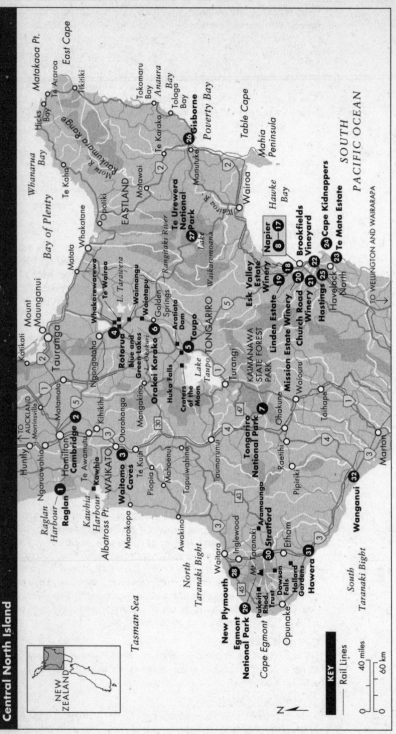

wine country; or in ▥ **Wellington** ㉝–㊽, with a side trip to the ▥ **Wairarapa.** You would have to fly into and out of New Plymouth in order to spend three days in ▥ **Mt. Taranaki**'s gardens and hiking in Egmont National Park. If surface treatment will do, you could take a day in Rotorua before dropping down the next morning to Napier for the rest of the time. Fly from there to your next stop.

IF YOU HAVE 6 DAYS

With almost a week, you can put together a more diverse experience of a couple of regions. Pick a path for moving from north to south and leave a half day or more for travel between Rotorua and Napier or Taranaki, then another half day plus for the trip down to Wellington if you have a car. Start in ▥ **Rotorua** ④, spending two to three days around the bubble and ooze, fishing, and going to a hāngi at night. Then continue either east to the art deco city of ▥ **Napier** ⑧–⑰ and ▥ **Hawke's Bay** ⑱–㉕ and the surrounding wine country, or west to ▥ **Taranaki** for gardens, mountain walks, and beaches for the rest of the time. Or from Rotorua you could head south to ▥ **Taupo** ⑤ and **Tongariro National Park** ⑦ for serious outdoor activities: fishing, canoeing, rafting, and hiking. The ▥ **Whanganui River region** is another outdoors option, though you'll need to set aside at least two full days to see its remote river settlements. Going to Napier or Taupo would set you up for a stop in the ▥ **Wairarapa** for more spectacular countryside, one of the country's finest wildlife parks, and a wine tour in ▥ **Martinborough** ㊾. In six days you could also combine Taranaki, the Wairarapa, and Wellington, with one day each in the last two. Or chuck it all and head straight for ▥ **Gisborne** ㉖ and Eastland for six days of some of New Zealand's finest off-the-beaten-path travel.

When to Tour Central North Island and Wellington

The months from December through mid-April are the best for central and southern North Island. Everything is open (though not the few days between Christmas and New Year and over Easter) and the weather can be glorious. That said, Wellington and the exposed coastal regions do get more than their fair share of rain and southerly winds, so even in summer expect the odd very chilly day and slightly more frequent overcast days. Some say that Taranaki's Rhododendron Festival nearly always gets rained on, the answer to which is to skip the festival and go in late November for more than just rhodo blossoms. Of course if you want to do some skiing, August is the month to hit the slopes of Tongariro National Park and Egmont National Park, though the first major snows fall as early as June.

THE WAIKATO AND WAITOMO

Many think of the Waikato region as the heartland of the North Island—a fertile, temperate, agricultural district south of Auckland that boasts New Zealand's largest inland city (Hamilton) and some of its most important pre-European sites.

Polynesian sailors first landed on the region's west coast as early as the mid-14th century; by way of contrast, Europeans didn't settle here until the 1830s. By the 1860s, the Waikato's different Māori tribes had overcome their differences and united to elect a king in an attempt to resist white encroachment upon their lands. This Māori "King Movement," as it is known, is still a significant cultural and political force, centered in the small Waikato town of Ngaruawahia.

History intrudes only briefly as you speed down Highway 1 from Auckland: Ngaruawahia is the official residence of the reigning Māori monarch, but the ceremonial buildings are not open to the public; and

Hamilton is a city you can afford to miss if time is tight. Instead, visitors are funneled through Hamilton to three nearby attractions: the surfing hot spot of Raglan on the West Coast; attractive Cambridge, an agricultural town renowned as a horse-breeding center; and the extraordinary cave formations at Waitomo.

Raglan

❶ *176 km (110 mi) south of Auckland, 44 km (27 mi) west of Hamilton.*

It's hard to think of a more laid-back town in the country than Raglan. Set on sheltered Raglan Harbour, and in the lee of Mt. Karioi, the tiny town owes its easygoing ways to the legions of young surfers drawn to the legendary breaks at nearby Manu Bay and Whale Bay, both 8 km (5 mi) southwest of town. When the surf's up, drive out to the parking areas above the sweeping bays to see scores of surfers tackling what's reputed to be world's longest left-hand break.

The surfers have made Raglan cool, and along the tree-lined main street, Bow Street, barefoot dudes in designer shades pad in and out of the few hip café-bars or hang in the smattering of crafts and surf-wear shops. Families vacation here, too, frequenting the sandy beaches on either side of the harbor entrance.

On hot days, the spectacular **Bridal Veil Falls** make an appealing target. A 10-minute shaded hike from the parking lot leads to a viewing platform above the 150-ft drop; from here, another 10-minute walk down a steep, stepped trail puts you on a wooden platform at the base of the falls. Bring your swimsuit and, if you dare, plunge into the very cold water. The falls are 20 km (12 mi) south of Raglan; take the Kawhia road from town.

OFF THE
BEATEN PATH

KAWHIA – With time on your hands, explore the minor road from Raglan to this isolated, coastal harbor settlement 55 km (34 mi) to the south. It's a fine route, skirting the eastern flank of Mt. Karioi and passing the turnoff for the Bridal Veil Falls, though take care, since much of the road is gravel. Kawhia was landfall in AD 1350 for some of the Waikato's earliest Polynesian settlers, the Tainui people, and permission is sometimes granted (inquire at the harborside museum) to visit the local *marae* (meetinghouse). What most come for, however, are the Te Puia hot springs at Ocean Beach, east of town. There's road access to the beach (or it's a two-hour walk from Kawhia). Since you can only find the springs by digging into the sand a couple of hours either side of low tide, you should check the tide tables in Raglan before you set off.

Dining and Lodging

$$ ✕ **Vinnie's World of Eats.** In this historic kauri cottage, you can tuck into anything from Mexican food to curries to pizzas. A wide range of salads and snacks covers the odd-hours appetites. ⊠ *7 Wainui Rd.,* ☎ *07/825–7273. AE, MC, DC, V.*

$ 🏠 **Raglan Backpackers & Waterfront Lodge.** Many rate this supremely
★ agreeable, budget-price, harborside lodge the best of its type in the country. An "outdoor living" ideal, it has small, very simple rooms that open on to a pretty, wood-decked interior courtyard (complete with hammock). From the lounge you can wander onto the lawn and barbecue area. The shared bathroom facilities are spotless, and there's a well-equipped self-catering kitchen. If you're feeling adventurous, ask for a surfing lesson. ⊠ *6 Nero St.,* ☎ *07/825–0515. 8 rooms, 1 eight-bed backpackers' dorm. Laundry facilities; no a/c. No credit cards.*

Outdoor Activities and Sports

If you're itching to hit the waves, stop by **Raglan Surf Co.,** a top surfing store. It stocks equipment by all the leading brands and rents surf boards, wet suits, and boogie boards. It's open daily, and the friendly staff will pass along helpful local surf tips. ⊠ *3 Wainui Rd.,* ☎ *07/825–8988,* WEB *www.raglansurfco.com.*

Cambridge

❷ *150 km (94 mi) southeast of Auckland, 23 km (14 mi) southeast of Hamilton, 85 km (53 mi) northwest of Rotorua.*

Cambridge is a place most people drive through in a hurry—en route to Rotorua from Auckland—and then wish they had stopped. Even a quick glance reveals that this is a charming town, with its historic buildings and rural English atmosphere.

The best way to check out its lovely trees and its crafts and antiques stores is simply to leave your car and take a walk along Victoria, Empire, and Commerce streets. Cambridge is also regarded as New Zealand's Kentucky, and, in fact, the Thoroughbred industry has become the most prominent local feature.

☾ **New Zealand Horse Magic** at Cambridge Thoroughbred Lodge is a must for anyone interested in horse racing or the Thoroughbred industry. Experienced presenters tailor shows for each audience, easily moving from expert-level information to antics for any kids who might be in the group. (Be sure to call ahead for a show reservation.) Numerous breeds of horses can be seen, including a Lippizaner. Kids can go for a short ride while you have a cup of coffee and muffins. Auctions, which are interesting to drop in on if you're in the area, are held in March, May, August, and November. ⊠ *State Hwy. 1, 6 km (4 mi) south of Cambridge,* ☎ *07/827–8118,* WEB *www.cambridgethoroughbredlodge. co.nz.* ☜ *$12.* ☉ *Tues.–Sun. tour and show at 10:30.*

Dining and Lodging

$–$$ ✕ **Fran's Café and Continental Cake Kitchen.** Snag a table in the main room, or wander past the kitchen to the courtyard out back. Once you're settled, choose from a big selection of imaginative homemade sandwiches, pasta, quiches, or salads, such as the grilled vegetables with balsamic vinegar. Vegetarians, note: Fran makes her own hummus and falafel. Don't forget to order a cuppa (Kiwi coffee or tea—Fran's doesn't have a license to sell wine) and a piece of cake. ⊠ *62 Victoria St.,* ☎ *07/827–3946. AE, DC, MC, V. BYOB.*

$$$ ✕▥ **Souter House.** If ever a place was worth a detour from the main
★ highway, this has to be it. This beautifully restored Edwardian villa, listed by the New Zealand Historic Places Trust, offers both superb guest rooms and exceptional dining. Seven studios and two honeymoon suites are tastefully furnished with fine paintings and antiques. In the dining room, choose from dishes such as New Zealand king salmon with a ginger-soy glaze and Asian greens. The wine list's selection of top New Zealand and international vintages is very reasonably priced. ⊠ *19 Victoria St.,* ☎ *07/827–3610,* FAX *07/827–4885,* WEB *www. souterhouse.co.nz. 7 rooms, 2 suites. Dining room; no a/c, no smoking. AE, DC, MC, V. CP.*

Waitomo Caves

❸ *80 km (50 mi) southwest of Hamilton, 65 km (41 mi) southwest of Cambridge, 150 km (95 mi) west of Rotorua.*

★ The **Waitomo Caves** are parts of an ancient seabed that was lifted and then spectacularly eroded into a surreal underground landscape of limestone formations, gushing rivers, and contorted caverns. Many of the caves are still unexplored, although an increasing number are accessible on adventurous underground activity trips involving rafting, caving, and rappelling. But you don't need to be Indiana Jones to appreciate the magnificent underground structures. Two of the caves are open to the public for guided tours: the Aranui and the Waitomo, or Glowworm, Cave. **Waitomo Cave** takes its name from the Māori words *wai* and *tomo,* "water" and "cave," since the Waitomo River vanishes into the hillside here. You ride through in a boat. In the grotto the larvae of *Arachnocampa luminosa,* measuring between 1 and 2 inches, live on cave ceilings. They snare prey by dangling sticky filaments, which trap insects attracted to the light the worm emits by a chemical oxidation process. A single glowworm produces far less light than any firefly, but when they are massed in great numbers in the dark, their effect is a bit like looking at the night sky in miniature.

Aranui Cave, 2 km (1 mi) beyond Waitomo Cave, is a very different experience. Eons of dripping water have sculpted a delicate garden in pink-and-white limestone. The cave is named after a local Māori, Te Rutuku Aranui, who discovered the cave in 1910 when his dog disappeared inside in pursuit of a wild pig. Each cave tour lasts 45 minutes. Glowworm Cave is high on the list of every bus tour, so try to avoid visiting between 11 and 2, when groups arrive from Auckland. ⊠ *Te Anga Rd.,* ☎ *07/878–8227,* 🕸 *www.new-zealand.com/ WaitomoCaves.* 🎫 *Waitomo Cave $20, both caves $30.* ⊗ *Waitomo Cave tour Nov.–Easter, daily every ½ hr 9–5:30; Easter–Oct., daily every hr 9–5; Aranui Cave tour daily at 10, 11, 1, 2, and 3.*

☾ At the visitor center of Waitomo Caves Village the **Museum of Caves** provides an entertaining and informative look at the formation of the caves and the life cycle of the glowworm, with a number of interactive displays designed especially for children. ⊠ *Waitomo Caves Village,* ☎ *07/878–7640,* 🕸 *www.waitomo-museum.co.nz.* 🎫 *$5, combined ticket for Waitomo Cave plus museum $24.* ⊗ *Daily 8:30–5.*

The **Waitomo Walkway** is a 5-km (3-mi), 2½-hour walk that begins across the road from the Museum of Caves and follows the Waitomo River. The track passes through forests and impressive limestone outcrops, and though it is relatively easy, you have to walk back to Waitomo Caves Village on the same path. For an alternative to the complete walk, take Te Anga Road from the village, turn left onto Tumutumu Road, park at **Ruakuri Reserve,** and walk the short (30-minute) final section of the track. There's a natural rock tunnel on the way, and many people come out here after dusk for a free view of the local glowworms—bring a flashlight.

OFF THE
BEATEN PATH
TE ANGA–MAROKOPA ROAD – This classic backcountry road works its way west out of Waitomo toward the coast. It makes for a spectacular detour—or the scenic long way to Taranaki—winding past stunning vistas. Some 26 km (16 mi) out of Waitomo, stop at the Mangapohue (mang-ah-po-*hoo*-ay) Natural Bridge. From the parking area, there are two approaches to the bridge. One to the right climbs over a hill, dropping into a valley strewn with boulders embedded with oyster fossils—the remains of a seismic shift that thrust up the seabed millions of years ago. The natural bridge rises off to the left of the boulders. The other path follows a stream through a gorge it has carved out. The gorge walls climb ever higher until they meet and form the bridge that closes

over the path. The circular walk—going out on one path, returning on the other—only takes 15 to 20 minutes to complete.

About 5 km (3 mi) farther along the road to Marokopa, **Piripiri Caves** beckon with their interesting fossil legacy—the marks of giant oysters that resided here during the area's onetime subaqueous existence. The approach and entrance to the caves are steep and slippery, so wear appropriate shoes or boots, and bring a jacket for the cool air and a powerful flashlight to cut through the gloom.

A couple of miles farther still, you can view the 120-ft **Marokopa Falls** from a small roadside platform or walk down a trail (15 minutes roundtrip) to get closer. And a few miles beyond the falls, the Māori-run pub at **Te Anga** is a good place to stop for refreshment.

The road splits at Te Anga, heading north to Kawhia or southwest for 14 km (9 mi) to the small hamlet of **Marokopa**, where there's a stupendous lookout point over the coast's black-sand beaches. At Marokopa you are 50 km (31 mi) from Waitomo; time either to turn back or keep on south on a more difficult (mostly gravel) stretch for an incredibly scenic route to the Taranaki region. If you're in for the duration, fill up your gas tank before turning off State Highway 1 for Waitomo.

Outdoor Activities and Sports

Most of Waitomo's adventure tours contain some element of blackwater rafting, that is, floating through the underground caverns on inflated inner tubes, dressed in wet suits and equipped with cavers' helmets. Be prepared for the pitch-black darkness and the freezing cold water: your reward is an exhilarating trip gliding through vast glowworm-lit caverns, clambering across rocks, and jumping over underground waterfalls. Waitomo Caves Visitor Information Centre (⊠ Museum of Caves, ☎ 07/878–7640) can advise on which of the various tours is most suitable—some involve steep rappelling or tight underground squeezes. Adventurous types will be able to cope with the basic trip offered by one of the longest-standing companies, **Black Water Rafting** (⊠ Black Water Rafting, Waitomo Caves, ☎ 07/878–6219 or 0800/228–464, WEB www.blackwaterrafting.co.nz). Trips finish with welcome hot showers and a mug of soup back at base. The cost is $69 per person for three hours, $140 per person for five hours, and includes free admission to the Museum of Caves. Departure times vary, depending on demand.

The Waikato and Waitomo A to Z

BUS TRAVEL

InterCity Coachlines runs buses several times daily between Auckland and Hamilton, with onward services to Cambridge. For Waitomo, take the bus from Auckland to Otorohanga, 50 minutes south of Hamilton, where there is also a train station. From here, the Waitomo Shuttle makes the half-hour trip from Otorohanga to Waitomo six times daily, connecting with all major bus and train arrivals. Outside of these times, you must pay taxi rates (around $30) for the shuttle service. One Newmans bus per day loops from Auckland to Rotorua via Waitomo for $33. The Waitomo Wanderer bus service makes the two-hour trip between Rotorua and Waitomo daily, once each way. Fares are $30 one-way or $55 round-trip.

➤ Bus Stops: **Cambridge** (⊠ Lake Street Bus Stop). **Waitomo** (⊠ Juno Hall).

➤ Bus Lines: **InterCity** (☎ 09/913–6100, WEB www.intercitycoach.co.nz). **Waitomo Shuttle** (☎ 0800/808–279). **Waitomo Wanderer** (☎ FAX 07/349–2509).

CAR TRAVEL

Traveling by car is generally the most convenient way to see this region; some towns, like Raglan, aren't served by the regional bus lines and can only be reached by car. Access to the Waikato region is straight down Highway 1 from Auckland—count on 90 minutes to Hamilton. Cambridge is another 20 minutes southeast on Highway 1. For Raglan, take Highway 23 west, a 40-minute drive. For Waitomo (1 hr from Hamilton), take Highway 3 south and turn off onto Highway 37 past Otorohanga. Some roads are narrow and winding, so you'll need to stay alert.

EMERGENCIES

➤ EMERGENCY SERVICES: **Fire, police, and ambulance** (☎ 111).

TOURS

BOAT TOURS

Raglan Harbour Cruises has daily boat trips throughout summer around the inlets and bays of Raglan's lovely harbor. Tickets are $15 and reservations are advised.

➤ CONTACT: **Raglan Harbour Cruises** (☎ 07/825–0300).

BUS TOURS

Newmans offers a one-way bus tour from Auckland to the Waitomo Caves and on to Rotorua, or from Rotorua to the Waitomo Caves, ending in Auckland, including a brief stop at a historic battle site, a barbecue lunch, and admission to the Waitomo Caves. You'll be picked up at your Auckland accommodation and dropped at your Rotorua accommodation, or vice versa. Cost is $136 per person.

➤ CONTACT: **Newmans** (☎ 09/913–6200, WEB www.newmanscoach. co.nz).

VISITOR INFORMATION

Cambridge and Raglan both have visitor centers open weekdays from 9 to 5, weekends from 10 to 4. The Waitomo Caves visitor bureau has slightly longer daily hours, extending until 8 PM in summer.

You'll find a helpful regional resource in Tourism Waikato's Web site, www.waikatonz.co.nz.

➤ TOURIST INFORMATION: **Cambridge Visitor Information Centre** (✉ Queen and Victoria Sts., ☎ 07/823–3456). **Raglan Visitor Information Centre** (✉ 4 Wallis St., ☎ 07/825–0556). **Waitomo Caves Visitor Information Centre** (✉ Museum of Caves, ☎ 07/878–7640, WEB www.waitomocaves.co.nz).

ROTORUA, LAKE TAUPO, AND TONGARIRO NATIONAL PARK

New Zealand's most famous tourist attraction, Rotorua (ro-to-*roo*-ah) sits smack on top of the most violent segment of the Taupo Volcanic Zone, which runs in a broad belt from White Island in the Bay of Plenty to Tongariro National Park, south of Lake Taupo. The region's spurting geysers, sulfur springs, and bubbling mud pools have spawned an unashamedly touristy town that is largely undistinguished save for its dramatic surroundings. True, Rotorua has tidied up its act considerably in the past few years, particularly by landscaping the streets and lakefront, but the air in "Sulphur City" doesn't always encourage lingering outdoors. Drive outside the city limits, however, and you'll find yourself in magnificent, untamed country, where lakes coddle some of the largest rainbow trout on earth.

Fishing is big business, both in Rotorua and at Lake Taupo to the south. The region's lakes are some of the few places where tales of the "big one" can actually be believed. Meanwhile, the town of Taupo on the northeastern shore of Lake Taupo has blossomed into one of the country's major outdoor activity centers—with everything from rafting to skydiving—and is worth a visit in its own right to see even more examples of the region's geothermal wonders. South of the lake rise the three volcanic peaks that make up Tongariro National Park. This is a year-round magnet for skiers and trampers. Even if you don't have much time, skirting the peaks provides a rewarding route on your way south to Wanganui or Wellington.

Rotorua

❹ *85 km (53 mi) south of Cambridge, 200 km (125 mi) southeast of Auckland.*

It's one of the most extraordinary areas in the country. Everywhere you turn, the earth bubbles, boils, spits, and oozes. Drainpipes steam, flower beds hiss, rings tarnish, and cars corrode. The rotten-egg smell of hydrogen sulfide hangs in the air, and even the local golf course has its own mud-pool hot spots, where a lost ball stays lost forever.

It's also a historic region. There is a well-established Māori community here tracing its ancestry back through the Te Arawa tribe to the great Polynesian migration of the 14th century. For hundreds of years, the local Māori settled by Lake Rotorua and harnessed the unique geological phenomena, cooking and bathing in the hot pools and erecting buildings on the warm ground. Māori culture is still stamped indelibly on the area, and most visitors take the opportunity to attend a hāngi (a traditional feast) followed by a Māori concert.

The town you see today at Rotorua is almost entirely a product of the late-19th-century fad for spa towns, from which era date the elaborate bathhouse and formal gardens. In fact, the "Great South Seas Spa," as Rotorua was known, was among the very earliest tourist ventures in the country, with tours of the geothermal oddities being offered as far back as the 1860s. In keeping with those times, the **Lakeland Queen** paddle steamer (☎ 07/348–6634, WEB www.lakelandqueen.co.nz) sets off daily from the lakefront piers for hour-long cruises of Lake Rotorua.

The **Government Gardens** occupy a small lakeside peninsula that fronts the modern street grid, and they are the most attractive part of Rotorua. The Māori call this area Whangapiro (fang-ah-*pee*-ro, "evil-smelling place")—an appropriate name for these bizarre gardens, where sulfur pits bubble and fume behind manicured rose beds and bowling lawns. The focus of interest here is the extraordinary neo-Tudor Bath House. Built as a spa at the turn of the 20th century, it is now Rotorua's **Art and History Museum.** One room on the ground floor is devoted to the eruption of Mt. Tarawera in 1886. You can see a number of artifacts that were unearthed from the debris and a remarkable collection of photographs of the silica terraces of Rotomahana before they were destroyed in the eruption. ⊠ *Arawa St.,* ☎ *07/349–4350,* WEB *www.rotoruamuseum.co.nz.* ☎ *$8.50.* ⊗ *Oct.–Mar., daily 9:30–6; Apr.–Sept., daily 9:30–5.*

Close to the Government Gardens you'll find the soothing, naturally heated **Polynesian Spa.** A wide choice of mineral baths is available, from large communal pools to family pools to small, private baths for two. You can also treat yourself with massage or spa treatments, and the Lake Spa has exclusive bathing in four shallow rock pools overlooking Lake Rotorua. ⊠ *Hinemoa St.,* ☎ *07/348–1328,* WEB *www.*

polynesianspa.co.nz. ✉ *Family or adult pool $12, private pool $12 per ½ hr, lake spa $30.* ⊙ *Daily 6:30 AM–11 PM.*

At the northern end of town on the shores of the lake stands **St. Faith's,** the Anglican church for the Māori village of Ohinemutu (which was one of the area's original settlements). The interior of the church, which is richly decorated with carvings inset with mother-of-pearl, deserves attention at any time, but it's at its best during Sunday services, when the sonorous, melodic voices of the Māori choir rise in hymns. The service at 8 AM is in the Māori language; the 10 AM service is in both Māori and English. ✉ *Memorial Dr.*

Whakarewarewa (*fa*-ka-*ree*-wa-*ree*-wa) is one mouthful of a name—locals just call it Whaka. This is the most accessible and popular of the Rotorua region's thermal spots—partly because it's closest to town—but it is also the most varied, as it provides an insight into Māori culture. The reserve is divided between two different groups; both groups give you some firsthand exposure to the hot pools, boiling mud, and native culture. **The New Zealand Maori Art & Crafts Institute** (✉ Hemo Rd., ☎ 07/348–9047, WEB www.nzmaori.co.nz) has a carving school that hosts workshops and, on the grounds, the Pohutu Geyser and some silica terraces. Don't miss the Nocturnal Kiwi House, where you might spot one of the birds that are the national emblem. Between November and April the institute is open daily from 8 to 6; from May through October it's open from 8 to 5. Entry costs $18. For another introduction Māori traditions, visit the **Whakarewarewa Thermal Village & Reserve** (✉ Tryon St., ☎ FAX 07/349–3463, WEB www.whakarewarewa.com). On the guided tours of this living village, you'll see thermal baths, boiling mineral pools, and cooking demonstrations using steam vents. Nature walks and horse treks are also available. The village opens daily from 8:30 to 5, with nearly a dozen tours ($18). Whakarewarewa is 3 km (2 mi) along Fenton Street from the Rotorua Visitor Centre, heading toward Taupo.

The **Blue and Green lakes** are on the road to Te Wairoa and Lake Tarawera. The Green Lake is off-limits except for its viewing area, but the Blue Lake is a popular picnic and swimming area. To get to them, take Highway 30 east (Te Ngae Road) about 15 minutes and turn right onto Tarawera Road at the signpost for the lakes and buried village. The road loops through forests and skirts the edge of the lakes.

At the end of the 19th century, **Te Wairoa** (tay why-*ro*-ah, "the buried village") was the starting point for expeditions to the pink-and-white terraces of Rotomahana, on the slopes of Mt. Tarawera. As mineral-rich geyser water cascaded down the mountainside, it formed a series of baths, which became progressively cool as they neared the lake. In the latter half of the 19th century these fabulous terraces were the country's major attraction, but they were destroyed when Mt. Tarawera erupted in 1886. The explosion, heard as far away as Auckland, killed 153 people and buried the village of Te Wairoa under a sea of mud and hot ash. The village has been excavated, and of special interest is the *whare* (*fah*-ray, "hut") of the *tohunga* ("priest") Tuhoto Ariki, who predicted the destruction of the village. Eleven days before the eruption, two separate tourist parties saw a Māori war canoe emerge from the mists of Lake Tarawera and disappear again—a vision the tohunga interpreted as a sign of impending disaster. Four days after the eruption, the 100-year-old tohunga was dug out of his buried whare still alive, only to die in the hospital a few days later. A path circles the excavated village, then continues on as a delightful trail, the lower section of which is steep and can be slippery in places. Te Wairoa is 14 km (9 mi) southeast of Rotorua, a 20-minute drive. ✉ *Tarawera Rd.,* ☎ *07/362–8287,* WEB *www.buriedvillage.co.nz.* ☎ *$12.* ☉ *Daily 9–5:30.*

From the shores of Lake Tarawera, the **M.V. Reremoana,** a restored lake cruiser, makes regular scenic runs. The two-hour cruise is especially recommended; it departs daily at 11, stopping at Te Ariki, the base of Mt. Tarawera, where you can picnic or swim or walk across the isthmus to Lake Rotomahana. Forty-five-minute cruises also depart from the landing at 1:30, 2:30 and 3:30 with a full commentary. The Tarawera landing is on Spencer Road, 2 km (1 mi) beyond the Buried Village. A sign points to LAUNCH CRUISES and the *Reremoana*'s parking lot. ✉ *Tarawera Launch Cruises,* ☎ *07/362–8595,* WEB *www. purerotorua.com.* ☎ *2-hr cruise $27, 45-min cruise $17.50.*

When Mt. Tarawera erupted in 1886, destroying Rotomahana's terraces, not all was lost. A volcanic valley emerged from the ashes—

★ **Waimangu**—extending southwest from Lake Rotomahana. It's consequently one of the world's newest thermal-activity areas, encompassing the boiling water of the massive Inferno Crater, plus steaming cliffs, bubbling springs, and bush-fringed terraces. A path (one–two hours) runs through the valley down to the lake, where a shuttle bus takes you back to the entrance. Or add on a lake cruise as well. Waimangu is 26 km (16 mi) southeast of Rotorua; take Highway 5 south (Taupo direction) and look for the turn after 19 km (12 mi). ✉ *Waimangu Rd.,* ☎ *07/366–6137,* WEB *www.waimangu.co.nz.* ☎ *$20, including cruise $45.* ☉ *Daily 8:30–5.*

If you've only got time for one visit to a thermal area around Rotorua,

★ make it to **Waiotapu** (why-oh-*ta*-pu)—a freakish, fantastic landscape of deep, sulfur-crusted pits; jade-color ponds; silica terraces; and a steaming lake edged with red algae and bubbling with tiny beads of carbon dioxide. Be smart and get here early: the **Lady Knox Geyser** erupts precisely at 10:15 daily—but not through some miracle of Mother Nature. Soap powder is poured into the vent of the geyser, which reduces the surface tension, so that the boiling water below erupts, on schedule, to gasps of delight. Having seen the geyser, which is set apart from the main thermal area, you then drive back to the main entrance for the spectacular one- to two-hour circular walk. Waiotapu is 30 km (19 mi) southeast of Rotorua—follow Highway 5 south (Taupo direction) and look for the signs. ✉ *State Hwy. 5,* ☎ *07/366–6333,* WEB *www. geyserland.co.nz.* ☎ *$15.* ☉ *Daily 8:30–5.*

Dining and Lodging

In addition to some solid restaurants, Rotorua provides the best opportunities to experience a Māori hāngi (feast). The **Tamaki Tours** (☎ 07/346–2823) hāngi takes place at a Māori village, **Te Tawa Ngahere Pa.** A coach picks you up at your hotel, and on the way to the village you get briefed on Māori protocol. Once there, you are formally welcomed before the important part—eating the food. The cost, including pickup, is $58. Hāngis at the **Sheraton** (☎ 07/349–5200, $49) have a long-standing reputation for serving authentic-tasting food and having good concerts. The **Lake Plaza** hāngi (☎ 07/348–1174, $47) has an equally strong reputation. Here you can watch the food being lifted out of the hāngi—usually an hour before the food is served, but call ahead to confirm.

$$$ ✕ **Poppy's Villa Restaurant.** This colorful colonial villa is Rotorua's big-occasion restaurant, yet prices are relatively moderate. The menu covers standout seafood, particularly New Zealand salmon and mussels. Other excellent choices might include rack of lamb with a simple rosemary glaze or cervena with poached pear in a beet-based sauce.

It's not all meat—vegetarians are also well looked after. ⊠ *4 Marguerita St.,* ☎ *07/347–1700. AE, DC, MC, V. No lunch.*

$$$ ✕ **You and Me.** Chef-owner Hiroyuki Teraoka's cuisine reflects his particular background: Japanese-born and French-trained, he gives a mainly French style some Japanese input. The menu shifts to take advantage of seasonal vegetables, but tuna and salmon are standards, with dishes such as seared yellowfin tuna with a black vinaigrette. ⊠ *1119 Pukuatua St.,* ☎ *07/347–6178. AE, DC, MC, V. BYOB. Closed Sun. Aug.–Feb. and Sun.–Mon. Mar.–July.*

$–$$ ✕ **The Fat Dog Café and Bar.** The eclectic but homely decor attracts young, old, and everyone in between. Settle in among fish tanks, lots of oak, and a few lounges for a cheap and cheerful meal. On the psychedelic blackboard menu that lights up the place like a rainbow, look for lasagna, Thai curry, or bar favorites like nachos. ⊠ *69 Arawa St.,* ☎ *07/347–7586. AE, DC, MC, V. Licensed and BYOB.*

$–$$ ✕ **Pig & Whistle.** The name winks at this 1940s city landmark's pre-
★ vious incarnation—as a police station. Sip a cold beer in the courtyard while waiting for the Scotch fillet steak, served with mushrooms, bacon, salad, and scalloped potatoes. After finishing off with sticky date pudding with butterscotch sauce and ice cream, you may be tempted with a quiet snooze under the enormous elm tree outside. There's live music every Friday and Saturday night. ⊠ *Corner of Haupapa and Tutanekai Sts.,* ☎ *07/347–3025. AE, DC, MC, V.*

$$$$ 🏨 **Royal Lakeside Novotel.** The Royal Lakeside has the handiest position of any of the large downtown hotels—it overlooks the lake and is just a two-minute walk from the restaurants and shops. Furnishings are sleek and contemporary, and the guest rooms are decently sized, though you'll want to specify a lake view when booking. ⊠ *Tutanekai St.,* ☎ *07/346–3888,* 🖷 *07/347–1888,* 🌐 *www.novotel.co.nz. 199 rooms. Restaurant, brasserie, pool, sauna, spa, bar, concert hall; no-smoking rooms. AE, DC, MC, V.*

$$$$ 🏨 **Solitaire Lodge.** Set high on a peninsula that juts out into Lake
★ Tarawera, this plush retreat is surrounded by lakes, forests, and volcanoes. Contemporary furnishings and artwork fill the luxuriously equipped suites; the best room is the Tarawera Suite, which has spectacular 180-degree views. Check out the volcanoes from the telescopes in the library-bar, or settle down in a shaded garden nook and sip a drink. The surroundings are perfect for hiking, boating, and fishing, and the lodge has boats and fishing gear. Smoking is not permitted indoors. ⊠ *Ronald Rd., Lake Tarawera,* ☎ *07/362–8208,* 🖷 *07/362–8445,* 🌐 *www.nz.com/travel/solitaire. 8 suites, 1 villa. Restaurant, spa, boating, fishing, bar. AE, DC, MC, V. MAP.*

$$$ 🏨 **Princes Gate Hotel.** Across the road from the Government Gardens, this ornate timber hotel was built in 1897 on the Coromandel Peninsula. It was brought here in 1917, and efforts have been made to re-create a turn-of-the-20th-century feeling. The decor may be a bit too floral for some tastes, but rooms are reasonably large and very comfortable and have been upgraded to incorporate all modern conveniences, from TVs to hair dryers. Best of all, though, is the sheer look of the place—pull up a cane chair on the wooden deck, look across to the Government Gardens, and imagine yourself transported back in time. ⊠ *1057 Arawa St.,* ☎ *07/348–1179,* 🖷 *07/348–6215,* 🌐 *www. scenic-circle.co.nz. 50 rooms. 2 restaurants, pool, hot tub, bar; no a/c. AE, DC, MC, V.*

$$ 🏨 **Cedar Lodge Motel.** These spacious, modern two-story units, about 1 km (½ mi) from the city center, are a good value, especially for families. All have a kitchen and lounge room on the lower floor, a bedroom on the mezzanine floor above, and at least one queen-size and one single bed, and some have a queen-size bed and three singles.

Every unit has its own hot tub in the private courtyard at the back. Gray-flecked carpet, smoked-glass tables, and recessed lighting are clean and contemporary. Request a room at the back, away from Fenton Street. ✉ *296 Fenton St.,* ☎ *07/349–0300,* FAX *07/349–1115. 15 rooms. Laundry facilities; no a/c. AE, DC, MC, V.*

$$ 🏠 **Eaton Hall.** Simplicity's the watchword at this central B&B. The rooms are hardly on the cutting edge of fashion (everything is pink, lilac, and cream—a bit like Grandma's), but the price and location are right, and a big English-style breakfast sets you up for the day. All rooms have a sink, though if you need more space (and your own shower and toilet) ask for Room 9 or 10. ✉ *39 Hinemaru St.,* ☎ FAX *07/347–0366,* WEB *www.eatonhallbnb.cjb.net. 10 rooms. Hot tub; no a/c. AE, DC, MC, V. BP.*

$ 🏠 **Hot Rock Backpackers.** A youthful buzz and a popular bar give this place a high profile. It's by Kuirau Park, a few minutes' walk from the center of town. The dorm rooms sleep anywhere from 4 to 12 people, but there are also several doubles and a pair of family rooms. If you're sore from hiking or hauling luggage, all the more reason to hit the geothermal pools. ✉ *1286 Arawa St.,* ☎ *07/347–9469,* WEB *www.acb. co.nz/hot-rock. 13 rooms, 18 dorm rooms. Kitchens, 3 pools (2 indoor), bar, lounge, Internet, laundry facilities. MC, V.*

$ 🏠 **Kiwi Paka YHA.** A 10-minute walk out of town is this lodge overlooking the thermal Kuirau Park. You can take advantage of the area's natural heating by soaking in the thermal pool for free. Rooms range from shares for four or five people to single rooms for under $30. Meals at the café are a steal as well. ✉ *60 Tarewa Rd.,* ☎ *07/347–0931,* WEB *www.kiwipaka-yha.co.nz. 83 rooms. Café, pool, bar. MC, V.*

$ 🏠 **Motel Monterey.** There's much to be said for driving right into Rotorua to the Monterey, a very central two-story motel with a touch of yesteryear about it. Accommodations are simple, the walls are bare, and the kitchens in each unit are a little old-fashioned, but there's a lovely, sunny rear garden with heated pool, private mineral pool, and barbecue area. ✉ *Whakaue St.,* ☎ *07/348–1044,* FAX *07/346–2264. 15 units. Kitchens, pool, outdoor hot tub; no a/c. AE, DC, MC, V.*

$ 🏠 **Rotorua Motor Lodge.** This exceptionally clean motor lodge is a hands-down great deal: for around $50 you can book a unit with full kitchen facilities, comfortable beds, and a dining area. It's across from a beautiful golf course, just a few minutes from both central Rotorua and Whakarewarewa. ✉ *418 Fenton St.,* ☎ *07/348–9179,* FAX *07/346–3474. 26 rooms. Kitchens, cable TV, 4 pools. AE, MC, V.*

Outdoor Activities and Sports

EXTREME ADVENTURE

The folks in Rotorua keep coming up with ever more fearsome ways to part adventurers from their money (and their wits). Try white-water sledging with **Kaitiaki Adventures** (☎ 0800/338–736, www.kaitiaki. co.nz): $120 gets you up to two hours shooting rapids on a buoyant, plastic water raft the size of a boogie board. You get a wet suit, helmet, fins, and gloves—you provide the "go for it attitude."

There's bungy-jumping (the New Zealand spelling for bungee-jumping), of course, but you would be better off waiting for the spectacular natural sites at Taupo and Queenstown rather than jumping from the 140-ft-high crane in Rotorua. So go Zorbing instead: the "zorbonaut" (that's you) is strapped into a huge plastic ball and rolled head-over-heels 200 yards down a hill. For the full washing-machine effect, go for a "wet" Zorb, with water sloshing around inside the ball. You'll find **Zorb Rotorua** (☎ 07/332–2768) outside of town on Western Road, near the Agrodome. Zorbing costs $40 a ride, $50 for two rides, or $60 for a tandem ride. **Rotorua Swoop** (☎ 07/357–4747) sounds innocuous enough—that is until you're strapped into the hang-gliding harness, raised 120 ft off the ground, and the rip cord is pulled. Is that the earth whizzing by at 130 kph (80 mph)? It most certainly is. The Swoop takes place out at the Agrodome complex and costs $40 a ride.

FISHING

If you want to keep the trout of a lifetime from becoming just another fish story, it pays to have a boat with some expert advice on board. Expect to pay about $70–$80 per hour for a fishing guide and a 20-ft cruiser that will take up to six passengers. The minimum charter period is two hours, and fishing gear and tackle are included in the price. A one-day fishing license costs $15 per person and is available on board the boat. In Rotorua fishing operators include **Clark Gregor** (☎ 07/347–1123, WEB www.troutnz.co.nz), who arranges boat fishing and fly-fishing with up to 10 anglers per trip. With **Bryan Colman** (☎ 07/348–7766, WEB www.troutfishingrotorua.com) you can troll Lake Rotorua or try fly-fishing on the region's many streams, including a private-land source. He takes up to five people at a time. A trip with **Gordon Randle** (☎ 07/349–2555) is a bit less expensive than the usual rates, at about $65 per hour. *See* Chapter 6 for more fishing information.

RAFTING AND KAYAKING

The Rotorua region has a number of rivers with Grade 3 to Grade 5 rapids that make excellent white-water rafting. For scenic beauty—and best for first-timers—the Rangitaiki River (Grades 3–4) is recommended. For experienced rafters who want a challenge, the Wairoa River has exhilarating Grade 5 rapids. The climax of a rafting trip on the Kaituna River is the drop over the 21-ft Okere Falls, among the highest to be rafted by a commercial operator anywhere. The various operators all offer similar trips on a daily schedule, though note that different rivers are open at different times of year, depending on water levels. All equipment and instruction is provided, plus transportation to and from the departure points (which can be up to 80 km [50 mi] from Rotorua). Prices start at around $65 for the short (one-hr) Kaituna run; a half day on the Rangitaiki costs from $90. Many operators also offer combination trips. **Kaituna Cascades** (☎ 07/357–5032 or 0800/524–8862, WEB www.kaitunacascades.co.nz) organizes one-day or multiday expeditions. **Raftabout** (☎ 07/345–4652 or 0800/723–822, WEB www.raftabout.co.nz) focuses on day trips, some pairing rafting with other extreme sports like jet-boating or a bungy-jumping. **River Rats** (☎ 07/347–6049 or 0800/333–900, WEB www.riverrats.co.nz) also offers day trips to the main rivers as well as adventure packages. **Wet 'n' Wild Adventure** (☎ 07/348–3191 or 0800/462–7238, WEB www.wetnwildrafting.co.nz) has multi-adventure and double-trip options. One-day itineraries cover the Rangitaiki, Wairoa, and Kaituna rivers. *See* Chapter 6 for further rafting information.

Gentler natures should opt for a serene paddle on one of Rotorua's lakes. **Adventure Kayaking** (☎ 07/348–9451, WEB www.adventurekayaking.co.nz) has a variety of tours, from half a day spent paddling on Lake Rotorua ($55) to a full day on Lake Tarawera ($75) including a swim in a natural hot pool. Especially magical is the twilight paddle ($65) on Lake Rotoiti that incorporates a dip in the Manupirua hot pools (which you can't otherwise reach).

Shopping

The **New Zealand Maori Arts & Crafts Institute** (⊠ Hemo Rd., ☎ 07/348–9047, WEB www.nzmaori.co.nz) was established in 1963 to preserve Māori heritage and crafts. At the institute you can watch wood-carvers and flax-weavers at work and see New Zealand greenstone (jade) being sculpted into jewelry. The gift shop sells fine examples of this

SPELLBOUND IN MIDDLE EARTH

SOME OF THE MOST STRIKING elements of the *Lord of the Rings* film trilogy weren't created by special-effects workshops or camera trickery—they were the astonishing views of New Zealand's countryside. The stark and ominous mountains, bucolic fields, and lush forests made a powerful impression on viewers unfamiliar with New Zealand's landscapes. While the movie's sets were cleared at the end of 2000 after 15 months of principal photography, the matchless scenery alone evokes the character of Middle Earth. The film crew traveled all over the country, so there are plenty of opportunities to see the amazing locations for yourself. For a full-blown official tour package, contact Newmans South Pacific Vacations (✉ 6033 W. Century Boulevard, Suite 970, Los Angeles CA 90045, ☎ 800/421–3326, WEB www.newmansvacations.com).

On the North Island you can visit a handful of hobbit homes in rural Matamata (www.hobbitontours.com). The volcanic peaks and blasted terrain of Tongariro National Park provided the setting for Mordor. Tackle one of the park's walking trails to see the otherworldly hot springs, lava rocks, and craggy peaks like Ruapehu, the films' Emyn Muil. Take the spectacular Tongariro Crossing trek to pass Ngauruhoe, the volcano the hobbits Frodo and Sam braved as Mount Doom.

Wellington, the film production's home base, is also the hometown of the director, Peter Jackson. Here the orcs, trolls, and the horrible Balrog all came to life. The Mines of Moria, the hellacious bridge of Khazad-dûm, and Cirith Ungol were created by Weta Workshop and the production company Three Foot Six (named for the height of a hobbit). You can follow the path of the heroic hobbit foursome of Frodo, Sam, Merry, and Pippin to Bree, actually the suburb of Seatoun. There you can grab a bite at the Chocolate Fish Café, a regular haunt of the stars. The White House restaurant and Brava, both in the city, were also favorite actor hangouts.

The Hutt Valley, east of Wellington, saw plenty of hobbit action; it's easily reached by car, public transit, or even bicycle. During filming a huge polystyrene castle towered over a quarry by the Western Hutt road. Unsuspecting drivers would pass by Minas Tirith and the fortress of Isengard, where the wizard Gandalf was betrayed and imprisoned. Stay on Highway 2 to reach the beautiful Kaitoke Regional Park, used for the elven city of Rivendell, and a perfect place to picnic on the riverbank.

On the South Island, Highway 6 unrolls south to glacier country. Stop at Franz Josef and look for Mount Gunn, where the beacon burned. Carving through the magnificent landscape, the road leads on to Wanaka, where the ghastly ringwraiths gave chase to Arwen and Frodo.

The first sight of the White Mountains, or Remarkables, at Queenstown is breathtaking; this gorgeous region was the background for the Ithilien Camp, the giant statues of the Pillars of Argonath, and a host of other scenes. From nearby Glenorchy, you can hire a horse and ride to Paradise, seen as the elven Lothlórien forest. Farther south, near Te Anau, explore the brooding silence of the lake district. This region, shot for the Midgewater Marshes, is also prime trout-fishing territory.

Despite the trilogy's epic adventures and battles, New Zealand's misty mountains and sweeping parklands remain untainted. Gandalf, Frodo, and Sam may be long gone, but you never know—the horse in that nearby meadow may have belonged to a ringwraith.

— Bob Marriott

work, plus many other items, from small wood-carved kiwis to decorative flax skirts of the kind worn in the Māori cultural shows.

Taupo

⑤ *82 km (51 mi) south of Rotorua, 150 km (94 mi) northwest of Napier, 335 km (210 mi) west of Gisborne.*

The neat and tidy town of Taupo is the base for Lake Taupo, the largest lake in New Zealand. It's a beautiful spot, its placid shores backed by volcanic mountains, and in the vicinity is more of the geothermal activity that characterizes this zone (and, unlike Rotorua, most of the natural sites are free to visit). Water sports are popular here—notably sailing, cruising, and waterskiing—but most of all Taupo is known for its fishing. The town is the rainbow-trout capital of the universe: the average Taupo trout weighs in around 4 pounds, and the lake is open year-round. Meanwhile, the backpacker crowd converges upon Taupo for its plethora of adventure activities: the town is celebrated for its skydiving and bungy-jumping opportunities, and there's also whitewater rafting and jet-boating available on the local rivers.

At **Huka Falls,** the Waikato River thunders through a narrow chasm and over a 35-ft rock ledge. The fast-flowing river produces almost 50% of the North Island's required power, and its force at this point is extraordinary, with the falls dropping into a seething, milky-white pool 200 ft across. The view from the footbridge is superb, though for an even more impressive look, both the Huka Jet and the Otuni paddleboat (☞ Outdoor Activities and Sports *and* Rotorua, Lake Taupo, and Tongariro National Park A to Z, *below*) get close to the maelstrom. The falls are 3 km (2 mi) north of town; turn right off Highway 1 onto Huka Falls Road.

The construction of the local geothermal project had an impressive— and unforeseen—effect. The underground dynamics were so drastically altered that boiling mud pools, steaming vents, and large craters appeared in an area now known as **Craters of the Moon.** A marked walkway snakes for 2 km (1 mi) through the belching, sulfurous landscape, past boiling pits and hissing crevices. Entrance (during daylight hours) is by donation. The craters are up Karapiti Road, across from the Huka Falls turnoffs on Highway 1, 3 km (2 mi) north of Taupo.

The Waikato River is dammed along its length, the first construction being the **Aratiatia Dam,** 10 km (6 mi) northeast of Taupo (turn right off Highway 5). The river below the dam is virtually dry for most of the time, but three times a day (at 10, noon, and 2), and four times a day in summer (Oct.–Mar., also at 4), the dam gates are opened and the gorge is dramatically transformed into a raging torrent. Watch the spectacle from the road bridge over the river or from one of two lookout points a 15-minute walk downriver through the bush. The whole thing lasts 30 minutes, after which the dam gates close, the river subsides, and the gorge returns to serenity.

⑥ Even if you think you have seen enough bubbling pools and fuming craters to last a lifetime, the captivating thermal valley of **Orakei Korako** is likely to change your mind. Geyser-fed streams hiss and steam as they flow into the waters of the lake, and there is an impressive multicolor silica terrace, believed to be the largest in the world since the volcanic destruction of the terraces of Rotomahana. At the bottom of Aladdin's Cave, the vent of an ancient volcano, a jade-green pool was once used exclusively by Māori women as a beauty parlor, which is where the name *Orakei Korako* (a place of adorning) originated. The valley is 37 km (23 mi) north of Taupo (take Highway 1 out of town) and takes around 25 minutes to reach by car; you could always see it en route to or from Rotorua, which lies another 68 km (43 mi) northeast of the valley. ☎ 07/378–3131, WEB *www.orakeikorako.co.nz.* ⊠ *$19.* ⊙ *Sept.–May, daily 8:30–4:30; June–Aug., daily 8:30–4.*

Dining and Lodging

$$$ ✕ **Villino's.** Kiwi gal Carolyn Obel and her German-born husband, Alex, spent time eating their way around Italy before settling down in picturesque Taupo, which explains the Italian influence on the menu. Alex's heritage shows in dishes like peppered wild venison with German braised red cabbage, egg noodles, and blue cheese poached pear. But mostly, the food is good, modern Mediterranean—innovative salads, antipasto, pasta, and risotto. The wine list is far reaching, with some interesting overseas vintages. ⊠ *45 Horomatangi Rd.,* ☎ *07/377–4478. AE, DC, MC, V.*

$$–$$$ ✕ **The Replete Food Company.** The food is served at the counter from display cabinets, and there's no wine license, but the trump card here is a delicious daily menu. *Panini* (Italian flatbread) is filled with various goodies, including eggplant with an Indian-spiced salsa. The Thai chicken curry is legendary, as is the Complete Replete breakfast—honey-cured bacon, poached eggs, and grilled mushrooms. You can choose some tools for your own kitchen from the adjoining shop; if you're in town for a while, ask about the cooking classes. ⊠ *45 Heu Heu St.,* ☎ *07/377–3011. AE, DC, MC, V.*

$$$$ ✕🖫 **Huka Lodge.** Secluded in parklike grounds at the edge of the
★ Waikato River, this Huka is the standard by which New Zealand's other sporting lodges are judged. The large, lavish guest rooms, decorated in muted grays and whites, are arranged in blocks of two or three. All have sliding glass doors that open to a view across lawns to the river. In the interest of tranquillity, they're not equipped with telephones, televisions, or radios. At dinner, a formal, five-course affair, study the wine list for an extensive view of New Zealand's best vintages—the wine cellar holds more than 50,000 bottles. Meals are served either at a communal dining table or, on request, at one of a dozen private dining areas (including the wine cellar or on the outdoor terrace). The lodge can arrange practically any activity under the sun, including helicopter rides. ⊠ *Huka Falls Rd. (Box 95, Taupo),* ☎ *07/378–5791,* FAX *07/378–0427,* WEB *www.hukalodge.co.nz.* *20 rooms, 1 cottage. Restaurant, spa, tennis court, fishing, bar, lounge, library. AE, DC, MC, V. MAP.*

$$ 🖫 **Cascades Motor Lodge.** Set on the shores of Lake Taupo, these attractive brick-and-timber rooms are large, comfortable, and smartly decorated. The two-story "luxury" apartments, which sleep up to seven, have a lounge room, bedroom, kitchen, and dining room on the ground floor in an open-plan design, glass doors leading to a large patio, and a second bedroom and bathroom on the upper floor. Studio rooms have one bedroom. All rooms are equipped with a jet bath. Room 1 is closest to the lake and a small beach. ⊠ *Lake Terr., 3 km (2 mi) south of Taupo, just beyond the Hwy. 5 (Napier) turnoff,* ☎ *07/378–3774,* FAX *07/378–0372,* WEB *www.cascades.co.nz.* *22 rooms. Pool, laundry facilities; no a/c. AE, DC, MC, V.*

Outdoor Activities and Sports

BUNGY JUMPING

If you're not heading to the South Island and Queenstown—spiritual home of bungy jumping—then Taupo is your best bet. **Taupo Bungy** (⊠ 202 Spa Rd., off Tongariro St., 1 km [½ mi] north of town, ☎ 0800/ 888–408, WEB www.taupobungy.co.nz) provides jumps from an awesome cantilevered platform projecting out from a cliff 150 ft above the Waikato River. You can go for the "water touch" or dry versions. Even if you have no intention of "walking the plank," go and watch the jumpers from the nearby lookout point. The jumps cost $100 a shot; they're available daily from 9 to 5.

FISHING

There's great fishing in the Taupo area and an attendant number of guides with local expertise. The season's height runs from October to April. Costs are usually $70–$80 per hour, including all equipment. **Mark Aspinall** (☎ 07/378–4453) leads fly-fishing trips for rainbow and brown trout. **Grant Bayley** (☎ 07/377–6105) arranges lake fishing and fly-fishing trips. **Richard Staines** (☎ 07/378–2736) offers Lake Taupo fishing charters. A luxury cruiser on Lake Taupo costs about $150 per hour; for more information, contact **Chris Jolly Outdoors** (☎ 07/378–0623, WEB www.chrisjolly.co.nz). *See* Chapter 6 for more fishing information.

JET-BOATING

For high-speed thrills on the Waikato River take a trip on the **Huka Jet** (☎ 07/374–8572, WEB www.hukajet.co.nz), which spins and skips its way between the Aratiatia Dam and Huka Falls. Departures are every 30 minutes from Karepoto Road throughout the day; cost is $69 per person.

RAFTING

The Grade 5 Wairoa and Mohaka rivers are accessible from Taupo, as are the Rangitaiki and more family-friendly Tongariro. Different rivers are open at different times of year, depending on water levels, and operators all run similarly priced trips, starting at around $85 per person. Call **Rapid Sensations** (☎ 07/378–7902 or 0800/227–238, WEB www.rapids.co.nz), who provide transportation, wet suits, equipment, and much-needed hot showers at the end. *See* Chapter 6 for more rafting information.

SKYDIVING

On a tandem sky-dive, you're attached to a professional sky diver for a breathtaking leap. Depending on altitude, free-fall can last from a few seconds to close to a minute. **Great Lake Skydive Centre** (☎ 0800/373–335, WEB www.freefly.co.nz) is one local operator. **Taupo Tandem Skydiving** (☎ 0800/275–934, WEB www.skydive.net.nz) is another option. Call at least one day in advance to arrange your jump—which goes ahead weather permitting—and expect to pay at least $169 per person per jump.

SOAKING

Trade in adrenaline for mellowness during a few hours spent at the **Taupo Hot Springs** (✉ Hwy. 5, 3 km [2 mi] southeast of Taupo [Napier Rd.], ☎ 07/377–6502, WEB www.taupohotsprings.com), a favored bathing spot for more than a century. Naturally occurring hot springs have been corralled into three interlinked pools and twin hot tubs. There's a water slide and barbecue and picnic area if you'd like to make a day of it. The pool cost is $8, the water slide $5; bathing gear and towel rentals are available. The complex is open daily from 7:30 AM until 9:30 PM. A new complex is on the drafting board, and construction was slated to start by early 2003.

Tongariro National Park

❼ *110 km (69 mi) southwest of Taupo.*

Tongariro is the country's first national park, established on sacred land donated by a Māori chief. Southwest of Lake Taupo, the park is dominated by three active volcanic peaks: Tongariro, Ngauruhoe, and Ruapehu, which at 9,175 ft is the highest North Island mountain. Ruapehu last erupted in 1996, spewing forth ash and showers of rocks.

Tongariro's spectacular combination of dense *rimu* pine forests, crater lakes, barren lava fields, and bird life makes it the most impressive and popular of the island's national parks. It has numerous walking trails, ★ the most famous the so-called **Tongariro Crossing,** a 16-km (10-mi)— six- to seven-hour—hike that traverses the mountain from one side to the other and is generally considered one of the finest walks in the country. You'll need to be reasonably fit to tackle it as some of the steep inclines and the harsh volcanic terrain can be punishing on a hot day. The longest hikes in the park are the three-day Northern Circuit and the four-day Round-the-Mountain Track, though you can just as well tackle short half-hour to two-hour walks if all you want is a flavor of the region. Wherever you hike, be prepared for rapidly changing weather conditions with warm and waterproof clothing. Also, be careful not to get too close to steam vents; the area around them is scorchingly hot. If you want to stay in the wilderness overnight, there are trailside huts throughout the park.

Highway 1 skirts the east side of the park, but the most direct access is from Highway 47, on the north side; Highway 48, which leads to Whakapapa Village, branches off from here, about 10 km (6 mi) before the confusingly named village of National Park, which sits at the junction of Highways 4 and 47, just outside the park proper. At National Park village you'll find motels, cafés, a gas station, and other services.

The only settlement—with the only services—within the national park is **Whakapapa Village,** on the north side of Mt. Ruapehu. The closest town to the second ski area, Turoa, is the ski resort of **Ohakune,** just beyond the southern boundary of the park—take Highway 49, which runs between Highways 1 and 4.

For displays about Tongariro National Park, and helpful tramping and skiing advice, stop off at the **Whakapapa Visitor Centre.** This is also the best place to buy maps and guides, including the very useful Department of Conservation park map—essential for trampers—and individual local walk leaflets. ⊠ *Whakapapa Visitor Centre, Hwy. 48, Mt. Ruapehu,* ☏ *07/892–3729.* ⊙ *Daily 8–5.*

Dining and Lodging

$$$ ✕⌷ **The Grand Chateau.** Built in 1929 in a French chateau style, this property really catches the eye as you drive into Whakapapa Village. It's a comfortable base for hiking or skiing. In the premium rooms there's plenty of space and some fine mountain views. Meals are taken in the Ruapehu Restaurant—serving traditional New Zealand cuisine with a modern slant—or there's a less formal café. The hotel can arrange guided tramps on all the best-known routes in the park. ⊠ *Hwy. 48,* ☏ *07/892–3809 or 0800/733–944,* ℻ *07/892–3704,* WEB *www.chateau. co.nz. 64 rooms. Restaurant, café, cable TV, hot tub, 9-hole golf course, tennis court, bar; no a/c. AE, DC, MC, V.*

Outdoor Activities and Sports

While trekkers flood to the Tongariro Crossing, that famed track is not the only activity around. The **Mt. Ruapehu ski slopes** add up to New Zealand's most extensive skiing and snowboarding terrain. The **Whakapapa** ski area, on the north side of the mountain, has more than 30 groomed trails, including excellent beginners' slopes. **Turoa,** on the south side, has a half-pipe. Its ski season is generally longer than Whakapapa's, from June through October. Both areas can provide lessons and top-notch rental equipment. Lift passes cost $56 for ac-

cess to the whole mountain. The area's Web site, WEB www.mtruapehu.
com, includes snow reports, trail maps, and other info.

Rotorua, Lake Taupo, and Tongariro National Park A to Z

AIR TRAVEL

Air New Zealand has daily flights that link Rotorua with Auckland,
Christchurch, and Wellington, with further connections throughout New
Zealand. Origin Pacific flies between Rotorua and Auckland every day
but Saturday.

➤ CARRIERS: **Air New Zealand** (☎ 0800/737–000, WEB www.
airnewzealand.co.nz). **Origin Pacific** (☎ 0800/302–302, WEB www.
originpacific.co.nz).

AIRPORT

Rotorua Airport, with the olfactorily evocative code ROT, is about
10 km (6 mi) from the city center. Taxi fare to the city is approximately $18.

➤ AIRPORT INFORMATION: **Rotorua Airport** (✉ Hwy. 33, ☎ 07/345–
6176).

BUS TRAVEL

InterCity buses run five times daily between Auckland and Rotorua,
and there are three daily services from Auckland to Taupo. (Some of
InterCity's routes are done by Newmans buses.) Rotorua is something
of a transportation hub: it's easy to reach Taupo, Hamilton, Tauranga,
Wellington, Gisborne, and Napier by bus.

It's more difficult to reach Tongariro National Park by public transportation, though there is a daily summer InterCity/Newmans bus
service (mid-October–April) between Taupo, Whakapapa Village, and
the village of National Park. To tackle the Tongariro Crossing one-day
walk—a one-way track between Mangatepopo and Ketetahi—call
Tongariro Track Transport for bookings. Its bus to the trailhead leaves
Whakapapa Visitor Centre daily at 8 AM. In addition, many of the motels and lodges in National Park village can arrange transport to the
track.

➤ BUS STOPS: **Rotorua** (✉ Tourism Rotorua Visitor Information Centre, 1167 Fenton St.). **Taupo** (✉ Gasgoine St.).

➤ BUS INFORMATION: **InterCity** buses (☎ 09/913–6100, WEB www.
intercitycoach.co.nz). **Tongariro Track Transport** (☎ 07/892–3897).

CAR TRAVEL

Rotorua is about three hours from Auckland. Take Highway 1 south
past Hamilton and Cambridge to Tirau, where Highway 5 breaks off
to Rotorua. Taupo is four hours from Auckland (take Highway 1 the
whole way) and 70 minutes from Rotorua. For Tongariro National Park,
the main approach is along Highway 4 on the park's western side, turn
off at National Park for Whakapapa and the northern ski slopes, or
at Raetihi for Ohakune and the south.

EMERGENCIES

➤ EMERGENCY SERVICES: **Fire, police, and ambulance** (☎ 111).

TOURS

ADVENTURE TOURS

Mount Tarawera 4WD Tours has a sensational half-day, four-wheel-
drive trip to the edge of the Mt. Tarawera crater. Departures are available at 8:30 and 1:30; the tour costs $110.

The Waimangu Round Trip is probably the most complete tour of Rotorua. It includes an easy 5-km (3-mi) hike through the Waimangu Thermal Valley to Lake Rotomahana, where a cruiser takes you past steaming cliffs to the narrow isthmus that divides the lake from Lake Tarawera. After crossing the lake, the tour visits the Buried Village and ends with a dip in the Polynesian Pools in Rotorua. The trip costs $140; reserve a place with the Rotorua visitor center.

➤ CONTACTS: **Mount Tarawera 4WD Tours** (☎ 07/348–2814, WEB www.mt-tarawera.co.nz). **Waimangu Round Trip** (☎ 07/347–1197).

BOAT TOURS AND LAKE CRUISES

Cruises on Lake Taupo all feature a similar itinerary, usually involving a couple of hours out on the lake visiting local bays and modern Māori rock carvings.

The *Barbary* is a 1920s wooden yacht believed once to be the property of Errol Flynn. Departures are at 10 and 2 ($25) and summer evenings at 5 PM ($20).

Otuni, an old "side-wheel" paddle steamer, visits the Huka Falls for $20; an evening glowworm cruise ($25) takes you through starlit gorges.

➤ CONTACTS: *Barbary* (☎ 07/378–3444). *Otuni* (☎ 07/378–5828).

BUS TOURS

Carey's Tours has the largest selection of bus and boat tours in Rotorua and Taupo, with various combinations taking you out to every conceivable sight and attraction in the area. Prices start at $50 for a half-day Waimangu valley trip to $125 for a full day touring all the major thermal areas.

➤ CONTACT: **Carey's Tours** (✉ 1108 Haupapa St., Rotorua, ☎ 07/347–1197, WEB www.careystours.co.nz).

HELICOPTER TOURS

New Zealand Helicopters Rotorua offers a choice of scenic flights to Tarawera, including a 20-minute trip ($270) and a 40-minute trip with a mountain landing ($299).

➤ CONTACT: **New Zealand Helicopters Rotorua** (☎ 07/348–1223, WEB www.nzhelicopters.co.nz).

TRAIN TRAVEL

Tranz Rail runs one daily service from Auckland to Rotorua: the Geyserland Connection, a combination train and bus ride. The trip takes just over four hours. For Tongariro National Park, either the daily Tranz Rail *Overlander* or *Northerner* service stops at National Park village and Ohakune.

➤ TRAIN INFORMATION: **Tranz Rail** (☎ 0800/802–802, WEB www.tranzscenic.co.nz).

VISITOR INFORMATION

All of the local tourism offices open daily from 8 until at least 5. The Rotorua bureau stays open until 5:30, and in addition to an information office it has a café, a film-processing service, a tour-reservation desk, a map shop operated by the Department of Conservation, and a lost-luggage facility.

Destination Lake Taupo, a regional tourism organization, maintains a helpful Web site, www.laketauponz.com. The Department of Conservation's Web site, www.doc.govt.nz, includes a good rundown on Tongariro National Park.

➤ TOURIST INFORMATION: **Taupo Visitor Information Centre** (✉ 30 Tongariro St., Taupo, ☎ 07/376–0027). **Tourism Rotorua Visitor Information Centre** (✉ 1167 Fenton St., Rotorua, ☎ 07/348–5179, WEB www.rotoruanz.com). **Whakapapa Visitor Centre** (✉ Hwy. 48, Mt. Ruapehu, ☎ 07/892–3729).

NAPIER AND HAWKE'S BAY

New Zealand prides itself on natural wonders. By that way of thinking, Napier is an exception. This city of 50,000, situated about two-thirds of the way down the east coast of the North Island, is best known for its architecture. After an earthquake devastated Napier in 1931, citizens rebuilt it in the fashionable art deco style of the day. Its well-kept uniformity of style makes it an exceptional sort of period piece. There's a similar aspect to Napier's less-visited twin city, Hastings, just to the south, which was also remodeled after the earthquake. After stretching your legs in either place, you can relax on a brief wine-tasting tour—the region produces some of New Zealand's best. In addition, the mild climate and beaches of Hawke Bay make this a popular vacation area for New Zealanders. (*Hawke* Bay is the body of water; *Hawke's* Bay is the region.) You also should make a point of trying to visit the gannet colony at Cape Kidnappers—which you can see only between October and March.

Napier

150 km (94 mi) southeast of Taupo, 345 km (215 mi) northeast of Wellington.

The focus of any visit to Napier is its art deco buildings, many of which lie between Emerson, Herschell, Dalton, and Browning streets. Art deco was born at the 1925 International Exposition of Modern Decorative and Industrial Arts in Paris. The style is bold and geometrical, often using stainless steel to represent the sleekness of the machine age as it was seen in the 1920s, 1930s, and beyond. In Napier, the elements that remain are often found above the ground floor, so any walk will involve looking up frequently. The buildings aside, Napier's charming seafront also makes for a rewarding stroll. Marine Parade is lined with Norfolk pines, formal gardens, and children's attractions and is backed by pastel-color houses; there is a town beach, though you should note that the waves and currents here make swimming dangerous.

❽ One of Napier's notable buildings is the **ASB Bank,** at the corner of Hastings and Emerson streets. The Māori theme on the lintels above the main entrance is echoed in the ceiling inside the building.

❾ The **Criterion Hotel** (✉ Hastings St.) is typical of the Spanish Mission style, which Napier took on due to its success in Santa Barbara, California, where an earthquake had similarly wreaked havoc just a few
❿ years before the New Zealand catastrophe. Along **Emerson Street** and its pedestrian mall, **Hannahs,** the **Bowman's Building, McGruers,** and the **Hawke's Bay Chambers** are among the city's finest art deco examples.

⓫ **Dalton Street** has its treasures as well. South of the intersection with Emerson Street, the pink **Countrywide Bank Building,** with its balcony, is one of Napier's masterpieces. **Hildebrand's,** at Tennyson Street, has an excellent frieze, which is best viewed from across Dalton. Hildebrand was a German who migrated to New Zealand—hence the German flag at one end, the New Zealand at the other, and the wavy lines in the middle to symbolize the sea passage between the two countries.

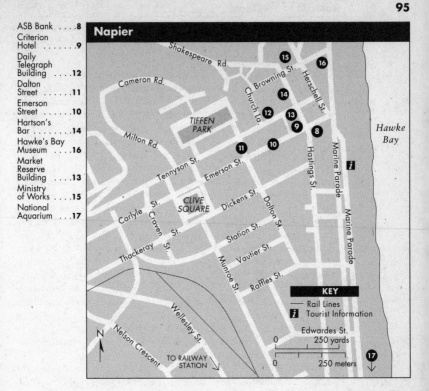

①② The **Daily Telegraph Building** (⊠ Tennyson St. and Church La.) is another Napier classic. If you can turn back the clock in your mind and

①③ imagine the city littered with heaps of rubble, you would see the **Market Reserve Building** (⊠ Tennyson and Hastings Sts.) as the first to rise following the earthquake. Hartson's Music Shop survived the quake,

①④ then turned into **Hartson's Bar** (⊠ Hastings St. between Browning and Tennyson Sts.), the facade of which has altered little since its change in ownership replaced songs with suds.

①⑤ The **Ministry of Works** (⊠ Browning St.), with its decorative lighthouse pillar at the front, takes on the almost Gothic menace that art deco architecture sometimes has (like New York's Chrysler Building).

A little over a kilometer (½ mi) north of the central area stands one of the finest deco buildings, commonly known as the **Rothmans Building** (⊠ Bridge St.). The magnificent 1932 structure has been totally renovated and its original name reinstated: the National Tobacco Company Building.

①⑥ Using newspaper reports, photographs, and audiovisuals, the **Hawke's Bay Museum** re-creates the suffering caused by the earthquake. It also houses a unique display of artifacts of the Ngati Kahungunu Māori people of the east coast—including vessels, decorative work, and statues. ⊠ *65 Marine Parade,* ☎ *06/835–7781.* ⊡ *$5.* ☉ *Nov.–Apr., daily 9–6; May–Oct., daily 10–4:30.*

☙ ①⑦ Napier's waterfront aquarium has undergone long-term refurbishment during its restyling as New Zealand's **National Aquarium.** The facility provides hands-on environmental and ecological displays alongside a collection of sharks, rays, tropical fish, saltwater crocodiles, turtles, and piranha. Completion was expected during 2002; phone for details, or inquire about progress at Napier Visitor Information Centre. ✉ *Marine Parade,* ☎ *06/834–1404,* ⅦEB *www.nationalaquarium.co.nz.*

Dining and Lodging

$$$–$$$$ ✕ **Pierre sur le Quai.** Whet your appetite by watching the chefs at work preparing sophisticated dishes such as a bouillabaisse with scampi, mussels, calamari, fish, and prawns. The wine list holds the cream of the local vineyards' crops, plus some superb imports. Crisp white tablecloths, high ceilings, and adept service emphasize the classy tone. ✉ *60 West Quay,* ☎ FAX *06/834–0189. AE, DC, MC, V.*

$$$ ✕ **Restaurant Indonesia.** The interior of this tiny Hawke's Bay insti-
★   tution may be a bit gloomy, but the food is a revelation. Try a large selection of the Dutch-Indonesian food by sharing a *rijsttafel,* which consists of 13 sampling dishes. Other favorites: marinated prawn *satay* (grilled skewers) and *babi panggang* (grilled pork loin with a sweet-and-sour sauce based on onions, pineapple, and lemon juice). ✉ *409 Marine Parade,* ☎ *06/835–8303. AE, DC, MC, V.*

$$$$ 🏨 **The County Hotel.** Built in 1909 as the headquarters of the Hawke's Bay County Council, this is one of the few Napier buildings that survived the 1931 earthquake. You can't help but feel that you're stepping back in time—brass fittings, wood paneling, and art deco–style lights in the rooms are betrayed only by TVs and fax and modem plugs. Each room has a spacious white-tile bathroom with shower, and some have a clawfoot tub as well. ✉ *12 Browning St., Napier,* ☎ *06/835–7800,* FAX *06/835–7797,* ⅦEB *www.countyhotel.co.nz. 18 rooms. Restaurant, bar, library; no a/c. AE, DC, MC, V.*

$$$ 🏨 **Anleigh Heights.** High on a hillside overlooking Hawke Bay sits this landmark town house. Built in 1900, it's a fine example of Edwardian timber architecture. The guest lounge—once a ballroom—is half paneled in English oak, and the pick of the rooms is the north-facing Colenso Suite, with its large bathroom and sunny aspect. Two of the rooms have only showers and no baths. ✉ *115 Chaucer Rd., North Napier,* ☎ *06/835–1188,* FAX *06/835–1032. 4 rooms, 2 with bath. Dining room, lounge; no a/c, no room phones, no room TVs. AE, DC, MC, V. BP.*

$$ 🏨 **Edgewater Motor Lodge.** Motels and inns line Marine Parade, and the Edgewater is a prime choice here. The small studio units on the ground floor would suffice for a night or two, but for more space and comfort opt either for a spic-and-span spa unit (with whirlpool bath and courtyard seating) or an upper-floor studio unit, with ocean views from a small private balcony. ✉ *359 Marine Parade,* ☎ *06/835–1148,* FAX *06/835–6600. 20 rooms. Pool, some in-room hot tubs, laundry facilities; no a/c. AE, DC, MC, V.*

$ 🏨 **Criterion Backpackers Inn.** On the top floor of the old Criterion Hotel, one of Napier's central art deco buildings, this lodging offers well-maintained rooms and secure storage. All rooms have washbasins; a few have bunks, but most have regular beds. There's a roomy lounge to relax in, a separate TV room, and computers for Internet access. ✉ *48 Emerson St.,* ☎ *06/835–2059,* FAX *06/835–2370. 27 rooms. Lounge, Internet, laundry facilities; no a/c, no room phones, no smoking. AE, MC, V.*

Shopping

Napier's Art Deco Trust maintains an **Art Deco Shop** in town, with everything from handcrafted jewelry, T-shirts, and ceramics to wine glasses, books, posters, and cards. ✉ *163 Tennyson St.,* ☎ *06/835–0022.*

Hawke's Bay

The natural world provides as vital an experience of Hawke's Bay as the human factor does. The gannet colony on the coast southeast of the city is a beautiful and fascinating spot. Then there is the wine—Napier's surrounding countryside grows some of New Zealand's most highly esteemed grapes, reds being of particular note. An area known as the Gimblett Gravels profits from its past as a riverbed; the stony soil retains heat, a boon to the grapevines.

⓲ **Esk Valley Estate Winery** is terraced on a north-facing hillside, ensuring it full sun. Wine maker Gordon Russell produces chardonnay, sauvignon blanc, merlot, and blends with cabernet sauvignon, merlot, cabernet franc, and malbec in various combinations, including a rare and expensive red simply called the Terraces. Look for the reserve version of any varietal to find out what he has done with the best grapes from given years. The winery is 12 km (8 mi) north of Napier, just north of the town of Bay View before Highways 2 and 5 split. ✉ *Main Rd., Bay View,* ☎ *06/836–6411.* ⏰ *Nov.–Mar., daily 10–5; Apr.–Oct., daily 9:45–5; tours by appointment.*

⓳ Tucked into the Esk Valley, **Linden Estate** neighbors an ancient church. Wine maker Nick Chan produces top-quality wines; the chardonnay is excellent, and the mellow dominant reds have won medals. The gallery of New Zealand art gives added incentive to visit. ✉ *SH5, Napier-Taupo Hwy.,* ☎ *06/836–6806,* 🌐 *www.lindenestate.co.nz.* ⏰ *Daily 10–5.*

★ **⓴** Gardens surround the former seminary building of the **Mission Estate Winery** in the Taradale hills overlooking Napier. As the country's oldest wine maker, dating back to 1851, it should be added to your "must-see" list. Award-winning wines, including the Mission Jewelstone range, can be bought or tasted at the cellar door. Join one of the tours for a look at the underground cellar and a discussion of the Mission's history. A gallery sells local handmade pottery and crafts. If you stay for a meal, get a seat on the terrace for a terrific view of the vineyard and Napier. To reach the vineyard, leave Napier by Kennedy Road, heading southwest from the city center toward Taradale. Just past Anderson Park, turn right into Avenue Road and continue to its end at Church Road. ✉ *198 Church Rd., Greenmeadows,* ☎ *06/845–9350,* 🌐 *www.missionestate.co.nz.* ⏰ *Mon.–Sat. 8:30–5:30, Sun. 11–4.*

㉑ The **Church Road Winery** is owned by Montana, the country's largest wine company, but it operates pretty much as a separate entity. The wines are labeled Church Road: their chardonnay is a nationwide restaurant staple, and the many variations on the cabernet sauvignon and merlot themes are all worth sampling. A wine tour with tasting costs $5; be sure you're wearing covered footwear. The complex has a unique wine museum and beautifully restored cellars, as well as an indoor-outdoor restaurant. ✉ *150 Church Rd., Taradale, Havelock North,* ☎ *06/877–2053,* 🌐 *www.churchroad.co.nz.* ⏰ *Daily 9–5; tours at 10, 11, 2, and 3.*

㉒ **Brookfields Vineyard** is one of the most attractive wineries in the area, befitting its status as a premier producer. The gewürztraminer and pinot gris are usually outstanding, but the showpiece is the reserve cabernet sauvignon/merlot, a powerful red that ages well. The winery restaurant is casual and very good. From Napier take Marine Parade toward Hastings and turn right on Awatoto Road. Follow it to Brookfields Road and turn left. Signs will point to the winery. ✉ *Brookfields Rd., Meeanee, Taradale,* ☎ *06/834–4615,* 🌐 *www.brookfieldsvineyards.co. nz.* ⏰ *Daily 10:30–4:30.*

㉓ **Te Mata Estate** is one of New Zealand's top wineries, and Coleraine, a rich but elegant cabernet-merlot blend named after the much-photographed home of the owner, John Buck, is considered the archetypal Hawke's Bay red. Elston Chardonnay and Cape Crest Sauvignon

Blanc show similar restraint and balance. If there's any viognier open (it's made only in tiny quantities), try it—it's excellent. From Napier head south on Marine Parade through Clive and turn left at the Mangateretere School. Signs from there will lead you to Te Mata Road and the estate. ⊠ *Te Mata Rd. (Box 8335, Havelock North)*, ☎ *06/877-4399*, WEB *www.temata.hb.co.nz.* ☼ *Weekdays 9–5, Sat. 10–5, Sun. 11–4; tours Christmas holidays–Jan., daily at 10:30.*

★ ㉔ **Cape Kidnappers** was named by Captain James Cook after local Māori tried to kidnap the servant of Cook's Tahitian interpreter. The cape is the site of a large **gannet colony.** The gannet is a large white seabird with black-tipped flight feathers, a golden crown, and wings that can reach a span of 6 ft. When the birds find a shoal of fish, they fold their wings and plunge straight into the sea at tremendous speed. Their migratory pattern ranges from western Australia to the Chatham Islands, about 800 km (500 mi) east of Christchurch, but they generally nest only on remote islands. The colony at Cape Kidnappers is believed to be the only mainland gannet sanctuary in existence. Between October and March, about 15,000 gannets build their nests here, hatch their young, and prepare them for their long migratory flight.

You can walk to the sanctuary along the beach from Clifton, which is about 24 km (15 mi) south of Napier, but not at high tide. The 8-km (5-mi) walk must begin no earlier than three hours after the high-tide mark, and the return journey must begin no later than four hours before the next high tide. Tidal information is available at Clifton and at Napier Visitor Information Centre. A rest hut with refreshments is available near the colony.

Because of these tidal restrictions, one easy way to get to the colony is to take a **Gannet Beach Adventures** (☎ 06/875–0898, WEB www.gannets.com) tractor-trailer, which is pulled along the beach starting from Clifton Reserve, Clifton Beach. Tractors depart approximately two hours before low tide, and the trip ($25) takes 4–4½ hours. If tides prevent the trip along the beach, the only other access is across private farmland. **Gannet Safaris** (☎ 06/875–0888) runs a four-wheel-drive bus to Cape Kidnappers from Summerlee Station, just past Te Awanga. A minimum of four is required for this tour ($38 each), which takes three hours. Advance booking is essential for all gannet colony tours.

㉕ **Hastings** is Napier's twin city in Hawke's Bay, and it is worth at least driving through on your way to or from the wineries—it's just 18 km (11 mi) south of Napier, down Highway 2. True, the town doesn't have the same concentrated interest of Napier, but buildings in the center exhibit similar art deco flourishes—the 1931 earthquake did a lot of damage here too. Where Hastings stands out is in its Spanish Mission buildings, a style borrowed from California, which produced such beauties as the **Municipal Theater** (⊠ Hastings St.) and the **Westermans Building** (⊠ Russell St.). Out of town, 3 km (2 mi) to the southeast, the village of Havelock North provides access to **Te Mata Peak,** a famed local viewpoint where it's possible to gaze right across the plains to Napier and the rumpled hills behind. The summit is a 15-minute (signposted) drive from Havelock North.

More of Hawke's Bay's wineries are sited closer to Hastings than Napier, particularly **Vidal Estate Winery** (⊠ 913 St. Aubyn St. E, Hastings, ☎ 06/876–8105), a sister winery of Esk Valley Estate that consistently produces some of New Zealand's finest reds. **Huthlee Estate Winery** (⊠ 84 Montana Rd., Bridge Pa, ☎ FAX 06/879–6234), a family-owned vineyard and winery, specializes in reds. At the distinctive, modern **Trinity Hill** winery (⊠ 2396 State Hwy. 50, ☎ 06/879–7778,

WEB www.trinityhillwines.com) you can taste the results of the stony Gimblett soil, including notable chardonnay and Bordeaux-style reds. Wines with the Shepherds Croft label are suited for early drinking. Have a glass in the gardens or by the courtyard fountain.

Dining and Lodging

$$–$$$ ✕ **Brookfields Vineyard Restaurant.** Executive chef Rick Rutledge-Manning, one of New Zealand's top cooks, orchestrates a contemporary menu to complement the Brookfields wines. Each dish has a recommended vintage by the glass or bottle. For instance, a *hapuka* (grouper) cake goes nicely with the 2001 riesling. ⊠ *Brookfields Rd., Meeanee,* ☎ *06/834–4389. AE, DC, MC, V. No dinner.*

$$–$$$ ✕ **Corn Exchange.** Big and bustling, this eatery was once a storehouse for local produce. A wood-fired pizza oven dominates the kitchen; you could try the Mafia, covered with pepperoni, olives, roasted peppers, and red onion. Beyond pizza, try the likes of seared lamb with saffron-infused potatoes, roasted onion pannacotta, and a cherry jus. ⊠ *118 Maraekakoho Rd., Hastings,* ☎ *06/870–8333. AE, DC, MC, V.*

$$–$$$ ✕ **Te Awa Farm Winery.** Profiting from the Gimblett Gravels terrain, this vineyard produces single-estate-grown wines. The vintages are carefully matched with the restaurant's menu, in pairings such as the Longlands 2000 cabernet sauvignon/merlot blend with lamb smoked over cabernet sauvignon vines, served with grilled vegetables and mesclun with mint vinaigrette. ⊠ *2375 State Hwy. 50, Hastings,* ☎ *06/879–7602. Reservations essential. AE, DC, MC, V. No dinner.*

$$ ✕ **Rose & Shamrock.** The developers of this Irish pub were so keen on authenticity, they sent their architect on a three-week tour of Ireland. The result seems to have spirited over from Dublin. The pints mix with old-fashioned but honest pub fare like grilled beef sirloin, or a generous platter of seafood, much of it battered and deep-fried. ⊠ *Napier Rd., Havelock North,* ☎ *06/877–2999. AE, DC, MC, V.*

$$ ✕ **Sileni Estates.** At the pair of restaurants in the Sileni Estates winery, each dish comes with a suggested wine match. For instance, a 2001 Sémillon pairs off with a Hawke's Bay tuna carpaccio with avocado and chili puree, while an intense dessert wine accompanies a chocolate pot and blackberry parfait. ⊠ *2016 Maraekakaho Rd., Bridge Pa, Hastings,* ☎ *06/879–8768. AE, DC, MC, V.*

$$$$ ✕🏨 **Mangapapa Lodge.** This restored lodge, built in 1885, was once
★   the home of the Wattie family, who made their fortune with fruit farming and canning. Reflecting this background, 20 acres of working orchards surround the house. Inside, a dozen guest suites are luxuriously and individually furnished in soft colors and snowy white damask coverlets. Some rooms have four-posters; all have under-floor heating. The manicured gardens include a grass tennis court, a heated swimming pool, and sauna. The chefs incorporate local produce into the daily five-course dinner menu, with dishes such as seared scallops with a crab and mango salad and citrus beurre blanc. The thorough wine list includes superb wines from Hawke's Bay wine country. ⊠ *466 Napier Rd., Havelock North,* ☎ *06/878–3234,* FAX *06/878–1214,* WEB *www. mangapapa.co.nz. 12 rooms. Restaurant, cable TV, tennis court, pool, sauna, spa, croquet, bicycles, bar, Internet. AE, DC, MC, V. BP.*

$$$ 🏨 **Hawthorne Country Lodge.** Susan Brooks, Hawthorne's owner, is
★   intent on creating a homey atmosphere; she's combined the elegant chandeliers, fireplaces, and polished floors with chintz and throw rugs. The five individually decorated rooms all have private verandas and fine linen. You can have breakfast at the communal dining-room table or in your room. Dinners can also be arranged in the lodge, except in December and January. The house is 6 km (4 mi) south of Hastings. ⊠

420 State Hwy. 2, Hastings South, ☎ *06/878–0035,* FAX *06/878–0035,*
WEB *www.hawthorne.co.nz. 5 rooms. No a/c. AE, MC, V. BP.*

Napier and Hawke's Bay A to Z

AIR TRAVEL

Air New Zealand has several flights daily between Napier and Auckland, Wellington, and Christchurch. The flights from Napier to Auckland or Wellington take about an hour; the trip to Christchurch lasts roughly two hours.

➤ CARRIER: **Air New Zealand** (☎ 0800/737–000, WEB www. airnewzealand.co.nz).

AIRPORT

The Hawke's Bay Airport (NPE) is 5 km (3 mi) north of Napier. Shuttle taxis run into town.

➤ CONTACT: **Hawke's Bay Airport** (✉ Main Rd.).

BUS TRAVEL

Newmans and InterCity operate daily bus services between Napier and Auckland, Taupo, Rotorua, and Wellington. There are also frequent local services between Napier and Hastings. For tickets and information, go to the Napier Visitor Information Centre; buses stop on Munroe Street.

➤ BUS INFORMATION: **InterCity** (☎ 09/913–6100 or 04/499–3261, WEB www.intercitycoach.co.nz). **Newmans** (WEB www.newmanscoach.co.nz).

CAR TRAVEL

The main route between Napier and the north is Highway 5. Driving time from Taupo is two hours, five hours if you're coming straight from Auckland. Highway 2 is the main route heading south; it connects Hastings and Napier. Driving time to Wellington is five hours.

Highway 50, the Napier–Hastings road, can help you steer clear of traffic by avoiding central Hastings; it then joins Highway 2 before Napier. Several wineries are on or near the 50, so you may want to designate a driver.

EMERGENCIES

➤ EMERGENCY SERVICES: **Fire, police, and ambulance** (☎ 111).

TOURS

ARCHITECTURE TOURS

The Art Deco Trust has a couple of excellent and informative guided walking tours of Napier. From October through June, a one-hour walk starts daily at 10 AM from the Napier Visitor Information Centre. A longer afternoon walk, starting at the Art Deco Shop, includes slide and video presentations. This is offered daily from October through June and on Wednesday and weekends from July through September. Both walks cost $10. Or take the Trust's self-guided Art Deco Walk; leaflets ($2.50) are available at its shop or at the visitor center. To really submerge yourself in the 1930s look, join Deco Affair Tours in a 1934 Buick for a drive around Napier; the costumed guides lead tours of various lengths, including a cocktail-hour jaunt.

➤ CONTACTS: **Art Deco Trust** (✉ Art Deco Shop, 163 Tennyson St., ☎ 06/835–0022, WEB www.hb.co.nz/artdeco). **Deco Affair Tours** (✉ Box 190, Napier, ☎ 025/241–5279, FAX 06/835–4491).

WINE TOURS

Bay Tours runs a daily four-hour tour of area wineries for $45 a person, where you can sample some of the boutique wines unavailable to independent travelers. Lunch at one of the winery restaurants is usually available, too (at your own cost).

➤ CONTACT: **Bay Tours** (✉ Napier Visitor Information Centre, Marine Parade, ☎ 06/843–6953, WEB www.baytours.co.nz).

VISITOR INFORMATION

Both the Napier and Hastings visitor centers open from 8:30 to 5 on weekdays. On weekends, Napier's center is open from 9 to 5; in Hastings, the bureau is open from 10 to 3. Hawke's Bay Tourism, a regional organization, puts up the www.hawkesbaynz.com Web site.

➤ TOURIST INFORMATION: **Hastings Visitor Information Centre** (✉ Russell St. N, Hastings, ☎ 06/873–5526). **Napier Visitor Information Centre** (✉ 100 Marine Parade, Napier, ☎ 06/834–1911).

GISBORNE AND EASTLAND

Traveling to Eastland takes you well away from the tourist track in the North Island. For some people, that is reason enough to make the trip. Once here, you will find rugged coastline, accessible beaches, dense forests, gentle nature trails, and small, predominantly Māori communities. Eastland provides one of the closest links with the nation's earliest past. Kaiti Beach, near the city of Gisborne, is where the *waka* (long canoe) *Horouta* landed, and nearby Titirangi was named by the first Māori settlers in remembrance of their mountain in Hawaiki, their Polynesian island of origin. Kaiti Beach is also where Captain Cook set foot in 1769—the first European landing in New Zealand.

Gisborne's warm climate and fertile soil make the region one of New Zealand's top wine areas. Often overshadowed by Hawke's Bay (and its formidable PR machine), Gisborne has about 7,000 acres under vine, and it is the country's largest supplier of chardonnay grapes. It has in fact been dubbed the chardonnay capital of New Zealand, which makes that the variety to concentrate on if you go tasting.

This is an easygoing area, with friendly people and a different pace of life than in other parts of the North Island. It has some of the finest and often almost deserted surfing beaches in the country; the region is also ideal for walking, fishing, horse trekking, and camping.

Gisborne

26 *210 km (130 mi) northeast of Napier, 500 km (310 mi) southeast of Auckland.*

The Māori name for the Gisborne district is Tairawhiti (tye-ra-*fee*-tee)—the coast upon which the sun shines across the water—and, in fact, Gisborne is the first city in New Zealand to see sunrise. Although the city (population 30,000) is hardly large, you will need a day or so to get around town properly. Most of the historical sights and other attractions are too spread out to explore them all by foot, and you'll need a car to get into the spectacular countryside nearby.

The **Tairawhiti Museum,** with its Māori and Pākehā (European) artifacts and an extensive photographic collection, provides a good introduction to the region's Māori and colonial history. A maritime gallery covers seafaring matters, and there are changing exhibits of local and national artists' work. Outside the museum, the colonial-style **Wyllie Cottage,** built in 1872, is the oldest house in town. ✉ *18 Stout St.,* ☎ *06/867–3832.* ☜ *Free.* ☉ *Weekdays 10–4, weekends 1:30–4.*

Cook Landing Site National Historic Reserve has deep historical significance for New Zealanders, but not so much to keep an international visitor amused. A statue of Captain James Cook, who first set foot on New Zealand soil here on October 9, 1769, stands on Kaiti Beach, across the river southeast of the city center. The beach itself, at low tide, attracts interesting bird life. ☒ *Esplanade on south end of Turanganui River.*

The **Titirangi Domain** on Kaiti Hill has excellent views of Gisborne, Poverty Bay, and the surrounding rural areas. Titirangi was the site of an extensive *pā* (fortified village), the origins of which can be traced back at least 24 Māori generations. The **Titirangi Recreational Reserve**, part of the Domain, is a great place for a picnic or a walk. The Domain is south of Turanganui River. Pass the harbor and turn right onto Esplanade, then left onto Crawford Road, right onto Queens Drive, and follow it to several lookout points in the Domain.

Te Poho o Rawiri Meeting House is one of the largest Māori marae in New Zealand, and the interior has excellent, complex traditional carving. On the side of the hill stands the 1930s Toko Toro Tapu Church. You'll need permission to explore either site; contact the Gisborne-Eastland Visitor Information Centre (☒ 209 Grey St.). ☒ *Kaiti Hill,* ☎ *06/868–5364.* ☒ *Small donation suggested.*

Matawhero Wines is a Gisborne original—both in style and longevity. Gewürztraminer is a specialty for owner Denis Irwin, but you can also taste chenin blanc, chardonnay, cabernet-merlot blends, and pinot noir, often from earlier vintages. The vineyard is 3 km (2 mi) southwest of Gisborne; follow State Highway 35 out of town. ☒ *Riverpoint Rd.,* ☎ *06/868–8366.* ☉ *Mon.–Sat. 11–4.*

Millton Vineyard has an attractive garden area, making it a logical place to sit with a picnic lunch and sip some barrel-fermented chardonnay. The award-winning Opou Riesling is also recommended. James and Annie Millton grow their grapes organically and biodynamically, following the precepts of philosopher Rudolf Steiner. ☒ *Papatu Rd., Manutuke,* ☎ *06/862–8680,* 🖳 *www.millton.co.nz.* ☉ *Nov.–Apr., Mon.–Sat. 10–5; Mar.–Oct., by appointment.*

OFF THE BEATEN PATH   **EASTWOODHILL ARBORETUM** – Inspired by the gardens seen on a trip to England in 1910, William Douglas Cook returned home and began planting 160 acres. His brainchild became a stunning collection of more than 500 genera of trees from around the world. Eastwoodhill is a place of seasonal change seldom seen in New Zealand. In spring and summer daffodils mass yellow, magnolias bloom in clouds of pink and white, and cherries, crab apples, wisteria, and azalea all add to the spectacle. The main tracks in the park can be walked in about 45 minutes. Maps and self-guided tour booklets are available. Drive west from Gisborne center on Highway 2 toward Napier and turn at the rotary onto the Ngatapa–Rere Road before leaving town. Follow it 35 km (22 mi) to the arboretum. ☒ *Ngatapa–Rere Rd.,* ☎ *06/863–9800,* 🖳 *www. eastwoodhill.org.nz.* ☒ *$8.* ☉ *Daily 9–5.*

Dining and Lodging

$$–$$$$ ✕ **Wharf Café Bar Restaurant.** At a former storage shed overlooking the Gisborne Wharf, find a seat at a sunny outdoor table for a breakfast of fresh fish wrapped in streaky bacon, with scrambled eggs and grilled tomato. Things stay lively through the evening, when you could try seared cervena with a kūmara and potato mash. The wine list leans to local and other New Zealand producers. ☒ *60 The Esplanade,* ☎ *06/868–4876. AE, DC, MC, V.*

$$$ ✕ **The Marina Restaurant & Bar.** The high-ceiling dining room of this large colonial house exudes gentility; light filters through stained glass

and you can look out towards the river. An upended wooden rowboat serves as an interesting wine rack. Seafood is the specialty; look for the sushi platter, which includes maki sushi rolls, sashimi, and tempura salmon "cigars." ⊠ *Marina Park*, ☎ 𝔽𝔸𝕏 *06/868–5919. AE, DC, MC, V. Closed Sun. No lunch.*

$$$ ✕ **The Works Café & Winery.** Set in a building that was once part of
★ the Gisborne Freezing Works, dating from 1906, this restaurant is delightfully different. The decor harks back to the industrial past, with a large drive shaft and pulleys on the brick walls; the staff is notably friendly and knowledgeable. The menu builds on all kinds of local products, from cheeses to fruit to *kina* (sea urchin). One excellent choice is the char-grilled beef fillet served with green beans, aïoli, and a merlot jus. Wrought-iron gates at the back lead to a boutique winery, where you'll find a small range of wines sold exclusively here. ⊠ *Kaiti Beach Rd.*, ☎ *06/863–1285. AE, DC, MC, V.*

$–$$ ✕ **Verve Café.** This funky little midtown coffee bar is a popular stop for backpackers from around the world. The decor is eclectic, the reading matter interesting, and the food honest and generous. Owner-chef Russell Walsh turns out handmade pasta and smokes fish to order. The cakes are suitably decadent, and, best of all, the coffee is terrific; sip a cup while you surf the net. ⊠ *121 Gladstone Rd.*, ☎ *06/868–9095. AE, DC, MC, V. BYOB. No dinner Sun.*

$$$$ ⊞ **Katoa Country Lodge.** Beautiful gardens enhance the Katoa's hill-
★ side setting, the scents of lavender, honeysuckle, and clematis underscoring the sense of tranquillity. The main house's lounge has an outside deck that opens onto the gardens, and the rural views are outstanding. You're welcome to join the warmly attentive hosts, Charles and Zona Averill, for dinner or eat alone; either way you'll be pampered with the best local produce and New Zealand wine. You can stay either in the elegantly furnished main lodge or in one of the three self-contained cottages. ⊠ *Taurau Valley Rd., Manutuke, 17 km (11 mi) west of Gisborne*, ☎ *06/862–8764*, 𝔽𝔸𝕏 *06/862–8786. 6 rooms. Pool, lounge; no a/c. MC, V. FAP.*

$$$ ⊞ **Cedar House.** A sedate residential neighborhood ensures quiet at this large Edwardian B&B. Gracious interiors keep the pace with modern amenities. The entrance hall has wood paneling, and bay windows overlook the garden; the lounge, meanwhile, has a TV, VCR, and CD player. Bedrooms are stocked with crisp linens, fresh flowers, and magazines. The house is a short walk from shops, cafés, and the river. ⊠ *4 Clifford St.*, ☎ *06/868–1902*, 𝔽𝔸𝕏 *06/867–1932*, 𝕎𝔼𝔹 *www.cedarhouse.co.nz. 4 rooms. Lounge; no a/c, no room phones, no room TVs. AE, DC, MC, V. BP.*

$$$ ⊞ **Tunanui Station Cottages.** During the hour's drive south from Gisborne to reach Tunanui, you'll go through Eastland's hill country and past some truly spectacular coastal views. Tunanui Station is a 3,000-acre sheep and cattle station; Leslie and Ray Thompson host guests in a 90-year-old restored three-bedroom cottage and a four-bedroom farmhouse. Both houses are thoughtfully equipped. The cottage has a deep-rooted appeal, with a lovely kauri table made by a local craftsman and rimu tongue-and-groove flooring, while the farmhouse has more room and better views over the Mahia peninsula. Both have kitchen facilities, so bring food for cooking on-site. You can also arrange to have breakfast fixings provided or to have dinner ($40) at the owners' nearby home. Ray will take experienced horseback riders out onto the station to see the farm at work. ⊠ *1001 Tunanui Rd., Opoutama, Mahia*, ☎ *06/837–5790*, 𝔽𝔸𝕏 *06/837–5797. 1 cottage, 1 farmhouse. Dining room, kitchenettes; no a/c. No credit cards.*

$$–$$$ ⊞ **Wairakaia Farmstay.** Rodney and Sarah Faulkner's colonial homestead, set in a large informal garden, anchors a 1,600-acre property with mixed crops, cows, and—surprise—sheep. During a stay here, you're free to wander the farm's hills or head out to explore the area's white-sand beaches and wineries. Bedrooms are large and well furnished. A three-course dinner, including local wine, can be arranged for $40. ✉ *Wairakaia Station, State Hwy. 2 (R.D. 2), 24 km (15 mi) south of Gisborne,* ☎ FAX *06/862–8607. 3 rooms. Tennis court; no a/c, no room phones, no room TVs. AE, MC, V. BP.*

$ 🏨 **Sycamore Lodge Backpackers.** The various room configurations here have some valued common denominators: they're modern and very clean and have washbasins. Special facilities, such as a wheelchair shower, accommodate travelers with disabilities. You can hang out in one of the lounges, outfitted with cable TV, Internet access, and a pool table or stake out a bench in the picnic area. Children are welcome. ✉ *690 Gladstone St.,* ☎ *06/868–1000,* FAX *06/868–4000. 5 single rooms, 13 double rooms, 2 dorm rooms. 2 lounges, Internet; no a/c, no room phones, no smoking. MC.*

Outdoor Activities and Sports

FISHING

Albacore, yellowfin tuna, mako sharks, and marlin are all prized catches off the East Cape from January to April. Fishing operators include **Tolaga Bay East Cape Charters** (☎ 06/862–6715), in Tolaga Bay, just north of Gisborne, whose skipper, Bert Lee, has had more than 35 years' experience in recreational fishing. Trips start at $95. **Surfit Boat Charters** (☎ 06/867–2970, WEB www.surfit.co.nz) is based in Gisborne. Fishing trips start at $105 per person. If you fancy being lowered in a shark cage to come face to face with the great white pointer, you can take the plunge for $165.

GOLF

The **Poverty Bay Golf Course** (✉ corner of Lytton and Awapuni Rds., Gisborne, ☎ 06/868–6113), an 18-hole championship course, ranks in the top five courses in the country. The greens fee is $25.

Gisborne–Opotiki Loop

Soak in the beauty and remoteness of Eastland driving the Provincial Highway 35 loop between Gisborne and Opotiki, the northwest anchor of the East Cape. Rolling green hills drop into wide crescent beaches or rock-strewn coves. Small towns appear here and there along the route, only to fade into the surrounding landscape. It is one of the country's ultimate roads less traveled. Some scenic highlights are **Anaura Bay,** with rocky headlands, a long beach favored by surfers, and nearby islands; it is between **Tolaga Bay** and **Tokomaru Bay,** two former shipping towns. Tolaga Bay has an incredibly long wharf stretching over a beach into the sea, and Cooks Cove Walkway is a pleasant amble (two-hour round-trip) through the countryside past a rock arch. In **Tikitiki** farther up the coast, an Anglican church is full of carved Māori panels and beams. Tikitiki has a gas station.

East of the small town of **Te Araroa,** which has the oldest *pohutukawa* (po-hoo-too-*ka*-wa) tree in the country, the coast is about as remote as you could imagine. At the tip of the cape (21 km [13 mi] from Te Araroa), the East Cape Lighthouse and fantastic views are a long, steep climb from the beach. **Hicks Bay** has another long beach. Back toward Opotiki, **Whanarua** (fahn-ah-*roo*-ah) **Bay** is one of the most beautiful on the East Cape, with isolated beaches ideal for a picnic and a swim. Farther on, there is an intricately carved Māori marae (meetinghouse) called Tukaki in **Te Kaha.**

If you plan to take your time along the way, inquire at the **Gisborne–Eastland Visitor Information Centre** (⊠ 209 Grey St., Gisborne, ☎ 06/868–6139) about lodging. There are motels at various points on the cape, and some superbly sited motor camps and backpackers' lodges, though you'll need to be well stocked with foodstuffs before you set off. Driving time on the loop—about 330 km (205 mi)—is about five hours without stops. You can, of course, drive the loop the other way—from Opotiki around the cape to Gisborne: to get to Opotiki from the north, take Highway 2 from Tauranga and the Bay of Plenty.

Outdoor Activities and Sports
Remember to keep inside any posted flags when swimming.

JET-BOATING

Motu River Jet Boat Tours (☎ 07/315–8107), based in Opotiki, combines the thrills and spills of speeding along the Motu River with the opportunity to learn about the ecology and history of the region. The trip lasts about two hours and costs $85.

Te Urewera National Park

★ ② *163 km (101 mi) west of Gisborne.*

Te Urewera National Park is a vast, remote region of forests and lakes straddling the Huiarau Range. The park's outstanding feature is the glorious **Lake Waikaremoana** ("sea of rippling waters"), a forest-girded lake with good swimming, boating, and fishing. The lake is circled by a 50-km (31-mi) walking track; the three- to four-day walk is popular, and in the summer months the lakeside tramping huts are often heavily used. For information about this route, contact the Department of Conservation Visitor Centre at Aniwaniwa, on the eastern arm of Lake Waikaremoana. You'll be able to pick up walking leaflets and maps, and ask advice about the many other shorter walks in the park, like that to the **Aniwaniwa Falls** (30 minutes round-trip) or to **Lake Waikare-iti** (five to six hours round-trip). The motor camp on the lakeshore, not far from the visitor center, has cabins, chalets, and motel units. In summer a launch operates sightseeing and fishing trips from the motor camp. There are areas of private Māori land within the park, so be sure to stay on marked paths. Access to the park is from Wairoa, 100 km (62 mi) southwest of Gisborne down Highway 2. It's then another 63 km (39 mi) from Wairoa along Highway 38 to Lake Waikaremoana. ⊠ *Department of Conservation Visitor Centre, Aniwaniwa,* ☎ *06/837–3803,* WEB *www.doc.govt.nz.*

Gisborne and Eastland A to Z

AIR TRAVEL
Air New Zealand Link flies daily to Gisborne from Auckland and Wellington. Flights on these routes last about an hour.
➤ CARRIER: **Air New Zealand Link** (☎ 0800/737–000, WEB www.airnewzealand.co.nz).

AIRPORT
Gisborne Airport (GIS) is about 5 km (3 mi) from town. You can catch a taxi to the city center for $10.
➤ CONTACT: **Gisborne Airport** (⊠ Aerodrome Rd., ☎ 06/867–1608).

BUS TRAVEL
There's one bus service a day to Gisborne with Newmans and Inter-City from either Auckland, via Rotorua, or from Wellington, via Napier. These trips take a solid day.

➤ Bus Stop: **Gisborne** (✉ Gisborne–Eastland Visitor Information Centre, Grey St.).
➤ Bus Information: **InterCity** (☎ 09/913–6100 in Auckland; 04/499–3261 in Wellington; 🕸 www.intercitycoach.co.nz). **Newmans** (🕸 www.newmanscoach.co.nz).

CAR TRAVEL

Gisborne is a long way from almost anywhere, though the coastal and bush scenery along the way makes the drive wholly worthwhile. The most direct route from the north is to follow State Highway 2 around the Bay of Plenty to Opotiki, Eastland's northern gateway, then continue to Gisborne through the Waioeka Gorge Scenic Reserve. The drive from Auckland to Gisborne takes seven hours. South from Gisborne, you will pass through Wairoa, about 90 minutes away, before passing Napier, Hawke's Bay, and Wairarapa on the way to Wellington, about 7½ hours by car.

Some roads in Te Urewera park are gravel. If you're driving the Gisborne–Opotiki loop, keep in mind that there are very few gas stations along the way.

EMERGENCIES
➤ Emergency Services: **Fire, police, and ambulance** (☎ 111).

VISITOR INFORMATION
The Gisborne tourist office is open daily from 9 to 5:30.
➤ Tourist Information: **Gisborne–Eastland Visitor Information Centre** (✉ 209 Grey St., Gisborne, ☎ 06/868–6139, 📠 06/868–6138, 🕸 www.gisbornenz.com).

NEW PLYMOUTH AND TARANAKI

On a clear winter day, with a cover of snow, Mt. Taranaki (its Māori name; Mt. Egmont is its English moniker) towers above its flat rural surroundings and seems to draw the sky right down to the sea. No less astonishing in other seasons, the solitary peak is similar in appearance to Japan's Mt. Fuji. It is the icon of the Taranaki region, and the province has shaped itself around the mountain. Northeast of Taranaki, the provincial seat of New Plymouth huddles between the monolith and a rugged coastline, and smaller towns dot the road that circles the mountain's base. For visitors, the Taranaki mountain and the national park that surrounds it, known as Egmont National Park, are often the center of attention. You can hike up the mountain and around it, ski on it (for a short period), and stay the night on it.

The Taranaki region is one of the most successful agricultural areas in the country because of layers of volcanic ash that have created superb free-draining topsoil, and a mountainous coastal position that ensures abundant rainfall. What serves farmers serves gardeners as well. Some of the country's most magnificent gardens grow in the rich local soil, and the annual Rhododendron Festival, held late in the year, celebrates the area's horticultural excellence.

Taranaki has plenty of other ground-level delights, too. By the water's edge—along the so-called Surf Highway (Highway 45)—you can surf, swim, and fish, and several museums delve into Taranaki history, which is particularly rich on the subject of the Māori. You could take in most of the area in a couple of days, but that will keep you on the run. Just getting from place to place around the mountain takes time. Most people use New Plymouth as a base, though Stratford also has comfortable accommodations, and there are B&Bs, motels, and motor camps spread throughout the region.

The weather is constantly in flux—locals say that if you can't see Mt. Taranaki it's raining, and if you can it's going to rain. Day in and day out, this meteorological mix makes for stunning contrasts of sun and clouds on and around the mountain.

New Plymouth

28 *375 km (235 mi) south of Auckland, 190 km (120 mi) southwest of Waitomo, 163 km (102 mi) northwest of Wanganui.*

New Plymouth is a center both for one of New Zealand's most productive dairy regions and the nation's gas and oil industries. This natural wealth means that even when New Zealand's economy is in hard times, the people of New Plymouth retain a sense of optimism. Prior to the arrival of Europeans in 1841, several Māori pā (fortified villages) were in the vicinity. In the mid-1800s, Māori-European land disputes racked Taranaki, and open war broke out in New Plymouth in 1860. Formal peace between the government and Māori was made in 1881, after which New Plymouth began to form its current identity. Today's city is second-best to its surroundings, but its few surviving colonial buildings and serene parkland are well worth half a day's exploration. The cafés and stores along the main drag, Devon Street (East and West), provide as cosmopolitan an experience as you'll find this far west.

The jewels of New Plymouth are most definitely **Pukekura Park** and the connected **Brooklands Park,** whose valley lawns, lakes, groves, and woodland lend real character to the city. Pukekura has water running throughout, and it's a real pleasure to hire a rowboat (from near the lakeside teahouse) and explore the small islands and nooks and crannies of the main lake. The park also has a fernery—caverns carved out of the hillside that connect through fern-cloaked tunnels—and botanical display houses, whose flowering plant collections are some of the most extensive in the country.

Brooklands was once a great estate, laid out in 1843 around the house of Captain Henry King, New Plymouth's first magistrate. During the land wars of the 1860s local Māori burned down the manor house, and the brick fireplace is all that remains of it, standing alone in the sweeping lawns among trees. Today, Brooklands is best known for its amazing variety of trees, mostly planted in the second half of the 19th century. There are giant copper beeches, pines, walnuts, and oaks, and the Monterey pine, magnolia *soulangeana,* ginkgo, and native *karaka* and *kohekohe* are all the largest of their kind in New Zealand. Take a walk along the outskirts of the park on tracks leading through native, subtropical bush. This area has been relatively untouched for the last few thousand years, and 1,500-year-old trees are not uncommon. A *puriri* tree near the Somerset Street entrance—one of 20 in the park—is believed to be more than 2,000 years old.

For a reminder of colonial days, visit Brooklands' former hospital, the **Gables,** built in 1847, which now serves as an art gallery and medical museum. The adjacent zoo is an old-fashioned example of how to keep birds and animals, but it is still a favorite of children. Brooklands has a rhododendron dell and a stadium used for a variety of shows throughout the year. ⊠ *Park entrances on Brooklands Park Dr. and Liardet, Somerset, and Rogan Sts.,* ☎ *06/759–6060.* ☐ *Free.* ☉ *Daily dawn–dusk; teahouse Wed.–Mon. dawn–dusk; display houses daily 8:30–4.*

The new **Puke Ariki** complex is due to open in June 2003. The complex encompasses a heritage and research center along with rich and unique cultural collections. There will be touring exhibitions in addition to permanent displays on local history. ✉ *Puke Ariki Landing, St. Aubyn St.,* ☎ *06/758–4544,* WEB *www.pukeariki.com.* ⛁ *Free.* ⊙ *Mon.–Tues. and Fri. 9–6, Wed. 9–9, weekends 9–5.*

The Queen Elizabeth II National Trust is a publicly funded organization established to conserve privately held native landscapes. The two New Zealand gardens in the trust are in Taranaki: in New Plymouth, **Tupare,** and south of the mountain in Kaponga, **Hollard Gardens** (☞ Egmont National Park, *below*). Complete with Tudor-style houses, Tupare is truly an English-style garden. Built in 1927, the estate of Sir Russell and Lady Matthews sits on a steep hillside that plunges down to the rushing Waiwhakaiho (why-fah-kye-ho) River. Russell Matthews, a road-building contractor, cleverly enlisted his crew during the off-season to build the impressive terraces, garden walls, and pools that define Tupare. There are numerous rhododendrons and azaleas, to be expected in Taranaki, with underplantings of hellebores, daffodils, and bluebells, creating a glorious floral vision in spring. Tupare is also noted for its autumnal foliage display. ✉ *487 Mangorei Rd.,* ☎ *06/758–6480.* ⛁ *$5.* ⊙ *Sept.–Mar., daily 9–5; Apr.–Aug., by appointment only. Some paths may be closed in winter for maintenance.*

★ The world-renowned **Pukeiti Rhododendron Trust** spreads over 900 acres of lush native rain forest adjacent to Egmont National Park on the northwest slope of the mountain. The Pukeiti (poo-kay-*ee*-tee) collection of 2,500 hybrid and species rhododendrons is the largest in New Zealand. Many of these varieties were first grown here, like the giant winter-blooming *R. protistum var. giganteum* Pukeiti, collected from seed in 1953 and now standing 15 ft tall—or the beautiful Lemon Lodge and Spring Honey hybrids that bloom in spring. Kyawi, a large red rhodie, is the very last to bloom, in April (autumn). Rhododendrons aside, there are many other rare and special plants to enjoy at Pukeiti. All winter long the Himalayan daphnes fragrance the pathways. Spring- to summer-growing candelabra primroses can reach up to 4 ft, and for a month around Christmas, spectacular 8-ft Himalayan *cardiocrinum* lilies bear heavenly scented 12-inch white trumpet flowers. This is a wonderful bird habitat, so keep your eyes and ears open for them, too. Pukeiti is 20 km (12½ mi) southwest of New Plymouth center. ✉ *2290 Carrington Rd.,* ☎ *06/752–4141.* ⛁ *$8.* ⊙ *Oct.–Mar., daily 9–5; Apr.–Sept., daily 10–3.*

To get a shadowy feeling for part of the Māori past in New Plymouth, pay a visit to **Koru Pa,** the former stronghold of the Nga Mahanga a Tairi *hapū* (subtribe) of the Taranaki iwi. The bush has taken it back in large measure, but you can still make out the main defensive ditch and stonewalled terraces that drop a considerable way from the highest part of the pa, where chiefs lived, down to the Oakura River. Part of the reserve has a picnic site. Take Highway 45 southwest out of New Plymouth to the beach suburb of Oakura, 17 km (10 mi) away, and turn left onto Wairau Road. Take it to Surrey Hills Road, where another left will take you to the pā site.

OFF THE   **TARANAKI–WAITOMO** – Mt. Taranaki is an ever-receding presence in your
BEATEN PATH   rear-view mirror as you head northeast up the Taranaki coast from New
                Plymouth on Highway 3. The highway provides the most direct route to
                Waitomo Caves and Hamilton, turning inland at Awakino, 90 km (56 mi)
                from New Plymouth. The Awakino Gorge, between Mahoenui and the
                coast, is breathtaking. Sheep have worn trails that seem to hang on the

sides of precipitous green hills that are broken here and there with marvelous limestone outcrops. From Awakino, you could be in Waitomo within the hour if you stick to the main highway, but a far more enjoyable route is to follow the minor road north, at the turnoff just beyond Awakino. This runs for 58 km (36 mi) to Marokopa (☞ Waitomo Caves *in* the Waikato and Waitomo, *above*). It's a gravel road for the most part but a reasonable trip provided you take care. The drive is through attractive sheep country, passing through the Manganui Gorge, and with a possible 4-km (2½-mi) detour down the Waikawau Road to the stunningly isolated Waikawau Beach. The sweep of black sand here, backed by high cliffs, is reached through a hand-dug drover's tunnel. Total driving time from Awakino to Marokopa, including a picnic stop, is around three hours, plus another hour from Marokopa to Waitomo.

Dining and Lodging

$$–$$$ ✕ **André L'Escargot Restaurant and Bar.** New Plymouth's oldest commercial building houses what many consider the town's finest restaurant. The menu updates classic southern French preparations in dishes such as duck leg confit encrusted with thyme and garlic, served on grilled vegetables and bean puree. ⊠ *37–43 Brougham St.,* ☎ *06/758–4812. AE, DC, MC, V. Closed Sun.*

$$–$$$ ✕ **Macfarlane's Caffe.** One of the new generation of New Zealand restaurants, this lively place energizes the dining scene in Inglewood, a town midway between New Plymouth and Stratford. Enticing choices could include the chicken parmigiano, filled with shaved ham and creamy Havarti and coated with Parmesan bread crumbs, with a rich tomato sauce. ⊠ *Kelly and Matai Sts., Inglewood, 20 km (12½ mi) east of New Plymouth,* ☎ *06/756–6665. AE, DC, MC, V.*

$$–$$$ ✕ **Steps Restaurant.** The thoroughly pleasant old-house atmosphere
★ in this cozy 30-seater will get you out of the travel-meal rut. Lunches are thoroughly relaxed, with down-home, friendly service and a mixture of classical and mod dishes that use mostly local produce. Dinner brings equally delicious food like the tower of grilled eggplant, red pepper, goat feta, and sun-dried tomato with a balsamic vinegar glaze. The wine list is well priced. Ask for a courtyard table on warm nights. ⊠ *37 Gover St.,* ☎ *06/758–3393. AE, DC, MC, V. Licensed and BYOB. Closed Sun.–Mon. No lunch Sat.*

$$$ ☷ **Henwood House.** This refurbished century-old homestead, now a B&B, is 6 km (4 mi) from town and thus extremely peaceful. The variety of rooms includes one with a balcony and fireplace. Head to the country-style kitchen for breakfast; in the evening, relax in the rather grand guest lounge. ⊠ *314 Henwood Rd.,* ☎ ꜰᴀx *06/755–1212. 5 rooms, 3 with bath. Lounge; no a/c, no room phones, no room TV. AE, MC, V. BP.*

$$ ☷ **Devon Hotel.** This hotel is easy to find, just a short drive (or 20-minute walk) north of the city center. The economy rooms are on the small side, but do look over a pretty internal courtyard; the larger, regular rooms are better equipped (with refrigerators and minibars) and have either sea or mountain views, though those at the front face on to a busy main road. ⊠ *390 Devon St. E,* ☎ *06/759–9099,* ꜰᴀx *06/758–2229. 110 rooms. Restaurant, some minibars, some refrigerators, pool, bar; no a/c, no smoking. AE, DC, MC, V.*

Outdoor Activities and Sports

BEACHES

Some of the coastal waters can be quite wild, so it's wise to swim at patrolled beaches. **Fitzroy Beach** has lifeguards in summer and is easily accessible from New Plymouth, just 1½ km (¾ mi) from city center. The adjoining **East End Beach** also has lifeguards. **Ngamotu Beach,** along Ocean View Parade, is calm and suitable for young children. And not for nothing is the road around the coast between New Plymouth and Hawera known as the **Surf Highway**—virtually any beach en route has consistently good waves. Fitzroy and East End are both popular with surfers, as are **Back Beach** and **Bell Block,** though the favored surf beach by those in the know is that at **Oakura,** 17 km (10 mi) southwest of town.

BOATING

Happy Chaddy's Charters' launch starts with the guide announcing, "Hold on to your knickers, because we're about to take off"—then the old English lifeboat rocks back and forth in its shed (with you on board), slides down its rails, and hits the sea with a spray of water. The trip lasts an hour, during which time you'll see seals and get a close-up view of the Sugar Loaf Islands just offshore from New Plymouth. ⊠ *Ocean View Parade,* ☎ *06/758–9133.* ⊡ *$20, chartered fishing trip $10 per person per hr (minimum 8 people).*

Egmont National Park

㉙ *North Egmont Visitor Centre is 26 km (16 mi) south of New Plymouth; Dawson Falls Visitor Centre is 68 km (42 mi) southwest of New Plymouth.*

Stately **Mt. Taranaki** rises 8,309 ft right out of the sea; it's difficult not to be drawn toward it. The lower reaches are cloaked in subtropical forests; above the tree line lower vegetation allows you to look out over the paddocks and seascape below. The mountain is surrounded, and protected, by Egmont National Park. The three main roads to the mountain turn off State Highway 3 and are all well signposted. The first, as you drive south from New Plymouth, is Egmont Road and leads to the **North Egmont Visitor Centre** (⊠ Egmont Rd., ☎ 06/756–0990), where it's worth dropping in to learn something about the mountain and its lush vegetation. The second road up the mountain (Pembroke Rd.) takes you to the Mountain House and, a little farther on, to **Stratford Plateau,** the mountain's ski slope, from which there are some stunning views. The third road (Manaia Rd.) leads to the southernmost **Dawson Falls Visitor Centre** (⊠ Manaia Rd., ☎ 025/430–248).

There are signposted local walks of varying difficulty from each of the three main mountain areas. For just a taste of the scenery, the best short walks are from the Dawson Falls Visitor Centre, where there are five popular routes—taking 1 to 2½ hours—including the forest tramp (one-hour round-trip) to the 50-ft-high **Dawson Falls** themselves. Ascents to the summit of Mt. Taranaki are also achieved relatively easily in summer from the North Egmont Visitor Centre and take anywhere from 7 to 10 hours round-trip. You must be properly equipped, keeping in mind that the weather conditions can change extremely quickly, and let the visitor center know in advance of your intentions. If you are really serious about getting out and striding, consider taking from three to five days to walk around the entire mountain. The circuit is well signposted, and there are accommodation huts at one-day intervals along the way, the cost for which is usually $10 for adults per night. There are also budget bunkhouses ($15 per night) at Dawson Falls and North Egmont. Advance bookings for all hiking accommodation are essential; contact the visitor centers.

★ Surrounded by dairy farms, **Hollard Gardens,** near the southern entrance to Egmont National Park, was conceived in 1927 when Bernard and Rose Hollard sectioned off a piece of their land and started building the impressive collection of plants now under the care of the Queen

Elizabeth II National Trust. The 14-acre garden was created in two stages: the old garden, dating from 1927, is a woodland area with narrow, winding paths, intensely planted with rhododendrons, azaleas, camellias, and other related plants. The broad lawns, paths, and mixed borders of the new garden, established in 1982, contain a comprehensive blend of exotics and natives. Brochures at the information shelter detail two self-guided walking tours and help locate some of the treasures. The main season for flowering is from September through March. ✉ *Upper Manaia Rd. off Opunake Rd., Kaponga, 8 km (5 mi) south of Dawson Falls,* ☎ *06/764–6544.* ✍ *$5.* ☉ *Sept.–Mar., daily 9–5; Apr.–Aug., by appointment only.*

Dining and Lodging

$$$$ ✕▥ **Dawson Falls Lodge.** This lodge's position on the southern slopes of Mt. Taranaki gives it unforgettable, panoramic views of the coastline and native bush. The interior is styled on an old Swiss inn; you can unwind in front of a roaring fire or in the sauna and alpine plunge pool. The rooms, each with individual touches, have wood panelling and carved and painted headboards. The Chalet bar and restaurant provide an intimate space for a drink or something from the daily menu of rib-sticking dishes such as beef medallions with a rosemary jus. Activities include visiting local gardens, horse riding, fishing, and golf, or you can take a scenic flight over the mountain. ✉ *Manaia Rd. off Opunake Rd., Dawson Falls,* ☎ FAX *06/765–5457. 11 rooms. Restaurant, gym, bar, lounge; no a/c. AE, DC, MC, V. MAP.*

$$–$$$ ✕▥ **Mountain House Motor Lodge.** Hosts Keith and Berta Anderson run a group of comfortable motel and hotel rooms whose terrific location helps make them the best lodging on the east side of Mt. Taranaki. Tracks from the lodge ascend the lower reaches of the mountain, and the ski slope is a 20-minute drive away. Six rooms stand apart from the main building and are equipped with kitchenettes. Berta brings her Swiss background to the menu; the honeyed quail with port sauce and the roast lamb shank with spaetzle might make it hard to finish the Black Forest cake. ✉ *Pembroke Rd., East Egmont, Stratford,* ☎ FAX *06/765–6100,* WEB *www.mountainhouse.co.nz. 10 rooms. Restaurant, sauna, bar; no a/c. AE, DC, MC, V.*

$$ ▥ **Anderson's Alpine Residence.** A few minutes' drive down the road from the Mountain House, you'll find the Andersons' other venture, a Swiss alpine-style B&B. The trio of rooms includes a deluxe Top Room, with glorious mountain views from a separate lounge area. The lodge has a log staircase, wood-burning fire, and wooden deck; the walls are decorated with Keith Anderson's paintings of Taranaki. ✉ *922 Pembroke Rd., Stratford,* ☎ *06/765–6620,* FAX *06/765–6100,* WEB *www. mountainhouse.co.nz. 3 rooms. No a/c, no smoking. AE, DC, MC, V. CP.*

Stratford

③⓪ *41 km (27 mi) southeast of New Plymouth.*

Stratford is the main town on the eastern side of Mt. Taranaki, and the principal supply base for the mountain. Its streets are named after characters from Shakespeare's works, and it has the only glockenspiel in New Zealand, which chimes three times a day. As the town sits at the junction of Highways 3 and 43 you're more than likely to pass through at some stage during any exploration of Taranaki. Its shops and food stores will give you a local sense of New Zealand's agricultural life, and in the valley to the east are some of the country's most interesting private gardens.

★ **Aramaunga** ("path between the mountains") has a double draw: the garden itself and Gwyn Masters, its sprightly creator. Over the past 50 years, Mrs. Masters has transformed a farm paddock into a garden with a personality to match her own. Most visitors comment on the wisteria, from the century-old specimen on the front of the cottage to other wisteria that climbs into the treetops along with various clematis species to throw bursts of color where it's least expected. At the beautifully mixed garden beds, ask to see the true red Gwynneth Masters hybrid rhododendron that she developed from seed. Cross one of the bridges over the flower-ringed pond for a glorious view back across the water, gardens, and cottage. Aramaunga is open to the public by appointment; there is a small entry fee. ⊠ 669 Beaconsfield Rd., ☎ 06/765–7600.

OFF THE BEATEN PATH	**STRATFORD–TAUMARUNUI –** Highway 43, heading northeast from Stratford, gives a real glimpse of the rural heart of New Zealand, winding through high farmland on the way to Taumarunui (the northern access point for the Whanganui river region). It's 145 km (90 mi), a three- to four-hour trip, nearly all on a paved, though narrow, road: fill up with gas in Stratford before you set off. Highlights on the way include the Kaieto Café, a scenically sited rest stop halfway along, on top of the Tahora saddle; and, starting just after Tahora, the dramatic, lush Tangarakau Gorge. The gorge is the only gravel section of the road—21 km (12 mi) of slow driving.

Lodging

$$$ 🏠 **Te Popo.** Tucked away on a back road northeast of Stratford, this peaceful homestead is set on 6 acres of lovely gardens. Tūī, wood pigeons, bellbirds, and fantails visit the gardens year-round, and glowworms shine at dusk. The spacious guest rooms have wood-burning fireplaces and private garden views. Breakfast is served in a sunny conservatory; dinner can be arranged separately. Te Popo is a 15-minute drive from Stratford center on good country roads. You can visit the gardens separately by appointment ($3), but it's well worth staying the night. ⊠ 636 Stanley Rd., Midhirst (R.D. 24, Stratford), ☎ FAX 06/762–8775. 3 rooms. No a/c, no room phones, no room TVs. MC, V. BP.

Hawera

③ 29 km (18 mi) south of Stratford.

This quiet country town, a hub for the farming community, can give you a close look at the local history and way of life. For the more adventurous there are adrenaline-pumping water sports on the Waingongoro River.

The **Tawhiti Museum** is a labor of love for Nigel Ogle, who bought an old cheese factory in 1975 and proceeded to fill it up with life-size figures from Taranaki's past. He creates the fiberglass figures from molds of local people, giving them a far more lifelike look than those in other museums. On the first Sunday of each month, the museum's Tawhiti Bush Railway springs into life, rattling through a variety of outdoor displays that highlight the historical logging operations in Taranaki. Take Tawhiti Road northeast out of Hawera and continue 4 km (2½ mi) to the museum. ⊠ 401 Ohangai Rd., ☎ 06/278–6837. 🖾 $6.50. ☉ Sept.–May, Fri.–Mon. 10–4; June–Aug., Sun. 10–4.

Just up the road from the Tawhiti Museum you'll find the astonishing **Turuturumokai Pā,** one of the most impressive Māori citadels in the province. Defense ditches and walls ring the former village, and the top is pocked with storage pits. ✉ *Turuturu Rd. near Ohangai Rd.* 🎫 *Free.* ☉ *Daily dawn–dusk.*

Outdoor Activities and Sports

Whitewater sledging is one of New Zealand's up-and-coming adventure sports; you'll have your nose nearly to the water as you maneuver your sledge head-first down rapids. **Dam Dropping** runs daily trips on the Waingongoro River, leaving from the Powerco Aquatic Centre on Waihi Road, Hawera. The trips cost between $40 and $80; they provide the equipment. ✉ *Box 502, Surf Hwy., Hawera,* ☎ FAX *06/278–4452,* WEB *www.kaitiaki.co.nz.*

New Plymouth and Taranaki A to Z

AIR TRAVEL

Air New Zealand operates flights four times daily between Auckland and New Plymouth and four times daily into Wellington.

➤ CARRIER: **Air New Zealand** (☎ 0800/737–000, WEB www.airnewzealand.co.nz).

AIRPORT

New Plymouth Airport (NPL) is about 12 km (7½ mi) from the city center. A taxi to town costs just over $20. Withers Coachlines runs a door-to-door shuttle service for $14 per person.

➤ CONTACTS: **New Plymouth Airport** (✉ 192 Airport Dr., ☎ 06/755–0500). **Withers Coachlines** (06/751–1777).

BUS TRAVEL

New Plymouth is served twice daily by InterCity buses from Auckland, via Hamilton. A daily bus from Wellington, via Wanganui, also stops at Hawera and Stratford on its way to New Plymouth. Buses arrive at and depart from the New Plymouth Travel Centre on Queen Street. There is no public transportation to Mt. Taranaki, though there are private shuttle-bus services to destinations like North Egmont Visitor Centre or Stratford's Mountain House—call the Travel Centre for details.

➤ CONTACTS: **InterCity** (☎ 09/913–6100, WEB www.intercitycoach.co.nz). **New Plymouth Travel Centre** (✉ 32 Queen St., ☎ 06/759–9039).

CAR TRAVEL

New Plymouth looks well out of the way on the map, but it is only 4½ hours from Auckland and 5 hours from Wellington. From the north, head to Te Kuiti near Waitomo caves, and then simply continue on State Highway 3. Leaving Taranaki heading south, take State Highway 3 to Wanganui. Staying on Highway 3, keep traveling to Sanson, where you have the option of heading east—still on Highway 3—through Palmerston North, the Manawatu Gorge, and on to the Wairarapa region; or following State Highway 1 down the west coast to Wellington. The roads in this region are generally in good condition.

EMERGENCIES

➤ EMERGENCY SERVICES: **Fire, police, and ambulance** (☎ 111).

TOURS

SCENIC FLIGHTS

Taranaki Scenic Flights' most popular tour is to the snowcapped summit of Mt. Taranaki ($75). You can also take a trip along the coastline, around the city, or out to the Maui offshore gas field. Beck Helicopters offers all kinds of service for $225 per person per half hour.

➤ CONTACTS: **Beck Helicopters** (✉ Mountain Rd., ☎ 0800/336–644). **Taranaki Scenic Flights** (✉ New Plymouth Airport, ☎ 06/755–0500).

VISITOR INFORMATION

All of the visitor centers listed below are open daily, with the exception of the Dawson Falls center between March and mid-November, which it opens only from Wednesday through Sunday.

The regional tourism board maintains a Web site, www.taranakinz.org, with plenty of local listings and event information.

➤ TOURIST INFORMATION: **Dawson Falls Visitor Centre** (✉ Manaia Rd., ☎ 025/430–248). **Hawera Information Centre** (✉ 55 High St., ☎ 06/278–8599). **New Plymouth Information Centre** (✉ St. Aubyn St., ☎ 06/758–4544, ℻ 06/758–5485, 𝕎𝔼𝔹 www.newplymouthnz.com). **North Egmont Visitor Centre** (✉ Egmont Rd., Egmont Village, ☎ 06/756–0990). **Stratford Information Centre** (✉ corner of Miranda St. and Prospero Pl., ☎ 06/765–6708, 𝕎𝔼𝔹 www.stratfordnz.co.nz).

WANGANUI AND THE WHANGANUI RIVER

The attractive river town of Wanganui marks the starting point of one of the North Island's most distinctive, yet unsung, journeys—following the historic trail that lies along the slow-moving Whanganui River, the longest navigable waterway in the country (as opposed to the Waikato, which is the longest river). You'll need to put aside time to make the trip, since this is not country you can rush through, especially if you plan to kayak in, or tramp around, the middle section of the river, which is encompassed by the isolated Whanganui National Park. Three days gives you enough leeway to see the best of the river and park, though even with just a day to spare you can visit the historic settlements along the meandering Whanganui River Road, which winds alongside the river from Wanganui.

Note: The town is Wanganui, and the river, region, and national park are Whanganui (with an "h") The difference is the result of an ongoing debate over Māori and European influence in the region. Just to confuse the issue further, both are pronounced the same—local Māori don't pronounce "wh" as "fa," as is the case elsewhere in New Zealand.

Wanganui

③② *163 km (102 mi) southeast of New Plymouth, 193 km (121 mi) north of Wellington, 225 km (141 mi) southwest of Taupo.*

Local Māori trace their occupation of the land around the Whanganui River back as far as the 10th century AD. With the European settlement of the garrison town of Wanganui in 1840, and subsequent appropriation of much of the land, conflict was inevitable. Land rights have always been an issue here, though today's town is making a determined effort to put past troubles behind it. Set on the banks of the Whanganui River, the compact town center shows off a series of revitalized streets and heritage buildings that hark back to colonial times and trading days. A stroll along Victoria Avenue, with its Victorian gaslights, wrought-iron seats, and avenue of palm and plane trees, gives you a pretty good idea of the whole. In summer (December–March), a profusion of hanging baskets and window boxes enhances its appeal.

For an overview of the Māori history, drop into the **Whanganui Regional Museum,** by Queens Park, which contains some wonderful *waka* (canoes), as well as Māori carvings, decorative ornaments, cloaks of kiwi feathers, greenstone clubs, tools, bone flutes, and ceremonial portraits. The museum also re-creates the 19th-century town in a series of traditional shop windows, filled with relics and curios. ✉ *Watt*

St., ☎ 06/345–7443, WEB *www.wanganui-museum.org.nz.* ✉ *$2.* ⊘ *Mon.–Sat. 10–4:30, Sun. 1–4.*

For a taste of the old days on the river, catch a ride on the restored paddle steamer, the *Waimarie*, built in 1899. This worked the river for 50 years before sinking in 1952, but painstaking restoration has made the craft shine like new. Two-hour cruises offer a stately ride up the Whanganui River from Wanganui—just don't wear anything white, as the coal-burning steamer throws out flecks of soot. ✉ *Whanganui River Boat Centre, Taupo Quay,* ☎ 06/347–1863, WEB *www.riverboat.co.nz.* ✉ *$25.* ⊘ *Jan.–Mar., cruises daily; call for schedule at other times.*

Dining and Lodging

$$–$$$ ✗ **Zanzibar.** Sunny colors indoors and a plant-filled courtyard make this well-regarded restaurant a pleasant place to sit in any weather. Look for generously sized fresh spins on the classics, like lamb stuffed with roast peppers and garlic with a basil–pine nut risotto. ✉ *Victoria Court, 92 Victoria Ave.,* ☎ 06/345–5900. *AE, MC, V. Licensed and BYOB. Closed Sun.*

$$ ✗ **Victoria's Restaurant.** Brushed apricot walls and green carpet give this friendly eatery a summery feel, which is appropriate for both of its menu manifestations. Lighter café fare could include a smoked chicken, Camembert, and cranberry sauce *panini* (sandwich). At dinner you might try South Island salmon poached with ginger and spring onions. ✉ *13 Victoria Ave.,* ☎ 06/347–7007. *AE, DC, MC, V. Licensed and BYOB. No lunch Sat.–Mon., no dinner Mon.*

$–$$ ✗ **Amadeus Riverbank Café.** Join the loyal local following at this café run by sisters Angie and Nevanah Cawley. The meals, starting with substantial breakfasts like bacon and eggs or New York–style bagels with plain, sweet, or savory cream cheese schmears, arrive with a smile as sparkling as the river view. ✉ *69 Taupo Quay, Suite 6,* ☎ 06/345–1538. *MC, V. Licensed and BYOB. No dinner Sat.–Thurs.*

$$$ ✗🖼 **Rutland Arms.** This renovated Victorian inn in the center of Wanganui is the top choice in town, with just eight guest rooms upstairs making the most of the spacious interior. The rooms have comfortable beds, repro period furniture, and bright bathrooms; downstairs, the bar has character with a traditional English look and a wide choice of imported beers. You can eat here, surrounded by the horse brasses and other agricultural paraphernalia, or in the sunny courtyard. The roasted pork fillet coated in hazelnuts, served with mashed potatoes, sliced apple, and a black-currant and cider sauce, is superb. ✉ *Victoria Ave. and Ridgeway St.,* ☎ 06/347–7677, FAX 06/347–7345, WEB *www.rutland-arms.co.nz. 8 rooms. Restaurant, bar. AE, DC, MC, V. CP.*

$$$–$$$$ 🖼 **Arlesford House.** This elegant country home is built almost entirely of native timber and surrounded by beautifully landscaped gardens. Hosts June and George Loibl prepare delicious, leisurely breakfasts; afterward you can relax by the pool or play tennis, croquet, or pétanque. Rooms are large, light, and airy, with king-size beds and inviting armchairs. ✉ *State Hwy. 3 (R.D. 4, Westmere),* ☎ 06/347–7751, FAX 06/347–7561, WEB *www.arlesfordhouse.co.nz. 4 rooms. Tennis court, pool, croquet; no a/c. AE, DC, MC, V. BP.*

The Whanganui River

The town of Wanganui sits at the southern end of the Whanganui River, whose source lies 329 km (206 mi) north on the flanks of Mt. Tongariro. Between the two are 239 rapids, several sheer-sided gorges, isolated lowland forest scenery, rolling farmland, and a whole series of historic sites and Māori communities that preserve the ways of New Zealand's early river life. Most visitors planning on seeing the river by kayak do so from the northern town of Taumarunui, 170 km (106 mi) north of Wanganui along Highway 4, or from Whakahoro, a put-in point 60 km (38 mi) to the south of Taumarunui. Local tour operators can arrange one- to five-day river trips downstream to Pipiriki, gateway community to Whanganui National Park.

An alternative for those with less time, or less inclination to travel by kayak, is to concentrate on the southern section of the river by following the **Whanganui River Road** from Wanganui town. Built in 1934 to provide access to communities that had been somewhat isolated since the ending of regular riverboat services, the road runs for 79 km (49 mi) north, as far as Pipiriki. It's a narrow backcountry road, unpaved in stretches, though perfectly doable with care. But many choose instead to take the early morning Rural Mail bus, which gets you to Pipiriki and back in a day and allows sightseeing stops on the outward and return journeys. You'll see the remains of giant, fossilized oyster shells at **Oyster Cliffs** (28 km [17 mi] from Wanganui). You'll next arrive at the tidy Māori village of **Koriniti** (47 km [29 mi]), with its well-kept ceremonial buildings and small Anglican church. The restored **Kawana Flour Mill** (56 km [35 mi]) and colonial miller's cottage is always open, if you'd like a glimpse of bygone rural life. At the farming settlement of **Ranana** (60 km [37 mi]), a Roman Catholic church from the 1890s is still used today. And there is the larger St. Joseph's Church and Catholic Mission at pretty **Hiruharama** (66 km [41 mi]), better known locally as Jerusalem. Drive up the track to see the carved Māori altar inside the church. Finally, at **Pipiriki** (79 km [49 mi]) it's possible to arrange jet-boat tours, short canoe trips, and overnight stays at some of the idiosyncratic lodges and farm stays in the area.

Lodging

$$$ ⊡ **The Flying Fox.** Even the arrival is exceptional at this truly unique
★ lodging. You'll reach it by its namesake Flying Fox—a simple aerial cable car—which deposits you high above the west bank of the Whanganui River. There you'll find a pair of cottages, each accommodating two to four people. They're distinctly eco-friendly, from their construction using recycled materials to their facilities, such as the wood- and gas-fired showers and an outdoor clawfoot tub. Inside, they're warmly comfortable, with rug-covered brick floors, tie-dyed throws, carved screens, wood-burning stoves, and wind chimes. Meals hinge on mostly organic and homegrown ingredients—avocados from the owner's trees, smoked eel from the river, seasonal produce, and homemade ice cream, bread, and muffins. If you choose to self-cater, the rate lowers a bit. Camping is available in a secluded bush clearing. ✉ *Whanganui River Rd., Koriniti,* ☎ FAX *06/342–8160,* WEB *www. theflyingfox.co.nz. 2 cottages. Kitchens; no a/c, no room phones, no room TVs. MC, V. MAP.*

Outdoor Activities and Sports

CANOEING AND KAYAKING

The main season for Whanganui River trips is between October and Easter, with the busiest period being in the summer holidays from Christmas through January. Transport is either in open, two-seater, Canadian-style canoes or in kayaks, with options ranging from one-day picnic trips to five-day camping expeditions. Operators can supply all equipment, transfers, and the necessary campsite passes; and trips can either be guided and catered, or independently undertaken (you supply your own food). Your first call should be to one of the operators to discuss itineraries. No experience is necessary, and the Whanganui is considered a safe river—it's definitely not "white-water" adventure. Prices vary considerably according to the length and style of the trip, but you can expect to pay from around $40 for a simple one-day trip and in the $500–$600 neighborhood for a fully inclusive three-day trip. **Canoe Safaris** (☎ 06/385–9237, WEB www.canoesafaris.co.nz) leads two- to five-day trips on the Whanganui; their "big boats," six-person open canoes, are built on the lines of the Canadian fur trapper boats. The price includes all equipment, including a waterproof camera bag. **Rivercity Tours** (☎ 06/344–2554, WEB www.rivercity_tours.co.nz) guides an all-inclusive, family-friendly overnight trip, as well as a four-day excursion. It also rents two-person canoes for $40 per day.

Wanganui and the Whanganui River A to Z

BUS TRAVEL

InterCity buses have four or five daily services between Wellington and Wanganui. The ride takes about half a day. Three buses a day make the daylong trip between Auckland and Wanganui. There's also daily service to Wanganui from New Plymouth; the trip takes roughly three hours.

Rivercity Tours operates the Rural Mail bus service on weekdays, leaving Wanganui at 7:30 AM and arriving in Pipiriki around 11:30 AM. The bus returns to Wanganui that afternoon; you should bring your own picnic lunch, but they'll provide tea and coffee. The cost is $30 per person round-trip.

➤ BUS STOP: **Wanganui** (✉ 156 Ridgeway St.).

➤ BUS LINES: **InterCity** (☎ 09/913–6100 or 04/472–5111, WEB www. intercitycoach.co.nz). **Rivercity Tours** (☎ 06/344–2554).

CAR TRAVEL

Wanganui is three hours' drive from Wellington; take Highway 1 north to Sanson and Highway 3 west from there. The Whanganui River Road is a minor route—you can expect it to take two hours to drive from Wanganui to Pipiriki, longer if you stop to sightsee on the way. To reach the kayak starting points, take Highway 4 north from Wanganui; it's a three-hour drive to Taumarunui, via Raetihi. A minor road connects Pipiriki to Raetihi, so you could always drive north up the Whanganui River Road, cut east along the minor road to Raetihi, and then make a quick return down Highway 4 to Wanganui.

TOURS

BOAT TOURS

In Pipiriki, call ahead to ensure a space on the popular jet-boat tour to the Bridge to Nowhere, a concrete bridge across the lush Mangaparua Gorge that is the only surviving remnant of a pioneering settlement abandoned in 1942. The four-hour tour includes a speedy ride up- and downriver (complete with spins and turns), an easy 40-minute bushwalk to the bridge, and entertaining tales of local life. Bring your own picnic. Cost is $75 per person.

Wairua Hikoi Tours offers one-day guided kayak journeys with a Māori slant. Local guides share their experiences of river life and customs. You'll spend around five hours on the river, departing from Hiruharama (Jerusalem); cost is $75 per person.

➤ CONTACTS: **Bridge to Nowhere Jet Boat Tours** (✉ Whanganui River Rd., ☎ 06/385–4128, WEB www.bridgetonowhere.co.nz). **Wairua Hikoi Tours** (☎ 06/345–3485).

VISITOR INFORMATION

The Wanganui tourist bureau is open weekdays 8:30–5 and weekends 10–2. Its Web site includes information on the Whanganui River.

➤ TOURIST INFORMATION: **Wanganui Visitor Information Centre** (✉ 101 Guyton St., ☎ 06/349–0508, WEB www.destinationwanganui.com).

WELLINGTON

Wedged between the sea and hills that rear up almost 3,000 ft, Wellington contains some striking juxtapositions. Colored roofs cascade down the steep hillsides, creating a vibrant collage against a spectacular green backdrop. An old brick monastery peers down on a jigsaw of masts and sails in the marina, which in turn flanks the splendid Te Papa museum. From a waterfront constructed on land reclaimed from Port Nicholson, high-rise buildings gaze over what must surely be one of the finest natural harbors in the world. Ferries skim over the harbor on their runs to the South Island or over to Eastbourne, with its sheltered beaches and village-style shopping. At the northern end of the harbor the WestpacTrust Stadium dominates the skyline; it stages all kinds of events ranging from rugby matches to rock concerts.

Wellington has been the nation's capital since 1865; the Parliament buildings stand close by the lively city center. Lambton Quay, Willis Street, and Cuba Street are bustling shopping areas, Courtenay Place the center of the entertainment district, and Civic Square the heart of the city. There is a fine selection of restaurants and public houses, while cafés crowd on to busy pavements. Just north of the Parliamentary district is Thorndon, the oldest part of the city, notable for its many historic wooden houses. At the southern end, Norfolk pines line the broad sweep of Oriental Bay with its small beach and a wide promenade, backed by some fine art deco buildings and apartments.

Exploring Wellington

Wellington is an easy city to get around on foot, although some of its tangles of streets can get confusing. The following walking tour includes city views, formal gardens, literary history, some fine examples of 19th-century architecture, and the seat of government. It ends right in the heart of downtown Wellington with a visit to the city's two major museum collections.

A Good Walk

Begin at the **Kelburn Cable Car** ㉝ terminus in Cable Car Lane off Lambton Quay, opposite Grey Street. Taking the cable car is a good way to get up high to see the city's layout—and end up walking down many of the hills instead of up them.

Leave the Kelburn Terminal and double back on your immediate right through the Uplands Road entrance to the **Wellington Botanic Garden** ㉟. Take the furthest right of the three paths and head downhill about 10 minutes, taking in views over the harbor and city. You'll pass a Henry Moore bronze and then reach the **Lady Norwood Rose Garden** ㊱, with more than 100 rose cultivars spilling out their blossoms and fragrance between November and the end of April.

Tear yourself away from the roses and walk to the right around the enclosed Anderson Park, following the sign to Bolton Street Memorial Park, site of the city's historic cemeteries. At the end of this short road, turn right to see the **John Seddon Memorial** ㊲, dedicated to the remarkable early 20th-century prime minister. Close to the memorial, a track, with three flights of steps, zigzags down the hill beneath a stand of pohutukawa trees. At the bottom, cross Bowen Street, walk downhill, take the path to your left, and climb narrow old **Ascot Street** ㊳, with its wonderful old city cottages.

When you pack your MCI Calling Card, it's like packing your loved ones along too.

Your MCI Calling Card is the easy way to stay in touch when you travel. Use it to call to and from over 125 countries. Plus, every time you call, you can earn frequent flier miles. So wherever your travels take you, call home with your MCI Calling Card. It's even easy to get one. Just visit **www.mci.com/worldphone** or **www.mci.com/partners**.

EASY TO CALL WORLDWIDE

1. Just enter the WorldPhone® access number of the country you're calling from.

2. Enter or give the operator your MCI Calling Card number.

3. Enter or give the number you're calling.

Australia ◆	1-800-881-100
China	108-12
Hong Kong	800-96-1121
India	000-127
Japan ◆	00539-121▶
Kenya	080011
Morocco	00-211-0012
South Africa	0800-99-0011

◆ Public phones may require deposit of coin or phone card for dial tone.
▶ Regulation does not permit intra-Japan calls.

EARN FREQUENT FLIER MILES

Find America *with a Compass*

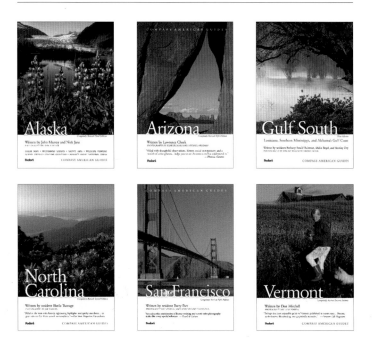

Written by local authors and illustrated throughout
with spectacular color images, Compass American
Guides reveal the character and culture of more than
40 of America's most fascinating destinations. Perfect
for residents who want to explore their own backyards
and for visitors who want an insider's perspective
on the history, heritage, and all there is to see and do.

Fodor's COMPASS AMERICAN GUIDES

At bookstores everywhere.

Turn right into **Tinakori Road** ㊲. Another fact of early life in Wellington is illustrated by No. 306, the pasta shop. Pressed for want of level ground, the citizens of early Wellington tended to build tall, narrow houses. This example—one room wide and five stories high—took things to extremes. Just below the house, make a short detour to see the three superbly kept timber houses side by side in Upton Terrace. Behind a green fence a few steps farther down Tinakori Road is Premier House, the official residence of the prime minister.

Continue down Tinakori Road past the former Shamrock Public House, which now houses an Indian restaurant and an antiques shop. Just beyond the Hobson Street Bridge look for 25 Tinakori Road, the **Katherine Mansfield House** ㊵, where the celebrated writer was born (as Kathleen Beauchamp) and lived the first five years of her life.

Turning back along Tinakori Road to the Hobson Street overpass, and on the far side of the motorway, turn right to walk through the elms of Katherine Mansfield Memorial Park. Turn left around the rather stern compound of the U.S. Embassy, and walk down Murphy Street, which becomes Mulgrave Street, to **Old St. Paul's Cathedral** ㊶, one of the country's wooden Gothic Revival gems. Continue down Mulgrave Street and turn right at Archives House into Aitken Street. The modern building on the right is the **National Library** ㊷, housing the nation's largest collection of books. Cross Molesworth Street and walk through the gate to the various **Parliament Buildings** ㊸ on the far side. Left of Parliament House, the **Executive Office Building** ㊹, alias the Beehive, is the strange-looking office space for government officials. Walk down the hill from the Beehive to the tremendous wooden **Original Government Buildings** ㊺.

The wide street curving behind the bronze lions is Lambton Quay. As its name suggests, this was once Wellington's waterfront. All the land between your feet and the present-day shoreline has been reclaimed, and brass markers at intervals on the sidewalk show just how much of downtown Wellington stands on reclaimed land. From this point, the shops of the city center are within easy walking distance along Lambton Quay, and if you cut off to the left down Brandon or Panama Street you'll reach Customhouse Quay and the present-day harborside. At Queens Wharf, the **Museum of Wellington, City and Sea** ㊻ occupies a former warehouse. Walk along and around the wharf—past happening bar-restaurants like Shed Five and Dockside—and up the steps into Frank Kitts Park, site of many an outdoor concert. Your route continues through the small park, down around the rowing club basin, and across the wooden bridge on Cable Street into **Civic Square** ㊼, an expanse containing the library, town hall, City Gallery, cafés, and some thought-provoking public sculpture. From the bridge, you'll have glimpsed the imposing (and locally unloved) shell of the national museum, **Te Papa–Museum of New Zealand** ㊽; reach it on foot by following Cable Street from Jervois Quay, which is the main road in front of Civic Square.

Timing

You could briskly walk the route outlined above in four hours, stopping to take in the views and glancing at the most important monuments and buildings. But this sort of timing—half a day—wouldn't give you the opportunity to tour the Parliament buildings or scour the main museums. In a seven-hour day, incorporating lunch downtown, you could hope to walk the tour and visit Te Papa—the one must-see—though really Wellington deserves two days. In this case, do the cable car, Botanic Gardens, and Parliament area on one day; and save downtown, shops, and museums for day two.

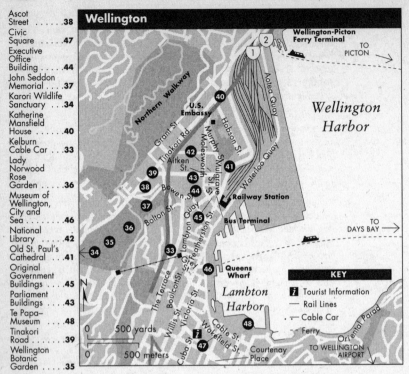

Sights to See

38 **Ascot Street.** The tiny, doll-like cottages along Ascot were built in the 1870s, and this remains the finest example of a 19th-century streetscape in Wellington. There is a bench at the top of the street that has been thoughtfully provided in the shady courtyard if you need to catch your breath. ⊠ *Off Glenmore St. and Tinakori Rd. northeast of Wellington Botanic Garden, Thorndon.*

Bolton Street Memorial Park. Soon after its foundation in 1840, the new city needed a cemetery. Burials until 1892 were conducted on this site (now a landscaped park) and divided into Anglican, Roman Catholic, and Jewish plots. The surviving gravestones, now mottled with age and entwined by roses and shrubs, provide a snapshot of early colonial life and death. ⊠ *Bolton St. northeast of Wellington Botanic Garden, Thorndon.*

★ **City Gallery.** Whether it's the latest exhibition of New Zealand's avant-garde artists, an international collection visiting the gallery, the Open City film series, or just the gallery's café, there are plenty of reasons to put Wellington's eyes-and-ears-on-the-arts into your schedule. It is an excellent representation of New Zealand's thoughtful, contemporary cultural set—something that you won't see much of in the countryside. The gallery has no permanent collection, so everything here is transitory. You may be in town during a show of New Zealand and Australian contemporary art, with artists such as Colin McCahon, Michael Parekowhai, Michael Stevenson, or John Drawbridge. The film series plays everything from John Huston to New Zealand documentaries scored with music played by the National Symphony Orchestra. ⊠ *Civic Sq., Wakefield St.,* ☎ *04/801–3952,* WEB *www.city-gallery.org. nz.* ⊑ *Free to New Zealand exhibits, otherwise $4–10, depending on the exhibit.* ◷ *Daily 10–5.*

47 **Civic Square.** Wellington's modernistic Civic Square is the most visible symbol of the cultural vitality of Wellington. Reminiscent of an Italian piazza, it is a delightful sanctuary from the traffic, with its outdoor cafés, benches, lawns, and harbor viewpoints. The ☞ **City Gallery**, perhaps the nation's finest art space, the library, and the concert venue town hall are all just steps apart. Architect Ian Athfield's steel *nikau* palms are a marvel, and Māori artist Para Matchitt contributed the impressionistic sculptures flanking the wide wooden bridge that connects the square to the harbor. ⊠ *Wakefield, Victoria, and Harris Sts.*

44 **Executive Office Building.** It would be difficult to imagine a more complete contrast in architectural styles than that of the stately Parliament House and the Executive Office Building. Known for obvious reasons as the Beehive, it contains the offices of government ministers and their staffs. ⊠ *Molesworth St.*

37 **John Seddon Memorial.** This monument is dedicated to the colorful and popular liberal politician who served as prime minister from 1893 to 1906. Under Seddon's leadership, New Zealand became the first country to give women voting rights and to pay its citizens an old-age pension. ⊠ *Bolton Street Memorial Park, northeast end of Wellington Botanic Garden, Thorndon.*

40 **Katherine Mansfield House.** Here at 25 Tinakori Road the writer, née Kathleen Beauchamp, came into the world (1888) and lived the first five years of her life. Mansfield left to pursue her career in the wider world of Europe when she was 20, but many of her short stories are set in Wellington. A year before her death in 1923, she wrote, "New Zealand is in my very bones. What wouldn't I give to have a look at it!" The house, which has been restored as a typical Victorian family home, contains furnishings, photographs, videos, and tapes that elucidate Mansfield's life and times. ⊠ *25 Tinakori Rd., Thorndon,* ☎ *04/473-7268.* ☜ *$5.50.* ⊙ *Daily 10–4.*

33 **Kelburn Cable Car.** The Swiss-built funicular railway makes a short but sharp climb to Kelburn Terminal, from which there are great views across parks and city buildings to Port Nicholson. Sit on the left side during the six-minute journey for the best scenery. ⊠ *280 Lambton Quay, at Grey St. and Upland Rd.,* ☎ *04/472-2199.* ☜ *$1.50 one-way, $2.50 round-trip.* ⊙ *Departures about every 10 mins, weekdays 7 AM–10 PM, weekends 9 AM–10 PM.*

★ **36** **Lady Norwood Rose Garden.** On a fine summer day you couldn't find a better place to go for a sniff and a smile. The rose garden is in fact the most popular part of the ☞ **Wellington Botanic Garden.** Situated on a plateau, the formal circular layout consists of 106 beds, each planted with a single variety of modern and traditional shrubs. Climbing roses cover a brick-and-timber colonnade on the perimeter. Adjacent to the rose beds, the Begonia House conservatory is filled with tender plants and has a teahouse serving light meals. ⊠ *North end of Wellington Botanic Garden, Tinakori Rd. (for parking lot),* ☎ *04/801-3071.* ☜ *Donation requested.* ⊙ *Begonia House daily 10–4, main gardens daily sunrise–sunset.*

★ **46** **Museum of Wellington, City and Sea.** Housed in the refurbished 1892 Bond Store (where goods were stored until duty was paid), this excellent museum explores the experience of the original Māori tribes who fished the harbor shores and of the Europeans who settled here in 1840. Three floors of well-presented exhibits include displays about life, leisure, work, crime, and education in 19th-century Wellington; coverage of the city's precarious position on a geological fault line; and a history of Cook Strait crossings to the South Island. The crossings exhibit incorporates a short film about the *Wahine*, the interisland ferry that foundered in the harbor in 1968, with the loss of 51 lives. ⊠ *The Bond Store, Queens Wharf,* ☎ *04/472–8904,* WEB *www.bondstore.co. nz.* ☒ *$5.* ☉ *Weekdays 10–5, weekends 10–5:30.*

㊷ National Library. This modern building houses the nation's largest collection of books, as well as the remarkable Alexander Turnbull Library. The latter contains an extensive Pacific history section, including accounts of every important European voyage of discovery since Magellan. A collection of sketches of New Zealand made by early visitors is displayed in changing exhibitions. ⊠ *Molesworth and Aitken Sts., Thorndon,* ☎ *04/474–3000,* WEB *www.natlib.govt.nz.* ☒ *Free.* ☉ *Weekdays 9–5, Sat. 9–1.*

㊶ Old St. Paul's Cathedral. Consecrated in 1866, the church is a splendid example of the English Gothic Revival style executed in native timbers. Even the trusses supporting the roof transcend their mundane function with splendid craftsmanship. The hexagonal oak pulpit was a gift from the widow of Prime Minister Richard Seddon. ⊠ *Mulgrave St., Thorndon,* ☎ *04/473–6722.* ☒ *Free.* ☉ *Mon.–Sat. 10–5.*

㊺ Original Government Buildings. This second-largest wooden structure in the world is now home to Victoria University's law faculty. It's an extraordinary conceit—built in 1876 and designed to look like stone, it was instead entirely fashioned from kauri timber. Inside are historic exhibits about the building and a Department of Conservation (DOC) information center, though it's the exterior that most captivates. ⊠ *15 Lambton Quay,* ☎ *04/472–7356.* ☒ *Free.* ☉ *Weekdays 9–4:30, weekends 10–3.*

㊸ Parliament Buildings. Following a $150 million renovation program, the three structures that compose the Parliament Buildings are open for public tours. The eye-catching pink Gothic Revival structure is the **Parliamentary Library,** a soaring, graceful building compared with the ponderous gray bulk of the **Parliament House** next door. Tours of the buildings explain the parliamentary process in detail. The **Debating Chamber,** where legislation is presented, debated, and voted on, is a copy of that in the British Houses of Parliament at Westminster, right down to the Speaker's mace and the dispatch boxes. There's fine Māori artwork in the **Māori Affairs Select Committee Room,** at the front of Parliament House; and your tour may even step into the Executive Office Building, known popularly as the **Beehive.** ⊠ *Molesworth St.,* ☎ *04/471–9999,* WEB *www.ps.parliament.govt.nz.* ☒ *Free.* ☉ *Tours depart on the hr weekdays 10–4, Sat. 10–3, Sun. 1–3.*

Premier House. The official residence of New Zealand's Prime Minister was a simple cottage when first erected in 1843, though it's increased in size and grandeur somewhat since then. Prime Ministers remained in residence until 1935, when the new Labour government, caught up in its reforming zeal, turned it into a dental clinic. The house had fallen into disrepair by the early 1990s. Since then renovations have restored it to its proper status—and allowed the Prime Minister of the day to move back in. The house isn't open to the public. ⊠ *260 Tinakori Rd., Thorndon.*

★ ☽ **㊽ Te Papa–Museum of New Zealand.** Don't think gloomy portals and crumbling exhibits—this bright, lively museum remains one of New Zealand's major attractions. This is hardly because there is a lack of modern, interactive museums elsewhere but because Te Papa is such a good introduction to the country's people, cultures, landforms, flora, and fauna. Unusual exhibits can make you feel an earthquake by standing in a house that rocks and shakes or take you into a marae

(Māori meetinghouse) where a *pōwhiri* (Māori greeting involving song and speeches) welcomes you. You can also explore an outdoor forest area with moa (the extinct, ostrichlike native bird) bones and glow-worms or delve into the stories of New Zealand's early European mi-grants. In the Time Warp area, a sort of theme park where most activities have additional fees, you can simulate a bungy jump, or leap three generations ahead to Wellington in 2055. Four discovery centers allow children to weave, hear storytelling, and learn a bit of Māori through song. Eateries in the complex come with an impeccable pedi-gree, having been set up by a team of top chefs. ⊠ *Cable St.,* ☎ *04/ 381–7000,* WEB *www.tepapa.govt.nz.* ⊡ *Free, some exhibits cost up to $8.* ☉ *Fri.–Wed. 10–6, Thurs. 10–9.*

㊴ Tinakori Road. The lack of suitable local stone combined with the col-lapse of most of Wellington's brick buildings in the earthquake of 1848 ensured the almost exclusive use of timber for building here in the sec-ond half of the 19th century. Most carpenters of the period had learned their skills as cabinetmakers and shipwrights in Europe, and the sturdy houses in this street are a tribute to their craftsmanship. Two notables are the tall and narrow No. 306 and ☞ **Premier House.**

★ ㉟ Wellington Botanic Garden. In the hills overlooking downtown is a con-centration of beautifully varied terrain. Woodland gardens under na-tive and exotic trees fill the valleys, water-loving plants line a pond and mountain streams, dry and craggy slopes are studded with succulents and rock-loving plants, and lawns spread over flatter sections with beds of bright seasonal bulbs and annuals. The lovely ☞ **Lady Nor-wood Rose Garden** is in the northeast part of the garden. **Carter Ob-servatory and Planetarium,** the only one of its kind in New Zealand, has public displays and programs, including evening telescope viewings, which are great opportunities for those from the northern hemisphere to learn about the southern night sky. If you don't want to walk the hill up to the garden, the ☞ **Kelburn Cable Car** can take you. Or take the No. 12 bus (direction: Karori) from Lambton Quay to the main (Glen-more Street) entrance. ⊠ *Tinakori Rd. for parking lot; main entrances on Upland Rd. (for cable car) and Glenmore St.,* ☎ *04/801–3071 gar-dens; 04/472–8167 observatory and planetarium.* ⊡ *Main gardens free, Carter observatory $7, planetarium $10.* ☉ *Main gardens daily sunrise–sunset; observatory and planetarium Mon., Wed., Fri. 10–5; Tues., Thurs., Sat. 10–5 and 6:30 PM–10:30 PM; Sun. noon–5.*

Around Wellington

㉞ Karori Wildlife Sanctuary. Just minutes from downtown Wellington, this 252-acre valley is being groomed as a safe haven for some of New Zealand's endangered species. After clearing the land of pests and predators and installing a predator-proof fence, rare native wildlife such as the little spotted kiwi, bellbird, and weka were released into the area. Two former city reservoirs were transformed into a wetlands area. More native plants and animals will be progressively introduced according to a carefully planned program. You can walk along well-developed bush tracks and stroll around the lakes, or join one of the volunteer-led guided tours. ⊠ *31 Waiapu Rd., Karori,* ☎ *04/920–9200,* WEB *www. sanctuary.org.nz.* ⊡ *$6.* ☉ *Mar.–Oct., weekdays noon–5, weekends 10–5; Nov.–Feb., weekdays noon–8, weekends 10–8.*

★ Maori Treasures. A visit to this exceptional Māori enterprise can re-sult in a wonderful, firsthand look at Māori arts and culture. Based on the Waiwhetu marae in Lower Hutt, the complex showcases arti-sans at work carving, weaving, or fashioning instruments. You might hear someone playing the nose flute or get your hands on a woven cloak; you could even participate in a weaving workshop. Guided tours give a thorough introduction to the various art forms. These cost $45 and include a courtesy shuttle to and from Wellington. Artwork produced in the studio hangs in the café and is for sale in the gift shop. ⊠ *58 Guthrie St., Lower Hutt,* ☎ *04/939–9630,* WEB *www.maoritreasures. com.* ⊙ *Daily 9–4; tours weekdays at 10 and 1:30.*

★ **Otari Native Botanic Garden.** Anyone with even the slightest interest in native New Zealand flora should spend an afternoon at Otari, just outside the city. Devoted to gathering and preserving indigenous plants, Otari's collection is the largest of its kind. With clearly marked bush-walks and landscape demonstration gardens, it aims to educate the public and thereby ensure the survival of New Zealand's unique plant life. While in the garden, you'll learn to dissect the forest, from the various *blechnum* ferns underfoot to the tallest trees towering overhead. An aerial walkway crosses high above the bush to offer an unusual vantage point over the gardens. Look and listen for the native birds that flock to this haven: the bellbird (*korimako*), gray duck (*parera*), New Zealand wood pigeon (*kereru*), silvereye (*tauhou*), and tūī, among others. Cultivated borders highlight everything from Wellington coast plants to grasses and alpine rock garden plants. Take the No. 14 Wilton bus from downtown (20 minutes) and ask the driver to let you off at the gardens. ⊠ *Wilton Rd., Wilton,* ☎ *04/475–3245,* WEB *www. owb.co.nz.* ▣ *Free.* ⊙ *Daily dawn–dusk.*

Southward Museum. This is in fact the largest collection of vintage and veteran cars in the southern hemisphere, with more than 250 vehicles, among them Bugattis; a Hispano-Suiza; one of only 17 Davis three-wheelers ever made; gangster Micky Cohen's armor-plated 1950 Cadillac; and a Cadillac once owned by Marlene Dietrich. The motorcycle collection, which has a number of early Harley-Davidsons and Indians, is almost as impressive. The museum is just off Highway 1, a 45-minute drive north of Wellington. ⊠ *Otaihanga Rd., Paraparaumu,* ☎ *04/297–1221,* WEB *www.southward.org.nz.* ▣ *$5.* ⊙ *Daily 9–4:30.*

OFF THE BEATEN PATH	**AKATARAWA VALLEY –** A drive through these steep, bush-clad hills may require extra attention, but it will lead you to a number of lovely out-of-the-way spots. About 35 minutes out of Wellington on State Highway 2, take the Brown Owl turnoff north of Upper Hutt onto the clearly marked valley road. You'll first come to **Harcourt Holiday Park** (☎ FAX 04/526–7400), which has motel units, cabins, and tent sites in gorgeous bush surroundings. Carry on over the bridge at the junction of the Hutt and Akatarawa rivers that heads into the valley. On the left look for **Trenance Organic Farm** (☎ 04/526–6788) and **Bluebank** (☎ FAX 04/526–9540); both grow delicious blueberries and farm the large flightless emus. Continue on to **Efil Doog Garden of Art** (☎ 04/526–7924, www.efildoog-nz.com), where Shirley and Ernest Cosgrove tend 11 acres of gardens with interesting sculptures. The grounds are magnificent at rhododendron time. The winding road crosses some wonderful old trestle bridges over the Akatarawa river before reaching **Staglands Wildlife Reserve** (☎ 04/526–7529, www.staglands.co.nz), where friendly animals abound and the birds will eat out of your hand. The road leaves the valley and ends at the Waikanae traffic lights on State Highway 1, 45 minutes north of Wellington. Both the Akatarawa and Hutt rivers are stocked with trout, and there are many peaceful fishing spots along the banks. You can get more information on this area from the **Upper Hutt Information Centre** (⊠ 6 Main St., ☎ 04/527–2141, WEB www.upperhuttcity.com). Keep in mind that the road is narrow and has one-way bridges, so you'll need to be especially alert.

Dining

$$$–$$$$ ✕ **Dockside and Shed Five.** These two restaurants may be separate establishments, but they share a building and a specialty: they're in a redeveloped waterfront warehouse and both focus on seafood. Look for the likes of West Coast whitebait with shoestring potatoes and lemon mayo at Shed Five and Cajun blackened pork with a balsamic tomato salsa at Dockside. ✉ *Dockside: Shed 3, Queens Wharf, Jervois Quay,* ☎ *04/499–9900. AE, DC, MC, V;* ✉ *Shed Five: Shed 5, Queens Wharf, Jervois Quay,* ☎ *04/499–9069. AE, DC, MC, V.*

$$$–$$$$ ✕ **Il Casino.** Owner Remiro Bresolin has been given a Hall of Fame award by his peers for his huge contribution to the Wellington restaurant scene. The food is northern Italian and quite authentic. Chef Franco Zanotto makes most of the pasta himself and milks top ingredients for his flavorful sauces. The wine list reads like the efforts of the New Zealand–Italy friendship society, and the service is correct in the old-fashioned way, with a dash of Kiwi friendliness. ✉ *108 Tory St.,* ☎ *04/385–7496. AE, DC, MC, V.*

$$$–$$$$ ✕ **Logan Brown.** If there's a run on this 1920s bank building now, it will be on the finely tuned menu and the attentive service. Starters might include crispy duck livers with apple and mint coleslaw; for a main course, consider seared cervena and kūmara dumplings. An excellent wine list includes many rare imports, plus New Zealand's very best, and the separate bar stays open late. ✉ *Cuba St. at Vivian St.,* ☎ *04/ 801–5114. AE, DC, MC, V. No lunch weekends.*

$$$–$$$$ ✕ **Roxburgh Bistro.** This intimate restaurant remains a steadfast fa-
★ vorite among locals who appreciate good food—and not a few reviewers. Chef-owner Mark Limacher might offer a seared duck breast with brown and oyster mushrooms sautéed in walnut oil, or perhaps an appetizer of smoked salmon with cucumber, mango, and tamarind–lemongrass dressing. The cheese selection caters to individual local products, and the comprehensive wine list is well priced. ✉ *18 Marjoribanks St.,* ☎ *04/385–7577. AE, DC, MC, V. Closed Sun.–Mon. No lunch Sat.*

$$$–$$$$ ✕ **White House.** The spectacular views across Oriental Bay and the har-
★ bor from this early 20th-century beach cottage may rouse you to take a walk along the waterfront. But first fortify yourself with an outstanding meal, such as a grilled cervena steak with truffle essence and what the menu calls an "orgy" of mushrooms, followed by a Grand Marnier soufflé. ✉ *232 Oriental Parade,* ☎ *04/385–8555. AE, DC, MC, V. Closed Sun. No lunch Sat.*

$$$ ✕ **Chameleon.** In the open kitchen of this contemporary space, you can see the chefs whip up luscious, innovative meals, such as roast saddle of rabbit with Savoy cabbage and tempura sweetbreads, followed by a Grand Marnier chocolate tart. ✉ *Hotel Inter-Continental, Featherston and Grey Sts.,* ☎ *04/472–2722. AE, DC, MC, V.*

$$–$$$ ✕ **Boulcott Street Bistro.** Having settled into life as a Wellington dining institution, this old colonial-style house conveys both experience and warmth. Chef John Allred concocts dishes like herb- and pepper-crusted salmon with creamed sweet corn and red peppers. Conversation hovers over desserts like roasted apricots with almond ice cream and macaroon crisps. The wine list is excellent. ✉ *99 Boulcott St.,* ☎ *04/499–4199. Reservations not accepted for dinner. AE, DC, MC, V. No lunch weekends.*

$$–$$$ ✕ **Turners Steak House.** Wellington's best-known steak house has been going for more than 30 years; it serves not only succulent cuts of beef but also some vegetarian choices. It's an all-around no-frills place; the steaks come with few trimmings and the tables are covered with classic gingham cloths. Mainly New Zealand wines are stocked and there is optional BYOB, wine only. You're more likely than not to overhear

ALL IN GOOD TASTE

A **POETIC GOURMET** once called New Zealand "the little green garden at the bottom of the world." It's a good description. Vegetables, fruit, and animals thrive in this Pacific paradise's temperate climate.

Internationally, the country's early food fame was earned for its butter and lamb, but these two staples have now been joined by a large number of other edibles. The hairy brown fruit known in most countries as a kiwi but in New Zealand as a kiwifruit (or, more recently, by the export marketing name *zespri*) has been a huge worldwide success.

Though many countries have incorporated dishes enjoyed by their original inhabitants into their everyday cuisine, there's not a lot of Māori influence on mainstream New Zealand cuisine. The best-known Māori meal is a *hāngi,* which involves cooking the food over heated stones buried in the earth. It's a method that doesn't translate easily to a European-style kitchen, though a few chic restaurants try to approximate it. One native vegetable, considered sacred to the Māori, is a common sight on most New Zealanders' tables: the *kūmara,* New Zealand's own sweet potato. It's eaten boiled, baked, or mashed, or whipped into elaborate concoctions by fine Kiwi chefs. Look for kūmara *rösti,* a sweet-potato fritter, in top urban restaurants.

At the bottom of the South Island and on Stewart Island, you might be offered muttonbird, also known as *titi,* which was eaten by local Māori for centuries and is eaten by local New Zealanders of all stripes today. It's a young seabird, cured for eating, and is salty and extremely fatty—definitely an acquired taste.

Meat cuts in New Zealand follow both American and European traditions. One exclusively local meat is *cervena,* the registered name for farmed venison. Not all restaurants use the term, so it pays to ask. Occasionally, the venison listed will be wild and will have a gamier flavor.

Several unique species of shellfish are caught around the coast. *Pipi* and *tuatua* are both similar to clams, but you are unlikely to come across another near-relation, the *toheroa,* in your restaurant travels. Dwindling stocks mean harvesting has been largely banned for some years, and it looks to remain so far into the future.

The registered name for the New Zealand farmed mussel is the Greenshell mussel. It is larger than its North American counterparts and is slightly sweet and succulent. Oysters are available in several species. Those from Bluff are considered the best, although Nelson Bay's come a close second. Rock oysters are rare. Most common are the Pacifics, which are sometimes (but not always) watery and insipid.

Whitebait, the juvenile of several fish species, are much smaller than their European equivalents. They are eaten whole, usually mixed into an omelet-like fritter. Another local delicacy from the sea is the roe of the *kina,* or sea egg, which is similar to a sea urchin. You'll see it for sale at roadside stalls and occasionally in innovative restaurants.

When you're visiting restaurants, be aware that many vegetables have two names, used interchangeably. Eggplants are often called aubergines here, and zucchini are also known as courgettes. The vegetable Americans know as a bell pepper is a capsicum in New Zealand.

Finally, if you're looking to to start a good-natured argument with a Kiwi, suggest that it was the Australians who invented that cream-topped, fruit-and-meringue concoction, the Pavlova. Though it's known for sure to be named for Russian ballerina Anna Pavlova, the question of where it originated is the source of constant trans–Tasman Sea rivalry.

American English around you. ✉ *155 Willis St.,* ☎ *04/385–0630. AE, DC, MC, V.*

$$ ✕ **Café L'Affaré.** This open-fronted, bustling café rotates around a coffee-roasting operation, where customers can see (and smell) beans undergoing their metamorphosis. Nearly everything served is made on the premises, including a range of delicious breads. A rug-covered children's area is well stocked with toys and other means of distraction for little ones. The all-day breakfast is hugely popular, but you could also opt for a classic Caesar salad or grilled chili squid. ✉ *27 College St.,* ☎ *04/385–9748. AE, MC, V. Closed Sun.*

$$ ✕ **Eden Wharf Café & Bar.** A bright, modern approach directs both the decor and the menu here. Try the New Orleans–style blackened fish with melon and sun-dried tomato salsa; then nibble on lemon tart while absorbing the soothing sea view. ✉ *301 Evans Bay Parade,* ☎ *04/386–1363. AE, DC, MC, V.*

$$ ✕ **Fog City Restaurant.** A roaring fire keeps this suburban restaurant warm on colder evenings, and a broad view of chef Steve Morris's kitchen team in action provides the predinner entertainment. Try a deeply satisfying dish like the chicken breast wrapped in bacon with dauphinoise potatoes, stuffing, gravy, and cranberry sauce, followed by a mini-Pavlova. ✉ *Marsden Village, 153 Karori Rd., Karori,* ☎ *04/476–8100. AE, DC, MC, V. Closed Sun.–Mon. No lunch.*

$$ ✕ **Tugboat on the Bay.** New Zealand's last steam tug is now moored in the Freyberg Lagoon, having found a berth as a restaurant. Walk the gangplank of the *Tapuhi II* to be greeted by an old-fashioned helmeted diver's suit; great waterside views will be truly at your elbow. The chef recommends the salmon Wellington: salmon fillets and scallops with spinach, wrapped in puff pastry and baked. ✉ *Oriental Bay,* ☎ *04/384–8884. AE, DC, MC, V.*

$–$$ ✕ **The Back-Bencher Pub & Café.** Right across the way from the Par-
★ liament buildings is this landmark watering hole, where politicians seek out a cold beer after a hot debate. The walls have become a gallery of political cartoons and puppets tweaking government characters and well-known sports figures. The menu makes for an equally entertaining perusal, and prices are reasonable. Try the lamb shanks with caramelized onions, garlic mashed potatoes, and rosemary jus. Just don't slurp your soup; you could be sitting next to the Prime Minister. ✉ *34 Molesworth St.,* ☎ *04/474–3065. AE, DC, MC, V.*

$–$$ ✕ **Dixon Street Gourmet Deli.** This city-center delicatessen stocks every-
★ thing you need for a superior picnic: homemade breads and bagels, meats, cheeses, pickles, preserves, chocolates, and local smoked fish. If you prefer to dine in, you can do that, too. Staff members delight in steering visitors toward the city's best sights. ✉ *45–47 Dixon St.,* ☎ *04/384–2436. AE, DC, MC, V.*

$–$$ ✕ **The Lido.** This busy corner café across from the tourist information center is a fun, funky place that turns out some clever combinations. For lunch try the pumpkin and pine-nut fritters topped with guacamole or a salmon and Brie omelet. It regularly stays open late. ✉ *Victoria and Wakefield Sts.,* ☎ *04/499–6666. Reservations not accepted. AE, DC, MC, V. No dinner Mon.*

$–$$ ✕ **The Malthouse.** This comfy, wood-paneled bar and restaurant has 30 beers on tap, many naturally brewed by microbreweries around the country. Choose your mood—eat outdoors on the balcony, inside in the lounge, or split the difference in the conservatory. Go for pub standbys like shepherd's pie, made with lean lamb and topped with creamy mashed potatoes and cheese. ✉ *47 Willis St.,* ☎ *04/473–0731. AE, DC, MC, V. Closed Sun.*

$–$$ ✕ **Vista.** For a breezy meal, head here for an outdoor table with an Oriental Bay view. Breakfast items, like the Italian omelet with ham, tomato, mozzarella, and fresh basil, can be ordered all day. The lighter bites, like Greek salad, are good bets too. ⊠ *106 Oriental Parade,* ☎ *04/385–7724. AE, DC, MC, V. Closed Mon. and June–Aug.*

Lodging

$$$$ ▥ **Hotel Inter-Continental.** Wellington's only five-star hotel, formerly
★ the Parkroyal, claims an ideal spot in the heart of the business district and a stone's throw from the waterfront. The foyer of this landmark high-rise building's interior is spacious and welcoming, the guest rooms modern and stylish. White duvets on the king-size beds stand out against the dark wood furniture and fittings. The restaurant, Chameleon, racks up awards. ⊠ *Featherston and Grey Sts.,* ☎ *04/472–2722,* F̄ĀX̄ *04/472–4724,* W̄ĒB̄ *www.intercontinental.com. 232 rooms. Restaurant, café, in-room data ports, indoor pool, sauna, gym, 2 bars, laundry service, convention center; no-smoking floors. AE, DC, MC, V.*

$$$–$$$$ ▥ **City Life Wellington.** This contemporary all-suite hotel has an excellent location, right in the middle of the city. And if you can snag a suite at a weekend or special summer rate, you've got one of the best-value lodgings in town. Guests have a wide selection of cream-and-white studios and spacious one-, two-, and three-bedroom suites enlivened by Asian-style area rugs. Facilities are similar in all suites and include self-catering kitchens, washers, dryers, and dishwashers (though the rooms are also serviced). Despite the location, you don't get street noise in the rooms. Breakfast is only included in the special weekend rate. ⊠ *300 Lambton Quay, The Terrace,* ☎ *04/472–8588 or 0800/368–888,* F̄ĀX̄ *04/473–8588,* W̄ĒB̄ *www.dynasty.co.nz. 65 suites. In-room data ports, in-room VCRs, kitchenettes, gym. AE, DC, MC, V.*

$$$ ▥ **Eight Parliament Street.** Walk through the door of this traditional wooden house, just five minutes from the Parliament Buildings, and you'll find a distinctly original, contemporary look. Brightly colored linen, funky sculpted mirrors, and commissioned New Zealand artwork offset cool cream drapes. Small bathrooms are spic-and-span, and there's a washer and dryer for guests' use. Breakfast might be smoked salmon and scrambled eggs or fresh fruit, yogurt, and espresso; you can have it outside in the sheltered courtyard. ⊠ *8 Parliament St., off Hill St., Thorndon,* ☎ *04/499–0808,* F̄ĀX̄ *04/479–6705,* W̄ĒB̄ *www. boutique-bb.co.nz. 3 rooms, 1 with bath. Laundry facilities; no a/c, no smoking. MC, V. BP.*

$$$ ▥ **Shepherds Arms Speights Ale House.** New Zealand's oldest hotel, the Shepherds Arms has been refurbished to approximate its original state. The rooms' four-poster beds, deep-blue carpets, and burgundy curtains signal their 19th-century roots, and in keeping with this they're also fairly small, especially the three single rooms, which share a bathroom. Head down to the bar to mix with the local after-work crowd. Old photos on the wall show what Wellington looked like in the hotel's early days. By Wellington standards the hotel is a bit out of town—about four minutes' walk to the Parliament Buildings and about 10 to the main shopping district. ⊠ *285 Tinakori Rd., Thorndon,* ☎ *04/472–1320,* F̄ĀX̄ *04/472–0523,* W̄ĒB̄ *www.shepherds.co.nz. 12 rooms, 9 with bath. Restaurant, bar; no a/c, no smoking. AE, DC, MC, V.*

$$–$$$ ▥ **Halswell Lodge.** For restaurant, theater, and cinema going, you can't beat the location, right by the eastern end of Courtenay Place. And you'll find it hard to beat the prices, too, as there's a room for most budgets. Standard hotel rooms at the front of the building are small and functional. Motel units, with studios or two bedrooms, are set farther back, each with kitchenette. Three of these have jet baths.

Finally, there's the newly restored 1920s villa at the rear of the property; its six superior rooms come with cane chairs, burnished wood decor, antique wardrobes, and restored fireplaces. Guests here can use the villa kitchen to prepare light meals. ✉ *21 Kent Terr.,* ☎ *04/385–0196,* FAX *04/385–0503,* WEB *www.halswell.co.nz. 25 rooms, 11 motel units. Some kitchenettes, laundry facilities; no a/c. AE, DC, MC, V.*

$$ ⌂ **Tinakori Lodge.** You can stay on the same road as the Prime Minister at this Victorian timber villa. The rooms are nicely furnished with comfortable beds, and there's a bright conservatory and small garden at the rear, facing a bush reserve. A buffet breakfast is laid out each morning; the city center is a 10-minute walk away. ✉ *182 Tinakori Rd., Thorndon,* ☎ *04/473–3478,* FAX *04/939–3475,* WEB *www. tinakorilodge.co.nz. 8 rooms, 5 with bath. No a/c, no room phones, no room TVs. AE, DC, MC, V. BP.*

$
★ ⌂ **Downtown Backpackers.** In a classic backpackers' location opposite the train station, this hostel stands out by virtue of its amenities and its well-kept landmark art deco building. Most of the rooms, which range from singles to six-person shares, have private baths. The extensive communal areas include a café, kitchen, bar, and pool room; computers are at the ready if you'd like to jump on the Web. Check out the old Māori carved fireplace surround in the bar; you won't see anything better in the national museum. ✉ *Corner of Bunny St. and Waterloo Quay,* ☎ *04/473–8482,* FAX *04/471–1073,* WEB *www. downtownbackpackers.co.nz. 60 rooms, 54 with bath. Café, kitchen, billiards, bar, laundry facilities, Internet; no a/c, no room phones, no room TVs. AE, DC, MC, V.*

Nightlife and the Arts

For a current listing of cultural events in Wellington, check the *Dominion Post* newspaper and the weekly *Capital Times.* The free booklet *Wellington What's On,* available from the Visitor Information Centre, also has seasonal listings of cultural events. **Ticketek** (☎ 04/ 384–3840) sells tickets for local performances.

The Arts

Wellington's art scene, traditionally a strong suit, continues to amplify. The major arts event in town is the **New Zealand International Festival,** held in March every two years (in even-numbered years) at venues across the city. This attracts a huge array of international talent in the fields of music, drama, dance, the visual arts, and media. Advance information and a festival program are available from the Festival Office (☎ 04/473–0149, WEB www.nzfestival.telecom.co.nz). Many events fill up quickly, so book ahead.

Wellington is the home of the **New Zealand Ballet Company,** the **National Opera of New Zealand,** and the **New Zealand Symphony Orchestra.** The **Michael Fowler Centre** and the adjacent **Town Hall** (✉ Civic Square, Wakefield St., ☎ 04/801–4242) are the main venues for theater and music. The **St. James Theatre** (✉ 77-83 Courtenay Pl., ☎ 04/ 802–4060, WEB www.stjames.co.nz) and the **Opera House** (✉ 111-113 Manners St., ☎ 04/384–3840) present drama, ballet and opera.

The **Circa Theatre** is a good bet to catch contemporary New Zealand pieces along with established masterworks from Pinter to Wilde. ✉ *1 Taranaki St.,* ☎ *04/801–7992,* WEB *www.circa.co.nz.*

The **Downstage Theatre** holds frequent performances of stage classics, contemporary drama, comedy, and dance. ✉ *Hannah Playhouse, Courtenay Pl. and Cambridge Terr.,* ☎ *04/801–6946,* WEB *www. downstage.co.nz.*

Nightlife

Wellington's after-dark scene splits between several main areas. The funky cafés of Cuba Street stay open most of the night for pre- and post-bar and club coffees; some put on regular gigs, too. Courtenay Place is where most of the drinking action is, with a selection of brash Irish pubs, sports bars, grand salons, and upscale establishments. In the downtown business district—between Lambton Quay and Manners Street—a couple of brewpubs and a few taverns cater to the after-work mob. Down by the harbor, a flashy crowd hangs out in several warehouse-style bars, which absolutely rock weekends.

Downtown, make an early start at the **Arizona Bar** (✉ Grey and Featherston Sts., ☎ 04/495–7867), a western-theme bar on the ground floor of the Hotel Inter-Continental. At the **Loaded Hog** (✉ 14–18 Bond St., ☎ 04/472–9160) you get microbrew beers, live music several nights a week, and an outdoor deck. The **Malthouse** (✉ 47 Willis St., ☎ 04/499–4355), upstairs in a renovated historic building, brews its own beers and has conservatory-style seating looking down on the street.

Of Courtenay Place's Irish spots, try **Molly Malone's** (✉ Taranaki St. and Courtenay Pl., ☎ 04/384–2896), a large, traditional bar with regular live music and a rowdy crowd, particularly on weekends. A restaurant serves pub grub while the upstairs bar has an outside balcony for people-watching. You can also check out the crowd from **Kitty O'Shea's** (✉ 28 Courtenay Pl., ☎ 04/384–7392) outside veranda; there is regular traditional live music.

The well-lived-in **Grand** (✉ 69–71 Courtenay Pl., ☎ 04/801–7800), once a brewery and then a distillery, has exposed brick walls, timber floors, and four levels with everything from a 400-person main bar to a garden bar to a 10-table poolroom. **CO2** (✉ 28 Blair St., at Courtenay Pl., ☎ 04/384–1064) is smallish and, true to its name, serves only sparkling wine.

On the waterfront, the two big draws are the bars at **Shed Five** (✉ Shed Five, Queens Wharf, Jervois Quay, ☎ 04/499–9069) and **Dockside** (✉ Shed 3, Queens Wharf, Jervois Quay, ☎ 04/499–9900). In good weather, everyone spills outside for the best close-up harbor views in Wellington. Later on, move across to **Chicago** (✉ Jervois Quay, ☎ 04/473–4900) on Queens Wharf, a spacious sports bar that sees boisterous post-game parties, live bands, dancing, and late-night pool sessions.

The best place to catch local rock music is **Bar Bodega** (✉ 286 Willis St., ☎ 04/384–8212). Touring acts most often play the **James Cabaret** (✉ 5 Hania St., ☎ 04/382–9097).

Shopping

Department Store

For more than a century, **Kirkcaldie & Stains** (✉ 165–177 Lambton Quay, ☎ 04/472–5899) has maintained an impeccable standard of customer service. With the lovely early 19th-century facade and posh selection, it's Wellington's answer to Harrod's.

Districts

The main **downtown shopping area,** for department stores, clothes, shoes, books, outdoor gear, and souvenirs, is the so-called Golden Mile—from Lambton Quay, up Willis, Victoria, and Manners streets. The principal shopping center is **Harbour City** on Lambton Quay, though there are also varied store outlets in **Capital on the Quay,** a mall on Lambton Quay, and the **Old Bank Arcade** (corner of Lambton Quay and Customhouse Quay). For ethnic-gift stores, boutiques, secondhand shops, and crafts, visit trendy **Cuba Street.**

Markets

The **Wellington Market** (⊠ Taranaki and Cable Sts., ☎ 04/801–8991) is the place to find souvenirs, New Zealand crafts, and collectibles and also has a great Asian food court. It's open Friday–Sunday 10–5:30. **James Smiths Corner** (⊠ 55 Cuba St., ☎ 04/801–8812) has a second-floor market area selling ethnic crafts, jewelry, and gifts; downstairs are more mainstream stores and a food court. It's open daily 9–5.

Specialty Stores

BOOKS AND MAPS

Arty Bee's Books (⊠ 17 Courtenay Pl., ☎ 04/385–1819) is a friendly store for secondhand books and sheet music. **Parson's Books & Music** (⊠ 126 Lambton Quay, ☎ 04/472–4587) may not be the largest book-store in town, but it's one of the most intriguing—strong on New Zealand writing and travel, and also featuring comprehensive classical record-ings, and a small upper-floor café.

OUTDOOR CLOTHES AND EQUIPMENT

Wellington is a fine place to stock up on camping supplies before hit-ting the great outdoors. **Kathmandu** (⊠ 34 Manners St., ☎ 04/801–8755) carries its house brand of clothing and equipment. **Mainly Tramp-ing** (⊠ 39 Mercer St., ☎ 04/473–5353) is a good bet for backpacks and other gear. **Ski & Snowboard Centre–Gordons** (⊠ corner Cuba and Wakefield Sts., ☎ 04/499–8894) focuses on snow sport equipment and clothing.

SOUVENIRS

Art Works (⊠ 117 Customhouse Quay, ☎ 04/473–8581, WEB www. artworksnz.co.nz) has a rich stock of gift possibilities, especially crafts. Look for blown glass, Māori carvings, paua shell ornaments, and merino wool and opossum fur clothing.

Wellington A to Z

AIR TRAVEL

The domestic carriers serving Wellington are Air New Zealand, Ori-gin Pacific, and Soundsair. The international carriers are Air New Zealand and Qantas, but here international means over to Australia; other overseas flights go through Auckland's airport. There are gen-erally a half dozen flights to Australia daily. Air New Zealand, between its Link and national services, connects Wellington to more than 20 other New Zealand cities daily for very reasonable fares. Origin Pa-cific has flights from Wellington to all major New Zealand cities daily. Soundsair flies between Wellington and Picton several times a day.

➤ CARRIERS: **Air New Zealand** (☎ 0800/737–000, WEB www. airnewzealand.co.nz). **Origin Pacific** (☎ 0800/302–302, WEB www. originpacific.co.nz). **Qantas** (☎ 0800/808–767, WEB www.qantas.com. au). **Soundsair Ltd** (☎ 04/801–0111, WEB www.soundsair.co.nz).

AIRPORTS

Wellington International Airport (WLG) lies about 8 km (5 mi) from the city.

➤ AIRPORT INFORMATION: **Wellington International Airport** (⊠ Stew-art Duff Dr., Rongotai, ☎ 04/385–5123).

TRANSFERS

Co-operative Shuttle operates a 10-seater bus between the airport and any address in the city ($10 for one person, $14 for two). The bus meets

all incoming flights; tickets are available from the driver. A taxi ride
costs about $25.

➤ CONTACT: **Co-operative Shuttle** (☏ 04/387–8787).

BY BIKE

If the sun is shining and the wind is still, cycling is an ideal way to explore the city and its surrounding bays. Penny Farthing Cycles rents
out mountain bikes for $35 per day or $140 per week, including helmets.

➤ BIKE RENTALS: **Penny Farthing Cycles** (✉ 89 Courtenay Pl., ☏ 04/
385–2772).

BOAT AND FERRY TRAVEL

The Interisland Line runs a couple of passenger-and-vehicle ferry services between Wellington and Picton: the Interislander and the Lynx.
Both services have one or two departures each way, daily. The Interislander service takes longer than the Lynx and is less expensive. Its
standard one-way adult fare is $49; a medium-size sedan costs between
$88 and $175 depending on the time of year. The three-hour crossing
takes in the lower North Island coastline and the scenic Marlborough
Sounds. Its ships have bars and restaurants, a children's area, and a
movie theater.

The Lynx ferry service takes 135 minutes. A standard one-way adult
ticket costs between $32 and $63. Taking a medium-size sedan costs
between $100 and $199.

Significantly discounted fares are available for both services, but these
special rates can only be booked from within New Zealand. Most car
rental agencies have North Island–South Island transfer programs for
their vehicles; you can drop one car off in Wellington and pick up another in Picton on the same contract.

There are separate terminals for each service; a free bus from the railway station connects the two. The Interislander ferry terminal is about
3 km (2 mi) from the city. A free bus leaves Platform 9 at the Wellington Railway Station for the ferry terminal 40 minutes before sailings.
The Lynx terminal is at Waterloo Quay in central Wellington.

➤ BOAT AND FERRY LINE: *Interisland Line* (☏ 0800/802–802 or 04/
498–3302, WEB www.interislandline.co.nz).

BUS TRAVEL

InterCity and Newmans buses provide daily departures to all major
North Island destinations. They also connect with the Interisland Line
that operates the ferries to Picton in the South Island.

➤ BUS DEPOT: **Wellington Railway Station** (✉ Bunny St. and Waterloo Quay, ☏ 04/498–3000).

➤ BUS INFORMATION: **InterCity** (☏ 04/472–5111, WEB www.
intercitycoach.co.nz). **Newmans** (☏ 04/499–3261, WEB www.
newmanscoach.co.nz).

BUS TRAVEL WITHIN WELLINGTON

Wellington's bus and trolley-bus network is operated by several companies, though it's easy to find out information on routes and fares by
calling the public transport information service known as Ridewell. The
main terminals for services are at the railway station and from Courtenay Place. The City Circular Bus departs every 10 minutes on a circular loop through the center passing all the main sights and attractions.
For all trips in the inner city, the fare is $2.

STARpass tickets ($8) allow a day's unlimited travel on all area buses;
a $5 gives you a day's bus travel within the city center. For maps and

timetables, go to the visitor information center at Victoria and Wake-field streets, the railway station on Bunny Street, or the Wellington Regional Council Centre on Wakefield Street.

➤ CONTACT: **Ridewell** (☎ 04/801–7000, WEB www.wrc.govt.nz/timetables).

CAR RENTAL

Avis, Budget, and Hertz have offices at Wellington airport.

➤ AGENCIES: **Avis** (☎ 04/801–8108). **Budget** (☎ 04/802–4548). **Hertz** (☎ 04/384–3809).

CAR TRAVEL

The main access to the city is via the Wellington Urban Motorway, which starts just after the merging of Highways 1 and 2, a few miles north of the city center. The motorway links the city center with all towns and cities to the north.

You won't need or, most likely, want a car to explore Wellington's center, but it's convenient to have one to get out to surrounding areas like the Hutt Valley and Akatarawa. Central Wellington is rife with narrow one-way streets, and there's very little on-street parking. Non-residents should resort to parking lots. Rush hours usually last from 7:30 to 9:30 AM and 4 to 6:30 PM.

EMBASSIES AND HIGH COMMISSIONS

➤ AUSTRALIA: **Australian High Commission** (⊠ 72–78 Hobson St., Thorndon, ☎ 04/473–6411), open weekdays 8:45–12:15.

➤ CANADA: **Canadian High Commission** (⊠ 61 Molesworth St., Thorndon, ☎ 04/473–9577), open weekdays 8:30–4:30.

➤ UNITED KINGDOM: **British High Commission** (⊠ 44 Hill St., Thorndon, ☎ 04/924–2888), open weekdays 9:30–noon and 2–3:30.

➤ UNITED STATES: **United States Embassy** (⊠ 29 Fitzherbert Terr., Thorndon, ☎ 04/462–6000), open weekdays 10–noon and 2–4.

EMERGENCIES

➤ EMERGENCY SERVICES: **Fire, police, and ambulance** (☎ 111).

➤ HOSPITAL: **After-Hours Medical Centre** (⊠ 17 Adelaide Rd., Newtown, ☎ 04/384–4944), open 24 hours. **Wellington Hospital** (⊠ Riddiford St., Newtown, ☎ 04/385–5999).

MONEY MATTERS

➤ CURRENCY EXCHANGE: **Thomas Cook** (⊠ 358 Lambton Quay, ☎ 04/472–2848).

TAXIS

Wellington is only a small city, but a taxi ride can save your legs on the long haul around the harbor or up the steep hills to Kelburn and the Botanic Gardens. Most city rides cost $8–$10. There are taxis outside the railway station, as well as on Dixon Street and along Courtenay Place and Lambton Quay.

TOURS

BOAT TOURS

The Dominion Post Ferry, a commuter service between the city and Days Bay, on the east side of Port Nicholson, is one of the best-value tours in the city. On the way to Days Bay you can stop at Matiu Somes Island; this former quarantine station makes an unusual picnic spot on a warm afternoon. Days Bay itself has a seaside village atmosphere, local crafts shops, and great views of Wellington. Weekdays the catamaran departs from Queens Wharf at 6:30 AM, 7:25, 8:15, 10, noon, 2:15, 4:30, 5:30 and 6:30 PM. The return boats leave Days Bay roughly 30

minutes later. The sailing schedule is cut back on weekends and holidays. The one-way fare to Days Bay is $7.50; the cost if you include a Somes Island stop is $16.50 round-trip. You can pick up tickets at the ferry terminal between 8 and 5; otherwise, tickets can be bought on board.
➤ CONTACT: **Dominion Post Ferry** (✉ Queens Wharf, ☎ 04/499–1282, WEB www.eastbywest.co.nz).

PRIVATE GUIDES

Wally Hammond, a tour operator with a great anecdotal knowledge and a fund of stories about Wellington, offers a 2½-hour minibus tour of the city and Marine Drive. This can be combined with a half-day Kapiti Coast Tour, which includes a visit to the Southward Car Museum. The city tour costs $25, the combined tour $80.
➤ CONTACT: **Wally Hammond** (☎ 04/472–0869, WEB www. wellingtonsightseeingtours.com).

TRAIN TRAVEL

The terminal for all TranzRail train services is Wellington Railway Station on Bunny Street, 1½ km (about 1 mi) from the city center. The Overlander train connects Auckland and Wellington, going daily once each way on the 11-hour trip. The Northerner route also runs between Auckland and Wellington, but it makes the trip overnight.

TranzMetro operates electric suburban train services to Wellington from the Hutt Valley, Palmerston North, and Masterton.
➤ TRAIN STATION: **Wellington Railway Station** (✉ Bunny St. and Waterloo Quay, ☎ 04/498–3000).
➤ TRAIN LINES: **TranzMetro** (☎ 04/801–7000, WEB www.tranzmetro. co.nz). **TranzRail** (☎ 0800/802–802, WEB www.tranzrailtravel.co.nz).

TRAVEL AGENCIES

➤ LOCAL AGENT: **Thomas Cook** (✉ 108 Lambton Quay, ☎ 04/473–5167).

VISITOR INFORMATION

The city's visitor bureau is open on weekdays from 8:30 to 5:30, weekends 9:30 to 4:30. In addition to its Web site, check out the City Council site, www.wcc.govt.nz, for information on Wellington's services, sights, and activities.
➤ TOURIST INFORMATION: **Wellington Visitor Information Centre** (✉ Civic Administration Bldg., Victoria and Wakefield Sts., ☎ 04/801–4000, WEB www.wellingtonnz.com).

THE WAIRARAPA

Wellington residents call the Rimutaka Range to the north of the city "the Hill," and for years it has been both a physical and psychological barrier that has allowed the Wairarapa region to develop at its own pace, in its own style. The hill has also kept tour buses away, and as a result landscapes such as the Pinnacles—cliff faces carved by the wind into shapes reminiscent of a cathedral—are uncrowded and easy to reach. There are great hikes and walks in the area. Times are changing quickly, however. An expanding wine trail in the southern Wairarapa is drawing people in increasing numbers. For the time being, however, the Wairarapa is still an uncrowded place to discover.

Martinborough

49 *70 km (44 mi) north of Wellington.*

Martinborough is the hub of the Wairarapa's wine industry, and as a result this small town is attracting interest from developers keen to cash

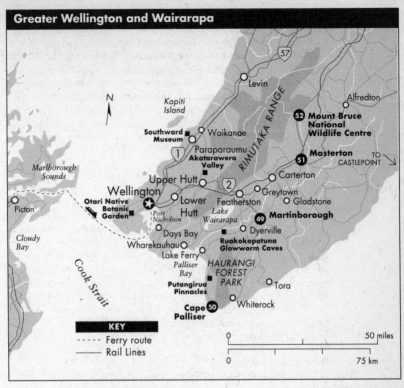

Greater Wellington and Wairarapa

KEY
- - - - Ferry route
―――― Rail Lines

in on growing tourist numbers. So far changes have been tasteful, with people refurbishing historic places and opening their homes as B&Bs. The town gets its name from founder John Martin, who planned the streets in a Union Jack pattern stretching out from a square that remains the center of activity. Most restaurants and shops are on or close to the square. There's also a wine taster's shortcut: the **Martinborough Wine Centre,** which stocks a thorough selection of local vintages for sipping and purchasing, plus books and wine accessories. ⊠ *6 Kitchener St.,* ☎ *06/306–9040,* WEB *www.martinboroughwinecentre.co.nz.* ⊙ *Daily 9–5.*

Local records indicate that grapes have been raised in the region since the turn of the 20th century. The present industry dates from 1979, and the popularity of Martinborough wine has grown tremendously since the mid- to late 1980s; there are now more than 20 vineyards in the immediate vicinity. That said, many local producers have small outputs, which means that some local varieties can be scarce everywhere but here, and prices tend to be higher than in other New Zealand wine regions. A number of the wineries are within a 10-minute walk of town, and there is a wine-trail horse-carriage tour as well. As in Hawke's Bay, red grape varieties seem to have the best go in the area's soil, with pinot noir being the most exceptional. Keep in mind that from year to year, any given winery's varieties may change depending on grape quality. Below is a short list of the region's best wineries.

Dry River (⊠ Puruatanga Rd., ☎ 06/306-9388, FAX 06/306-9275) is undoubtedly the country's hottest small (read: tiny) producer. Wines are sold out by mail order within hours of release; you'll need an appointment to visit. **Ata Rangi Vineyard** (⊠ Puruatanga Rd., ☎ 06/306–

9570, WEB www.atarangi.co.nz) makes exceptional chardonnay, pinot noir, and Célèbre (a cabernet-merlot-shiraz blend), again in small quantities. Tastings are held October through April, weekdays 1 to 3, weekends 11 to 5. **Martinborough Vineyard** (⊠ Princess St., ☎ 06/306–9955, WEB www.martinborough-vineyard.co.nz), open daily 11 to 5, is a larger but equally fine regional winery—the first to convince the world of the Wairarapa's pinot noir potential. Martinborough's chardonnay is also exceptional. **Palliser Estate** (⊠ Kitchener St., ☎ 06/306–9019, WEB www.palliser.co.nz) has come out with some of the best local whites. The sauvignon blanc and pinot noir are both distinguished by their intense flavors. Palliser is open daily 10–4.

OFF THE
BEATEN PATH

RUAKOKOPATUNA GLOWWORM CAVES – The glowworm display here is not quite as impressive as the one at Waitomo, but the sense of adventure is much greater—nobody will tell you to duck when you're approaching a low-hanging rock, so be careful. You'll walk right through a cave following a freshwater stream: expect to get wet feet, and take a flashlight. Once you have found a cluster of glowworms, turn your flashlight off for the best display, then switch it on again as you walk deeper into the cave. And keep in mind that as you stay in the cave longer, your eyes will adjust to the darkness, allowing you to see more lights. Take Jelicoe Street from Martinborough 7 km (4½ mi), turn left at Dry River Road, and drive another 8 km (5 mi) to a sign for the caves. Entrance is free, and it is best to call ahead for permission before you go, as the caves are on private property. ☎ 06/306-9393.

Dining and Lodging

$$$ ✕🏨 **Martinborough Hotel.** This restored wooden 1890s hotel, with a
★ flower-filled internal courtyard, sits right on Martinborough's square. Rooms are each decorated uniquely with a mix of antique and contemporary furnishings, such as four-poster beds and writing tables. Some bathrooms have clawfoot tubs. Upstairs rooms in the main building open onto the veranda, and garden rooms look out on to roses and lavender bushes. There's an attractive, wood-floored bistro whose kitchen has a way with steak and salmon: try the fillet steak, barbecued and served with a Stilton and olive polenta, or an herb-crusted salmon with seared scallops and creamed spinach. ⊠ *The Square,* ☎ *06/306-9350,* FAX *06/306-9345,* WEB *www.martinborough-hotel.co. nz. 16 rooms. Restaurant, cable TV, bar, Internet. AE, DC, MC, V. BP.*

Palliser Bay and Cape Palliser

🔟 *Southwest of Martinborough: 25 km (16 mi) to Lake Ferry, 40 km (25 mi) to Putangirua Pinnacles, 60 km (37 mi) to Cape Palliser.*

To witness Wairarapa's most remote, blustery scenery—and to see the North Island's southernmost point, Cape Palliser—you need to make the drive southwest from Martinborough. It's 25 km (16 mi) through rolling sheep country to the coast at the little settlement of **Lake Ferry** on Palliser Bay. The lake in question, called Onoke, is a salt lagoon formed by the long sandbank here. Vacation homes, fishing spots, and remarkable sunsets over the bay bring in the weekend Wellingtonian crowd.

Just before Lake Ferry, turn left (coming from Martinborough) at the sign for Cape Palliser and drive another 15 km (9 mi) around Palliser Bay to Te Kopi, where the **Putangirua Pinnacles Scenic Reserve** is protected from the hordes by its relative isolation. The spectacular rocks have been formed over the last 120,000 years as rains have washed away an ancient gravel deposit, and pinnacles and towers now soar hundreds of feet into the air on both sides of a stony riverbank. An hour-long round-trip walk from the parking area takes you along the riverbank and close up to the base of the pinnacles. If you're feeling adventurous, there is a three- to four-hour bushwalk involving some steep climbs and wonderful vistas of the coast—as far off as the South Island on a clear day. The Pinnacles are an hour's drive from Martinborough.

The road to Cape Palliser deteriorates after the Pinnacles and is unpaved in places. It's a dramatic, bleak ride, though not particularly hard, provided you take care. After 20 km (12 mi), the road ends at **Cape Palliser** itself, where 250 wooden steps climb up to the candy-striped lighthouse. The views from here, up and down the wild coastline, are terrific. Below the lighthouse, splashing in the surf and basking on the rocks, are members of the North Island's only resident **fur seal colony.** You'll be able to get pretty close for photos, but not too close—these are wild animals and fiercely protective of their young. Best advice: don't get between seals and pups, or seals and the ocean.

Dining and Lodging

$$$$ ✕🏠 **Wharekauhau.** This Edwardian-style lodge set on a 5,000-acre
★   working sheep station has luxury lashed by nature. On a hot summer afternoon this is one of the most peaceful places on earth; on a windy, wet morning it's like something out of *Wuthering Heights*. Self-contained guest cottages are scattered around the main lodge; each has a king-size bed, a small patio, and an open fireplace. On the farm you can take in the workings of the sheep station and walk around the gloriously remote coastline. Trout fishing is also an option, as are tours to the seal colony at Palliser Bay. The dining room's seasonally changing menus highlight the best of local produce—especially lamb and fish—accompanied by fine Martinborough wines. The lodge is 40 minutes' drive south of Featherston on the rugged coast at the northern end of Palliser Bay; from Featherston, take the minor road along the west side of Lake Wairarapa. ⊠ *Western Lake Rd., Palliser Bay (R.D. 3, Featherston),* ☎ *06/307–7581,* 𝖥𝖠𝖷 *06/307–7799,* 𝖶𝖤𝖡 *www.wharekauhau. co.nz. 12 cottages. Dining room, tennis court, pool, gym, lounge, Internet; no a/c, no smoking. AE, DC, MC, V. MAP.*

$ ✕🏠 **Lake Ferry Hotel.** The North Island's southernmost pub sits almost on the beach, with breathtaking views across Cape Palliser to the South Island's Kaikoura ranges. The menu would do credit to a city hotel, particularly the superb seafood. The rooms are no-frills, but having a drink on the deck at sunset is an unbeatable experience. ⊠ *Lake Ferry,* ☎ *06/307–7831,* 𝖥𝖠𝖷 *06/307–7891. 8 rooms, 1 with bath. Restaurant; no a/c, no room phones, no TVs, no smoking. MC, V. BP.*

Masterton

🔢 *40 km (25 mi) northeast of Martinborough, 230 km (144 mi) southwest of Napier.*

Masterton is Wairarapa's major population center, but—in common with the other towns strung out along Highway 2 from Wellington, like Featherston, Greytown, and Carterton—you will find little of interest beyond its suitability as an exploring base. Visitors are best advised to make for the coast, an hour's drive east of Masterton through lovely hill country, where **Castlepoint** is perhaps the most spectacular site on the entire Wairarapa coast. Here, Castle Rock rises a sheer 500 ft out of the sea; below, in **Deliverance Cove,** seals sometimes play. There's a fantastic walk to the peninsula lighthouse, and surfers rate highly the beach break at Deliverance Cove.

There are enjoyable bushwalks in beautiful forests laced with streams at **Tararua Forest Park,** which also has picnic facilities. The Mt. Holdsworth area at the east end of the park is particularly popular for tramping. To get there turn off State Highway 2 onto Norfolk Road, 2 km (1 mi) south of Masterton.

★ ❺❷   Nearby **Mount Bruce National Wildlife Centre** makes a fine introduction to the country's wildlife, particularly its endangered bird species. An easy-to-walk trail (one hour round-trip) through the bush takes you past aviaries containing rare, endangered, or vulnerable birds, including the *takahē,* a flightless bird thought to be extinct until it was rediscovered in 1948. The real highlight, though, is the nocturnal habitat containing foraging kiwis, the country's symbol, which are endearing little bundles of energy. It takes a while for your eyes to adjust to the artificial gloom, but it's worth the wait. Don't miss the eel feeding (daily at 1:30 PM), when the reserve's stream writhes with the New Zealand long-finned eel. ⊠ *State Hwy. 2, 30 km (19 mi) north of Masterton,* ☎ *06/375–8004,* WEB *www.mtbruce.doc.govt.nz.* ⊠ *$8.* ☉ *Mar.–Oct., daily 9:30–4; Nov.–Apr., daily 9:30–5.*

Shopping

For a unique souvenir, visit the **Paua Shell Factory and Shop** (⊠ 54 Kent St., Carterton, ☎ 06/379–6777), 15 km (9 mi) south of Masterton. Paua (akin to abalone) has been collected by the Māori for food since ancient times. The rainbow-color shell interiors are highly prized (used by the Māori to represent eyes in their statues) and here are polished and processed, then turned into jewelry and other gifts.

The Wairarapa A to Z

CAR TRAVEL

A car is essential for getting around the Wairarapa. State Highway 2 runs through the region from north and south, between Napier and Wellington. From Wellington you'll drive through Upper Hutt, over the Rimutaka Range, then into the gateway town of Featherston. Highway 53 will take you to Martinborough; turn southwest here on Lake Ferry Road for Lake Ferry and Cape Palliser. Masterton is farther north along State Highway 2. The journey from Wellington to Martinborough takes 1½ hours; Masterton is another half hour. From Napier, Masterton is about three hours.

TOURS

HORSE-AND-CARRIAGE TOURS

The Horse and Carriage Establishment runs tours around the vineyards. The cost is $45 per person for a two-hour tour; advance booking is essential. The company also has twilight carriage drives, mystery tours, and horse and carriage hire for any specific journey.
➤ CONTACT: **Horse and Carriage Establishment** (⊠ Martinborough, ☎ 025/477–852).

VISITOR INFORMATION

The Wairarapa bureau opens on weekdays 8:30–5:30, weekends 9–4. The Martinborough office is open daily 10–4.
➤ TOURIST INFORMATION: **Martinborough Visitor Information Centre** (⊠ Kitchener and Broadway Sts., Martinborough, ☎ 06/306–9043). **Tourism Wairarapa** (⊠ 5 Dixon St., Masterton, ☎ 06/378–7373, WEB wairarapa.co.nz).

4 UPPER SOUTH ISLAND

Natural wonders never cease—not on the South Island. Nor do the opportunities for adventure: sea-kayaking, glacier hiking, trekking, fishing, mountain biking, rafting, and rock climbing. If you'd rather kick back while you feast your senses, you can fly over brilliant glaciers and snowy peaks, watch whales from on deck, or taste some of the region's delicious wines. Add New Zealand hospitality, and you can't go wrong.

Updated by
Bob Marriott

THE CLOSE PASSAGE across Cook Strait separates the North Island from the South Island, but the difference between the two is far greater than the distance suggests. Whether you're seeing the South Island from aboard a ferry as it noses through the rocky entrance to Marlborough Sounds or through the window of a plane, the immediate impression is that the landscape has turned feral: the mellow, green beauty of the North Island has given way to jagged snowcapped mountains and rivers that sprawl across vast, rocky shingle beds. The South Island has been carved by ice and water, a process still rapidly occurring. Locals will tell you that you haven't seen rain until you've been drenched by a storm on the West Coast, where annual precipitation is ambitiously measured in meters.

The top half of the South Island is a fair introduction to the contrasts of New Zealand's less populated island. The Marlborough Province occupies the northeast corner, where the inlets of Marlborough Sounds flow around verdant peninsulas and sandy coves. Marlborough is now the largest wine-growing region in New Zealand, with more than 7,200 acres of vineyards. Predominant varieties grown are sauvignon blanc, chardonnay, riesling, pinot noir, pinot gris, cabernet sauvignon, and merlot. Marlborough is relatively dry and beautifully sunny, and in summer the inland plains look something like the American West, with mountains rising out of grassy flats. Throughout Upper South Island, you'll notice commercial foresting of the hills—Californian *Pinus radiata* (Monterey pine) mature rapidly in New Zealand soil. Their 25-year harvest cycle is one of the shortest in the world, a fact duly noted by Japanese lumber concerns.

The northwest corner of the island, the Nelson region, is a sporting paradise with a mild climate that allows a year-round array of outdoor activities. Sun-drenched Nelson, a lively town with fine restaurants and a vibrant network of artists and craftspeople, is the gateway to an area surrounded by great national parks and hiking tracks (trails). Abel Tasman National Park, to the west of the city, is ringed with spectacularly blue waters studded with craggy rocks; these outcroppings guard coves and sands that are the stuff of dreams. To the southwest is Kahurangi National Park, home of the Heaphy Track, one of the world's great walks, while Nelson Lakes National Park lies to the south.

After the gentler climate of Marlborough and Nelson, the wild grandeur of the West Coast comes as a surprise. This is Mother Nature with her hair down, flaying the coastline with huge seas and drenching rains and littering its beaches with evocative pieces of bleached driftwood. When it rains, you'll feel like you're inside a fishbowl; then the sun bursts out, and you'd swear you're in paradise. (With such changeable weather, it's essential to check local conditions before heading out for an excursion.) It's a country that has created a special breed of people, and the rough-hewn and powerfully independent locals—known to the rest of the country as coasters—occupy a special place in New Zealand folklore.

These three regions, which ring the north and west coasts of the South Island, offer an immense variety of scenery, from the siren seascapes of Marlborough Sounds and rocky Kaikoura to the mellow river valleys of Golden Bay and Abel Tasman National Park to the West Coast's colliding rain forests and glaciers, where the Southern Alps soar to 12,000 ft within 32 km (20 mi) of the shore.

Note: For more information on bicycling, fishing, hiking, and sea-kayaking in Upper South Island, *see* Chapter 6.

Pleasures and Pastimes

Dining

The top of the South Island is where you'll find some of the country's best seafood, fruit, and wine. In Marlborough check out at least one winery restaurant—there's no better way to ensure that your meal suits what you're drinking. Salmon and Greenshell mussels are both farmed in the pristine Marlborough Sounds, and local crops—besides grapes—include cherries, wasabi, and garlic. In Kaikoura try crayfish. The region is named after the delicacy (*kai* means food in Māori; *koura* means lobster), and you'll find it not only in restaurants but occasionally sold in makeshift vans or roadside sheds. On the West Coast, try whitebait fritters—a sort of omelet starring masses of baby fish, called *inanga* by Māori. One warning: restaurants and cafés around the glaciers can be quick to close their doors at night. Be there by 8:30, or you might go hungry.

CATEGORY	COST*
$$$$	over $25
$$$	$20–$25
$$	$15–$20
$	under $15

per person for a main course at dinner

Lodging

North Islanders might disagree, but you may find New Zealand's friendliest people in the rural areas of the South Island. And the best way to get to know them is to stay with them. Bed-and-breakfasts, farm stays, and homestays, all a variation on the same theme, abound in the South Island in some spectacular coastal or mountain settings. Your hosts will feed you great breakfasts and help with advice on where to eat and what to do locally. Other choices include luxury lodges and hotels, or inexpensive motel rooms—there are plenty of the latter.

CATEGORY	COST*
$$$$	over $200
$$$	$125–$200
$$	$80–$125
$	under $80

All prices are for a standard double room.

Mountains and Glaciers

The South Island is piled high with mountains. The massive Southern Alps mountain chain virtually slices the island lengthwise, and many outlying ranges spring up farther north. Most of the mountains are easily accessible. You can walk on and around them, ski, or catch a helicopter to land on a glacier and tramp around. Much of the skiing in the upper half of the South Island is reasonably challenging for intermediate skiers—the more advanced should look farther south.

Trekking and climbing are as challenging as you care to make them. Department of Conservation tracks and huts are spread around the region, and you can get details on hundreds of hikes from department offices or information centers. Even if you just want to take a casual, scenic walk, the opportunities are endless. In some places, such as the Kaikoura Coast Track, pioneering farmers have banded together to create farm-to-farm hiking trails. These take you through otherwise inaccessible mountains, bush, and coastal areas.

Wildlife

The West Coast is the habitat for some very interesting creatures. Tuatara, the last reptile of its kind, live on the protected Stephens Island in Marlborough Sounds. South by Lake Moeraki, you may see fiord-land crested penguins, and you'll have an even better chance of spotting New Zealand fur seals. On the other side of the island, along the Kaikoura Coast, you can get very close to whales, dolphins, and seals in the wild. There's abundant bird life up and down the coasts as well.

Wine

It took only a couple of decades for Marlborough to establish itself as one of the world's great wine-making regions. The local sunny-day–cool-night climate means grapes come off the vines plump with flavor, and that translates into wines with aromas that positively burst out of the glass. It's an exciting feistiness that some American connoisseurs consider too unbridled—but the wine is delicious, and you should seriously consider bringing a few bottles home. At any of the smaller wineries, it's quite likely you'll share your first taste of their labors with the wine makers themselves.

Exploring Upper South Island

Most people come to Marlborough and Nelson on the ferry to Picton, the northern entrance to the South Island. From here the choices open up before you. In four days you can see much of the northernmost part of the island. To undertake a walk on the Queen Charlotte, Abel Tasman, or Heaphy tracks, you'll need more time. For the West Coast three days is a bare minimum—it takes a half day just to get there.

Great Itineraries

Numbers in the text correspond to numbers in the margin and on the Upper South Island map.

IF YOU HAVE 2 DAYS

Spend a day touring the wineries in and around ☒ **Blenheim** ④. On the second day head down to ☒ **Kaikoura** ⑤, stopping at Winterhome garden on the way (call ahead for an appointment). Alternately, you could head straight from the ferry to ☒ **Nelson** ⑥, taking the first day in town and the second in ☒ **Abel Tasman National Park** ⑰, or the second visiting Nelson's wineries while following one of its unique arts-and-crafts or heritage trails.

IF YOU HAVE 4 DAYS

With four days you confront the kind of conundrum that makes trip planning for the South Island difficult. You can see the top of the island: relaxing ☒ **Nelson** ⑥, the wineries of ☒ **Blenheim** ④, the beautiful beaches and forests of ☒ **Abel Tasman National Park** ⑰ (perhaps all four days hiking one of Abel Tasman's tracks or the Queen Charlotte Track in the Marlborough Sounds). Or you can head straight for four days with the glaciers and wildlife of the West Coast.

IF YOU HAVE 7 DAYS

You *could* try to cover three of the major areas in this chapter—Marlborough, Nelson, and the West Coast, or Marlborough, Nelson, and Kaikoura, but allowing three or four days each for two areas is a better plan. Spend a day or two at the wineries, a day or two on the Marlborough Sounds sea-kayaking or walking, perhaps swinging through **Havelock** ③ on the way to or from the beautiful Kenepuru and Pelorus sounds, and then head to ☒ **Nelson** ⑥ or the West Coast.

Or spend the first three days in and around Nelson, looking at arts and crafts, following a heritage trail, tasting wine, and taking in ☒ **Abel Tasman National Park** ⑰ and **Golden Bay–Takaka** ⑱ area; then head to the West Coast. On the way down, stop at the town of Punakaiki for the

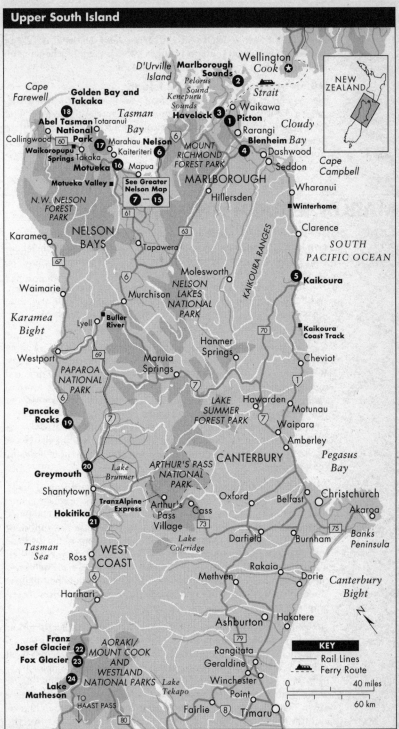

Upper South Island

Cape Farewell

Golden Bay and Takaka **18**

Abel Tasman National Park

Collingwood

Waikoropupu Springs

Motueka **16**

Takaka

17

Marahau

Kaiteriteri

Totaranui

Mapua

Motueka Valley

See Greater Nelson Map **7** — **15**

61

N.W. NELSON FOREST PARK

Karamea

NELSON BAYS

Waimarie

Karamea Bight

Westport

PAPAROA NATIONAL PARK

Pancake Rocks **19**

Greymouth **20**

Shantytown

TranzAlpine Express

Hokitika **21**

Tasman Sea

Ross

WEST COAST

Harihari

Franz Josef Glacier **22**

Fox Glacier **23**

Lake Matheson **24**

AORAKI/ MOUNT COOK AND WESTLAND NATIONAL PARKS

TO HAAST PASS

80

D'Urville Island

Marlborough Sounds

Pelorus Sound

Kenepuru Sounds

Havelock **3**

Tasman Bay

Nelson **6**

60

MOUNT RICHMOND FOREST PARK

MARLBOROUGH

Hillersden

63

Tapawera

Molesworth

NELSON LAKES NATIONAL PARK

Murchison

Lyell

Buller River

Maruia Springs

7

Hanmer Springs

6

LAKE SUMMER FOREST PARK

7

69

ARTHUR'S PASS NATIONAL PARK

Lake Brunner

Arthur's Pass Village

Cass

73

Lake Coleridge

Oxford

Darfield

Methven

Rakaia

CANTERBURY

Hawarden

Waipara

Amberley

Belfast

Burnham

Ashburton

79

Rangitata

Geraldine

Winchester

Point

Fairlie

8

Timaru

Lake Tekapo

Wellington

Cook Strait

Waikawa

Picton **1**

Rarangi

Blenheim **4**

Dashwood

Seddon

Cloudy Bay

Cape Campbell

Wharanui

Winterhome

Clarence

SOUTH PACIFIC OCEAN

Kaikoura **5**

70

Kaikoura Coast Track

Cheviot

1

Motunau

Pegasus Bay

Christchurch

Akaroa

75

Banks Peninsula

Dorie

Canterbury Bight

Hakatere

2

1

3

NEW ZEALAND

KEY

— Rail Lines

Ferry Route

0   40 miles

0   60 km

coastal phenomenon called **Pancake Rocks** ⑲. You could overnight at ⚇ **Greymouth** ⑳ or ⚇ **Hokitika** ㉑ before continuing to Westland National Park to get yourself on the ⚇ **Franz Josef Glacier** ㉒ or ⚇ **Fox Glacier** ㉓. Then head south to Haast, which has great beaches, and on to Wanaka or Queenstown via the Haast Pass.

When to Tour Upper South Island

Nelson and Marlborough are pleasant year-round, but beach activities are best from December to mid-April. Between December and early February is the busiest time on walking tracks, with New Zealanders setting out on their own vacations. Snow covers the mountains from June through October, which is a beautiful sight from seaside Kaikoura. The pleasures of winter weather around the West Coast glaciers—clear skies and no snow at sea level—are so far a well-kept local secret.

MARLBOROUGH AND KAIKOURA

The Marlborough Sounds were originally settled by seafaring Māori people, who in their day kept to the coastal areas, living off the abundant fruits of the sea. It's no wonder they didn't venture inland, because these coastal areas are spectacular. The Māori named the area Te Tau Ihu O Te Waka a Māui ("the prow of Maui's canoe"), as legend has it that from his canoe the trickster demigod Maui fished up the North Island with the jawbone of a whale. Consequently the North Island is called Te Ika a Māui—"the fish of Maui."

Captain James Cook met the Māori settlers around 1770, when he stopped in the sounds to repair his ships and take on fresh provisions. Whalers later set up shop in Queen Charlotte Sound, but it wasn't until the 1840s that *Pākehā* (foreigners) came to the Wairau and Awatere valleys around Blenheim. Thirty years later, the unwittingly prescient Charles Empson and David Herd began planting red muscatel grapes among local sheep and grain farms. Their modest viticultural torch was rekindled in the next century by the Freeth family, and by the 1940s Marlborough wineries were producing port, sherry, and Madeira most successfully.

At the same time, commercial wineries were growing up around Auckland and Hawke's Bay. But the volume of their grape production didn't meet their needs. In 1973 New Zealand's largest wine company, Montana, planted vines in Marlborough to increase the supply of New Zealand grapes. Other vintners followed suit, and within a decade today's major players—like Hunter's, whose founder, Ernie Hunter, almost single-handedly launched the Marlborough name—had established the region's international reputation. Marlborough now boasts New Zealand's single largest area under vine, and many local growers sell grapes to wine makers outside the area.

Down the coast from Blenheim, Kaikoura is another area that the Māori settled, the predominant tribe being Ngai Tahu. True to their seafaring heritage, they are active in today's whale-watching interests. Ngai Tahu was one of the first major Māori tribes to receive compensation from the New Zealand government—to the tune of $170 million—along with an apology for unjust confiscation of their lands and fishing areas. The tribe has extensive interests in tourism, fishing, and horticulture. Kaikoura's name denotes its original significance for the Māori—"to eat crayfish." These clean-tasting, clawless lobsters are a delight, and there are no better reasons to come to Kaikoura than to eat *kaikoura* and to take in the refreshing ocean air.

Picton

❶ *29 km (18 mi) north of Blenheim, 110 km (69 mi) east of Nelson.*

The maritime township of Picton lies at the head of Queen Charlotte Sound and is the arrival point for ferries from the North Island, as well as a growing number of international cruise ships. It plays a major role in providing services and transport by water taxi to a multitude of remote communities in the area of islands, peninsulas, and waterways that make up the Marlborough Sounds Maritime Park. With such an expansive watery environment, it is not surprising that Picton is a yachting mecca and has two sizable marinas, at Picton Harbour and at the adjacent Waikawa Bay. Along with the port of Havelock, these make up the second-largest marina complex in New Zealand. For information on deep-sea fishing out of Picton, *see* Chapter 6.

There's plenty to do in the township, with crafts markets during summer, historical sights to see, and walking tracks to scenic lookouts over the sounds. The township wraps around the harbor and is easy to traverse on foot. It has a good number of restaurants—seafood gets top billing—within easy reach of relatively reasonable inns.

❷ Picton is the base for cruising in the **Marlborough Sounds,** the labyrinth of waterways that was formed when the rising sea invaded a series of river valleys at the northern tip of the South Island. Backed by forested hills that at times rise almost vertically from the water, the sounds are a wild, majestic place edged with tiny beaches and rocky coves and studded with islands where such native wildlife as gannets and the primitive tuatara have remained undisturbed by introduced species. Māori legend says the sounds were formed when a great warrior and navigator called Kupe fought with a giant octopus. Its thrashings separated the surrounding mountains, and its tentacles became parts of the sunken valleys. These waterways are the country's second favorite for boating after the Bay of Islands, but for isolation and rugged grandeur they are in a class of their own.

Much of the area around Picton is a national park, and it has changed little since Captain Cook found refuge here in the 1770s. There are rudimentary roads on the long fingers of land jutting into the sounds, but the most convenient access is invariably by water. One of the best ways to discover the area is by hitching a ride in Havelock aboard the Pelorus Mail Boat, *Adventurer,* which delivers mail and supplies to outlying settlements scattered around Pelorus Sound.

To get your feet on the ground in and around the sounds, you can take any number of hikes on the **Queen Charlotte Track.** Starting northwest of Picton, the trail stretches 67 km (42 mi) south to north, playing hide-and-seek with the sounds along the way. Tramp through lush native forests filled with bird life, and stop here and there to swim or to pick up shells on the shore. Unlike along tracks such as the Abel Tasman in Golden Bay, there are no Department of Conservation huts to stay in, just a few points on the way for camping. There are other types of accommodation on the walk, however, from backpacking options to lodges, resorts, and homestays. Boats such as the *Cougar Line* can drop you off at various places for one- to four-day walks (guided or unguided), or you can kayak or bike parts of it.

For local and Queen Charlotte Track information, contact the **Picton Visitor Information Centre** (✉ Picton Foreshore, ☎ 03/573–7477, ℻ 03/573–5021). The **Department of Conservation** (✉ Box 161, Picton, ☎ 03/520–3002, 🆆🅴🅱 www.doc.govt.nz) is also a good resource.

Dining and Lodging

$$–$$$$ ✕ **Americano Restaurant.** Hanging ferns and blue-and-yellow table settings make this a cheerful spot. Try the succulent fresh fish of the day, served grilled, panfried, or poached in wine, lemon and lime juice, or the rib-eye steak with a creamy garlic sauce. Wind down with either the rich fudge cake or a drink at the upstairs bar. ⊠ *31 High St.,* ☎ *03/573–7040. AE, MC, V. BYOB. No lunch.*

$–$$ ✕ **Expresso House.** This sunny, friendly place rapidly established a reputation for both terrific quality and value. The lunch menu includes open sandwiches like spicy chicken on rye bread with lemon-caper sauce and made-from-scratch, regularly changing soups (try any with Thai flavors). At night the restaurant hits a bistro stride, with dishes like oven-baked local salmon with dill cream sauce or heartier options like Dutch sausage with *kūmara* (sweet potato) mash. There's a good selection of local wines, but you can BYOB as well. ⊠ *58 Auckland St.,* ☎ *03/573–7112. MC, V. Closed Wed.*

$$$$ ⌂ **Craglee Lodge.** On a hillside overlooking the emerald waters of the
★ Bay of Many Coves, this three-level complex is a perfect place to unwind. It's swathed in *punga* (tree ferns) and native bush and serenaded by bellbirds and *tūī.* Gary Lowe serves healthy fare from the sea and the region's produce and stocks some outstanding local wines. All the comfortable, contemporary en-suite rooms open onto balconies overlooking the bay. The two well-maintained tracks from the lodge are worth climbing for two reasons: the stunning views from Kenepuru Saddle and the free packed lunch. Take a 45-minute *Cougar Line* water taxi ride, possibly accompanied by dolphins, to get to this remote spot. ⊠ *Bay of Many Coves, Queen Charlotte Sound (Private Bag 407, Picton),* ☎ *03/579–9223,* FAX *03/579–9923,* WEB *www.lodgings. co.nz/craglee.html. 5 rooms, 2 with bath. Restaurant, outdoor hot tub, boating, fishing, lounge; no a/c, no room phones, no room TVs, no smoking. AE, DC, MC, V. FAP.*

$$$–$$$$ ⌂ **Punga Cove Resort.** A baker's dozen of chalets are tucked into the bush at this Queen Charlotte Track crossroads. The smaller A-frames have balconies, while a couple of larger, more luxurious two-bedroom chalets have wraparound decks; all share the serene vistas of Camp Bay and Endeavour Inlet. You can rent kayaks and dinghies on site, fishing trips can be arranged, and there is a small grocery market. Access is quickest by the *Cougar Line* water taxi, 45 minutes from Picton. Otherwise, a two-hour-plus drive winds along Queen Charlotte Sound Drive to the turnoff at Link Water, where you come through the spectacular scenery of the Kenepuru Sound via some 15 km (10 mi) of gravel road— this is wonderfully off the beaten path. ⊠ *Punga Cove, Endeavour Inlet, Queen Charlotte Sound (Rural Bag 408, Picton),* ☎ *03/579–8561 or 0800/809–697,* FAX *03/579–8080,* WEB *www.pungacove.co.nz. 13 chalets. Restaurant, pool, 2 bars; no a/c. AE, DC, MC, V.*

$$–$$$ ⌂ **The Gables.** Just a few minutes' walk from the ferry terminal you'll find this 1924 house, now a B&B. Enjoy a pre-dinner drink with hosts Annette and Peter Gardiner in the lounge, where there is a piano, a TV, and even a harp. Breakfast may include smoked-salmon pancakes with bananas or bacon and eggs. Two individual cottages behind the main house are ideal if you'd prefer more privacy. ⊠ *20 Waikawa Rd., Picton* ☎ *03/573–6772,* FAX *03/573–8860,* WEB *www.thegables.co.nz. 3 rooms, 2 cottages. Lounge; no a/c, no room phones, no TV in some rooms, no smoking. AE, MC, V. BP.*

$$ ⌂ **Ocean Ridge Seaside Holiday Apartment.** From this secluded spot overlooking Port Underwood Sound, you might catch sight of fur seals, penguins, dolphins, or even an orca. Every room in this contemporary, self-catered apartment has a sea view. The space includes a lounge, dining area, fully equipped kitchen, and three large bedrooms

each with private bath; the basic fee covers one bedroom, and each additional bedroom adds another $75. Several hiking trails wind through the 54-acre property. Port Underwood Road is partially unpaved, so allow 45 minutes from Blenheim, turning off at Tuamarina, or from Picton via Waikawa Bay. Also, you'll need to bring in your own groceries. ⊠ *Port Underwood Rd., Ocean Bay (Private Bag, Blenheim)*, ☎ *03/579–9474,* FAX *03/579–9474,* WEB *www.nmb.quik.co. nz/roush. 3 rooms. Outdoor hot tub, hiking, beach; no a/c, no kids under 10, no smoking. MC, V.*

$ 🖳 **Atlantis Backpackers.** Particularly convenient for divers, this hostel neighbors a dive shop and school, and it has its own indoor heated swimming pool for scuba training. It's close to the ferry terminal (free pickup can be arranged), and its rooms are clean and modern. ⊠ *Auckland St. and London Quay, Picton*, ☎ FAX *03/573–7390,* WEB *www.atlantishostel. co.nz. 8 single rooms, 9 double rooms, 2 dorms, 3 family units. Kitchen, pool, lounge, Internet, laundry facilities; no a/c, no room phones, no room TV, no smoking. MC, V.*

Outdoor Activities and Sports

Divers World (⊠ Auckland St. and London Quay, ☎ 03/573–7323, WEB www.pictondiversworld.co.nz) is a registered Scuba Schools International (SSI) training establishment with some of the best-value diving in the country. Dive trips depart daily, including one to the wreck of the cruise liner *Mikhail Lermontov* in the Outer Sounds.

En Route To take the long way to Blenheim, **Port Underwood Road** is yet another unbelievably scenic road in a country full of unbelievably scenic roads. There are picnic areas north of Waikawa before you reach the eastern coastal bays, and a couple more near Rarangi. Get on Waikawa Road north out of Picton and continue through the town of Waikawa; then turn south at Opihi Bay. You could also pick up the road driving north out of Rarangi.

Heading west out of Picton toward the town of Havelock, **Queen Charlotte Drive** rises spectacularly along the edge of Queen Charlotte Sound. It cuts across the base of the peninsula that separates this from Pelorus Sound, then drops into a coastal plain before coming to Havelock. Beyond town the road winds through forested river valleys before it rounds the eastern side of Tasman Bay and reaches Nelson. To start the drive from the InterIslander ferry terminal in Picton, turn right after leaving the parking lot and follow the signs.

About a third of the way to Havelock, **Governor's Bay** is a gorgeous spot for a picnic, a stroll along the forested shore.

Havelock

❸ *35 km (22 mi) west of Picton.*

Arguably the Greenshell mussel capital of the world, Havelock is at the head of the **Kenepuru and Pelorus sounds,** and trips around the sounds on the Pelorus Mail Boat, *Adventurer,* depart here. Locals will forgive you for thinking you've seen what the Marlborough Sounds are all about after crossing from the North Island to the South Island on the ferry—that's just a foretaste of better things to come. Small, seaside Havelock (population 400) is good to potter around in, looking at crafts and tucking into some of those mussels.

Dining

$–$$ ✗ **Mussel Boys Restaurant.** Outside, giant fiberglass mussels play rugby on the roof. Inside, the real things are served two ways—steamed for three minutes in the whole shell (steamers) and on the half shell (flats). Choose a light sauce for both steaming and topping: white wine, garlic, and fresh herbs; coconut, chili, and coriander; or even pesto with tomato and Parmesan cheese. Sauvignon blanc from nearby Marlborough perfectly pairs with almost any dish on the menu. ✉ *73 Main Rd.,* ☎ *03/574–2824. AE, DC, MC, V. Closed May–Sept.*

Blenheim

❹ *29 km (18 mi) south of Picton, 120 km (73 mi) southeast of Nelson, 129 km (80 mi) north of Kaikoura.*

Most people come to Blenheim (pronounced *bleh*-num by the locals) for one reason—wine. Most years, Marlborough boasts the highest total sunshine hours in New Zealand, and this daytime warmth combines with crisp, cool nights to give local grapes a long, slow ripening period. The smooth river pebbles that cover the best vineyards are a bonus—they reflect heat onto the ripening bunches. All these factors together create grapes with audacious flavors. Whites reign supreme. Cabernet sauvignon has mostly been pulled out following disappointing results, but recent examples of pinot noir have been pretty impressive.

In 1973 the Montana company paid two Californian wine authorities to investigate local grape-growing potential. Both were impressed with what they found. It was the locals who were skeptical—until they tasted the first wines produced.

There is no reason to race around to all the wineries here—if you do, chances are good that your taste buds won't serve you very well by the time you get to the 39th tasting room. Those mentioned below are among the country's notables, but you won't go wrong if you stop at any of the vineyards around Blenheim. Tastings are generally free. More than half of the wine bottled here is exported, particularly to the United Kingdom, although a few forward-thinkers are targeting the United States. If you've never tried a Marlborough wine, you have some great discoveries ahead of you.

The streets where most wineries are located are arranged more or less in a grid, which makes getting around relatively straightforward. Pick up a map of the Marlborough wine region at the **Marlborough Visitor Information Centre** (✉ The Old Railway Station, Sinclair St., along State Hwy. 1, ☎ 03/577–8080, ℻ 03/577–8079).

Not all the plantings around Blenheim are of grapevines, however. The gardens of **Winterhome** beautifully demonstrate the rules of traditional garden design and structure. Precise lines and patterns create a gracefully unified whole. Dwarf boxwood hedges surround a large, sunken garden filled with fragrant, white Margaret Merril roses, while a pathway takes you past sweeps of lavender boldly punctuated by evergreen spires. Benches appear in carefully chosen places: in a cool spot at the end of a long pathway or overlooking the Pacific. The views are orchestrated, too, framed with greenery or the span of an arched gateway. Be sure to stop in for a fabulous meal at the nearby restaurant, the **Store** (☞ Dining and Lodging, *below*). ✉ *State Hwy. 1, Kekerengu, 64 km (40 mi) south of Blenheim,* ☎ *03/575–8674,* ℻ *03/575–8620.* 🎫 *Small entry fee.* ☉ *By appointment.*

Wineries

Allan Scott Wines. Allan Scott helped establish the big-selling Stoneleigh label for Corbans, the country's second-biggest wine company, before launching his own company in 1990. Now he makes well-respected sauvignon blanc, chardonnay, pinot noir, and riesling. The tasting room is adjacent to a pleasant indoor-outdoor restaurant (open for lunch

NEWS FROM THE GRAPEVINE

NEW ZEALAND WINE is on a roll. Nine times in the last 12 years this tiny country has taken the sauvignon blanc trophy at London's annual International Wine and Spirits Competition. Similar accolades are being won all over the world, yet the history of top wine production here can be counted in decades, not generations.

There are nearly 400 wineries here, but only three produce more than 2 million liters. Because even the largest companies are small by international standards, management remains close to the wine-making process—with outstanding results. Passion for the product is evident in all the country's wineries, regardless of their size.

The country's long, narrow shape means that there are major differences between the grape-growing regions. This geographic diversity means that most of Europe's great grapes have found a second home somewhere in the country.

- Sauvignon blanc, particularly from Marlborough, is the export star. It's now noted for tropical fruit characters like passion fruit and pineapple.

- Chardonnay grows well all over the country. Left to its own devices, it has a citric, melonlike flavor, but wine makers love to work their magic on it. Barrel fermentation adds a graininess, and wood-aging gives it spiciness and, sometimes, a hint of vanilla.

- Riesling is a gentle variety, with a floral, lightly scented bouquet and fruity taste. Most local versions have at least a touch of sweetness.

- Gewürztraminer is the most distinctive grape variety of them all, with a superspicy bouquet reminiscent of litchis and cloves. Many of the best Kiwi examples come from Gisborne, but a couple of exceptional versions have come out of Hawke's Bay and Martinborough.

- Originally from Alsace, pinot gris is an up-and-coming variety in New Zealand. At its best, it produces wine with delightfully grainy character and loads of honest flavor.

- Deutz, the international Champagne house, has established itself in Marlborough, another major success story.

- In the red corner, cabernet sauvignon is well suited to warmer parts of New Zealand. Most years, it performs best in Hawke's Bay and on Waiheke Island, in Auckland's Hauraki Gulf, but when conditions are right, good examples have also come from West Auckland and as far south as Nelson. It is often blended with merlot and cabernet franc.

- Merlot was first used in blends, to fill what was seen as a "flavor hole" in the mid-palate of Kiwi cabernet. Now more and more wine makers are bottling it on its own. It has leather-coffee-tobacco undertones that are often summed up as "British gentleman's club."

- Long considered a stumbling block, pinot noir has recently been working well for many wine makers across the country. It's often described in red-fruit terms, with notes of strawberries, cherries, and plums.

In an increasingly heated wine trade, vintners are pulling out all the corks to bring their vintages to the public's attention. But are they corks? In fact, the time-honored bottle stopper is under attack by some New Zealand estates. Frustrated by faulty natural cork, a handful of top wine makers have made the move to screw caps—so you shouldn't automatically shudder if there's no corkscrew required.

only). ✉ *Jackson's Rd., R.D. 3, Blenheim,* ☎ *03/572–9054,* FAX *03/572–9053,* WEB *www.allanscott.com.* ☉ *Daily 9:30–5.*

Cloudy Bay Vineyards. From the start, Kevin Judd produced first-class sauvignon blanc, and an equally impressive chardonnay was added to the portfolio soon afterward. That was the intention of Australia's Cape Mentelle Vineyards when it got Cloudy Bay up and running in 1985. Its sauvignon blancs are consistently highly rated for their notes of citrus, pear, and passion fruit; these are generally ready for immediate drinking. The chardonnay is more complex and can take medium-term cellaring. ✉ *Jackson's Rd., Blenheim,* ☎ *03/520–9140,* FAX *03/520–9040,* WEB *www.cloudybay.co.nz.* ☉ *Daily 10–4:30; tours by appointment.*

Highfield Estate. Arches, tiles, and a terra-cotta plaster finish mark this building as an unashamed imitation of Tuscan style. From its hilltop there are spectacular views all the way to the North Island. The small but select range of wines spans sauvignon blanc, pinot noir, chardonnay, and riesling. At the superb restaurant, try the Monte Cristo sandwich with rhubarb-plum sauce, along with a fine merlot—it almost matches the view for excellence. ✉ *Brookby Rd., R.D. 2, Blenheim,* ☎ *03/572–9244,* FAX *03/572–9257,* WEB *www.highfield.co.nz.* ☉ *Daily 10–5.*

Hunter's Wines. Ernie Hunter's marketing skills pushed Marlborough into the international spotlight; after his tragic death, his wife, Jane, with wine maker Gary Duke, forged ahead and expanded the vineyard to 2½ times its original size. They have a reputation for remarkable wines, including an oak-aged sauvignon blanc, and have won dozens of awards. Likewise, the winery's restaurant is worth seeking out (☞ Dining and Lodging, *below*). ✉ *Rapaura Rd., Blenheim,* ☎ *03/572–8489,* FAX *03/572–8457,* WEB *hunters.co.nz.* ☉ *Daily 9:30–4:30.*

Seresin Estate. Named for owner Michael Seresin, a New Zealand–born filmmaker, this estate stands out by virtue of its organic viticulture. Wine makers Brian Bicknell and Gordon Ritchie pursue high standards of environmentally friendly cultivation, and they test less-utilized varietals in addition to their plantings of sauvignon blanc, chardonnay, pinot gris, pinot noir, and riesling. They also produce extra-virgin olive oil from their acres of olive trees. The unusual signature handprint label was inspired by early French cave drawings. ✉ *Bedford Rd., Blenheim,* ☎ *03/572–9408,* FAX *03/572–9850,* WEB *www.seresin.co.nz.* ☉ *Nov.–Mar., daily 10–4:30; Apr.–Oct., weekdays 10–4:30*

Vavasour Wines. An almost instant hit among Marlborough's mid-1980s start-ups, the small, extremely conscientious wine-making operation at Vavasour produces sensitively balanced whites and reds. Based on the quality of a given year's harvest, grapes will be used either for Reserve vintages available in limited quantities or the medium-price-range Dashwood label. Vavasour is in its own microclimate, in the Awatere Valley south of Blenheim. You won't taste as many varieties here, but what you taste will be interesting and very well crafted. ✉ *Redwood Pass Rd., Awatere Valley, 20 km (12 mi) south of Blenheim,* ☎ *03/575–7481,* FAX *03/575–7240,* WEB *www.vavasour.com.* ☉ *Oct.–Mar., daily 10–5; Apr.–Sept., Mon.–Sat. 10–4; tours by appointment.*

Wairau River Wines. Phil and Chris Rose were the first contract grape growers in Marlborough. Now they produce a very good range of classic Marlborough-grown wines under their own label. The tasting room is made from mud bricks; it also serves as a restaurant, concentrating on local produce. Try the multi-award-winning sauvignon blanc and, if it's available, the startlingly good, sweet riesling, made in some years from grapes infected with the mold the French call the "noble rot." ✉ *Rapaura Rd. and State Hwy. 6, Blenheim,* ☎ *03/572–9800,* ℻ *03/572–9885,* WEB *www.wairauriverwines.com.* ☉ *Daily 10–5.*

Dining and Lodging

\$\$\$\$ ✗ **Bellafico Caffé & Wine Bar.** Start the day here with fresh fruit on crunchy granola, or savory waffles with sliced banana, maple syrup, and crispy bacon. Later, choose a pizza—with chorizo, olives, tomato, and basil, for one—or share a meze platter with smoked beef, gherkins, tapenade, pickles, and cheese. The kitchen uses wild venison whenever it can get it and if you're a meat lover, you can follow that with sautéed pork medallions and red cabbage with orange-walnut marmalade. ✉ *17 Maxwell Rd.,* ☎ *03/577–6076. AE, DC, MC, V.*

\$\$\$–\$\$\$\$ ✗ **Bacchus.** Marcel Rood has cooked at Michelin-starred restaurants in Europe and done the rounds of top kitchens in New Zealand. Now he's settled in wine country—and loving it. His restaurant has a romantic and sumptuous feel, with rich burgundy walls and lots of velvet. A fountain (of Bacchus—who else?) occupies center stage in the small courtyard, and inside an open fire keeps things cozy in winter. Marcel makes good use of New Zealand produce in dishes like bacon-wrapped beef fillet on kūmara mash. ✉ *3 Main St.,* ☎ ℻ *03/578–8099. AE, MC, V. No lunch.*

\$\$\$–\$\$\$\$ ✗ **Rocco's.** Skeins of garlic and dozens of chianti bottles hang from the roof trusses here; in winter an open fire with a spit provides both warmth and atmosphere. Try the spaghetti alla marinara, with mussels, prawns, scallops, fish, and garlic butter—the fish is fresh off the boat. The helpings are more than generous, but you're welcome to share dessert. Look for the delicious Marlborough cherries marinated in brandy and served with vanilla ice cream. The wine list covers most of the local labels and includes several Italian imports. ✉ *5 Dodson St.,* ☎ ℻ *03/578–6940. AE, DC, MC, V. Closed Sun.*

\$\$\$ ✗ **d'Urville Wine Bar and Brasserie.** On the ground floor of the Hotel d'Urville, this long, narrow restaurant serves everything from a cup of coffee to a delightful dinner based on local produce. Local seafood is a strong suit, with dishes such as Marlborough mussels steamed in a fragrant, herbal black bean and tomato broth. ✉ *52 Queen St.,* ☎ *03/577–9945. AE, DC, MC, V. No lunch weekends.*

\$\$\$ ✗ **Hunter's Vineyard Restaurant.** Dining at a vineyard is a great way
★ to appreciate how seriously the best New Zealand wine makers have food in mind when they create their wine. Local produce stars at this pleasant indoor-outdoor eatery. Marlborough Greenshell mussels, steamed open in Hunter's Riesling with wild thyme and garlic, are a great match for a glass of that same riesling. Dishes like double-braised lamb shanks with rosemary potatoes may tempt you to try one of the Hunter's reds. They're leaner and greener than North Island examples, but they go well with the local food. ✉ *Rapaura Rd.,* ☎ *03/572–8803. AE, DC, MC, V. No dinner Mon.–Wed.*

\$\$\$ ✗ **Paysanne.** This bright and breezy central restaurant is a popular meeting place for Blenheimites. The food is modern New Zealand café style, which means you can choose from a simple snack to a full-blown three-courser. The pizzas, fresh out of the wood-fired oven, have a big local following—tandoori chicken is the biggest-selling topping. At night, look for the likes of pan-seared pork paupiette, stuffed with roasted pear and mint, served with sweet potato rösti (shredded and fried) and wilted spinach. ✉ *The Forum, Market Place,* ☎ *03/577–6278. AE, DC, MC, V. No lunch Sun.*

\$\$–\$\$\$ ✗ **The Store.** Susan and Richard Macfarlane of Winterhome have
★ branched out and built a one-stop store and café below their notable

gardens. The space uses natural wood and displays interesting pot plants, barrels, and an open fireplace. On this dramatic perch at the edge of the Pacific, the waves almost reach the open deck. From a blackboard menu, choose a lunch of fresh seafood or chicken and avocado salad, with a glass of local wine. ⊠ *State Hwy. 1, Kekerengu, 64 km (40 mi) south of Blenheim,* ☎ *03/575–8600,* FAX *03/575–8620. MC, V.*

$–$$ ✕ **Paddy Barry's Bar and Restaurant.** Locals come here for a chat and a beer, and the menu is casual, straightforward, and very well priced. In other words, it's a good place to come down from traveler's stomach and overenthusiastic gourmandizing—a local peril. Pair a plate of battered and fried seafood with a well-poured Guinness. You'll find Guinness *in* the food, too, in the form of a beef 'n' Guinness hot pot. ⊠ *51 Scott St.,* ☎ *03/578–7470. AE, DC, MC, V.*

$$$ ✕ The Marlborough. The art deco–inspired furnishings and contemporary New Zealand art throughout this hotel are enhanced by a color scheme that seems to emulate the region's ripening produce, its brilliant sun, and the blue-green waters of the Marlborough Sounds. The hotel is on the edge of town, opposite the Wairau River on the road to Nelson. Most rooms are deluxe, with high, *rimu*-wood ceilings and super-king-size beds; two standard rooms have queen-size beds. Suites have whirlpool baths. The restaurant is worth seeking out for dishes like pan-fried terakihi (a whitefish) over winter greens with a zingy, peppery sauce. It's open to nonguests for dinner only; you'll need to make a reservation. ⊠ *20 Nelson St.,* ☎ *03/577–7333,* FAX *03/577–7337,* WEB *www. themarlborough.co.nz. 24 rooms, 4 suites. Restaurant, some in-room hot tubs, pool, bar; no a/c, no smoking. AE, DC, MC, V.*

$$$$ The Hotel d'Urville. Every room is unique in this modern boutique hotel
★ in the old Public Trust building. You could choose the Raja Room, with its sari-draped main bed and a carved Javanese day bed; the room with an African theme; or the sensory trip of the Color Room. One room matches the overall travel theme of the hotel and is based on the exploits of Dumont d'Urville, who made voyages to the Pacific and the Antarctic in the 1820s and 1830s. There is a separate, relaxing house bar as well as the excellent restaurant (☞ *above*). ⊠ *52 Queen St., Blenheim,* ☎ *03/577–9945,* FAX *03/577–9946,* WEB *www.durville.co.nz. 11 rooms. Restaurant, bar; no a/c, no smoking. AE, DC, MC, V.*

$$$$ Le Grys Vineyard Cottage. If wine has brought you to Marlborough, you could truly immerse yourself with a stay in the heart of a vineyard. Waterfall Lodge, a mud-brick cottage, sits next to a brook in the midst of rows of grapevines. Its rooms are light and homey; the main bedroom has a canopied queen-size bed. Le Grys focuses on sauvignon blanc, chardonnay, and pinot noir; naturally, a wine tasting is part of the welcome. Various activities can also be arranged. ⊠ *Conders Bend Rd., Renwick, 12 km (7 mi) west of Blenheim,* ☎ *03/572–9490,* FAX *03/572–9491,* WEB *www.legrys.co.nz. 1 cottage. Indoor pool; no a/c, no room phones, no room TVs, no smoking. MC, V. BP.*

$$$$ Timara Lodge. This 1923 house was built as a rural retreat; its craftsmanship, skilled used of native timber, and luxurious decor evoke an elegant past. The gardens extend over 20 acres with rhododendrons, camellias, and a carpet of spring bulbs. One of the hosts doubles as the chef, preparing terrific meals based on local ingredients, such as a rack of lamb with baked eggplant, beetroot relish, and mint aïoli. Wine tours, trout fishing, sea-kayaking, golf, skiing, even whale-watching (an hour and a half away in Kaikoura) can be arranged for you. ⊠ *Dog Point Rd., R.D. 2, Blenheim,* ☎ *03/572–8276,* FAX *03/572–9191,* WEB *www.timara.co.nz. 4 rooms. Pond, pool, tennis court; no room TVs, no kids, no smoking. AE, DC, MC, V. MAP.*

Kaikoura

5 *129 km (81 mi) south of Blenheim, 182 km (114 mi) north of Christchurch.*

The town of Kaikoura sits on a rocky protrusion on the east coast, backed by an impressive mountainous upthrust. There is plenty of local crayfish to be had at roadside stalls, which is an excellent reason to come here, but an even better one is sighting the sperm whales that frequent the coast in greater numbers than anywhere else on earth. The sperm whale, the largest toothed mammal, can reach a length of 60 ft and a weight of 70 tons. The reason for the whales' concentration in this area is the abundance of squid—among other species, the giant squid of seafaring lore—which is their main food. Scientists speculate that the whales use a form of sonar to find the squid, which they then bombard with deep, powerful sound waves generated in the massive cavities in the fronts of their heads. Their hunting is all the more remarkable considering that much of it is done at great depths, in darkness. The whales' food source swims in the trench just off the continental shelf, barely a kilometer (½ mi) off Kaikoura. You are most likely to see the whales between October and August.

Fyffe House is Kaikoura's oldest surviving building, erected soon after Robert Fyffe's whaling station was established in 1842. Built on whalebone piles, the house provides a look at what life was like when people aimed at whales with harpoons rather than cameras. ⊠ *62 Avoca St.,* ☎ *03/319–5835.* ☞ *$5.* ☉ *Daily 10–5.*

The Kaikoura Peninsula has two **walks**—not to be confused with the Kaikoura Coast Track—that are particularly worthwhile, considering the town's spectacular coastal scenery: the cliff-top walk, from which you can look over seal colonies, and the longer shoreline walk, which takes you much closer to the colonies. Consult the town's information center about tides to avoid getting flooded out of certain parts of the walks. ⊠ *Walks start at end of Fyffe Quay.*

★ **Lavendyl Lavender Farm.** Just off the main highway a few minutes' drive north of the town center, rows of lavender stretch out against the stunning backdrop of Mt. Fyffe and the Seaward Kaikouras. Mike and Maureen Morris run a working 5-acre farm; the blooms are harvested in late January and early February. Walk through the heaven-scent gardens, and then head for the shop, where bunches of lavender hang from the ceiling. If you can't tear yourself away, you can stay overnight (☞ *Dylan's Country Cottages, below*). ⊠ *Postmans Rd.,* ☎ *03/319–5473,* WEB *www.lavenderfarm.co.nz.* ☞ *$2.* ☉ *Daily 10–4.*

On the first Saturday of October Kaikoura celebrates its annual **Seafest,** during which the best of this coastal area's food, wine, and beer is served up while top New Zealand entertainers perform on an outdoor stage. Tickets are available from the town's information center.

Dining and Lodging

$$$–$$$$ ✕ **White Morph Restaurant.** Once the first bank of Kaikoura, this
★ building now sees runs on seafood specialties. Crayfish is always on the menu, but there are plenty of alternatives, such as wild venison, lamb loin, ostrich, and at least one vegetarian dish. The desserts are to die for, too. Locally made gilded mirrors and marine art fill the walls, but the best scenes are the seaside views from the front windows. ⊠ *92–94 the Esplanade,* ☎ *03/319–5676. AE, DC, MC, V.*

$$–$$$$ ✕ **The Craypot.** This casual and modern café relies strongly, as the name suggests, on the local delicacy. Crayfish isn't cheap, but this kitchen sure knows how to prepare it. Other types of seafood also figure large

on the menu, and if you feel like a change you can choose from several variations on the steak, chicken, and lamb themes. Homemade desserts are worth leaving room for. In summer you can get a table outdoors; in winter an open fire roars at night. ✉ *70 West End Rd.,* ☎ *03/319–6027. AE, DC, MC, V.*

\$\$–\$\$\$ ✕ **Hislops Café.** Homey and wholesome Hislops is a few minutes' walk north of town and well worth the trip, especially when the sun streams in the windows. In the morning you'll find tasty eggs and bacon, plus baked whole-grain bread served with marmalade or honey. The imaginative lunch and dinner menus are all based on organic ingredients. On fine days eat outside on the veranda. It's open all day, every day. ✉ *Main Hwy.,* ☎ *03/319–6971. AE, DC, MC, V.*

\$\$ ✕🖭 **Donegal House.** The name refers to owner Murray Boyd's home county; life-size statues of his ancestors stud the parklike grounds. The units are all modern and spacious, but the real attraction is the Irish bar and restaurant, where posters and photographs of "Auld Oireland" cover the paneled walls. Tuck into local crayfish with garlic or fresh lime and caper butter, followed by a Guinness or three while you listen to traditional music. ✉ *School House Rd.,* ☎ 🅵🅰🆇 *03/319–5083,* 🆆🅴🅱 *www.donegalhouse.co.nz. 10 rooms. Restaurant, pond, pub; no a/c, no room phones, no room TVs, no smoking. AE, MC, V. BP.*

\$\$\$ 🖭 **Old Convent.** It's easy to get into the habit of staying at this former convent. Built in 1911, it's now protected by the Historic Trust, and the interiors still reveal its past. The lounge, for instance, used to be a chapel and still has a cathedral ceiling and an ornate wrought-iron stairwell that winds down to a reception area. Rooms have high ceilings and ornately flowered carpet; some have fireplaces. The two queen bedrooms have great views over the Kaikoura Ranges. The owners, John and Dominique Rooth, speak French, Dutch, and Spanish between them. The convent is a few minutes' drive out of town, but a courtesy car is available. ✉ *Mt. Fyffe Rd.,* ☎ *03/319–6603 or 0800/365–603,* 🅵🅰🆇 *03/ 319–6660,* 🆆🅴🅱 *www.theoldconvent.co.nz. 17 rooms, 15 with bath. Restaurant, croquet, bicycles, some pets allowed; no a/c, no room phones, no room TVs, no smoking. AE, DC, MC, V. BP.*

\$\$ 🖭 **Dylan's Country Cottages.** A pair of timber-clad cottages perch at the edge of the Lavendyl Lavender Farm. Both make special use of their gardens; Kowhai's private garden virtually extends its living room, while Mahoe has an open-air bath and shower (in addition to its standard bath). The cottages' upstairs bedrooms have balconies looking onto the Seaward Kaikoura mountains; their living rooms, kitchens, dining areas, and bathrooms are downstairs. Breakfast is delivered to the door. ✉ *Postmans Rd., R.D. 1,* ☎ *03/319–5473,* 🅵🅰🆇 *03/319–5425,* 🆆🅴🅱 *www. dylanscottages.co.nz. 2 cottages. Kitchens; no a/c, no room phones, no room TVs, no smoking. MC, V. BP.*

\$\$ 🖭 **White Morph Motor Inn.** A waterfront view is hard to ignore—even more so on the rugged Kaikoura coast. This contemporary motel-style inn is in a great spot just opposite the beach, and its two foremost suites get the best views of the sea. Of the 19 self-contained units, 12 are studios, 4 are luxury suites with king-size beds and double whirlpool baths, and 3 others are two-bedroom apartments with lounges and kitchens downstairs, two bedrooms upstairs. Upstairs rooms have decks from which you can enjoy views of the magnificent Kaikoura Ranges, and downstairs units have courtyards. You can book local activities from here, and the inn's restaurant is in a historic building next door. ✉ *92– 94 the Esplanade,* ☎ *03/319–5014,* 🅵🅰🆇 *03/319–5015,* 🆆🅴🅱 *www. whitemorph.co.nz. 12 rooms, 4 suites, 3 apartments. Some kitchens, minibars, microwaves; no a/c, no smoking. AE, DC, MC, V.*

\$ 🖭 ⚠ **Kaikoura Holiday Park.** A short walk from town, this well-priced, nicely laid-out site has spotless facilities. There are both cabins and campsites, plus an on-site caravan. Four of the cabins have showers; all of the campsites have electricity. There's even a TV in the communal kitchen. The breathtaking view of the Seaward Kaikouras is priceless. ⊠ *69 Beach Rd.,* ☎ 𝔽𝔸𝕏 *03/319–6275,* 𝕎𝔼𝔹 *www.holidayparks.co.nz. 6 cabins, 30 campsites. Grills, kitchen, playground, laundry facilities; no a/c, no room phones, no room TVs, no smoking. MC, V.*

Outdoor Activities and Sports

Whale-watching and swimming with dolphins or seals are both extremely popular in December and January, so either avoid Kaikoura at those times or book well in advance. To keep your feet on terra firma, the three-day Kaikoura Coast Track is a great way to see a spectacular mix of rugged coastline, pioneering farms, and mountain scenery.

HIKING

The descendants of two Scottish pioneering families—the Caverhills and Macfarlanes, who settled the huge 57,000-acre Hawkswood Range in 1860—have opened up their farms and homes to travelers. The three-day **Kaikoura Coast Track** walk combines uncrowded hiking—10 people at a time maximum—and farm hospitality. Take binoculars to search out sea life like whales and dolphins.

Warm, clean cottages with kitchens and hot baths or showers are at the end of each day's hike. You can have a meal with your hosts on weekdays or buy fresh farm produce to prepare yourself. Breakfast and lunches are also available. The first night is at Hawkswood in the historic sheep station setting of the **Staging Post,** where host J. D. Macfarlane has a passion for Shakespeare and old stagecoaches. Accommodations are in rustic mud-brick or log cabins. A challenging five- to six-hour walk the next day will take you to **Ngaroma,** Heather and Bruce Macfarlane's 3,000-acre sheep and cattle farm. The Loft has a large lounge with a log fire and rooms that each sleep up to four people. The next day's hike is along the beach, passing an ancient buried forest before heading across farmland to an area of regenerating bush. Around the dinner table at **Medina,** where you'll spend the third night in either Te Whare or the Garden Cottage (better for couples), you might meet David Handyside's father, Miles, who settled the 1,600-acre sheep and cattle farm in 1945. The final day, a demanding four- to five-hour walk takes you over the 2,000-ft-plus Mt. Wilson, with its breathtaking views of the Waiau River and the Kaikoura Ranges.

The fee for walking the track is $120 per person, and a guided walk can be arranged. If you opt to have all meals included and need bedding, the total cost is $181 per day. Bookings are essential. The track is a ¾-hour drive south of Kaikoura on State Highway 1. Shuttles or buses can drop you at the gate. ⊠ *Medina, R.D. Parnassus, North Canterbury,* ☎ *03/319–2715,* 𝔽𝔸𝕏 *03/319–2724,* 𝕎𝔼𝔹 *www.kaikouratrack. co.nz.* ☉ *Daily Oct.–Apr.*

SWIMMING WITH DOLPHINS AND SEALS

On seal and dolphin encounters, guides can prime you with information on the local species as you get an incomparable up-close view. Wet suits and other gear are provided. Fur seals are common, and you might also spot an octopus or crayfish. Pods of dusky dolphins stay in the area year-round; you may even see them doing aerial jumps and flips. **Top Spot Seal Swims** (☎ 03/319–5540) has two trips daily November–April, $50 per person. **Seal & Swim Kaikoura** (☎ 03/319–6182, 𝔽𝔸𝕏 03/319–6186, 𝕎𝔼𝔹 www.kaikoura.co.nz/sealswim) has three trips daily November–April, $50 per person. **Dolphin Encounters** (☎ 03/319–6777, 𝔽𝔸𝕏 03/319–6534, 𝕎𝔼𝔹 www.dolphin.co.nz) arranges dolphin swims two or three times a day year-round for $95 per person.

WHALE-WATCHING

Whale Watch™ Kaikoura Ltd. Whale Watch is owned by the Ngai Tahu *iwi* (tribe). Since arriving in the Kaikoura area in AD 850, Ngai Tahu, the predominant South Island Māori iwi, claims to have lived and worked based on a philosophy of sustainable management and sensible use of natural resources. Having worked these waters since 1987, Whale Watch skippers can recognize individual whales and adjust operations, such as the boat's proximity to the whale, accordingly. Allow 3½ hours for the whole experience, 2½ hours on the water.

Book in advance: 7 to 10 days November–April, 3 to 4 days at other times. Trips depend on the weather, and should your tour miss seeing a whale, which is rare, you will get up to an 80% refund of your fare. Take motion-sickness pills if you suspect you'll need them: even in calm weather, the sea around Kaikoura often has a sizable swell. ⊠ *Whaleway Station, Box 89, Kaikoura,* ☎ *03/319–6767 or 0800/655–121,* FAX *03/319–6545,* WEB *www.whalewatch.co.nz.* ⌨ *$110. AE, MC, V.*

Wings over Whales. If you'd rather get above the action, take a half-hour whale-viewing flight. From a nine-seater Islander, you'll have a bird's-eye view of the giant sperm whales' immensity. While searching for other whales' telltale water spouts, the pilot and copilot provide informative commentary on the creatures' habits. The trick is to stay glued to your window—which isn't hard, because at least half the time, with the plane banked in an almost perpetual circle, gravity ensures that your face is just about stuck to it. Children's fares are significantly less than the standard fee, just $75. ⊠ *Peketa Airfield, State Hwy. 1, Kaikoura,* ☎ *03/319–6580 or 0800/226–269,* FAX *03/319–6668,* WEB *www.whales.co.nz.* ⌨ *$135. AE, DC, MC, V.*

Marlborough and Kaikoura A to Z

AIR TRAVEL

The very scenic flight from Wellington to Blenheim takes about a half hour. Air New Zealand Link has 10 departures to and from Wellington daily. From Wellington, Soundsair makes the half-hour trip to Picton a few times daily from May to October and at least seven times a day from October through April.

➤ CARRIERS: **Air New Zealand Link** (☎ 04/474–8950, WEB www.airnewzealand.co.nz). **Soundsair** (☎ 03/573–6184, 04/801–0111, or 0800/505–005, WEB www.soundsair.co.nz).

AIRPORTS

Blenheim Airport (BHE) is quite close to town; you can hop a shuttle bus for a roughly 10-minute ride into Blenheim. Soundsair operates Picton's Koromiko Airport (PCN); this is also within 10 minutes of town and has shuttle bus service.

➤ CONTACTS: **Blenheim Airport** (☎ 03/572–9899). **Koromiko Airport** (☎ 04/801–0111).

BOAT AND FERRY TRAVEL

InterIsland Line runs vehicle and passenger ferries between Wellington and Picton. The one-way adult fare ranges from $24 to $49 depending on the time of year. The fare for a medium-size sedan ranges from $88 to $175. The crossing takes about three hours and can be very rough. InterIsland's slightly more expensive ferry, the *Lynx,* also runs the whole year and does the journey in 135 minutes. There are two departures in each direction every day, and bookings should be made in advance, particularly during holiday periods. The one-way adult fare ranges from $32 to $63, and the fare for a medium-size sedan ranges from $100 to $199, again depending on time of travel. The ferry docks in Picton at the town wharf.

➤ BOAT AND FERRY INFORMATION: **InterIsland Line** (☎ 0800/802–802, WEB www.theinterislander.co.nz).

BUS TRAVEL

InterCity runs service between Christchurch and Kaikoura, Picton, and Blenheim a couple of times a day. The ride between Christchurch and Blenheim takes about five hours, from Christchurch to Picton closer to six hours. A trip between Kaikoura and Christchurch runs 2 hours and 40 minutes. Blenheim, Picton, and Kaikoura don't have separate bus depots. At Blenheim, buses stop at the train station; at Picton, they use the ferry terminal as a hub. In Kaikoura, southbound buses stop at the parking lot by the Craypot restaurant, northbound buses at the Sleepy Whale.

➤ BUS LINE: **InterCity** (☎ 03/577–8080, WEB www.intercitycoach.co.nz).

CAR RENTAL

Most rental agencies have North Island–South Island transfer programs for their vehicles: leave one car off in Wellington and pick another one up in Picton on the same contract. It is common practice, quickly and easily done. If you initiate a rental in Picton, Avis, Budget, and Hertz have offices at the ferry terminal.

➤ AGENCIES: **Avis** (☎ 03/573–6363). **Budget** (☎ 03/573–6081). **Hertz** (☎ 03/573–7224).

CAR TRAVEL

Driving your own car is the most unrestricted way of seeing the area, but you'll need to take extra care on the roads, as even the highways can be quite narrow. One-way bridges are common in this area, and occasionally these include railway tracks. You may also find yourself behind a slow-moving sheep truck for a while before finding a place to pass. Allow plenty of time for travel and enjoy the ride—the countryside around the main roads is often beautiful. If you plan to do a wine tasting or two, remember that driving under the influence is not tolerated and generally carries a hefty fine at least. Blenheim is a 25-minute drive from the ferry terminal in Picton and just less than a two-hour drive from Nelson to the west and Kaikoura to the south.

EMERGENCIES

➤ EMERGENCY SERVICES: **Fire, police, and ambulance** (☎ 111).

TOURS

BOAT TOURS

The Pelorus mail boat, *Adventurer,* a small launch that makes a day-long trip around Pelorus Sound, is one of the best ways to discover the waterway and meet its residents. The boat leaves from Havelock, west of Picton, Tuesday, Thursday, and Friday at 9:30 AM and returns in the late afternoon. The fare is $70. For reservations, contact Beachcomber Cruises or the Havelock Outdoor Centre.

Beachcomber Cruises can take you to and from any point on the Queen Charlotte Walkway for one-day or longer unguided walks. Boats depart at 10:15 and 2:15 from the Picton waterfront and charge around $32.

The Cougar Line runs scheduled trips from Picton through the Queen Charlotte Sounds four times daily, dropping passengers (sightseers included) at accommodations, private homes, or other points. A Queen Charlotte drop-off and pickup service costs $50 for multiday hikes, $48 for day hikes that end at Furneaux Lodge. Water-taxi service to area lodges costs from $15 to $45, depending on distances.

Marlborough Sounds Adventure Company has one- and four-day guided kayak tours of the sounds, leaving from Picton, as well as kayak rentals for experienced paddlers. The cost is $85 for a one-day guided tour and $445 for a three-day guided tour, including water transportation, food, and camping equipment. A kayak rental costs $50 per person per day.

Mussel Farm Cruises will take you into the largely untouched Kenepuru and Pelorus sounds, which are part of the labyrinth of waterways comprising the Marlborough Sounds. The world's largest production of Greenshell mussels is done in the sounds, and guides Ed Knowles and John Laird run a daily four-hour cruise from Havelock to visit farms where the mussels are at varying stages of development. You can even get in and swim with them. The 40-ft M.V. *Mavis* is a 1919 kauri-wood launch. The tours cost $49.

➤ TOUR INFORMATION: **Beachcomber Cruises** (✉ Beachcomber Pier, Town Wharf [Box 12, Picton], ☎ 03/573–6175, FAX 03/573–6176). **Cougar Line** (✉ Picton Wharf, ☎ 03/573–7925 or 0800/504–090, FAX 03/573–7926, WEB www.cougarlinecruises.co.nz). **Havelock Outdoor Centre** (✉ 65A Main Rd., Havelock, ☎ FAX 03/574–2114). **Marlborough Sounds Adventure Company** (✉ The Waterfront, London Quay, Picton, ☎ 03/573–6078, FAX 03/573–8827, WEB www.marlboroughsounds.co.nz). **Mussel Farm Cruises** (✉ Havelock Outdoor Centre, 65A Main Rd., Havelock, ☎ FAX 03/574–2114).

FISHING TOURS

The Sounds Connection, a family-run tour company, offers half-day and full-day fishing trips. They leave from Picton; a half day runs $59. They'll supply all the necessary gear and fillet your catch.

➤ TOUR INFORMATION: **The Sounds Connection** (✉ 10 London Quay, Picton, ☎ 03/573–8843, FAX 03/573–7726, WEB www.soundsconnection.co.nz).

WALKING AND HIKING TOURS

To see the glorious Marlborough Sounds, try a four- or five-day fully catered and guided inn-to-inn walk on the Queen Charlotte Track with Southern Wilderness. The four-day walk includes all land and water transport, as well as overnight stays in three Sounds resorts—Punga Cove Resort, Furneaux Lodge, and the Portage. Experienced guides give informative talks on the area's rich natural and human history. Advance bookings are essential; trips cost $999. There's also a two-day hike on the Nydia Track for $578 per person. Marlborough Sounds Adventure Company guides trampers on the Queen Charlotte Walkway as well, with three-day ($650) or four-day ($845) trips.

➤ TOUR INFORMATION: **Marlborough Sounds Adventure Company** (✉ The Waterfront, London Quay, Picton, ☎ 03/573–6078, FAX 03/573–8827, WEB www.marlboroughsounds.co.nz). **Southern Wilderness** (✉ 67 George St., Blenheim, ☎ 03/578–4531, FAX 03/578–4533, WEB www.southernwilderness.com).

WINERY TOURS

Sounds Connection runs daily tours from October through July to visit a handful of Marlborough's main wineries. Southern Wilderness leads one- and two-day winery treks, including walks through vineyards, wine tastings, and meals at winery restaurants.

➤ CONTACTS: **The Sounds Connection** (✉ 10 London Quay, Picton, ☎ 03/573–8843, FAX 03/573–7726, WEB www.soundsconnection.co.nz). **Southern Wilderness** (✉ 67 George St., Blenheim, ☎ 03/578–4531, FAX 03/578–4533, WEB www.southernwilderness.com).

VISITOR INFORMATION

The visitor information centers in Blenheim, Kaikoura, Picton are all open daily.

➤ TOURIST INFORMATION: **Kaikoura Information and Tourism Centre** (✉ West End, ☎ 03/319–5641, FAX 03/319–6819, WEB www.kaikoura. co.nz). **Marlborough Visitor Information Centre** (✉ The Old Railway Station, Sinclair St., Blenheim, ☎ 03/577–8080, FAX 03/577–8079, WEB www.destinationmarlborough.com). **Picton Visitor Information Centre** (✉ Picton Foreshore, ☎ 03/573–7477, FAX 03/573–5021, WEB www. picton.co.nz).

NELSON AND THE NORTHWEST

Set on the broad curve of its bay with views of the Tasman Mountains on the far side, Nelson makes a strong case for itself as one of the top areas in New Zealand for year-round adventure. To the west beckon the sandy crescents of Abel Tasman National Park and Golden Bay. To the south, mellow river valleys and the peaks and glacial lakes of Nelson Lakes National Park draw hikers, mountaineers, and cross-country skiers. There's a climatic allure as well; Nelson has more hours of sunlight than any other major city in the country. New Zealanders are well aware of these attractions, and in December and January the city is swamped with vacationers. Apart from this brief burst of activity, you can expect to have the roads and beaches mostly to yourself.

Nelson

❻ *116 km (73 mi) west of Blenheim.*

Relaxed, hospitable, and easy to explore on foot, Nelson has a way of making you feel like you should stay longer, no matter how many days you're here. You can make your way around the mostly two-story town in a day, poking into crafts shops and stopping at cafés, but two days is a practical minimum, especially if you need a respite in the midst of a busy itinerary. Use Nelson as a base for a variety of activities within an hour's drive of the town itself.

To get your bearings in town, start at the visitor center on the corner of Trafalgar and Halifax streets. The heart of town is farther up **Trafalgar Street,** between two parallel roads, Bridge Street and Hardy Street. These areas are fringed with shops, some of them with walk-through access back on to Trafalgar Street. A weekend crafts market is held at the Montgomery parking lot. There are a few shops in Nile Street and Selwyn Place, but the majority are on Trafalgar, Hardy, and Bridge streets. For a dose of greenery, the **Queens Gardens** are on Bridge Street between Collingwood and Tasman.

The Suter Te Aratoi o Whakatu exhibits both historical and contemporary art; it's a good place to see a cross section of work from an area that has long attracted painters, potters, woodworkers, and other artists. Many of them come for the scenery, the lifestyle, and the clay, and, as a result, Nelson is considered the ceramics center of New Zealand. In recent years the gallery has increased its emphasis on painting and sculpture. Exhibits change every three or four weeks. ✉ *Queens Gardens, Bridge St.,* ☎ *03/548–4699,* WEB *www.thesuter.org. nz.* 🎫 *$2.* ☉ *Daily 10:30–4:30.*

★ Wacky and wonderful, the **World of Wearable Art (WOW)** gives you the chance to see outfits from Nelson's annual wearable art contest. In one gallery, mannequins wear the inventive ensembles; the elaborate sets, props, sound, and psychedelic lighting make this a must-see.

An adjoining gallery exhibits a superb collection of restored classic cars, ranging from a pink Cadillac to sleek sports tourers. Here, too, the displays are revved up with special effects. All together, the complex more than lives up to the acronym. ⊠ *95 Quarantine Rd., Annesbrook,* ☎ *03/548–9299,* WEB *www.worldofwearableart.com.* ☜ *$15.* ☉ *Oct.– Mar., daily 9–6:30; Apr.–Sept., daily 10–5.*

If you're going to be in town in September, call ahead to find out when the annual **Montana New Zealand Wearable Art Awards** will be held. At this extravaganza—the brainchild of Nelson resident Susie Moncrieff— entries from around the world can be outrageous and sometimes quite inspired.

Nelson's iffy architectural "highlight" is **Christ Church Cathedral,** which sits on a hilltop surrounded by gardens. Work on the church began in 1925 and dragged on for the next 40 years. During construction the design was altered to withstand earthquakes, and despite its promising location at the end of Trafalgar Street, it looks like a building designed by a committee. ⊠ *Cathedral Sq.* ☜ *Free, tower $4.*

Dining and Lodging

$$$$ ✕ **The Boat Shed.** The name is no gimmick: this genuine boat shed perches on wooden piles with the tide lapping below. Chef Luke McCann brings a nice Asian touch to New Zealand and Mediterranean dishes. Look for salads with black and white sesame seeds and pickled vegetables or panfried scallops with garlic, a white wine and lemon cream sauce, and a bacon and sage croquette. Crayfish are priced according to size; beef, lamb, and vegetarian dishes cater to those without a piscatory palate. ⊠ *350 Wakefield Quay,* ☎ *03/546–9783. AE, DC, MC, V.*

$$–$$$ ✕ **Amadeus Café Restaurant & Bar.** Whispering ceiling fans and white marble table tops give this café a gracious tone. The chef-owner hits Central European notes with dishes such as pork schnitzel with Black Forest ham and mushroom duxelles. You can also pore over the glass cases full of pastries, or relax with a cold beer or an excellent coffee. The music changes throughout the day, with everything from classical music to Dean Martin to Edith Piaf. ⊠ *284 Trafalgar Sq.,* ☎ *03/545– 7191. AE, DC, MC, V.*

$$–$$$ ✕ **Appelman's.** The paneled walls and beamed ceilings make the dining room in this renovated colonial house particularly inviting. The excellent chef looks to European classics; popular demand ensures that the chateaubriand for two is in no danger of being taken off the menu. The sharp wine list slips some Australian labels in with the local vintages. ⊠ *294 Queen St., Richmond, 6½ km (4 mi) southwest of Nelson,* ☎ *03/544–0610. AE, DC, MC, V. No lunch.*

$–$$$ ✕ **Broccoli Row.** If you've got a rendezvous on a warm evening, make a
★   beeline for the intimate courtyard here; it's surrounded by plant-covered trellises. The vegetarian and seafood menu could yield a blue-nose (a local fish) brochette, grilled with fresh herbs and using rosemary as the skewer. Finish with the delicious hazelnut, chocolate, and date meringue torte. ⊠ *5 Buxton Sq.,* ☎ *03/548–9621. AE, DC, MC, V. Closed Sun.*

$$$ ▥ **Cambria House.** Built for a sea captain, this 1860 house, now a B&B,
★   mixes old and new, from the original kauri doors to the high-speed Internet access. The decor pairs antiques with rimu-wood paneling and modern fabrics. Each bedroom has an en-suite bathroom with shower; two have a shower and separate bathtub. You can settle in with coffee or a drink by the wood-burning fireplace or on the garden deck. The house is near the town center. ⊠ *7 Cambria St.,* ☎ *03/548–4681,* FAX *03/546–6649,* WEB *www.cambria.co.nz. 7 rooms. Internet; no a/c, no kids, no smoking. AE, MC, V. BP.*

$$$ 🖭 **Cathedral Inn.** Abandoning the corporate world didn't require a sec-
ond thought for hosts Peter and Lesley Cavanagh. Their luxurious lodge,
a transformed 1878 deanery, appears almost Mediterranean from the
outside—the front courtyard has turquoise and terra-cotta colors—but
inside you'll find solid colonial-style furniture made from native rimu
and kauri wood, as well as wrought-iron and brass bedsteads. You can
join the other guests around the recycled *matai*-wood table for break-
fast. The inn is a short walk through Christ Church Cathedral's gar-
den to shops and restaurants. ⊠ *369 Trafalgar St.,* ☎ *03/548–7369,*
FAX *03/548–0369,* WEB *www.cathedralinn.co.nz. 7 rooms. No a/c, no kids,
no smoking. AE, DC, MC, V. BP.*

$$$ 🖭 **A Little Manor.** This little historic A-frame home, on land first sur-
veyed in 1864, seems to defy the modern-day neighborhood around
it. The place is full of antiques, not to mention the original clawfoot
bath and open fire. (Guests share the bathroom.) The sunny upper deck
and lower garden are well secluded. There are a pantry full of good-
ies (such as homemade jams and sauces), a dining area, and a reading
room. The B&B is just a short walk to cafés, restaurants, art galleries,
and pottery studios. ⊠ *12 Nile St. W,* ☎ *03/545–1411,* FAX *03/545–
1417. 2 rooms with shared bath. Kitchenette, 2 lounges; no a/c, no smoking. AE, DC, MC, V. BP.*

$$$ 🖭 **Mapledurham.** This colonial-style homestead in the nearby town of
 ★   Richmond, presided over by Deborah Grigg, is as friendly and com-
fortable a place as you'll find in the Nelson area. The garden around
the house and fresh flowers in your room make it an especially pleas-
ant place to come to at the end of the day. Take advantage of the pri-
vate trellised courtyard at the back of the garden or the shade of the
veranda. The full breakfast, with eggs and venison as well as fresh fruit
and juices, makes a great start to the day. ⊠ *8 Edward St., Richmond,*
☎ FAX *03/544–4210,* WEB *www.mapledurham.co.nz. 3 rooms. No a/c,
no room phones, no smoking. MC, V. BP.*

$$ 🖭 **Aloha Lodge.** A stone's throw from Tahunanui Beach, this modern
B&B has luxury accommodations at a reasonable price. The design of
the lodge is Asian, even in its garden, which is landscaped using the
principles of the Chinese design philosophy *feng shui.* An ample breakfast is served in the outer courtyard or the spacious dining room. You
can reach Tahunanui on a five-minute drive from Nelson via Haven
Road. ⊠ *19 Beach Rd., Tahunanui,* ☎ *03/546–4000,* FAX *03/546–
4420. 17 rooms, 4 suites. No a/c, no smoking. AE, DC, MC, V. BP.*

Outdoor Activities and Sports

There is hiking and sea-kayaking aplenty in the glorious coastal Abel
Tasman National Park west of Nelson. For information on stream fishing in the Nelson Lakes district, *see* Chapter 6.

Shopping

There are artist's studios and crafts shops in various parts of town. More
than 300 artists live in the Nelson area, working full-time in various
media: ceramics, glassblowing, wood turning, fiber, sculpture, and
painting. Not surprisingly there are 16 arts-and-crafts trails to follow,
for which there is a brochure at the information center. There is also
a colorful Saturday- and Sunday-morning crafts market.

At **Gael Montgomerie Fine Woodturning** (⊠ 117 Nile St., ☎ FAX 03/
546–6576, WEB www.gaelmontgomerie.co.nz), just a short way out of
the center of town, you'll meet a woman whose passion for her craft
is captured in every wood grain of her meticulously honed and oiled
work. Check out her ornamental or practical—but never plain—
kitchenware.

★ From the collectible family of penguins to the bold platters and vases, the style of the **Hoglund Art Glass Blowing Studio** (✉ Lansdowne Rd., Richmond, ☎ 03/544–6500) is unmistakable. Ola and Marie Hoglunds' clean designs show the influence of their native Scandinavia but are also in keeping with a growing trend in Pacific-style art—with vivid colors and inspiration from New Zealand's environment.

The skilled craftspeople of the **Jens Hansen Workshop** (✉ 320 Trafalgar Sq., ☎ 03/548–0640) create thoughtfully designed, well-made gold and silver jewelry. Contemporary pieces are handmade at the workshop-showroom, and many are set with precious stones or *pounamu* (jade) from the west coast of the South Island.

The 19th-century, two-story cottage of the **South Street Gallery** (✉ 10 Nile St. W, ☎ 03/548–8117) overflows with ceramic art, sculpture, and housewares. The gallery represents 23 Nelson artisans with a national reputation; some are gaining international recognition. Upstairs a number of West Coast artists display their work.

Around Nelson

Though Nelson's a bustling city, it manages to retain a certain rural feel. With the Tasman Bay before it and the foothills of the Bryant and Richmond ranges behind, there are open countryside and vineyards within easy reach of the city center.

❼ The **Nelson Provincial Museum,** on the grounds of **Isel Park,** exhibits a small but outstanding collection of Māori carvings. The museum also has a number of artifacts relating to the so-called Maungatapu murders, grisly goldfields killings committed near Nelson in 1866. To get to the Isel Park from Nelson, follow Rutherford Street out of town—the street was named for the eminent nuclear physicist Ernest Rutherford, who was born and raised nearby. On the outskirts of the city, take the right fork onto Waimea Road and continue as it becomes Main Road. Turn left into Marsden Road, where a sign points to the park. ✉ *Isel Park, Stoke, 7 km (4½ mi) south of Nelson,* ☎ *03/547–9740.* 🎫 *$2.* ◷ *Tues.–Fri. 10–4, weekends 2–5.*

Isel House, near the Nelson Provincial Museum, was built for Thomas Marsden, one of the region's prosperous pioneers. It was Marsden who laid out the magnificent gardens surrounding the house, which include a towering California redwood and a 140-ft Monterey pine. The house itself contains the Marsden family's impressive porcelain and furniture. ✉ *Isel Park, Stoke,* ☎ *03/547–5222.* 🎫 *Donation.* ◷ *Sept.–May, weekends 2–4.*

❽ **Broadgreen** is a fine example of a Victorian cob house. Cob houses, made from straw and horsehair bonded together with mud and clay, are commonly found in Devon, the southern English home county of many of Nelson's pioneers. The house is furnished as it might have been in the 1850s, with patchwork quilts and kauri furniture. ✉ *276 Nayland Rd., Stoke,* ☎ *03/546–0283.* 🎫 *$3.* ◷ *Daily 10:30–4:30.*

❾ **Waimea Estates** is one of the newer names on the Nelson scene, but it's making big waves. The range includes chardonnay, riesling, and—unusual in this region—a couple of variations on the cabernet sauvignon and merlot themes. A café next to the tasting room serves interesting dishes, mostly using local produce. ✉ *22 Appleby Hwy., Appleby,* ☎ *03/544–4963,* 🌐 *www.waimeaestates.co.nz.* ◷ *Café 10–6 daily, wine tastings by appointment.*

❿ Andrew Greenhough and Jennifer Wheeler's **Greenhough Vineyard and Winery** in the optimistically named suburb of Hope has established a

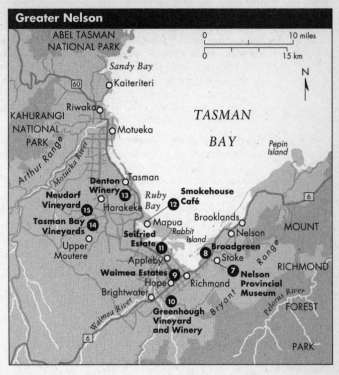

Greater Nelson

big reputation for quality in a short time. Sauvignon blanc, chardonnay, pinot noir, and the occasional supersweet dessert wine are all worth trying. ⊠ *Patons Rd., Hope,* ☎ *03/542–3462.* ✆ *Jan.–Feb., daily 1–5; Mar.–Dec., weekends 1–5 or by appointment.*

⓫ **Seifried Estate** is a 25-minute drive from Nelson's main center, on the way to Motueka. Hermann Seifried produces fine sauvignon blanc, chardonnay, and especially riesling. A large, sunny restaurant is next door to the tasting room. ⊠ *Redwood Rd., Appleby,* ☎ *03/544–1555,* WEB *www.seifried.co.nz.* ✆ *Daily 10–5.*

★ ⓬ It might be hard to resist stopping at the **Smokehouse Café,** operated by Vivienne and Tom Fox, who buy their fish right off local boats, fillet it, marinate it according to a secret recipe, smoke it—and offer samples. Especially if you're headed south, you won't find a better lunch along the way than a slab of smoked snapper, salmon, or albacore tuna with a loaf of crusty bread from the bakery in Motueka. Match this with the great view over the estuary, and it's little wonder the café won the Taste Nelson Award for three years running, starting in 2000. You can't miss the big blue corrugated iron building. ⊠ *Mapua Wharf,* ☎ *03/540–2280,* WEB *www.smokehouse.co.nz.* ✆ *Apr.–Oct., daily 9–5:30; extended hrs Nov.–Mar.*

⓭ The hilltop **Denton Winery** has terrific views of the surrounding countryside. Richard Denton gave up a pressure career in the computer industry to grow grapes and make wine. Now he and his wife, Alex, an artist, run this pleasant winery and café and produce a range of wines that get better with every vintage. Syrah is one unusual variety that has won praise; more in tune with the area are chardonnay, pinot noir, and sauvignon blanc. ⊠ *Awa Awa Rd., off Marriages Rd., Upper Moutere,* ☎ FAX *03/540–3555,* WEB *www.dentonwinery.co.nz.* ✆ *Oct.–Dec. and Feb.–Apr., daily 11–5; Jan., daily 11–6.*

⑭ Expatriate Californian Philip Jones doesn't follow established flavor patterns at his equipment-crammed **Tasman Bay Vineyards.** His best wines have great flavor concentration and many have won major awards. Fifteen acres of grapes—sauvignon blanc, chardonnay, pinot gris, and pinot noir—surround the winery. Most of the wines are made from their estate vineyards, although some grapes are brought in from Marlborough. Except for the three-month window for tasting, the winery is open only for sales. ⊠ *Best Rd., Upper Moutere,* ☎ FAX *03/543–2031.* ☾ *Tastings Dec.–Feb., daily noon–4.*

⑮ Despite its tiny size, **Neudorf Vineyard** has established an international reputation for chardonnay, but riesling, sauvignon blanc, pinot gris, and pinot noir are also highly regarded. Owners Tim and Judy Finn are enthusiastic about their region's attributes and will talk at length about local food and wine. The top wines wear the Moutere designation on the label. ⊠ *Neudorf Rd., Upper Moutere,* ☎ *03/543–2643,* WEB *www.neudorf.co.nz.* ☾ *Sept.–May, daily 10–5.*

En Route West of Mapua, on the way to Motueka, Highway 60 loops around quiet little sea coves that, for all but the warmest months of the year, mirror the snow-frosted peaks on the far shore. The tall vines along the roadside are hops, used in beer brewing.

Motueka

⑯ *50 km (31 mi) west of Nelson.*

Motueka (mo-too-*eh*-ka) is an agricultural center—tobacco, hops, kiwi fruit, and apples are among its staples. South of town, the Motueka River valley is known for trout fishing, rafting, and its sporting lodges. About 15 km (9 mi) northeast of town on the edge of the national park, ★ **Kaiteriteri Beach** is one of New Zealand's best-known beaches, famous for its golden sand and great for a swim.

Lodging

$$$$ 🏠 **Motueka River Lodge.** One of New Zealand's exclusive retreats, this lodge offers tranquillity, marvelous scenery, and a superb standard of comfort. Owned and operated by former Londoner Mick Mason and Cordon Bleu–trained Fiona Mason, the lodge is on 80 acres bordering the Motueka River, with magnificent mountain views. The interior of the rustic house is accented with antiques collected around the world. You can hike and raft nearby, but the lodge's specialty is fishing, especially dry fly-fishing for brown trout in the wild river country. The activities are restricted outside the October–April fishing season. ⊠ *Motueka Valley Rd., Motueka,* ☎ *03/526–8668,* FAX *03/526–8669,* WEB *www.motuekalodge.co.nz. 5 rooms. Dining room, hot tub, tennis court, lounge, fishing; no a/c, no room phones, no room TVs, no kids. AE, DC, MC, V. FAP.*

$$$ 🏠 **Doone Cottage.** At this charming 130-year-old cottage, hosts Stan and ★ Glen Davenport have welcomed homestay guests for more than 20 years. They're relaxed and friendly and have a great sense of humor. Guest rooms and the private garden chalet are all done in flowery chintzes and frilly cushions. Glen spins and weaves wool; her on-site studio has sweaters, rugs, and wall hangings for sale. You can arrange to have dinner here. Five streams and the Motueka River, a trout-fishing hot spot, are just a short walk away. The cottage is also within easy reach of Golden Bay and Abel Tasman and Nelson Lakes national parks. ⊠ *Motueka Valley Rd., R.D. 1, Motueka,* ☎ FAX *03/526–8740,* WEB *www.doonecottage. co.nz. 2 rooms, 1 chalet. Hot tub; no a/c, no room phones, no room TVs, no kids, no smoking. MC, V. BP.*

Outdoor Activities and Sports

FISHING

You won't lack for places to land some whopping brown trout. Tony Entwistle leads fly-fishing excursions to local rivers as well as to remote backcountry areas, which involve hiking or helicopter trips. The cost for one angler starts at $700. Peter Carty and Zane Murfin of Brown Trout Heaven Guiding also tackle both easily accessible and wilderness rivers, starting at $695 per day. Fishing season in this area runs from October through April.

➤ CONTACTS: **Peter Carty** (✉ Chalgrave St., Murchison, ☎ FAX 03/523–9525, WEB www.browntroutheaven.co.nz). **Tony Entwistle** (✉ 5 Mason Pl., Nelson, ☎ FAX 03/544–4565, WEB www.TonyEntwistlesFlyFishing.co.nz). **Zane Murfin** (✉ Box 75, St. Arnaud, Nelson Lakes, ☎ FAX 03/521–1017, WEB www.TonyEntwistlesFlyFishing.co.nz).

RAFTING

Rapid River Adventure Rafting has rafting trips down the Gowan and Buller rivers (both Grade III–IV). Choose from a half-day ($80) or full-day ($140) trip. ✉ 73A Brook St., Nelson, ☎ FAX 03/545–7076.

Ultimate Descents Rafting Adventure Company. Don Allardice, one of New Zealand's leading white-water adventurers, along with Deane Parker, guide on the Buller (Grade III–IV) and the Karamea (Grade V) rivers. Choose from half-day ($95), full-day ($155), or a variety of multiday trips. ✉ 51 Fairfax St., Murchison, ☎ 03/523–9899 or 0800/748–377, FAX 03/523–9811, WEB www.rivers.co.nz.

En Route If you don't intend to visit the Abel Tasman National Park and Golden Bay and are headed for the West Coast, turn south onto Highway 61 at the Rothmans Clock Tower in Motueka, following the sign to Murchison. The road snakes through **Motueka Valley** alongside the Motueka River, which is edged with poplars and yellow gorse, with the green valley walls pressing close alongside. If this river could talk, it would probably scream, "Trout!" After the town of Tapawera, turn south on State Highway 6 and continue to the West Coast.

Abel Tasman National Park

⑰ *77 km (48 mi) northwest of Motueka, 110 km (69 mi) northwest of Nelson.*

Beyond the town of Motueka, Highway 60 passes close to Kaiteriteri Beach, then turns inland to skirt Abel Tasman National Park. Its coastline is a succession of idyllic beaches backed by a rugged hinterland of native beech forests, granite gorges, and waterfalls. The cove and inlets at **Anchorage**, to mention one part of the park, are spectacular.

Abel Tasman has a number of walking trails, from both Totaranui at its north end and Marahau in the south. The most popular is the two- to three-day **Coastal Track**, open year-round. Launches from **Abel Tasman National Park Experiences** (☞ Hiking, *below*) will drop off and pick up hikers from several points along the track. A popular way to explore the clear waters and rock-strewn coastline is by sea kayak. The main accommodations base for the national park is Motueka.

Dining and Lodging

$$$ ✕▥ **Awaroa Lodge.** Relax in an idyllic part of the spectacular Abel Tasman National Park, surrounded by native bush, just two minutes' walk to the beach. You can sea-kayak to the lodge or walk, as the Abel Tasman Track passes right through the property. To reach the lodge by boat, contact **Aqua Taxis** (☎ 03/527–8083), which leaves from Marahau daily, or fly direct from Nelson with **Tasman Bay Aviation** (☎ 03/

547–2378). Choose from standard doubles with private decks or fully self-contained chalets. Much of the wood used to build and to finish the interiors has been recycled from the local bush. The attached restaurant, with its chunky wooden furnishings and open adobe fireplace, serves stylish regional cuisine; most of the produce is grown organically on the property. ✉ *Awaroa Bay, Abel Tasman National Park, Motueka,* ☎ *03/528–8758,* 🖷 *03/528–6561,* WEB *www. awaroalodge.co.nz. 4 rooms, 10 chalets. Restaurant. AE, MC, V.*

$$–$$$ 🛏 **Abel Tasman Marahau Lodge.** With Abel Tasman National Park 200 yards in one direction and the Marahau beach 200 yards in the other, this location is hard to resist. The boutique lodge has spacious fully self-contained chalets, clustered in groups of two or four with native gardens between them. Units are finished in natural wood and have high cathedral ceilings, clean-lined wooden furniture, New Zealand wool carpets, queen- or king-size beds, and balconies from which to take in the park's natural beauty. Rates do not include breakfast, but the lodge has a communal kitchen. Staff can give information about and make reservations for sea-kayaking, water-taxis, and hiking options. ✉ *Marahau, R.D. 2, Motueka,* ☎ *03/527–8250,* 🖷 *03/527–8258,* WEB *abeltasmanmarahaulodge.co.nz. 12 rooms. Kitchen, outdoor hot tub, sauna; no a/c. DC, MC, V.*

Outdoor Activities and Sports

HIKING

Bushwalk in the park on your own—it's called freedom walking—or opt for a guided walk. The **Department of Conservation Field Centre** (✉ 62 Commercial St., Takaka, ☎ 03/525–8026) provides trail maps.

Abel Tasman National Park Experiences are the original operators of day excursions to this park. They offer several kinds of bushwalks, trips to beaches, launch cruises, and sea-kayaking. They also run three- and five-day hiking or hiking-kayaking treks around the park. ✉ *265 High St., Motueka,* ☎ *03/528–7675 or 0800/223–582,* 🖷 *03/528–0297,* WEB *www.abeltasman.co.nz.*

SEA-KAYAKING

Ocean River Adventure Company has a variety of guided sea-kayaking trips in Abel Tasman National Park, lasting from one to five days. Guided trips cost from $92 per person per day, "freedom" rentals from $99 per person with a two-day minimum rental. ✉ *Marahau, R.D. 2, Motueka,* ☎ *03/527–8266,* 🖷 *03/527–8006,* WEB *www.seakayaking. co.nz.*

The **Sea Kayak Company** offers a range of guided kayaking options through the pristine waters of the national park to beaches and campsites often inaccessible to hikers. These include a one-day discovery tour ($95), a two-day "More than Beaches" tour ($295), and three- and five-day tours ($380 and $720, respectively). All tours are fully catered and all equipment is supplied, down to the Department of Conservation camp passes. ✉ *506 High St., Motueka,* ☎ *03/528–7251 or 0508/ 252–925,* 🖷 *03/528–7221,* WEB *www.seakayaknz.co.nz.*

Golden Bay and Takaka

⑱ *55 km (35 mi) northwest of Motueka, 110 km (70 mi) west of Nelson.*

From the Montueka-Nelson area, a spectacular hill road rises up about 2,500 ft before plunging again to sea level to reach the tiny township of Takaka, a jumping-off point for Kahurangi National Park. The gorgeous stretch of coastline that begins at Takaka is known, deservedly, as **Golden Bay.** Alternating sandy and rocky shores curve up to the sands of Farewell Spit, the arcing prong that encloses the bay. Other than a 19th-century lighthouse, the Spit is pure, raw nature. Fault-lines slash the cliffs, and the area is a favorite for all kinds of birds. In short, it's solitude at its very best. Dutch navigator Abel Tasman anchored here briefly just a few days before Christmas 1642. His visit ended abruptly when four of his crew were killed by the then-resident Māori iwi (tribe), Ngāti Tumata Kokiri. Bitterly disappointed, Tasman named the place Moordenaers, or Murderers' Bay, and sailed away without ever setting foot on New Zealand soil. If you have time to explore it, Golden Bay is a delight—a sunny, 40-km (25-mi) crescent with a relaxed crew of locals who firmly believe they live in paradise.

Eight kilometers (5 miles) west of Takaka is **Waikoropupu Springs,** known as Pupu Springs. This is the largest spring system in New Zealand, and clear cold water bubbles into the Waikoropupu Valley after traveling underground from its source at the nearby Takaka River. Dated tourist brochures still available in the area show people swimming in the springs, but this is now frowned upon—alas—because of the impact it has on the delicate flora within the springs. It's best to leave the bathing suit in the car and take a leisurely stroll around the valley on the 90-minute Pupu Walkway. Take your time and go quietly—the better to spot *tūī*, bellbirds, wood pigeons, and other bird life. The road from Takaka is well marked.

Less well known but no less fascinating is the **Labyrinth,** a system of twisting tunnels and gullies carved into the rocks by long-receded river systems. The phenomenon went unnoticed for years and until recently was simply part of grazing land. Now the delightfully eccentric and totally enthusiastic Dave Whittaker has proclaimed himself to be "keeper of the rocks" and has opened the place to the public. You will find rocks shaped like crocodiles and other reptiles, plus a natural maze. Dave has hidden a few gnomes and other fairy-tale creatures around the park, which is great for kids. There's also a troll bridge, an Asian garden, and a picnic site. ⊠ *Off Abel Tasman Dr.,* ☎ *03/525–8434.* ⊠ *$5.* ☉ *Daily 12:30–5.*

Lodging

$$$ ⊞ **Westhaven Retreat.** If it's remote luxury you're after, this peninsula retreat is for you. It's set on 1,000 acres of regenerating native forest surrounded by the Tasman Sea and the Whanganui Inlet. Austrian-born Bruno and Monika Stompe literally carved the accommodations out of the environment; access roads were built by Bruno, once an industrial engineer. Rooms in the main house have rimu-wood paneling and a neutral color scheme; the separate cottage is modern, roomy, and bright. Lunch and dinner can be added on. On-site you'll find a menagerie of farm animals, including more than 40 gentle llamas. There's at least 40 km (25 mi) of gravel road between you and the nearest neighbor. If you're leery of the gravel roads, inquire about helicopter access or about being picked up at Nelson Airport, Motueka, or Takaka. ⊠ *Te Hapu Rd., Collingwood,* ☎ *03/524–8354,* FAX *03/524–8354. 3 rooms, 1 cottage. Hiking, beaches; no a/c, no room phones, no room TV, no smoking. AE, DC, MC, V. BP.*

$$ ⊞ **Anatoki Lodge.** This spacious, contemporary motel is close to Takaka center. Owners Gaye and Garth Prince can help point out the main attractions and best places to eat in the area. The lodge has spacious studios and one- and two-bedroom units; each opens out to a private patio and grass courtyard. ⊠ *87 Commercial St.,* ☎ *03/525–8047,* FAX *03/525–8433. 5 studios, 4 one-bedrooms, 1 two-bedroom. Indoor pool, convention center; no a/c, no smoking. AE, MC, V. CP.*

Outdoor Activities and Sports

BEACHES

Golden Bay has miles of swimming beaches. **Paton's Rock** is one of the best near Takaka. Check the tides before taking the 10-minute drive from town, as swimming is best with a full tide. Farther out, less suitable for swimming but spectacular for its coastal landscapes, is **Wharariki Beach.** You'll find massive sand dunes, and among these you're likely to come across fur seals sunbathing. They are, of course, wild seals, and if you get too close to them, they might charge or even bite, so keep a 15-ft distance. To get here, drive past Collingwood and follow the signs. Go as far as the road will take you, and then walk over farmland on a well-defined track for 20 minutes. As these are quite remote beaches, there are no lifeguards on duty.

FISHING

For information on deep-sea fishing in Golden Bay out of Takaka, *see* Chapter 6.

HIKING

The wild **Kahurangi National Park** has a diversity of walks and treks. This vast patch of land includes in its compass great fern-clad forests, rivers, rolling hills, snowcapped mountains, and beaches pounded by West Coast surf. The most famous walk is the **Heaphy Track.** It is known primarily as a "free walk"—a slight misnomer in that trekkers need to pay a nominal fee to camp or use huts ($7–$14) during the four- to six-day experience. It is best to purchase these tickets in advance from information centers at Nelson, Motueka, or Takaka. Tickets in hand, all you really need to do is get to the track and start walking toward Karamea on the West Coast. Huts along the way have gas cooking and heating facilities, water, and toilets. You'll need to carry your own food and bedding. And be prepared for weather of all kinds at all times of year—bring rain gear and warm clothing even in summer (and insect repellent for the sand flies!). The east entrance to the park is 35 km (23 mi) west of Takaka, south of the town of Collingwood.

The **Department of Conservation Golden Bay Area Office** (⊠ 62 Commercial St., Takaka, ☎ 03/525–8026, WEB www.doc.govt.nz) provides local trail maps.

If you'd like some expert company on hikes around the national park, **Kahurangi Guided Walks** (☎ 03/525–7177, WEB www.kahurangiwalks. webnz.co.nz) runs easy one-day treks (from $80) on routes known to locals but virtually untouched by visitors. One goes to a remote historic hut, known as Chaffey Cottage, where a couple lived for 40 years. A more strenuous, three-day walk ($390) goes to the rarely visited Boulder Lake. You can also choose a five-day hike on the Heaphy Track ($800).

Kahurangi National Park Bus Services (☎ 03/525–9434, FAX 03/525–9430, WEB www.nelson.net.nz/kahurangi) offers transport to the track from Takaka on demand for $100 (drop-off and pickup). It also provides general charter services and scheduled services between Golden Bay, Abel Tasman, and Nelson. From Nelson, **Intercity** (☎ 03/548–1538) runs buses at 7:30 AM each day; the ride costs $44.

HORSE TREKKING

Cape Farewell Horse Treks has a range of treks, from trips around a farmyard for kids to overnighters down the West Coast. The sturdy, hand-picked standard Thoroughbred horses know exactly where they're going—even if you don't. For great views of Farewell Spit, ask about the Pillar Point Light trek. Book ahead in summer. ⊠ *Wharariki Beach Rd., Puponga,* ☎ *03/524–8031,* WEB *www.horsetreksnz.com.*

Nelson and the Northwest A to Z

AIR TRAVEL

Air New Zealand links Nelson with Christchurch, Queenstown, Dunedin, the West Coast town of Hokitika, and all major cities on the North Island.

➤ CARRIER: **Air New Zealand** (☎ 03/546–9300, WEB www. airnewzealand.com).

AIRPORTS

Nelson Airport (NSN) is 10 km (6 mi) south of the city.

➤ AIRPORT INFORMATION: **Nelson Airport** (✉ Trent Dr., ☎ 03/547–3199).

AIRPORT TRANSFER

Super Shuttle buses meet all incoming flights and can take you wherever you need to go in town; the cost is $8 to the city for one passenger, $5 each for two. Taxi fare into town is about $14.

➤ CONTACT: **Super Shuttle** (☎ 03/547–5782).

BUS TRAVEL

InterCity buses leave daily for Nelson from the ferry terminal in Picton. The trip takes about three hours. From Nelson, InterCity runs the length of both the west and east coasts daily.

➤ BUS DEPOT: **Nelson** (✉ 27 Bridge St., ☎ 03/548–1538).
➤ BUS LINE: **InterCity** (☎ 03/548–1538, WEB www.intercitycoach.co.nz).

CAR RENTAL

➤ MAJOR AGENCIES: **Avis** (✉ Nelson Airport, Trent Dr., Nelson, ☎ 03/547–2727). **Budget** (✉ Nelson Airport, Trent Dr., Nelson, ☎ 03/547–9586). **Hertz** (✉ Nelson Airport, Trent Dr., Nelson, ☎ 03/547–2299).

CAR TRAVEL

Nelson is about a two-hour drive from the ferry in Picton. The distance is 145 km (90 mi), but the winding roads don't allow for fast open-road driving.

From Nelson, Highway 6 runs southwest to the West Coast, down the coast to the glaciers, then over the Haast Pass to Wanaka and Queenstown. If you're going to the West Coast, allow at least seven hours for the 458-km (284-mi) journey from Nelson to Franz Josef. The same applies if you plan to drive from Nelson to Christchurch, 424 km (265 mi) to the southeast, whether you drive through the mountains of Nelson Lakes National Park or through Blenheim and Kaikoura.

Driving is the most convenient way to get around the region, although even the highways can be narrow and winding. Highway 6 is a main artery, but if you're going to the West Coast, the 63 down the Wairau Valley is a scenic alternative. Provincial Highway 60 splits from Highway 6 about 6 km (4 mi) out of Nelson near Richmond to reach the Abel Tasman area. Note that towns marked on maps are often tiny—blink and you'll miss them—and it can be a long way between gas stations.

EMERGENCIES

➤ EMERGENCY SERVICES: **Fire, police, and ambulance** (☎ 111).

TOURS

ACTIVITY TOURS

Bay Tours Nelson runs daily tours of wine trails, half- and full-day arts-and-crafts tours, and scenic adventure tours by arrangement. Trips include the city and its immediate district and also go farther afield to Motueka and Kaiteriteri Beach and south to Nelson Lakes National Park.

➤ CONTACT: **Bay Tours Nelson** (✉ 48 Brougham St., Nelson, ☎ 03/ 545–7114 or 0800/229–868, FAX 03/545–7119, WEB www.baytoursnelson. co.nz).

NATURE TOURS

A trip with the Original Farewell Spit Safari is an absolute must if you are in Golden Bay. Each of the two tour itineraries takes you out along the Farewell Spit, a 35-km (22-mi) protected sandbar with a 19th-century lighthouse. There's a tremendous seabird population here; one tour will take you to a gannet colony. (This is a truly unique opportunity, since the company is the only one with a Department of Conservation licence to visit the gannets.) Costs run between $58 and $75.

➤ CONTACT: **Original Farewell Spit Safari** (✉ Tasman St., Collingwood, ☎ 03/524–8257, FAX 03/524–8939, WEB www.farewellspit.co.nz).

WALKING TOURS

Abel Tasman National Park Experiences guides day trips and three- and five-day treks in the beautiful coastal park. Spend nights in comfortable lodges and eat well, without having to carry a big pack. The rates for a five-day kayaking and hiking trip or five-day guided walk are from $1,080, depending on the season; the three-day kayaking and hiking trip or three-day guided walk each start at $720.

➤ CONTACT: **Abel Tasman National Park Experiences** (✉ 265 High St., Motueka, ☎ 03/528–7801 or 0800/221–888, FAX 03/528–6087, WEB www.abeltasman.co.nz).

VISITOR INFORMATION

The visitor information centers in Nelson, Motueka, and Takaka are all open daily.

➤ TOURIST INFORMATION: **Golden Bay Visitor Information Centre** (✉ Willow St., Takaka, ☎ 03/525–9136, WEB www.nelsonnz.com). **Motueka Visitor Information Centre** (✉ Wallace St., ☎ 03/528–6543, FAX 03/ 528–6563). **Nelson Visitor Information Centre** (✉ Trafalgar and Halifax Sts., ☎ 03/548–2304, WEB www.nelsonnz.com).

THE WEST COAST

Southwest of Nelson, the wild West Coast region is a land unto itself. The mystical Pancake Rocks and blowholes around Punakaiki (poon-ah-*kye*-kee) set the scene for the rugged, sometimes forlorn landscape to the south. Early *Pākehā* (European) settlers lived a hardscrabble life, digging for gold and farming where they could, constantly washed by the West Coast rains. The towns along the way don't have much of interest in their own right, but they are good bases from which to explore the coast, mountains, lakes, and forests of the region.

At the glacier towns of Franz Josef and Fox, the unique combination of soaring mountains and voluminous precipitation means that the massive valleys of ice descend straight into rain forests—interestingly enough, a combination also found on the southwest coast of South America. South of the glaciers, the road follows the seacoast, where fur seals and fiordland crested penguins inhabit fantastical beaches and forests. On sunny days the Tasman Sea along the stretch between Lake Moeraki and Haast takes on a transcendent shade of blue.

For all its beauty, this is not the most hospitable of New Zealand's provinces. The people are friendly and welcoming, but the landscape and weather can make things difficult if you don't have an adventurous streak. Locals pride themselves on their ability to coexist with the wild, primeval landscape on their doorstep. Be prepared for rain, fog, and cold nights. The meteorological mix can, unfortunately, mean that the glacier flight that you planned at Franz Josef or Fox won't fly the day that you're there. If you do end up here on a rainy day, keep in mind that you might wake up the next morning to have brilliant sunshine lighting up the region's glorious scenery.

If you're driving to the West Coast from Nelson or Motueka, Highway 6, beyond Murchison, parallels the broad **Buller River** as it carves a deep gorge from the jagged mountain peaks. Nineteen kilometers (12 miles) south of Murchison, the **Newtown Hotel,** no longer licensed, teeters on the brink of the gorge, surrounded by a wild junkyard of obsolete farm machinery. The Buller once carried a fabulous cargo of gold, but you'll have to use your imagination to reconstruct the days when places such as Lyell, 34 km (21 mi) past Murchison, were bustling mining towns. Not far from here is New Zealand's longest swaying footbridge, the **Buller Gorge Swing Bridge. Hawk's Crag,** where the highway passes beneath a rock overhang with the river wheeling alongside, is the scenic climax of the trip along the Buller. Before the town of Westport, turn left to continue along Highway 6.

Punakaiki

269 km (168 mi) southeast of Nelson.

Punakaiki is just a small collection of shops at first glance. In fact, the big attraction is not the town. From the visitor center, an easy 10-minute walk leads to a fantastic maze of limestone rocks stacked high above
⓳ the sea. These are the surreal **Pancake Rocks,** the outstanding feature of the surrounding **Paparoa National Park.** At high tide, a blowhole spouts a thundering geyser of spray. Aoraki (Mt. Cook) is sometimes visible to the south. ☎ *03/731–1895.*

Greymouth

⓴ *44 km (28 mi) south of Punakaiki.*

The town of Greymouth (said like the anatomical feature) is aptly named—at first take it's a rather dispirited strip of motels and industrial buildings. But the **Jade Boulder Gallery** is a great place to pick up a distinctive souvenir. The gallery exhibits the work of Ian Boustridge, one of the country's most accomplished sculptors of greenstone, the jade that is highly prized by the Māori. (The area is particularly rich in this stone.) You're in a Ngai Tahu iwi (tribe) area and as part of the tribe's 1997 Treaty of Waitangi settlement, the government recognized Ngai Tahu as having sole rights to collect and sell the precious jade in its natural form. Earrings start at about $10, and sculpture can cost up to $100,000. You'll find that the stone can manifest itself in a number of colors, including deep blues, rusts, even creams, depending on what minerals and conditions have worked their magic. The Jade Rock Café, with its distinctive bright yellow furniture and some eye-catching art work, is part of the complex. ✉ *1 Guinness St.,* ☎ *03/768–0700,* WEB *www. jadeboulder.com.* ☉ *Nov.–Apr., weekdays 8:30 AM–9 PM, weekends 9– 9; May–Oct., weekdays 8:30–5, weekends 9–5.*

On the southern outskirts of Greymouth, **Shantytown** is a lively reenactment of a gold-mining town of the 1880s. Except for the church and the town hall, most of the buildings are replicas, including a jail, a blacksmith shop, a railway station, and a barbershop. The gold-digging displays include a water jet for blasting the gold-bearing quartz from the hillside, water sluices, and a stamper—battery-powered by a 30-ft waterwheel—for crushing the ore. You can pan for gold—there's even a good chance of striking "color." ✉ *Rutherglen,* ☎ *03/762–6634,* WEB *www.shantytown.co.nz.* ✎ *$10.50.* ☉ *Daily 8:30–5.*

Lodging

$$$$ ★ 🏨 **Lake Brunner Sporting Lodge.** Set on the southern shore of Lake Brunner, a 40-minute drive southeast of Greymouth, this lodge, first established in 1868, is an enticing retreat at a price that is relatively low by the standards of New Zealand's elite lodges. Rooms are large and well equipped, with the emphasis on comfort rather than opulence. The best rooms are at the front of the villa, overlooking the lake. Brown trout can be easily seen in the clear waters of the surrounding rivers; fly-fishing is the main sport, but good spin fishing is also available at certain times of the year. (There's a catch-and-release policy.) The lodge is surrounded by untouched forests, which you can explore on a guided environmental tour. The kitchen turns out seasonal dishes with a local bent, such as roast lamb with ratatouille. ✉ *Mitchells, R.D. 1, Kumara, Westland,* ☎ 𝐅𝐀𝐗 *03/738–0163,* 𝐖𝐄𝐁 *www.lakebrunner.com. 11 rooms. Dining room, fishing, mountain bikes, library; no a/c, no room phones, no room TV, no smoking. AE, DC, MC, V. FAP.*

$$–$$$ 🏨 **Rosewood.** Rhonda and Stephan Palten run this B&B in a restored 1920s home close to the town center. Original oak paneling and stained-glass windows remain, and there are cozy seats in the bay windows. Stephan's a chef, so expect a very good breakfast of fresh rolls, bacon, and eggs "any way you want them." Two rooms share a bathroom. ✉ *20 High St.,* ☎ *03/768–4674,* 𝐅𝐀𝐗 *03/768–4694,* 𝐖𝐄𝐁 *www.rosewoodnz. co.nz. 5 rooms, 3 with bath. No a/c, no smoking. MC, V. BP.*

Hokitika

㉑ *41 km (26 mi) south of Greymouth.*

Hokitika won't exactly wow you, but if you're finding the drive down to the glaciers a bit long, it is a convenient stopover. There are crafts shops in town if you have time for browsing, or a few local bushwalks, and the beach is littered with some very interesting driftwood.

One annual Hokitika event worth stopping for is the **Wildfoods Festival,** where you'll find a plethora of gourmet bushtucker (food from the bush) from the West Coast's natural food sources. Bite into such delectables as *huhu* grubs (they look like large maggots), worm sushi, whitebait patties (far more mainstream), and snail caviar, and follow it all with gorse wine, moonshine, or Monteith's bitter beer. The mid-March fest attracts crowds of up to 20,000, six times the local population. Entertainment includes lively performances by members of the Hokitika Live Poets Society at the tree stump by Billy Tea Hut (where else). It can get rowdy at night at the barn dance, which seems to spill through the town. Of course, a good dump of West Coast rain will quiet things down—until the next year. Take your gum boots.

Lodging

$$$ 🏨 **Teichelmann's Central Bed & Breakfast.** Named for Dr. Ebenezer Teichelmann, the surgeon-mountaineer-conservationist who built the original part of the house, this is the most comfortable place in town. It's been a bed-and-breakfast for 30 years, and its warm, friendly atmosphere has a lot to do with hosts Frances Flanagan and Brian Ward, who are happy to make suggestions for local activities. Furnishings are a combination of antique and country-cottage style, using plenty of native wood. The rimu bookcase is full of literature about the area. ✉ *20 Hamilton St.,* ☎ *03/755–8232,* 𝐅𝐀𝐗 *03/755–8239,* 𝐖𝐄𝐁 *www. teichelmanns.co.nz. 6 rooms, 5 with bath. No a/c, no room phones, no room TVs, no kids under 10, no smoking. MC, V. BP.*

Westland National Park

North end 146 km (91 mi) south of Hokitika.

The top of Westland National Park begins at the Franz Josef glacier field. These glaciers—New Zealanders say "glassy-urs"—are formed by the massive precipitation of the West Coast—up to 300 inches per annum—which descends as snow on the névé, or head, of the glacier. The snow is compressed into ice, which flows downhill under its own weight. There are more than 60 glaciers in the park; the most famous **㉓** and accessible are at Franz Josef and Fox. The **Fox Glacier** is slightly larger and longer than that at Franz Josef, but you'll miss nothing important if you see only one. Both glaciers have separate townships, and **㉒** if you are spending the night, **Franz Josef Glacier** is marginally preferable. There are parking areas outside both towns from which you can walk about 30 minutes to reach the glaciers' terminal faces. Both parking lots are sometimes visited by mischievous keas (*kee*-ahs)—mountain parrots—that take delight in destroying the rubber molding around car windows. Their beaks are like can openers. Keas are harmless to humans, but please don't feed them.

Trails from the parking lots wind across the rocky valley floor to the glacier faces, where a tormented chorus of squeaks, creaks, groans, and gurgles can be heard as the glacier creeps down the mountainside at an average rate of up to 3 ft per day. Care must be taken here, since rocks and chunks of ice frequently drop from the melting face.

These being New Zealand glaciers, there is much to do besides admire them. You can fly over them in helicopters or planes and land on the stable névé, or hike on them with guides. Remember that these structures are dynamic and always in motion—an ice cave that was visible yesterday might today be smashed under tons of ice that used to be just uphill of it. Likewise some of the fascinating formations that you see on the surface of the glacier were fairly recently at the very bottom of it higher up in the valley. Danger comes with this unstable territory; guides know the hazardous areas to avoid.

For the most part, flights are best made early in the morning, when visibility tends to be clearest. Seasonal variables around the glaciers are a surprising thing. Summer is, of course, warmer and by far the busiest season. But there is a lot more rain and fog that can scuttle "flight-seeing" and hiking plans. Winter is in fact a well-kept secret in these parts. In winter, snow doesn't fall at sea level in Franz Josef or Fox. Skies are clearer, which means fewer canceled flights and glacier hikes and more of the dazzling sunshine that makes views of the mountains so spectacular.

㉔ Outside the town of Fox Glacier, **Lake Matheson** has one of the country's most famous views. A walking trail winds along the lakeshore, and the snowcapped peaks of Aoraki and Mt. Tasman are reflected in the water. Allow at least an hour for the complete walk from town to the "view of views." The best time is early morning, before the mirrorlike reflections are fractured by the wind. From town, turn and walk toward the sea where a sign points to Gillespies Beach; then turn right again to reach the lake.

Lake Moeraki sits in the midst of Westland National Park, 90 km (56 mi) south of Fox Glacier. There isn't a town here; it's the site of a thoughtfully designed wilderness lodge. The immediate area's public access is **Monro Beach.** The 45-minute walk to the beach takes you through spectacular, fern-filled native forest to a truly remarkable beach: rock clusters jut out of incredibly blue waters, and rivers and streams flow over the sand into the Tasman Sea. You might arrive at a time when spunky little fiordland crested penguins are in transit from the sea to their stream- or hillside nests. Early morning and late afternoon are good but not sure bets to find them.

Two kilometers (1 mile) south of the trail entrance on the beach is a seal colony, which you will smell before you see it. If you venture that way, be sure to keep about 16½ ft away from the seals (the legal dis- tance), and don't block their path to the sea. A spooked seal will bowl you over on its lurch for the water and may even bite, so be extremely respectful of their space. Sculpted dark gray rocks also litter the beach to the south, and seals like to lie behind and among them, so look care- fully before you cross in front of these rocks.

Monro Beach is an utter dream, not least if you collect driftwood or rocks. On the road 2 km (1 mi) or so south of it, there is a lookout over the rock stacks at **Knights Point.** Farther south still, between Mo- eraki and Haast, the walkways and beach at **Ship Creek** are another stop for ferny forests and rugged coastline. Sand flies here can be vo- racious, so bring insect repellent and hope for a windy day.

Dining and Lodging

$$$ ✕ **Blue Ice Café.** This café is a departure both in cuisine and decor from the steak-and-chips joints so common on the West Coast. Along with pizza and a light menu of salads, lasagna, and the like, you'll find Green- shell mussels, pork ribs, rack of lamb, and *cervena* (farmed venison). Coffee and desserts such as hot kūmara custard pudding or fudge cake are delicious. With a 2 AM license, Blue Ice keeps buzzing late during the tourist season, and if it's warm enough you can dine outside on the deck. ⊠ *South end of Main Rd., Franz Josef,* ☎ *03/752–0707. MC, V. No lunch May–Oct.*

$$$$ ✕▥ **Franz Josef Glacier Hotels.** The largest hotel in the glacier region, this complex is split into two sites about 1 km (½ mi) apart at the north end of Franz Josef village. The rooms are a cut above average in size and furnishings, but be sure to ask for a room with glacier views— particularly stunning as the sun rises over the Southern Alps and lights up the glaciers. Larger suites with upgraded facilities are also available, and the hotel has a choice of three restaurants, none of which serve lunch. Entrées go beyond the basic lamb with choices such as grilled salmon with bok choy and dill aïoli. ⊠ *State Hwy. 6, Franz Josef,* ☎ *03/752–0729 or 0800/228–228,* 🆑 *03/752–0709,* 🆆🅴🅱 *www.scenic-circle. co.nz. 177 rooms. 3 restaurants, 2 hot tubs, 4 bars, laundry facilities; no a/c. AE, DC, MC, V.*

$$$$ ▥ **Wilderness Lodge Lake Moeraki.** A superb setting and a team of eco-
★ guides make this lodge an ideal place to get absorbed in the environ- ment. Built in the rain forest, 30 km (21 mi) north of the town of Haast on Highway 6, it's on the banks of the Moeraki River. On-site natu- ralists will take you along while they feed eels, and you may see fur seals and fiordland crested penguins. On organized night walks, they'll point out glowworms and the southern constellations. Rates include the use of canoes and mountain bikes, plus two short guided activi- ties. Longer guided hikes, fishing guides, lunch, and dinner drinks are an extra charge. ⊠ *Private Bag, Hokitika,* ☎ *03/750–0881,* 🆑 *03/750– 0882,* 🆆🅴🅱 *www.wildernesslodge.co.nz. 22 rooms. Fans, beach, boat- ing, fishing, laundry service; no smoking. AE, DC, MC, V. MAP.*

Outdoor Activities and Sports

FISHING

For information on fishing around Franz Josef and Fox, *see* Chapter 6.

ON AND ABOVE THE GLACIERS

The walks to the glacier heads mentioned above are the easiest way of seeing the glaciers. But joining a guided walk and getting up close to the glaciers' ice formations—the shapes created by the glaciers' movement and the streams of water running through them—is unforgettable.

Flying over the glaciers is also quite thrilling, and that thrill comes at considerable expense. The ultimate combination is to fly by fixed-wing plane or helicopter to the top or middle of the glacier and get out and walk on it. Fixed-wing landings on the snow atop the ice fields are fabulously scenic, but you have only 10 minutes out of the plane. Heli-hikes give you the most time on the ice, two to three hours of snaking up and down right in the middle of a stable part of the glacier. If you've never flown in a helicopter, the experience can be nearly heart-stopping, as the pull of the rotors lifts you up and into the glacial valleys. As you make your way to a landing spot, the pilot banks the helicopter so that the only things between you and the mass of ice below you are a sheet of glass and centrifugal force. It's a wild ride.

Alpine Guides Fox Glacier has half- or full-day guided walks on Fox Glacier, the only safe way to experience the ethereal beauty of the ice caves, pinnacles, and crevasses on top of the glaciers. The 3½- to 4-hour walk travels about 2 km (1 mi) up the glacier. The climb requires some fitness; a half day costs $42, a full day $70. Arguably the best option is to heli-hike, combining a helicopter flight onto and off of Fox Glacier and walking for two hours on the ice with a guide ($195). Or try the full-day ice-climbing excursion with mountaineering equipment provided ($180). Tours are given daily at 9:30 and 2. ⊠ *Box 38, Fox Glacier,* ☎ *03/751–0825,* FAX *03/751–0857,* WEB *www.foxguides. co.nz.*

Aoraki Aero Services has fixed-wing ski planes that fly over the glaciers. Landings amid craggy peaks in the high-altitude ski slopes are otherworldly. The 40-minute ($210) and one-hour ($270) flights both cover Fox and Franz Josef glaciers; the longer one includes a circuit of Aoraki and lands on Tasman Glacier. ⊠ *Franz Josef,* ☎ *03/752–0714; 0800/800–737 for Franz Josef; 0800/800–702 for Fox;* FAX *03/752–0786;* WEB *www.aorakiaero.co.nz.*

Franz Josef Alpine Guides provides a comprehensive guide service with a half-day walk ($45), a full-day trip ($90), or a heli-hike tour ($230). An all day ice-climbing adventure with all equipment provided costs $175. ☎ FAX *03/752–0047,* WEB *www.franzjosefglacier.com.*

The **Helicopter Line** operates several scenic flights over the glaciers from heliports at Franz Josef and Fox. The shortest is the 20-minute flight over Franz Josef Glacier ($160 per person); the longest is a 40-minute flight that includes a landing on the head of the glacier and a circuit of Aoraki and Mt. Tasman ($300). Two-and-a-half-hour heli-hikes are yet another option ($230). ⊠ *Main St. (Box 45, Franz Josef),* ☎ *03/752– 0767 or 0800/807–767,* FAX *03/752–0769,* WEB *www.helicopter.co.nz.*

The West Coast A to Z

BUS TRAVEL

InterCity buses run the length of the West Coast daily; buy tickets at local stations. The trip from Nelson runs about seven hours.
➤ BUS DEPOTS: **Franz Josef** (⊠ Main Rd.). **Greymouth** (⊠ Mawhera Quay).
➤ BUS LINES: **InterCity Franz Josef** (☎ 03/752–0164, WEB www. intercitycoach.co.nz). **InterCity Greymouth** (☎ 03/768–5101, WEB www.intercitycoach.co.nz).

CAR TRAVEL

The north end of the West Coast is roughly a four-hour drive from Nelson on Highway 6 or a five- to six-hour drive over Arthur's Pass on Highway 7 from Christchurch, the very top of which is harrowing to say the least. Hokitika and Greymouth are about 256 km (166 mi) from Christchurch.

To continue south out of the region, beyond Lake Moeraki, take Highway 6 along the south coast to Haast, where it turns inland to Wanaka and Queenstown. The driving time between Moeraki and Wanaka is about five hours.

EMERGENCIES

➤ EMERGENCY SERVICES: **Fire, police, and ambulance** (☎ 111).

TRAIN TRAVEL

The West Coast in general is poorly served by the rail network, but one glowing exception is the *TranzAlpine Express,* which ranks as one of the world's great rail journeys. This passenger train crosses the Southern Alps between Christchurch and Greymouth, winding through beech forests and mountains that are covered by snow for most of the year. The bridges and tunnels along this line, including the 8-km (5-mi) Otira Tunnel, represent a prodigious feat of engineering. The train is modern and comfortable, with panoramic windows as well as dining and bar service. The train departs Christchurch daily at 9 AM and arrives in Greymouth at 1:25 PM; the return train departs Greymouth at 2:25 PM and arrives at Christchurch at 6:35 PM. The one-way fare is $87, round-trip $119.

➤ TRAIN INFORMATION: **TranzAlpine Express** (☎ 0800/802–802, WEB www.tranzscenic.co.nz).

VISITOR INFORMATION

Two regional tourism organizations maintain helpful Web sites: Tourism West Coast (www.west-coast.co.nz) and Glacier Country Tourism Group (www.glaciercountry.co.nz). The visitor information centers at Franz Josef and Greymouth are both open daily, although the Franz Josef bureau shortens its hours slightly in winter and the Greymouth office has shorter hours on weekends.

➤ TOURIST INFORMATION: **Fox Glacier Visitor Centre** (⊠ State Hwy. 6, ☎ 03/751–0807). **Franz Josef Glacier Visitor Information Centre** (⊠ State Hwy. 6, Franz Josef, ☎ 03/752–0796, WEB www.doc.govt.nz). **Greymouth Information Centre** (⊠ Mackay and Herbert Sts., Greymouth, ☎ 03/768–5101, www.westcoastbookings.co.nz).

5 CHRISTCHURCH AND LOWER SOUTH ISLAND

This is it—picture-postcard New Zealand, where the country's tallest mountains are reflected in crystal-clear lakes and sheer rock faces tower above the fjords. The choice of activity is yours. You can enjoy some of the world's most dramatic views in complete peace and quiet or leap—literally, if you'd like—from one adrenaline rush to the next.

A S THE KEA FLIES, it's only 130 km (80 mi) from the eastern shores of South Island to its highest peak, 12,283-ft Aoraki (Mt. Cook). As many as 60 glaciers are locked in the Southern Alps, slowly grinding their way down to lower altitudes, where they melt into running rivers of uncanny blue-green hues. Aoraki/Mount Cook National Park is a UNESCO World Heritage Area, and the alpine region around it contains the Tasman Glacier, New Zealand's longest.

Updated by
Mere Wetere

The wide-open Canterbury Plains separate the mountains from the ocean. This is some of New Zealand's finest pastureland, and the higher reaches are sheep station territory, where life and lore mingle in South Island's cowboy country. This is the territory where young Samuel Butler dreamed up the satirical *Erewhon*—the word is an anagram of "nowhere." The station he lived on is now on a horse-trekking route.

Trekking is one of the things that Southland does best. The southwest corner of the island, where glaciers over millennia have cut the Alps into stone walls dropping sheer into fjords, is laced with walking tracks that take you into the heart of wild Fiordland National Park. The Milford Track is the best known—it has been called the finest walk in the world since a headline to that effect appeared in the London *Spectator* in 1908. If you're not keen on walking all the way to the Milford Sound, drive in and hop on a boat and take in the sights and sounds from on deck.

Christchurch was built on the fortunes made from the Canterbury region's sheep runs. People call it the most English city outside England, and, indeed, Christchurch was founded in 1850 by the Canterbury Association, a group of leading British churchmen, politicians, and peers who envisioned a settlement that would serve as a model of industry and ideals, governed by the principles of the Anglican faith. Whatever the historical reasons, the earthy gentility of Christchurch makes it a pleasant foil for the wilds of South Island.

Gold, on the other hand, fueled Dunedin's glory days. Following the Central Otago strike of 1861 thousands of tons of gold were shipped out of the city's port, but not before some of it went into building some of New Zealand's finest buildings in the city. Southwest of Dunedin, hanging off the bottom of South Island, Stewart Island is a study in remoteness. Commercial fishing settlements give way to bushland that the kiwi bird—so rare elsewhere in the country—still haunts. Expansive views across the Foveaux Strait from time to time alight with the *aurora australis,* the spectacular southern hemisphere equivalent of the northern lights.

Note: For more information on outdoor activities in lower South Island, *see* Chapter 6.

Pleasures and Pastimes

Bungy Jumping

Don't worry, New Zealanders aren't going to pressure you into jumping off a bridge with an elastic cord tied to your ankles. But if you have an overwhelming desire to bungy (the Kiwi spelling for bungee), this is the place to do it. The cost of the jump usually includes a "been there–done that" T-shirt and even a video of your daredevil act.

Dining

Christchurch has a fairly wide range of eateries, from cosmopolitan restaurants to earthy vegetarian cafés. The region has a thriving wine industry, as does the Waipara district.

The small fishing town of Bluff is known for two reasons in New Zealand—it is the southernmost tip of the South Island, and it gives its name to an oyster. The Bluff oyster is one of the country's great delicacies, so pick up a dozen fresh ones from a fish shop if you can, or try them in a restaurant. As for Dunedin and Queenstown, you'll find a good variety of restaurants because of the former's student population and the latter's influx of international visitors.

CATEGORY	COST*
$$$$	over $30
$$$	$23–$30
$$	$15–$22
$	under $15

*per person for a main course at dinner

Hiking

South Island's southwestern wilderness areas are the stuff of legendary tramping. The Milford Track, the Kepler, the Routeburn, the Hollyford—it doesn't get any better than these. The variety on these treks is astonishing; you'll see mountains, fjords, waterfalls, and rain forests.

Lodging

No matter where you stay in Christchurch, you're sure to find some of the best lodging in New Zealand, from luxury hotels and lodges to very fine B&Bs. The rest of lower South Island is blessed with great views; you'll almost always be able to find a place to stay overlooking a lake, river, or mountainous landscape. If you can forego luxury, basic but comfortable cabins can often be found in the most beautiful places. Farm stays are often set on lush green grasslands.

CATEGORY	COST*
$$$$	over $200
$$$	$125–$200
$$	$80–$125
$	under $80

*All prices are for a standard double room including tax.

Exploring Christchurch and Lower South Island

Great Itineraries

Touring the lower half of South Island requires making difficult choices. Do you want to walk the Milford Track, or does the remote Stewart Island appeal more? Will you go away disappointed if you miss Queenstown, the adventure capital, or would you just as soon station yourself in the snowy reaches of Aoraki? The Otago Peninsula has its own spectacular scenery and the charming city of Dunedin. The scenic coastal highway from Dunedin to Invercargill presents the exciting and wild Catlins coast to explore. And then there is Christchurch and side trips from the city to the precipitous Banks Peninsula.

To see it all would take a good three weeks, if you intend to do it justice and stay sane. Short of that, treat each of these areas as two- to three-day segments, mix them up to suit your fancy, and take into account travel time of three to five hours between each.

Numbers in the text correspond to points of interest on the Canterbury Region and the Southern Alps; Christchurch; and Southland, Otago, and Stewart Island maps.

IF YOU HAVE 3 DAYS

Spend the first or last day in ⊞ **Christchurch** ①–⑬, strolling through the beautiful **Christchurch Botanic Gardens** ⑤, poking around the **Arts**

Centre ⑧, perhaps heading out to **Mona Vale** ⑪ for afternoon tea. Then choose whether to drive to ⛰ **Aoraki (Mt. Cook)** ⑲, or fly to ⛰ **Queenstown** ㉓, or to ⛰ **Stewart Island** for two days. If you pick Aoraki, explore some of South Canterbury one day, making sure to stop at ⛰ **Lake Tekapo** ⑱, and take in the view from inside the Church of the Good Shepherd. You could spend the night here or at Aoraki/Mount Cook Village. On the next day take a flight over the mountain or onto the **Tasman Glacier** ㉑, followed by a walk into the Hooker Valley or up Mt. Sebastopol.

IF YOU HAVE 6 DAYS

Spend two days in ⛰ **Christchurch** ①–⑬, using the second to see the **International Antarctic Centre** ⑩ or ride the **Christchurch Gondola** ⑫. You could otherwise take the whole day and go to the town of ⛰ **Akaroa** ⑭ on the Banks Peninsula, drive up the summit of the volcanic dome, then take a road down to one of the bays on the other side of the peninsula. On the third day fly to ⛰ **Queenstown** ㉓. Depending on how active you are, you could easily spend three days here throwing yourself off a bridge, heli-skiing, and jet-boat riding. Next head to **Milford Sound** ㉗ via the scenic alpine township of Te Anau where the Kepler Track begins, to take in the amazing spectacle of sheer cliffs, deep water, and dense native bush. You could spend an adventurous day in ⛰ **Wanaka** ㉒, stopping in at Stuart Landsborough's Puzzling World or getting familiar with this gorgeous alpine area by kayaking, rafting, or skydiving. From here you could easily tack on a trip to the stunning West Coast, driving over the scenic Haast Pass to get there.

IF YOU HAVE 8 DAYS

With eight days you have the luxury of taking your time. You could spend four of them on the Milford or Kepler tracks, a couple more in ⛰ **Wanaka** ㉒ and ⛰ **Queenstown** ㉓, plus a couple more in ⛰ **Christchurch** ①–⑬ or **Dunedin** ㉘. Or you could feel like you're skirting the edge of the earth by driving to Dunedin to explore the fascinating Otago Peninsula and view its wildlife, **Larnach Castle** ㉙, and **Taiaroa Head** ㉚, then continuing south along the rugged Catlins coast to **Invercargill** ㉛ and on to the southernmost ⛰ **Stewart Island,** where you can spend three or four days doing some serious bushwalking and looking for kiwi birds in the wild. Or just go alpine and spend all of your time around Aoraki, Wanaka, and Queenstown.

When to Tour Christchurch and Lower South Island

This is the part of New Zealand that gets cold with a capital C in winter, so if you're coming for warm weather stay away between May and September. For skiing, snowboarding, and other winter sports, this is *the* time to come. From July through September you can be assured of snow around Queenstown and Wanaka, where the ski scene is pretty lively. In the height of summer—from December into February—popular places like Queenstown can get so crowded that they lose the relaxed, laid-back atmosphere New Zealand is famous for. If you hold off until April or May, leaves turn yellow and red, and the nearby mountains have a smattering of early season snow. You'll have the Alps more to yourself, and some lodgings offer bargains.

CHRISTCHURCH

Your first impression of Christchurch may take you aback—the city seems to be under the grand delusion that it is somewhere in southern England. The drive from the airport into town takes you through pristine suburbs of houses lapped by flowers and past playing fields where children flail at one another's legs with hockey sticks. The heart of this

The Canterbury Region and the Southern Alps

TO KAIKOURA

70

Cheviot

Hanmer
Springs 16

Maruia
Springs

7

Motunau

7

LAKE
SUMMER
FOREST PARK

15 Waipara

SOUTH
PACIFIC OCEAN

Pegasus
Bay

Amberley

NEW
ZEALAND

CANTERBURY

Woodend

Christchurch
1 — 13

Little
Akaloa

Okains
Bay

Lake
Brunner

ARTHUR'S PASS
NATIONAL
PARK

Belfast

Sumner

Pigeon
Bay

14 Akaroa

Oxford

Templeton

Lyttelton

Akaroa
Harbor

Arthur's
Pass 17

Cass

Lincoln

75

Banks
Peninsula

TO
GREYMOUTH

Craigieburn
Forest Park

73

Burnham

Lake
Ellesmere

Hokitika

Castle Hill
Conservation Area

Darfield

6

Ross

Lake
Coleridge

72

Southbridge

Rakaia River

Rakaia

Dorie

WEST
COAST

Methven

1

Harihari

Canterbury
Plain

Ashburton

Hakatere

Canterbury
Bight

Franz
Josef

AORAKI/
MOUNT COOK
NATIONAL
PARK

Rangitata

Geraldine

Winchester

Fox
Glacier

Lake
Tekapo 18

Fairlie

79

Pleasant
Point

Timaru

Aoraki
(Mt. Cook) 19

Pareora

Tasman
Glacier 21

AORANGI
The Hunters Hills

Aoraki/
Mount Cook
Village 20

Ben Ohau Range

Lake
Pukaki

Morven

80

Lake Pukaki

Twizel

KEY
Rail Lines

8

Lake Ohau

Lake
Benmore

83

Kurow

Oamaru

0   50 miles

0   75 km

Omarama

Otematata

TO
QUEENSTOWN

pancake-flat city is dominated by church spires; its streets are named Durham, Gloucester, and Hereford. And instead of the usual wild New Zealand torrents, there bubbles, between banks lined with willows and oaks, the narrow Avon River, suitable for punting.

With a population approaching 350,000, Christchurch is the largest South Island city and the only one with an international airport. It is also the forward supply depot for the main U.S. Antarctic base at McMurdo Sound, and if you come in by plane, you are likely to see the giant U.S. Air Force transport planes of Operation Deep Freeze parked on the tarmac at Christchurch International Airport.

Exploring Christchurch

The inner city is compact and easy to explore by foot; the central sights are easy to reach during an afternoon's walk. Outside the city boundaries, there are a number of special-interest museums and activities about 20 minutes away by car. There are also side trips into the Canterbury Plains countryside and to the Akaroa Peninsula, the remnant of an ancient volcanic dome whose steep, grassy walls drop to the sea.

A Good Walk

Start in Cathedral Square, the city's hub, before the landmark **Christchurch Cathedral** ⑨. By climbing up the cathedral's tower, you can survey the city before hitting its streets and parks. Back down in the square, you'll see the statue of Robert Godley, dubbed "the founder of Canterbury," along with the War Memorial and the old post office, built in 1879. You can't miss the tall, conical metal sculpture, the *Chalice*, which commemorates both the new millennium and the 150th anniversary of the founding of Christchurch. Forty-two leaves represent native trees while complex shapes, intertwined with the leaves, reflect elements of the cathedral's architecture. Take Worcester Boulevard out of the square, passing the Edwardian Regent Theatre and the **Southern Encounter Aquarium & Kiwi House** ⑬. One block west, you'll pass a statue of Antarctic explorer Robert Falcon Scott, then cross the Avon River on a bridge with ornate iron balustrades. Turn left on Cambridge Terrace to follow the Avon upstream. A hitching post and gas lamp mark one of the city's oldest gentlemen's clubs, the Canterbury Club. A short distance away, by the Hereford Bridge, is the redbrick Old Library Chambers (1876). The next bridge over the river is the imposing **Bridge of Remembrance** ②. Trees representing each of Christchurch's sister cities cluster next to the bridge.

The belfry of the Victorian Gothic **St. Michael and All Saints Anglican Church** ③ rises across the river as you continue along the tree-shaded bank. Passing Montreal Street, you'll find the **Antigua Boatshed** ④. This may inspire you to try your hand at punting; otherwise, you can walk up Rolleston Avenue with the **Christchurch Botanic Gardens** ⑤ on your left. These gardens form the southern part of **Hagley Park,** a magnificent wooded area. Across from the park loom the gray Gothic buildings of the **Arts Centre** ⑧, a great place to stop for a pick-me-up. Next to the center is the newly opened **Christchurch Art Gallery Te Puna O Waiwhetu** ⑦. You can walk a further 45 minutes to Victoria Square by continuing north up Rolleston Street.

TIMING

The core of this walk, from Cathedral Square to the Arts Centre and Canterbury Museum area, takes about an hour, not including the time you may spend checking out exhibits, browsing in shops, or punting on the Avon. If you're planning a visit to the Southern Encounter, try to be there for the salmon and trout feeding time at 1 PM. Your best

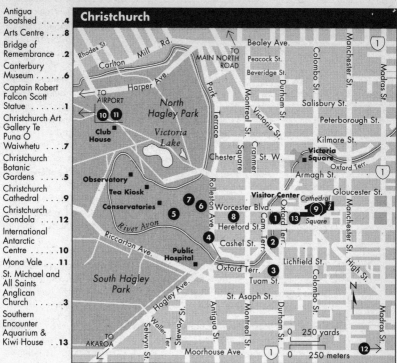

chance to see the Wizard riffing in front of the cathedral will be in summer, around 1.

Sights to See

4 **Antigua Boatshed.** Built for the Christchurch Boating Club in 1882, this is the only boat shed that remains of the half dozen that once stood along the Avon. Canoes may be rented for short river trips. ✉ *2 Cambridge Terr.,* ☎ *03/366–5885.* 🛶 *Canoe $6 per hr, rowboat $20 per hr.* ⏱ *Oct.–Mar., daily 7–5:30; Apr.–Sept., daily 10–4.*

★ **8** **Arts Centre.** Why Canterbury University gave up its former quarters seems a mystery. The collection of Gothic Revival stone buildings it used to inhabit represents some of New Zealand's finest architecture. In the college days of Ernest Rutherford (1871–1937), the university's most illustrious pupil, classes were held in what is now the Arts Centre. At Arts Centre Information you'll find "Rutherford's Den," the modest stone chamber where the eminent physicist conducted experiments in what was then a new field, radioactivity. It was Rutherford who first succeeded in splitting the atom, a crucial step in the harnessing of atomic power. In 1908 Rutherford's work earned him the Nobel prize—not for physics but for chemistry. Now a dynamic multimedia presentation depicts Rutherford and daily life at Canterbury.

The Arts Centre houses more than 40 specialty shops and studios, as well as art galleries, theaters, and art-house cinemas. It is also an excellent place to stop for food, coffee, or a glass of wine—there are four cafés and a wine bar. At the **Saturday and Sunday Market** you'll find jewelry, prints, bric-a-brac, and handmade clothing and crafts. This market is a seeding ground for talented artisans: many former stall holders are now resident in the center or running successful businesses in other parts of the city or country. Free live entertainment kicks off at noon and goes until 2 PM. For a $5 guided tour of the center led by the "town crier"—hear ye, hear ye—you should meet at the clock tower at 11 AM weekdays. ⊠ *Worcester Blvd. between Montreal St. and Rolleston Ave.,* ☎ *03/366–0989 or 03/366–0980; 03/363–2836 tours;* WEB *www.artscentre.org.nz.* ☼ *Shops and galleries daily 10–5.*

NEED A BREAK?

The Arts Centre has five eateries in its stone buildings and quadrangles. **Dux de Lux** (☎ 03/366–6919) is a sprawling, upbeat, popular cafeteria-style restaurant in a mock-Tudor building. The blackboard menu offers vegetarian items and seafood: quiches, crepes, sandwiches, breads and dips, pizzas, and a range of crisp salads. The courtyard is a great spot on a sunny day, especially with a beer from the brewery next door. The **Backstage Bakery** turns out specialty breads daily. Just follow your nose—it's right in the center of the complex. The **Boulevard Bakehouse** is great for coffee and a sweet. There is another café half a block down from the Bakehouse, and **Le Café** (⊠ 41 Hereford St., ☎ 03/366–6919) is the most refined of the five, a very pleasant place to taste New Zealand wine alongside bistro fare. All but the Le Café wine bar have outdoor seating in season.

② Bridge of Remembrance. Arching over the Avon, this bridge was built in memory of the soldiers who crossed the river here from King Edward Barracks, just down Cashel Street, on their way to the battlefields of Europe during World War I. ⊠ *Avon River at Cashel St.*

☾ ⑥ Canterbury Museum. When this museum was founded in 1867, its trading power with national and international museums was in moa bones. These Jurassic birds roamed the plains of Canterbury and are believed to have been hunted to extinction by early Māori settlers. The museum still houses one of the largest collections of artifacts from the moa hunting period. You'll also find a reconstruction of an early Christchurch streetscape and a natural-history discovery center that's great for kids. The Hall of Antarctic Discovery charts the links between the city and the U.S. bases on the frozen continent from the days of Captain Scott; Christchurch is still used as a forward supply depot for U.S. Antarctic bases. ⊠ *Rolleston Ave. and Worcester Blvd.,* ☎ *03/366–5000.* ▨ *Donation requested.* ☼ *Oct.–Mar., daily 9–5:30; Apr.–Sept., daily 9–5.*

① Captain Robert Falcon Scott statue. "Scott of the Antarctic" (1868–1912), who visited Christchurch on his two Antarctic expeditions, is just across Worcester Boulevard from the information center. The statue was sculpted by his widow, Kathleen Lady Kennett, and inscribed with his last words, written as he and his party lay dying in a blizzard on their return journey from the South Pole. ⊠ *Worcester Blvd. and Oxford Terr.*

⑦ Christchurch Art Gallery Te Puna O Waiwhetu. With the opening of this new exhibition space in spring 2003, Christchurch will claim the largest gallery in the South Island. It will include nine exhibit areas, as well as an auditorium, education facilities, and an outdoor sculpture garden. A lively schedule of shows focusing on Canterbury, New Zealand, and international art is in the works. The permanent collection spans art from the mid-17th century to the present day, with a particularly rich selection of regional art. The museum's Māori name, given by Ngai Tuahuriri, the Māori tribe of this area, refers to an artesian spring on the site and means "the wellspring of star-reflecting waters." ⊠ *Worcester Blvd. and Montreal St.,* ☎ *03/941–7970,* WEB *www.christchurchartgallery.org.nz.* ▨ *Free.* ☼ *Daily 10–6.*

★ ⑤ Christchurch Botanic Gardens. Think big. These superb gardens are known for the magnificent trees that were planted in the 19th century.

Many are the largest specimens found in the country—or even in their native lands. Pick up the Historic Tree Walk brochure for a self-guided Who's Who tour of the tree world. There are a number of specialty gardens as well. In spring spend time in the woodlands, in the rock garden, or at the primrose garden. In summer the rose garden is a display of every conceivable way to grow these beauties, and the water garden calls out for attention. In autumn that magnificent perennial border and the herb garden continue to amaze. And as the weather cools, the hips of species roses begin to redden. Spend time in the conservatories to discover tropical plants, cacti, and ferns on days when you'd rather not be outside. Any time of the year, be sure to go to the New Zealand plants area, where you can see plant life that you won't find in other countries. A small information center has displays and books. ✉ *Rolleston Ave.,* ☎ *03/366–1701.* 🎫 *Free.* 🕓 *Daily 7 AM–dusk, conservatories daily 10:15–4.*

❾ Christchurch Cathedral. The city's dominating landmark was begun in 1864, 14 years after the arrival of the Canterbury Pilgrims. Though consecrated in 1881, it wasn't completed until 1904. Carvings inside commemorate the work of the Anglican missionaries, including Tamihana Te Rauparaha, the son of a fierce and, for the settlers, troublesome Māori chief. Free guided tours begin daily at 11 and 2. For a view across the city to the Southern Alps, climb the 133 steps to the top of the bell tower. The cathedral is known for its boys' choir, which can be heard singing evensong at 5:15 on Tuesday and Wednesday and at 4:30 on Friday, except during school holidays. **Cathedral Square,** the city's focal point, buzzes with an arts-and-crafts market, food stalls, and street musicians. Gradual upgrades of the Square have been pursued since 1991; one of the more recent developments includes the addition of a designated marketplace.

If it's close to 1 PM when you emerge from the cathedral, look for the bearded gentleman with long hair, who's easy to spot because of the crowd that instantly forms around him. This is the **Wizard,** who offers funny and irreversial dissertations on just about any controversial subject—especially religion, politics, sex, and women's issues. Originally a free-lance soapbox orator, the Wizard (whose real name is Ian Channel) became so popular that he is now employed by the city council—one of his frequent targets. Don't be too disappointed if he's not around; his appearances have become less frequent in recent years, and he doesn't come out in winter, between May and October. ✉ *The Square,* ☎ *03/366–0046.* 🎫 *Tower $3.* 🕓 *Oct.–Mar., daily 8:30–7; Apr.–Sept., daily 9–5.*

★ ⑫ Christchurch Gondola. East of the city in the Port Hills, the gondola is the best vantage point from which to overlook Christchurch, the Canterbury Plains, and Lyttelton Harbour. At the top, you can wander through the **Time Tunnel,** which gives a brief history of the region. Best of all, sit with a glass of local wine at the Summit Cafe Brasserie and watch the sunset. Remember to ride the tram with your back to the mountain for the best views of the Southern Alps. If you don't have a car, you can hop a bus from the city center. The **Best Attractions Direct** bus includes the gondola on its run. ✉ *10 Bridle Path Rd., Heathcote,* ☎ *03/384–0700,* 🌐 *www.gondola.co.nz.* 🎫 *$15.* 🕓 *Daily 10–late evening.*

Hagley Park. Once cultivated Māori land, Hagley Park was developed by Pākehā settlers in the mid-1800s, with imported plants given trial runs in what would become the Botanic Gardens (☞ Christchurch Botanic Gardens, *above*). Now the park is divided into four sections, which together include walking and jogging tracks, cycling paths, and self-guided historic tours. Hagley Park North draws people to its tennis and pétanque courts; Little Hagley Park is classified as a heritage area. Hagley Park South is another good spot for sports, and the Botanic Gardens are perfect for strolling. ⊠ *Main entrance: Armagh St. at Rolleston Ave.*

★ ⏲ ⑩   **International Antarctic Centre.** Ever since Scott wintered his dogs at nearby Quail Island in preparation for his ill-fated South Pole expedition of 1912, Christchurch has maintained a close connection with the frozen continent. Dedicated to the past, present, and future of Antarctic exploration, this complex includes intriguing interactive displays, in which you can feel firsthand the Antarctic conditions, for example, as well as photographs and exhibits showing the sophisticated clothing and hardware that modern-day scientists use to carry out their work at the Antarctic bases. The audiovisual show is superb. You can also ride in a Hägglund, the actual tracked vehicle used for Antarctic programs. The 15-minute tour-ride tackles a specially designed adventure course; it leaves from the front of the complex daily, every 20 minutes from 9:20 on. The Centre is within walking distance of the airport— you can also catch a free shuttle from there—and about a 20-minute drive from central Christchurch. ⊠ *Orchard Rd.,* ☎ *03/358–9896,* WEB *www.iceberg.co.nz.* ⊟ *$18, Hägglund tour ride $10, joint ticket $26.* ⊘ *Oct.–Mar., daily 9–8; Apr.–Sept., daily 9–5:30.*

⑪   **Mona Vale.** One of Christchurch's great historic homesteads, the turn-of-the-last-century riverside Mona Vale makes for a lovely outing from the city. Come for lunch or Devonshire tea and make believe that your estate lies along the Avon as you stroll under the stately trees and through the well-tended fuchsia, dahlia, herb, and iris gardens. If the mood really takes you, go for a punt ride (a gondola-like boat) and contemplate your travels from the water. ⊠ *63 Fendalton Rd., 2 km (1 mi) from city center,* ☎ *03/348–9659 or 03/348–9666.* ⊟ *Free.* ⊘ *Grounds Oct.–Mar., daily 8–7:30; Apr.–Sept., daily 8:30–5:30; tea Sun.–Fri. at 10 AM and 3; smorgasbord lunch Sun. (reservations essential).*

❸   **St. Michael and All Saints Anglican Church.** St. Michael's dates from the city's earliest days. The first settlers sent out by Christchurch's founding Canterbury Association were known as the Canterbury Pilgrims, and their churches were focal points for the whole community. Built in 1872, the white-timber St. Michael's is an outstanding building. One of the bells in the wooden belfry came from England aboard one of four ships that carried the Canterbury Pilgrims. ⊠ *Oxford Terr. and Durham St.* ⊘ *Daily noon–2.*

⏲ ⑬   **Southern Encounter Aquarium & Kiwi House.** Fish and rare kiwi birds in the heart of Christchurch? The giant aquarium has an enormous variety of New Zealand fish species—from rocky tidal-pool creatures to those from lakes, rivers, and the briny deep. In some displays you can actually touch the critters if you want to. Watch divers feed giant eels or carpet sharks, cod, skates, and other rarely seen deep-water fish. Move on to get a glimpse of the kiwi; the shy, nocturnal national symbol is now hard to find in the wild, but here you can watch them foraging in a natural setting. For the gold diggers there's even a replica gold-mining town. ⊠ *Cathedral Sq.,* ☎ *03/359–0581,* WEB *www.southernencounter.co.nz.* ⊟ *$10.* ⊘ *Daily 9–5.*

Victoria Square. Once the city's commercial hub, Victoria Square now surrounds a modern governmental seat with 19th-century buildings. On its north side sits the striking Town Hall, with its auditorium, theater, and conference spaces. The stone ramp sloping from the square down to the river was used for watering horses; you'll also see

Christchurch's oldest iron bridge, a floral clock, and statues of Queen Victoria and Captain Cook. ⊠ *Armagh and Colombo Sts.*

OFF THE BEATEN PATH

GETHSEMANE GARDENS – As you might guess from the name, this suburban spot is a born-again Christian garden, where lush plants form religious symbols or texts. As you approach, take note of the 90-ft-long trellis fences and rock walls that spell GETHSEMANE. Inside, four meticulous knot gardens shape a Star of David, Star of Bethlehem, and two parallel Jerusalem crosses. The path through a fragrant, rose-filled maze spells JESUS, and the Prayer Garden includes the Lord's Prayer written in box hedges. In the St. Cecilia Chapel, you can pray to grow plants of your own like these. The garden is a 20-minute drive east of central Christchurch along Ferry Road. ⊠ *27 Revelation Dr., at top of Clifton Terr., Sumner,* ☎ *03/326–5848.* 🎟 *$5.* ⊘ *Daily 9–5.*

Dining

$$$–$$$$ ✕ **Cook'n with Gas.** This place was hot from the moment the kitchen team first lit up the stoves. Now with several awards in their belts, the chefs continue to create innovative dishes such as green-lipped mussels steamed in Stella Artois and slow-roasted pork belly with mashed white beans and pickled roast courgettes in tomato relish, a house specialty. The wine and beer lists focus on New Zealand and Australia but include a few bottles from farther afield. ⊠ *23 Worcester Blvd.,* ☎ *03/377–9166. AE, DC, MC, V. Closed Sun. No lunch.*

$$$–$$$$ ✕ **50 on Park.** Don't miss the breakfasts at this light and airy street-
★ side restaurant in the George Hotel—they're legendary. Start with the likes of baked semolina with char-grilled grapefruit and spiced rhubarb compote. Move on to chive waffles with roasted tomatoes and smoked bacon, or house-smoked salmon on English muffins with béarnaise sauce. Later in the day you can choose from dishes like lime-scented scallops and scampi or roasted *cervena* (farmed venison) with broad bean mash. ⊠ *50 Park Terr.,* ☎ *03/371–0250. AE, DC, MC, V.*

$$$–$$$$ ✕ **Pescatore.** In the intimate George Hotel, overlooking Hagley Park, you can try contemporary dishes using distinctively New Zealand ingredients. Look for Kaikoura crayfish with baby spring vegetables and champagne sauce or char-grilled tuna with red onion confit and a gingery kūmara (native sweet potato) *dauphinoise.* ⊠ *50 Park Terr.,* ☎ *03/371–0257. AE, DC, MC, V. No lunch.*

$$$–$$$$ ✕ **Sign of the Takahe.** From this dining room atop the Cashmere Hills, you'll have superb views over Canterbury and Christchurch. The Scottish castlelike restaurant, a longtime local favorite, maintains its silver-service style, though the menu has turned to Pacific Rim cuisine, with crayfish as the house specialty. Between courses, admire the heraldic display—it's the southern hemisphere's largest. ⊠ *200 Hackthorne Rd., Cashmere Hills,* ☎ *03/332–4052. AE, DC, MC, V.*

$$–$$$$ ✕ **Saggio di vino.** As the name suggests, wine is the raison d'être for
★ this long-established Christchurch vinotheque. The extensive list includes around 300 library choices, both local and imported. The menu isn't large, but it includes seasonal daily specials along with classics like carpaccio and fettuccine with pesto. Staff members are adept at recommending any of the 60 wines on the standard menu, by the glass or full bottles to accompany specific dishes. ⊠ *185 Victoria St.,* ☎ *03/ 379–4006. AE, DC, MC, V. No lunch Sat.*

$$–$$$ ✕ **Barringtons Big Steak Pub.** Serious carnivores will be supremely happy in the woody surroundings of this fun-time steak house. As the name suggests, the meaty meals are massive—some of the steaks weigh in at more than a kilogram (that's around 2 pounds). Beef reigns supreme, but you can also order ostrich, venison, and other red meat. A range of light meals for under $10 tend to those with smaller appetites. ⊠ *256 Barrington St.,* ☎ *03/337–5192. AE, DC, MC, V.*

$$–$$$ ✕ **Pedro's.** New Zealand's only Spanish restaurant has had a loyal following for more than two decades, and the menu hasn't changed a lot in all that time. Not that it has needed to—two favorites with the many regulars are *huevos a la flamenca* (eggs with chili-hot chorizo) and a whole roasted shoulder of baby lamb (for which you have to be seriously hungry). The decor is woody, simple, and, like the food, probably hasn't changed much since the doors were opened for the first time. ⊠ *143 Worcester Blvd.,* ☎ *03/379–7668. AE, DC, MC, V. Closed May–Aug.*

$$–$$$ ✕ **Sala Sala.** Generally considered to be Christchurch's top Japanese restaurant, Sala Sala wins praise for its ability to pair wines with its dishes. Diners can choose from sushi, *teppan yaki* (show time at the table), or traditional set meals. The last gives the chefs the opportunity to demonstrate their considerable skills. You might not recognize all the ingredients, but you can rest assured they will be fresh and delicious. ⊠ *184–186 Oxford Terr.,* ☎ *03/366–6755. AE, DC, MC, V. No lunch weekends.*

$–$$ ✕ **Zydeco.** Cajun fans suffering chili withdrawal will find a pretty good facsimile of what they're used to at this long-established central-city eatery. The 'gator on one wall and accordions on another set the scene for a menu chock-full of New Orleans classics like gumbo, jambalaya, and prawns (okay, they're not crawfish, but they're close) with andouille (sausage). ⊠ *113 Manchester St.,* ☎ *03/365–4556. AE, DC, MC, V. Licensed and BYOB.*

$ ✕ **The Cocoa Club.** This quirkily decorated restaurant (painted brick, antique tiles, brightly colored artwork) can surprise you with unusual combinations—fish crackling with shrimp paste and sweet pork relish, salmon with artichokes and fennel. That sort of innovation sounds expensive, but the prices are, in fact, pretty reasonable. ⊠ *705 Gloucester St.,* ☎ *03/381–2496. AE, MC, V. Licensed and BYOB. Closed Sun.–Mon. No lunch.*

$ ✕ **Main Street Café and Bar.** If you lived in Christchurch and liked hearty
★   vegetarian cooking, you'd probably end up at this bohemian storefront haunt once a week. The rich pumpkin and kūmara balls with peanut sauce or a choice of three mixed salads with a piece of homemade bread will help you get out of a vacation-food rut. The espresso's great, the desserts phenomenally delicious, and there's even a bar next door with a selection of international beers. ⊠ *840 Colombo St., at Salisbury St.,* ☎ *03/365–0421. AE, DC, MC, V.*

Lodging

$$$$ ▦ **Bangor Country Estate.** Don't hurry when you stay at this 1854 colo-
★   nial mansion; instead, let the long, meandering, tree-lined drive set the pace. Antiques and fine art fill the entranceway's sweeping staircase, the stately dining room, and the reception floor. The six rooms, two of which are detached from the main house, are each a study in elegance. The J. Hamilton Suite, for example, has a huge mahogany bed and clawfoot marble tub. Rates include full breakfast, predinner drinks, afternoon tea, and a marvelous five-course dinner. The estate is just south of Christchurch, 25 minutes from Christchurch International Airport. Pickup from the airport can be arranged. ⊠ *Bangor Rd., Darfield,* ☎ *03/318–7588,* ℻ *03/318–8485,* ⅦⅢ *www.bangor.co.nz. 6 rooms. Dining room, pool, tennis court, archery, croquet, 2 lounges; no smoking. AE, DC, MC, V. MAP.*

$$$$ ☐ **Charlotte Jane.** Once a girls' school, this magnificent 1891 villa now
★ sees pampered guests instead of disciplined students. The centrally located house brims with beautiful elements: the Victorian veranda, a
stained-glassed window above the entrance depicting the *Charlotte Jane*
(one of the first four ships to bring settlers to Christchurch in 1850),
a native kauri and *rimu* wood staircase, a rimu-paneled dining room,
and period furniture throughout the 10 beautiful guest rooms. Just across
the courtyard, a converted 1930s house holds two more suites, a rimu-
lined bar, and a restaurant. Delicious breakfasts are served whenever
you wish. ✉ *110 Papanui Rd.,* ☎ *03/355–1028,* FAX *03/355–8882,* WEB
*www.charlotte-jane.co.nz. 12 rooms. Restaurant, in-room VCRs, bar,
library, laundry service; no-smoking rooms. AE, DC, MC, V. BP.*

$$$$ ☐ **The George.** The adage that great things come in small packages
★ holds true for the George. In the spacious, modern guest rooms a
crisp, monochromatic color scheme weaves through everything from
the bedside notepads to the luxe bathroom products. Lovely details con-
tinually crop up, such as the magnificent brass handles on the entrance
door and the verdigris brass bannister. Adjacent to the Avon River and
Hagley Park, it's just a short walk to the Arts Centre and downtown
shopping. The two on-site restaurants are topflight. ✉ *50 Park Terr.,*
☎ *03/379–4560,* FAX *03/366–6747,* WEB *www.thegeorge.com. 57 rooms.
2 restaurants, massage, tennis court, health club, laundry facilities, laundry service, free parking. AE, DC, MC, V.*

$$$$ ☐ **The Weston House.** This fine, neo-Georgian building, registered by
the New Zealand Historic Places Trust, was built in the early 1920s
for a prominent Christchurch lawyer named George Weston. The restored house now combines its elegant style with plush modern amenities. The pair of spacious suites have private access; there's also a guest
lounge, dining area, and a secluded garden where you can take breakfast or just relax. ✉ *62 Park Terr.,* ☎ *03/366–0234,* FAX *03/366–5454,*
WEB *www.westonhouse.co.nz. 2 suites. Lounge, Internet, laundry service. AE, DC, MC, V. BP.*

$$$–$$$$ ☐ **Centra.** A contemporary hotel where business travelers, vacation-
ers, and conference delegates converge, the Centra can fulfill your of-
fice-with-a-view wishes. In this converted bank building, guests stay
in what once were offices; ceiling-to-floor windows afford panoramic
views of the cityscape. Rooms' shapes and sizes are anything but stan-
dard. The hotel is in the central business district, just a minute or two
on foot from Cathedral Square. The Streetside Bar is arguably the best
place in Christchurch to have a business drink. ✉ *Cashel and High
Sts.,* ☎ *03/365–8888,* FAX *03/365–8822,* WEB *www.centra.com.au. 199
rooms, 2 suites. Restaurant, health club, bar, business services, meet-
ing rooms. AE, DC, MC, V.*

$$$–$$$$ ☐ **The Chateau on the Park.** One of the older Christchurch hotels, this
★ French-chateau–style property is surrounded by 5 acres of delightful,
landscaped gardens next to Hagley Park. The main building has an in-
door water garden that wraps around the main entrance and foyer. Rooms
are spacious, and all have a view of part of the greenery. ✉ *189 Deans
Ave.,* ☎ *03/348–8999,* FAX *03/348–8990,* WEB *www.chateau-park.co.nz.
190 rooms, 6 suites. 2 restaurants, minibars, pool, bar, laundry service.
AE, DC, MC, V.*

$$$–$$$$ ☐ **Inter-Continental Christchurch.** This plush hotel is set in a prime lo-
cation overlooking Victoria Square and the river. The rooms are large
and luxurious, colored in rich tones of burgundy, gold, and blue. In
summer the best views are from rooms overlooking Victoria Square,
but in the winter popularity switches to those with views of the snow-
capped Alps to the west. The hotel is especially well equipped with restau-
rants and bars. A pianist plays in the glass-roof atrium—the heart of

this hotel—at lunch or in the evening. The Canterbury Tales restaurant, which specializes in innovative New Zealand cookery, and the Japanese restaurant, Yamagen, which has teppan yaki and traditional fare, are among the city's finest. ✉ *Kilmore and Durham Sts.,* ☎ *03/365–7799,* FAX *03/365–0082. 298 rooms. 3 restaurants, sauna, gym, bicycles, 3 bars, car rental. AE, DC, MC, V.*

$$$ 🏨 **Millennium.** Right at the city's heart, on Cathedral Square, this glossy complex blends an interesting mix of European and Asian touches. In the rooms, for instance, Italian lamps stand beside Asian ginger jars. From the lounge you'll have a magnificent view over the busy square. ✉ *14 Cathedral Sq., Central Christchurch* ☎ *03/365–1111 or 0800/ 358–888,* FAX *03/365–7676,* WEB *www.millenniumchristchurch.co.nz. 162 rooms, 17 suites. 2 restaurants, café, in-room data ports, minibars, sauna, health club, bar, business services, valet parking. AE, DC, MC, V.*

$$$ 🏨 **Riverview Lodge & Churchill Suites.** This grand Edwardian house
★ overlooking the Avon is one of the finest bed-and-breakfasts in Christchurch. With native timber in details throughout the house—such as solid kauri stairs and doors—it offers superbly comfortable, historic accommodations. All rooms are upstairs, and the three front rooms provide great views of the river. The Turret Room has a charming alcove from which to enjoy the view while snuggled in the antique chaise lounge. In an adjacent two-story, Edwardian town house are two spacious suites, each with a lounge and kitchen. The lower-floor suite has one bedroom and French doors that open out to a secluded garden. The upper floor has two bedrooms. The city center is a pleasant (and safe at night) 15-minute walk along the river, which allows you to leave the car behind. ✉ *361 Cambridge Terr.,* ☎ *03/365–2860,* FAX *03/365– 2845. 4 rooms, 2 suites. Boating, bicycles. MC, V. BP.*

$$–$$$ 🏨 **Turret House.** Built in 1905 as a family home for a retired farmer— and now run by retired farmers—this lodge has fittingly comfortable, well-maintained rooms and a friendly atmosphere. All rooms are furnished differently, and prices vary accordingly. For a couple, the medium-size rooms offer a good combination of space and value. If you happen to be interested in rugby, the hosts are both keen on the sport and will be happy to fill you in on the latest. ✉ *435 Durham St.,* ☎ *03/365–3900,* FAX *03/365–5601,* WEB *www.turrethouse.co.nz. 8 rooms. MC, V. CP.*

Nightlife

Christchurch's after-dark action has picked up over the years. The 24-hour **Christchurch Casino** has blackjack, American roulette, baccarat, gaming machines, and other ways to try your luck. Dress is smart-casual or better; you will be turned away at the door if you arrive in jeans. There are free shuttles to and from local hotels and motels. ✉ *30 Victoria St.,* ☎ *03/365–9999.*

For dancing and dining into the wee hours, your best bet is to head to the myriad bars and cafés along the popular **Oxford Terrace strip** by the Avon River. Many of the venues spill out onto the footpath. The **Coyote** (✉ *126 Oxford Terr.,* ☎ *03/366–6055*) serves good food during the day and then transforms into one of the city's popular bars, with partying 'til the break of dawn.

For some natural suds in the city center try the **Loaded Hog** bar and restaurant (✉ *Manchester and Cashel Sts.,* ☎ *03/366–6674*). This brewery produces excellent beers like Hogs Dark and Hogs Gold. Check out the amusing caricatures of pop culture icons. If you just want to kick back over a coffee or a glass of wine, try **Bar Santé in the Square** (✉ *14 Cathedral Sq.,* ☎ *03/365–1111*).

The **Bard** (✉ Oxford Terr. and Gloucester St., ☎ 03/377–1493) is said to be Christchurch's only authentic English pub with live entertainment, English ales on tap, and hearty pub meals.

Outdoor Activities and Sports

Bicycling

Mainland Mountainbike Adventures organizes off-road tours in the Canterbury region as well as customized tours around the South Island. The day tours, such as the not-too-challenging half-day ride through Bottle Lake Forest ($70), are a good introduction to mountain biking. More experienced bikers can sign up for the tougher multiday trips, which include food, accommodation, and transport. ✉ *11 Nirvana St., Christchurch*, ☎ *03/329–8747 or 027/229–5349,* WEB *www. mountainbiketours.co.nz.*

Horse Trekking

Around Christchurch, the Canterbury Plains and encircling mountain ranges provide a dramatic setting for riding. *See* Chapter 6 for operators and trip information.

Shopping

The best **Arts Centre** shopping is at the **Saturday and Sunday Market,** which has various Kiwi goods, including handmade sweaters and woolens. Inside the Arts Centre buildings, the **Galleria** consists of more than two dozen shops and studios for artisans and crafts workers, from potters to weavers to some very good jewelry makers. The quality of work varies considerably from shop to shop, but this is one of the few places where many crafts workers are represented under one roof. Other boutiques dot the complex as well; all are open daily. ✉ *Worcester Blvd.,* ☎ *03/379–7573.*

Kathmandu sells a complete and colorful range of outdoor gear and maps. ✉ *235 High St.,* ☎ *03/366–7148.*

Riccarton Mall is South Island's largest shopping mall. It has more than 90 stores. ✉ *129 Riccarton Rd.,* ☎ *03/348–4119.*

Untouched World is an offbeat store that brings together all that's hip and natural in New Zealand. Apart from its own line of stylish, outdoorsy clothing, you'll find New Zealand artwork, handcrafted jewelry, organic produce, aromatherapy and essential oils, natural skin-care products, and great gift ideas. The attached restaurant serves organic food, wine, and beer. ✉ *155 Roydvale Ave., Burnside,* ☎ *03/357–9399.*

Christchurch A to Z

AIR TRAVEL
CARRIERS

Qantas and Air New Zealand link Christchurch with cities on both North and South islands, including Auckland. Flying time between Christchurch and Auckland is an hour and 15 minutes. Air New Zealand also flies from Christchurch to Queenstown, a roughly one-hour flight time.

➤ CARRIERS: **Air New Zealand** (☎ 03/379–5200, WEB www. airnewzealand.com). **Qantas** (☎ 0800/808–767 within New Zealand, WEB www.qantas.com.au).

AIRPORT
Christchurch Airport (CHC) is 10 km (6 mi) northwest of the city.
➤ AIRPORT INFORMATION: **Christchurch International Airport** (✉ Memo-

rial Dr., Harewood, ☎ 03/358–5029, WEB www.christchurch-airport. co.nz).

TRANSFERS

Super Shuttle buses meet all incoming flights and charge about $12 per passenger to city hotels. Depending on the number of people traveling, the fare is reduced. Metro buses operate between the airport and Cathedral Square from 6:45 AM to 9:15 PM daily. The fare is $4. A taxi to the city costs about $30.

➤ CONTACTS: **Metro** (✉ Litchfield and Colombo Sts., ☎ 03/366–8855, WEB www.metroinfo.org.nz). **Super Shuttle** (☎ 03/357–9950).

BIKE TRAVEL

Christchurch's relative flatness makes for plenty of easy biking, and the city has cultivated good resources for cyclists. White lines and sometimes red-colored tarmac denote cycling lanes on city streets, and holding bars are at the ready near intersections. You can pick up a route map from the city council; there's a particularly nice, paved cycling path along the Avon. Cyclone Cycles rents out mountain bikes; City Cycle Hire rents touring bikes.

➤ CONTACTS: **City Cycle Hire** (✉ 73 Wrights Rd., ☎ 03/339–4020, WEB www.cyclehire-tours.co.nz). **Cyclone Cycles** (✉ 245 Colombo St., ☎ 03/332–9588).

BUS TRAVEL

InterCity operates a daily bus service between Christchurch and Dunedin, Aoraki/Mount Cook Village, Nelson, and Queenstown. The Coast to Coast Shuttle bus goes daily to Arthur's Pass Village and Greymouth from Christchurch.

➤ BUS DEPOT: **Christchurch Travel Centre** (✉ 124 Worcester St.).
➤ BUS LINES: **Coast to Coast Shuttle** (☎ 0800/800–847). **InterCity** (☎ 03/377–0951, WEB www.intercitycoach.co.nz).

BUS TRAVEL WITHIN CHRISTCHURCH

Christchurch's city bus system may look confusing, but luckily it has a thorough Web site and a helpful hot line. Tickets cost between $1 and $2 depending on your destination; with multitrip tickets you'll get a dozen rides for the cost of nine. You can also get between a handful of top sights on the double-decker Red Buses, which leave from Cathedral Square. Day passes cost $10.

➤ INFORMATION: **Christchurch Metro Services** (☎ 0800/324–636, WEB www.metroinfo.org.nz). **Red Bus** (☎ 0800/733–287, WEB www.redbus. co.nz).

CAR RENTAL

All the major car rental companies have bureaus at the Christchurch International Airport.

➤ CONTACTS: **Avis** (✉ Christchurch International Airport (☎ 0800/655–111 or 03/358–9634). **Budget** (✉ corner of Lichfield St. and Oxford Rd., ☎ 09/366–0072 or 09/357–9150). **Hertz** (✉ 46 Lichfield St., ☎ 03/366–0549 or 03/358–6757). **National** (✉ 143 Victoria St., ☎ 03/366–5574 or 03/366–5027). **Nationwide Rental Cars** (✉ 524 Wairakei Rd., ☎ 09/401–0389 or 0800/803–003).

CAR TRAVEL

Highway 1 links Christchurch with Kaikoura and Blenheim in the north and Dunedin in the south. Driving time for the 330-km (205-mi) journey between Christchurch and Aoraki/Mount Cook Village is 5 hours; the trip between Christchurch and Dunedin lasts 5½ hours. Driving time for the 192-km (119 mi) journey from Christchurch to Kaikoura is three hours.

Getting in and out of town is quite easy, as a clear lattice of streets leads to the city center. However, central Christchurch is a warren of one-way streets; it's best to leave your car in a parking lot while exploring this area. Peak traffic times here run from 8 to 9 AM and 3 to 7 PM.

EMERGENCIES

While Christchurch does not have an all-night pharmacy, Urgent Pharmacy stays open from 9 AM to 11 PM.

➤ EMERGENCY SERVICES: **Christchurch Hospital** (✉ Riccarton St., ☎ 03/364–0640). **Fire, police, and ambulance** (☎ 111). **Urgent Pharmacy** (✉ corner of Bealy Ave. and Colombo St., ☎ 03/366–4439).

TOURS

ADVENTURE TOURS

Taking the High Country Explorer is definitely one of the best and most action-packed ways of getting into the Canterbury Plains, the Southern Alps, and experiencing the world-famous TranzAlpine train journey. The full-day trip takes you on a one-hour bus trip, a 15-km (9-mi) jet-boat cruise, and a 65-km (40-mi) four-wheel-drive safari, before setting you on the TranzAlpine back to Christchurch. The scenery is spectacular, the boat ride a thrill, and your safari guide will discuss the region's human and natural history, flora and fauna, and geography and geology. After the two-hour train trip back to Christchurch railway station, a coach or shuttle will take you to your accommodations. A full-day trip is $275 per person.

➤ CONTACT: **High Country Explorer** (✉ 6 Fraser Pl., Rangiora, ☎ 03/377–1391, FAX 03/313–6494, WEB www.high-country.co.nz).

BOAT TOURS

Punting on the Avon is perfectly suited to the pace of Christchurch. You can hire punts with expert boatmen at the Worcester Street Bridge, near the corner of Oxford Terrace, daily from 10 to 6 in summer and from 10 to 4 the rest of the year. A 20-minute trip costs $10.

➤ CONTACT: **Punting on the Avon** (✉ Worcester Blvd. bridge landing, ☎ 03/379–9629).

PRIVATE GUIDES

Jack Treagar, great-great-grandson of early settler Thomas Jackson Hughes, provides a personal historic tour of Christchurch. It covers Lyttleton, Sumner, and the Canterbury Provincial Council buildings, takes just over three hours, and costs $53. The tour includes an elegant morning tea and entry to the Timeball Station at Lyttleton.

➤ CONTACT: **Jack Treagar** (☎ 03/322–7844 or 021/320–951).

SIGHTSEEING TOURS

Canterbury Leisure Tours offers day trips to Kaikoura, Hanmer Springs, Akaroa, Arthur's Pass, and Aoraki (Mt. Cook). It also offers a range of half-day tours and activities, including wine trails, night tours, sheep-farm visits, and golfing excursions.

Canterbury Trails Ltd. runs several tours from Christchurch. Among their itineraries is a full-day tour to Akaroa and Banks Peninsula, which includes a dolphin-sighting cruise. Longer tours include trips to Arthur's Pass National Park and Hanmer Springs—as well as spectacular luxury-lodge tours, which go farther afield.

➤ CONTACTS: **Canterbury Leisure Tours** (✉ 260 Port Hills Rd., ☎ 03/384–0999 or 0800/484–485, WEB www.leisuretours.co.nz). **Canterbury Trails, Ltd.** (✉ 5 Dannys La., Christchurch, ☎ 03/337–1185, FAX 03/337–5085, WEB www.canterburytrails.co.nz).

Guided walking tours ($8) of the city depart daily at 9:45 and 12:45 from the Christchurch–Canterbury Visitor Information Centre (☞ Visitor Information, *below*) and depart at 10 and 1 from the red-and-black kiosk in Cathedral Square. The tours take about two hours.

TRAIN TRAVEL

InterCity operates a daily TranzAlpine Express train to Arthur's Pass Village and Greymouth, departing at 9 AM. The train goes through gorgeous scenery with striking colors at any time of year, from the tawny vineyards of the Canterbury Plains through granite canyons to the jade green, wild West Coast bush. The trip takes a little over four hours.
➤ TRAIN STATION: **Christchurch Railway Station** (⊠ Troup Dr., ☎ 0800/802–802).
➤ TRAIN LINE: **Tranzrail** (☎ 03/377–0951 or 0800/802–802, WEB www.tranzscenic.co.nz).

TRAM TRAVEL

The historic Christchurch Tramway serves as an attraction in its own right and doubles as a way to get around when those feet tire. A city circuit takes in Cathedral Square, Worcester Boulevard, Rolleston Avenue, Armagh Street, and New Regent Street. It stops close to all major attractions, including the Arts Centre, Botanic Gardens, and Canterbury Museum. A full-day pass costs $10 and is valid for up to two days.
➤ CONTACT: **Christchurch Tramway** (☎ 03/366–7830, WEB www.tram.co.nz).

VISITOR INFORMATION

The visitor information center is open weekdays 8:30–5, weekends 8:30–4.
➤ TOURIST INFORMATION: **Christchurch–Canterbury Visitor Information Centre** (⊠ Chief Post Office Building, Cathedral Sq., ☎ 03/379–9629, WEB www.christchurchtourism.co.nz).

SIDE TRIPS FROM CHRISTCHURCH

If you have more than a day or two to spend in the Christchurch area, head out to the countryside for a change of pace. East of the city, you can explore the wonderful coastline of the Banks Peninsula. Looking north, consider stopping in Waipara and its wineries if you're en route to or from Kaikoura. Hanmer Springs' thermal baths are good for a relaxing soak. Plan an entire day for any of these side trips.

Akaroa and the Banks Peninsula

⑭ *82 km (50 mi) east of Christchurch.*

Bearing the shape of a long-dormant volcanic cone, the Banks Peninsula—that nub that juts into the Pacific southeast of Christchurch—has a coastline indented with small bays, where sheep graze almost to the water's edge. It's best known for the town of Akaroa, which was chosen as the site for a French colony in 1838. The first French settlers arrived in 1840 only to find that the British had already established sovereignty over New Zealand by the Treaty of Waitangi. Less than 10 years later, the French abandoned their attempt at colonization, but the settlers remained and gradually intermarried with the local English community. Apart from the *rue* (street) names and a few surnames, there is little sign of a French connection anymore, but the village has a splendid setting. A half day will get you to and from Akaroa, including a drive up to the edge of the former volcanic dome, but take a full day if you want to do other exploring of the peninsula. The main route to Akaroa is Highway 75, which leaves the southwest corner of Christchurch as Lincoln Road. The 82-km (50-mi) drive takes about 90 minutes. If you'd rather not drive, the **Akaroa Shuttle** (☎ 0800/500–929) runs between the Christchurch–Canterbury Visitor Information Centre and Akaroa. Buses depart daily from Christchurch December through April at 9, 10, and 4. They depart from the **Akaroa Information Centre** (✉ Rues Lavaud and Balguerie, ☎ 03/377–1755, WEB www.akaroa.com) at 8:30, 2:15, and 4:30. From May through November, the shuttle departs Christchurch daily at 10 and leaves from Akaroa at 4, but there are often extra scheduled trips that vary—check the latest timetables. The cost is $15 one-way or $25 round-trip.

The best way to get the feel of Akaroa is to stroll along the waterfront from the lighthouse to Jubilee Park. The focus of historic interest is the **Akaroa Museum,** which has a display of Māori greenstones and embroidery and dolls dating from the days of the French settlement. The museum includes Langlois-Eteveneaux House, the two-room cottage of an early French settler, which bears the imprint of his homeland in its architecture. ✉ *Rues Lavaud and Balguerie,* ☎ *03/304–7614.* ☞ *$2.50.* ◷ *Daily 10:30–4:30.*

The picture-book **Church of St. Patrick,** near the Akaroa Museum, was built in 1864 to replace two previous Catholic churches—the first destroyed by a fire, the second by a storm. ✉ *Rue Pompallier.* ◷ *Daily 8–5.*

The contrast of the rim of the old volcanic cone and the coves below is striking. An afternoon drive to the summit and then a drop into one of the coves leaves you with a feeling like you've found your own corner of the world. At **Okains Bay,** a small settlement lies at the bottom of Okains Bay road, which winds down from the summit and ends at a beach sheltered by tall headlands. There's a cave in the rocks on the right and a path above it that leads to the remnants of a pier, now just a cluster of tilting pilings in the water. Sheep paddocks rise on either side of the sand, cradling it in green. There's a small general store that doubles as a post office back in the village, as well as a tiny old church to poke your head into if you're curious.

Another way to get to the feel of the peninsula is to have an afternoon cold one with locals at **Hilltop Tavern.** ✉ *Hwy. 75 at Summit Rd., Akaroa,* ☎ *03/325–1005.*

Dining and Lodging

$$$$ ✕ **Harbour 71.** Eclectic spins on New Zealand produce, meat, and seafood, along with a seaside location, make for sought-after reservations here. Subtle Asian influences spark sauces and enhance the flavors of salmon, lamb, or beef. Look through the New Zealand wines on the list to find some of the local labels. ✉ *71 Beach Rd.,* ☎ *03/304–7656. AE, MC, V. Closed Wed.–Thurs. Mar.–Nov.*

$$$–$$$$ ▦ **Oinako Lodge.** Surrounded by a garden, a five-minute walk from the town and harbor of Akaroa, this charming Victorian manor house still has its original ornamented plaster ceilings and marble fireplaces. The exterior paint may be weathered, a casualty of the sea air, but the building's elegance is still plainly evident. You'll find fresh flowers in the spacious and pleasantly decorated rooms; half have whirlpool baths. ✉ *99 Beach Rd., Akaroa,* ☎ FAX *03/304–8787,* WEB *www.oinako. co.nz. 6 rooms. Dining room, lounge. AE, DC, MC, V. BP.*

Outdoor Activities and Sports

The 35-km (22-mi) **Banks Peninsula Track** crosses beautiful coastal terrain. From Akaroa you hike over headlands and past several bays, waterfalls, and seal and penguin colonies, and you might see Hector's dolphins at sea. Two-day ($120) and four-day ($180) tramps are available between October 1 and April 27. Overnight in cabins with fully equipped kitchens, which you might share with other hikers. Rates include lodging, transport from Akaroa to the first hut, landowners' fees, and a booklet describing the features of the track. No fear of overcrowding here—the track is limited to accommodate 12 people at a time and booking well ahead is essential. ⊠ *Box 50, Akaroa,* ☎ *03/ 304–7612,* WEB *www.bankstrack.co.nz.*

Waipara

⑮ *57 km (35 mi) north of Christchurch.*

The attractive rural township of Waipara is about 45 minutes north of Christchurch heading toward Kaikoura. The area was once renowned for its profusion of moa (an enormous, extinct, flightless bird) bones. It used to be dotted with swamps—perhaps the reason the Māori named it Waipara, meaning "muddy water"—into which hundreds of moa tumbled over the centuries. That same geological history has given Waipara a different soil type from the rest of Canterbury and Waipara is consequently one of the country's most exciting wine-making regions. A handful of Waipara's wineries run pleasant restaurants as well.

The huge, cathedral-like **Canterbury House Winery** (⊠ 780 Glasnevin Rd., Amberley, ☎ 03/314–6900) is probably the most serious in the area. Family-run **Pegasus Bay** (⊠ Stockgrove Rd., Waipara, ☎ FAX 03/ 314–6869) also has one of the region's best reputations.

Waipara is also a departure point for the **Weka Pass Railway,** which drives through farmlands and interesting rock formations in a train pulled by a vintage locomotive. It runs twice a day on the first and third Sunday of each month and public holidays. ⊠ *McKenzies Rd.,* ☎ *03/366–2325,* WEB *www.wekapassrailway.co.nz.* ⊡ *$12.*

Dining and Lodging

$$$-$$$$ ✕ **Waipara Springs Winery.** At one of the valley's oldest wineries, you can stop for lunch along with a wine tasting. The café, in converted farm buildings, serves light dishes such as omelets and antipasti. Watch for the daily specials, which tend to be a bit more adventurous than the standard menu, and match well with the vineyard's sauvignon blanc, cabernet sauvignon, and their top chardonnay. ⊠ *State Hwy. 1,* ☎ *03/314–6777,* WEB *www.waiparasprings.co.nz. AE, DC, MC, V. Closed mid-June–Aug. No dinner.*

$$-$$$ ✕ **Norwester Café & Bar.** Sophisticated dining in rural places is one of life's great pleasures, especially when it involves the best regional produce. You can enjoy such a meal here either outdoors or inside the 1928 bungalow; the decor's colors reflect the Canterbury landscape. Lunch offers an eclectic mix of both casual and stylish dishes, while evening is formalized with the Classic After 5 menu. The espresso is superb, and you can compliment your meal with one of the fabulous local wines. ⊠ *95 Main North Rd., Amberley, 7 km (4½ mi) south of Waipara,* ☎ *03/314–9411. AE, DC, MC, V.*

$$$$
★ ⊞ **Mountford Vineyard.** At this stylish home stay you can settle into the Canterbury Plains amid the chardonnay and pinot noir grapes of a working vineyard. Former railway buildings have been transformed into a gracious, Mediterranean-style complex with a large, white-pebbled central courtyard overlooking the rows of grapes. The heart of the building is the dining room, with its handcrafted wrought-iron fixtures, slate floors, and high ceiling. The spacious guest rooms, done in sage and white, have lime-wash kauri furniture and exposed beams;

both have balconies. ✉ *Omihi Rd. (State Hwy. 1), Waipara,* ☎ *03/ 314–6819,* FAX *03/314–6820. 2 rooms. Dining room, lounge. AE, DC, MC, V. MAP.*

Hanmer Springs

⑯ *120 km (75 mi) northwest of Christchurch.*

Long before Europeans arrived in New Zealand, Māori travelers knew the Hanmer Springs area as Waitapu (sacred water). Early settlers didn't take long to discover these thermal springs, which bubble out into a serene alpine environment, just a two-hour drive from Christchurch. More than 100 years ago European visitors would "take the water" for medicinal purposes, but nowadays you will find it far more pleasant to lie back and relax in the water than to drink the stuff. From Christchurch follow Highway 1 north to Highway 7 at Waipara, 57 km (35 mi) from the city. The drive then continues through the small town of Culverden, where Highway 7A turns toward Hanmer Springs, which is well signposted.

The **Hanmer Springs Thermal Reserve** remains the number one reason to visit the area and now consists of 10 thermal pools, one freshwater pool, an activity pool, a children's slide, and a hydroslide. The reserve also has massage, a sauna and steam room, and a restaurant. ✉ *Amuri Ave.,* ☎ *03/315–7511,* WEB *www.hotfun.co.nz.* ◻ *$10, private pool $15 per person per ½ hr (minimum 2 people), sauna $17 per ½ hr, hydroslide $5.* ☉ *Daily 10–9.*

The forest around Hanmer Springs, planted by convict labor in the early 1900s, has a distinctly European look. You'll find European larch, Austrian pine, European alder, and other varieties. The **Hurunui Visitor Information Centre** (✉ Amuri Ave., ☎ 03/315–7128, WEB www.hurunui. com) has maps and fact sheets detailing several walks.

THE SOUTHERN ALPS

The Canterbury Plains, which ring Christchurch and act as a brief transition between the South Pacific and the soaring New Zealand Alps, are the country's finest sheep pastures, as well as its largest area of flat land. But although this may be sheep- and horse-trekking heaven, the drive south along the plain is mundane by New Zealand standards until you leave Highway 1 and head toward the Southern Alps. By contrast, the drive to Arthur's Pass quickly takes you up into the hills, and Route 73 is a good way to get to Westland and the glaciers at Fox and Franz Josef, but it would be the long way to Queenstown.

Arthur's Pass

⑰ *153 km (96 mi) northwest of Christchurch.*

Arthur's Pass National Park is another of New Zealand's spectacular alpine regions, and hiking opportunities abound. On the way to the pass, the **Castle Hill Conservation Area** is littered with interesting rock formations. You'll find the parking lot for Castle Hill on the left several miles past Lake Lyndon. Along with nearby Craigieburn Forest Park, Castle Hill gets less rainfall than Arthur's Pass National Park. Craigieburn itself has wonderful beech and fern forests.

Arthur's Pass National Park has plenty of half- and full-day hikes and 11 backcountry tracks with overnight huts for backpacking in a gorgeous setting: waterfalls, gorges, alpine herbs and flowers, grasslands, and stunning snowcapped peaks. The landscape and vegetation change dramatically according to the altitude and rainfall, from the drier beech forests and tussock grasslands on the eastern side to the dense forestation on the steep western slopes, which get five times more rain. Above the tree line you'll find snowfields and, between November and March, masses of wildflowers, including giant buttercups. Around the summit you'll also have a good chance of seeing *kea,* the South Island's particularly intelligent and curious birds. More information on the park is available on the Department of Conservation's Web site, www.doc.govt.nz.

The pass is the major mid-island transit to the West Coast. The west side of the pass is unbelievably steep—be warned that this may be the most hair-raising paved road you'll ever drive. The village of Arthur's Pass itself isn't much to speak of, and in foul weather it looks rather forlorn. There are a restaurant and a store for basic food supplies.

Lodging

$$$$ ⊞ **Wilderness Lodge Arthur's Pass.** That pot of gold at the end of the
★ rainbow is in fact a Southern Alps lodge surrounded by spectacular peaks, beech forests, and serene lakes. This back-to-nature lodge shares 6,000 acres with a sheep farm and nature reserve in a valley called Te Ko Awa a Aniwaniwa (Valley of the Mother of Rainbows) by its first Māori visitors. From a hillside perch it overlooks the Waimakariri River, which has carved a gaping swath through the pass. Rooms have balcony views of this incredible area. By taking advantage of the walks and guided nature day trips, staying here constitutes a superb short course in rare, high-country ecology and sheep farming. Longer, guided trips in the region, which can introduce you to limestone caves, a glacier basin, or rare alpine plants, can also be arranged. ⊠ *130 km (81 mi) west of Christchurch on State Hwy. 73 (Box 33, Arthur's Pass 8190), Canterbury,* ☎ *03/318–9246,* FAX *03/318–9245,* WEB *www.wildernesslodge.co.nz. 20 rooms. Boating, fishing, lounge, library, laundry service. AE, DC, MC, V. MAP.*

Lake Tekapo

⑱ *227 km (141 mi) west of Christchurch.*

As you approach the snowy peaks of the Southern Alps, the long, narrow expanse of Lake Tekapo is one of the most photographed sights in New Zealand. Its extraordinary milky-turquoise color comes from rock flour—rock ground by glacial action and held in a soupy suspension. On the east side of the lakeside power station is the tiny **Church of the Good Shepherd,** which strikes a dignified note of piety in these majestic surroundings. A nearby memorial commemorates the sheepdogs of the area, who made farming this vast countryside possible in the early pioneering days and still do so today. As you drive into the small town, you'll notice a knot of restaurants with tour buses parked outside. It's rather an off-putting image if you've come for peace and quiet, but it's relatively easy to keep the township at your back and your eyes turned on the lake and mountains—and get a tasty meal. This is also a good alternative place to stay the night on a trip to Aoraki, as the options here are more varied and less expensive than those in Aoraki/Mount Cook Village.

At the **Tekapo Information Centre** (⊠ Main Hwy., ☎ 03/680–6686) you can pick up a walking-track map and hike the **Domain to Mt. John Lookout** track. In a couple of hours you can be well above the township, enjoying views of the Mackenzie Basin, Southern Alps, and Lake Tekapo.

Dining and Lodging

$$$–$$$$ ✗ **Reflections Café.** You'll have great views of the lake from almost every table at this rustically decorated restaurant. Red meat is treated well; Reflections consistently wins awards for its beef and lamb dishes. Salmon from a nearby hatchery is also notably delicious. ⊠ *Lake Tekapo Scenic Resort, State Hwy. 8*, ☎ *03/680–6808. AE, DC, MC, V.*

$$–$$$$ ✗ **Kohan Japanese Restaurant.** Masato Itoh runs the only Japanese restaurant in town, which gives him guaranteed access to tour loads of tourists from his home country. Choose from sushi, sashimi, and tempura; one popular snack is salmon *don*, served on steamed rice. The restaurant has some of the best views over Lake Tekapo. ⊠ *State Hwy. 8*, ☎ *03/680–6688. AE, DC, MC, V. No dinner Sun.*

$$$ ✗ **The Garden Courtyard.** An impressive buffet appears three times a day in this pleasant dining room. Lunch and dinner selections always include six entrées and another half dozen vegetable dishes, as well as soups, salads, and several desserts. The salmon is reliably good, and if you've caught your own, the restaurant kitchen will cook it for you. At other times of the day, a snack menu offers burgers, burritos, and the like, all for well under $10. ⊠ *The Godley, State Hwy. 8*, ☎ *03/680–6848. AE, DC, MC, V.*

$ ✗ **Breadcrumb Bakery.** Mark Gillespie doesn't get a lot of sleep. He's at his busy bakery-café before dawn most mornings, baking most of Breadcrumb's offerings. These include seven or eight different breads, croissants, and 12 different kinds of pies. Sandwiches have yummy fillings like seafood, chicken and mayonnaise, or bacon and eggs, and the scones are legendary. Just in case that's not enough, Mark will rustle up a full breakfast (bacon, two eggs, tomato), and charge around $8 for it. ⊠ *State Hwy. 8*, ☎ *03/680–6655. No credit cards. No dinner.*

$$$$ 🏠 **Lake Tekapo Lodge.** Top New Zealand craftsmen created this luxurious, earth-brick complex, whose arresting decor competes for attention with the stunning views of Lake Tekapo and the Southern Alps. Arched, studded antique church doors open into a beamed entrance area where fine art mixes with farming paraphernalia. Wrought-iron embellishments run throughout the building, with most furnishings made of oak or elm. The front rooms open out to a covered veranda, the garden, and the best views. ⊠ *24 Aorangi Crescent*, ☎ *03/680–6566,* 𝔽𝔸𝕏 *03/680–6599,* 𝕎𝔼𝔹 *www.laketekapolodge.co.nz. 4 rooms. Dining room, lounge, Internet. AE, DC, MC, V.*

$$–$$$ 🏠 **The Chalet.** The Chalet's six fully self-contained apartments stretch
★ beside the turquoise waters of Lake Tekapo. Most rooms have adobe plaster walls, native timbers, and refreshing color schemes, along with an individual thematic streak. The best are those with spacious living rooms and lake views; two of the rooms have no appreciable views but open onto a small patio area and lovely alpine gardens. You can arrange a customized local expedition with the host, an experienced hunting, fishing, and nature guide. Tekapo township is a scenic five-minute walk away. ⊠ *Pioneer Dr. (Box 2)*, ☎ *03/680–6774,* 𝔽𝔸𝕏 *03/680–6713. 6 units. Hiking, fishing, laundry service. MC, V. BP.*

Outdoor Activities and Sports

STARGAZING

Star Gazing (⊠ Box 8, Lake Tekapo, ☎ 03/680–6565, 𝕎𝔼𝔹 www.stargazing.co.nz) beside Lake Tekapo or at Aoraki/Mount Cook National Park is a most pleasurable and educational way to better understand the southern hemisphere skies. Astronomer Hideyuki Ozawa expertly interprets the night sky while you await a shooting star to make a wish upon.

Shopping

The main street of Lake Tekapo is the place to go for necessary gear for an Aoraki (Mt. Cook) trip. Though Tekapo has its share of typical souvenir shops, too, there are a few exceptions. **Tekapo High Country Crafts** (⊠ Main Rd., ☎ 03/680–6895) features the unique work of local artists such as Olive Small, who creates framed pictures of the Mackenzie Country using natural wool as her medium. **Studio 25** (⊠ 25 Murray Pl., ☎ 03/680–6514) displays and retails the enchanting watercolors of talented artist Shirley O'Connor.

Aoraki (Mt. Cook)

⑲ *330 km (205 mi) southwest of Christchurch.*

You will know you have reached the **Mackenzie Country** after you cross Burkes Pass, and the woodland is suddenly replaced by high-country tussock grassland, which is dotted with lupines in the summer months. The area is named for James ("Jock") Mackenzie, one of the most intriguing and enigmatic figures in New Zealand history. Mackenzie was a Scot who may or may not have stolen the thousand sheep that were found with him in these secluded upland pastures in 1855. Arrested, tried, and convicted, he made several escapes from jail before he was granted a free pardon nine months after his trial—and disappeared from the pages of history. Regardless of his innocence or guilt, there can be no doubt that Mackenzie was a master bushman and herdsman. A commemorative obelisk marks Mackenzie Pass.

Above this grassy basin towers **Aoraki (Mt. Cook),** the tallest of the 22 peaks over 10,000 ft in **Aoraki/Mount Cook National Park.** At approximately 12,283 ft, it is the highest peak between Papua New Guinea and the Andes. The mountain's Māori name is Aoraki, after one of three brothers who were the sons of Rakinui, the sky father. Legend has it that their canoe was caught on a reef and frozen, forming South Island. In these parts, South Island's oldest Māori name is Te Waka O Aoraki (Aoraki's canoe) and the highest peak is Aoraki, himself frozen by the south wind, then turned to stone. The officially recognized names of this mountain, the national park, and many other South Island places have been changed to their original Māori names as part of a 1998 settlement between the government and the major South Island Māori tribe, Ngai Tahu.

Aoraki was dramatically first scaled in 1894 by three New Zealanders—Fyfe, Graham, and Clarke—just after it was announced that an English climber and an Italian mountain guide were about to attempt the summit. In a frantic surge of national pride, the New Zealand trio resolved to beat them to it, which they did on Christmas day. The mountain is still considered a difficult ascent. In the summer of 1991 a chunk of it broke away, but fortunately there were no climbers in the path of the massive avalanches. High Peak, the summit of the mountain, is now about 66 ft lower, but its altered form makes for a much more difficult ascent.

⑳ The national park surrounds **Aoraki/Mount Cook Village** (population 300), which consists of a visitor center, a grocery store, and a couple of hotels. Lodging here is controlled by a single company, and it tends to be quite pricey. Unless you really want to be very close to the mountain, Lake Tekapo is a great option; other nearby townships like Fairlie or Twizel also have good accommodations.

If the sun is shining, the views are spectacular, and even unambitious walks are inspiring. If the cloud ceiling is low, however, you may wonder why you came. Because the mountain weather is notoriously changeable, and because a lengthy detour is required to reach the village, be sure to contact the **Aoraki/Mount Cook National Park Visitor Centre** (☎ 03/435–1186) or the weather phone (☎ 03/435–1171) to check conditions. A network of hiking trails radiates from the Aoraki/Mount Cook National Park Visitor Centre, offering everything from easy walking paths to full-day challenges. There are some especially lovely wildflowers to search out, such as the Mount Cook lily, really the world's largest buttercup.

A unique hands-on educational experience is to take a half-hour hike to the fast-growing 2-square-km (1-square-mi) **Terminus Lake of the Tasman Glacier.** Fed by the glacier and the Murchison River, the lake was only formed in the past couple of decades, due to the retreat of the glacier. Rock flour, a powdery white residue, gives the water a milky color. From Terminus Lake, which is officially growing by a foot a week, you can examine up close the terminal face of the glacier, which is 3 km (2 mi) wide. A trip with Glacier Explorers (☞ Tours *in* Southern Alps A to Z, *below*) can take you by boat to explore some of the large floating icebergs that have calved (fallen away) from the Tasman Glacier. It's an eerie experience skimming across the milky-white water and closing in on icebergs—even riding *through* where they have melted—to touch rocks caught in the ice.

Another main activity is "flightseeing." From the airfield at Mount Cook Village, helicopters and fixed-wing aircraft make spectacular scenic flights across the Southern Alps. One of the most exciting is the one-hour trip ② aboard the ski planes that touch down on the **Tasman Glacier** after a gorgeous scenic flight. The 10-minute stop on the glacier doesn't allow time for much more than a snapshot, but the sensation is tremendous. The moving tongue of ice beneath your feet—one of the largest glaciers outside the Himalayas—is 27 km (17 mi) long and up to 2,000 ft thick in places. The intensity of light on the glacier can be dazzling, and sunglasses are a must. During winter the planes drop skiers on the glacier at 10,000 ft, and they ski down through 13 km (8 mi) of powder snow and fantastic ice formations. With guides, this run is suitable even for intermediate skiers.

Dining and Lodging

$$$$ ✗⊡ **The Hermitage.** Famed for its stupendous mountain views, this rambling hotel reopened in 2001 after a substantial revamp. The improved layout now gives most of the rooms terrific views, and the foyer looks directly out to Aoraki. As the name suggests, the Panorama Room takes in the scenery, too. Its menu leans toward Pacific Rim cuisine; try the whitebait fritters if they're in season, or crayfish. (Reservations are essential here.) Be sure to keep your car in the hotel's parking, safe from the beaks of the cheeky local keas. ⊠ *Aoraki/Mount Cook Village,* ☎ *03/435–1809,* FAX *03/435–1879,* WEB *www.mount-cook.com. 164 rooms. 2 restaurants, café, sauna, bar, shops. AE, DC, MC, V.*

Outdoor Activities and Sports

CLIMBING AND MOUNTAINEERING

The Aoraki/Mount Cook National Park area is ideal for rock climbing; summer is the best climbing season. **Adventure Consultants** (⊠ Box 97, Wanaka, ☎ 03/443–8711, WEB www.adventureconsultants.co.nz), a group specializing in the world's top peaks, guides ascents of Aoraki as well as the challenging climbs up Mount Tasman. They also give multiday mountaineering, alpine climbing, and ice climbing courses. Experienced climbers and beginners alike can sign up for the appropriate level of **Alpine Guides'** (⊠ Box 20, Mt. Cook, ☎ 03/435–1834, WEB www.alpineguides.co.nz) 7- to 10-day mountaineering courses, which begin around $2,100.

FARM STAYS AND RURAL NEW ZEALAND

I T'S A TIRED CLICHÉ, but it's true: you can't truly experience New Zealand if you stay only in the cities and towns. As you leave metro Auckland, heading north or south, you'll quickly realize that this is still a country that relies heavily on agriculture. New Zealand was built on sheep farming, with dairy, beef, and, more recently, deer farming also playing their parts. Today there are 47 million sheep and fewer than 4 million humans in this green, clean country! Sheep are, quite simply, everywhere.

In past years, the farming sector had what some people regarded as a charmed (though not necessarily easy) life, with favorable trading terms with Britain and financial subsidies from the government. But over the past 20 or 30 years, the agricultural sector has had its fair share of knocks. Export markets are tougher, and government assistance has dried up. Farmers have looked for ways to supplement their incomes, and one of these has been to open up their homes and properties to overseas guests. Because of New Zealand's burgeoning popularity as a travel destination, it's a match made in heaven. Farmers get an economic boost—and a chance to meet the world—and visitors get a chance to get up close to the heart of this predominately agricultural country. If you're especially keen on experiencing farm life here, look into the schedules of local A and P shows, held annually in most large agricultural communities.

The country has about 3,000 farm stays and rural homes open to visitors. Their aim, first and foremost, is to provide country hospitality and the opportunity to meet and talk to New Zealanders who make a living from the land. On arrival to a farm stay you'll usually be met by your hosts, given a welcoming cup of coffee or tea, and then taken on a tour by foot or four-wheel-drive of the property's main attributes. Be prepared to talk farming, Kiwi-style. These people love what they do and take pride in it. For many it's been a way of life for generations.

Some farm stays emphasize a hands-on experience. Don't be surprised if you're given the chance to partake in a sheep muster or to help with milking the cows at 5 AM. And don't worry, the "farmwork" is voluntary.

An added bonus of heading to a farm is that you'll probably be completely surrounded by spectacular countryside—the kind of scenery that draws visitors to New Zealand in the first place. An extended stay out in the country gives you the pleasure of really getting to know the local landscape. With most farm stays you'll have the chance to walk or tramp in the nearby wilderness or go horseback riding, rafting, kayaking, and fishing. You'll go off on your adventures fortified by a full, cooked breakfast. And, in many of the best farm stays and country lodges, a three-course dinner with wine will await you at the end of your active day. Best of all, the cost of a farm stay tends to be far lower than the rates for comparable accommodations in crowded resort areas.

FLIGHTSEEING

Flightseeing gives you an unparalleled view of the mountains, with the added thrill of landing on a glacier for a short walk. The light can be intensely bright in such dazzlingly white surroundings, so be sure to bring sunglasses. Generally, the best time for flights is early morning. Ski planes are flown by **Mount Cook Ski Planes** (☎ 03/435–1026, WEB www.skiplanes.co.nz). The **Helicopter Line** (☎ 03/435–1801, WEB www.new-zealand.com/THL) can fly you around Aoraki (Mt. Cook) and take you up for a glacier landing. Or take a breathtaking 50-minute scenic flight to see Aoraki, the Tasman, Murchison, Fox, and Franz Josef glaciers, and the rain forests on the west side of the Main Divide with **Air Safaris** (☎ 03/680–6880, WEB www.airsafaris.co.nz). Flights start at $230 per adult; helicopter flights start at $165.

HIKING

The hiking trails spooling out from the visitor center range in difficulty and length, from the 10-minute Bowen Track to the 5½-hour climb to the 4,818-ft summit of Mt. Sebastopol. Seven tracks can be done in running shoes and don't require hiking experience; the rest of the park's trails require some hiking experience. The Mueller Hut route is a popular climb taking about three hours. A new 28-bed hut will open in 2003. The rewarding Hooker Valley walk, a four-hour round-trip, will take you across a couple of swingbridges to the Hooker Glacier terminus lake.

HORSE TREKKING

Pukaki Horsetreks (✉ Pukaki Canal Rd., Twizel, ☎ 025/280–7353; 0800/245–549 in New Zealand) has half-hour to half-day guided trips ($65 per half day) in winter and half-hour to two-day treks in summer up Mt. Ruataniwha, which overlooks Lake Ohau in the Mackenzie Basin.

The Southern Alps A to Z

AIR TRAVEL

CARRIERS

Air New Zealand no longer flies to Aoraki/Mount Cook National Park, but you can call its airport to see if a charter flight is available.
➤ CONTACT: **Mount Cook Airport** (☎ 0800/800–737).

BUS TRAVEL

InterCity operates a daily bus service between Christchurch and Queenstown via Mount Cook Village, with a one-hour stop at the Hermitage Hotel for lunch. The Coast to Coast Shuttle bus goes to Arthur's Pass Village from Christchurch.
➤ CONTACTS: **Coast to Coast Shuttle** (☎ 0800/800–847). **InterCity** (☎ 03/377–0951, WEB www.intercitycoach.co.nz).

CAR TRAVEL

Arthur's Pass is a 2½- to 3-hour drive southwest out of Christchurch on Highway 73. The pass is the main artery to the West Coast; be aware that its western side is extremely steep and quite unnerving for the uninitiated.

The 330-km (205-mi) drive from Christchurch straight through to Aoraki/Mount Cook Village takes four hours. Take Highway 1 south out of Christchurch. At the tiny town of Rangitata turn right onto Highway 79 to Lake Tekapo. Pass through Lake Tekapo and look on the right for Highway 80 to Aoraki/Mount Cook Village.

TOURS

ADVENTURE TOURS

Mid Southern Tracks organizes and provides experienced guides for fishing trips, hunting safaris, and nature tours both locally and to destinations all over New Zealand.

➤ CONTACT: **Mid Southern Tracks** (✉ Pioneer Dr. [Box 2, Lake Tekapo], ☎ 03/680–6774).

BOAT TOURS

Glacier Explorers leave from the Hermitage Hotel, the visitor center, or the Mount Cook YHA for guided boat trips on the Tasman Glacier Lake. Lake Tekapo Adventures & Cruises offers fishing and boat cruises on the startlingly blue Lake Tekapo.

➤ CONTACTS: **Glacier Explorers** (✉ Box 18, Aoraki/ Mount Cook Village, ☎ 03/435–1809 or 03/435–1077, WEB www.glacierexplorers.co. nz). **Lake Tekapo Adventures & Cruises** (✉ Tekapo Information Centre, Main St., Lake Tekapo, ☎ 03/680–6721 or 03/680–6629, WEB www. laketekapo.co.nz).

SCENIC FLIGHTS

See Outdoor Activities and Sports *in* Aoraki (Mt. Cook) for information on flightseeing.

TRAIN TRAVEL

InterCity operates the daily TranzAlpine Express train from Christchurch to Arthur's Pass Village departing at 9 AM. A coach meets this train to take you on to Greymouth and elsewhere in the West Coast.

➤ CONTACT: **Tranzrail** (☎ 03/377–0951 or 0800/802–802, WEB www. tranzscenic.co.nz).

VISITOR INFORMATION

All of the regional visitor bureaus are open daily year-round, with slightly longer hours in summer. Some of the smaller offices, such as those in Tekapo and Twizel, may curtail their hours if necessary.

➤ TOURIST INFORMATION: **Aoraki/Mount Cook National Park Visitor Centre** (✉ Aoraki/Mount Cook Village, ☎ 03/435–1186, WEB www.doc. govt.nz). **Arthur's Pass Visitor Centre** (✉ Box 8, Arthur's Pass, ☎ 03/ 318–9211). **Lake Tekapo Information** (✉ Main Rd., Lake Tekapo, ☎ FAX 03/680–6686). **Mt. Cook–Mackenzie Visitor Information Centre** (✉ Wairepo Rd., Twizel, ☎ 03/435–3280; WEB www.mtcook.org.nz).

SOUTHLAND

Most of Southland, the western lobe of lower South Island, is taken up by two giant national parks, Fiordland and Mt. Aspiring. Fiordland, the name generally given to the southwest coast, is a majestic wilderness of rocks, ice, and beech forest, where glaciers have carved mile-deep notches into the coast. The scenic climax of this area—and perhaps of the whole country—is Milford Sound. A cruise on the sound is a must. But if you really want to take in the raw grandeur of Fiordland, hike one of the many trails in the area, among them the famous four-day Milford Track, what some call the finest walk in the world. The accommodations base and adventure center for the region is Queenstown.

Wanaka

㉒ *70 km (44 mi) northeast of Queenstown, 87 km (54 mi) south of Haast Pass.*

Set on the southern shore of Lake Wanaka, with some of New Zealand's most impressive mountains stretched out behind it, Wanaka is the welcome mat for Mt. Aspiring National Park. It is a favorite of Kiwis

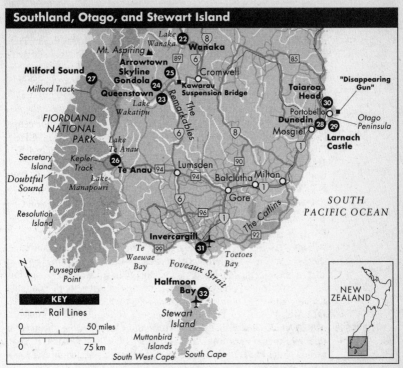

on vacation, an alternative of sorts to Queenstown. The region has numerous trekking opportunities, a choice of ski areas, and a diverse selection of other outdoor activities. The town has a couple of unusual cultural attractions as well, if you arrive on a rainy day.

Since Wanaka doesn't reach Queenstown's levels of international publicity, it draws fewer tourists and thus manages to retain an almost sleepy-village atmosphere for most of the year. The town generally fills up only during the December to January summer vacations and in the middle of the ski season.

Spectacularly sited on the shores of Lake Wanaka, **Rippon Vineyard** is one of the most photographed in the country. Lois and Rolfe Mills planted a "fruit-salad" vineyard in the mid-1970s and spent the next few years sorting out which varieties best suited the region. Now their portfolio includes sparkling wine, riesling, gewürztraminer, chardonnay, sauvignon blanc, and fine (but expensive) pinot noir. Head west from Wanaka along the lake on Mt. Aspiring Road for 4 km (2½ mi). ✉ *Mt. Aspiring Rd. (Box 175),* ☎ *03/443–8084,* 🌐 *www.rippon.co. nz.* ☉ *Dec.–Apr., daily 11–5; July–Nov., daily 1:30–4:30.*

On your way into town on Highway 6 you'll pass the **New Zealand Fighter Pilots Museum.** The museum is a tribute to New Zealand fighter pilots, of whom the country contributed more per capita than any other nation in World Wars I and II. The collection of planes includes aircraft used during the World Wars, such as the British Spitfire and rarities such as the Russian Polikarpov I-16. If you're visiting around Easter, check out the biennial international air show Warbirds over Wanaka, where you can see some of these magnificent aircraft in flight. The museum anticipates moving in either 2003 or 2004. ✉ *Hwy. 6,* ☎ *03/ 443–7010,* 🌐 *www.nzfpm.co.nz.* ✉ *$8.* ☉ *Daily 9–4.*

☺ Don't make **Stuart Landsborough's Puzzling World** your first stop in Wanaka—you may get hooked trying to solve one of the myriad brain-teasers and not leave until closing. The complex includes the amazing Tumbling Towers and Tilted House, which is on a 15-degree angle (is the water really running uphill?), as well as the Leaning Tower of Wanaka. The maze can be as demanding as you want to make it by setting individual challenges. Most people spend from 30 minutes to one hour in the maze and, understandably, a little less time in the Fol-lowing Faces room: it's an eerie feeling to have so many famous peo-ple watch your every move. The place to take your time is the popular Puzzle Centre. Just take on the puzzle of your choice, order a cup of coffee, and proceed to get worked up. The place is 2 km (1 mi) east of town—just look for the cartoonlike houses on funny angles. ⊠ *Hwy. 89,* ☎ *03/443–7489.* ☒ *Puzzle Centre free; Tilted House and Holo-gram Hall $4; Tilted House, Hologram Hall, Leaning Tower of Wanaka, and Maze $6.* ☉ *Daily 8:30–5:30.*

Dining and Lodging

$$$–$$$$ ✕ **White House.** Mediterranean and North African flavors influence these simple dishes, served without pretension—recent listings have in-cluded harissa chicken, loaded with Moroccan spices. There's outdoor seating in summer. Come for a meal, or you can just sit with a cuppa—coffee, that is. ⊠ *Dunmore and Dungarvon Sts.,* ☎ *03/443–9595. AE, DC, MC, V.*

$–$$$$ ✕ **Kai Whaka Pai.** Fun, funky surroundings set the scene for an eclec-tic menu that ranges from casual standbys (nachos, kebabs) to more formal plates like cervena (farmed venison) with a red currant and Dijon mustard sauce. While reservations aren't mandatory, they're a good idea, since this place stays busy year-round. ⊠ *Helwick and Ardmore Sts.,* ☎ *03/443–7795. AE, DC, MC, V.*

$$–$$$ ✕ **Toscana.** Italy rules in this tiny restaurant. Properly thin-crusted piz-zas are cooked in a wood-fired oven, and the toppings are authentic (what—no pineapple?) and delicious. Some pastas are made on the premises; main-course meats include venison, ostrich, and wild boar. The wine list mixes Otago bottles with Italian imports. ⊠ *76 Golf Course Rd.,* ☎ *03/443–1255. AE, MC, V. Closed Oct.–Apr. No lunch.*

$$$$ ▣ **Whare Kea Lodge.** This spectacular luxury lodge overlooks the west-ern shores of Lake Wanaka. The lodge's name means "house of the kea," for the alpine parrot, a mischievous local you're sure to meet. Floor-to-ceiling windows ensure you won't miss any of the surroundings—it looks as though you could reach out and touch the lake. The table d'hôte fo-cuses on New Zealand produce and wines. ⊠ *Mt. Aspiring Rd.,* ☎ *03/ 443–1400,* FAX *03/443–9200,* WEB *www.wharekealodge.com. 6 rooms. Dining room, lounge. AE, MC, V. MAP.*

$$$ ▣ **Mount Aspiring Hotel.** Close to the lake and 2 km (1 mi) from town, this family-run motor inn has a friendly and casual atmosphere. The rooms' natural color schemes—with timber walls and green car-pets—work well with the views. Upstairs rooms have private terraces from which you can enjoy the scenery. ⊠ *Mt. Aspiring Rd.,* ☎ *03/443–8216,* FAX *03/443–9108,* WEB *www.wanakanz.com. 36 rooms. Restau-rant, bar. AE, DC, MC, V.*

Outdoor Activities and Sports

FISHING

Locals will tell you that fishing on Lake Wanaka and nearby Lake Hawea is better than the more famed Taupo area. You won't want to enter that argument, but chances are good you'll catch fish if you have the right guide. **Harry Urquhart** (☎ 03/443–1535) has trolling excur-sions for rainbow trout, brown trout, and quinnat salmon on Lake Hawea, and he has fly-fishing trips as well. **Gerald Telford** (☎ 03/443–

9257, WEB www.flyfishhunt.co.nz) will take you fly-fishing, including night fishing. For more information on trout fishing around Wanaka, *see* Chapter 6.

RAFTING AND KAYAKING

At **Pioneer Rafting** you can finally do some white-water rafting at a calm pace. Lewis Verduyn is New Zealand's leading eco-rafting specialist, with many years' experience as a white-water rafter. Lewis had his share of adrenaline pumping high-grade trips and then got tired of missing out on what he sees as the real adventure, the environment he was tearing past. His highly informative eco-rafting adventure, suitable for most ages, retraces a historic pioneer log-raft route. Both full-day ($145) and half-day ($95) trips are available. ⊠ *Box 124, Wanaka,* ☎ *03/443–1246 or 025/295–0418.* ☉ *Sept.–Apr.*

Exploring this beautiful region's rivers with **Alpine River Guides** Geoff Deacon is a must while in Wanaka. Unlike many of the large-scale operations of neighboring Queenstown, this company caters to smaller groups, which means a lot of attention for beginners. You'll learn how to glide for a rest into a calm eddy, to wave surf, and to safely charge down the center of the white water. You *will* spill, and for this reason all your gear, right down to the polypropylene underwear, is provided. The full-day trip costs $120 per person. ⊠ *11 Mt. Iron Dr., Wanaka,* ☎ *03/443–9023 or 025/382–475,* WEB *www.alpinekayaks.co.nz.*

SKYDIVING

New Zealand is definitely the place to experiment with wild adventures, and with **Tandem Skydive Lake Wanaka** (⊠ Wanaka Airport, Hwy. 6, Wanaka, ☎ 03/443–7207 or 025/796–877, WEB www.skydivenz. com) you're in capable hands. The 9,000-ft jump over gorgeous scenery is $225, and you can have a video of your exploits for $45 and photos on the ground and as you exit the plane for $20.

WALKING AND TREKKING

You could stay for a week in Wanaka, take a different walk into the bush and mountains each day, and still come nowhere near exhausting all options. If you have time for only one walk, **Mt. Iron** is relatively short and rewarding. A rocky hump carved by glaciers, its summit provides panoramic views of Lakes Wanaka and Hawea, plus the peaks of the Harris Mountains and Mt. Aspiring National Park. The access track begins 2 km (1 mi) from Wanaka, and the walk to the top takes 45 minutes. To avoid going over old ground, descend on the alternative route down the steep eastern face.

Mt. Roy is a daylong commitment. A track starts at the base of the mountain, 6 km (4 mi) from Wanaka on the road to Glendhu Bay. The round-trip journey takes about six hours. The track is closed from early October to mid-November.

For maps and information on these and other local walks, contact the **Department of Conservation** (⊠ Ardmore St., ☎ 03/477–0677).

Queenstown

㉓ *70 km (44 mi) southeast of Wanaka, 530 km (330 mi) southwest of Christchurch.*

Set on the edge of a glacial lake beneath the sawtooth peaks of the Remarkables, Queenstown is the most popular tourist stop on South Island. Once prized by the Māori as a source of greenstone, the town boomed when gold was discovered in the Shotover, which quickly became famous as "the richest river in the world." Queenstown could easily have become a ghost town when gold gave out—except for its location. With ready access to mountains, lakes, rivers, ski slopes, and the glacier-carved coastline of Fiordland National Park, the town has become the adventure capital of New Zealand. Its shop windows are crammed with skis, Polartec, Asolo walking boots, and Marin mountain bikes. Along Shotover Street, travel agents tout white-water rafting, jet-boating, caving, trekking, heli-skiing, parachuting, and parapenting (rappelling). New Zealanders' penchant for bizarre adventure sports reaches a climax in Queenstown, and it was here that the sport of leaping off a bridge with a giant rubber band wrapped around the ankles—bungy jumping—took root as a commercial enterprise. Taking its marvelous location for granted, Queenstown is mostly a comfortable, cosmopolitan base for the outdoor activities around it.

Some of the best views of the town and the mountains all around are from the **Queenstown Gardens,** on the peninsula that encloses Queenstown Bay. The **Skyline Gondola** whisks you to the heights of Bob's Peak, 1,425 ft above the lake, for a panoramic view of the town and the Remarkables. You can also walk to the top on the **One Mile Creek Trail.** The summit terminal has a cafeteria, a buffet restaurant, and *Kiwi Magic,* a rather silly 25-minute aerial film that uses stunning effects to provide a tour of the country. There's also a luge ride—start with the scenic track, and then work your way up to the advanced track. If even that isn't exciting enough, you can bungy jump or rappel from the summit terminal (☞ AJ Hackett Bungy *in* Outdoor Activities and Sports, *below*). ⊠ *Brecon St.,* ☎ *03/442–7860,* WEB *www.skyline.co.nz.* ☜ *Gondola $14, Kiwi Magic $8, luge ride $4.50.* ☉ *Daily 10–10; Kiwi Magic screens every hr on the hr, 11–9.*

At **Gibbston Valley Wines,** the best-known vineyard in central Otago, the world's southernmost wine-producing region, you can taste wines in a cool, barrel-lined cave. The showcase wine here is pinot noir, named a world champion pinot noir in the 2001 International Wine Challenge, but there are rieslings and a pinot gris to sip as well. In 2001 they added a cheesery, where you can watch sheep's-milk and goat's-milk cheeses being made. The attached restaurant offers tempting preparations of mostly local produce and plenty of wines by the glass. ⊠ *State Hwy. 6, Gibbston, 10 km (6 mi) east of Queenstown,* ☎ *03/442–6910,* WEB *www.gvwines.co.nz.* ☜ *Wine-cave tour and tasting $8.50, less for larger groups.* ☉ *Tasting room daily 10–5, cave tours on the hr daily 10–4, restaurant daily noon–3.*

The **Chard Farm** vineyard perches on a rare flat spot on the edge of the Kawarau Gorge, not far from Gibbston Valley. The portfolio includes a couple of excellent chardonnays, sauvignon blancs, gewürztraminers, pinot gris, and three variations of pinot noir. They're also venturing into the champagne method. ⊠ *Chard Rd. (R.D. 1, Gibbston),* ☎ *03/442–6110,* WEB *www.chardfarm.co.nz.* ☉ *Daily 10–5.*

Dining and Lodging

$$$–$$$$ × **The Boardwalk.** You might want to eat here just for the view, as the restaurant looks over Lake Wakatipu toward the Remarkables from the second floor of the steamer wharf building. Nothing can quite beat that, but the menu makes a good attempt. Seafood is the strong suit, with dishes such as the Provençal classic bouillabaisse and kingfish layered between grilled Mediterranean vegetables. Reservations are recommended. ⊠ *Steamer Wharf,* ☎ *03/442–5630. AE, DC, MC, V.*

$$$–$$$$ × **The Bunker.** Log fires, leather armchairs, and a clubby atmosphere make the Bunker especially cozy. Whet your appetite with an aperitif at the bar before heading downstairs for a meal that might include a salad of smoked cervena (farmed venison) served with a chili, pear, and

plum chutney, or something more traditional like duck confit. ⊠ *Cow La.,* ☎ *03/441–8030. Reservations essential. AE, DC, MC, V.*

$$$–$$$$ ✕ **Gourmet Express.** This sunny spot at the front of a shopping center is popular for breakfast, when pancakes with maple syrup, eggs any way you want, and heart-starting coffee are all on call. Later in the day, come here for sandwiches, hamburgers, and a huge selection of salads, casseroles, and omelets—a good number incorporating chili in some shape or form. The wine list emphasizes local bottles. ⊠ *Bay Centre, Shotover St.,* ☎ *03/442–9619. AE, DC, MC, V.*

$$$–$$$$ ✕ **H.M.S. Britannia.** The timber floors and fishing nets on the walls and the seaward-leaning menu give an impression of shipboard dining. Choose from prawns, crayfish, calamari, or mussels, all prepared in predictable but flavorful ways. This is one of the few eateries in town that can take a booking for up to 20 people and seat them at one large table. Lunch is available by arrangement only. ⊠ *The Mall,* ☎ *03/442–9600. AE, DC, MC, V.*

$$$–$$$$ ✕ **The 19th.** No restaurant has a better situation—this bright and breezy eatery sits at the end of the wharf that juts out into Lake Wakatipu. The regularly changing menu could include panfried calamari with roasted plum tomatoes, garlic, and calamata olives or linguine tossed with sun-dried tomato pesto. ⊠ *Steamer Wharf,* ☎ *03/442–4006. AE, DC, MC, V.*

$$–$$$ ✕ **The Bathhouse.** It was exactly that—a 1911 Victorian bathhouse, right on the beach. Now, it's a casual café in the mornings and afternoons, and a full-fledged restaurant for dinner. The surroundings remain Victorian, but the kitchen is up-to-date, offering starters like duck confit with bacon tart Tatin and a selection of generous mains—loin of wild venison filled with wild mushrooms is typical. ⊠ *Marine Parade,* ☎ *03/442–5625. AE, DC, MC, V. Closed Mon.*

$ ✕ **Naff Caff.** The café that opens earliest is happily also Queenstown's best place for coffee. If all the adventure activities here have you racing, you can get a delicious breakfast egg-and-bacon panini to go. At lunch, look for tasty combos like pesto, chicken, and tomato on *ciabatta* or fougasse breads. Salads are imaginative, and muffins and a cake are baked daily. ⊠ *1/66 Shotover St.,* ☎ *03/442–8211. AE, DC, MC, V. No dinner.*

$$$$ 🏨 **Blanket Bay.** Blanket Bay can claim to be next door to Paradise (val-
★ ley). Here an immense schist lodge faces Lake Wakatipu, surrounded by thousands of acres of sheep-station land. At the heart of the lodge is the Great Room, with a grand fireplace, vaulted wharf-timber beams, and antique wooden floors. Floor-to-ceiling windows open out to views of the lake and Humboldt Mountains. All five lakeside rooms have a balcony or terrace. The three suites have stone fireplaces and large bathrooms with a steam shower and a separate tub. The two chalets echo the main lodge's structure and luxuries. The decor throughout is sumptuous; hues of maroon and gold complement native timbers and stone. Blanket Bay is a 35-minute drive from Queenstown. ⊠ *Blanket Bay, 3 km (2 mi) south of Glenorchy,* ☎ *03/442–9442,* FAX *03/442–9441,* WEB *www.blanketbay.com. 5 rooms, 3 suites, 4 chalet suites. 2 dining rooms, in-room data ports, hot tub, steam room, gym, boating, fishing, bar; no kids under 13, no smoking. AE, DC, MC, V. MAP.*

$$$$ 🏨 **Millennium Queenstown.** This hotel occupies the site where American scientists first sighted Venus, in 1870. One of the conditions of building it was leaving intact the rock from which the planet was sighted. Of more tangible importance are the comfortable, well-equipped rooms and the Observatory Restaurant, which adds an international touch to New Zealand fare. ⊠ *Franklin Rd. and Stanley St.,* ☎ *03/441–8888,* FAX *03/441–8889,* WEB *www.cdlhotels.co.nz. 217 rooms, 3 suites. Restaurant, minibars, sauna, gym, bar, baby-sitting. AE, DC, MC, V.*

$$$$ ☆ ▣ **Nugget Point.** Poised high above the Shotover River, this stylish retreat conjures up an intimate atmosphere while providing the amenities of a large hotel. Rooms are luxuriously large, and each has a balcony, a kitchenette, and a bedroom separate from the living area. Check out the open-air whirlpool perched on the edge of Shotover Valley—great with a glass of champagne. The lodge is a 10-minute drive from Queenstown on the road to Coronet Peak, one of the top ski areas in the country. ⊠ *Arthur's Point Rd.,* ☎ *03/442–7273,* ℻ *03/442–7308,* WEB *www.nuggetpoint.co.nz. 35 rooms. Restaurant, kitchenettes, minibars, pool, outdoor hot tub, sauna, spa, tennis court, squash, bar. AE, DC, MC, V.*

$$$$ ▣ **Stone House.** On the hillside overlooking Queenstown and the lake, this handsome, historic 1874 cottage has been reinvigorated by its enthusiastic owners. The guest lounge has a large, welcoming open fire, and there is an outdoor hot tub where you can appreciate the alpine night sky. The rooms run to country florals, with feather duvets on the beds; three have a shower only. Smoking is not permitted inside the house, and children are not accommodated. ⊠ *47 Hallenstein St.,* ☎ *03/442–9812,* ℻ *03/441–8293,* WEB *www.stonehouse.co.nz. 4 rooms, 1 with bath. Outdoor hot tub, lounge, laundry service. MC, V. BP.*

$$$–$$$$ ☆ ▣ **Heritage Queenstown.** On Fernhill, just a few minutes from the town center, the Heritage is more peaceful than other local hotels and has great views of the Remarkables and Lake Wakatipu. The hotel was built almost entirely out of South Island materials, including central Otago schist and wooden beams from old local railway bridges. Rooms are notably spacious and are fitted with writing tables and comfortable sitting areas. ⊠ *91 Fernhill Rd.,* ☎ *03/442–4988,* ℻ *03/442–4989,* WEB *www.dynasty.co.nz. 137 rooms, 41 suites. Restaurant, minibars, pool, gym, hot tub, sauna, bar. AE, DC, MC, V.*

$ ▣ **The Black Sheep Backpacker's Lodge.** You can get an eyeful of the Remarkables from this backpacker hangout. A bar's on hand for those needing liquid courage after a particularly nerve-racking excursion. If you're coming and going at odd hours, this may be your best bet as it's open 24 hours. ⊠ *13 Frankton Rd.,* ☎ *03/442–7289,* WEB *www. blacksheepbackpackers.co.nz. 6 rooms, 14 dorm rooms. Kitchen, billiards, bar, lounge, Internet, laundry facilities. MC, V.*

Nightlife

Queenstown's exciting daytime activities are not matched by its nightlife. The clubs and bars are mostly in the center of town, within easy walking distance of one another. Bars start to close around 11 PM, but the nightclubs stay open late into the night.

Bardeux (⊠ The Mall, ☎ 03/442–8284) is a stylish wine bar, good for an intimate, subdued evening. If you want to dance until the wee hours, check out **Chicos** (⊠ The Mall, ☎ 03/442–8439). The **Edge** nightclub (⊠ Camp St., ☎ 03/442–6253) also offers late-night dancing. And for a hip, funky nightspot with a Pacific feel, try **Surreal** (⊠ Rees St., ☎ 03/441–8492).

Outdoor Activities and Sports

BUNGY JUMPING

AJ Hackett Bungy, the pioneer in the sport, offers a variety of jumps in the area. Kawarau Bridge is the original jump site, 23 km (14 mi) from Queenstown on State Highway 6. Daredevils who graduate from the 143-ft plunge might like to test themselves on the 230-ft Skippers Canyon Bridge. Top that with the Nevis Highwire Bungy, suspended 440 ft above the Nevis River, from which you jump in a specially designed bungy chair. If you're short on time, head to the Ledge, the jumping point by the Skyline Gondola; from April through September you can hurl yourself off by moonlight. Prices start at $125 for the Kawarau or Ledge jump (including T-shirt) and extra fees for photos and videos. Be sure to check the age, height, and weight requirements. A new, partially underground visitor center is under development at the Kawarau site; it includes a new viewing deck, and should be open in summer 2003. ⊠ *The Station, Camp and Shotover Sts.,* ☏ *03/442–1177 or 03/442–7100,* WEB *www.ajhackett.com.* ⊙ *Apr.–Sept., daily 9:30–4:30; Oct.–Mar., daily 9–5.*

FISHING

For information on trout fishing guides around Queenstown, *see* Chapter 6.

HIKING

For information on hiking the Milford and Kepler tracks, *see* Te Anau *and* Milford Sound, *below,* and Chapter 6.

HORSE TREKKING

Moonlight Stables has a choice of full- or half-day rides with spectacular views of the mountains and rivers around the Wakatipu-Arrow Basin. Ride across its 800-acre deer farm. Both novice and experienced riders are welcome. Transportation from Queenstown is provided. The company operates a clay-bird shooting range, and you can shoot in combination with the ride. ⊠ *Box 784, Queenstown,* ☏ *03/442–1229,* WEB *www.moonlightcountry.co.nz.* ⊠ *½-day trip $55 per person, from $115 including shooting and 20 clay targets.*

JET-BOAT RIDES

With **Dart River Safaris** you can get a nonpareil look at rugged Mt. Aspiring National Park, one of the most spectacular parts of South Island. The Safari route includes jet-boating on the upper and lower Dart River, along with a bit of walking. The longer Heritage Trail takes smaller groups on a jet-boat and walking trip with a historic focus. Shuttle buses depart daily from Queenstown for the 45-minute ride to the boats. ⊠ *Box 76, Queenstown,* ☏ *03/442–9992,* WEB *www.dartriverjet.co.nz.* ⊠ *$145–$299.*

Shotover Jet leads high-speed, heart-stopping rides in the Shotover River canyon, during which the boat pirouettes within inches of canyon walls. If you want to stay relatively dry, sit beside the driver. The boats are based at the Shotover Bridge, a 10-minute drive from Queenstown. If you don't have transport, a shuttle makes frequent daily runs. Reservations are essential. ⊠ *Shotover River Canyon, Queenstown,* ☏ *03/442–8570,* WEB *www.shotoverjet.co.nz.* ⊠ *$85.*

RAFTING

Kawarau Raft Expeditions runs various half-, full-, and 3-day whitewater rafting trips in the Queenstown area year-round. The most popular is the Grade 3½–Grade 5 ride along the Shotover River, an unforgettable journey that ends with the rafts shooting through the 560-ft Oxenbridge Tunnel. ⊠ *35 Shotover St., Queenstown,* ☏ *03/442–9792,* WEB *www.rafting.co.nz.* ⊠ *$129–$894.*

For something even more physical on the river, **Serious Fun River Surfing** lets you jump on a body board and speed down the rapids that way. You'll enjoy the experience best if you have a reasonable level of fitness. Transport to and from Queenstown hotels is provided. Excursions run daily year-round, conditions permitting. ⊠ *33 Watts Rd., Sunshine Bay, Queenstown,* ☏ *03/442–5262,* FAX *03/442–5265.* ⊠ *$109.*

Arrowtown

㉕ *22 km (14 mi) northeast of Queenstown, 105 km (66 mi) south of Wanaka.*

Another gold-mining town, Arrowtown lies northeast of Queenstown. It had long been suspected that there was gold along the Arrow River, and when in 1862 William Fox, an American, was seen selling large quantities of the precious metal in nearby Clyde, the hunt was on. Others attempted to follow the wily Fox back to his diggings, but he kept giving his pursuers the slip, on one occasion even abandoning his tent and provisions in the middle of the night. Eventually a large party of prospectors stumbled on Fox and his team of 40 miners. The secret was out, miners rushed to stake their claims, and Arrowtown was born.

After the gold rush ended, the place was just another sleepy rural town until tourism created a new boom. This village at the foot of the steep Crown Range, with weathered timber shop fronts and white stone churches shaded by ancient sycamores, was simply too gorgeous to escape the attention of the tour buses. These days it has become a tourist trap, but a highly photogenic one, especially when autumn gilds the hillsides. On a stroll along the main street, Buckingham Street, you can stop in the old post and telegraph office, still open for business.

In a less-visited part of the town is the former **Chinese settlement.** Chinese miners were common on the goldfields in the late 1860s, but local prejudice forced them to live in their own separate enclave. A number of their huts and Ah Lum's Store, one of the few Chinese goldfield buildings to survive intact, have been preserved. ⊠ *Bush Creek (west end of town).* 🖼 *Free.* ⊘ *Daily 9–5.*

Kawarau Suspension Bridge is where bungy jumpers make their leaps— a spectacle well worth the short detour. As a promotional stunt, the AJ Hackett company once offered a free jump to anyone who would jump nude, but there were so many takers the scheme had to be abandoned. The bridge is on Highway 6, not far from Arrowtown.

Lodging

$$$$ **Millbrook Resort.** A 20-minute drive from Queenstown, this glamorous resort has a special appeal for golfers: an 18-hole championship golf course that was designed by New Zealand professional Bob Charles. A luxurious spa, opened in late 2001, pampers you whether or not you've taken advantage of the extensive exercise options. Accommodations range from rooms in the resort's main hotel to villas and multi-bedroom cottages. Standard rooms have private balconies and fireplaces. The villas, done in cream and cornflower blue, have kitchens, laundry facilities, and large lounge–dining rooms. ⊠ *Malaghans Rd.,* ☎ *03/441–7000,* 🖷 *03/441–7007,* 🕸 *www.millbrook.co.nz. 13 villas, 70 villa suites, 51 rooms, 24 cottage apartments. 2 restaurants, café, some kitchens, indoor pool, outdoor hot tubs, massage, saunas, spa, 18-hole golf course, tennis court, health club, hiking, mountain bikes, bar, baby-sitting. AE, DC, MC, V.*

Te Anau

㉖ *175 km (109 mi) southwest of Queenstown.*

Lake Te Anau (tay-*ah*-no), which is 53 km (33 mi) long and up to 10 km (6 mi) wide, is the second-largest lake in New Zealand after Lake Taupo. The town of Te Anau, on the southern shores of the lake, serves as a base for a wide range of local activities in Fiordland National Park, the largest national park in New Zealand. Fiordland takes its name from the deep sea inlets, or sounds, on its western flank. This is the

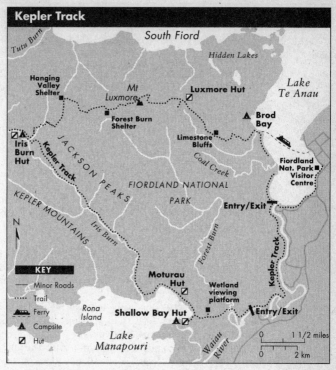

Kepler Track

most rugged part of the country. Parts of the park are so remote that they have never been explored, and visitor activities are mostly confined to a few of the sounds and the walking trails. The township of Te Anau has a few attractions and activities worth checking out if you have some lingering time on your way into or out of the park.

At **Te Anau Caves,** boats and walkways take you through a maze of caves containing underground whirlpools, waterfalls, and gushing streams. On the cave walls, myriad glowworms shine like constellations in a clear night sky. The caves can only be reached by water, and the entire trip takes 2½ hours. Real Journeys arranges daily caving trips year-round, with an additional daily tour from May through September. ⊠ *Real Journeys, Lake Front Dr.,* ☎ *03/249–7416,* WEB *www.realjourneys.co.nz.* ☞ *$44–$52.*

The lakeshore **Te Anau Wildlife Centre** gives you the chance to preview some of the wildlife you're likely to encounter when tramping in Fiordland. The center houses one of New Zealand's rare flightless birds, the *takahe,* which was at one time thought to be extinct. The lakeside walk to the center makes for a pleasant afternoon or evening stroll. ⊠ *Manapouri Rd., 1 km (½ mi) west of Te Anau,* ☎ *03/249–7921.* ☞ *Donation requested.* ☉ *Daily 8:30–4:30.*

From Te Anau, you can set out on sightseeing trips by bus, boat, or plane to Milford and Doubtful sounds, or take off on one of the park's world-class hiking tracks. Of these tracks, the most accessible to town is the Kepler Track.

★ The 67-km (42-mi) **Kepler Track** loops from the south end of Lake Te Anau; it skirts the lakeshore, climbs up to the bush line, passes limestone bluffs and the Luxmore Caves, goes through extensive beech forest, and has incredible views of the mountains and of South Fiord. An alpine crossing takes you to the high point near the peak of **Mt. Lux-more**. It's a moderate walking track that takes three to four days to complete. And for those on a tight schedule it's possible to take day hikes to the Luxmore and Moturau huts.

The track was opened in 1988 to take pressure off the increasing numbers of people walking the Routeburn and Milford tracks. It has some very good-quality trails and huts and is relatively easy, with only one steep climb to the alpine section by Mt. Luxmore. Trampers should beware, however, of high wind gusts while crossing the exposed saddle above the bush line. During winter and spring the alpine section may be impassable because of snow.

The track starts just 4 km (2½ mi) from Te Anau town. Although it can be walked in either direction, most people walk it counterclockwise, following the shores of the lake for 90 minutes and then climbing steeply to the Luxmore Hut. This high-standard 40-bunk hut is a 50-minute walk from where the track climbs above the tree line. The next day most people tackle the six- to seven-hour mountain-ridge walk to Iris Burn Hut. This exposed stretch of the walk offers spectacular mountain and lake views but should not be attempted in extreme weather conditions. Keep your eyes open here for the kea, New Zealand's large and sociable mountain parrot. The following day involves a 17-km (10½-mi) walk through beech forest and riverside clearings before you meet up with the shores of Lake Manapouri. The track follow the shoreline for two more hours and then reaches the lodgings for the third night, the Moturau Hut. The final day is mostly easy walking on flat terrain. The walk takes four to five hours, passes by rivers and forests, and crosses a wetland by boardwalk.

In summer, from late October through late April, the huts are serviced and cost $15 per night for adults. During winter, when huts are unserviceable, this charge drops to $5. Inquiries and reservations can be made through **Real Journeys** (☎ 03/249–7416 or 0800/656–501, WEB www.realjourneys.co.nz). You can also make a reservation with the **Great Walks Booking Office** (☎ 03/249–8514).

Dining and Lodging

$$$$ ✕ **Keplers Restaurant.** Described by many locals as the only serious restaurant in town, Keplers has quite a reputation to maintain. The ambience is relaxing, the view magnificent. Tandoori prawns are the most popular starter, and beef Wellington is a big seller. Crayfish arrives live in the kitchen every day and is offered simply grilled (highly recommended) or with Mornay sauce. As nighttime falls, candles add a romantic air. ✉ *5 Town Centre,* ☎ *03/249–7909. AE, DC, MC, V.*

$$$$ ✕ **Settlers Steakhouse.** The curtains are red, the carpet is red—and most of the meals feature red meat. Choose your own steak, perhaps rump steak or a T-bone, and the chef will cook it just the way you want it. It's not all beef, though—you can also choose from grilled lamb, venison, local salmon, cod, or crayfish tail. ✉ *Town Centre,* ☎ *03/249– 8454. AE, DC, MC, V. Closed June–July.*

$$$–$$$$ ✕ **Hollyford Boulevard.** With seating for more than 100 indoors and out, this is Te Anau's biggest eatery. Bright colors, metal and wicker chairs, and lots of light wood give it a modern look. At dinner, local delicacies like blue cod, mussels, and venison are complemented by an extensive wine list. For lunch, try the Parma Zinger, a citrusy combination of oranges, grapes, and prosciutto, or the Vege Stack with grilled mushrooms, New Zealand Brie, and roasted peppers. Breakfast and lunch are done over the counter, while dinner has table service. ✉ *63 Milford Rd.,* ☎ *03/249–7334. DC, V. Closed June–early Sept.*

$-$$ ✕ **La Toscana.** The wine-color walls in this cheap-and-cheerful café put you in the mood for the well-priced selection of Tuscan soups, pastas, and pizzas. You won't find geographically confused toppings like tandoori chicken or ham and pineapple—the kitchen keeps things pretty authentic. Sensibly, both pastas and pizzas are available in medium or large sizes, but remember to keep dessert in mind—the *torta di cioccolata* (chocolate cake) is a local legend. ⊠ *108 Town Centre,* ☎ *03/249–7756. AE, MC, V. No lunch.*

$$$-$$$$ 🏨 **Holiday Inn Te Anau.** On the shores of Lake Te Anau, within two minutes of the downtown area, this luxurious hotel has spacious lounges, extensive gardens, individual villas, and the feel of a tropical resort, minus the palm trees. The hotel is popular with hikers who are soaking up a bit of pampering on their way to the Milford Track. The McKinnon's Restaurant serves delectable South Island seafood and game. ⊠ *64 Lake Front Dr.,* ☎ *03/249–9700,* FAX *03/249–7947. 80 rooms, 15 villa rooms, 15 suites. Restaurant, in-room data ports, minibars, pool, sauna, spa, bar, baby-sitting, laundry service. AE, DC, MC, V.*

$$$ 🏨 **The Cats Whiskers.** Hosts Irene and Terry Maher have created a home-away-from-home atmosphere at their lakefront B&B, complete with a resident cat. It's a 10-minute walk from the town center. A courtesy car can take you to any of the local restaurants. ⊠ *2 Lake Front Dr.,* ☎ *03/249–8112,* FAX *03/249–8112. 4 rooms. MC, V. BP.*

$$$ 🏨 **The Village Inn.** Close to the lake and the town's central shopping area, this inn has a facade of a carefully reconstructed pioneer village. Behind these shop and business fronts are thoroughly modern hotel rooms and suites, including some family-size units. ⊠ *Mokoroa St.,* ☎ *03/249–7911,* FAX *03/249–7003,* WEB *www.thevillageinn.co.nz. 50 rooms. Restaurant, minibars, bar, laundry facilities. AE, DC, MC, V.*

Outdoors Activities and Sports

CRUISING

Peaceful Doubtful Sound is three times as long as Milford Sound and sees far fewer visitors. **Real Journeys** (⊠ Lake Front Dr., ☎ 03/249–7416, WEB www.realjourneys.co.nz) runs a range of combined bus and boat trips there. Tours include a 2-km (1-mi) bus trip down a spiral tunnel to the Lake Manapouri Power Station machine hall, an extraordinary engineering feat built deep beneath the mountain. On the sound itself, you may see bottlenose dolphins or fur seals. Most people take a 9½-hour day trip from Lake Manapouri; there's a bus connection to Te Anau. Between October and May you can overnight on the sound, aboard the *Fiordland Navigator.* Rates for the day excursion are $190 per person, and for the overnight cruise, $289–$395.

FLYING

Air Fiordland offers a range of scenic flights on its fixed-wind aircraft to Milford Sound ($230) and Doubtful Sound ($165). It also has combined packages offering the option of flying to Milford Sound and then taking a cruise boat or kayaking before returning to either Te Anau or Queenstown. The company also runs flights to Mt. Cook and Mt. Aspiring from Queenstown. ⊠ Box 38, Te Anau, ☎ 03/249–7505, FAX 03/249–7080, WEB www.airfiordland.co.nz.

Waterwings Airways offers scenic flights with a floatplane that takes travelers to some of the region's most inaccessible areas. The company has a Catch a Crayfish package, which allows passengers to be flown to a licensed crayfishing vessel on Doubtful Sound. After cruising along the rugged coastline observing seals, penguins, and (most days) dolphins, passengers then enjoy a champagne lunch eating the crayfish they are guaranteed to catch. They can also take crayfish home. The four-hour trip costs $475 per person, and a minimum of three passengers is required. Waterwings Airways offers a range of other scenic flights, including a 10-minute trip over Lake Te Anau, Lake Manapouri, and the Kepler Track and longer flights over Doubtful, Dusky, and Milford sounds. ⊠ *Box 222, Te Anau,* ☎ *03/249–7405,* fax *03/249–7939.*

HIKING

Information and maps for the plethora of hikes near Te Anau, including the Kepler Track, can be obtained from the **Fiordland National Park Visitor Centre.** ⊠ *Lake Front Dr.,* ☎ *03/249–7924,* fax *03/249–7613,* WEB *www.doc.govt.nz.*

En Route   The **Milford Road,** from Te Anau to Milford Sound, winds through deep, stony valleys where waterfalls cascade into mossy beech forests. The 120-km (75-mi) road starts with a fast 29-km (18-mi) stretch along the shores of Lake Te Anau to Te Anau Downs. This is where the ferry leaves for those wishing to hike the Milford Track.

Past Te Anau Downs, the road cuts away from the lake and after 20 km (12½ mi) enters **Fiordland National Park.** On its way to the Divide, some 85 km (53 mi) from Te Anau, the road passes some great photo ops at **Mirror Lakes, Knobs Flat,** and **Lake Gunn.** The Divide, a watershed between rivers flowing both east and west, marks the starting point for the **Routeburn Track,** one of New Zealand's designated Great Tramps. Four kilometers (2½ miles) past the Divide, the road passes the turnoff for another fine trail, the **Hollyford Track.** From here you can take the 3-km (2-mi) walk to **Lake Marion,** which is a good alternative if you are on a tight schedule and unable to do the more extensive tramps in the area.

The Milford road continues 4 km (2½ mi) to the **Homer Tunnel.** Work on the tunnel started in 1935 as a Depression-era government work project. After the lengthy tunnel, the road descends sharply for 16 km (10 mi) before reaching the small settlement at Milford Sound. Allow at least 2½ hours for the trip from Te Anau.

Milford Sound

㉗ *120 km (75 mi) northwest of Te Anau, 290 km (180 mi) west of Queenstown.*

★ Fiordland National Park's greatest appeal and busiest attraction is **Milford Sound,** the sort of overpowering place where poets run out of words and photographers out of film. Hemmed in by walls of rock that rise from the waterline sheer up to 4,000 ft, the 13-km-long (18-mi-long) inlet was carved by a succession of glaciers as they gouged a track to the sea. Its dominant feature is the 5,560-ft pinnacle of **Mitre Peak,** which is capped with snow for all but the warmest months of the year. Opposite the peak, Bowen Falls tumbles 520 ft before exploding into the sea. On a clear day this is a spectacular place. Luxuriant rain forest clings to the sheer precipices that are washed with waterfalls. But Milford Sound is also spectacularly wet: the average annual rainfall is around 20 ft, and it rains an average of 183 days a year. In addition to a raincoat you'll need insect repellent—the sound is renowned for its voracious sand flies.

Still, even in heavy rain and storms Milford Sound is magical. Rainfall is so excessive that a coat of up to 20 ft of fresh water floats on top of the surface of the saltwater sound. This creates a unique underwater environment similar to that found at a much greater depth in the open ocean. You can observe this at the **Milford Deep Underwater Observatory,** moored a 15-minute boat ride from Milford at Harrison Cove. From the underwater windowed gallery you'll see rare red

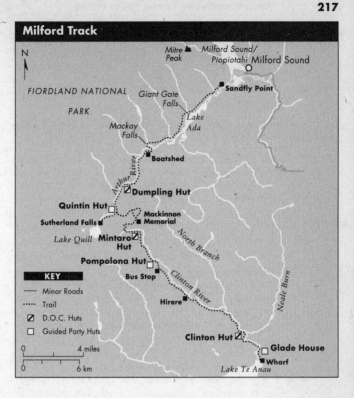

Milford Track

N

Mitre Peak

Milford Sound/ Piopiotahi Milford Sound

FIORDLAND NATIONAL

PARK

Giant Gate Falls

Sandfly Point

Lake Ada

Mackay Falls

Arthur River

Boatshed

Dumpling Hut

Quintin Hut

Mackinnon Memorial

Sutherland Falls

North Branch

Lake Quill

Mintaro Hut

Pompolona Hut

Bus Stop

Clinton River

Neale Burn

Hirere

KEY

— Minor Roads

···· Trail

☑ D.O.C. Huts

☐ Guided Party Huts

Clinton Hut

Glade House

Wharf

Lake Te Anau

0   4 miles

0   6 km

and black coral and a range of deepwater species. The 30-minute visit and round-trip boat trip from Milford take about one hour. Several boating companies, such as Real Journeys and Mitre Peak Cruises, make regular trips to the observatory. ✉ *Box 20, Milford Sound,* ☎ *03/249–9442,* 🌐 *www.milforddeep.co.nz.* ☉ *Oct.–Apr., daily 9:30–5:30; May–Sept., daily 10–2.*

★ If you plan to walk the **Milford Track**—a wholly rewarding, four-day bushwalk through Fiordland National Park—understand that it is one of New Zealand's most popular hikes. The 53½-km (33-mi) track is strictly one-way, and because park authorities control access, you can feel as though you have the wilderness more or less to yourself. Independent and guided groups stay in different overnight huts. Be prepared for rain and snow, but also for what many call the finest walk in the world. This is still wild country, largely untouched by humanity. Mountains rise vertically for several thousand feet out of valleys carved by glaciers. Forests tower above you, and myriad cascading waterfalls plunge into angry, fast-flowing rivers.

The trailheads for the track are remote. Both guided and unguided walks begin with a two-hour ferry ride from Glade Wharf on Lake Te Anau and end with a ferry taking you from Sandfly Point over to the Milford Sound dock. Because of the good condition of the track, the walk is rarely demanding. Much of the first day's shortish hike to the Clinton Hut entails walking along river valleys through lovely beech forests. The second day's four- to five-hour hike to the Mintaro hut is also mostly easy, but the crossing of the Mackinnon Pass on the third day can be a challenge. It involves a steady climb and then a rapid descent, some of it on a lengthy, wooden staircase, past roaring rivers and waterfalls. The view from the Mackinnon Pass, however, is stunning. Also on day three, be sure to take the detour at Quintin Hut to view the world's fifth-highest waterfall, Sutherland Falls, which plunges 1,900 ft in three leaps. It's possible to walk behind the curtain of water as the waterfall reaches the valley floor, a truly unforgettable experience. Your last day entails the lengthy 21-km (13-mi) hike from Quintin Lodge to the track end at Sandfly Point. It requires an early start, but this last leg provides a glorious finale, since—especially after a rain—Arthur River and the many waterfalls flow abundantly.

Because the track is often blocked by snow in winter, there is a restricted hiking season from November until mid-April.

To hike independent of a tour group, call the **Great Walks Booking Desk** at the Fiordland National Park Visitor Centre (⊠ Lake Front Dr., Te Anau, ☎ 03/249–8514, FAX 03/249–8515, WEB www.doc.govt.nz). You'll need to book well in advance—up to a year if you plan to go in December or January. Freedom walking, without a guide, requires that you bring your own food, utensils, bedding, and other equipment. You stay in clean, basic Department of Conservation huts. The hut cost from November to April, the prime booking time, runs $105.

Going with a guide requires deep pockets (the service costs $1,690, $1,490 in low season) and provides comfortable beds and someone who does the cooking. Food and wine are flown in by plane or helicopter to the remote lodgings, which are equipped with generators to provide electric power. Trampers enjoy quality meals, hot showers, and evening entertainment. As meals and bed linen are provided, guided walkers need not carry a lot of gear. The guided tramp package ends with a night's accommodation at Mitre Peak Lodge in Milford Sound and a cruise on Milford Sound the next day. Also included in the fee is transport to and from Queenstown. Book your guided walk with **Ultimate Hikes.** ⊠ Box 259, Queenstown, ☎ 03/441–1138 or 0800/659–255, FAX 03/441–1124, WEB www.ultimatehikes.co.nz.

Lodging

Accommodations are scant at Milford Sound, and it's best to stay in Queenstown or Te Anau and make your visit a very long day trip.

$ 🖬 **Milford Sound Lodge.** Just 1 km (½ mi) out of the Milford settlement, off the main Milford–Te Anau road, this backpacker hostel offers basic but relatively fresh accommodations. In the past few years the guest rooms were completely revamped, from the heating system to the mattresses and curtains. The range of rooms includes twin and double units with linen for $56 a person, four-person bunk rooms at $22 per bed, and dormitories for six people also at $22 a bed. All bathrooms are shared. The lodge serves inexpensive breakfast and dinner, or people can cook for themselves in the on-site kitchen. ⊠ Milford Sound, ☎ 03/249–8071, FAX 03/249–8075, WEB www.milfordlodge.com. 23 rooms with shared bath. Restaurant, laundry facilities. MC, V.

Outdoor Activities and Sports

CRUISING

The view from the water is mind-bendingly beautiful, which accounts for the popularity of cruising here. It's essential to book ahead between mid-December and March. Some include a visit to the **Milford Sound Underwater Observatory** (☞ above). All boats leave from the Milford wharf area. If you can, avoid the midday sailings, as they link with tour buses and are most crowded. Milford Sound Red Boat Cruises and Real Journeys run over a dozen cruises a day between them, with extra options in summer.

Real Journeys (⊠ Lake Front Dr., Te Anau, ☎ 03/249–7416 or 0800/656–501, WEB www.realjourneys.co.nz) organizes daily nature cruises on the *Milford Wanderer* and its companion the *Milford Mariner*, both designed along the lines of trading scows. These cruise the full length of the Milford Sound to the Tasman Sea, with views of waterfalls, rain forest, mountains, and wildlife. The staff keeps things lively with barbecues, on-board games, and anecdotes of the sound's history. The ride costs $60. A pair of modern cruisers run shorter daily sightseeing trips ($45). The *Mariner* and *Wanderer* are also used for overnight cruises. The *Mariner* has private cabins, starting at $275, while the *Wanderer* has bunk berths ($175).

Milford Sound Red Boat Cruises (✉ Milford Sound Wharf, ☎ 03/441–1137, WEB www.redboats.co.nz) offers frequent daily scenic cruises on Milford Sound or to the Milford Deep Underwater Observatory. The basic tour, which lasts less than two hours, loops through the sound to the Tasman Sea; the fare starts at $45.

KAYAKING

Milford Sound Sea Kayaks (✉ Box 19, Milford Sound, ☎ 03/249–8500; 0800/476–726 in New Zealand; WEB www.kayakmilford.co.nz) offers guided kayaking on the sound that includes a hike along part of the Milford track. Prices range from $85 to $139 per person. No experience is required.

SCENIC FLIGHTS

You can avoid the four-hour bus journey from Queenstown to Milford by taking a "flightseeing" option. This combines a round-trip flight from Queenstown to Milford with a scenic cruise. Flights are weatherdependent. **Milford Sound Scenic Flights** (☎ 03/442–3065 or 0800/207–206, www.milfordflights.co.nz) start with one-hour flights for $199. The **Helicopter Line New Zealand** (☎ 03/442–3034, WEB www.new-zealand.com/THL) will get you buzzing over the Milford Sound; the Milford Sound Fantastic trip has three landings and costs $545.

Southland A to Z

AIR TRAVEL

Queenstown is linked directly with Auckland by Air New Zealand and to Christchurch by Air New Zealand Link. Both routes have at least three daily flights. On a clear day the views are spectacular; in winter, snow sometimes closes the airport.

➤ CARRIER: **Air New Zealand** (☎ 03/441–1900 or 0800/737–000, WEB www.airnewzealand.com).

AIRPORT

Queenstown Airport (ZQN) is 9 km (5½ mi) east of town.

➤ AIRPORT INFORMATION: **Queenstown Airport** ✉ Frankton Rd., Queenstown, ☎ 03/442–3505, WEB www.queenstownairport.co.nz).

TRANSFERS

Super Shuttle Queenstown meets all incoming flights and charges $12 for one person (and increasingly less depending on the number of people in a group) to hotels in town. Taxi fare is about $20.

➤ CONTACTS: **Alpine Taxi** (☎ 03/442–6666). **Queenstown Taxis** (☎ 03/442–7788 or 0800/788–294). **Super Shuttle Queenstown** (☎ 03/442–3639).

BUS TRAVEL

It may take a full day, but you can take buses to and from the Southland. InterCity coaches make daily trips from the Franz Josef and Fox glaciers through Wanaka to Queenstown. Another daily InterCity route links Christchurch, Mt. Cook, Wanaka, and Queenstown. InterCity also goes down the South Island's eastern flank from Christchurch to

Queenstown via Dunedin. Newmans, meanwhile, runs a daily bus service from Christchurch through Mount Cook to Queenstown. Hazlett Tours covers a route from Queenstown to Invercargill Monday through Saturday.

Within the Southland, InterCity and Newmans buses both shuttle daily between Queenstown, Te Anau, and Milford Sound. Wanaka Connections sends buses between Wanaka and Queenstown several times a day for $25 each way.

In Queenstown, Newmans, Hazlett, and InterCity buses stop at the Clock Tower building on Camp Street. In Te Anau, both bus lines stop on Miro Street; Wanaka's bus stop is on Ardmore Street.

➤ CONTACTS: **Hazlett Tours** (☎ 03/442–0099). **InterCity** (☎ 03/442–8238, WEB www.intercitycoach.co.nz). **Newmans** (☎ 09/913–6188, WEB www.newmanscoach.co.nz). **Wanaka Connections** (✉ 86 Ballantyne St., Wanaka, ☎ 03/443–9122, WEB www.wanakaconnexions.co.nz).

CAR TRAVEL

Driving is certainly the best way to get around this region, but be prepared for rugged country and frequent heavy rain, particularly around Milford Sound. Rental car companies may discourage driving on some of the tougher rural roads. Highway 6 enters Queenstown from the West Coast; driving time for the 350-km (220-mi) journey from Franz Josef is eight hours. From Queenstown, Highway 6 continues south to Invercargill—a 190-km (120-mi) distance that takes about three hours to drive. The fastest route from Queenstown to Dunedin is via Highway 6 to Cromwell, south on Highway 8 to Milton, then north along Highway 1, a distance of 280 km (175 mi), which can be covered in five hours.

It takes approximately an hour and a half to drive between Queenstown and Wanaka; the drive between Queenstown and Te Anau generally lasts a little over two hours.

EMERGENCIES

Queenstown has a late-night pharmacy, Wilkinson's Pharmacy, which stay open until 10 PM.

➤ EMERGENCY SERVICES: **Fire, police, and ambulance** (☎ 111). **Wilkinson's Pharmacy** (✉ Corner of the Mall and Rees St., ☎ 03/442–7313).

TOURS

ADVENTURE TOURS

Real Journeys has a wide choice of fly-drive-cruise tour options to Milford and Doubtful sounds from Queenstown, Te Anau, and Milford.

Outback New Zealand offers four-wheel-drive "safari" trips to old gold-rush settlements (or their remains), such as Skippers Canyon, Seffertown, and Macetown. Another offroading trip takes you to see some of the areas filmed for the *Lord of the Rings* trilogy. The straightforward tours cost about $85, but you can add on helicopter rides, bungy jumping, rafting, and jet-boat rides at an extra cost.

➤ CONTACTS: **Outback New Zealand** (✉ Box 341, Queenstown, ☎ 03/442–7386, FAX 03/442–7346, WEB www.outback.net.nz). **Real Journeys** (✉ Lake Front Dr., Te Anau, ☎ 03/249–7416 or 0800/656–501, FAX 03/249–7022; ✉ Steamer Wharf, Queenstown, ☎ 03/442–7500, WEB www.realjourneys.co.nz).

BUS TOURS

The Double Decker is an original London bus that makes a 2½-hour circuit from Queenstown to Arrowtown and the bungy-jumping platform on the Karawau River. Tours ($27) depart Queenstown daily at 10 and 2 from the Mall.

➤ CONTACT: **Double Decker** (☎ 03/442–6067).

Ultimate Hikes provides guided walks on the Milford Track. The walk costs $1,690 and $1,490 in the low season.

➤ CONTACT: **Ultimate Hikes** (✉ Box 259, Queenstown, ☎ 03/441–1138 or 0800/659–255, FAX 03/441–1124, WEB www.ultimatehikes.co.nz).

VISITOR INFORMATION

In addition to the visitor centers listed below, there are some local tourism organizations whose Web sites can be helpful. A Lake Wanaka site (www.lakewanaka.co.nz) provides information on local businesses, events, and attractions. Destination Fiordland (www.fiordland.org.nz) covers Te Anau, Milford and Doubtful sounds, and more.

The Fiordland National Park's visitor bureau hours vary a bit seasonally. Queenstown's visitor center opens daily from 7 AM to 7 PM.

➤ TOURIST INFORMATION: **Fiordland National Park Visitor Centre** (✉ Box 29, Lakefront Dr., Te Anau, ☎ 03/249–8900). **Queenstown Visitor Information Centre** (✉ Clocktower Centre, Shotover and Camp Sts., ☎ 03/442–4100, WEB www.queenstown-nz.co.nz). **Wanaka Visitor Information Centre** (✉ The Log Cabin, Ardmore St., ☎ 03/443–1233, FAX 03/443–1290).

DUNEDIN, OTAGO, AND INVERCARGILL

The province of Otago stretches southeast of Queenstown to the Pacific. Flatter than Southland—as most of the world is—it looks more like parts of North Island. Its capital, Dunedin (dun-*ee*-din), is one of the unexpected treasures of New Zealand: a harbor city of steep streets and prim Victorian architecture, with a royal albatross colony on its doorstep. Invercargill is the southern anchor of the province, essentially a farm service community and for visitors a gateway to Fiordland or a stopover on the way to Stewart Island.

Dunedin

28 *280 km (175 mi) east of Queenstown, 362 km (226 mi) south of Christchurch.*

Clinging to the walls of the natural amphitheater at the west end of Otago Harbour, South Island's second-largest city is blessed with inspiring nearby seascapes and wildlife. Its considerable number of university students gives the city a vitality far greater than its population of 120,000 might suggest. And its size makes it easy to explore on foot—with the possible exception of Baldwin Street, the world's steepest residential street.

Dunedin is the Gaelic name for Edinburgh, and the city's Scottish roots are evident. It was founded in 1848 by settlers of the Free Church of Scotland, a breakaway group from the Presbyterian Church. Today it has the only kilt shop in the country and the first and only (legal) whiskey distillery—and a statue of Scottish poet Robert Burns. The city prospered mightily during the gold rush of the 1860s. For a while it was the largest city in the country, and the riches of the Otago goldfields are reflected in the bricks and mortar of Dunedin's handsome Victorian townscape, most notably in the Italianate **Municipal Chambers** building in the Octagon.

The **Octagon,** at the center of town, is the city's hub. A **statue of Robert Burns** sits in front of **St. Paul's Cathedral,** a building part Victorian Gothic, part modern. On Stuart Street at the corner of Dunbar, take notice of the late-Victorian **Law Courts.** Their figure of Justice stands with scales in hand but without her customary blindfold (though the low helmet she wears probably has the same effect).

The **Dunedin Public Art Gallery,** opened in 1996, has notably lovely display spaces. Natural light streams into the glass ceiling foyer, while the galleries are distinguished by native-wood parquet flooring and hand-crafted wrought iron. The collection includes European masters such as Turner and Gainsborough, as well as New Zealand and Otago artists. A special gallery highlights Dunedin native Frances Hodgkins, whose work won acclaim in the 1930s and '40s. The museum also regularly mounts innovative contemporary shows. ✉ *30 The Octagon,* ☎ *03/474–3240.* ▨ *Free.* ⊙ *Daily 10–5.*

The 1906 **Dunedin Railway Station,** a cathedral to the power of steam, is a massive bluestone structure in Flemish Renaissance style, lavishly decorated with heraldic beasts, coats of arms, nymphs, scrolls, a mosaic floor, and even stained-glass windows portraying steaming locomotives. This extravagant building earned its architect, George Troup, the nickname Gingerbread George from the people of Dunedin and a knighthood from the king. The station has far outlived the steam engine and for all its magnificence receives few trains these days. ✉ *Anzac Ave. at Stuart St.,* ☎ *03/477–4449.* ⊙ *Daily 7–6.*

The **First Presbyterian Church** on the south side of Moray Place is perhaps the finest example of a Norman Gothic building in the country. ✉ *415 Moray Pl.*

🐚 The **Otago Museum** is a great opportunity to see a Victorian-style gallery. In the 19th century, displays were lit with natural light, so museums often had huge skylight windows. In this museum's 1877 building, you can visit the "Animal Attic," a restored, magnificent kauri-timbered gallery with skylights. The museum's first curator was a zoologist, and many of the original animals collected from 1868 are still on display. Other galleries focus on Māori and Pacific Island artifacts, animal and insect specimens, and nautical items, including ship models and a whale skeleton. Discovery World adds a hands-on element. ✉ *419 Great King St.,* ☎ *03/474–7474,* ⊞ *www.otagomuseum.govt.nz.* ▨ *Free, Discovery World $6.* ⊙ *Daily 10–5.*

The 35-room Jacobean-style **Olveston** mansion was built between 1904 and 1906 for David Theomin, a wealthy businessman and patron of the arts who amassed a handsome collection of antiques and contemporary furnishings. The house and its furnishings are undoubtedly a treasure from an elegant age, but, apart from some paintings collected by Theomin's daughter, there is very little in it to suggest that it's in New Zealand. Even the oak staircase and balustrade were prefabricated in England. The one-hour guided tour is recommended. ✉ *42 Royal Terr.,* ☎ *03/477–3320.* ▨ *$12.* ⊙ *Daily 9–5; tour daily at 9:30, 10:45, noon, 1:30, 2:45, and 4.*

When walking Dunedin's central streets, you can't miss the tantalizing aroma coming from a favorite institution: the Cadbury chocolate 🐚 factory, which produces most New Zealand–made chocolate. At **Cadbury World** you can watch chocolate candy in the making; keep an eye out for the chocolate waterfall. ✉ *280 Cumberland St.,* ☎ *03/467–7800,* ⊞ *www.cadbury.co.nz.* ▨ *$14.* ⊙ *Daily 9–4.*

For more taste-bud indulging, head to **Speight's Heritage Centre** for a tour of the Southland's top brewery, which dates back to 1876. You'll be shown the various stages of the gravity-driven brewing process and learn the trade's lingo such as "wort" and "grist." And, of course, you'll have a chance to taste the results. ✉ *200 Rattray St.,* ☎ *03/477–7697.* ▨ *$12.* ⊙ *Tours daily at 10, 11:45, and 2.*

Dining and Lodging

$$$–$$$$ ✕ **The Ale House Bar & Restaurant.** A rugged interior with heavy wood furniture, old brewing equipment, and a huge schist fireplace makes the Speight's brewery restaurant quite welcoming. Its hub, naturally, is the bar, whose brass footrest invites you to pull up a stool and relax. The menu includes a "drunken" steak (steak marinated in dark, malty porter) and beer-battered fish. Of course, you'll get recommendations for the best Speight's ale for your meal. ⊠ *200 Rattray St.,* ☎ *03/471–9050. AE, DC, MC, V.*

$$$–$$$$ ✕ **Bell Pepper Blue.** Michael Coughlin, one of the country's most re-
★ spected chefs, brings an inventive flair to his dishes. You might find char-grilled cervena (farmed venison) with soy- and sesame-roasted pota-toes and a mushroom confit or salmon with chili-mint butter. The set-ting, inside a converted pub, is casual and attractive. ⊠ *474 Princes St.,* ☎ *03/474–0973. AE, DC, MC, V. Closed Sun. No lunch.*

$$$–$$$$ ✕ **Palms Restaurant.** The watchful eye of a statue of Queen Victoria guards this notable spot. Delicious local beef, lamb, cervena, and salmon are matched by imaginative vegetarian dishes. Bottles from cen-tral Otago lead the wine list. ⊠ *84 Lower High St.,* ☎ *03/477–6534. AE, DC, MC, V. No lunch.*

$$–$$$ ✕ **Two Chefs.** With terra-cotta walls and a log fire, this restaurant has a cozy, intimate feel. The tempting menu might include jasmine tea–smoked salmon with roasted Jerusalem artichokes, steamed scallops, and a chili-and-tomato compote. The thoughtfully pruned wine list in-cludes Cloudy Bay and Pelorus vintages. ⊠ *428 George St.,* ☎ *03/477–9117. AE, DC, MC, V. Closed Sun. No lunch.*

$–$$$ ✕ **Abalone.** An extralong bar dominates this quirkily decorated restau-rant, but the emphasis is as much on food as ingestion of the more liq-uid kind. And it's not only the decor that's quirky—recent menus have seen cervena (farmed venison) medallions with a beet sauce on crispy noodles and lamb rumps with ratatouille and a blue cheese crepe. Staff members are adept at recommending wines. ⊠ *44 Hanover St.,* ☎ *03/477–6877. AE, DC, MC, V. Closed Sun. No lunch Sat.*

$$$$ ✕🏨 **Corstorphine House.** This restored Edwardian mansion, surrounded by private gardens, exudes luxurious gentility. The interior's lavishness extends from the public areas, with their carved fireplaces and custom-made furniture, to the thematic suites. Each room's name—such as the Egyptian Room or the French Room—points to its decor. Bathrooms have up-to-date pluses such as de-misting mirrors. Organic produce grown on the property appears in the conservatory restaurant's contemporary dishes, such as polenta with sage, walnuts, and artichokes or roasted pork loin with pumpkin and fig gnocchi. ⊠ *23a Milburn St.,* ☎ *03/487–6676,* 𝔽𝔸𝕏 *03/487–6672,* 𝕎𝔼𝔹 *www.corstorphine.co.nz. 8 suites. AE, DC, MC, V. MAP.*

$$$$ ✕🏨 **Southern Cross Hotel.** Originally named the Grand Hotel and built in 1883, this central hotel was then considered one of the finest guest houses in the southern hemisphere. Today, although it has been completely modernized, much of the ornate Victorian architecture and detail is still in evidence, not least in the casino. Even if you don't want to try your luck, it's well worth walking up the sweeping staircase to ogle the chandeliers and the ornate plaster ceilings. The Carlton Restau-rant is a good place for seafood and a thorough selection of central Otago wines. ⊠ *Princess and High Sts.,* ☎ *03/477–0752,* 𝔽𝔸𝕏 *03/477–5776. 144 rooms, 8 suites. 3 restaurants, in-room data ports, health club, 2 bars, casino. AE, DC, MC, V.*

$$$–$$$$ ✕🏨 **Lisburn House.** Listed with the Historic Trust, this Victorian-
★ Gothic inn is a romantic retreat set amid lovingly tended gardens. Many of its 1865 details are intact, such as the decorative Irish brickwork and fishtail slate roof tiles. Inside, there are high molded plaster ceil-

ings, an impressive turn-of-the-20th-century stained-glass entrance, and a welcoming fireplace. The three sumptuous bedrooms each have four-poster queen beds. At the Claddagh Restaurant, you may have the rare opportunity to try wild venison, with a port and juniper jus— exquisite. ⊠ *15 Lisburn St., Caversham,* ☎ *03/455–8888,* FAX *03/455– 6788,* WEB *www.lisburnhouse.co.nz. 3 rooms. Dining room, in-room VCRs, lounge. AE, DC, MC, V. BP.*

$$–$$$ ⊡ **Hulmes Court Bed & Breakfast.** In an 1860 home built for one of the founders of the Otago Medical School, this friendly B&B maintains its scholarly ties: the host, Norman Wood, employs University of Otago graduates. The complex has spread to include a 1907 home right next door. Rooms are characterized by their architectural elements, such as large bay windows; nearly half have shared baths. It's just a short walk to the center of town. Children are welcome, and there is a resident cat named Solstice. ⊠ *52 Tennyson St.,* ☎ *03/477–5319,* FAX *03/ 477–5310,* WEB *www.hulmes.co.nz. 14 rooms, 8 with bath. In-room VCRs, mountain bikes, lounge, Internet. AE, DC, MC, V. CP.*

The Arts

The **Marshall Seifert Gallery** (⊠ 1 Dowling St., ☎ 03/477–5260) is housed in an turn-of-the-20th-century, triangular-shape building with a dizzying spiral staircase. It's overflowing with rare and collectible fine art, antiques, prints, and contemporary New Zealand art.

Milford Galleries (⊠ 18 Dowling St., ☎ 03/477–8275, WEB www. milfordgalleries.co.nz) is the largest fine art-dealer gallery in New Zealand. The gallery carries the work of every major New Zealand artist, including the large-scale abstract expressionist paintings of Neil Frazer and Elizabeth Rees's telling oil studies of New Zealand machismo. Ask about the gallery's lectures on New Zealand art history.

En Route   If you're driving along the coast north of Dunedin, stop to see the striking **Moeraki Boulders.** These giant spherical rocks are concretions, formed by a gradual buildup of minerals around a central core. Some boulders have sprung open, revealing—no, not alien life forms—interesting calcite crystals. The boulders stud the beach north of the town of Moeraki and south as well at Katiki Beach off Highway 1, about 60 km (37 mi) above Dunedin, or 40 km (25 mi) south of Oamaru.

Otago Peninsula

The main areas of interest on the claw-shape peninsula that extends northeast from Dunedin are the albatross colony and Larnach Castle. On the return journey to Dunedin, the Highcliff Road, which turns inland at the village of Portobello, is a scenic alternative to the coastal Portobello Road. Allow an hour to drive from the city.

㉙ Set high on a hilltop with commanding views from its battlements, **Larnach Castle** is the grand baronial fantasy of William Larnach, an Australian-born businessman and politician. The castle, built in the mid-1870s, was a vast extravagance even in the free-spending atmosphere of the gold rush. Larnach imported an English craftsman to carve the ceilings, which took 12 years to complete. The solid marble bath, marble fireplaces, tiles, glass, and even much of the wood came from Europe. The mosaic in the foyer depicts Larnach's family crest and the modest name he gave to his stately home: the Camp. Larnach rose to a prominent position in the New Zealand government of the late 1800s, but in 1898, beset by a series of financial disasters and possible marital problems, he committed suicide in Parliament House. (According to one romantic version, Larnach's third wife, whom he married at an advanced age, ran off with his youngest son; devastated,

Larnach shot himself.) There are 35 acres of grounds around the castle that include a rhododendron garden; a rain-forest garden with kauri, rimu, and *totara* trees; statues of *Alice in Wonderland* characters; an herbaceous walk; and a South Seas Walkway lined with palms and aloe plants. ✉ *Camp Rd.,* ☎ *03/476–1616,* WEB *www.larnachcastle. co.nz.* 🎟 *$14.* ☉ *Daily 9–5.*

㉚ Taiaroa Head, the eastern tip of the Otago Peninsula, is the site of a breeding colony of royal albatrosses. Among the largest birds in the world, with a wingspan of up to 10 ft, they can take off only from steep slopes with the help of a strong breeze. Except for here, at Taiaroa Head, and at the Chatham Islands to the east, the birds are found only on windswept islands deep in southern latitudes, remote from human habitation. Under the auspices of the **Trust Bank Royal Albatross Centre,** the colony is open for viewing from October through August, with the greatest number of birds present shortly after the young hatch around the end of January. Between March and September parents leave the fledglings in their nests while they gather food for them. In September, the young birds fly away, returning about eight years later to start their own breeding cycle. From the visitor center you go in groups up a steep trail to the Albatross Observatory, from which you can see the birds through narrow windows. They are only rarely seen in flight. Access to the colony is strictly controlled, and you must book in advance.

Also overlooking the albatross colony is the **"Disappearing" Gun at Fort Taiaroa,** a 6-inch artillery piece installed during the Russian Scare of 1888. When the gun was fired, the recoil would propel it back into its pit, where it could be reloaded out of the line of enemy fire. The gun has been used in anger only once, when it was fired across the bow of a fishing boat that had failed to observe correct procedures before entering the harbor during World War II.

✉ *Taiaroa Head,* ☎ *03/478–0499,* WEB *www.albatross.org.nz.* 🎟 *1½-hr tour (including fort) $27, 1-hr tour (excluding fort) $23.* ☉ *Nov.–Mar., daily 9–dusk; Apr.–Oct., daily 10–dusk; tours late Nov.–Aug., daily 10:30–4, every ½ hr Nov.–Mar., hourly Apr.–Oct.*

If you'd like to observe the world's most endangered penguin in its natural habitat, visit the **Yellow-Eyed Penguin Conservation Reserve,** where a network of tunnels has been disguised so you can get up close to this rare and protected species. Experienced guides will interpret the birds' behavior and seasonal habits as you creep through the tunnels. ✉ *Harrington Point,* ☎ *03/478–0286.* 🎟 *$27.* ☉ *Daily 9–5.*

To learn about the Southland's underwater species, check out the aquarium at the **New Zealand Marine Studies Centre.** You can spot octopi, sea horses, and sharks in the viewing tanks, or get your hands on a starfish in the touch tanks. There are also displays on marine conservation and current research, as well as educational tours. The center is run by the University of Otago Marine Sciences Department; the enthusiastic guides can regale you with locally specific information. ✉ *Hatchery Rd., Portobello,* ☎ *03/479–5826,* WEB *www.otago.ac.nz/MarineStudies.* 🎟 *$7.* ☉ *Daily noon–4:30.*

Lodging

$$$$ ★ 🏨 **Larnach Lodge.** It's hard to beat this setting—panoramic sea views, 35 acres of gardens, the Larnach Castle next door, and astounding luxury theme suites. The Scottish Room, for instance, has classic tartan bedcovers and curtains, heavy brass bedsteads, and a Robbie Burns rug, while the Enchanted Forest Room has 19th-century William Morris wallpaper. Breakfast is served in the former castle's tables. More affordable rooms with shared facilities are available in the converted 1870 coach house. ⊠ *Camp Rd.,* ☎ *03/476–1616,* FAX *03/476–1574,* WEB *www. larnachcastle.co.nz. 12 rooms. MC, V. BP.*

En Route The **Southern Scenic Route,** 440 km (273 mi) of mostly paved road, stretches from Balclutha, south of Dunedin, through the Catlins—known for its stands of native forest and glorious coastline—on through Invercargill to Milford Sound in Fiordland. Pick up a Southern Scenic Route Brochure at the Dunedin visitor center.

Invercargill

③① *182 km (113 mi) south of Queenstown, 217 km (135 mi) southwest of Dunedin.*

Originally settled by Scottish immigrants, Invercargill has retained much of its turn-of-the-20th-century character, with a broad main avenue and streetscapes with richly embellished buildings. You'll find Italian and English Renaissance styles, Gothic stone tracery, and Romanesque designs in a number of well-preserved buildings. The city also has botanic gardens. The pyramid-shape **Southland Museum and Art Gallery** houses the largest public display of live tuatara—New Zealand's extremely rare ancient lizard. It has also established the world's most successful captive breeding program. ⊠ *108 Gala St.,* ☎ *03/218–9753,* WEB *www.southlandmuseum.co.nz.* ⬚ *Donation.* ☉ *Weekdays 9–5, weekends 10–5.*

Dining and Lodging

$$$$ ✕ **Donovan's.** In one of the half dozen dining rooms in this restored Edwardian home, you can try purely 21st-century dishes. Chicken could be served with a roasted plum and tomato-chili jam, and pork loin drizzled with mango-bourbon sauce might be accompanied by a kūmara and green pea puree. ⊠ *220 Bainfield Rd.,* ☎ *03/215–8156. AE, DC, MC, V. Closed Sun.*

$$$$ ✕ **The Rocks.** Exposed brick walls and terra-cotta tiles increase the noise level in this compact suburban eatery, but they add a pleasantly rustic feel. The kitchen makes good use of local seasonal ingredients, and the plates get crowded with interesting combinations such as rosemary-infused cervena (farmed venison) with a beet-and-red-onion confit. ⊠ *101 Dee St., at Courtville Pl.,* ☎ *03/218–7597. AE, DC, MC, V. Closed Sun. No dinner Tues.–Wed., no lunch Sat.*

$$$ 🏨 **Ascot Park Hotel.** This rambling complex is a welcome sight if you've just battled the rugged, gravel roads of the Catlins. The hotel is the largest in town; its rooms are spacious and modern, with small balconies. An on-site restaurant offers traditional and contemporary New Zealand fare. ⊠ *Tay St. and Racecourse Rd.,* ☎ *03/217–6195,* FAX *03/217–7002. 64 rooms, 24 motel units, 2 suites, 4 studio rooms. Restaurant, minibars, pool, hot tub, sauna, gym, bar. AE, DC, MC, V.*

$$ 🏨 **Homestead Villa Motel.** The Homestead's large, fully self-contained units have contemporary furnishings and decor. All have whirlpools. The U-shape motor lodge is a 10-minute walk from the city center and five minutes to the Southland Museum and Art Gallery. ⊠ *Avenal and Dee Sts.,* ☎ *03/214–0408 or 0800/488–588,* FAX *03/214–0478. 25 units. Kitchenettes, laundry. AE, DC, MC, V.*

En Route In the tiny township of **Bluff,** you can taste the coveted namesake oyster. An annual oyster and seafood festival, held in late April at the town's wharf, wallows in seafood delicacies; oyster-opening and -eating competitions and cook-offs are part of the fun. You'll also find the curious Kiwi icon, the **Paua Shell House** (⊠ *Gore St.*). *Paua* is a kind of abalone; the home's walls gleam with the iridescent shells. The house is open most days and a donation is requested. Bluff is also the main jumping-off point for Stewart Island.

Dunedin and Otago A to Z

AIR TRAVEL

Both Qantas and Air New Zealand link Dunedin and Christchurch; the flight takes just under an hour. Air New Zealand also flies regularly from Dunedin to Auckland and Wellington. From Invercargill, Air New Zealand offers direct flights to Christchurch, while Stewart Island Flights hops over to Stewart Island.

➤ CARRIERS: **Air New Zealand** (☎ 03/477–5769, WEB www.airnewzealand.com). **Qantas** (☎ 03/477–4146 or 0800/800–146, WEB www.qantas.com.au). **Stewart Island Flights** (☎ 03/218–9129, WEB www.stewartislandflights.com).

AIRPORTS

Dunedin Airport, with the rather unfortunate code of DUD, lies 20 km (13 mi) south of the city. Invercargill's airport (IVC) is just 3 km (2 mi) from city center.

➤ AIRPORT INFORMATION: **Dunedin International Airport** (✉ 25 Miller Rd., Momona, ☎ 03/486–2879, WEB www.dnairport.co.nz). **Invercargill Airport** (✉ 106 Airport Ave., ☎ 03/218–6920, WEB www.invercargillairport.co.nz).

Taxi fare from Dunedin's airport to city center is about $55–$60. Atomic Shuttles require an advance reservation for trips between the airport and Dunedin but the fare is much lower, at $25.

Taxis from Invercargill Airport into town cost $8; the Spitfire Shuttle runs $7 per person.

➤ CONTACTS: **Atomic Shuttles** (☎ 03/477–4449). **Spitfire Shuttle** (☎ 03/214–1851).

BUS TRAVEL

InterCity makes two daily runs between Christchurch and Dunedin, plus an extra run on Friday and Sunday. One daily InterCity bus continues on from Dunedin to Invercargill; another shuttles between Dunedin and Invercargill on Friday and Sunday.

➤ BUS DEPOTS: **Dunedin** (✉ 205 St. Andrew's St.). **Invercargill** (✉ Railway station).

➤ BUS INFORMATION: **InterCity** (☎ 03/477–8860 or 0800/664–545, WEB www.intercitycoach.co.nz).

CAR TRAVEL

Driving time along the 283 km (177 mi) between Queenstown and Dunedin (via Highway 6 and Highway 1) is four hours.

The main route between Dunedin and Invercargill is Highway 1—a 3½-hour drive. A slower, scenic alternative is along the Catlins coast, which takes a full day for the journey.

EMERGENCIES

Dunedin has a late-night pharmacy, open until 10 PM.

➤ EMERGENCY SERVICES: **Fire, police, and ambulance** (☎ 111). **Urgent Pharmacy** (✉ 95 Hanover St., Dunedin, ☎ 03/477–6344).

TOURS

Lynette Jack, an outstanding personal guide-driver, draws on an extensive knowledge of Invercargill and the surrounding area to illuminate local history while you explore gardens, beaches, historic homes, and even a smelter. A two-hour tour costs $45 per person.

➤ CONTACT: **Lynette Jack Scenic Sights** (⊠ 22 Willis St., ☎ 025/338–370 or 03/215–7741).

WILDLIFE TOURS

Natures Wonders Naturally, a family-run company based at a working farm in a stunning location, uses an all-terrain vehicle to get you to hard-to-reach parts of the Otago Peninsula. You'll visit shag (cormorant) and seal colonies and may even catch up with some yellow-eyed penguins coming ashore. The one-hour trip starts at $30.

Twilight Tours offers various minibus tours of Dunedin and its surroundings, including a daily tour that focuses on the albatrosses, penguins, and seals of the Otago Peninsula. This is a good way to see the rare yellow-eyed and little blue penguins if you don't have a car. The tour costs $50, not including admission to the albatross colony.

Another way to get to know about the prolific wildlife of this area is to take a boat trip to Taiaroa Head with Monarch Wildlife Cruises. A basic guided hour-long cruise includes visits to the breeding sites of the northern royal albatross, New Zealand fur seals, and three species of shags (cormorants). If you are lucky, an albatross will fly over your boat—a spectacular sight with that huge wingspan. Longer trips make landing stops at the penguin reserve or the Taiaroa visitor center. The basic cruise costs $27.

➤ CONTACTS: **Monarch Wildlife Cruises** (⊠ Wharf and Fryatt Sts., Dunedin, ☎ 03/477–4276, WEB www.wildlife.co.nz). **Natures Wonders Naturally** (⊠ Harrington Point, Portobello, ☎ 03/478–1150, FAX 03/478–0714, WEB www.natureswondersnaturally.com). **Twilight Tours** (⊠ Box 963, Dunedin, ☎ 03/474–3300).

VISITOR INFORMATION

In addition to the tourist bureau Web sites listed below, you may want to check out the following: www.southernscenicroute.co.nz for information on the spectacular drive; www.southland.org.nz, maintained by a regional tourism group; and Bluff's www.bluff.co.nz.

The Dunedin visitor center keeps regular business hours daily, with extended hours in summer. The Invercargill visitor bureau opens weekdays 9 to 5, 10 to 5 on weekends, also extending until 6 PM in summer.

➤ TOURIST INFORMATION: **Dunedin Visitor Information Centre** (⊠ 48 The Octagon, ☎ 03/474–3300, FAX 03/474–3311, WEB www.cityofdunedin.com). **Invercargill Visitor Information Centre** (⊠ Southland Museum and Art Gallery, 108 Gala St., ☎ 03/214–6243, FAX 03/218–4415, WEB www.invercargill.org.nz).

STEWART ISLAND

The third and most southerly of New Zealand's main islands, Stewart Island is separated from South Island by the 24-km (15-mi) Foveaux Strait. Its original Māori name, Te Punga o Te Waka a Maui, means "the anchor stone of Maui's canoe." Māori mythology says the island's landmass held Maui's canoe secure while he and his crew raised the great fish—the North Island. Today it is more commonly referred to by its other Māori name, Rakiura, which means "the land of the glowing skies"—referring both to the spectacular sunrises and sunset and to the southern sky's equivalent of the northern lights.

The island covers some 1,700 square km (650 square mi). It measures about 75 km (46 mi) from north to south and about the same distance across at its widest point. On the coastline, sharp cliffs rise from a succession of sheltered bays and beaches. In the interior, forested hills rise gradually toward the west side of the island. Seals and penguins frequent the coast, and the island's prolific bird life includes a number of species rarely seen in any other part of the country. In fact, this is the surest place to see a kiwi: the Stewart Island brown kiwi, or tokoeka, the largest of New Zealand's kiwis. Unlike its mainland cousins, these kiwis can be seen during the day as well as at night. It's a rare and amusing experience to watch these pear-shape birds scampering about on a remote beach as they feed on sand hoppers and grubs.

Archaeologists' studies of 13th-century Māori middens (refuse heaps) indicate that the island was a rich, seasonal resource for hunting, fishing, and gathering seafood. A commonly eaten delicacy was and, interestingly, still is the *titi*, also known as the sooty shearwater or mutton bird.

In the early 19th century, explorers, sealers, missionaries, and miners settled the island. They were followed by fishermen and sawmillers who established settlements around the edges of Paterson Inlet and Halfmoon and Horseshoe bays. In the 1920s the Norwegians set up a whaling enterprise, and many descendants of these seafaring people remain. Fishing, aquaculture, and tourism are now the mainstays of the island's economy.

Even by New Zealand standards, Stewart Island is remote, raw, and untouched. Roads total about 20 km (13 mi), and apart from the tiny township of Oban at **Halfmoon Bay** on Paterson Inlet, the place is practically uninhabited. The appeal is its seclusion, its relaxed way of life, and—despite the once busy whaling and lumber-milling industry—its untouched quality.

In spring 2002, about 85% of Stewart Island was designated as **Rakiura National Park,** encompassing areas that were formerly nature reserves and the like. More than 200 walking tracks thread through the park, and a dozen huts give shelter for overnight stays. One of the best spots for bird-watching is **Ulva Island,** a one-hour launch trip around the coast from Halfmoon Bay. ✉ *Department of Conservation Visitor Centre, Main Rd., Oban,* ☎ *03/219–1130,* ⓦⒺⒷ *www.doc.govt.nz.*

Dining and Lodging

$$$–$$$$ ✕ **Church Hill Cafe Bar & Restaurant.** Deanne McPherson specializes in preparing tantalizing cuisine from the sea's bounty, as well as local favorites like roasted mutton bird. The wine list has some great New Zealand choices and outdoor dining is recommended, as are reservations. ✉ *36 Kamihi Rd., Oban,* ☎ *03/219–1323. AE, DC, MC, V.*

$$–$$$$ ✕ **Lighthouse Wine Bar.** There's nothing like the aroma of wood-fired pizza after a day out kayaking or hiking. Appreciating their customers' ferocious appetites, the owners turn out hearty meals based on local produce. Look for the Big Glory pizza, topped with smoked salmon, marinated mussels, Brie, and avocado, or the Thai-spiced seafood chowder. The wine list has some choice picks, like the Cloudy Bay Sauvignon Blanc. The trick is that the restaurant doesn't have a phone, so you'll have to book the night before or get there just as it opens. ✉ *Main Rd., Oban,* ☎ *no phone. AE, MC, V. Closed Mon. Jan.–Apr.; Mon.–Tues. Sept.–Dec.; and May–Aug.*

$ ✕ **Justcafé.** American Britt Moore has set up her cybercafé in paradise. Stop in for great coffee, muffins, quiche, and cold smoked-salmon sandwiches—and surf the net while you nibble and sip. ✉ *Main Rd., Oban,* ☎ *03/219–1422. No credit cards.*

$$$$ 🏠 **The Bach.** This secluded "self-catering" home works well for couples, with a loft for extra visitors. The place is thoroughly supplied, from beach towels to a CD player. There are plenty of nice design touches, too, such as the paua-shell inlay in the bathroom. The open-plan design makes the most of the sea views, and there's a deck with a barbecue, suited for alfresco meals. If you don't feel like cooking, the owners are nearby and can shuttle you into town. ⊠ *Leask Bay Rd., Halfmoon Bay,* ☎ *03/219–1394. 1 house. AE, DC, MC, V.*

$$$$ 🏠 **Port of Call.** Phillippa Fraser-Wilson and Ian Wilson are sixth-generation Stewart Islanders who have opened the doors of their stunningly appointed home to visitors. This modern B&B overlooks Halfmoon Bay and the Foveaux Strait and is just a few minutes' drive from Oban. There is a historic 1840 stone house on the property, the second oldest of its kind in New Zealand. Ian provides a water-taxi service and customized trips around the island. ⊠ *Leask Bay Rd., Halfmoon Bay, Oban,* ☎ *03/219–1394,* 🖷 *03/219–1394,* 🌐 *www.portofcall.co.nz. 1 room. Lounge. AE, DC, MC, V. CP.*

$$$ 🏠 **Glendaruel.** At this B&B a short walk from town, you'll have private views over Golden Bay. The owners fell in love with the island years ago and couldn't bring themselves to leave; they'll bring that enthusiasm to your stay. The upstairs room is the larger of the two but both are perfectly comfortable. Continental or cooked breakfasts are available, as is dinner by arrangement. ⊠ *38 Golden Bay Rd., Oban,* ☎ 🖷 *03/219–1092,* 🌐 *www.glendaruel.co.nz. 2 rooms. AE, MC, V. BP.*

$$$ 🏠 **Goomes Bed & Breakfast.** Peter and Jeanette Goomes epitomize the
★   idea of island hospitality. Peter's Portuguese and Rakiura Māori background makes him a truly all-around islander, and he's got a wealth of local history to share. Jeanette can rustle up the appropriate gear—like gum boots that fit—if you're off to explore. The tasteful decor and sea views make this a lovely place to stay. ⊠ *Halfmoon Bay,* ☎ *03/ 219–1057,* 🖷 *03/217–6585. 2 rooms. MC, V. BP.*

Outdoor Activities

If you're feeling restless on a bad-weather day, you can use the island's gym in the **community center** (⊠ Ayr St., ☎ 03/219–1477) for a small fee.

FISHING

For information on deep-sea fishing out of Halfmoon Bay, *see* Chapter 6.

HIKING

In addition to several day hikes, Stewart Island offers some outstanding multiday treks. The **Rakiura Track,** one of New Zealand's Great Walks, loops out from Oban, skirting several bays. The tramp takes three days. Another popular trek is the **North West Circuit,** a 10- to 12-day walk from Halfmoon Bay that circles the north coast and then cuts through the interior to return to its starting point. The island's climate is notoriously changeable, and walkers should be prepared for rain and mud. For information on walks, contact the **Department of Conservation Visitor Centre** (⊠ Main Rd., Oban, ☎ 03/219–1130, 🌐 www.doc.govt.nz).

SEA-KAYAKING

Stewart Island Sea Kayak Adventures. Some of the best and most remote sea-kayaking, arguably in the world, abounds around Stewart Island. Paterson Inlet is 100 square km (38 square mi) of bush-clad, sheltered waterways, mostly uninhabited. It has 20 islands, four Department of Conservation huts, and two navigable rivers. Winter is generally the best kayaking season, weather-wise. Rentals start at $90 for two days. ⊠ Argyle St., Oban, ☎ 🖷 03/219–1080.

Stewart Island A to Z

Note that there are no banks or ATM machines on Stewart Island. Since some establishments don't accept credit cards, be sure to have enough cash on hand. Some larger businesses will cash traveler's checks.

AIR TRAVEL

Stewart Island Flights has three scheduled flights daily between In-vercargill and Halfmoon Bay. The scenic 20-minute flight costs $150 round-trip; for the best views ask to sit up front with the pilot.

➤ CARRIER: **Stewart Island Flights** (☎ 03/218–9129, WEB www. stewartislandflights.com).

AIRPORT

The island's bare-bones Ryan's Creek Airstrip is about 2 km (1 mi) from Oban. You can't drive out to the airstrip, but the cost of the shut-tle from town is included in the airfare.

BOAT TRAVEL

Stewart Island Marine runs the *Foveaux Express* and the *Southern Ex-press* between the island and Bluff, the port for Invercargill. The fare is $45 one-way and $84 round-trip; the crossing lasts one hour. There's a morning departure and an afternoon departure daily year-round from both Bluff and Halfmoon Bay.

➤ BOAT INFORMATION: **Stewart Island Marine** (☎ 03/212–7660, FAX 03/ 212–8377, WEB www.foveauxexpress.co.nz).

EMERGENCIES

➤ EMERGENCY SERVICES: **Fire, police, and ambulance** (☎ 111).

TOURS

ADVENTURE TOUR

Stewart Island Flights and Seaview Water Taxis jointly offer a flying, hiking, and boating adventure called "Coast to Coast." For $155 per person (with a three-person minimum) you can view the east and west coasts of the island including Paterson Inlet and Mason Bay. The trip includes an easy four-hour hike on the North West Circuit and a water-taxi ride on the meandering Freshwater River. It's an interchangeable trip, so you can fly-hike-boat or boat-hike-fly. There is also the option of an overnight at Mason Bay in a Department of Conservation hut.

➤ CONTACTS: **Seaview Water Taxis** (✉ Box 128, Stewart Island, ☎ FAX 03/219–1014). **Stewart Island Flights** (☎ 03/218–9129, WEB www. stewartislandflights.com).

BOAT TOURS

Stewart Island Sea Kayak Adventures has assembled a crack guiding team to lead kayaking tours around the island. The guides have a strong background in the island's history, and they can arrange flexible mul-tiday itineraries. Water taxis can take kayaks to more remote areas. Fees range from $85 for a day trip to $310 for a three-day tour.

Want to learn more about aquaculture, visit salmon and mussel farms, or just get a better idea of the fascinating marine life in Stewart Island's waters? The Seabuzzz Experience offers one- and two-hour trips in a glass-bottom boat. Rates start at $25.

Thorfinn Charters owner Bruce Story has an excellent knowledge of the area's natural and human history. Five-hour trips aboard a launch will show you the most scenic parts of Paterson Inlet, and there's a good chance of spotting rare seabirds. Tours run $70 per person.

Talisker Charters gives you the opportunity to sail around Stewart Is-land up to Fiordland in a motor sailing ketch, from half-day trips for $50 to live-aboard cruises for $110 per day. Peter Tait's extensive knowledge of the southern waters is rivaled only by his wife Iris's fa-miliarity with the local ecology—and her cooking.

➤ CONTACTS: **Seabuzzz Experience** (✉ Argyle St., ☎ 03/219–1282, FAX 03/219–1382, WEB www.seabuzzz.co.nz). **Stewart Island Sea Kayak**

Adventures (✉ Innes Backpackers, Argyle St., Oban, ☎ FAX 03/219–1080). **Talisker Charters** (✉ Box 66, Stewart Island, ☎ FAX 03/219–1151, WEB www.taliskercharter.co.nz). **Thorfinn Charters** (☎ 03/219–1210, WEB www.thorfinn.co.nz).

WALKING TOURS

Kiwi Wilderness Walk leads all-inclusive trips from the mainland for a few days' hiking and kayaking around Stewart Island, usually between November and April. The rate is $1,295.

For a unique Rakiura Māori interpretation of Ulva Island's flora and fauna, contact Ulva's Guided Walks. Ulva Amos gives half-day and full-day tours of the island she was named after; the cost, including water-taxi fare, starts at $65.

➤ CONTACTS: **Kiwi Wilderness Walk** (✉ 136 Palmerston St., Riverton, ☎ 03/234–8886, FAX 03/234–8816). **Ulva's Guided Walks** (✉ Box 85, Stewart Island, ☎ 03/219–1216, WEB www.ulva.co.nz).

WILDLIFE TOURS

For a guided, twilight kiwi-spotting trip, including a short boat ride and hike, contact Bravo Adventure Cruises. The excursion costs $60 and is given on alternate nights. You'll need sturdy footwear, warm clothing, and a flashlight.

For information and bookings on shuttles, water taxis, and boat trips around Paterson Inlet, contact Oban Tours.

Thorfinn Charters arranges half- and full-day nature tours, which include a cruise to the Titi Islands and a guided walk on Ulva Island. You'll have the chance to see several kinds of rare birds, as well as three kinds of penguins. The trip cost starts at $70.

Also see Ulva's Guided Walks *in* Walking Tours, *above.*

➤ CONTACTS: **Bravo Adventure Cruises** (✉ Box 104, Stewart Island, ☎ FAX 03/219–1144). **Oban Tours** (✉ Main St. [Box 180, Stewart Island], ☎ FAX 03/219–1456). **Thorfinn Charters** (☎ 03/219–1210, WEB www.thorfinn.co.nz).

VISITOR INFORMATION

Stewart Island's visitor bureau is open daily year-round, with the exception of May through October, when it is open only from 10 to noon on weekends.

➤ CONTACT: **Stewart Island Visitor Information Centre** (✉ Main Rd., Halfmoon Bay, ☎ 03/219–0009, FAX 03/219–0003, WEB www.stewartisland.co.nz).

6 ADVENTURE VACATIONS

Bicycling

Cross-Country Skiing

Diving

Fishing

Hiking

Horse Trekking

Rafting

Sailing

Sea-Kayaking

By David
McGonigal,
Doug
Johansen, and
Jan Poole

FOR SOME OF THE MOST VIBRANT experiences in New Zealand, head out to explore the magnificent outdoors. The mountains and forests in this clean, green land are made for hiking and climbing, the rivers for rafting, and the low-traffic roads for bicycling. The rugged coastline looks wonderful from the deck of a small vessel or, even closer to the water, a sea kayak. And this is the country that invented jet-boating.

These activities are commonly split into soft and hard adventures. Hard adventure requires some physical stamina, although you usually don't have to be perfectly fit; in a few cases, prior experience is a prerequisite. In soft adventures the destination is often the adventurous element—you can sit back and enjoy the ride.

With most adventure tour companies, the guides' knowledge of flora and fauna—and love of the bush—is matched by a level of competence that ensures your safety even in dangerous situations. The safety record of adventure operators is very good. Be aware, however, that most adventure-tour operators require you to sign waivers absolving the company of responsibility in the event of an accident or a problem. Courts normally uphold such waivers except in cases of significant negligence.

You can always choose to travel without a guide, but in unfamiliar territory you'll learn more about what's around you by having a knowledgeable local by your side. The material in this chapter complements information in the rest of the book on what to do in different parts of the country. If you're interested in a multiday excursion, such as a fishing tour or tramp, you'll often need to book at least several weeks in advance. For a day's shot at an extreme-sport activity, such as bungy jumping or jet-boating, you'll generally need to make a reservation only a day in advance, or even on the same day.

Bicycling

Cycling is an excellent way to explore a small region, allowing you to cover more ground than on foot and to observe far more than you would from the window of a car or bus. Cycling rates as hard adventure because of the amount of exercise you get.

New Zealand's combination of spectacular scenery and quiet roads is ideal for cycling. Traditionally, the South Island, with its central alpine spine, has been more popular, but Auckland is where most people arrive, and the North Island has enough back roads and curiosities—the Waitomo Caves and the coast beyond, the stunning Coromandel Peninsula, and the hot mud pools of sulfurous Rotorua—to fill days. The average daily riding distance is about 60 km (37 mi), and support vehicles are large enough to accommodate all riders and bikes if circumstances so demand. Rides in the South Island extend from the ferry port of Picton to picturesque Queenstown, the center of a thriving adventure day-trip industry. New Zealand Pedaltours operates on both islands, with tours of 9–22 days. On Adventure South trips, you'll get away from the main roads as they head for quiet South Island back roads on trips for 5–21 days. Mercury Mountain Biking organizes half-day and full-day guided tours.

Season: October–March.
Locations: Countrywide.
Cost: Mountain biking from $40 for half-day guided tour; multiday tours at least $1,365.

Tour Operators: Adventure South (✉ Box 33153, Christchurch, ☎ 03/332–1222, FAX 03/332–4030, WEB www.advsouth.co.nz). **Mercury Mountain Biking** (✉ 8 Kaudu Dr., Whitianga, ☎ 07/866–4993). **New Zealand Pedaltours** (✉ Box 37–575, Parnell, Auckland, ☎ 09/302–0968; 888/222–9187 in the U.S.; FAX 09/302–0967; WEB www.pedaltours.co.nz).

Cross-Country Skiing

Cross-country skiing is arguably the best way to appreciate the winter landscape, and New Zealand's is spectacular. Going cross-country, you'll get away from the downhill hordes and feel like you have the mountains to yourself. Cross-country skiing is hard adventure—the joy of leaving the first tracks across new snow and the pleasure afforded by the unique scenery of the ski slopes is tempered by the fatigue that your arms and legs feel at the end of the day. Multiday tours are arranged so that you stay in lodges every night.

Aoraki (Mt. Cook) and its attendant Murchison and Tasman glaciers offer wonderful ski touring, with terrains to suit all skiers. Tours typically commence with a flight to the alpine hut that becomes your base; from there the group sets out each day for skiing and instruction.

Season: July–September.
Locations: Aoraki, South Island.
Cost: Around $420 for two days, $1,080 for five days.
Tour Operator: Alpine Recreation Canterbury (✉ Box 75, Lake Tekapo, ☎ 03/680–6736, FAX 03/680–6765, WEB www.alpinerecreation.com).

Diving

The Bay of Islands, in the Northland arm of the North Island, is perhaps New Zealand's best diving location. In the waters around Cape Brett, you can encounter moray eels, stingrays, grouper, and other marine life. Surface water temperatures rarely dip below 15°C (60°F). From September through November, underwater visibility can be affected by a plankton bloom. Knight Diver Tours makes the rounds at the Poor Knights Islands Marine Reserve, which is a great place to see colorful subtropical fish and underwater caves and tunnels. While the outfit does not give PADI training courses, it can take noncertified people on guided dives. One of the highlights of Bay of Islands diving is the wreck of the Greenpeace vessel *Rainbow Warrior,* which French agents sank in 1985. It is about two hours from Paihia by dive boat. Paihia Dive Hire and Charter organizes dives to the wreck, now an artificial reef; it also offers PADI courses.

The clear waters around New Zealand make for good diving in other areas as well, such as the Coromandel Peninsula, where the Mercury and Aldermen islands have interesting marine life. With Cathedral Cove Dive, you can dive in the Cathedral Cove Marine Reserve; PADI courses are available. Whangamata, with three islands just off the coast, also has very good diving.

Remember that you cannot fly within 24 hours of scuba diving.

Season: Year-round.
Locations: Bay of Islands and the Coromandel Peninsula, North Island.
Cost: A two-dive day trip without rental gear runs about $80, with gear around $150. Contact diving outfitters for price information for overnight packages.
Tour Operators: Cathedral Cove Dive (✉ R.D. 1, Whitianga, ☎ 07/866–3955, WEB www.hahei.co.nz/diving). **Knight Diver Tours** (✉ 30 Whangarei

Heads Rd., Whangarei, ☎ 09/436–2584 or 0800/766–756, ℻ 09/436–2758, ꟿ www.poorknights.co.nz). **Paihia Dive Hire and Charter** (✉ Box 210, Paihia, Bay of Islands, ☎ 09/402–7551, ℻ 09/402–7110, ꟿ www.divenz.com).

Fishing

Fishing in New Zealand is as good as it gets. Don't pass up an opportunity to drop a line in the water, whether you're looking for the joy of being away from it all in some remote spot, the simplicity of sitting on a wharf or a rock in the sun with a line in hand, or the adrenaline rush when a big one strikes and the reel starts screaming.

Most harbor towns have reasonably priced fishing charters available. They are generally very good at finding fish, and most carry fishing gear you can use if you do not have your own. Inland areas usually have streams, rivers, or lakes with great trout fishing, where guides provide their knowledge of local conditions and techniques. With the aid of a helicopter, you can get into places few people have ever seen. Catch-and-release practices are becoming more prevalent, especially in wilderness areas. As for equipment, visitors can bring their own gear into the country except for flies, which are forbidden. Equipment can also be rented or provided by a guiding company once you're there.

Freshwater Fishing: Trout and salmon, natives in the northern hemisphere, were introduced into New Zealand in the 1860s and 1880s. Rainbow and brown trout in particular have thrived in the rivers and lakes, providing arguably the best trout fishing in the world. Salmon do not grow to the size that they do in their native habitat, but they still make for good fishing. There is free access to all water. You may have to cross private land to fish certain areas, but a courteous approach for permission is normally well received.

The three methods of catching trout allowed in New Zealand are fly-fishing, spinning or threadlining, and trolling. In certain parts of the South Island using small fish, insects, and worms as bait is also allowed. Deep trolling using leader lines and large-capacity reels on short spinning rods is widely done on Lakes Rotoma, Okataina, and Tarawera around Rotorua and on Lake Taupo, with the most popular lures being tobies, flatfish, and cobras. Streamer flies used for trolling are normally the smelt patterns: Taupo tiger, green smelt, ginger mick, Jack Sprat, Parsons glory, and others. Flies, spoons, or wobblers used in conjunction with monofilament and light fly lines on either glass fly rods or spinning rods are popular on all the other lakes.

The lakes in the Rotorua district—Rotorua, Rotoiti, and Tarawera are the largest—produce some of the biggest rainbow trout in the world, which get to trophy size because of an excellent food supply, the absence of competition, and a careful and selective breeding program. In Lake Tarawera, fish from 6 to 10 pounds can be taken, especially in the autumn and winter, when bigger trout move into stream mouths before spawning.

The season around Rotorua runs from October 1 to June 30. In the period between April and June, just before the season closes, flies work very well on beautiful Lake Rotoiti. From December to March fly-fishing is good around the stream mouths on Lake Rotorua. The two best areas are the Ngongotaha Stream and the Kaituna River, using nymph, dry fly, and wet fly. Lake Rotorua remains open for fishing when the streams and rivers surrounding the lake are closed.

Lake Taupo and the surrounding rivers and streams are world renowned for rainbow trout—the lake has the largest yields of trout in New Zealand, an estimated 500 tons. Trolling on Taupo and fishing the rivers flowing into it with a guide are almost surefire ways of catching fish. Wind and weather on the lake, which can change quickly, will determine where you can fish, and going with local knowledge of the conditions on Taupo is essential. The streams and rivers flowing into the lake are open for fly-fishing from October 1 to May 31. The lower reaches of the Tongariro, Tauranga-Taupo, and Waitahanui rivers, and the lake itself, remain open year-round. Lake Waikaremoana in Urewera National Park southeast of Rotorua, is arguably the North Island's most scenic lake, and its fly-fishing and trolling are excellent. As it's well off the beaten track, though, it's not frequented by guides.

The South Island has excellent rivers with very clear water. Some of them hardly ever see anglers, and that untouched quality is particularly satisfying. South Island's best areas for trout are Marlborough, Westland, Fiordland, Southland, and Otago.

The Canterbury district has some productive waters for trout and salmon—along with the West Coast it is the only part of New Zealand where you can fish for salmon, the quinnat or Pacific chinook salmon introduced from North America. Anglers use large metal spoons and wobblers on long, strong rods with spinning outfits to fish the Waimakariri, Waitaki, Rakaia, Ashburton, and Rangitata rivers around Christchurch, often catching salmon of 20 to 30 pounds.

Trout fishing is normally tougher than in the North Island, with trout being a little smaller on average. But occasionally huge browns are caught. You can catch brown and rainbow trout in South Island lakes using flies or by wading and spinning around lake edges or at stream mouths.

Saltwater Fishing: No country in the world is better suited than New Zealand for ocean fishing. Its coastline—approximately as long as that of the mainland United States—has an incredible variety of locations, whether you like fishing off rocks, on reefs, surf beaches, islands, or harbors. Big-game fishing is very popular, and anglers have taken many world records over the years. All the big names are here—black, blue, and striped marlin, both yellowfin and bluefin tuna, and sharks like mako, thresher, hammerhead, and bronze whaler.

The most sought-after fish around the North Island are snapper (sea bream), kingfish, *hapuka* (grouper), *tarakihi,* John Dory, *trevally, maomao,* and *kahawai,* to name a few. Many of these also exist around the top of the South Island. Otherwise, the South Island's main catches are blue cod, butterfish, hake, *hoki,* ling, *moki,* parrot fish, pigfish, and trumpeter, which are all excellent eating fish.

Perhaps the most famous angler to fish New Zealand's waters was adventure novelist Zane Grey, who had his base on Urupukapuka Island in the Bay of Islands. On the North Island, the top areas are the Bay of Islands, the nearby Poor Knights Islands, Whangaroa in Northland, the Coromandel Peninsula and its islands, and the Bay of Plenty and White Island off its coast. The South Island does not have an established deep-sea game-fishing industry as yet.

Licenses: Different districts in New Zealand require different licenses, so it pays to check at the local fish and tackle store to make sure you are fishing legally. (For example, Rotorua is not in the same area as nearby Lake Taupo.) Fees are approximately $60 per year, but at most tackle stores you can purchase daily or weekly licenses. They can also advise you about local conditions, lures, and methods. No license is needed for saltwater fishing.

Publications: *How to Catch Fish and Where,* by Bill Hohepa, and *New Zealand Fishing News Map Guide,* edited by Sam Mossman, both have good information on salt- and freshwater fishing countrywide.

Season: Generally from October through June in streams and rivers; year-round in lakes and at sea.

Locations: Countrywide.

Cost: Big-game fishing: $275 per person per day. Heli-fishing: from $545 per person, per day. Trolling and fly-fishing for lake trout: from $75 per hour (one–four people), on rivers and streams from $75 per hour. Costs for fishing charters vary widely; contact operators for specifics.

North Island Freshwater Operators:Bryan Colman Trout Fishing (⊠ 32 Kiwi St., Rotorua, ☎ 07/348–7766, WEB www.TroutFishingRotorua. com). **Chris Jolly Outdoors** (⊠ Box 1020, Taupo, ☎ 07/378–0623, FAX 07/378–9458, WEB www.chrisjolly.co.nz). **Clark Gregor Trout Fishing** (⊠ 33 Haumoana St., Rotorua, ☎ 07/347–1123, FAX 07/347–1313, WEB www.troutnz.co.nz). **Lake Tarawera Launch Services** (⊠ The Landing, Lake Tarawera [R.D. 5, Rotorua], ☎ 07/362–8595, FAX 07/362–8883). **Mark Draper Fishing and Outdoors** (⊠ Box 445, Opotiki, Bay of Plenty–East Cape, ☎ FAX 07/315–8069, WEB www.tsuribaka-fishing.co. nz/markdraper).

North Island Saltwater Operators: Blue Ocean Charters (⊠ The Coronation Pier, Wharf St., Tauranga, ☎ 07/578–9685, FAX 07/578–3499, WEB www.blueoceancharters.co.nz). **Earl Grey Fishing Charters** (⊠ 23 Mission Rd., Keri Keri, Bay of Islands, ☎ 09/407–7165, FAX 09/407–5465, WEB www.earlgreyfishing.co.nz). **Tairua Dive & Fishing** (⊠ The Esplanade, Tairua, ☎ 07/864–8054). **Te Ra–The Sun** (⊠ Whangamata Harbor, Whangamata, Coromandel Peninsula, ☎ 07/865–8681).

South Island Freshwater Operators: Chris Morris (⊠ Southwest Wilderness Experience, c/o Fox Glacier Post Office, Franz Josef, ☎ FAX 03/752–0047). **Daniel Jackson** (⊠ 142 Thorp St., Motueka, ☎ 03/528–7756). **Dave Hetherington** (⊠ Alpine Adventure, Main Rd., Franz Josef Glacier, ☎ 03/752–0793, FAX 03/752–0764). **Fish Fiordland** (⊠ Box 31, Manapouri, ☎ 03/249–8070, FAX 03/249–8470, WEB www.fishfiordland.co. nz). **Fishing & Hunting Amongst Friends** (⊠ Box 312, Wanaka, ☎ FAX 03/443–9257, WEB www.flyfishhunt.co.nz). **Fly Fishing New Zealand Ltd.** (⊠ Box 1061, Queenstown, ☎ 03/442–5363, FAX 03/442–2734, WEB www. wakatipu.co.nz). **Harvey Maguire** (⊠ 334 Littles Rd., Queenstown, ☎ 03/442–7061, WEB www.flyfishing.net.nz).

South Island Saltwater Operators: Bounty Charters (⊠ 8 Kotuku Rd., Kaikoura, ☎ 03/319–6682, FAX 03/319–5542, WEB www.virtual-kaikoura. com). **Cat O Nine Tails** (⊠ Barry Shirtcliss, 6A Parkers Rd., Nelson, ☎ 03/548–0202, WEB www.catonine.co.nz). **Thorfinn Charters** (⊠ Bruce Story, Box 43, Halfmoon Bay, Stewart Island, ☎ FAX 03/219–1210, WEB www.thorfinn.co.nz). **Toa Tai Charters** (⊠ 144 Waikawa Rd., Picton, ☎ 03/573–7883, FAX 03/573–7882, WEB www.soundsfishing.co.nz).

Hiking

There isn't a better place on earth for hiking—called tramping here—than New Zealand. If you're looking for short tramps, you may want to head off on your own. "Freedom walking" means that you tramp without a guide and carry all your own food and equipment. For long treks, however, it can be a big help to go with a guide. With their knowledge of the native bush, guides can point out and discuss the country's fascinating flora and fauna. (They often have great senses of humor, too). Book trips at least three weeks in advance.

Particularly in the peak months of January and February, trails can be crowded enough to detract from the natural experience. One advantage of a guided walk is that companies have their own tent camps or huts, with such luxuries as hot showers and cooks. For the phobic, it's worth mentioning one very positive feature: New Zealand has no snakes or predatory animals, no poison ivy, poison oak, leeches, or ticks. In the South Island, especially on the West Coast, in central Otago, and in Fiordland, be prepared for voracious sand flies—some call it the state "bird." Pick up insect repellent in New Zealand—their repellent fends off their insects.

New Zealand's Department of Conservation (DOC) oversees a group of nine routes called Great Walks, which are outstanding both for their facilities and their incredible scenery. These routes are the Abel Tasman Coastal Track; the Heaphy Track; the Kepler Track; the Lake Waikaremoana Track; the Milford Track; the Rakiura Track; the Routeburn Track; the Tongariro Northern Circuit; and the Whanganui Journey. (The Whanganui Journey, while technically a Great Walk, traces a canoeing trip.) Most of the Great Walks are moderately difficult and take at least three days to complete. There are also more than 50 routes the DOC dubs "major tracks," many of which go through national parks. These range from day hikes to challenging multiday tramps. The most recent addition to the roster is the South Island's Hump Ridge Track, opened in 2001.

One of the top areas in the North Island for hiking and walking is the rugged Coromandel Peninsula, with 3,000-ft volcanic peaks clothed with semitropical rain forest and some of the best stands of the giant kauri tree, some of which are 45 ft around, and giant tree ferns. There is also gold-mining history on the peninsula, though the flicker of miners' lamps has given way to the steady green-blue light of millions of glowworms in the mines and the forest. Kiwi Dundee Adventures, Ltd., has a variety of hiking trips that cover all aspects of the peninsula, as well as New Zealand–wide eco-walks away from the usual tourist spots.

Tongariro National Park in central North Island has hiking with a difference—on and around active volcanoes rising to heights of 10,000 ft, the highest elevation on the island. It is a beautiful region of contrasts: deserts, forests, lakes, mountains, and snow. Outdoor Experiences is the only company with a Department of Conservation concession to guide the famous Tongariro Crossing.

The three- to six-day walks on the beaches and in the forests of the northern South Island's Marlborough Sounds' Queen Charlotte Walkway and in Abel Tasman National Park are very popular, relatively easy, and well suited to family groups: your pack is carried for you, and you stay in lodges. Another option is the Alpine Recreation Canterbury 15-day minibus tour of the South Island, with two- to six-hour walks daily along the way. It provides an extensive and scenic cross section, with visits to three World Heritage areas and six national parks and discussions of natural history. Of course, it misses the magic of completing a long single walk.

If you want to get away from the more standard hiking routes, check out the very northwest corner of the South Island, Cape Farewell and the Farewell Spit, the longest naturally occurring sand spit in the world. The area has magnificent coastline and the lush rain forest of the Kahurangi National Park.

The most famous New Zealand walk, the Milford Track—a three- to four-day trek through the South Island's Fiordland National Park—

covers a wide variety of terrains, from forests to high passes, lakes, a glowworm grotto, and the spectacle of Milford Sound itself. As the track is strictly one-way (south to north), you rarely encounter other groups and so have the impression that your group is alone in the wild. Independent and escorted walkers stay in different huts about a half day's walk apart. Escorted walkers' huts are serviced and very comfortable; independent walkers' huts are basic, with few facilities. There are other walks in the same area: the Hollyford Track (five days), the Kepler Track (three days), the Greenstone Valley (three days), and the Routeburn Track (three days). Greenstone and Routeburn together form the Grand Traverse. *See* Chapter 5 for more information on the Milford and Kepler tracks.

If you want to get up close and personal with a mountain, Alpine Guides has a renowned seven-day course on the basics of mountaineering around Aoraki (Mt. Cook), the highest point in the New Zealand Alps. There is also a 10-day technical course for experienced climbers. New Zealand is the home of Sir Edmund Hillary, who, with Tenzing Norgay, made the first ascent of Mt. Everest, in 1953. The country has a fine mountaineering tradition, and Alpine Guides is its foremost training school.

Season: October–March for high-altitude walks, year-round for others.
Locations: Coromandel Peninsula and Tongariro National Park in North Island; Aoraki, Westland, Abel Tasman, and Fiordland national parks in South Island.
Cost: One- to three-day hikes range from $150 to $1,050. Prices for longer hikes and day tours vary widely; contact outfitters for specifics.
Tour Operators: Abel Tasman National Park Enterprises (⊠ 265 High St. [Box 351, Motueka], ☎ 03/528–7801, FAX 03/528–6087, WEB www. abeltasman.co.nz). **Alpine Guides Ltd.** (⊠ Box 20, Mt. Cook, ☎ 03/ 435–1834, FAX 03/435–1898, WEB www.alpineguides.co.nz). **Alpine Recreation** (⊠ Box 75, Lake Tekapo, ☎ 03/680–6736, FAX 03/680–6765, WEB www.alpinerecreation.co.nz). **Bush & Beach** (⊠ Shortland St. [Box 3479, Auckland], ☎ 09/575–1458, FAX 09/575–1454, WEB www. bushandbeach.co.nz). **Guided Walks New Zealand Ltd.** (⊠ Box 347, Queenstown, ☎ 03/442–7126, FAX 03/442–7128, WEB www.nzwalks. com). **Hollyford Track** (⊠ Box 360, Queenstown, Otago, ☎ 03/442– 3760, FAX 03/442–3761, WEB www.hollyfordtrack.co.nz). **Kiwi Dundee Adventures, Ltd.** (⊠ Box 198, Whangamata, Coromandel Peninsula, ☎ FAX 07/865–8809, WEB www.kiwidundee.co.nz). **Marlborough Sounds Adventure Company** (⊠ The Waterfront [Box 195, Picton], ☎ 03/573– 6078, FAX 03/573–8827, WEB www.marlboroughsounds.co.nz). **Milford Track guided walk** (⊠ Ultimate Hikes, Box 259, Queenstown, ☎ 03/ 441–1138 or 0800/659–255, FAX 03/441–1124, WEB www.ultimatehikes. co.nz). **Outdoor Experiences** (⊠ Vern Meyer, R.D. 1, Reporoa, ☎ 07/ 333–7099, WEB www.tongarironz.com). **Routeburn Track guided walk** (⊠ Ultimate Hikes, Box 568, Queenstown, ☎ 03/442–8200, FAX 03/ 442–6072, WEB www.ultimatehikes.co.nz). **Wild West Adventure Co.** (⊠ 8 Whall St., Greymouth, ☎ 03/768–6649 or 0800/223–456, FAX 03/ 768–9149, WEB www.nzholidayheaven.co.nz).

Horse Trekking

Operators all over New Zealand take people horseback riding along beaches, in native forests, on mountains, and up rivers through pine plantations to all sorts of scenic delights. Horse treks qualify as soft or hard adventure, depending on the itinerary. All of the outfitters listed here offer trips for inexperienced riders, and all provide the required protective headgear. Some companies will also supply suitable heeled footwear, but be sure to check with the outfitter about what you'll need to bring. On longer trips, you'll likely be expected to help with the horses and equipment.

In the North Island, Pakiri Beach Horse Rides & Overnight Safaris, north of Auckland, runs trips from several hours to several days, all incorporating a ride on the namesake beach. Rangihau Ranch, halfway between Whitianga and Tairua, leads short rides of an hour or two; the routes follow packhorse trails from the 1800s. They specialize in working with inexperienced riders. Pinetrek Ultimate Treks organizes part- or full-day trips into the rolling farmland near Whangamata.

In the South Island, the sweep of the Canterbury Plains around Christchurch—and the surrounding mountain ranges—creates some of New Zealand's most dramatic scenery. One of the best ways to explore the area is on horseback. Hurunui Horse Treks has a variety of rides, including 8- and 10-day horse treks into remote backcountry in groups of six or fewer, on which you'll stay in rustic huts (without electricity, showers, or flush toilets). The feeling of riding in so much open air, watching the trail stretch to the distant horizon, is unparalleled. Terrain varies from dense scrub to open meadows and alpine passes. Dart Stables, based in Glenorchy, near Queenstown, takes small groups out on trips ranging from two hours to three days.

Season: October–March.
Locations: Northland and the Coromandel Peninsula in the North Island, Nelson and Canterbury high country in the South Island.
Cost: Prices from $200 for a day trip; contact outfitters for specifics on shorter or multiday trips.
Tour Operators: Dart Stables Glenorchy (✉ Box 47, Glenorchy, ☎ 03/442–5688 or 0800/474–3464, FAX 03/442–6045, WEB www.glenorchy.co.nz). **Hurunui Horse Treks** (✉ 757 The Peaks Rd. [R.D., Hawarden, North Canterbury], ☎ FAX 03/314–4204, WEB www.hurunui.co.nz). **Pakiri Beach Horse Rides** (✉ Taurere Park, Rahuikiri Rd., Pakiri, Wellsford, ☎ 09/422–6275, FAX 09/422–6277, WEB www.horseride-nz.co.nz). **Pinetrek Ultimate Treks** (✉ 297a Main Rd., Tairua, ☎ 07/864–7078, FAX 07/864–9509). **Rangihau Ranch** (✉ Rangihau Rd., Coroglen, ☎ 07/866–3875, FAX 07/866–3837).

Rafting

The exhilaration of sweeping down into the foam-filled jaws of a rapid is always tinged with fear—white-water rafting is, after all, rather like being tossed into a washing machine. As you drift downriver during the lulls between the white water, it's wonderful to sit back and watch the wilderness unfold, whether it's stately *rimu* or *rata* trees overhanging the stream or towering cliffs with rain forest on the surrounding slopes. Rafting means camping by the river at night, drinking tea brewed over a fire, going to sleep with the sound of the stream in the background, and at dawn listening to the country's wonderful bird music. The juxtaposition of action and serenity gives rafting an enduring appeal that leads most who try it to seek out more rivers with more challenges. Rivers here are smaller and trickier than the ones used for commercial rafting in North America, and rafts usually hold only four to six people. Rafting companies provide all equipment—you only need clothing that won't be damaged by water (cameras are carried in waterproof barrels), a sleeping bag (in some cases), and sunscreen. Rafting qualifies as hard adventure.

In the North Island, near Rotorua, the Rangitaiki offers exciting Grade-IV rapids and some good scenery. Nearby, the Wairoa offers Grade V—

the highest before a river becomes unraftable—and the Kaituna River has the highest raftable waterfall in the world: a 21-ft free fall. The Tongariro River flows from between the active 10,000-ft volcanic peaks of Tongariro National Park into the south end of Lake Taupo, New Zealand's largest lake. The Tongariro (Grade III), as well as the mighty Motu River out toward the East Cape (Grade V), is great for rafting.

In the South Island, the great majority of activity centers on Queenstown. The most popular spot here is the upper reaches of the Shotover River beyond tortuous Skippers Canyon. In winter the put-in site for the Shotover is accessible only by helicopter, and wet suits are essential year-round, as the water is very cold. Some of the rapids are Grade V. The Rangitata River south of Christchurch is fed by an enormous catchment basin, and rafting is serious at all water levels.

Season: Mainly October–May.
Locations: Rotorua and Taupo in the North Island, Canterbury and Queenstown in the South Island.
Cost: $130 per person for three-hour trips; heli-rafting from $180 per person, three-day trips $900 per person.
Tour Operators: Challenge Rafting (⊠ Box 634, Shotover and Camp Sts., Queenstown, ☎ 03/442–7318 or 0800/423–836, FAX 03/441–8563, WEB www.raft.co.nz). **Kaituna Cascades** (⊠ Trout Pool Rd., Okere Falls, Rotorua, ☎ 07/345–9533 or 0800/524–8862, FAX 07/345–4199, WEB www.kaitunacascades.co.nz). **Queenstown Rafting** (⊠ 35 Shotover St., Queenstown, ☎ 03/442–9792 or 0800/723–8464, FAX 03/442–4609, WEB www.rafting.co.nz). **Rangitata Rafts** (⊠ Peel Forest, Geraldine, South Canterbury, ☎ 0800/251–251, ☎ FAX 03/696–3534, WEB www.rafts.co.nz). **Wet 'n' Wild Rafting Company** (⊠ 2 White St., Rotorua, ☎ 07/348–3191 or 0800/462–7238, FAX 07/349–6567, WEB www.wetnwildrafting.co.nz).

Sailing

Varied coastline and splendid waters have made sailing extremely popular in New Zealand. Admittedly, your role as a passenger on a commercial sailing vessel is hardly strenuous. You are likely to participate in the sailing of the vessel more than you would on a regular cruise line, but for all intents and purposes this is a soft adventure in paradise. The best sailing areas in New Zealand are undoubtedly from the Bay of Islands south to the Coromandel Peninsula and the Bay of Plenty. This coastline has many islands and a wrinkled shoreline that make for wonderful, sheltered sailing. With Tauranga Sailing School and Yacht Charters, you can sail out to some of the islands in the Bay of Plenty. You can take a piloted launch or, if you have the experience, captain a sailboat yourself.

The rugged Marlborough Sounds at the north end of the South Island are particularly beautiful when seen from the water. The islands and coves make wonderful overnight moorings; it's easy to understand why Captain James Cook felt this was his favorite part of the country. At the bottom of the South Island, Heritage Expeditions uses a Finnish-built, 236-ft, 19-cabin, ice-strengthened vessel, the *Akademik Shokalski,* to explore the islands of the southern Pacific Ocean and beyond to Antarctica, with one short voyage each season (November to mid-March) through the deeply indented coastline of Fiordland. It's a wonderful voyage for wildlife viewing, and you may see royal albatross, Hookers sea lions, elephant seals, and several penguin species.

Season: Year-round.
Locations: Bay of Islands in the North Island, lower South Island.
Cost: Bay of Islands from $690 to $830 per night depending on the craft; Doubtful Sound from $1,725 for five days; Fiordland National Park area from $3,510 for eight days; sub-Antarctic islands of Australia and New Zealand from USD$11,534 for up to one month.
Tour Operators: Catamaran Sailing Charters (✉ 46 Martin St., Nelson, ☎ 03/547–6666, FAX 03/547–6663, WEB www.sailingcharters.co.nz). **Heritage Expeditions** (✉ Box 6282, Christchurch, ☎ 03/338–9944, FAX 03/338–3311, WEB www.heritage-expeditions.com). **Tauranga Sailing School and Yacht Charters** (✉ 70 Omokoroa Rd., Tauranga, ☎ 07/548–0689, FAX 07/548–0649).

Sea-Kayaking

Unlike rafting, where much of the thrill comes from negotiating white water, sea-kayaking is soft adventure. The best areas are in Northland, the Coromandel Peninsula, the Whanganui River area, the top of South Island, Kaikoura, and as far south as Stewart Island.

With Cathedral Cove Kayaks, you can explore part of the Coromandel Peninsula coastline; on the sunset kayaking trip, the rock formations look especially gorgeous. Ross Adventures guides groups along the coast of Waiheke Island. On its nighttime trips you'll look for phosphorescence, when the water glows along your paddles or hands. Marlborough Sounds Adventure Company can introduce you to local sounds and islands on one- to three-day trips. There is also a three-hour twilight excursion. The tour with Ocean River Adventure Company in the sheltered waters of Abel Tasman National Park provides a waterline view of a beautiful coastline. Fiordland Wilderness Experience focuses on the Fiordland sounds, including Milford, Dusky, and Doubtful sounds. A couple of combination trips pair sea-kayaking with hiking or diving. Stewart Island Sea Kayak Adventures will give you a crack at kayaking in New Zealand's newest national park.

Season: December–May.
Locations: Northland, the Coromandel Peninsula, and Whanganui River in the North Island; Marlborough Sounds, Kaikoura, Abel Tasman National Park, and the Southland in the South Island.
Cost: From $60 for a half-day excursion; contact kayaking outfitters for price information for longer trips.
North Island Tour Operators: Bay of Islands Kayak Co. (✉ Box 217, Russell, ☎ FAX 09/403–7672). **Cathedral Cove Kayaks** (✉ 2 Margot Pl., Hahei, ☎ 07/866–3877, WEB www.seakayaktours.co.nz). **Ross Adventures** (✉ Box 106037, Auckland, ☎ 09/372–5550, FAX 09/357–0550, WEB www.kayakwaiheke.co.nz).
South Island Tour Operators: Fiordland Wilderness Experience (✉ 66 Quintin Dr., Te Anau, ☎ 03/249–7700 or 0800/200–434, FAX 03/249–7768, WEB www.fiordlandseakayak.co.nz). **Marlborough Sounds Adventure Company** (✉ The Waterfront [Box 195, Picton], ☎ 03/573–6078, FAX 03/573–8827, WEB www.marlboroughsounds.co.nz). **Ocean River Adventure Company** (✉ Abel Tasman National Park, Marahau [R.D. 2, Motueka], ☎ 03/527–8266, FAX 03/527–8006, WEB www.seakayaking.co.nz). **Stewart Island Sea Kayak Adventures** (✉ Box 32, Stewart Island, ☎ FAX 03/219–1080).

7 BACKGROUND AND ESSENTIALS

Portrait of New Zealand

Books and Movies

Chronology

Kiwi and Māori Vocabularies

FLORA AND FAUNA

NEW ZEALAND is a fascinating evolutionary case. Its islands are a chip off the onetime Gonwanaland supercontinent—a vast landmass that consisted of current-day South America, Africa, and Australia that started breaking up some 100 million years ago, well before the evolution of mammals. Since then, floating on its own some 1,920 km (1,200 mi) southeast of Australia, this cluster of islands might seem to have developed quietly on its own, away from the hungry, predatory jaws of the rest of the world.

But powerful forces of change have been constantly working on New Zealand. Plate tectonics created the rugged, 12,000-plus-ft mountains of the South Island. And the Pacific Rim's wild geothermal eruptions left their mark on the North Island. For eons volcanic activity has built mountainous cones and laid carpets of ash, making tremendously rich soil for the plant kingdom. The great, rumbling Mt. Ruapehu near Lake Taupo is a living reminder of this subterranean fury.

Global climatic variations haven't spared the islands, either, and on numerous occasions the Antarctic ice cap has edged north from the pole. In these times, glaciers covered the South Island and much of the North Island, significantly affecting the character of plant life. Some plants adapted, and some couldn't survive. Except for the northern portions of the North Island that weren't iced over—interestingly enough the rough extent of New Zealand's glorious kauri trees—after each glacial retreat the country's flora has recolonized the areas previously covered by ice in different ways.

Animals on the islands were, at least until the arrival of humans, almost like living fossils. The only mammal was a tiny bat, and there were no predators until the Māori first came, around AD 700. Bird life included the 12-ft flightless moa, which the Māori hunted to extinction. This happened relatively quickly, because the birds had never needed to develop evasive behavior to stay alive. The Māori brought dogs and rats, and Europeans brought deer, possums, goats, trout, and other fauna, some of which were used for their pelts, others for sport. In almost all cases, the exotic fauna have done tremendous damage to the landscape. And, of course, the human presence itself has dramatically altered the land. Early Māori farming practices involved burning, which reduced a portion of the forests. When Europeans settled the country, they brought sheep, cattle, and the grasses that their livestock needed to eat. And they cut down the forests for, among other uses, ship masts. The kauri served this purpose better than any other wood in the world and paid in numbers for that virtue.

None of this makes the forests that cover New Zealand any less exotic, or any less fascinating. Some plants have adapted growth cycles in which the plant completely changes appearance—lancewood is an example—some of them two or three times until they reach maturity. As a result, botanists at one time believed there to be two or three species where in fact there was only one. If you have never been in a rain forest, the sheer density of vegetation in various subtropical areas will be dazzling. There are species here that exist nowhere else on earth. And keep in mind that one-fifth of the country is set aside as parkland. In those wild woods, you will still find no predators, and native species are alive and well, in many cases making comebacks very dramatic indeed.

Here is a short list of plants and animals that you might encounter in New Zealand. The New Zealand forest has a different sound than any other, and it's the welcoming, chiming song of the **bellbird,** together with that of the *tūī*, that makes it unique.

It's a lot easier to get into the grips of a **bush lawyer** plant than out of them. It is a thorny, viney thing that grows in dense forest, climbing in and out of whatever it chooses.

The odd plant clumps fastened to the sides of trees throughout forests are **epiphytes,** not parasites. They grow on the trees but make their own living off water and other airborne particles. Some are orchids, a marvelous sight if you catch them in bloom.

The abundance of **ferns** may be what you most readily associate with the New Zealand bush. Two of the most magnificent are the *mamaku* and the *punga*. The former also goes by the English name black tree fern, and it is the one that grows up to 60 ft tall and is found countrywide, with the exception of the east coast of the South Island. The Māori used to cook and eat parts of the plant that are said to taste a bit like applesauce. The punga is shorter than the mamaku, reaching a height of 30 ft. Its English name, silver tree fern, comes from the color of the undersides of the fronds. Their silvery whiteness illuminates darker parts of the bush. The punga is the ferny emblem of New Zealand's international sports teams and Air New Zealand.

The **Hector's dolphin** is rare and confined to New Zealand waters. You might have the luck of seeing one near Kaikoura or off the Banks Peninsula. They have a distinctive rounded fin.

The *horoeka* (also called lancewood) tree is one of the freakish New Zealand natives par excellence. In its youth, its long, serrated, almost woody leaves hardly look alive, hanging down from their scrawny trunk. Horoekas inch their way skyward like this for as many as 20 years before maturing, flowering profusely, and bearing black berries.

The towering *kahikatea* (ka-*hee*-ka-*tee*-ah) is the tallest tree in the country, reaching as high as 200 ft with its slender and elegant profile. A mature tree bears a tremendous amount of berries, which Māori climbers used to harvest by ascending 80 branchless ft and more to pluck. These days wood pigeons are the prime consumers of the fruit.

There are still **kauri** trees in Northland and the Coromandel Peninsula that are as many as 1,500 years old, with a girth of at least 30 ft and height upward of 150 ft. The lower trunks of the trees are branchless, and branches on an old tree begin some 50 ft above the ground. Lumberjacks in the 1800s spared some of these giants, and their presence is awesome. Like so many other native trees, kauris are slow growers—a mere 80-year-old will stand just 30 ft tall. Kauris were valued for their gum

as well as their wood. The gum doesn't rot, so balls of gum of any age were usable to make varnish and paint. It is now illegal to cut down a kauri, and as a result the trees are making a solid comeback. Visitors with limited time can see impressive kauri trees in the Waitakere Ranges, just west of Auckland, but the oldest and largest examples are in the Waipoua Forest in Northland. The southernmost kauri trees are found just south of Katikati in the Bay of Plenty.

Much is said of the formidable South Island **kea** (*kee*-ah), a mountain parrot, which, because it has been accused of killing sheep, has in the last century barely escaped extinction. Its numbers are significant today, much to the dismay of campers and anyone who lives under a tin roof. Keas love to play, which means anything from ripping tents to shreds to clattering around on metal roofs at all hours to peeling out the rubber gaskets around car windows. They are smart birds, smart enough, perhaps, to delight in taking revenge on those who tried to wipe them out. Observe their behavior keenly; it may be the only way to maintain a sense of humor if harassed.

It takes effort and more than a fair share of luck to spot a **kiwi** in the wild. These nocturnal, bush-loving birds are scarce and shy, and their numbers had dwindled significantly with the felling of forests over the last 150 years. Predator eradication programs have helped them make a slight resurgence over the last few years. Along with the now-extinct giant moa and other species, the kiwi is one of the remarkable New Zealand natives that live (or lived) nowhere else on earth. If you're keen on seeing one in the feather, plan a trip to Stewart Island and hire a guide to take you on a search, or stop at a wildlife park. Your best chance of sighting one on the North Island is to pitch a tent in the Waipoua forest camping ground.

The *mohua,* or yellowhead, is a small insect-eating bird you'll only find in the forests of the South Island and Stewart Island. The bird is easily identifiable from the splash of bright yellow that covers its head and breast. The rest of the body is brown with varying tinges of yellow and olive.

The *manuka* is a small tree shrub found throughout the country in tough impenetrable thickets. Early settlers made a tea from the plant until something tastier came along. The tea tree's white or rosy blossoms attract bees in profusion, and they in turn produce the popular, strong-tasting manuka honey that you can find in stores just about everywhere.

The **nikau palm** is one of the country's most exotic-looking trees, growing to a height of about 30 ft. The Māori used different parts of the leaves both for food and for thatch in shelters.

Phormium tenax, also called New Zealand flax—even though it isn't a true flax—has been used in traditional and contemporary weaving. It favors damp areas and hillsides. Its thick, spiky, dark green leaves originate from a central saddle and can grow to 6 ft. The telltale flower stalk can reach 15 ft and bears dark red flowers. A number of varieties are ornamental and are very popular in New Zealand gardens.

The **pohutukawa** (po-hoo-too-ka-wa) tree is a sight both for its gnarly roots that like watery places and its red blossoms, which burst forth toward the end of December—hence its Kiwi name: New Zealand's Christmas tree.

Currently about 80 million in number, **possums** are an introduced species that is gobbling up New Zealand forests. Try as they may to get rid of them, Kiwis are having a rough go with the tree dwellers. Their nickname, "squash 'ems," comes from seeing so many splayed out on roads throughout the country.

The **pukeka** (poo-keh-ka) is a bird that kicks around on farms and roadsides often enough that you're likely to see plenty of them. They're blue, with a red bill, and they stand about 15 inches tall.

You'll get to know the **rangiora** (rang-ee-ohr-ah) plant better if you remember it as "bushman's friend"—its soft, silvery underside is the forest's best tissue for your underside.

There are a couple of species of **rata.** The northern rata is a parasite plant, climbing a host tree and eventually cutting off its light and water supplies. The rata and its host wage a long-term struggle, and the rata doesn't always win. The southern rata is a freestanding tree, yielding beautiful red lumber. Rata flowers are a pretty red themselves, resembling the pohutukawa tree's blooms but coming out about a month earlier in November.

If you're in the country in November, you'll first see evidence of the **rewarewa** (re-wa-re-wa) tree in its fallen blossoms on the ground. They are tightly woven, magenta bottle-brush-like flowers, with touches of chartreuse and black, that are some of the most enchanting in the country, in part for their uniqueness.

One of those ingenious New Zealand plants that goes through three distinct stages on its way to maturity, the **rimu** red pine is a valuable source of timber. It spends its first stage in life as a delicate treelet, with pale green, weeping branches that look something like an upright moss. It then turns itself into a conical shape before finishing its growth as a soaring, 100-plus-ft wonder with a branchless trunk and a rounded head. Charcoal from rimu was used in traditional Māori tattooing.

Supplejack vines just hang about in the forest, so dense in places that they make passage next to impossible. You'll often find that their soft, edible tips have been nipped off by the teeth of wild goats that Pākehā (Europeans) introduced. Believe it or not, this is a member of the lily family.

New Zealand's living dinosaur, the **tuatara,** is an ancient reptile found on protected islands such as Stephens Island in Marlborough Sounds. It feeds on insects, small mammals, and birds' eggs and has a vestigial third eye. The combination of its nocturnal habits and its rarity means that the likelihood of seeing one in the wild is virtually nil. Your best bet is to see one in captivity at a zoo. Auckland Zoo has a particularly good tuatara display in its Kiwi House.

Along with the bellbird, the **tūī** is the chanteuse extraordinaire that fills Aotearoa's woods with its magically clear melodies. You may have never thought of birds as actually singing, but you certainly will when you hear a tūī.

Weka (weh-kah) are funny birds. They can appear to be oblivious to what's going on around them as they walk about pecking at this or that, looking bemused. They are flightless rails, and they'll steal your food if you're camping, so hide it away. Generally speaking, they're pleasant to have around, particularly if you're looking for some entertainment.

Wetas are large insects, some species of which are only topped in size by the African goliath beetle. If you chance upon one, it is likely to throw its spiny back legs up in the air as a defense, giving it a particularly ferocious look. However, wetas are not as fearsome as they look, and in the unlikely event that you do get nipped, it will only result in a slight stinging sensation. The largest species is found on Little Barrier Island near Auckland. You may well see specimens in the wild in forests such as the Waitakere Ranges near Auckland, but if you like your fierce-looking insects safely behind glass they can be viewed at the Arataki Visitors Centre, west of Auckland.

You'll have no trouble figuring out that the **wood pigeon** is indeed a pigeon, but your jaw will drop at the size—they look like they've been inflated like balloons. They're beautiful birds.

— Stephen Wolf, Barbara Blechman,
and Stu Freeman

BOOKS AND MOVIES

Books

Because of the limited availability of many first-rate books on New Zealand outside the country, there is only so much that you'll be able to read before you go. So leave room in your suitcase for pickup reading once you arrive, and bring something home to make your trip linger longer. One caveat: because of economies of scale in the New Zealand publishing industry, books tend to be expensive. That's one reason to do some secondhand shopping; another is the stores' usually knowledgeable staff, which can make recommendations.

History

The *Oxford Illustrated History of New Zealand,* edited by Keith Sinclair, provides a comprehensive and highly readable account of the country's social, political, cultural, and economic evolution from the earliest Māori settlements up to 1989. James Belich's *Making Peoples* looks at New Zealand history from a 1990s perspective, with more emphasis on the Māori view than some earlier publications. His *Paradise Reforged: A History of the New Zealanders from the Beginning of the Twentieth Century* (2002) also pays particular attention to the Māori population. The *Colonial New Zealand Wars,* by Tim Ryan and Bill Parham, is a vivid history of the Māori-British battles. Lavishly illustrated with photographs of colonial infantry and drawings of Māori hill forts, flags, and weapons, the book makes far more compelling reading than the dry military history suggested by the title. Another highly readable military-historical book is James Belich's *The New Zealand Wars.* J. C. Beaglehole's *The Discovery of New Zealand* is an authoritative and scholarly analysis of the voyages of discovery, from the first Polynesians to the Europeans of the late 18th century.

Fiction

New Zealand's best-known short-story writer is **Katherine Mansfield** (1888–1923), whose early stories were set in and around the city of Wellington, her birthplace. *The Best of Katherine Mansfield* is a fine compilation of stories from five collections. Reading her journals will give you a sense of her passionate romantic side, and as much as she disliked the small-minded provincial qualities of New Zealand, she loved the country deeply.

New Zealand's most distinguished living writer is **Janet Frame.** Her works are numerous, from novels such as her successful *The Carpathians* to a three-part autobiography, which is a lyrical evocation of growing up in small-town New Zealand in the 1920s and 1930s and of the gradual awakening of a writer of great courage. Kiwi filmmaker Jane Campion adapted the middle of it for the screen into *An Angel at My Table.* **Maurice Gee** is another distinguished novelist. His *Plumb* won the James Tait prize for the best novel in Britain when it was published. *Plumb* reaches back to the early 20th century for its story of a renegade parson and his battle with old-world moral pieties. One particularly compelling scene is set in a mining town, where Plumb happens to be the man to hear the last testament of a notorious murderer. A more recent volume is *Ellie and the Shadow Man.* Gee is also known for his young adult fiction, in which he often plays out a fantasy–science fiction story in a New Zealand setting. Best examples include *Half Men of O* and *Under the Mountain.*

Two of the finest and most exciting writers at work in the country today are **Patricia Grace** and **Witi Ihimaera,** both Māori whose story collections and novels are on a par with the best fiction in the United Kingdom and the States. Grace's stories are beautifully and fluidly related, very much from inside her characters. Look for *The Dream Sleepers and Other Stories* and her novel *Mutuwhenua.* Ihimaera (ee-hee-may-ra) also uses very clear prose and Māori experience. His early novel *Tangi* opens with the death of a father and moves through the 22-year-old son's experience of loss and innocence to his acceptance of his role as a man. Māori elements of the story are fascinating both culturally and emotionally. Also look for his *Bulibasha* and *Nights in the Garden of Spain.*

Keri Hulme's internationally celebrated *The Bone People* won the Booker McConnell Prize in 1985. Set on the isolated West Coast of the South Island, this challenging, vital novel weaves Polynesian myth with Christian symbolism and the powerful sense of place that characterizes modern Māori writing. More recently, **Alan Duff**'s *Once Were Warriors* is a frank, uncompromising, and ultimately transcendent look at urban Māori society. Both the novel and the film were real sensations in New Zealand. The sequel, *One Night Out Stealing,* as well as *What Becomes of the Broken Hearted* and *Both Sides of the Moon,* has also been hugely successful. In a move to non-fiction, Duff addresses Māori issues in *Maori: The Crisis and the Challenge.*

Lloyd Jones, a hot current novelist, focuses on New Zealand while also looking beyond the country's borders. In *The Book of Fame* (2001), for instance, he fictionalizes the true story of New Zealand's All Blacks rugby team, who set out by steamer in 1905 to tour Great Britain. In *Here at the End of the World We Learn to Dance,* he brings tango music to the rural West Coast.

Margaret Mahy is a prolific children's-book writer; her books for kids under 10 include *Bubble Trouble* and *Down the Dragon's Tongue.*

On a lighter note, cartoonist **Murray Ball** has created an amusing look at Kiwi country life with his *Footrot Flats* series.

Poetry

100 New Zealand Poems by 100 New Zealand Poets, edited by New Zealand's current poet laureate, Bill Manhire, ranges from the country's earliest poems to the new poets of the 1990s. Greg O'Brien and Jenny Bornholdt's *My Heart Goes Swimming* is a charming selection of New Zealand love poems. A more wide-ranging and weighty collection is *An Anthology of New Zealand Poetry in English,* edited by Mark Williams, Greg O'Brien, and Jenny Bornholdt.

Garden Guides

If you are serious about visiting gardens while in New Zealand, any of the books listed below would be helpful. These are not typically stocked in U.S. bookstores or even on-line, so make a well-supplied store one of your first stops when you arrive. Hundreds of gardens are listed in Alison McRae's *Gardens to Visit in New Zealand* and Beverly Bridge's *Register of New Zealand Private Gardens Open to the Public, Volume 2.* They both give descriptions of gardens and list addresses, telephone numbers, and visiting times. *The Native Garden,* by Isobel Gabites and Rob Lucas, offers a superb vision of what constitutes a truly New Zealand garden, which of course is dominated by unique indigenous flora. Two other books are more limited in providing information but offer glossy photographs and make good souvenirs: Julian Matthews and Gil Hanly's *New Zealand Town and Country Gardens* and Premier Books' *Glorious New Zealand Gardens.* A superb monthly magazine, *New Zealand Gardener,* highlights several of the country's gardens in each issue. It is available at newspaper shops and bookstores countrywide.

Specialized Guidebooks

Strictly for wine lovers, *The Wines and Vineyards of New Zealand,* by Michael Cooper, is an exhaustive evaluation in words and pictures of every vineyard in the country. For travelers who plan to make hiking a major component of their vacations, *Tramping in New Zealand,* published by Lonely Planet, is an invaluable guide. *A Field Guide to Auckland* is a wonderful introduction to the natural and historic attractions of the Auckland region. It includes an overview of natural and human history and details of more than 140 interesting places to visits within easy distance of the city.

Art Books

Three companion volumes—on painting, sculpture, printmaking, photography, ceramics, glass, and jewelry—provide a superb introduction to New Zealand art: *100 New Zealand Paintings, Another 100 New Zealand Artists,* and *100 New Zealand Craft Artists.* Greg O'Brien's *Hotere: Out the Black Window* covers the work of one of the country's most respected artists.

Illustrated Books

Salute to New Zealand, edited by Sandra Coney, is a coffee-table book that intersperses lavish photographs with chapters by some of the country's finest contemporary writers. *Wild New Zealand,* published by Reader's Digest, is a pictorial account of the country's landscape, flora, and fauna, supplemented by an informative text with such a wealth of detail that it turns the sensory experience of the landscape into a cerebral one.

Movies

New Zealand director Peter Jackson dazzled moviegoers with the imagery and creativity of his home country with the first installment of *The Lord of the Rings* film trilogy. *The Fellowship of the Ring* won four Academy Awards in 2002, including a pair for Wellington-based Weta Workshop, which designed and achieved many of the film's effects. But one of the film's strongest effects was that of its amazing scenery—New Zealand's phenomenal mountain ranges and countryside standing in for Hobbiton, elvish forests, and the dreadful lands of Mordor and Mount Doom. Jackson's much-anticipated following two films, *The Two Towers* and *The Return of the King,* have Christmas 2002 and Christmas 2003 release dates, respectively.

Until now, New Zealand's film industry has had a relatively small output, but the quality of its films has been consistently quite high. Jane Campion's *The Piano* (1993) is a prime example, as are her earlier *An Angel at My Table* (1990) and *Sweetie* (1988), which was made in Australia. Roger Donaldson's 1977 thriller *Sleeping Dogs* was the first New Zealand

film released in the United States, followed by the equally worthy *Smash Palace* (1982). The tough, urban portrayal of *Once Were Warriors* (1995) is one of the most recent to make it across the Pacific. Its portrait of urban Māori life, unfortunately, makes New Zealand look a little too much like Los Angeles. *Scarfies,* a black comedy about Otago University students, received positive feedback at the 2000 Sundance Film Festival, following success in local cinemas. Christine Jeffs' haunting depiction of troubled family dynamics, *Rain* (2001), was filmed on the North Island coast. *The Last Samurai,* starring Tom Cruise, began filming around Taranaki in 2003.

Peter Jackson was making an impact on the industry long before *The Lord of the Rings.* His first foray into film was the splatter comedy *Bad Taste* (1987), followed by the intense murder drama *Heavenly Creatures* (1994), which introduced Kate Winslet to a worldwide audience. *The Frighteners* (1996), another dip into the horror pool, starred Michael J. Fox.

Hardly high culture, but still a major success for New Zealand's film and television industry, was the *Hercules* television series starring Kevin Sorbo. The show was axed in the United States in 1999 but its spin-off series, *Xena: Warrior Princess,* survived until 2001. Both series were filmed in West Auckland, doing its best to look like ancient Greece.

CHRONOLOGY

ca. AD 750 The first Polynesians arrive, settling mainly in the South Island, where they find the moa, a flightless bird and an important food source, in abundance.

950 Kupe, the Polynesian voyager, names the country Aotearoa, "land of the long white cloud." He returns to his native Hawaiki, believed to be present-day French Polynesia.

1300s A population explosion in Hawaiki triggers a wave of immigrants.

1642 Abel Tasman of the Dutch East India Company becomes the first European to sight the land—he names his discovery Nieuw Zeeland. But after several of his crew are killed by Māori, he sails away without landing.

1769 Captain James Cook becomes the first European to set foot on New Zealand. He claims it in the name of the British crown.

1790 Sealers, whalers, and timber cutters arrive, plundering the natural wealth and introducing the Māori to the musket, liquor, and influenza.

1814 The Reverend Samuel Marsden establishes the first mission station, but 11 years pass before the first convert is made.

1832 James Busby is appointed British Resident, charged with protecting the Māori people and fostering British trade.

1840 Captain William Hobson, representing the crown, and Māori chiefs sign the Treaty of Waitangi. In return for the peaceful possession of their land and the rights and privileges of British citizens, the chiefs recognize British sovereignty.

1840–41 The New Zealand Company, an association of British entrepreneurs, establishes settlements at Wanganui, New Plymouth, Nelson, and Wellington.

1852 The British Parliament passes the New Zealand Constitution Act, establishing limited self-government. The country's first gold strike occurs in Coromandel town in the Coromandel Peninsula.

1860–72 Māori grievances over loss of land trigger the Land Wars in the North Island. The Māori win some notable victories, but lack of unity ensures their ultimate defeat. Vast tracts of ancestral land are confiscated from rebel tribes.

1861 Gold is discovered in the river valleys of central Otago, west of Dunedin.

1882 The first refrigerated cargo is dispatched to England, giving the country a new source of prosperity—sheep. A century later, there will be 20 sheep for every New Zealander.

1893 Under the Liberal government, New Zealand becomes the first country to give women the vote.

1914 New Zealand enters World War I.

1931 The Hawke's Bay earthquake kills 258 and levels the city of Napier.

1939 New Zealand enters World War II.

1950 New Zealand troops sail for Korea.

1965 Despite public disquiet, troops are sent to Vietnam.

1973 Britain joins the European Economic Community, and New Zealand's loss of this traditional export market is reflected in a crippling balance-of-payments deficit two years later.

1981 Violent antigovernment demonstrations erupt during a tour by a South African rugby team.

1984 David Lange's Labour Government wins a landslide majority in the general election, at least partly due to its pledge to ban nuclear armed vessels from New Zealand waters.

1985 The Greenpeace ship *Rainbow Warrior* is sunk by a mine in Auckland Harbour, and a crewman is killed. Two of the French secret service agents responsible are arrested, jailed, transferred to French custody—then soon released.

Sir Paul Reeves is sworn in as the first Māori governor-general.

Relations with the United States sour when the government bans visits by ships carrying nuclear weapons. The U.S. government responds by ejecting New Zealand from the ANZUS alliance.

1986 Goods and Services Tax (GST) is introduced at 10% (later to be raised to 12.5%). Tourists are not exempt from the tax, although many exports and foreign exchange earners are.

1989 David Lange resigns as prime minister.

1990 The National Party replaces the Labour Party in government.

1993 The country votes for a major constitutional change, replacing the "first past the post" electoral system inherited from Britain with a "mixed-member proportional" (MMP) system. The election sees the National Party clinging to power within a coalition.

1995 New Zealand's *Black Magic* wins the America's Cup yachting regatta. The country goes into party mode over the win, which signals both a sporting triumph and a coming of age technologically.

Mt. Ruapehu in the North Island's Tongariro National Park bubbles and sputters, attracting interested onlookers from around the world.

New Zealanders' abhorrence of all things nuclear comes to the fore again with major floating protests against France's resumed nuclear testing in the South Pacific.

1996 Noisy Ruapehu spews debris into the air, covering nearby towns with a few inches of ash.

New Zealand elects its first MMP government, having voted for constitutional change three years earlier. New Zealand First holds the balance of power and goes into government with the National Party.

1997 New Zealand starts to feel the effect of weakening Asian currencies, particularly as the number of Korean and Japanese tourists falls.

Jenny Shipley becomes the country's first woman PM.

1998 The government introduces a controversial "work for the dole" scheme, in which people on unemployment benefit are required to work or train 20 hours a week or risk having their income slashed.

As the Asian economic crisis continues to bite, industrial strikes on Australia's waterfront also effect New Zealand's economy. The country's economic fundamentals remain strong, but these outside influences cause the N.Z. dollar to lose value against U.S. currency.

1999 The New Zealand cricketers record their first test-win over England at Lords, regarded as the spiritual home of the game. New Zealand goes on to win the series.

New Zealand contributes personnel and machinery to a United Nations peace-keeping force in Indonesia.

A Labour-Alliance coalition wins the general election, but a close vote means it still needs the support of the Green Party in matters of national importance. Helen Clark becomes New Zealand's second successive female prime minister.

2000 The airline Ansett New Zealand enters a franchise with Qantas Airways. The carrier operates as Qantas New Zealand, but the airline goes belly-up just months later.

New Zealand successfully defends the America's Cup, becoming the first country outside the United States to do so.

The lone, 125-year-old pine at the top of Auckland's One Tree Hill, one of the city's defining features, is removed.

2001 National carrier Air New Zealand runs into financial troubles and is bailed out by a $885 million taxpayer-financed rescue package.

Sir Peter Blake, a yachting champion who led New Zealand to win and retain the America's Cup, is murdered by pirates while on a conservation expedition in the Amazon.

2002 The movie *The Lord of the Rings: The Fellowship of the Ring,* directed by North Islander Peter Jackson and filmed entirely in New Zealand, wins four Academy Awards.

A simmering dispute over sponsorship and control of corporate facilities culminates with the International Rugby Board's dropping New Zealand as a sub-host of the 2003 Rugby World Cup. Australia becomes the event's sole host, and the rugby-mad New Zealand public is left fuming.

Internal wrangling sees the minor Government partner, the Alliance, split in half, though both sides continue to support Labour. After an early election, Labour has to rely on the support of several minor parties rather than a single coalition partner.

KIWI AND MĀORI VOCABULARIES

A Kiwi Glossary

Talking Kiwi is hardly a daunting prospect for people traveling abroad with the English language under their belt. You'll seldom be at a complete loss, and if a phrase does confuse you, the locals will delight in explaining its meaning. The word "kiwi" itself can be a source of confusion—it can mean the brown flightless bird that lives in New Zealand forests, the people of New Zealand, a furry fruit that is one of the country's best-known exports, a quick lottery ticket, or even a rugby league team. You'll have to figure it out in context. Despite being half a world away, New Zealanders are in many ways still fairly protective of the Queen's English and have resisted the Americanization of the language to a greater extent than their cousins in Australia. In newspapers and magazines you will read "colour" instead of "color" and "programme" instead of "program." New Zealanders are prone to shorten names and also to give nicknames, but this is not as prevalent as in Australia. And Kiwis have developed a few quirky terms of their own. Here are a few translations that will help:

Across the Ditch: Over the Tasman Sea in Australia
Aubergine: Eggplant
Aussi: An Australian
Bach: Vacation house (North Island) (pronounced *batch*)
Battle on: Try hard with limited success
Bludger: Someone who lives off other people's effort
Bush: The outdoors, wilderness
Capsicum: Bell pepper
Carpark: Parking lot
Chilly bin: A cooler
Choka (or choka block): Full
Courgette: Zucchini
Cuppa: Cup of tea or coffee
Crib: Vacation house (South Island)
Crook: Sick
Dag: Amusing person or happening
Dairy: Convenience or corner store
Devonshire tea: Cream tea with scones (served morning and afternoon)
En suite: Bathroom attached to your hotel room
Fair dinkum: It's really true

Fair go: Fair chance
Fair suck of the sav: Fair deal
Fanny: Woman's privates (considered obscene)
Flat white: Coffee with milk
Footie: Rugby football
Footpath: Sidewalk
Give a wide berth: Leave alone
Greenie: Conservationist
Home and hosed: Successful
Jandal: Open topped footwear
Loo: Toilet ("bathroom" is only for bathing)
Mainlander: Resident of the South Island
Metal road: Gravel road
Motorway: Freeway or highway
Mozzie: Mosquito
Mug: Good-hearted to the point of being foolish
Napkin or nappie: Diaper
Ocker: An Australian
Pavlova: A meringue cake
Pom or pommie: Native of England
Rubber: Eraser (also condom)
Sealed road: Paved road
Serviette: Napkin
Shout: Buy a round of drinks
Sink a few: Drink some beer
Smoko: Tea or coffee break
Take-aways: Food to go, takeout
Tall poppy: One who excels
Tea: Dinner (also the beverage)
Togs: Swimsuit
Track: Hiking trail
Tramping: Hiking
Up with the play: Knows what is going on
Ute: Pickup truck
Whinger: Whiner or moaner

A Māori Glossary

The use of the *Te Reo Māori* (Māori language) is experiencing a resurgence in contemporary New Zealand, with nearly 90% of Māori children enrolled in some form of Māori-language early-childhood education. This is a heartening outcome for a language that has stood for decades tenuously at the brink of extinction. Though the language was never officially legislated against, the great-grandparents of today's generation were beaten at school for speaking Māori. Not until the 1980s was government funding made available for Māori language education.

The realms of Māori language use are slowly moving out of the *marae* and into schools, parliament, and broadcasting. While you're in New Zealand, make a point to watch Sunday-morning television. It's the only time you'll see Māori language programs. Except for when you're involved in a specifically Māori activity or event, you won't be hearing it much in everyday use (though expressions like "kia ora" have made their way into general Kiwi speech).

Still, knowing how to pronounce Māori words can be important when trying to say place-names in New Zealand. Even if you have a natural facility for picking up languages, you'll find many Māori words to be quite baffling. The West Coast town of Punakaiki (pronounced poon-ah-*kye*-kee) is relatively straightforward, but when you get to places like Whangamata, the going gets tricky—the opening *wh* is pronounced like an *f*, and the accent is placed on the last syllable: "fahng-ah-ma-*ta*. Sometimes it is the mere length of words that makes them difficult, as in the case of Waitakaruru (why-ta-ka-ru-ru) or Whakarewarewa (fa-ka-*re*-wa-*re*-wa). You'll notice that the ends of both of these have repeats—of "ru" and "rewa," which is something to look out for to make longer words more manageable. Town names like Waikanea (*why*-can-eye) you'll just have to repeat to yourself a few times before saying them without pause.

The Māori *r* is rolled so that it sounds a little like a *d*. Thus the Northland town of Whangarei is pronounced "fang-ah-day," and the word *Māori* is pronounced "mo-dee," with the *o* sounding like it does in the word mould, and a rolled *r*. A macron indicates a lengthened vowel. In general, *a* is pronounced *ah* as in "car"; *e* is said as the *ea* in "weather." O is pronounced like "awe," rather than *oh*, and *u* sounds like the *u* of "June." *Ng*, meanwhile, has a soft, blunted sound, as the *ng* in "singing." All of this is a little too complicated for some *Pākehā* (non-Māori), who choose not to bother with Māori pronunciations. So in some places, if you say you've just driven over from "fahng-ah-ma-*ta*," the reply might be: "You mean 'wang-ah-*ma*-tuh.' " You can pronounce these words either way, but more and more non-Māori New Zealanders are saying Māori words as the Māori do.

Āe: Yes

Ahau: I, me

Aotearoa: Land of the long white cloud (New Zealand)

Atua: Spirit, god

Awa: River

Awhi: Help

Haere atu: Go away, farewell, depart

Haere mai: Welcome, come here

Haere rā: Farewell, good-bye

Haka: Fierce rhythmical dance made internationally famous by the country's rugby team, the All Blacks, and performed before each game

Hākari: Feast, gift

Hāngi: Earth oven, food from an earth oven

Hapū: Subtribe

Harakeke: Flax leaf (also used to refer to woven flax items)

Heitiki: Greenstone pendant

Hongi: Press noses in greeting

Hui: Gathering

Ika: Fish

Iwi: People, tribe

Kāhore: No

Kai: Food, eat, dine

Kai moana: Seafood

Karakia: Ritual chant, prayer, religious service

Kaumātua: Elder

Kete: Flax bag

Kino: Bad

Koha: Customary gift, donation

Kōhanga reo: Language nest, Māori preschool

Kōtiro: Girl

Kūmara: Sweet potato

Kura kaupapa: Total immersion Māori-language school

Mana: Influence, prestige, power

Manu: Bird

Manuhiri: Guest, visitor

Māoritanga: Māori culture, perspective

Marae: Traditional gathering place

Maunga: Mountain

Mauri: Life principle, source of vitality and mana

Mihi: To greet, congratulate

Moana: Sea, lake

Moko: Tattoo

Motu: Island

Pā: Fortress

Pai: Good

Pākehā: Non-Māori, European, Caucasian

Poi: Light ball attached to string

Rangatira: Chief, person of rank

Reo: Language

Roto: Lake

Taiaha: Long, two-handed weapon, blade at one end and point at the other
Tama: Boy
Tāne: Man
Tangata whenua: People of the land, local people
Taniwha: Spirits-monsters living in the sea and inland waters
Taonga: Treasure
Tapu: Sacred, under religious restriction, taboo
Tauiwi: Foreigner
Tino rangatiratanga: Chief's authority, self-determination
Toa: Warrior
Tohunga: Priest, expert
Tupuna: Ancestor
Wahine: Woman
Wai: Water, liquid
Waiata: Sing, song
Wairua: Soul, spirit
Waka: Canoe
Whai kōrero: Speech
Whakapapa: Genealogy, cultural identity
Whānau: Family
Whare: House
Whenua: Land, country

Greetings and Expressions

Kia ora: Hello
Tēnā koe (korua) (koutou): Hello to one person (to two people) (to three or more people)
Haere mai: Welcome
Haere rā: Good-bye (from the person staying to the one leaving)
E noho ra: Good-bye (from the person leaving to the person staying)
Ka pai: Good, excellent
Kei te pehea koe: How are you? (to one person)

Māori Place-Names

Kirikiriroa: Hamilton
Ōtautahi: Christchurch
Ōtepoti: Dunedin
Rakiura: Stewart Island
Tāmaki-makau-rau: Auckland
Te Ika-A-Māui: North Island
Te Waipounamu–Te-Waka-A-Aoraki: South Island
Whanganui-a-tara: Wellington

INDEX